THE SIGN

THE SIGN

ROBERT VAN KAMPEN

CROSSWAY BOOKS • WHEATON, ILLINOIS
A DIVISION OF GOOD NEWS PUBLISHERS

The Sign.

Copyright © 1992 by Robert Van Kampen.

Published by Crossway Books, a division of
Good News Publishers, 1300 Crescent Street, Wheaton, Illinois 60187.

Cover illustration: Michael Carroll

First printing, 1992

Printed in the United States of America

ISBN 0-89107-667-0

All Bible quotations, unless otherwise indicated, are taken from *New American
Standard Bible*, copyright © 1977 by the Lockman Foundation.

Library of Congress Cataloging-in-Publication Data
Van Kampen, Robert.
    The sign / Robert Van Kampen.
        p.   cm.
    Includes bibliographical references and indexes.
        1. End of the world.   2. Good and evil.   3. Prophecy—
Christianity.   I. Title.
BT876.V36 1992   236'.9—dc20   92-18465
ISBN 0-89107-667-0

00		99		98		97		96		95		94		93
15	14	13	12	11	10	9	8	7	6	5	4			

To Ezekiel Shachar,

the late commanding genius of
the first Israeli Paratrooper Regiment, Senior Master
of chess, brilliant student of the Hebrew Bible — I am proud to
dedicate this book to you, my very special friend. Although
completely unfamiliar with the claims of Christ until very late in
life, your passion for the Scripture and love of Messiah have had
an immeasurable impact upon me. All of Scripture was precious to
you, both the Old and New Testaments, and you saw Christ on
every page. Thank you, my dear friend, for your love and
inspiration, for your contribution to almost every phase of this
manuscript, and for what you continue to mean to me,
although separated until the Lord comes.
Come quickly, Lord Jesus.

TABLE OF CONTENTS

ACKNOWLEDGMENTS

After spending eight years in the writing of this book, the credit for the final product is broad based, as so many have given of their time and wisdom in helping me, encouraging me, writing for me, and protecting me in this endeavor. To each of you I wish to acknowledge your invaluable contribution.

My writers: Those who know me well know that I am anything but a writer — a talker, yes, a writer, no. And so, many thanks to David Douglass and Lane Dennis for your patience toward me, and for your faithfulness to this project, in spite of my unreadable scratchings and marginal notes with all the arrows. Your efforts contributed immeasurably to the clarity of the concepts developed herein.

My scholarly sources: Marve Rosenthal, Kevin Howard, Paul Teasdale, John MacArthur, and others who so faithfully kept my focus thoroughly biblical. Iron sharpeneth iron, and so these men were to me. Together we have had many lengthy and intense debates, more times than I care to admit — sometimes resulting in a twenty-page response to a single issue, with phone bills out of sight, and all long-distance. And yet, coming with kindness and gentleness, all your criticism and argument have been constructive with the sole purpose of finding biblical truth.

My artist: Tom Allen. The chart speaks for itself and is uniquely illustrated, right down to the separate and distinct individuals standing around the throne of God in the heavenlies. Tom, I personally thank you, dear friend, for your dedication to this project as your ministry to Christ.

My critics: In all things we are instructed to give thanks, and so to the most aggressive critics of the position defended in this volume,

I genuinely thank you. For without your aggressive verbal and written criticism, and the logical biblical defenses developed in response, I would have never have been so bold as to go into print with the confidence that I now have. Without you, this book would have been several hundred pages shorter, as many of the endnotes have been written as a result of the input my critics have provided me in advance. So I thank you for helping me to be forewarned and forearmed.

My church: To the adult class at my church that has listened to and waded through my thinking for at least the last five years, thank you for being unafraid of new concepts, Bereans to the core, choosing only to know Scripture more fully. I am grateful for your honest questions. One grows by being questioned, especially when those questioning do so from a genuine desire to learn. But most of all, thank you for your encouragement. How often my presentation of a particular issue was clarified for the book through organizing and teaching it to my class in advance. Thank you, my friends.

And, my family: Oh, such patience and support. I am forever grateful. You have individually worked through any number of the many preliminary drafts of this manuscript, partially out of interest in the subject, always out of love and concern for me. That in itself is worthy of note. Thank you, each one of you.

PREFACE

T his book is the result of the most exhaustive and rewarding work of my life, the culmination of some nine thousand hours of Bible study and research over the past eight years. The truths that God reveals about the end times are found in virtually all parts of Scripture, and careful study and comparison of countless passages is necessary to discover His full revelation concerning these times.

When this work began, I was determined to understand and harmonize all prophetic passages of Scripture according to their most natural and literal meanings, firmly believing that if a contradiction seemed to exist, God's full revelation about the subject had not yet been discovered. To this end I took a four- by eight-foot cork board and divided it into sections representing the events of the end times.* Using 3 x 5 cards, I wrote down the references of every prophetic passage I could find in both the Old and New Testaments and pinned them on the board where they seemed to belong.

For several years that board was in front of our fireplace, to the dismay of my wife but to the delight of friends interested in prophecy. The cards were rearranged over and over, until two things happened. First, a pattern emerged that had no evident contradictions or inconsistencies. Second, the cork board, what I called my warboard, began to come apart as the cards were moved time and time again in an effort

---

* For the meaning of "the end times" as used here, see the Glossary at the end of this book. The Glossary includes a wide range of definitions and explanations of technical terms and unfamiliar words and phrases. The reader is encouraged to consult the Glossary frequently, whenever words or phrases may be unclear. Occasionally the reader is referred to the Glossary immediately following a word or phrase in the text, especially where a clear understanding of a word or phrase is particularly important.

to find the pattern that accommodated all the prophetic passages. Finally the pinholes won the battle and the board ceased to exist!

The majority of study time was spent comparing Scripture to Scripture, checking and cross-checking to see if an interpretation was inconsistent with or should be modified by any other passage, and making sure that no significant truth was omitted or misrepresented. Every time I came across a new text that related to the area I was studying, I first tried to understand it as best I could within its own context, and then I tried to see how it might fit into the overall scheme on the board. Many times I failed to find a place for it and would stick the card off to the side until I could study the text further; or I would wait until another prophetic passage would give the passage in question a fresh perspective. As the work progressed, the contradictions, inconsistencies, and gaps became fewer and fewer. As of this writing, I have become confident that the overall picture is essentially complete and is not likely to be radically changed by honest scrutiny of other texts.

To stake my life on the absolute accuracy of every detail of this book would be foolish and presumptuous, especially in light of the vast amount of material in the following pages. Yet I can say truthfully that I have not intentionally avoided a single verse or word of Scripture I thought might weaken or undermine my conclusions. It goes without saying that some areas are not as clear or complete as they might be, and that some of the truths discovered are more implicit than explicit. But I have tried to make certain that even implicit interpretations are consistent with the explicit truths of Scripture, that they are defended as logically and honestly as possible, and that they are consistent with the work as a whole.

The Bible was written for all believers, the whole church of God, as well as for divinely-ordained preachers and teachers. Every church and every individual Christian should therefore be a "Berean" — someone who carefully holds up whatever is read or heard or promoted to the light of God's Word to see if it is true or not. Although Paul was an apostle and knew that he taught with God's authority, he was not offended but was greatly encouraged when members of the synagogue at Berea checked everything against Scripture that he and Silas taught (see Acts 17:10-12).

On the other hand, Paul admonished Timothy not to permit mere wrangling "about words, which is useless, and leads to the ruin of the hearers" (2 Tim. 2:14). Every Christian's purpose in studying God's

Word should be to better understand and more faithfully obey its truths, not to defend his or her own predisposition or tradition.

During the preparation of this volume, I had the opportunity to attend a national conference of evangelical Bible scholars and theologians. One of the scholars gave a lecture on Ezekiel 38 — 39, and because those two chapters are exceptionally relevant to the material in this book, I listened with special interest. But my expectations quickly turned to disappointment when this speaker stated that what Ezekiel wrote had no relevance to end-time events but related solely to the prophet's own time. In defense of his position, he quoted scholar after scholar, most of whom, I later discovered, were avowed liberals. As I recall, he did not so much as mention Ezekiel's statement that "It will come about in the last days" (38:16); nor did he seem to realize the significance of the national salvation of Israel prophesied at the end of the passage (39:22). Likewise, he completely overlooked the larger context of the passage — which is preceded by Ezekiel's "dry bones" vision, telling of Israel's return (in unbelief) to their homeland (chap. 37), and which is followed by a discourse concerning Israel in the millennial kingdom (chaps. 40-48). He used little other Scripture, if any, to support his views. Instead he relied largely on the conjectures of scholars who deny the inerrancy of Scripture and on variant renderings of Hebrew terms that bolstered his argument or that supposedly discredited orthodox interpretation. And all of this at a supposedly conservative symposium!

Although I have consulted with great benefit many commentaries, concordances, lexicons, Bible dictionaries and encyclopedias, and other scholarly works, the disappointing experience at that conference made me more determined than ever to keep the focus of this book on God's Book and on no other.

This volume is essentially a sequential history of prophetic events concerning the end times, based to a great extent on the clear timeline structure given for those events in the book of Daniel. I do not expect every genuine Christian to agree with what I say. This study, however, will acquaint the serious student of prophecy with a great deal of prophetic material that must be dealt with in a responsible manner, no matter what conclusions may be reached. I simply would ask those who disagree with the position arrived at in these pages to challenge my arguments and conclusions on the basis of Scripture, taking into account every Old and New Testament text that relates to the particular issue so as to leave no contradictions or discrepancies. In the meantime, until a better solution is found that accommodates *all* the passages without contradiction, I am comfortable with the positions taken in the pages that follow. This is the only system I know of that comes close to harmonizing all the relevant passages, not just some or most of them. On the other hand, if you are a skeptic, the following pages will at least acquaint you with many of the pieces of the prophetic puzzle that you must harmonize before truth can be genuinely known. If you can make *all* the pieces fit in a different sequence without sacrificing a literal hermeneutic, I applaud you and will respect your findings as I hope you will respect mine. My sole intent has always been truth and truth only, without contradiction.

Paul's words to Timothy should continually be on the mind of every believer: "All Scripture is inspired by God and profitable for teaching, for reproof, for correction, for training in righteousness; that the man of God may be adequate, equipped for every good work" (2 Tim. 3:16, 17). Yet Scripture does not reveal every detail of God's infinite truth (including His truth about the end times), just as it does not record every detail of Jesus' earthly life and ministry (cf. John 21:25). But God's Word *does* give us every truth necessary to understand what we, His people, need to know about the last days and how we should anticipate and prepare for those days.

Out of this study, several overriding truths have manifested themselves over and over. The first is God's unfathomable love for the nation of Israel — a sovereign and gracious love that extends undiminished from eternity past to eternity future; an omnipotent love that will unfailingly bring ultimate redemption to those of the natural line of Abraham which He has chosen to become the spiritual line of Abraham, after the nation has atoned for her sin. Apart from that momentous truth, the end times can be nothing but an enigma that baffles every attempt to comprehend it.

Second, I have come to believe with ever-deepening conviction that God's holiness will not allow Him to disregard the moral and spiritual compromise that characterizes so many churches and individual Christians today, and that this will grow still worse as the last days approach. God has in the past and will again deal severely with the natural line of Abraham (Israel), sometimes chastising them by means of ungodly nations — as He did with wicked "Assyria, the rod of [His] anger" (Isa. 10:5). How much more, then, will His holiness demand chastisement of unspiritual and disobedient Christians (part of the spiritual line of Abraham) who have so much more light through His completed Word and so much more capacity for righteousness by the power of His indwelling Spirit? The Bible is fearfully clear that all impurities in the church will be purged (1 Pet. 4:12, 13, 17, 18), in order that every believer might be presented to the divine Bridegroom "as a pure virgin" (2 Cor. 11:2), "blameless in the day of our Lord Jesus Christ" (1 Cor. 1:8).

The third and final truth is the unimaginable fierceness of God's final wrath on all who reject and oppose Him. God's wrath is not a popular subject today — we would much rather stress His love and long-suffering compassion. God is indeed a God of loving patience, "not wishing for any to perish but for all to come to repentance" (2 Pet. 3:9b). But just as surely Scripture reveals, in exactly that same passage, that Christ will come in judgment and destruction of the ungodly (2 Pet. 3:7). As we will see, the peoples who have been God's greatest enemies on earth and the greatest persecutors of His people will suffer the greatest outpouring of God's wrath for their wanton oppression of His chosen people. An even more sobering truth, however, is that *all* unbelievers, no matter how upright they may be by human standards, will face the Lord's wrath. And when it comes, there will be no doubt in any person's mind that the incredible affliction during the day of the Lord is neither from men nor from Satan but that it is the inescapable outpouring of God's holy judgment.

My hope for this study of the end times is that it will encourage others to search the Scriptures, using the basic principles of interpretation mentioned in the first chapter, to carry the work further, refining, expanding, and, if necessary, correcting it — in a way that is honoring to God and will be of help to His people. And as a result of searching the Scriptures in this way, my prayer is that we would come to a renewed assurance of the absolute truth and reliability of God's Word, that we would be challenged to carefully examine our lives, and that by God's grace we would seek to live a devout and holy life that honors our Lord in every way.

1

Introduction: Foundations for Understanding Prophetic Truth

To write a good fiction novel, one needs an exciting story line that keeps the reader riveted to the book. The material presented in this book could give any capable novelist (which I am not) everything necessary to write a best-seller. In fact, one might be inclined to think it is fiction. But the incredible events outlined here are all founded in truth and will in fact transpire as described in the following pages, not because of any claims that I might make, but because God's Word declares it. Although this book is not written in fictionalized form but as serious theology, the extraordinary events presented in the following pages *will* be played out, if not in our lifetimes, most probably in the lifetimes of our children or grandchildren.

THE STARTLING TRUTH

I began this work with no intention of being sensational, but only with a desire to discover God's truth about the end times by carefully examining all prophetic Scriptures and then harmonizing these in such a way that there would be no contradictions or inconsistencies.

What I found is more terrifying than anything I could have dreamed up. And it is fact, not fiction.

The most disheartening aspect of my writing, however, has been knowing beyond any doubt that the thrust of the book never will or can be accepted by the church at large. The church that enters the last days will undergo intense persecution that largely could be avoided if it had had correct understanding of those days. Scripture teaches that this church will, in general, be compromising and confused and that much of its affliction will come because of improper teaching and belief about the subjects discussed in this book.

If a volume such as this could somehow remedy the thinking of the church about the end times, many of the events and circumstances that Scripture foretells would never come to pass. But because God's Word is inerrant, its prophetic revelations are not simply possible but inevitable. For that very reason, the conclusions of this book will, by definition, never be accepted by many within the organized church today. In light of the many somber warnings the Bible gives to those who do not rightly understand the last days, my heart is heavy, especially for God's people.

But the church includes many individual believers who are willing to change or modify their beliefs if they can be convinced on the basis of clear, defendable arguments from Scripture. It is to such believers in particular that this book is addressed. If these believers, concerned more about truth than tradition, are better prepared to face the end times and to escape the major brunt of Satan's "great wrath" (Rev. 12:12) — when he is cast down to earth, enraged with both the natural and spiritual descendants of Abraham, and goes "off to make war with [all those] who keep the commandments of God and hold to the testimony of Jesus" (v. 17) — then this book will have served its purpose and the author will be grateful.

My great hope is that everyone who reads this book will understand to the fullest possible extent that the issues being dealt with relate to God's prophetic truth, not to religious fiction or imagination. Someday, perhaps very soon, our children or grandchildren, or even we ourselves, will face the actual events described in this book — events which, if anything, have been understated rather than overstated.

Please carefully think through the basically simple biblical truths on which this book is based. Especially keep in mind that God's promises have always been to the faithful remnant who truly believe in Him, and that only that remnant will be prepared, by His gracious power, to face and to overcome the end-time challenges and afflictions portrayed in the following pages. *Each reader must evaluate and decide for himself.*

MAJOR DISAGREEMENTS

Eschatology, the study of the end times in relation to biblical prophecy, has been debated from the time of the early church. One of the major purposes of Paul's two letters to believers at Thessalonica was to correct false, confusing, and disquieting ideas about Christ's second coming.

One of the most debated issues among twentieth-century evangelicals has been, and still is, the timing of the Rapture* — when Christ will take both living and dead believers to Himself — and how this relates to the terrifying events described in the book of Revelation. All Christians who believe that the Bible is the inerrant, infallible Word of God, and who believe that it is to be understood in its most natural and literal interpretation, agree that the momentous events of the end times will literally take place. In particular, all such Bible-believing Christians affirm that the specific events of the Rapture, the day of the Lord, and the thousand-year reign of Christ on earth (the Millennium) will actually occur in future history at God's preordained time.

But while Bible-believing Christians are in complete *agreement that these events will take place,* there are major *disagreements as to when and how they will happen, and whom they will involve.* The major disagreements are about such questions as:

— Will the church go through the great tribulation?

— When, in the sequence of end-time events, will the Rapture actually occur?

— When does the wrath of God begin? Does it extend through the entire "seventieth week"? Is it confined only to the final battle of Armageddon?

It is my conviction that Scripture gives specific answers to all the questions mentioned above, as well to many others, and it is my sincere hope that this volume will help clarify those answers.

---

* See the Glossary for an explanation of "the Rapture" and other theological terms used in this section. Although just introduced in this section, all of these terms will be explained fully in the following chapters.

For the most part, everyone agrees that Scripture clearly teaches that the church will be removed (raptured) *before* God's final wrath is executed on the unrighteous during the day of the Lord. The most explicit passages concerning the church's protection from the day of the Lord's wrath are found in Paul's letter to the Romans and in his first letter to the Thessalonians. He declares unequivocally that "having now been justified by His blood, we shall be *saved from the wrath of God* through Him" (Rom. 5:9), that Jesus "*delivers us from the wrath to come*" (1 Thess. 1:10), and that "*God has not destined us for wrath,* but for obtaining salvation [deliverance] through our Lord Jesus Christ" (1 Thess. 5:9; cf. Rev. 3:10, emphasis added). The real question is, what is God's wrath, and in contrast to this, what is the wrath of Satan who "has come down to you, having great wrath, knowing that he has only a short time" (Rev. 12:12)?

THE COMING PERSECUTION

On the other hand, although Christians will be delivered from God's wrath, Scripture is equally clear that believers are *not promised* freedom from persecution and tribulation, and that they can in fact *expect* persecution and tribulation to come for the very reason that they *are* Christians. As Jesus said, "If the world hates you, you know that it has hated Me before it hated you. If you were of the world, the world would love its own; but because you are not of the world, but I chose you out of the world, therefore the world hates you" (John 15:18, 19). But along with this, Jesus also promises in the last beatitude a double blessing for those who are persecuted for righteousness' sake (Matt. 5:10-12).

Paul both warned and encouraged fellow believers with these words: Let "no man . . . be disturbed by these afflictions; for you yourselves know that *we have been destined for this.* For indeed when we were with you, we kept telling you in advance that we were going to suffer affliction; and so it came to pass, as you know" (1 Thess. 3:3, 4, emphasis added; cf. v. 13). He explained to Timothy that believers, possibly even himself, could expect to be afflicted until the time "when the Lord Jesus shall be revealed from heaven with His mighty angels in flaming fire" (2 Thess. 1:7). He reminded Timothy that "in the last days difficult times will come" and that "indeed, all who desire to live godly in Christ Jesus will be persecuted" (2 Tim. 3:1, 12).

Peter gives a similar admonition: "Beloved, do not be surprised at the fiery ordeal among you, which comes upon you for your testing, as though some strange thing were happening to you; but to the degree that you share the sufferings of Christ, keep on rejoicing; so that also at the revelation of His glory, you may rejoice with exultation" (1 Pet. 4:12, 13; cf. vv. 3-7). The real question here is, does this persecution include any of the events associated with the last days, in particular the great tribulation by Antichrist?

This volume will harmonize both of these truths. As will be mentioned numerous times throughout this volume, just as Scripture makes abundantly clear that believers *will* escape God's wrath, it makes equally clear that believers are *not* promised escape from the wrath of the world and of Satan, especially from the persecution of God's elect during the great tribulation by Antichrist (Rev. 12:12). The prewrath position, which will be defined in more detail at the end of this chapter, is the system, then, that harmonizes both of those truths, without any biblical contradictions!

PRINCIPLES OF INTERPRETATION

To have validity, our method of interpretation (i.e., our hermeneutic) must be consistent and without contradiction, and it must never be governed by a theological predisposition or school of thought. In other words, if our hermeneutic is controlled by our theology, then the Bible can be twisted to say whatever our theology would have it say — which of course is what often happens in the study of the end times. Likewise, our method of interpretation will have a far-reaching effect on our theological conclusions. Thus, it is axiomatic that those who use a different method of interpretation (i.e., a different hermeneutic) will end up with basically different doctrines and theology. How important it is, then, that we be very clear about what our hermeneutic is — and, even more important, that we are in fact using the right principles of interpretation in order to properly understand the truth of God's Word.

The following principles of interpretation — none of them unique to this writer, but all of them held by careful students of Scripture throughout history — have been followed as honestly and consistently as possible.

The *first principle* is that *all Scripture is to be taken in its literal and normal sense*, allowing, of course, for obvious symbolism and figures of speech. Every passage must be taken at face value whenever possible.

Martin Luther called this the principle of literal interpretation, interpreting Scripture by its *sensus literalis*. Many of the greatest advances in the biblical scholarship of the Reformation resulted from the application of that single principle. In its simplest meaning and application, that principle means that we read and evaluate Scripture with the same normal understanding of words and symbolic language that we read any other serious book or carry on any serious conversation.

This principle has special relevance in the study of prophecy, and in fact finds strong confirmation in the way Old Testament prophecy was fulfilled in the life of Christ. For example, the Old Testament contains over three hundred prophecies concerning the first coming of Christ. Although many of those prophecies are virtual duplicates, at least sixty distinct facets of Christ's life and ministry were predicted, and all sixty, without exception, were *literally fulfilled*. It is then not only a matter of faith but of biblical principle to expect the many prophecies of Christ's second coming to be fulfilled with equal literalness and completeness. Prophecy that *is not* literally fulfilled is not true prophecy, and eventually it proves itself to be simply misguided human speculation.

When we use this principle, the Bible suddenly comes alive in a new way. We have a renewed confidence in the reliability of God's Word — that it is literally true, that it is something laymen can understand, and that the events described in its pages really will happen according to God's sovereign time and plan. No longer do we approach the Bible looking for an obscure spiritualized meaning, but rather for the literal understanding of events that will actually happen in history.

The *second principle* has to do with *the context of a word, phrase, or larger passage*. Sometimes that involves careful understanding of the complete Bible book being studied, carefully interpreting a given idea or principle in light of the overall thrust and nature of the book as well as in light of its immediate context. The context involves the persons or kind of persons being addressed in a passage and their historical setting and situation. I have never forgotten the truth of the simple rhyme, "A text taken out of context is no more than a pretext."

The *third principle*, equally important as the first two, is that of *comparing Scripture with Scripture*. A word, phrase, or concept should first of all be studied in light of its use in the Bible book being studied and then in light of its use in other passages of Scripture. When a given text is not explicit about a truth, no conclusion should be drawn about that truth until all relevant passages have been studied. Of course some passages are not as clear as others, and some truths are more implicit than explicit. When this is the case, those truths which are more implicit always need to be understood in light of those which are more explicit, and never the reverse. Likewise, the more important a truth is, the more carefully related truths should be compared and examined. Because Scripture is *always* its own best interpreter, careful comparison always adds depth and clarity to our understanding.

Fourth, antimonies are never acceptable, and the importance of this principle cannot be overstated. An antinomy is "a contradiction between two apparently equally valid principles or between inferences correctly drawn from such principles" (*Webster's Ninth New Collegiate Dictionary*). After all passages relating to a specific issue are carefully studied and compared, no interpretation is valid that does not genuinely harmonize with *all* the passages. If God's Word is inerrant, it cannot be self-contradictory. Some interpreters try to compare seeming scriptural antinomies to the parallel tracks of a railroad, which are clearly separated where one is standing but which seem to converge in the far distance — the meaning being that a contradiction today will someday, in the sweet bye and bye, come together and cease to contradict. The fact is, however, that once you arrive at the horizon and far beyond, those tracks continue to be separated and will *never* converge. In exactly the same way, ideas that are mutually exclusive can *never* be reconciled, no matter how far their implications are extrapolated. So if two passages seem to contradict, truth has not yet been discovered, and no position should be taken. Rather, keep looking. Eventually a higher common denominator will be found that perfectly harmonizes the critical passages in question. Then you have truth, but not before. It is essential to understand that there are no antimonies in God's Word.

Fifth, it is recognized that *many passages of Scripture, in both Testaments, have both near and far implications and applications.* In other words, prophecy often operates on two levels of fulfillment. On the first level, there is a divinely revealed "near" prediction relating to a soon-coming event. But on a second level, there is a corresponding "far" prediction that will be fulfilled at a later time, or in the events of the end times. The failure to recognize and apply this principle has caused immeasurable confusion among even the most godly and scholarly students of Scripture. Obviously, *misuse* of this principle, as of any other, will also cause confusion and misunderstanding. For a near/far interpretation to be valid, it must clearly be allowed for by the context and by the specific wording of the text itself, as well as be consistent with the rest of Scripture. Whenever such prophecies are dealt with in this volume, their near/far aspects will be established as carefully and as fully as this author knows how.

Several additional general comments on the basic issue of hermeneutics need to be made.

In relation to a given prophetic event or issue, careful study of various texts in the Old and New Testaments will reveal that the *different terminology and styles of the writers will describe the same event or issue with equal and consistent truthfulness*, though often not in the same detail or from the same perspective. Many examples will be seen as Scripture is compared to Scripture in our study of end-time events. But one needs only to look at the first coming of Christ to see the principle in operation. Psalm 22, written by David, gives the reader one perspective of the crucifixion of Christ, whereas Isaiah 53 gives another perspective of exactly the same event. And Daniel 9:26 simply says, "Messiah will be cut off and have nothing." Either the context or the similarity of the events described must be present for the student of prophecy to make the connection between the passages in question. But where a genuine connection exists, the different perspectives found in various passages bring a fuller understanding to the same event.

Our understanding of the end times will continue to increase as history continues to unfold and verify biblical prophecy. Many of the prophetic passages of the Old Testament were unclear to those who first heard or read them. God's people were not certain whether a given prophetic message related to their own times or to the future. As with near/far prophecies, the biblical language clarified some of the uncertainties. In regard to many passages, the modern student of prophecy has the great advantage of looking back, as it were, and learning from the fulfillment of prophecy as revealed in the New Testament, or as recognized in subsequent history. Daniel was told to "conceal these words and seal up the book until the end of time . . . for these words are concealed and sealed up until the end time" (Dan. 12:4, 9). When the end times come, therefore, the church will have a long historical base from which to gain understanding of many of the prophetic passages that hitherto were a mystery. *History has been, and will continue to be, a source of prophetic insight* for those who carefully study God's Word. Since Israel gained possession and control of her homeland in 1948, for instance, we have a perspective on prophecy that could only have been surmised before that momentous event.

In summary, in working on this volume I have tried diligently to be faithful to all of these principles of hermeneutics, never being satisfied with a conclusion or interpretation unless it is in complete harmony with every biblical text I have been able to find on the subject. And whenever clear biblical truth is found, never can we dare to stand in judgment of that truth; that truth always stands in judgment of each one of us! There can be no exceptions; no spiritualizing, no allegorizing, no culturalizing, no semiticizing, no rationalizing is ever permissible. God says what He means and means what He says; our only response is to bow in acceptance of His truth, however reassuring or unsettling we may find it to be.

THE PIVOTAL TEXTS

There are two texts in the New Testament that provide the direct teaching of Christ concerning the end times, and both of these taken together are essential for an understanding of these events. The first is the Olivet Discourse (found in Matthew 24 and 25), where Christ personally gives his most crucial message of the end times. But His most in-depth instruction about those times is not found in the Gospels but in the last book of the New Testament, Revelation. Although not usually associated with the direct teaching of Christ, Revelation nonetheless clearly does come directly from Christ for the purpose of instructing the church concerning the end times, as seen in the opening verse: "The Revelation of Jesus Christ, which God gave Him to show to His bond-servants, the things which must shortly take place" (Rev. 1:1).

Although God is, of course, the author of all Scripture, the Olivet Discourse and the book of Revelation have a special significance in that these messages were delivered in a more direct way by Christ Himself. And certainly if any two passages of Scripture should be totally consistent with each other and reflect a common approach to the same subject, these two passages should be. Even the Lord's command to teach this material to the churches is remarkably similar. The Gospel of Matthew concludes with Christ's great commission: "Go therefore and make disciples of all the nations, baptizing them in the name of the Father and the Son and the Holy Spirit, *teaching them to observe all that I commanded you*; and lo, I am with you always, even to the end of the age" (Matt. 28:19, 20, emphasis added). Very near the end of Revelation He says, "I, Jesus, have sent My angel to *testify to you these things for the churches*" (Rev. 22:16, emphasis added).

It should go without saying that the Olivet Discourse and the book of Revelation are absolutely pivotal for understanding the end times. They beautifully parallel and complement each other, and in a unique way the understanding of one is necessary for understanding the other. Of utmost importance is the Lord's explicit teaching from His own lips that both of these eschatological messages are to be taught *to His church.*

THE VARIOUS POSITIONS CONCERNING CHRIST'S RETURN

As noted above, in a broad sense all evangelicals who take a literal approach to prophecy believe that the Lord will rapture His people before He unleashes His wrath upon a wicked, unrepenting world. No other conclusion is possible, because it is *from* God's condemnation and wrath that believers are saved, or delivered. The greatest question of interpretation is in regard to *when* that wrath will begin.

Those who believe that the "seventieth week of Daniel"* corresponds to the day of the Lord, when God executes His wrath upon the earth, *must* believe then that the Rapture will occur *before the beginning* of that critical seven-year period. Thus, their position on the timing of the Rapture is referred to as "pretribulational," wherein the entire seventieth week is designated as the "tribulational period" and the time of God's wrath. For the sake of clarification, the reader should understand that Scripture never refers to either the wrath of God during the day of the Lord or Daniel's seventieth week as "the tribulational period." The term has been coined by men, and for this reason this author will always refer to the seventieth week as "the seventieth week," never as "the tribulational period."

Although the pretribulational rapture position is highly popular and influential, it is of recent origin — not much more than a hundred and fifty years old.[1] Without going into great detail here in the text, the common pretribulational view not only sees the entire seventieth

---

* The "seventieth week" refers to the final seven years described in Daniel and Revelation (each day of the seventieth "week" of Daniel corresponds to one year). See the Glossary for further explanation of the seventieth week and other terms occurring in this section such as "tribulation," "pretribulational," "amillennial," "Rapture," "prewrath," "day of the Lord," and others.

week as the wrath of God, but by necessity must also believe in two separate but related second comings of Christ — or in reality, a second and a third coming of Christ. The first future coming of Christ is said to be at His coming "for His church" (at the Rapture) before the seventieth week begins, and His second future coming "with the church" at the final battle of Armageddon at the end of the seventieth week.[2] As far as church history can determine, that view cannot be traced further back than about 1830.

On the other hand, there are many in the evangelical church who do not take prophecy in its most literal sense, and for this reason their view of end times is considerably different. This system, known as *amillennialism*, allegorizes prophetic Scripture, holding that there will be no physical, earthly millennial kingdom over which Christ will rule. The Olivet Discourse and the greater part of the book of Revelation are largely viewed as past historical events, with minimal end-time relevance. The second coming of Christ, therefore, is for the purpose of ending human history when the future eternity immediately begins. Thus there will be no future, literal, personal Antichrist who will seek to destroy the elect of God in the last days. This view has its roots in Roman Catholicism, having begun with Augustine in the fourth century, and was not the view of the church for the first three hundred years after the New Testament was completed. Because the hermeneutic of those holding to this position is opposite the hermeneutic of this writer, there is little biblical appeal I can make to those who hold this view, as any passages I would use in my appeal to you would be quickly "spiritualized" away. But before you cast your lot to this view, I would encourage you to read this entire book. If the first coming of Christ was fulfilled literally in every point, why not His second coming? Can prophecy that is not fulfilled literally be considered prophecy at all? Contrary to what many may believe or have been taught, what we believe about end times is critical — if not for our own well-being, then certainly for the well-being of our children or their children!

THE PREWRATH POSITION

On the other hand, it can be demonstrated from church history that the prewrath view on the timing of the Rapture, as carefully presented throughout this book, has been the most common position of biblical Christianity since the days of the early church. (See note 3 for a full discussion demonstrating the wide acceptance of the prewrath position among the early church fathers.)[3]

Simply stated, the prewrath view contends that *the church will go through the great tribulation by Antichrist during the end times, but will be raptured before the wrath of God, when Christ cuts short the persecution of Antichrist.* The great tribulation is the time that occurs after the mid-point of the seventieth week, when Antichrist has complete control of the earth (Matt. 24:15) and seeks to destroy all who will not worship him (Matt. 24:21, 22). This will be a time of putting to a proof those who name the name of Christ, as God permits the persecution by Antichrist to purify genuine but unfaithful believers in order to make them worthy to be the bride of Christ. As will be studied at some length in chapters 14-17 of this volume, Christ will "cut short" that time of great affliction by Antichrist and will gather His elect to Himself at the Rapture, on the same day that He unleashes His day-of-the-Lord destruction on the wicked world that remains, sometime during the second half of the seventieth week but before its completion.

This is what the Apostle Paul had in mind when he wrote to the church at Thessalonica concerning the end times. Thus Paul writes:

> We ourselves speak proudly of you among the churches of God for your perseverance and faith in the midst of all your persecutions and afflictions [tribulation][4] which you endure. This is a plain indication of God's righteous judgment so that you may be considered worthy of the kingdom of God, for which indeed you are suffering. For after all it is only just for God to repay with affliction those who afflict you, and to give relief[5] to you who are afflicted and to us as well when the Lord Jesus shall be revealed from heaven with His mighty angels in flaming fire, dealing out retribution to those who do not know God and to those who do not obey the gospel of our Lord Jesus. (2 Thess. 1:4-8)

Regardless of one's position on any doctrinal issue, however, the only position that can be truly respected is one that has been honestly and earnestly hammered out by intense study of God's Word on the subject, after having resolved all seeming inconsistencies and contradictions according to the hermeneutical principles mentioned above. In this writer's opinion, the prewrath position is the only one that can meet that stringent test, and I believe it will withstand the most careful scrutiny that is made with integrity.

THE DANGER OF PRECONCEIVED CONCLUSIONS

I am aware that the prewrath view of the end times as presented in this book stands in conflict with the other main views which are most influential among evangelical Christians today. As a result, the prewrath position has often been rejected out of hand — without serious consideration and without careful study of God's Word according to the principles outlined above. Unfortunately, some Bible scholars, pastors, and teachers (of various theological persuasions) are strongly inclined to base their eschatology largely on the traditional interpretations of a denomination or of a particular theological school of thought, and thereby fail to adequately consider whether the prewrath position may in fact be true. When they come to a text whose plain meaning does not fit those preconceived positions, they often semiticize it (i.e., consider it a Hebraism), spiritualize it, allegorize it, culturalize it, or rationalize it — and thereby fail to accurately understand what the passage really means.

Unfortunately, holding to preconceived conclusions can have serious consequences. It was rabbinical presuppositions and traditions that kept most of the Jewish religious leaders from accepting Jesus as the Messiah. It was also the disciples' predisposition to human ideas that prevented them from believing Jesus' predictions of His imminent arrest, affliction, death, and resurrection. It was because of his personal convictions based on traditional teaching about the Messiah that Peter contradicted His Lord to His face, only a few minutes after confessing Him as being the Messiah and Son of God (see Matt. 16:15-23).

These dangers were underscored further by the Apostle Paul in writing to the church at Thessalonica. No single book in the New Testament more clearly supports the prewrath position than does Second Thessalonians, a book devoted almost entirely to the timing of Christ's return. Paul begins with the warning, "Let no one in any way deceive you, for it [the day of the Lord, when the church is gathered together to Him] will not come unless . . ." (2 Thess. 2:3). With that warning in mind, Paul's statement near the end of the third chapter is of extreme importance in regard to eschatology, which is the overall focus of this letter. "And if anyone does not obey [listen to attentively] our instruction [words] in this letter," he warns, "take special note of that man and do not associate with him, so that he may be put to shame. And yet do not regard him as an enemy, but admonish him as a brother" (2 Thess. 3:14, 15).

In other words, anyone who teaches doctrine contrary to that which Paul clearly presents in this letter is to be ostracized by the church. The reason for the severity of that warning will become progressively clearer to the reader as the truth and significance of the prewrath position becomes better understood.

THE IMPORTANCE OF THE PREWRATH POSITION

If, as this volume strongly insists, Christ will not rapture His church until sometime *during* the great tribulation by Antichrist — rather than *before* the seventieth week or *before* the great tribulation by Antichrist begins — the significance for Christians is almost inestimable. It is absolutely true, of course, that a Christian's view of the end times in no way affects his salvation. But one's view of the end times will have exceeding importance for believers who must suffer or be in real danger of the worst human oppression of all time. In fact, the whole reason that this book is written is to help prepare those Christians — which may well include the author and many readers — for the cataclysmic days that lie ahead. Christians who experience any part of the events occurring during the seventieth week — from the relatively mild shudderings of the initial "birth pangs" to the unmerciful atrocities of the great tribulation by Antichrist — will need to know the full truth of those times if they are to remain faithful to their Lord and confident in His Word.

THE PURPOSE OF THIS BOOK

It is my great hope that the truths this book presents will be used of God to encourage and strengthen His children for personal faithfulness and holiness; for witnessing to the lost, especially to lost Jews; and for steadfastness in sound doctrinal teaching, especially in the areas of prophecy concerning the last days. As will be seen in the next chapter, what a believer thinks about the last days cannot but have a strong bearing on how he will live both before and during those days.

Despite the author's firm position that the views expressed here are in accord with a right interpretation of Scripture and are of immense importance to the church, the primary purpose of this volume is not to debate or refute other views, although that is not completely avoidable. But to the degree that other positions cannot be harmonized with Scripture, the admonition of Paul just mentioned above, concerning what is taught about the last days, must not be quickly overlooked or rationalized away. That is God's warning, not man's. And I realize that it is a two-edged sword that applies as fully to my own views as to those of anyone else.

The purpose of this book, then, is to acquaint readers with the biblical sequence and importance of the many events that will occur during the end times. The subject is so vast that although the statements and conclusions in this volume cover many areas and are extensively documented from Scripture, no claim is made for this being an exhaustive study of biblical eschatology. But readers will be thoroughly exposed to the sequence of events that I believe harmonizes, without contradiction or significant omission, all Scripture concerning the last days. All issues of significance are presented and dealt with in a systematic and logical order that not only should bring greater understanding of the end times but should shed light on passages that heretofore may have seemed perplexing and unexplainable.

The book will trace the momentous events of the end times — events that will *actually happen in history*, possibly in our own lifetime. Many of those events are extremely sobering, even frightening, but they are a part of God's revealed truth and must not be ignored. Paul warned the Thessalonian believers, "But you, brethren, are not in darkness, that the day should overtake you like a thief; for you are all sons of light and sons of day. We are not of night nor of darkness; so then let us not sleep as others do, but let us be alert and sober" (1 Thess. 5:4-6). If such counsel was important for the church of Paul's day, how much more important is it for our day, when so many end-time precursors have already taken place, as will be discussed in greater detail in chapter 10.

In the admonition just cited, Paul makes clear that believers have no excuse for being taken by surprise in the end times. But he makes just as clear that it is not only possible but certain that *untaught believers* can and will be caught by surprise. In His Olivet Discourse, Christ declared that "false Christs and false prophets will arise and will show great signs and wonders, so as to mislead, if possible, even the elect" (Matt. 24:24). Christ's people cannot be separated from His salvation, but they *can be*, and often are, led away from His absolute truth, His intimate fellowship, and His gracious and always-sufficient protection and provision.

The primary purpose of this book, therefore, is to edify believers about the end times and, most especially, to help spiritually prepare those who will be called to live through those cataclysmic times. To be forewarned is to be forearmed. The significance of that statement will be seen time and again as we progress through this volume.

THE FORMAT OF THIS BOOK

I have written this book with a view to making each chapter as readable as possible to the average churchgoer. A considerable amount of Scripture is quoted directly in the text, and references are given for much more, in order to establish every argument and conclusion as completely as possible on God's Word.

Some of the positions developed in the book involve the presentation of considerable amounts of information and technical defenses. For the most part these are covered at length in the endnotes, for those who wish to undertake more in-depth study. Many of the notes are therefore rather long, but they are of great importance in the defense of the positions discussed. Endnotes are also used to provide bibliographic documentation for material quoted or otherwise used in support of the text.

An extensive Glossary is also provided toward the end of the book. The reader is encouraged to refer to this whenever a technical term, phrase, or concept is unfamiliar.

A special feature of the book is the chart of the end times attached to the inside cover of the book. The chart may be easily removed for reference while reading the book. My hope is that the reader will find the chart to be an invaluable help while reading the book and in understanding the flow of events during the end times.

A CONCLUDING WORD

In concluding this chapter, I would re-emphasize how essential the subject matter of this book is for everyone who reads it. The issues being dealt with are not a matter of imagination or religious speculation, but of God's prophetic truth. Someday, perhaps in the near future, our children or grandchildren, or even we ourselves, will face the actual events described in the following pages. And what we think about the last days will have enormous consequences on how we will live both before and during those days.

My great hope is that God will, by His grace, use the truths presented in this book to encourage and strengthen His own, to call believers to faithfulness and godly living, to reach many who are lost — and above all to bring glory to His name.

A Warning to the Church

I t would be hard to overemphasize the urgency of the message of this book. What Christians believe about the end times, especially as those times seem so clearly to be drawing near, is of utmost practical as well as spiritual importance. Sadly, countless Christians in reality have abandoned any interest in the return of Christ, or are seriously mistaken in their understanding. Both kinds of Christians will be completely unprepared for the momentous events of the last days, as Satan wreaks havoc on the earth and attempts especially to pour out his vengeance on believers during the great tribulation of Antichrist.

But there is no reason to be unprepared. As this book attempts to show, the degree to which Christians will be persecuted by Antichrist and his ungodly forces in the last days (especially during the great tribulation) will be directly dependent on the degree to which we are spiritually prepared. For this reason the Lord has given us His Word — to provide everything we need to know for our understanding and preparation for the last days. Some of the most essential teaching concerning this is found in Christ's letters to the seven churches recorded in Revelation 2 and 3 — where Christ gives both warning and encouragement to His people on their preparedness for that unparalleled time of testing through persecution. We turn now to this timely message, with its "near" application to the church of the first century and its critically important "far" application to the end times.

THE SEVEN CHURCHES OF REVELATION

The book of Revelation begins with John's salutation to the seven churches, ending with this testimony: "Behold, He [that is, Christ Himself] is coming with the clouds, and every eye will see Him, even those who pierced Him; and all the tribes of the earth will mourn over Him" (1:7). The second to last passage in the book of Revelation closes in the same manner: "'Yes, I am coming quickly.' Amen. Come, Lord Jesus" (22:20). From beginning to end, that is what this prophetic book is all about — the return of Christ.

For this reason our Lord gave a series of messages to His beloved apostle John that were to be sent to seven churches that existed in Asia Minor (modern western Turkey) in the latter part of the first century. Christ begins His revelation to John by exhorting its readers, the churches of all ages, to carefully hear and faithfully obey "the words of the prophecy, and heed the things which are written in it" (1:3). Near the close of this last book of His revealed Word, the Lord reminds John: "I, Jesus, have sent My angel to testify to you these things for the churches. I am the root and the offspring of David, the bright morning star" (22:16). The book of Revelation is directed to "the churches" — not only to the seven churches in Asia Minor of John's day, but also to all churches throughout the world who will encounter the Satanically inspired and empowered trials and afflictions of the end times.

Through the mediation of specially-appointed angels, each letter was directed specifically to the church that bore its name (see 2:1 — 3:22). Yet each message includes a call to *all* believers from that day forward, especially to those who will be living in the end times, to think about and heed with the utmost seriousness the messages to all seven churches. "He who has an ear," Jesus admonished at the end of each letter, "let him hear what the Spirit says to the churches" (2:7; cf. 1:11, 17, 29; 3:6, 13, 22).

These seven letters exemplify perfectly the near/far type of prophecies explained in chapter 1 of this book, common in both the Old and New Testaments. The seven churches do not represent stages in church history, but rather depict historical New Testament churches that exemplify various characteristics found in churches during all periods of church history and, *as the language clearly states*, will particularly characterize the condition of the church in the final days.

THREE REPRESENTATIVE TYPES OF CHURCHES

As we study the letters carefully, it becomes evident that the seven churches can be grouped into three basic types — represented by Thyatira, Sardis, and Philadelphia — which are representative of all seven churches. But it is also clear that these three basic types are especially representative of the churches which will face the last days. These three types may be summarized as follows:*

THE FAITHFUL CHURCH — PHILADELPHIA

The church at Philadelphia was a spiritual jewel among the seven churches mentioned in Revelation 2 and 3. The letter to this church contains several admonitions but no warnings or rebukes. The Lord begins His commendation by saying, "I know your deeds. Behold, I have put before you an open door which no one can shut, because you have a little power, and have kept My word, and have not denied My name. Behold, . . . I have loved you" (Rev. 3:8, 9).

Christ continued to encourage those believers with the gracious promise: "Because you have kept the word of My perseverance, I also will keep you from the hour of testing, that hour which is about to come upon the whole world, to test those who dwell upon the earth" (3:10). Later in the epistle we learn the meaning of true perseverance. John beheld that

> another angel, a third one, followed them, saying with a loud voice, "If anyone worships the beast and his image, and receives a mark on his forehead or upon his hand, he also will drink of the wine of the wrath of God, which is mixed in full strength in the cup of His anger; and he will be tormented with fire and brimstone in the presence of the holy angels and in the presence of the Lamb. And the smoke of their torment goes up forever and ever; and they have no rest day and night, those who worship the beast

* These three basic types might also be thought of as a three-part continuum, with the *faithful church* (Philadelphia) at one end, the *dead church* (Sardis) at the other end, and the *compromising churches* (Ephesus, Smyrna, Pergamum, Thyatira, and Laodicea), representing varying degrees of compromise, in the middle.

and his image, and whoever receives the mark of his name." *Here is the perseverance of the saints* who keep the commandments of God and their faith in Jesus. (14:9-12, emphasis added)

Christ goes on to tell the Philadelphian overcomers that because of their perseverance, He "will keep [them] from the hour of testing" (Rev. 3:10b). "Keep" translates a Greek verb that carries the basic idea of protection *within* a sphere of danger, and "from" has the basic meaning of *deliverance* "out from," or "out from within."[1] In other words, God promises faithful churches that He will guard them while they are within this particular sphere of danger, in the context of "the hour of testing," promising them eventual safe deliverance "out from within" this danger.

What exactly is the sphere of danger that faithful churches are promised protection from? Most students of prophecy agree that "the hour of testing" can only refer to the great tribulation — the unparalleled affliction of man against man that Antichrist will unleash against those who refuse his mark. This hour of testing will end when Christ cuts short the great tribulation by Antichrist at His second coming (Matt. 24:22) and then wreaks His relentless retaliation on the wicked who remain on earth. "The Lord knows how to rescue the godly from temptation [from the Greek word translated "testing" in Rev. 3:10], and to keep the unrighteous under punishment for the day of judgment" (2 Pet. 2:9).[2]

Therefore, because of her perseverance — that is, her faithfulness to Christ by not denying His name through either worshiping the beast or its image or taking the mark of Antichrist — the faithful church is promised God's protection while within a sphere of great danger (i.e., during the great tribulation by Antichrist) and the eventual removal out from within that dangerous time.

At the end of the letter to the church at Philadelphia, we find this warning: "I [Christ] am coming quickly; hold fast what you have, in order that no one take your crown" (3:11). Because the book of Revelation was written almost half a century after the first coming of Christ, that reference can only be to His second coming. Revelation thus clearly gives "the churches" to which it was written the necessary language to understand that Christ's message to the church at Philadelphia was a near/far prophecy. The near term deals with the historical church that existed when the book was written but which disappeared not long afterward. The far term deals with the faithful churches that will encounter the end-time events revealed in the chapters of Revelation that immediately follow.

What then are the main characteristics we see in the *faithful church* and its experience during the end times? First, we see that the faithful church will persevere, will keep Christ's Word, and will not deny the name of Christ — in other words, she does not take the mark of the beast or worship his image (cf. 14:9). Second, because of her faithfulness, she receives the Lord's gracious promise that He will keep and protect her while *within* the sphere of danger (that is, during the hour of testing, the great tribulation), and that He will eventually deliver her *out from within* this danger — when He returns to "cut short" those days of terrible distress (Matt. 24:21, 22), rapture the church, and pour out His holy wrath on the unrighteous. Lastly, Christ promises that He will give the faithful church a crown and a place of great honor and intimate fellowship with God in His eternal Kingdom (Rev. 3:11, 12).

THE DEAD CHURCH — SARDIS

But when we turn to the church of Sardis, we see that not even the few genuine believers in this dead church are given any assurance of protection. Christ's letter to that church is in marked contrast to the one sent to Philadelphia. He had nothing but words of commendation for the members at Philadelphia, but almost none for those at Sardis.

The Lord told them, "You have a name that you are alive, but you are dead" (3:1) — that is, spiritually dead. They are the tares (counterfeit believers) who will have been sown in among the wheat (true believers) and will exist side by side with the wheat in the kingdom of heaven (the church) until God's time of harvest. Because they will have knowledge of the true gospel, Christ admonishes them, "Remember therefore what you have received and heard; and keep it, and repent" (v. 3a). But their spiritual lifelessness will prevent them from truly hearing spiritual truth. The Lord then adds the severe warning, "If therefore you will not wake up" — that is, repent and receive Him as Savior and Lord, "I will come like a thief, and you will not know at what hour I will come upon you" (v. 3b). Here again, Christ gives a warning to the dead church to awaken or face condemnation. And here again the context is His second coming, indicating that the warning also applies specifically to the churches in the end times.

The *unbelieving* members of the Sardis church will suffer the judgmental destruction of God's fury that will shortly follow, when God's day-of-the-Lord wrath is unleashed upon the unbelieving world at His second coming. During the last days they will be blind to the imminence of the day of the Lord, which will therefore come upon them "just like a thief in the night. While they are saying, 'Peace and safety!' then destruction will come upon them suddenly like birth pangs upon a woman with child; and they shall not escape" (1 Thess. 5:2, 3; cf. 2 Pet. 3:10).

The characteristics and experience of the *spiritually dead church* stand in sharp contrast to the perseverance of the faithful church. First, the dead church will be totally oblivious to the consequences of worshiping Antichrist (the beast) or his image and of taking his mark (Rev. 14:9). Many will do so without hesitation, still thinking themselves to be "good Christians," conforming to the world for the sake of survival instead of trusting in Christ. But, second, the consequences of this will be disastrous. When God's wrath is poured out on the satanic world kingdom ruled by Antichrist, it will come upon these unregenerate church members "like a thief in the night." Thus the end of the spiritually dead church stands in tragic contrast to the faithful church, which is promised God's *protection during the hour of testing* (the great tribulation) and safe *deliverance out from within that hour* just before the awesome day of the Lord.

THE COMPROMISING CHURCH — THYATIRA

But what of the *compromising church* — the church that is not spiritually dead but is less than spiritually faithful, the church that is composed of genuine believers who are alive in Christ but are not living in His will, the church that best characterizes the decaying church at large just before the end times begin?

This was the condition of the church at Thyatira. Many, perhaps most, believers in that church genuinely sought to be faithful and active in the things of the Lord. Christ highly commended them, saying, "I know your deeds, and your love and faith and service and perseverance" (2:19a). Many believers obviously were growing spiritually, and the Lord continued His praise by acknowledging that their "deeds of late are greater than at first" (v. 19b). But the church was also a compromising church.

Like many evangelical, conservative churches throughout history, compromising churches today are not careful about what is being taught the flocks — instead preferring teachers who rationalize, allegorize, spiritualize, culturalize, or semiticize Scripture, anything but taking it for what it says at face value. Jesus therefore goes on to say, "I have this against you, that you tolerate the woman Jezebel, who calls herself a prophetess, and she teaches and leads My bond-servants astray, so that they commit acts of immorality and eat things sacrificed to idols" (2:20).

The tragic revelation of that verse is that false teachers in the church were corrupting the gospel and causing many true believers, Christ's "bond-servants," to stray from right belief and right living. It is probable that the name Jezebel, though in the singular, represented a group of unregenerate church leaders, who, like the wicked Queen Jezebel of 1 Kings 16 and 2 Kings 9, were dedicated to undermining the work of God and corrupting the people of God. That certainly is the case in regard to the far-term application of this prophecy. There is a lesson to learn from this verse for believers in every age, most especially those in the end times. The lesson is that true salvation is not in itself a protection against false doctrine. The believer who is not regularly in God's Word and continually seeking the guidance and strength of God's Spirit is easy prey for those who teach falsehood under the guise of Christianity.

Satan, the great counterfeiter, deceives with half-truths, often using Scripture out of context, as He did with Jesus in the wilderness temptations (Matt. 4:1-11). If he believed that strategy would work with Jesus, he surely will use it against the followers of Christ, including those in the last days who will be facing great danger and will therefore be more vulnerable to deception and confusion. The church that believes biblical prophecies concerning the last days can only be understood allegorically, or that prophecy is in any way less than factual, will be easy prey for Satan's craftiness. The same will be true of churches that have been taught that these passages are to be taken literally but that they have no direct application to them — because they are trusting in the false assurance that they will be raptured away before those events occur. Once such churches discover their great folly, it will be too late to avoid the full brunt of Antichrist's persecution. True believers in those churches will not lose their salvation, but they will endure immeasurable persecution and suffering, from which faithfulness to their Lord and to His Word — like the Philadelphian church — would have otherwise protected them. Thus, genuine believers in compromising churches will experience what our Lord described in the Olivet Discourse as the "great tribulation, such as has not occurred since the beginning of the world until now, nor ever shall" (Matt. 24:21).

It is within the context of the great tribulation by Antichrist that Christ warns both the compromising church of Thyatira and the compromising church that enters the seventieth week, "Behold, I will cast her [the false teachers] upon a bed of sickness, and those who commit [spiritual] adultery with her into *great tribulation,* unless they repent of her deeds" (Rev. 2:22, emphasis added). Christ reveals that two things will happen to that church. First, the false teachers will be cast "upon a bed of sickness" because of their corruption of Christ's "bond-servants." Second, the true but unfaithful believers who have committed spiritual adultery by following those false teachers will suffer "great tribulation, unless they repent." Although they will not forfeit their salvation, they will be subject to the greatest satanic persecution of all times — that is, the affliction, as noted above, that Jesus calls the "great tribulation."

It is especially important to note here that the church definitely *will still be on earth during the great tribulation by Antichrist,* contrary to what many believe. This is shown clearly in Revelation 2:22 when Christ speaks first of the "great tribulation" that the compromising church will experience and then in verse 23 says that "all the churches will know that I am He who searches the minds and hearts." In other words, "all the churches" will be present to see the "great tribulation" (v. 22) of the compromising church at the hands of Antichrist and his ungodly forces; and "all the churches" will then realize who God is, the One "who searches minds and hearts" (v. 23), as they witness firsthand what is happening.

Finally, Christ's message to the church of Thyatira again clearly applies to the last days because of His unqualified promise to return and take them to Himself: "Nevertheless what you have, hold fast until I come" (2:25) — which corresponds perfectly to the second coming references He makes in His letters to Sardis (3:3) and Philadelphia (3:11). All three churches were cautioned about the coming of Christ, and for that reason it is clear that the messages to all three types of churches — the faithful church, the dead church, and the compromising church — are relevant to the end times.

The compromising churches that enter the last days are promised they will be spared God's day-of-the-Lord wrath (Rom. 5:9; 1 Thess. 1:10; 5:9), but not the persecution by Antichrist during his great tribulation of God's elect. They will experience this persecution because they will believe what they have been falsely taught, without testing the words of men against the Word of God. Before Christ terminates the affliction by Antichrist on the compromising churches, He will sovereignly and lovingly use that affliction to cleanse and purify those churches, "to make [them] stand in the presence of His glory blameless" (Jude 24). It is for this very reason that Peter admonishes those looking for the day of the Lord, "[S]ince you look for these things, be diligent to be found by Him in peace, spotless and blameless" (2 Pet. 3:14). Similarly, the writer of Hebrews states: "For those whom the Lord loves He disciplines, and He scourges every son whom He receives. It is for discipline that you endure; God deals with you as with sons" (Heb. 12:6, 7). God's holiness demands that Christ's bride, including the church, be made worthy by being absolutely holy and pure. Thus Paul chastised the compromising Corinthian church because, he said, "I am jealous for you with a godly jealousy; for I betrothed you to one husband, that to Christ I might present you as a pure virgin" (2 Cor. 11:2).

Likewise, Paul states in his first letter to the Corinthians that because they had been enriched in everything by Christ, who was confirmed in them, they should therefore be "awaiting eagerly the revelation of our Lord Jesus Christ, who shall also confirm you to the end, blameless in the day of our Lord Jesus Christ" (1 Cor. 1:7, 8). How much more should this admonition apply to the many compromising churches who will enter the end times!

Again we see the sharp contrast between the compromising and faithful churches. The *compromising church*, the typical church of the last days, will be tested and cleansed before she will be ready to assume the role of Christ's bride. It is not a question of their needing forgiveness of sin, which all true believers receive at the moment of salvation, but of freedom from their willing submission to sin's continuing influence and power. On the other hand, believers who are spiritually prepared (the *faithful church*) for Christ's coming to rescue and receive them into Heaven will also be spiritually prepared for Antichrist's coming to torment and torture them while they are still on earth. The faithful church will be protected from Antichrist and his attacks against the church, with the exception of those Christians who voluntarily waive that protection and risk their lives to win others to Christ before the time of salvation is past (see Matt. 10:16-23; cf. Rev. 6:9).

THREE ESSENTIAL TRUTHS

From Christ's references to His second coming in His letters to the three churches of Revelation 2 — 3 just discussed, we learn three truths about the churches that will enter the last days: (1) *Faithful churches* will be offered God's protection *within a sphere of danger* — that is, protection during the great tribulation by Antichrist, throughout which he will attempt to kill all those who do not worship the beast, Antichrist, or his image. As we have seen earlier, they will be delivered out from within that great tribulation just before the day of the Lord's wrath descends upon the unrighteous. (2) On the other hand, *spiritually dead churches* are told that if they do not repent and turn to Christ, they will lose all opportunity for salvation and will endure the full wrath of His day-of-the-Lord judgment, which will come upon them like a "thief in the night." (3) Genuine but unfaithful believers within the *compromising church*, however, are told that they will face the full brunt of the great tribulation by Antichrist — the fearful "hour of testing" — as a testimony to all the churches that Christ is the one and only true Lord who searches the hearts and minds of men, the one who rewards or punishes with perfect justice and righteousness, as He permits the persecution by Antichrist to purify and prepare His bride to stand pure and blameless in the day of our Lord Jesus Christ.

A FOREWARNING FROM THE LORD

When we take these truths seriously and literally as God intended, they should be terrifying to all who comprise spiritually dead and compromising churches. Yet for this very reason, these truths are just as much evidence of God's grace, as God forewarns His own through His Word to understand and be prepared for the terrible events to come.

In God's dealing with Sodom and Gomorrah we see this same principle and its relevance for the end times. Just before the complete and terrible destruction of Sodom and Gomorrah, an event yet unknown to Abraham, the Lord said to the angels who were visiting the patriarch, "Shall I hide from Abraham what I am about to do, since Abraham will surely become a great and mighty nation, and in him all the nations of the earth will be blessed? For I have chosen him, in order that he may command his children and his household after him to keep the way of the Lord by doing righteousness and justice; in order that the Lord may bring upon Abraham what He has spoken about him" (Gen. 18:17-19). In other words, the warning of the impending disaster upon Sodom and Gomorrah — and the reason for it — was given to Abraham not only for his own sake but also for the sake of those of "his children and his household after him to keep the way of the Lord by doing righteousness and justice."

Just as the destruction of Sodom and Gomorrah is used as an example of the terrible day of the Lord that will someday cut short the great tribulation by Antichrist, so God has carefully chosen to warn His elect church of that impending doom, "in order that [we] may command [our] children and [our] household after [us] to keep the way of the Lord by doing righteousness and justice."

It is for this reason that Christians are cautioned, over and over, to live godly lives, looking for the return of Christ. As the Apostle Peter writes:

> Since all these things are to be destroyed in this way, what sort of people ought you to be *in holy conduct and godliness, looking for and hastening the coming of the day of God*, on account of which the heavens will be destroyed by burning, and the elements will melt with intense heat. But according to His promise we are looking for new heavens and a new earth, in which righteousness dwells. Therefore, beloved, since you look for these things, *be diligent to be found by Him in peace, spotless and blameless.* . . . You therefore, beloved, knowing this beforehand, *be on your guard* lest, being carried away by the error of unprincipled men, you fall from your own steadfastness, but *grow in the grace and knowledge* of our Lord and Savior Jesus Christ. To Him be the glory, both now and to the day of eternity. Amen. (2 Pet. 3:11-14, 17, 18, emphasis added)

Peter's challenge to the believer could not be clearer. *All* believers are to look for the day of the Lord. *All* believers are to be "holy [in] conduct and godliness"; "diligent . . . spotless and blameless"; "on your guard"; "grow[ing] in the grace and knowledge of the Lord." And to the extent to which the believer falls short of this admonition, he will be unprepared for the events to come.

In the Olivet Discourse, Christ gives His people the same admonition to watch for the signs of His coming in order not to be surprised and unprepared: "Now learn the parable from the fig tree: when its branch has already become tender, and puts forth its leaves, you know that summer is near; even so you too, when you see all these things, recognize that He is near, right at the door" (Matt. 24:32, 33). The last comment of Christ in His Olivet Discourse, recorded in Luke 21, sums it all up: "Watch ye therefore, and pray always, that ye may be accounted worthy to escape all these things that shall come to pass, and to stand before the Son of man" (v. 36, KJV).

THREE CONCLUDING CONCERNS

This chapter began by stressing the urgency of the message of this book, and in the preceding pages we have seen the critical significance of this for believers in the past as well as in our own time. It would be hard to overemphasize the urgency of this message, especially as the end times seem so clearly to be drawing near. In concluding this chapter, then, I would draw our attention to these final concerns.

First, what we think about the end times is critically important. Many evangelical Christians have become "agnostic" about the Lord's return, without any interest or understanding concerning end-time events, having spiritualized or allegorized them all away so that they are no longer applicable to the church today. Many others have a sadly mistaken understanding that will leave them completely unprepared, thinking that the events outlined by Christ in His Olivet Discourse or given to John in the book of Revelation concern unrepentant Israel, not the church. To both of these, the Apostle Paul offers a severe warning to "Let no one in any way deceive you" (2 Thess. 2:3). This comes in his second letter to the Thessalonian church, which contains the clearest passage in all of Scripture about the timing of Christ's second coming.[3]

Second, to the degree to which the genuine Christian is prepared, he will either have the protection of God during the great persecution by Antichrist, or will feel the full brunt of Antichrist's fury in his attempt to kill all who will not bow down to him. A believer's theology concerning the last days, therefore, is of immense importance, especially for those who will actually live during those last days.

Third, *we can indeed be prepared*! God has graciously given us His Word to warn us, to instruct us, and to prepare us for the momentous events of the end times. He calls us, therefore, to understanding, to perseverance, to be "looking for and hastening the coming of the day of the Lord," and especially to godliness and holy living in hope and expectation as the end times draw near.

3

The Cosmic Conflict

The cataclysmic events of the end times are the last act of a great cosmic drama extending back through the ages to eternities past. And like any drama, the last act can be understood only in light of all the acts that have come before. But unlike any drama written by men, the cosmic conflict is directed by the Sovereign God of the universe, fulfilling His perfect will and proclaiming His eternal Truth.

This is the drama that starts before the birth of time and spans the ages of human history. This is the drama that explains every tragic experience of pain and sorrow, of sin and suffering, of sickness and death. This is the drama that will end in glorious victory, when God "shall wipe away every tear . . . and there shall no longer be any death . . . [nor] any mourning, or crying, or pain" (Rev. 21:4a), when Christ shall reign forever and ever (Dan. 7:27).

To understand the final act (the end times) of God's great cosmic drama, we need to understand the acts that have been played out before, even before the birth of human history. In this chapter, then, we will trace this cosmic conflict as it begins with Satan's willful rebellion against God, and Adam's willful disobedience in believing Satan's lie; as it unfolds in God's prophetic plan with His choice of Abraham, His chosen people, and His Redeemer and King; and as the last act is played out in the momentous events of the end times, the climactic day of the Lord, and the founding of His eternal kingdom upon earth. This is the cosmic drama — but more than just a drama, it is an actual conflict of cosmic proportions. We turn now to consider an overview of the cosmic conflict, and although many of the topics introduced in this chapter are covered in detail as the book unfolds, it is essential to begin first with a clear understanding of the larger context of the cosmic conflict in order to properly understand what will actually happen during the end times.

GOD'S SOVEREIGNTY

An immense conflict between God and Satan began at the birth of human history when the great archangel Lucifer rebelled against his Creator and Lord. That cosmic conflict has continued unabated since that day. And from the time that Adam was satanically seduced to join in the rejection of God in the Garden of Eden, the thoughts, actions, and lives of every human being (with the single exception of Jesus Christ) have manifested that heavenly conflict.

Yet the course and destiny of the universe are not at the mercy of a cosmic contest between the forces of good and evil with an outcome that is uncertain or unknown. There is indeed an immense and universal *conflict*, but it is not a *contest*, because the Victor was determined in eternity past, long before the conflict began. Nor is the conflict between essentially equal but opposite forces that struggle for supremacy. Good is that which is of God, whereas evil is a corruption of what was once good. And ultimately God will preserve everything that is His (the good) and defeat everything that is not (the evil).

All good in the universe is of the kingdom of God, and all evil in the universe is of the kingdom of Satan. Those are the only two spiritual realms that exist, and every spirit being, including man, belongs to one realm or the other. Those who belong to the realm of goodness (the kingdom of God) are those who are under willing submission to God. Those who belong to the realm of evil (the kingdom of Satan) are those who are under submission to Satan. This is true whether we are conscious of it or not.

The one realm, or kingdom, is righteous; the other is unrighteous.

The one is founded in truth; the other is founded in falsehood. The one is of light; the other is of darkness. The one is infinite; the other is finite. The one is eternal; the other will one day cease to exist. The one is ruled by God from Heaven and encompasses the entire universe, including the domain of the other kingdom. The ruler of the one is the Creator; the ruler of the other was created by Him. The ruler of the one is omnipotent, whereas the ruler of the other has only the power granted to him by his Creator. The ruler of the one is omniscient, whereas the ruler of the other has only the knowledge given to him by his Creator. The ruler of the one is omnipresent, whereas the other ruler's presence is limited to the sphere permitted by his Creator.

Even within his own realm, Satan is not sovereign. Because of his pride, Nebuchadnezzar learned that lesson the hard way. In desperation he cried out to God in the midst of living "with the beasts of the field," where he would stay until he recognized "that the Most High is ruler over the realm of mankind, and bestows it on whomever He wishes" (Dan. 4:32) and that "all the inhabitants of the earth are accounted as nothing, but He does according to His will in the host of heaven and among the inhabitants of earth; and no one can ward off His hand" (v. 35). Only after Nebuchadnezzar acknowledged God's absolute sovereignty was his kingdom restored to him. Satan can no more do with the world entirely as he pleases than he was able do with Job entirely as he pleased (see Job. 1:12; 2:6). Like all other created beings, Satan *has* nothing apart from God's sovereign provision, and he *does* nothing apart from God's sovereign permission.

Like all other created beings, Satan is finite and vulnerable. Evil is the only thing Satan can truly claim as his own; and that evil, vast and pernicious as it is, is circumscribed by divine limits — in degree, in extent, and in time. Satan's intelligence and power not only are *from* God but are *restricted by* God. Satan's conflict with God therefore could not be eternal, because Satan is not eternal. And because "with the Lord one day is as a thousand years, and a thousand years as one day" (2 Pet. 3:8), Satan's rebellion will be but a fleeting blip on the screen of God's eternity.

THE COSMIC CONFLICT BEGINS

The strife with Satan's Creator began at a particular time, and it will end at a particular time; and even during the intervening age, his sphere of influence is divinely proscribed. At God's already designated time, He will put an end to Satan's kingdom and an end to evil. At that same time He will cast Satan — and every creature, angelic and human, identified with Satan — into eternal punishment in the lake of fire, where "they will be tormented day and night forever and ever" (Rev. 19:20; 20:10; 21:8).

Before man fell, Satan fell, and his fall is inextricably related to the fall of man. As Ezekiel explains, Satan became proud of his angelic grandeur, thinking his majesty and intelligence were his by right (Ezek. 28:17). He was foolishly blinded with pride, and, not being omniscient, he believed that with the power he had received from the Creator he somehow could subdue the Creator. It was with that wicked design that the cosmic conflict began.

The supreme ambition of Satan became to usurp God's sovereignty over the earth, especially over man, who was made in God's image and given divine authority to rule the earth as God's steward (Gen. 1:26-28). At Creation, God placed but one restriction on Adam and Eve, warning them that "from the tree of the knowledge of good and evil you shall not eat, for in the day that you eat from it you shall surely die" (Gen. 2:17). Satan contested that warning, in essence calling God a liar. "You surely shall not die," Satan told Eve. "For God knows that in the day you eat from it your eyes will be opened, and you will be like God, knowing good and evil" (Gen. 3:4, 5). The death that came as a consequence of sin was not annihilation but separation from God, a trait that every descendant of Adam and Eve, except for Jesus Christ, would inevitably inherit.

When Adam and Eve chose to believe Satan's word above God's, they chose Satan's lordship above God's; and in that act of disobedience, by default, they lost their rulership over the earth and their spiritual relationship to God. Not only were Adam and Eve and all their posterity corrupted and alienated from God, but the entire world suffered curse and corruption because of their sin (Gen. 3:17; cf. Jer. 12:4; Rom. 8:20).

Because of Adam's sin, two deaths fell upon mankind. The first was spiritual death, which brought eternal, spiritual separation from God. God expelled mankind from His divine realm of spiritual life and light and cast them into the realm of Satan's spiritual death and darkness with the ultimate destiny of the lake of fire — that place where there is eternal separation from God and eternal existence in suffering. The second death caused by the Fall was physical (the separation of man's physical body from his eternal soul which lives forever), and is a consequence of the first.

By leading man into sin, Satan succeeded in dethroning man from his rulership over the earth and arrogantly claimed that authority to himself. He therefore now reigns as ruler of this present world and age (John 12:31; 14:30; 16:11; 2 Cor. 4:4; Eph. 2:1, 2). By Adam's willful act of disobedience, intending to serve himself rather than God, he succeeded in serving neither himself nor God but only Satan. "Just as through one man sin entered into the world, and death through sin," Paul explains, "so death [spiritual death, eternal separation from God] spread to all men, because all sinned" (Rom. 5:12). From that time forward mankind was destined to serve Satan, whose reign over the fallen earth and fallen man God has sovereignly tolerated for a limited period of time. Until God supernaturally reverts full Lordship of the earth to Himself, "the whole world lies in the power of the evil one" (1 John 5:19; cf. Luke 4:5, 6).

Just as Satan became spiritually blinded and condemned when he rebelled against God, in the same way he led fallen mankind into spiritual blindness and condemnation. "[T]he god of this world has blinded the minds of the unbelieving, that they might not see the light of the gospel of the glory of Christ, who is the image of God" (2 Cor. 4:4).

GOD'S PROPHETIC PLAN

God, however, made it known to Satan that his rule over mankind was temporary and that Satan's reign would, in God's sovereign time, be destroyed. While Adam and Eve were still in the Garden of Eden, God made clear to Satan how his defeat would come, saying, "I will put enmity between you and the woman, and between your seed and her seed; he shall bruise you on the head, and you shall bruise him on the heel" (Gen. 3:15). In other words, a male descendant of the woman would bring the ultimate downfall and destruction of Satan. That descendant would come from the line of Abraham (Gal. 3:16), just as God promised. "I will make you a great nation," God said to Abraham, "and I will bless you, and make your name great; and so you shall be a blessing; and I will bless those who bless you, and the one who curses you I will curse. And in you all the families of the earth shall be blessed" (Gen. 12:2, 3). Satan would manage to bruise that descendant, Jesus Christ, "on the heel," through the crucifixion of Christ at His first coming. But Christ rose from the dead, and eventually He will bruise

Satan on the head, returning authority over the earth back to its rightful ruler, God Almighty (Rev. 11:15). Ultimately Satan will be cast into
the eternal lake of fire, where he "will be tormented day and night forever and ever" (Rev. 20:10).

To redeem back certain men and women belonging to the kingdom
of Satan, and to reclaim back the corrupted earth from the reign of
Satan, God put into motion a prophetic plan — a simple but divinely
perfect plan upon which both the Old and New Testaments are
founded. Through this plan God will eventually reclaim His rule over
earth. But first He must secure for Himself a nation of believers living
on earth who will yield completely to the rule of His Son, Jesus Christ.
That future kingdom of Christ (the millennial kingdom, made up of
this nation of believers living on earth), will be a consummate recre-
ated order and dominion not unlike that of the Garden of Eden in
which Adam and Eve lived before the Fall.

How will God accomplish all of this? God has graciously revealed
in Scripture a great deal concerning His prophetic plan, the main
points of which may be seen in the six steps as summarized below:

(1) God Chose His Own People

The first step is that *God chose His own people to be the spiritual descendants of Abraham*. In his letter to Ephesus Paul explains that God chose
people (not a *nation*) to become His spiritual children, people who
would trust and obey Him. "He [God the Father] chose us in Him
[God the Son, Jesus Christ] before the foundation of the world," the
apostle says, "that we should be holy and blameless before Him [the
Father]. In love He predestined us to adoption as sons through Jesus
Christ to Himself, according to the kind intention of His will"
(Eph. 1:4, 5).

Later in that epistle Paul reminds the chosen children of God: "You
were [spiritually] dead in your trespasses and sins, in which you formerly walked according to the course of this world, according to the
prince of the power of the air, of the spirit that is now working in the
sons of disobedience. . . . But God, being rich in mercy, because of His
great love with which He loved us, even when we were dead in our
transgressions, made us [spiritually] alive together with Christ"
(Eph. 2:1, 2, 4, 5).

As seen earlier, the promises of God were given to Abraham,
through whom "all the families of the earth shall be blessed" (Gen.
12:3). However, God ordained that no one would become one of His

chosen saints merely because of Jewish ancestry (see point 3 of God's prophetic plan), but would be counted worthy before Him solely through the divinely bestowed faith He would give to those chosen by God (Eph. 2:8, 9; cf. Gen. 14:6; Heb. 11:1, 2). Only those who received this faith would be the spiritual descendants of Abraham. As Paul writes, "the promise to Abraham or to his descendants that he would be heir of the world was not through the Law, but through the right-eousness of faith" (Rom. 4:13); and again, "For by grace [God's unmer-ited favor] you have been saved through faith; and that [the faith] not of yourselves, it is the gift of God; not as a result of works, that no one should boast" (Eph. 2:8, 9). As Paul also explains, "They are not all Israel [and never had been] who are descended from Israel; neither are they all children because they are Abraham's descendants. . . . That is, it is not the children of the *flesh* [the natural line of Abraham] who are children of God, but the children of the *promise* [the spiritual line of Abraham] are regarded as descendants" (Rom. 9:6-8, emphasis added).

It is for this reason that Christ told the Jews who had professed to believe in Him, "If you are Abraham's children, do the deeds of Abraham. But as it is, you are seeking to kill Me, a man who has told you the truth, which I heard from God; this Abraham did not do. You are doing the deeds of your father. . . . You are of your father the devil, and you want to do the desires of your father" (John 8:39-41, 44). Paul therefore assures both Jews and Gentiles: "If you belong to Christ, then you are Abraham's offspring, heirs according to promise" (Gal. 3:29). Gentiles are included in the spiritual line of Abraham because "by their [Israel's] transgression salvation has come to the Gentiles" (Rom. 11:11).

God's chosen spiritual line was originally to come primarily from within the chosen physical line of the nation of Israel that He established through Abraham, but because that nation continued in unbelief and disobedience, "salvation has come to the Gentiles, to make them [Israel] jealous" (Rom. 11:11). Only after "the fulness of the Gentiles has come in . . . all Israel [the nation] will be saved" (vv. 25, 26).

When we speak of God's chosen people, then, we speak of all who are the spiritual descendants of Abraham, both Jews and Gentiles — all who have received the divinely bestowed gift of faith and who through faith trust and obey Him.

(2) God Chose Messiah (Christ)

The second step is that *God chose Messiah (Christ) to redeem His chosen people*. In his first epistle Peter reminded those "who are chosen" (1:1), "You were not redeemed with perishable things like silver or gold from your futile way of life inherited from your forefathers, but with precious blood, as of a lamb unblemished and spotless, the blood of Christ. For He was foreknown before the foundation of the world" (1:18-20). In other words, long before He created the world, God chose the Lamb, the Messiah, to redeem His elect back from the kingdom of Satan.

The coming Messiah's first purpose was to pay the penalty of sin for those whom God chose in Christ "before the foundation of the world" (Eph. 1:4). In this regard, Isaiah depicts Christ's work of redemption as if it had already come to pass: "Surely our griefs He Himself bore, and our sorrows He carried; yet we ourselves esteemed Him stricken, smitten of God, and afflicted. But He was pierced through for our transgressions, He was crushed for our iniquities; the chastening for our well-being fell upon Him, and by His scourging we are healed. All of us like sheep have gone astray, each of us has turned to his own way; but the Lord has caused the iniquity of us all to fall on Him. . . . As a result of the anguish of His soul, He will see it and be satisfied; by His knowledge the Righteous One, My Servant, will justify the many, as He will bear their iniquities" (Isa. 53:4-6, 11).

(3) God Chose the Nation Israel

The third step is that *God chose the nation Israel (the natural line of Abraham) through which Messiah (Christ) would come*. To redeem a chosen remnant of mankind back to God, a price had to be paid to satisfy His holiness and justice, a price so immeasurably high that it could be satisfied only through the shedding of the blood of an absolutely pure and sinless sacrifice. God sovereignly ordained that this sacrifice for the sin of the world would come through the nation of Israel, fathered by Abraham and divinely protected on earth in order that the sacrificial Messiah could not be cut off until He paid the necessary price for the redemption of this elect people of God's own choosing. This nation, then, is the natural line of Abraham — the Jews — the nation of Israel. For this reason, the Lord declared to Abraham, "I will make you a great nation, and I will bless you, and make your name great; and so you shall be a blessing; and I will bless those who bless you, and the one who curses you I will curse. And in you all the families of the earth shall be blessed" (Gen. 12:2, 3).

As seen in point 1 above, many Jews living in disobedience to God tried to claim the promises given to the spiritual line of Abraham. But Abraham's natural descendants merely formed the line through which the Redeemer would come. God's physical blessings of the people were given in response to their obedience to His law, but His spiritual blessings were bestowed solely as acts of His sovereign grace.

God's promise to Abraham was unconditional. But the natural line of Israel fathered by Abraham's descendants were free, *while on earth*, either to obey the God who chose them and receive His gracious blessings, or to disobey Him and receive their deserved curses. Through Moses, the Lord told Israel: "Now it shall be, *if you will diligently obey the Lord your God*, being careful to do all His commandments which I command you today, *the Lord your God will set you high above all the nations of the earth.* . . . But it shall come about, *if you will not obey the Lord your God*, to observe to do all His commandments and His statutes which I charge you today, that *all these curses shall come upon you and overtake you*" (Deut. 28:1, 15, emphasis added).

Although this chosen nation of God, the natural line of Abraham, would enjoy His special protection on earth until the Messiah would come and fulfill His mission, this nation — as a nation — *never* comprised the *spiritual* people of God, but only the natural line through which Messiah would come.

(4) God Chose When to Destroy Satan's Kingdom

The fourth step is, *God chose when He would destroy the kingdom of Satan, at a future time, during the day of the Lord*. God gave repeated promises and warnings to the nation of Israel that just before He comes to earth to reign over His chosen people He will first — in preparation for that day — destroy the kingdom of darkness — that is, the kingdom of earth over which Satan now rules. He gave the *promises* to the obedient, spiritual descendants of Abraham and the *warnings* to the disobedient, natural descendants of Abraham, who refused to trust in their true Messiah. That specific time will be "the day of the Lord," when God will unleash His unparalleled wrath on all ungodliness, utterly and eternally destroying Satan's usurped earthly kingdom and all of its inhabitants.

With terrifying vividness, the prophet Zephaniah describes that awful day:

Near is the great day of the Lord, near and coming very quickly; listen, the day of the Lord! In it the warrior cries out bitterly. A day of wrath is that day, a day of trouble and distress, a day of destruction and desolation, a day of darkness and gloom, a day of clouds and thick darkness, a day of trumpet and battle cry, against the fortified cities and the high corner towers. And I will bring distress on men, so that they will walk like the blind, because they have sinned against the Lord; and their blood will be poured out like dust, and their flesh like dung. Neither their silver nor their gold will be able to deliver them on the day of the Lord's wrath; and all the earth will be devoured in the fire of His jealousy, for He will make a complete end, indeed a terrifying one, of all the inhabitants of the earth. (Zeph. 1:14-18)

(5) GOD CHOSE WHEN TO SAVE THE NATION ISRAEL

The fifth step is that *God chose when He would save the nation Israel (the natural line of Abraham), after the seventieth week of Daniel* is complete.* From the beginning, the natural line of Abraham (Israel) was never synonymous with the elect people of God, the spiritual descendants of Abraham. Although many individual Jews have been and are among God's elect, nevertheless, as we have seen, "they are not all Israel who are descended from Israel; neither are they all children because they are Abraham's descendants. . . . That is, it is not the children of the flesh who are children of God, but the children of the promise are regarded as descendants" (Rom. 9:6-8).

Yet God determined that one day *all the nation of Israel* (the entire natural line of Abraham through which the Redeemer would come) will become "the children of promise," when "the fullness of the Gentiles [the end of the seventieth week] has come in; and thus all Israel will be saved" (Rom. 11:25, 26). But first, "'I will turn my hand against the little ones,'" God revealed to Zechariah, "'And it will come about in all the land . . . that two parts in it will be cut off and perish; but the third will be left in it. And I will bring the third through the fire, refine them as silver is refined, and test them as gold is tested. [Then]

---

* See the Glossary and chapter 5 for a full explanation and discussion of the "seventieth week of Daniel."

they will call on My name, and I will answer them; I will say "They are My people," and they will say "The Lord is my God"'" (Zech. 13:7b-9). That glorious day will occur only after the seventieth week of Daniel is complete, when God will bring the surviving remnant of that entire chosen nation into "everlasting righteousness" (Dan. 9:24).

As Ezekiel declared:

> Therefore, say to the house of Israel, "Thus says the Lord God, 'It is not for your sake, O house of Israel, that I am about to act, but for My holy name, which you have profaned among the nations where you went. . . . For I will take you from the nations, gather you from all the lands, and bring you into your own land. Then I will sprinkle clean water on you, and you will be clean; I will cleanse you from all your filthiness and from all your idols. . . . And I will put My Spirit within you and cause you to walk in My statutes, and you will be careful to observe My ordinances.'" (Ezek. 36:22, 24, 25, 27)

(6) GOD CHOSE WHEN TO MAKE CHRIST KING

The last step is that *God chose the precise time Christ would become King over all the earth.* Referring to this precise time, when God will restore Christ's reign over earth, Daniel declared: "Then I kept looking because of the sound of the boastful words which the horn [Antichrist] was speaking; I kept looking until the beast [Antichrist] was slain [at Armageddon], and its body was destroyed and given to the burning fire. . . . I kept looking in the night visions, and behold, with the clouds of heaven, One like a Son of Man [Christ] was coming, and He came up to the Ancient of Days [God Almighty] and was presented before Him. And to Him [Christ] was given dominion, glory and a kingdom, that all the peoples, nations, and men of every language might serve Him. His dominion is an everlasting dominion which will not pass away" (Dan. 7:11, 13, 14).

When the seventh trumpet is blown, just after the completion of the seventieth week and the subsequent salvation of the natural line of Israel several days later, the reign over earth will be reclaimed by God (Rev. 11:15). Several weeks later, after Antichrist and his armies are defeated by Christ and He has reclaimed the physical possession of earth, then the reign over earth will be given by the Ancient of Days to Christ. Then "the Lord [Christ] will be king over all the earth; in that day the Lord will be the only one, and His name the only one" (Zech. 14:9). Satan must and will do all he can to prevent that event, knowing it will bring to an end his rule over the earth and bring about his final and permanent defeat in the cosmic conflict.

When we bring these six steps together, the simplicity of God's divinely perfect plan is plain to see:

1. *God chose His own people* to be the spiritual descendants of Abraham.

2. *God chose Messiah (Christ)* to redeem His chosen people and destroy the kingdom of Satan.

3. *God chose the nation Israel* (the natural line of Abraham) through which Messiah (Christ) would come.

4. *God chose when He would destroy the kingdom of Satan* — at a future time, during the day of the Lord.

5. *God chose when He would save the nation Israel* (the natural line of Abraham) — but not before the seventieth week is complete.

6. *God chose when Christ would become King over all the earth* — but only after the salvation of the entire natural line of Abraham and the final defeat of Antichrist and his armies at the battle of Armageddon.

Simple as God's plan is, it is also costly beyond measure, as Jesus Christ, the only Son of God, shed His precious blood in atonement for our sin.

GOD'S PROPHETIC MAN

To accomplish the prophetic plan of God and the overthrow of Satan, Christ, the second person of the Godhead, became the seed of a woman and would come to earth at two different times in the history of mankind. At His first coming He permanently reversed the consequences of sin — that is, spiritual death, which is eternal separation from God — and paid the price for the redemption of a people of His own choosing from the kingdom of darkness ruled by Satan (Eph. 1:3 — 2:7). At His second coming He will bring judgment upon the kingdom of Satan and salvation to the remnant of the natural line of Abraham — to all those who, at the risk of their own lives, have refused to worship Antichrist or his image and who, by God's grace alone, somehow survive the seventieth week. This will be in direct contrast to Adam and Eve in the Garden and to their forefathers at the crucifixion of Christ. With the destruction of every living inhabitant of the kingdom of Satan, and with the salvation of the remnant of the natural line of Abraham, Satan's rule over earth will be brought to an end and Christ's millennial reign will begin.

CHRIST'S FIRST COMING

The first coming of Christ accomplished four specific things. First, Christ came as the Passover Lamb *to permanently pay the price of sin* — that price being the death of the perfect Lamb provided by God, paid through the shedding of His blood at Calvary.

Second, Christ came as the Passover Lamb *to permanently overcome the effect of sin* — that is, to set man free from spiritual death, eternal separation of man's soul from the presence of God.

Third, Christ came as the Passover Lamb *to permanently redeem those chosen to be His people*, the spiritual line of Abraham, back from the kingdom of darkness. What Christ accomplished through His death, therefore, is exactly what we find described in Romans where Paul wrote: "through one man sin entered into the world, and death through sin, and so death spread to all men, because all sinned . . . so through the obedience of the One [i.e., through Christ's atoning death] the many will be made righteous" (5:12, 19). "The blood of Jesus His Son cleanses us from all sin" (1 John 1:7). And because of this, those chosen (redeemed by the blood of Christ) are to look "for the blessed hope and the appearing of the glory of our great God and Savior, Christ Jesus; who gave Himself for us, that He might redeem us from every lawless deed and purify for Himself a people for His own possession, zealous for good deeds" (Titus 2:12-14).

The fourth essential purpose of Christ's first coming is that it *spelled the certain doom of Satan and his rule over the earth*. When Christ gave His life on the cross, Satan believed this would surely be his greatest victory, thereby eliminating Christ, the Redeemer, forever. But what was seen by Satan as his own certain victory became his own certain defeat when Christ was raised three days later. In fulfillment of Genesis 3:15, Satan did indeed bruise the heel of Christ; but by His death and resurrection Christ will bruise the head of Satan and secure the decisive victory in the end times. Christ therefore is the One who would be found worthy to ultimately judge the kingdom of Satan at His second coming. As Christ explained to the disciples just before His death: "For this purpose I came to this hour. . . . Now judgment is upon this world; now the ruler of this world shall be cast out" (John 12:27b, 31). Paul further explained this momentous truth, as recorded in Acts: "God is now declaring to men that all everywhere should repent, because He has fixed a day [the day of the Lord] in which He will judge the world in righteousness through a Man [Christ] whom He has appointed, having furnished proof to all men by raising Him from the dead" (Acts 17:30, 31).

With the second coming of Christ, the decisive victory secured through His death and resurrection will come to its ultimate consummation.

CHRIST'S SECOND COMING

With the second coming of Christ, the great cosmic drama comes to its most climactic moment. Words cannot begin to describe the awesome spectacle of Christ returning in great power and glory with His holy angels. The stunning reality of what is actually happening will be understood around the world in a moment, striking the lost with terror and the redeemed with unspeakable joy.

Of this climactic event, Scripture reveals at least four major objectives that Christ's return will fulfill.

First, God's Word predicts that *Christ will rescue His elect* when He appears, before He systematically and thoroughly destroys the inhabitants of the kingdom of Satan in His day-of-the-Lord judgment. This judgment is compared to the destruction by water of all mankind in Noah's day, when only he and his family were saved in the ark. It is also compared to the destruction of Sodom and Gomorrah by fire and brimstone in Lot's day, when only he and his family were allowed to escape (Matt. 24:37-39; Luke 17:26-30; 2 Pet. 2:4-9). Yet, like Noah and his family and Lot and his family, God will rescue the elect before he destroys the wicked. In Peter's words, "The Lord knows how to rescue the godly from temptation [testing], and to keep the unrighteous under punishment for the day of judgment" (2 Pet. 2:9).

Second, when Christ returns *He will destroy all the unrighteous* during the day of the Lord. The prophet Zephaniah foretold that "on the day of the Lord's wrath . . . all the earth will be devoured in the fire of His jealousy, for He will make a complete end, indeed a terrifying one, of all the inhabitants of the earth" (Zeph. 1:18). And as the prophet Isaiah wrote, God will in that day "punish the world for its evil, and the wicked for their iniquity" (Isa. 13:11a). Likewise, Peter explains, "But the present heavens and earth by His word are being reserved for fire, kept for the day of judgment and destruction of ungodly men" (2 Pet. 3:7).

Third, *Christ will reclaim for God the natural line of Abraham (Israel)* that survives the seventieth week of Daniel. He will return to earth "for the salvation of Thy people, for the salvation of Thine anointed" (Hab. 3:13). Then "'They will look on Me whom they have pierced; and they will mourn for Him'" (Zech. 12:10). "'And I will bring the third part [the surviving remnant of Israel] through the fire, refine them as silver is refined, and test them as gold is tested. They will call on My name, and I will answer them; I will say, "They are My people," and they will say "The Lord is My God"'" (Zech. 13:9). *Only* after the salvation of the remnant of Israel that survives the seventieth week will "the kingdom of the world . . . become the kingdom of our Lord, and of His Christ; and He will reign forever and ever" (Rev. 11:15).

Fourth and finally, *Christ will reclaim physical possession of the earth* when He defeats Antichrist and his armies at the final battle of Armageddon. As described vividly in Revelation:

And I saw heaven opened; and behold, a white horse, and He who sat upon it [Christ] is called Faithful and True; and in right-eousness He judges and wages war. . . . And I saw the beast [Antichrist] and the kings of the earth and their armies, assembled to make war against Him who sat upon the horse, and against His army. And the beast was seized, and with him the false prophet who performed the signs in his presence, by which he deceived those who had received the mark of the beast and those who worshiped his image; these two were thrown alive into the lake of fire which burns with brimstone. And the rest were killed with the sword which came from the mouth of Him who sat upon the horse, and all the birds were filled with their flesh. (Rev. 19:11, 19-21)

After that time, when Antichrist and his armies are defeated and killed at the battle of Armageddon, "the Lord [Christ] will be king over all the earth; in that day the Lord will be the only one, and His name the only one" (Zech. 14:9).

And so through Christ God will bring to fulfillment His purposes as determined in eternity past, to "accomplish all [His] good pleasure" (Isa. 46:10). His purpose and good pleasure, as outlined above are: (1) to redeem for Himself those elected before the foundation of the world (Eph. 1:4; cf. Rom. 8:29, 30); (2) to bring the chosen nation of Israel to Himself (Rom. 11:1, 2, 26, 27); (3) to bring an end to Satan's rule over the earth (Rev. 11:15) — to destroy the inhabitants and armies of the kingdom of Satan (Zeph. 1:18; cf. Rev. 19:11-21); and (4) to establish Christ as rightful King (Dan. 7:11-14, 26, 27; cf. Zech. 14:9) over an earthly kingdom in "a new heaven and a new earth" (Rev. 21:1-8).

SATAN'S COUNTERATTACK

Blinded by his unbounded pride, Satan has his own strategy. But in one sense it is no strategy at all, but rather a desperate attempt to counterattack God's plan, played out within the strict limits of God's sovereignty and with a preordained conclusion revealed unequivocally in God's Word. *History has already played out the failures of the first two phases of Satan's futile strategy*, which are briefly described below. Not being omniscient, Satan no doubt believes that his final strategy will become reality, even though its failure was long ago predicted in God's Word. That final scheme, which is yet to come, will be equally futile.

(1) DESTROY OR DISQUALIFY THE LINE OF CHRIST

Satan's first strategy — *his attempt to destroy or disqualify the line of Messiah (Christ)* — is history, the results of which are recorded carefully in Scripture. As soon as Satan became aware of God's intentions, his counteroffensive was to try to *disqualify* by deception or to *destroy* by Gentile nations the nation of Israel, from whom the Redeemer and King would come.

Through the nation of Israel God promised that "all the families of the earth shall be blessed" (Gen. 12:3), because "salvation [Christ, the Redeemer] is from the Jews" (John 4:22). God sovereignly designated Israel as the natural line through whom Christ would come. Likewise, He sovereignly destined that the surviving remnant of Israel in the end times would not bow down to the beast (the leader of Satan's final beast empire) or his image, and that they would put their faith in their true Messiah, at which time the power of Satan over the earth will be reclaimed by God. And for the very reason that they *are* God's chosen nation, the Jews have continually been the major target of Satan's fury throughout history.

History, especially as found in the Old Testament, gives abundant evidence of Satan's success in his attempt to deceive the natural line of Israel. Moses foresaw how Israel would disobey God and described the future condition of Israel with this vivid indictment: "You are grown fat, thick, and sleek — Then he [Israel] forsook God who made him, and scorned the Rock [the Messiah] of his salvation. They made Him jealous with strange gods; with abominations they provoked Him to anger. They sacrificed to demons [fallen angels] who were not God, to gods whom they have not known, new gods who came lately, whom your fathers did not dread. You neglected the Rock who begot you, and forgot the God who gave you birth" (Deut. 32:15-18).

But Satan did not totally succeed in deceiving Israel. God always had His remnant, the spiritual descendants of Abraham who would obey Him. As Paul explains,

> God has not rejected His people whom He foreknew. Or do you not know what the Scripture says in the passage about Elijah, how he pleads with God against Israel? "Lord, they have killed Thy prophets, they have torn down Thine altars, and I alone am left, and they are seeking my life." But what is the divine response to him? "I have kept for Myself seven thousand men who have not bowed the knee to Baal." In the same way then, there has also come to be at the present time a remnant according to God's gracious choice. (Rom. 11:2-5)

Thus, in every age God has preserved His remnant, which is composed of all those Jews from the natural line of Abraham, who are also from Abraham's spiritual line through obedience to God and trust in Him.

Unable to completely deceive God's chosen nation, Satan has simultaneously attempted to carry out his parallel strategy of Israel's complete destruction by the hands of Gentile nations. Thus when God chose His elect nation, through which Messiah would come, Satan began as it were to choose his own Gentile "elect nations," through which Satan would try to destroy Israel if he could not lead her into apostasy. As we shall see in detail in the coming chapters, these ungodly nations are made up of eight great empires — appropriately described as "beast empires" (Rev. 13:1, 2; 17:3; Dan. 7:3) — which Satan has used and will use in his attempt to eliminate the natural line of Israel. The first seven of those beast empires are now history. Now that Israel is again back in her own land with control of her holy city, Jerusalem, the eighth and last beast empire of Satan can become reality; and when it does, "this generation [that witnesses the eighth beast empire] will not pass away until all these things [end-time events] take place" (Matt. 24:34).

As will be seen in more detail in later chapters, certain similarities have dominated all of Satan's first seven beast empires. Most important has been their hatred for the true God of Abraham and for His chosen nation of Israel. Every one of those beast empires had a leader who at one time *attempted to annihilate the entire nation of Israel* — men, women, and children. Apart from God's protection of Israel, the nation of Israel would long ago have been destroyed.

(2) DESTROY OR DISQUALIFY CHRIST

Satan failed in his first strategy — in his attempt to destroy or disqualify *the natural line* of Messiah (Christ) before the birth of Christ. And so his second strategy — *his attempt to destroy or disqualify Christ Himself* — became all the more bold. And like the first strategy, the failure of his second strategy is also history, the results of which are also recorded carefully in Scripture.

Although his knowledge is limited, Satan clearly understood who Jesus Christ was (and is). Satan knew that God's incarnate Son came to redeem His own back from Satan's kingdom to become part of God's kingdom. As Paul writes in one of the great passages in the Bible on Christ's divinity: "Although He existed in the form of God, [Christ] did not regard equality with God a thing to be grasped, but emptied Himself, taking the form of a bond-servant, and being made in the likeness of men" (Phil. 2:6, 7). In so doing, Christ, the Messiah, became the seed of the woman, precisely as God announced to Satan immediately after the Fall: "And I will put enmity between you [Satan] and the woman, and between your seed and her seed" (Gen. 3:15).

Knowing that Christ had come to redeem God's elect from the kingdom of darkness and to reclaim the rightful rule over the world for God, Satan sought to obstruct Him in every way possible. He first attempted to take Jesus' life while He was still an infant, using King Herod as his evil instrument to slaughter all male children in and around Bethlehem who were under two years of age (Matt. 2:1-18). Failing in that, he attempted repeatedly through the Jewish leaders to kill Jesus during His earthly ministry (see Matt. 12:14; 26:4; John 5:18; 7:1). Also throughout Jesus' ministry, and especially at the beginning, Satan endeavored to disqualify Christ's redemptive work by tempting Him to disregard His Father's will and use His divine powers for His own human welfare and prestige (Matt. 4:1-10; cf. Heb. 2:18; 4:15). The writer of Hebrews explains that Christ "has been tempted in all things as we are, yet without sin" (Heb. 4:15).

A central part of Satan's strategy was to put a blemish on the perfect Lamb of God, thereby disqualifying Christ as being worthy to atone for the sins of the world. That purpose is most clearly seen in Satan's temptations of Jesus in the wilderness for forty days and nights. But that scheme was anticipated by God, for "Jesus was led up by the Spirit into the wilderness to be tempted by the devil" (Matt. 4:1). In other words, Christ's Heavenly Father directed the Holy Spirit to lead Christ into the wilderness *for the very purpose of confronting and confounding Satan's evil plan.*

The cosmic conflict between God and Satan is particularly significant in the third wilderness temptation. Satan's offer to Christ at that time was by far the most grandiose and all-encompassing, going directly to the heart of the issue: "The devil took Him [Jesus] to a very high mountain, and showed Him all the kingdoms of the world, and their glory; and he said to Him, 'All these things will I give You, if You fall down and worship me'" (Matt. 4:8, 9). Satan, "ruler of this world" (John 16:11), offered to give Christ rule over the earth without His having to pay the awful redemption price of the cross — the specific purpose for which Christ had come to earth. Had Christ succumbed to that temptation, He would have disqualified Himself as Redeemer of the spiritual descendants of Abraham. It is clear that Satan was *not* offering Christ *supreme* lordship over the world, but rather a subordinate role under Satan's sovereignty — because the condition for Christ's receiving that limited rulership was His acknowledgment and worship of Satan. Satan himself was so arrogantly self-deceived that he foolishly thought he could beguile his "competitor," the very Son of God, by what would have amounted to simple surrender. Equally foolish is the fact that the only thing Satan had to offer was reign over a corrupted and sinful kingdom of darkness — which, had Christ submitted to Satan, would have forever remained the kingdom of darkness. Christ, on the other hand, was looking to the day envisioned by Daniel, when He will be "given dominion, glory and a kingdom, that all the peoples, nations, and men of every language might serve Him. His dominion [will be] an everlasting dominion which will not pass away; and His kingdom is one which will not be destroyed" (Dan. 7:14).

Through Judas, whom Satan actually indwelt shortly before his betrayal of the Christ (Luke 22:3), Satan made a last attempt on Jesus' life. Christ knew, however, that the very purpose of His first coming was to die, and that without His death by His own choice and without His resurrection, the elect of God would remain in their sin forever, and the rule over earth would remain in the hands of Satan. When that death was imminent, He prayed in the Garden of Gethsemane, "Now My soul has become troubled; and what shall I say, 'Father, save Me from this hour'? But for this purpose I came to this hour. . . . Now judgment is upon this world; now the ruler of this world shall be cast out" (John 12:27, 31).

Therefore, when Jesus surrendered His own sinless life voluntarily on the cross (John 10:18; Matt. 27:50) and was raised from the dead just as He had predicted (Matt. 16:21; 28:6), Satan was forever foiled in his plan to kill the Redeemer and King. The inescapable consequence for Satan is that "now judgment is upon this world; now the ruler of this world shall be cast out" (John 12:31). In perfect fulfillment of the divine promise given in Genesis 3:15, Satan bruised Jesus' heel, as it were. "And being found in appearance as a man, He humbled Himself by becoming obedient to the point of death, even death on a cross" (Phil. 2:8). But through His death and resurrection, the doom of Satan was sealed and Satan's head would be "bruised" permanently (John 12:31; 16:11).

(3) DESTROY THE SUBJECTS OF CHRIST'S KINGDOM

Realizing he has no further opportunity to kill or disqualify the Redeemer and King, Satan's final strategy will be to rekindle and redouble his efforts to kill the King's intended subjects of the millennial kingdom over which he has promised someday to rule. In the last days the primary target of Satan's fury will be an obedient remnant of the natural line of Abraham (the "woman" of Rev. 12:17), which God Almighty has promised to save as a nation before He reclaims the absolute reign over the earth from Satan. As prophesied by Daniel, "Then the sovereignty, the dominion, and the greatness of all the kingdoms under the whole heaven will be given to the people of the saints of the Highest One; [then] His kingdom will be an everlasting kingdom, and all the dominions will serve and obey Him" (Dan. 7:27).

Since Christ's resurrection, this final strategy of Satan has been relentlessly pursued. Consequently, were it not for the restraining ministry of the archangel Michael (see Dan. 10:21; 12:1), Israel would long since have perished at Satan's hand. After the first coming of Christ, when the Gentiles were grafted into the spiritual descendants of

Abraham, they too became the target of Satan's wrath. But the primary focus of his fury has always been against the nation of Israel.

Through the first six beast empires, Satan attempted unsuccessfully to exterminate the nation of Israel, especially those Jews who resisted those empires. The last of the six was the ancient Roman Empire, which had wrested control of the land of Israel from the waning Greek empire. Because of Israel's persistent rebellion against Rome, Caesar ordered General Titus in A.D. 70 to utterly devastate Jerusalem and the Temple. Afterwards, just as Jesus had predicted, there was not one Temple stone left upon another (Matt. 24:2). During that horrifying campaign, Titus mercilessly slaughtered over a million inhabitants of Jerusalem — men and women, young and old, healthy and sick, even pregnant women and tiny babies. In the wake of that massacre virtually all other Jews in Israel fled or were driven out of the land, a time known to Israel as the *Diaspora*, and they would not return as a nation until 1948.

As we shall see later in this volume, the seventh beast empire was even more devastating to Jews than was Rome, even though the natural line of Abraham was scattered to the ends of the earth. Yet Antichrist's persecution of Jews in the eighth and last beast empire, especially during the great tribulation by Antichrist, will be far worse still, unimaginably more horrible than even the Nazi Holocaust. In the last days Antichrist's primary target will again be obedient Israel, the "woman" who will not bow down to him or his image.

But as the Apostle John makes clear, the secondary target of Satan's wrath will be the church, God's spiritual descendants of Abraham, both Jews and Gentiles alike:

> Woe to the earth and the sea, because the devil has come down to you, having great wrath, knowing that he has only a short time. . . . And the dragon was enraged with the woman [i.e., obedient Israel], and went off *to make war with the rest of her offspring, who keep the commandments of God and hold to the testimony of Jesus* [i.e., the church; see chapter 13]. . . . And it was given to him *to make war with the saints and to overcome them;* and authority over every tribe and people and tongue and nation was given to him. And all who dwell on the earth will worship him, *every one whose name has not been written from the foundation of the world in the book of life of the Lamb* who has been slain. (Rev. 12:12, 17; 13:7, 8, emphasis added)

THE FINAL CONFLICT

As mentioned in the opening of this chapter, the battle between God and Satan is not a *contest*, because its Victor and its outcome were determined in eternity past, long before the conflict began.

The book of Revelation vividly details the final confrontation of the cosmic conflict. This final showdown will begin near the end of the timeframe referred to in Scripture as the seventieth week of Daniel and will culminate during the thirty days that immediately follow the close of the seventieth week. Christ will open the seven seals because He alone is worthy (see Acts 17:30, 31) "to take the book, and to break its seals; for Thou wast slain, and didst purchase for God with Thy blood men from every tribe and tongue and people and nation" (Rev. 5:9) — an act which perfectly depicts the redemption of a person's own possession when the sealed deed is opened by its rightful owner (see Jer. 32:1-11).

As that final conflict is played out in the last days, Michael and his holy angels will cast Satan and his demonic angels out of Heaven and down to earth (Rev. 12:7-9), setting the stage for this final conflict. Then the restraining power of Israel's great protector, Michael himself, will be removed (2 Thess. 2:7) and a "loud voice in heaven" will declare: "Woe to the earth and the sea; because the devil has come down to you, having great wrath, knowing that he has only a short time" (Rev. 12:12).

Because of his own presence on earth and the removal of Michael's protection, Satan will gain great advantage over Israel and over the world at large. Consequently he will be utterly emboldened, and through his minion Antichrist and the false prophet, he will demand the world's worship exclusively for himself. This will be the test that all men, living on the face of the earth, will undergo — what John calls "the hour of testing . . . which is about to come upon the whole world, to test those who dwell upon the earth" (Rev. 3:10), and what Peter refers to in his first epistle as "the fiery ordeal among you, which comes upon you for your testing" (4:12). To enforce that demand, he will "cause as many as do not worship the image of the beast to be killed" (Rev. 13:15).

But God will not be silent or inactive. His angel will warn the entire earth that "If anyone worships the beast and his image, and receives a mark on his forehead or upon his hand, he also will drink of the wine of the wrath of God, which is mixed in full strength in the cup of His anger; and he will be tormented with fire and brimstone in the presence of the holy angels and in the presence of the Lamb" (Rev. 14:9, 10).

The battle lines will be drawn and the stage set for the final and absolutely decisive battle of Armageddon. During the sixth bowl judgment of God's day-of-the-Lord wrath, Satan will make a desperate but futile attempt to gain advantage for the final showdown at Armageddon, sending out "spirits of demons, performing signs . . . to the kings of the whole world, to gather them together for the war of the great day of God, the Almighty" (Rev. 16:14).

But as will be discussed in detail in chapter 20, the satanic armies of Antichrist, no matter how great a force he may muster, will be no match for the angelic armies of Christ. In very short order the armies of the kingdom of darkness will be totally and completely destroyed, Antichrist will suffer his final defeat and will be cast into the lake of fire, and Satan will be bound until the end of the Millennium a thousand years later.

God long ago ordained that His Son, Jesus Christ, would be both Redeemer and King, the eternal Victor in the cosmic conflict. Therefore the final outcome has never been in doubt. When Christ came into the world the first time, He reversed the consequences of spiritual and physical death for the children of His kingdom. When He comes the second time, it will be to judge the world that has blindly followed Antichrist and to reclaim for Himself the natural line of Abraham (Israel) after "the fulness of the Gentiles has come in" (Rom. 11:25). Then, in that day, "the Lord will be king over all the earth; in that day the Lord will be the only one, and His name the only one" (Zech. 14:9).

A FRAMEWORK FOR UNDERSTANDING

The preceding chapters have sought to provide the basic framework for understanding this cosmic conflict that lies at the very center of reality. The final outcome of that conflict we know is certain, for we know that true prophecy is certainty, not possibility! "For I am God, and there is no other; I am God, and there is no one like Me, declaring the end from the beginning and from ancient times things which have not been done, saying 'My purpose will be established, and I will accomplish all My good pleasure'" (Isa. 46:9, 10).

But until Satan's final defeat, every moment of our lives bears the ruinous effects of that conflict. Until then, every tragic experience of pain and sorrow, of sin and suffering, of sickness and death stems from this conflict. This understanding is essential as we live moment by moment — so that we will be conscious of the spiritual conflict that rages around us and, by God's grace, live a godly life of trust and obedience to the Savior. But understanding this is doubly important for those who will experience the momentous events of the end times — when Satan will unleash his fury as never before.

The chapters which follow, then, seek to provide this fuller understanding of the cosmic conflict, especially how this will be played out on the earth in the climactic events of the last days. Thus we turn to a careful, extensive and detailed study of the end times as revealed in God's Word — in order that, by God's grace, we might be better prepared for the events to come, more consistent in living a holy life for God's glory alone, and more faithful in proclaiming His truth to a lost world desperately in need of the Savior.

4

The Blessings and
the Curses

As the cosmic drama between Satan and God continued in the heavenlies, the corresponding drama unfolded on earth. And so God reached out to His people Israel, to graciously instruct, guide, and protect them, while Satan mounted his counteroffensive to draw them away from God with his own devices of evil.

At the heart of God's relationship with Israel are His eternal covenant and His law, given by God through Moses soon after delivering His people from bondage in Egypt. That law was a reflection of God's own holy and righteous nature, and its purpose was to *guide* His people into lives of moral and spiritual holiness and uprightness, to *preserve* the line in which their Redeemer and King would eventually come, and to *protect* them from the ungodly influences of a hostile world that was under Satan's control.

But even God's own law could have no benefit for the natural line of Abraham unless it was heeded. Therefore along with the law, God gave Israel a promise and a warning — the gracious promise of blessings if they obeyed His law, and the stern warning of curses if they disobeyed.

THE BLESSINGS OF OBEDIENCE

We see God's gracious promise of blessings beautifully recorded by Moses in the closing chapters of Leviticus:

> If you walk in My statutes and keep My commandments so as to carry them out, then I shall give you rains in their season, so that the land will yield its produce and the trees of the field will bear their fruit. . . . You will thus eat your food to the full and live securely in your land. I shall also grant peace in the land . . . you will chase your enemies, and they will fall before you by the sword; . . . I will turn toward you and make you fruitful and multiply you, and I will confirm My covenant with you. . . . Moreover, I will make My dwelling among you, and My soul will not reject you. I will also walk among you and be your God, and you shall be My people. (Lev. 26:3-7, 9, 11)

THE CONSEQUENCES OF DISOBEDIENCE

God's gracious promises touch every area of life, painting a glorious picture of abundance, peace, and contentment in intimate fellowship with God. But by contrast, the warnings, or curses, show the tragic consequences of disobedience. In the following passage, quoted at length, we see how carefully God spelled out the consequences of disobeying Him:

> But if you do not obey Me and do not carry out all these commandments, if, instead, you reject My statutes, and if your soul abhors My ordinances so as not to carry out all My commandments, and so break My covenant, I, in turn, will do this to you: I will appoint over you a sudden terror, consumption and fever that shall waste away the eyes and cause the soul to pine away; also, you shall sow your seed uselessly, for your enemies shall eat it up. And I will set My face against you so that you shall be struck down before your enemies; and those who hate you shall rule over you, and you shall flee when no one is pursuing you. If also after these things, you do not obey Me, then I will punish you seven times more for your sins. And I will also break down your pride of power; I will also make your sky like iron and your earth like bronze. And your strength shall be spent uselessly, for your land shall not yield its produce and the trees of the land

shall not yield their fruit. If then, you act with hostility against Me and are unwilling to obey Me, I will increase the plague on you seven times according to your sins. And I will let loose among you the beasts of the field, which shall bereave you of your children and destroy your cattle and reduce your number so that your roads lie deserted.

And if by these things you are not turned to Me, but act with hostility against Me, then I will act with hostility against you; and I, even I, will strike you seven times for your sins. I will also bring upon you a sword which will execute vengeance for the covenant; and when you gather together into your cities, I will send pestilence among you, so that you shall be delivered into enemy hands. . . .

Yet if in spite of this, you do not obey Me, but act with hostility against Me, then I will act with wrathful hostility against you; and I, even I, will punish you seven times for your sins. Further, you shall eat the flesh of your sons and the flesh of your daughters you shall eat. I then will destroy your high places, and cut down your incense altars, and heap your remains on the remains of your idols; for My soul shall abhor you. I will lay waste your cities as well, and will make your sanctuaries desolate; and I will not smell your soothing aromas. And I will make the land desolate so that your enemies who settle in it shall be appalled over it. You, however, I will scatter among the nations and will draw out a sword after you, as your land becomes desolate and your cities become waste. . . .

But you will perish among the nations, and your enemies' land will consume you. So those of you who may be left will rot away because of their iniquity in the lands of your enemies; and also because of the iniquities of their forefathers they will rot away with them. (Lev. 26:14-25, 27-33, 38, 39)

God's warnings to the natural line of Abraham about disobedience stand in stark contrast to His blessings promised for obedience. The curses become progressively worse (cf. Deut. 28:15-26) only as Israel persists in greater disobedience and fails to return to Him in obedience. First there would be natural affliction (Lev. 26:16), then human affliction (v. 17), and then divine affliction (vv. 18, 19). After that would come futility in their work (v. 20), decimation of their families and flocks (vv. 21, 22), and execution by their enemies (v. 25). If the statutes of God were still rejected, God would turn Jew against Jew (vv. 28, 29), destroy Israel's Temple and cities (vv. 30-32), and ultimately scatter her among the nations, where she would perish (vv. 33, 38, 39).

But beforehand, God determined He would always have an obedient remnant from within the natural line of Abraham, the spiritual descendants of Abraham. Although at times this obedient remnant seemed non-existent except for a few, it was always the heart of the natural line of Abraham. This remnant, then, was the thread that ran through the fabric of Israel — the thread through which the promises concerning Messiah would be fulfilled, thereby spelling certain doom to the ultimate plan of Satan in his conflict with God over the rule of mankind. Even Elijah pleaded with God against the disobedient nation of Israel: "'Lord, they have killed Thy prophets, they have torn down Thine altars, and I alone am left, and they are seeking my life.' But what is the divine response to him? 'I have kept for Myself seven thousand men who have not bowed the knee to Baal.' In the same way then, there has also come to be at the present time *a remnant* according to God's gracious choice" (Rom. 11:3-5, emphasis added; cf. 1 Kings 19:18; 2 Kings 19:4).

As every Sunday school child knows, however, God's chosen nation began to rebel against Him long before they even saw the Promised Land. Just a few short months after they had witnessed the miraculous parting of the Red Sea and had themselves passed through the waters on dry ground, the people of Israel forsook their Almighty God to worship an idol made with their own hands. Their rebellion continued in disbelief and disobedience when commanded by God to take possession of the Promised Land. Forty years later, after wandering in the wilderness as a consequence of their disobedience, God omnisciently revealed to Moses what would happen in the future:

> "Behold, you [Moses] are about to lie down with your fathers; and this people will arise and play the [spiritual] harlot with the strange gods of the land, into the midst of which they are going, and will forsake Me and break My covenant which I have made with them. Then My anger will be kindled against them in that day, and I will forsake them and hide My face from them, and they shall be consumed, and many evils and troubles shall come upon them; so that they will say in that day, 'Is it not because our God is not among us that these evils have come upon us?' But I

will surely hide My face in that day because of all the evil which they will do, for they will turn to other gods." (Deut. 31:16-18)

With such a somber and terrifying warning, one would think that every Hebrew would have done everything in his power to be obedient and faithful to his gracious but righteous God. Yet the very opposite would be true. After Israel entered the Promised Land and became established as a nation, they continued to disobey Him, and their punishment continued to become worse. The plight of the nation became so desperate that some even cannibalized their own children (Lev. 26:29). An especially gruesome part of that prediction was fulfilled during the days of Elisha, when the army of Ben-hadad, king of Aram (Syria), besieged the city of Samaria, which was then the capital of the northern kingdom of Israel (cf. 2 Kings 6:28-30).

But the curse on Israel for her disobedience would become progressively worse. God would cause her to be conquered and subjugated by powerful pagan enemies while she was still in the land of promise. He would then allow His nation to be taken captive out of the land and made to live as exiles in the lands of their conquerors. That punishment was fulfilled when the northern kingdom was conquered and dispersed by Assyria in 722-721 B.C. and the southern kingdom was conquered and dispersed by Babylon in 586 B.C.

During the reign of Hoshea, king of the northern kingdom (732-722 B.C.), "the king of Assyria invaded the whole land and went up to Samaria and besieged it three years. In the ninth year of Hoshea, the king of Assyria captured Samaria and carried Israel away into exile to Assyria, and settled them in Halah and Habor, on the river of Gozan, and in the cities of the Medes" (2 Kings 17:5, 6). Adding insult to injury, after the king of Assyria scattered the people of Israel, he repopulated the land with Babylonians (2 Kings 17:24).

During the one hundred and thirty-five years that followed, except for a few brief periods of faithfulness to the Lord, the kingdom of Judah, the southern kingdom, also became more and more corrupt and idolatrous. Although she was not conquered by the Assyrians, the southern kingdom of Judah was forced to pay tribute to the Assyrians for many years and suffered various indignities from her oppressors. In response to her disobedience, God eventually turned Judah over to the Babylonians, whose ruthless king, Nebuchadnezzar (605-562 B.C.), held the nation under long subjugation and finally ordered Jerusalem destroyed (587 B.C.). After being stripped of all its gold and other valuables, the Temple was also destroyed.

However bad the oppression of the foreign invaders may have seemed at the time, the ultimate curse upon Israel would be the worst:

> "Moreover, the Lord will scatter you among all peoples, from one end of the earth to the other end of the earth; and there you shall serve other gods, wood and stone, which you or your fathers have not known. And among those nations you shall find no rest, and there shall be no resting place for the sole of your foot; but there the Lord will give you a trembling heart, failing of eyes, and despair of soul. So your life shall hang in doubt before you; and you shall be in dread night and day, and shall have no assurance of your life." (Deut. 28:64-66)

THE GREAT *DIASPORA*

The final curse decreed by God was that He would scatter His own people "among all peoples, from one end of the earth to the other end of the earth" (Deut. 28:64a), where they would "find no rest" and would live in constant fear for their lives (Deut. 28:64-68; Lev. 26:33-39). This would only occur *after* their Messiah had come fulfilling God's promises to provide for His elect a Redeemer through the seed of Abraham (Gen. 12:3), and only *after* Israel's rejection of their Messiah (Matt. 21:12-19; cf. Psa. 118:22). This ultimate curse found its literal fulfillment in A.D. 70 when the human armies under General Titus utterly destroyed Israel because of the Jews' persistent rebellion against Rome. Thus Titus razed Jerusalem, slaughtered most of the inhabitants, turned the Temple into rubble, and caused virtually every surviving Jew in Jerusalem to flee "from one end of the earth to the other." This then was the beginning of the great *Diaspora*, the ultimate curse as foretold by Moses.

This tragic event was the direct consequence of an even more tragic event — namely, Israel's participation in the crucifixion of Christ (Zech. 13:7; cf. Dan. 9:26; Matt. 27:11-26). But in a sense it was an event that had been revealed by God to His people going as far back as the time of Moses. Thus God warned the nation through Moses: "'I will surely hide My face in that day because of all the evil which they will do, for they will turn to other gods'" (Deut. 31:18). Even more specifically, Zechariah the prophet had warned that the day would come when Israel would "strike the Shepherd [Christ] that the sheep [Israel] may be scattered" (Zech. 13:7). And Daniel likewise prophesied: "Then . . . the Messiah will be cut off and have nothing, and the people of the prince who is to come will destroy the city and the sanctuary" (Dan. 9:26a).

Christ was "cut off," then, when Israel rejected their Messiah and participated in His crucifixion. The destruction of the Temple, which came later in A.D. 70, was vividly foretold by Jesus before His death and resurrection. After overhearing the disciples admire the Temple's beautiful stones and lavish adornment, Jesus replied: "As for these things which you are looking at, the days will come in which there will not be left one stone upon another which will not be torn down" (Luke 21:6). The disciples naturally asked, "Teacher, when therefore will these things be? And what will be the sign when these things are to take place?" (Luke 21:7). Jesus' response to this, recorded in Luke, was specific:

> When you see Jerusalem surrounded by armies, then recognize that her desolation is at hand. Then let those who are in Judea flee to the mountains, and let those who are in the midst of the city depart, and let not those who are in the country enter the city; because these are days of vengeance, in order that all things which are written may be fulfilled. Woe to those who are with child and to those who nurse babes in those days; for there will be great distress upon the land, and wrath to this people, and they will fall by the edge of the sword, and will be led captive into all the nations; and Jerusalem will be trampled underfoot by the Gentiles until the times of the Gentiles* be fulfilled. (Luke 21:20-24)[1]

The final and complete dispersion of Israel came in the year A.D. 132 — when every Jew who remained was forcefully expelled from Jerusalem, its rebuilt buildings were destroyed, and the ground was literally plowed under, "trampled under foot," and used for growing crops.

At the time Jesus spoke the words just quoted above, Israel had been under Gentile domination for some six hundred years. After the destruction of Jerusalem, Israel was completely scattered throughout

* See the Glossary for a definition of "Gentiles, time of."

the world and will, in one way or another, be persecuted by Gentiles until the end of the age.

THE RESTORATION OF ISRAEL

But God's revelation does not end with Israel's unfaithfulness and her consequent "trembling heart, failing of eyes, and despair of soul [when] your life shall hang in doubt before you; and you shall be in dread night and day, and shall have no assurance of your life" (Deut. 28:65, 66). Instead, the Lord promised a glorious future for His nation — when one day, after He has restored them back to their land, He will lovingly bring His nation back to Himself:

> So it shall be when all of these things have come upon you, the blessing and the curse which I have set before you, and you call them to mind in all nations where the Lord your God has banished you . . . the Lord your God will bring you into the land which your fathers possessed, and you shall possess it; and He will prosper you and multiply you more than your fathers. Moreover the Lord your God will circumcise your heart and the heart of your descendants, to love the Lord your God with all your heart and with all your soul, in order that you may live. And the Lord your God will inflict all these curses on your enemies and on those who hate you, who persecuted you. And you shall again obey the Lord, and observe all His commandments which I command you today. Then the Lord your God will prosper you abundantly in all the work of your hand, in the offspring of your body and in the offspring of your cattle and in the produce of your ground, for the Lord will again rejoice over you for good, just as He rejoiced over your fathers. (Deut. 30:1, 5-9; cf. Lev. 26:44)

That prophecy gives a condensed overview of end-time events and their sequence — events which will be literally fulfilled and actually take place in the end times. First, Jews will return to the land that their forefathers possessed (Deut. 30:5). But because they will return still in unbelief, they will not recognize God's sovereign provision of that blessing, but will rather consider it to be their own achievement. Next, the nation of Israel will be restored to faith in her Lord (v. 6), the Messiah whom she has so long neglected. Finally, Israel's enemies will forever be destroyed (v. 7), and God's specially chosen nation will forever obey and serve her Savior and Lord (v. 8) when Christ physically rules over the earth. In a final and vain attempt to thwart God's plan, Satan will do everything in his power to destroy the nation of Israel before these things can happen, only to meet his final defeat.

The Lord promises through Zechariah that at that time "I will pour out on the house of David and on the inhabitants of Jerusalem the Spirit of grace and of supplication, so that they will look on Me whom they have pierced; and they will mourn for Him, as one mourns for an only son, and they will weep bitterly over Him, like the bitter weeping over a first-born" (12:10). Under the prompting of the Holy Spirit, repentant Jews in that day will cry out, "Come, let us return to the Lord. For He has torn us, but He will heal us; He has wounded us, but He will bandage us. He will revive us after two days; He will raise us up on the third day that we may live before Him" (Hos. 6:1, 2).

Along with Israel's restoration and salvation there is a further promise, one given to Israel through Zechariah. In some ways it is a promise that must be as frightening to Satan as was God's initial declaration of Satan's fate given in Genesis 3:15. After the national salvation of Israel and the total defeat of her greatest enemy (the final beast empire of Satan), "the Lord will be king over all the earth; in that day the Lord will be the only one, and His name the only one" (14:9), and "then the sovereignty, the dominion, and the greatness of all the kingdoms under the whole heaven will be given to the saints of the Highest One; *His kingdom will be an everlasting kingdom, and all the dominions will serve and obey Him*" (Dan. 7:27, emphasis added).

WHEN WILL THESE THINGS HAPPEN?

When will these things happen? No one knows the day or the hour when Christ will return (Matt. 24:36). At the same time, Jesus told us that we are to "learn the parable from the fig tree: when its branch has already become tender, and puts forth its leaves, you know that summer is near; even so when you see all *these things*, recognize that He is near, right at the door" (Matt. 24:32, 33; emphasis added). "Therefore be on the alert" (v. 42), Jesus admonished, and "for this reason you be ready too" (v. 44).

Jesus' words ring with urgency to every generation, but have a special immediacy for us today — now that the Jews once again have control of the land of Israel — and are returning to their homeland in vast numbers "from one end of the earth to the other end of the earth" (Deut. 28:64). What are "these things" to which Christ refers? When and how will they happen? The importance of "these things," as Christ Himself urged, cannot be overemphasized. Thus we will now carefully consider further "these things" to which Christ refers — the events that God revealed long ago in His Word would happen, those that have already taken place, and those that are yet to come.

5

The "Seventy Week" Prophetic Timetable

O nce we capture even a small sense of the momentous events
through which God Almighty will reclaim His rightful reign
over earth, we cannot help but ask, "When will these things
take place?" But even more basic than this question should be, "When
will God reclaim the nation of Israel for Himself?" The answer to this
question is the critical piece in God's prophetic plan for the overthrow
of Satan and for the reestablishment of God Almighty's rightful and
sovereign rule over the earth. As we shall see, the answer to the second question will bring about God's rightful reign over earth. There is
a cause and effect relationship here. The cause will be God's reclaiming Israel to Himself. The effect will be God's reclaiming His rightful
rule over earth. To answer this question, we turn to the book of Daniel,
which provides one of the crucial passages in the Bible for understanding God's prophetic timetable.

In the days of the prophet Daniel the nation of Israel had lost its
independence to Babylon (586 B.C.), one of the beast empires of Satan,
because of Israel's continued disobedience to God. Driven from the
Promised Land into Babylonian exile, Israel experienced the direct

effects of God's intensified curses, and she was again coming to recognize that God was indeed a God of His word. The Temple of Solomon had been destroyed, and the Jews began to realize that their great Defender was withdrawing the protection He had so often provided in the past. No one felt the nation's anguish or saw her guilt more than Daniel, who cried out to God in their behalf. "Indeed all Israel has transgressed Thy law and turned aside, not obeying Thy voice," Daniel prayed, "so the curse has been poured out on us, along with the oath which is written in the law of Moses the servant of God, for we have sinned against Him" (Dan. 9:11).

Exactly as God had foretold through Moses, the nation had been driven into exile (Deut. 28:36) as the curses of God became progressively worse. Seeing the tragic condition of Israel, Daniel poured out his heart in prayer, pleading with God Almighty to forgive and act on behalf of His chosen nation. In response, God sent His angel Gabriel, giving Daniel an answer that is one of the most critical prophetic passages in Scripture.

THE SEVENTY WEEKS OF DANIEL

The message from Gabriel outlines the prophetic future of Israel in terms of "seventy weeks," which refers here to seventy time periods of seven years each, or a total of 490 years. Gabriel's words give startling insight into specific prophetic events, some of which have since been fulfilled with literal precision, and others of which are yet to come, providing the framework for the end times:

> Seventy weeks have been decreed for your people [Israel, the natural line of Abraham] and your holy city [Jerusalem], to finish the transgression, to make an end of sin, to make atonement for iniquity, to bring in everlasting righteousness, to seal up vision and prophecy, and to anoint the most holy. . . . So you are to know and discern that from the issuing of a decree to restore and rebuild Jerusalem [destroyed by Babylon] until Messiah the Prince [Christ] there will be seven weeks and sixty-two weeks [a total of sixty-nine weeks or 483 years]; it will be built again, with plaza and moat, even in times of distress. Then after the sixty-two weeks the Messiah will be cut off [rejected and crucified] and have nothing, and the people of the prince [Titus] who is to come will destroy the city and the sanctuary. And its end will come

with a flood; even to the end [of the age] there will be war; deso-
lations are determined. And he [Antichrist] will make a firm
covenant with the many [Israel] for one week [seven years], but
in the middle of the week he will put a stop to sacrifice and grain
offering; and on the wing of abominations will come one who
makes desolate [Antichrist], even until a complete destruction,
one that is decreed, is poured out on the one who makes desolate
[at Armageddon]. (Dan. 9:24-27)

Gabriel answers Daniel's question by telling Daniel that Israel and
their holy city, Jerusalem, will have 490 more years of direct Gentile
domination before they will have atoned for their sin to God and
before everlasting righteousness will be brought to the nation. For this
reason, these four verses contain the basic truths necessary to form a
broad timeline of events, after which Israel, as a nation, will acknowledge her true Redeemer and King, Jesus Christ. Therefore, this small
passage is one of the most crucial eschatological passages in all of
Scripture. As we shall see, sixty-nine of those "weeks" are past, and
only the seventieth "week" (i.e., the seventieth seven-year period)
remains before "everlasting righteousness" can be brought to Israel.

"Seventy weeks" is more literally translated as "seventy sevens." In
the Hebrew language, "sevens" can refer to days, weeks, or years,
depending on the context, which in this case clearly is years (see Dan.
12:7, 11, 12; cf. Rev. 11:2, 3; 12:6, 14; 13:5). (In other words, a prophetic
"week" corresponds to seven years, with each day in the "week" representing one year.) Thus Gabriel revealed to Daniel that there would
be a period of sixty-nine seven-year periods (483 years) from the time
a decree would be given to "restore and rebuild Jerusalem" until
"Messiah the Prince" (Dan. 9:25). The decree referred to here was actually given in 445 B.C. by Artaxerxes Longimanus (see Neh. 2:5). And in
exact fulfillment of this prophecy, the time between the decree and the
coming of Christ to Jerusalem on Palm Sunday has been calculated as
being exactly 483 prophetic years of 360 days each.[1]

The events of the seventieth week, however, still lie in the future. In
addition to the passage quoted above, this last "week" (i.e., the last
seven-year period) is described in further detail in Daniel 12:11, 12.
Here we find the last half of the last seven years (along with the brief
period of time that follows the end of the seven years until the
Millennium begins) outlined in terms of *days*. Thus we see that the last
half of the seventieth week of Daniel is three and a half years, or 1,260

days (see Rev. 12:6, 14) and that there is an additional interval of seventy-five days (comprised of two time periods, one of thirty days and the second of forty-five days), both of which transpire before the Millennium begins:

> And from the time that the regular sacrifice is abolished, and the abomination of desolation is set up [at the midpoint of the final seven years], there will be 1290 [1,260 + 30] days. How blessed is he who keeps waiting and attains to the 1,335 [1,260 + 30 + 45] days! (Dan. 12:11, 12)

The sequence of events revealed in Daniel 9:24-27, then, provides a step by step outline of God's prophetic timetable. As we have already seen, the prophecy concerning the decree to "restore and rebuild Jerusalem" was fulfilled in 445 B.C., and the prophecy concerning the coming of "Messiah the Prince" on Palm Sunday was fulfilled 483 years later, just as prophesied. The other events predicted by Gabriel, which were to occur before the final seventieth week would begin in the last days, have been fulfilled with equal precision. Thus the prophecy that the Messiah would be "cut off" was fulfilled in Israel's rejection of their Messiah and their participation in His crucifixion and death; and the prophecy concerning the destruction of Jerusalem and the sanctuary was fulfilled in 70 A.D. by Titus, "the prince who is to come," as was predicted by Christ Himself (see Luke 19:41-44; cf. 21:12-24).

The first 483 years of Daniel's prophecy are now past. These years, which represent the first sixty-nine "weeks," came to an end on the week Christ made His triumphal entry into Jerusalem, just prior to being rejected and crucified. Shortly thereafter Israel was scattered to the four corners of the earth, without a homeland and without the holy city of Jerusalem when Titus "destroy[ed] the city and the sanctuary." The seven remaining years will transpire in the end times. But before this last "week" could take place, Israel needed to regain control of her Promised Land (which she did in 1948) and then the entire city of Jerusalem (which she did in 1967) — as seen by the fact that Daniel's prophetic passage concerning the seventy weeks pertains to both "your people [Israel as a nation] and your holy city [Jerusalem]" (Dan. 9:24). However, the nation's return to the land and her control of Jerusalem once again did not initiate the last seven-year period, but had to occur before that time could begin, as we will see later in this volume.[2]

With the first sixty-nine weeks of Daniel's prophecy completed long ago, and with Israel now back in her own homeland, the obvious question is, "When will the seventieth week begin?" In His Olivet Discourse, Christ tells His disciples that "when you see all these things [things associated with the seventieth week], recognize that He [Christ] is near, right at the door. Truly I say to you, this generation will not pass away until all these things take place" (Matt. 24:33, 34). "These things" referred to by Christ are the events which occur *during* the seventieth week and which must take place *before* the return of Christ. Therefore the seventieth week has tremendous significance to all who are "looking for the blessed hope and the appearing of the glory of our great God and Saviour, Christ Jesus" (Titus 2:13). But before "these things" can occur, there would be a mysterious time gap between the sixty-ninth and the seventieth weeks. Although the early church thought Christ would return in its own time, history, of course, has proved that the gap between the sixty-ninth and seventieth weeks would last for many centuries, not simply for a few years.

The long gap between the sixty-ninth and the seventieth weeks is not explained, or even hinted at in Daniel's revelation concerning the seventy weeks. For this reason Israel, and even the early church before the destruction of Jerusalem, had no way of knowing about, much less understanding, that highly significant truth. Other Old Testament prophecies, however, do give insight concerning that gap, and we turn to these now for further understanding.

WHY THE LONG GAP?

After God gave the nation of Israel the choice of receiving His blessings for their obedience or His curses in exchange for their disobedience, in their depravity they quickly chose the latter. They suffered one curse after another, each one becoming progressively worse because of their progressively increasing sin.

As we saw in the last chapter, God warned the nation of the ultimate curse, telling them through Moses: "You, however, I will scatter among the nations and will draw out a sword after you, as your land becomes desolate and your cities become waste. . . . But you will perish among the nations, and your enemies' land will consume you. So those of you who may be left will rot away because of their iniquity in the lands of your enemies; and also because of the iniquities of their forefathers they will rot away with them" (Lev. 26:33, 38, 39).

The divine King of Israel, the very Word of God incarnate, "came to His own, and those who were His own did not receive Him" (John 1:11). As already explained in the last chapter, that rejection triggered Israel's most terrible curse, the great scattering of her people throughout the world that began in A.D. 70. Most of Israel did not receive the Shepherd. Some even accused Him of casting out demons by the power of Satan, "Beelzebul the prince of the devils" — and by that act they committed the unpardonable sin (Matt. 12:24, 31). And because Israel rejected her Redeemer and King, Jesus Christ, God withdrew (or perhaps more appropriately, postponed) His offer of the kingdom to her as a nation. Therefore, from that time forward in His earthly ministry, Jesus began teaching the multitudes primarily in parables because, as He explained to the Twelve, "while seeing they do not see, and while hearing they do not hear, nor do they understand" (Matt. 13:13).

But God has not forgotten and will never forsake Israel. God's gracious plans for the people of His chosen nation are explained beautifully by the Apostle Paul in Romans:

> I say then, God has not rejected His people, has He? May it never be! . . . God has not rejected His people whom He foreknew. Or do you not know what the Scripture says in the passage about Elijah, how he pleads with God against Israel? . . . I say then, they did not stumble so as to fall, did they? May it never be! But by their transgression salvation has come to the Gentiles, to make them [Israel] jealous. Now if their transgression be riches for the world and their failure be riches for the Gentiles, how much more will their [Israel's] fulfillment be! . . . Quite right, they were broken off for their unbelief, and you [Gentile believers] stand only by your faith. Do not be conceited, but fear; for if God did not spare the natural branches [Israel], neither will He spare you [Gentile believers]. . . . For if you were cut off from what is by nature a wild olive tree, and were grafted contrary to nature into a cultivated olive tree, how much more shall these who are the natural branches be grafted into their own olive tree? *For I do not want you, brethren, to be uninformed of this mystery, lest you be wise in your own estimation, that a partial hardening has happened to Israel until the fulness of the Gentiles has come in; and thus all Israel will be*

saved; just as it is written, "The Deliverer will come from Zion, He will remove ungodliness from Jacob." (11:1, 2, 11, 12, 20, 21, 24-26, emphasis added)

And so the interlude between the sixty-ninth and seventieth weeks has brought in salvation for the Gentiles, in order to make the nation of Israel jealous because of her rejection of her true Messiah (Rom. 11:11-24). But it will not always be that way. Through Daniel the Lord declared, "Seventy weeks have been decreed for your people and your holy city, to finish the transgression, to make an end of sin, to make atonement for iniquity, to bring in everlasting righteousness . . ." (Dan. 9:24). And at the end of the seventy weeks Israel's estrangement from God will come to an end — when God shall bring in "everlasting righteousness," when "the fulness of the Gentiles has come in; and thus all Israel will be saved" (Rom. 11:25, 26). Until then, "a partial [spiritual] hardening has happened to Israel." Hosea explained to Israel that the Lord has decreed, "I will go away and return to my place until they [Israel] acknowledge their guilt and seek My face. In their affliction [during the seventieth week] they will earnestly seek me" (5:15).

Satan must do all in his power to prevent what God has clearly predicted He will do with Israel — namely, bring the entire nation back to Himself in salvation. When Israel as a nation comes to her Lord, as the Lord Himself has declared she will, then He alone "will be king over all the earth; in that day the Lord will be the only one, and His name the only one" (Zech. 14:9). As we will see in the following chapters, Satan therefore will use his eighth and final beast empire nation, ruled by his minion Antichrist, in a final but vain attempt to destroy God's elect nation of Israel and "the rest of her offspring [the church], who keep the commandments of God and hold to the testimony of Jesus" (Rev. 12:17) — hoping thereby to thwart God's plan for His people by leaving Him no earthly subjects over which to rule. All of this will occur during the seventieth week of Daniel; all of this, then, encompasses what we call the "end times."

THE SEVENTIETH WEEK

It will be during the seventieth week (the last seven years of the times of the Gentiles) that Satan will make that last great effort to preserve his domination over the earth. Speaking of that final effort of

Satan, which he will carry out through Antichrist, Daniel describes the final beast empire as

> ... dreadful and terrifying and extremely strong; and it had large iron teeth. It devoured and crushed, and trampled down the remainder with its feet; and it was different from all the beasts that were before it, and it had ten horns [kingdoms]. While I was contemplating the horns, behold, another horn, a little one [Antichrist], came up among them, and three of the first horns [kingdoms that will be directly controlled by Antichrist] were pulled out by the roots before it; and behold, this horn [Antichrist] possessed eyes like the eyes of a man, and a mouth uttering great boasts. (Dan. 7:7, 8)

> And he [Antichrist] will make a firm covenant with the many [Israel] for one week [seven years], but in the middle of the week he will put a stop to sacrifice and grain offering; and on the wing of abominations will come one who makes desolate [Antichrist, empowered directly by Satan], even until a complete destruction, one that is decreed [at Armageddon], is poured out on the one who makes desolate. (Dan. 9:27)

> Now at that time [the midpoint of the seventieth week] Michael, the great prince who stands guard over the sons of your people, will arise. And there will be a time of distress [the great tribulation by Antichrist] such as never occurred since there was a nation until that time. (Dan. 12:1)

Speaking of those same days, Jesus gives both a warning and promise in His Olivet Discourse:

> Therefore when you see the abomination of desolation which was spoken of through Daniel the prophet, standing in the holy place (let the reader understand) . . . then there will be a great tribulation, such as has not occurred since the beginning of the world until now, nor ever shall. And unless those days had been cut short, no life would have been saved; but for the sake of the elect [Jews and Gentiles] those days [of Antichrist's persecution] shall be cut short. (Matt. 24:15, 21, 22)

Because of Israel's recent return to and rule over her own homeland (including the entire city of Jerusalem), the present generation of the church is the first since the early church before the *Diaspora* of A.D. 70 that can look with well-founded expectation for the events that will initiate the seventieth week. Those final seven years of Gentile domination could now be imminent. But as we will see in the following chapters, Antichrist must first establish his eighth beast empire, or at least its three-nation power base that will drive the final beast empire of Satan. Such a formation could be assembled almost overnight. And when it is, Israel will then make a covenant (Dan. 9:27) with the powerful ruler of that empire — hoping to gain his protection, but having no idea that he is the Antichrist and that her alliance with him will prove to be a "covenant with death." It will be this "covenant with death" that initiates the end times, the seventieth week outlined in the book of Revelation and the Olivet Discourse of Christ. "These things" must occur before Israel has atoned for her iniquity, before "everlasting righteousness" can be brought into the natural line of Abraham, hardened because of their rejection of Messiah at His first coming.

One last comment. Throughout this chapter we have seen an important principle at work: those events prophesied in Daniel that have already been fulfilled (the first sixty-nine weeks) *were fulfilled with literal precision*. Thus we can expect the same to be true of the remaining events of the seventieth week. But more than this, we can expect this same principle to be at work in all of God's prophetic revelation. We will now look in greater depth at what God has revealed concerning both the prophetic events that have already been fulfilled and what these mean for the things that are to come.

The First Seven
Beast Empires

S atan's "beast empires" are at the center of his counter-strategy in the cosmic conflict between God and Satan as it is being waged here on earth. These empires are vividly described as beasts in both Revelation 17:3 and Daniel 7:3 — appropriately so because of their satanically inspired obsession to destroy the Jewish people through the centuries. Actually the term *beast*, especially in the book of Revelation, is used to describe both the empires of Satan and the leader of the final beast empire, Antichrist. This is true in the passage quoted below. However, careful understanding of the context will quickly determine which is in view — the beast empires of Satan or Antichrist. Thus John gives the church an overview of all the beast empires of Satan, as well as Antichrist, the leader of the final beast empire, when he writes:

> And he carried me away in the Spirit into a wilderness; and I saw a woman sitting on a scarlet beast [the beast empires of Satan], full of blasphemous names, having seven heads and ten horns. . . . Here is the mind which has wisdom. The seven heads

. . . are seven kings [of the first seven beast empires]; five have fallen, one is, the other has not yet come; and when he comes, he must remain a little while. And the beast [Antichrist] which was and is not, is himself also an eighth [king], and is one of the [first] seven [kings], and he goes to destruction. And the ten horns which you saw are ten kings, who have not yet received a kingdom, but they receive authority as kings with the beast [Antichrist] for one hour. (Rev. 17:3, 9-12)

THE EIGHT BEAST EMPIRES INTRODUCED

This passage is critical to the understanding of the beast empires that Satan has or will use throughout the course of history as his elect nations against the elect nation of God, Israel. The scarlet beast is symbolic of all eight of the beast empires of Satan. The first seven empires and their leaders are represented by the seven heads, and the final beast empire, the eighth, is represented by the ten horns. The eighth empire comprising the ten horns will be ruled by one of the prior seven heads of one of the previous seven beast empires, who will come back to life to rule over the final beast empire. John explains these truths in greater depth when he says that he "saw one of his [seven] heads as if it had been slain, and his fatal wound was healed. And the whole earth was amazed and followed after the beast [Antichrist]" (Rev. 13:3). A great deal more is said about this, particularly in chapter 11.

Although the seven heads represent seven different kings, these kings refer to specific kingdoms or beast empires Satan has already used in his attempt to destroy God's elect nation of Israel. At the time John wrote the book of Revelation, five of the eight beast empires were history, one was in existence at the time of his writing (c. A.D. 90), and one was yet to come, although its existence would be brief (v. 10). Following this seventh beast empire, there would still be one more, the eighth and final beast empire of Satan (v. 11). The ten kings who arise and receive authority with the beast (Antichrist) will comprise that eighth and final beast empire (v. 12), which God will destroy when He unleashes His day-of-the-Lord wrath at "the end of the age" (Matt. 13:40).

THE BEAST EMPIRES OF NEBUCHADNEZZAR'S DREAM

In the prophetic counterpart of the passage in Revelation quoted above, Daniel gives additional information about the identity of some of the eight beast empires of Satan. This additional insight comes through the interpretation of King Nebuchadnezzar's dream which God gave to Daniel. In this passage God's divinely revealed interpretation omits the first two empires mentioned in Revelation, focusing instead only on those empires which would dominate Israel and her holy city, Jerusalem, from Daniel's time on to the very last beast empire that will dominate Israel and Jerusalem during the seventieth week:

"You, O king [Nebuchadnezzar], were looking and behold, there was a single great statue; that statue, which was large and of extraordinary splendor, was standing in front of you, and its appearance was awesome. The head of that statue was made of fine gold, its breast and its arms of silver, its belly and its thighs of bronze, its legs of iron, its feet partly of iron and partly of clay. You continued looking until a stone was cut out without hands, and it struck the statue on its feet of iron and clay, and crushed them. Then the iron, the clay, the bronze, the silver and the gold were crushed all at the same time, and became like chaff from the summer threshing floors; and the wind carried them away so that not a trace of them was found. But the stone that struck the statue became a great mountain and filled the whole earth. . . .

"You, O king [Nebuchadnezzar], are the king of kings, to whom the God of heaven has given the kingdom, the power, the strength, and the glory; and wherever the sons of men dwell, or the beasts of the field, or the birds of the sky, He has given them into your hand and has caused you to rule over them all. You are the head of gold. And after you there will arise another kingdom inferior to you, then another third kingdom of bronze, which will rule over all the earth. Then there will be a fourth kingdom as strong as iron; inasmuch as iron crushes and shatters all things, so, like iron that breaks in pieces, it will crush and break all these in pieces. And in that you saw the feet and toes, partly of potter's clay and partly of iron, it will be a divided kingdom; but it will have in it the toughness of iron, inasmuch as you saw the iron mixed with common clay. And as the toes of the feet were partly of iron and partly of pottery, so some of the kingdom will be strong and part of it will be brittle. And in that you saw the iron mixed with common clay, they will combine with one another in the seed of men; but they will not adhere to one another, even as iron does not combine with pottery. And in the days of those kings the God of heaven will set up a kingdom which will never be destroyed, and that kingdom will not be left for another people; it will crush and put an end to all these kingdoms, but it will itself endure forever." (Dan. 2:31-35, 37-44)

This passage in Daniel identifies four distinct beast empires (gold, silver, bronze, iron), and a final empire (iron mixed with clay) that is in direct continuity with the fourth (i.e., the iron that forms the legs extends down into the feet and toes where it becomes mixed with clay). The empires spoken of here began with King Nebuchadnezzar (605-562 B.C.) and include those that Satan would use from Daniel's time onward until the last beast empire that would dominate Israel during the seventieth week. Thus at the time of Daniel two empires were already past (i.e., the first two mentioned in Revelation 17:10, 11), and the head of gold from Nebuchadnezzar's dream corresponds to the third empire referred to in Revelation.[1]

THE BEAST EMPIRES OF DANIEL'S VISION

We need to look briefly at one further prophecy from the book of Daniel which fits in perfectly with the two passages just quoted above. This is the vision of Daniel as recorded in chapter 7 and which correlates directly to the passages in both Revelation 17 and Daniel 2:

Daniel said, "I was looking in my vision by night and behold . . . four great beasts [beast empires] were coming up from the sea, different from one another. The first was like a lion and had the wings of an eagle. . . . And behold, another beast, a second one, resembling a bear. . . . After this I kept looking, and behold, another one, like a leopard. . . . After this I kept looking in the night visions, and behold, a fourth beast, dreadful and terrifying and extremely strong; and it had large iron teeth. It devoured and crushed, and trampled down the remainder with its feet; and it was different from all the beasts [beast empires] that went before it, and it had ten horns [the eighth beast empire]. While I was contemplating the horns, behold, another horn, a little one [Antichrist], came up among them, and three of the first horns were pulled out by the roots before it; and behold, this horn possessed eyes like the eyes of a man, and a mouth uttering great boasts." (vv. 2-8)

The correlation between the beast empires in this vision of Daniel and in Nebuchadnezzar's dream of the statue is immediately apparent — with (1) the lion corresponding to the gold empire, (2) the bear to silver, and (3) the leopard to bronze. Likewise there is a fourth empire with ten horns, which becomes the final empire led by the little horn, which again corresponds directly to the fourth empire of Nebuchadnezzar's statue (legs of iron) that extends down to the final empire (ten toes of iron mixed with clay). And as we shall see, especially in the next chapter, the correlation of all three passages provides clear insight into the composition of Satan's final beast empire that will seek to destroy the nation of Israel and all who profess the name of Christ during the last days of the seventieth week.

By the time of Nebuchadnezzar, the curse of God had intensified against the Jews because of the nation's continued disobedience to the law of God. When the book of Daniel was written, Nebuchadnezzar had already destroyed the city of Jerusalem and the Temple, and many Israelites, including Daniel, had been taken into exile in Babylon. Part of the purpose of Nebuchadnezzar's dream (Dan. 2) and Daniel's later vision (Dan. 7) was to inform the Jews that their trouble had only begun and that the curse of God for their disobedience would become progressively worse as clearly foretold in the writings of Moses (see chapter 4 of this book). Thus God revealed to Daniel there would be more kingdoms that would oppress Israel, each one becoming steadily worse, before God would "set up a kingdom which will never be destroyed, and that kingdom will not be left for another people; it will crush and put an end to all these kingdoms [beast empires], but it will itself endure forever" (2:44).

THE FIRST SIX BEAST EMPIRES IDENTIFIED

The first six beast empires of Satan span the time from before the birth of Israel as a nation to when John penned the book of Revelation. The accurate identification of these first six empires is essential in order to identify both the seventh empire and Satan's final empire in the last days.

One of the crucial factors in identifying the seventh and eighth beast empires concerns how each of the first six empires fits into the table of nations found in Genesis 10. This table tracks the ancestry of Noah after the Flood through his three sons Shem, Ham, and Japheth — the father of all the nations of the world today. The many references in this book to Semitic, Hamitic, or Japhethite peoples pertain to the descendants of Shem, Ham, and Japheth respectively. As we shall see in the next chapter, the biblical descriptions of the people that will comprise the final beast empire leave no doubt about their ancestry (even if there may be some uncertainty about their exact geographic location today). We will therefore return to the table of nations in the next chapter for a precise explanation of how this relates to the eighth beast empire. In this section, then, we will simply note which line (Shem, Ham, or Japheth) each of the first six beast empires is descended from, as part of the identification of each empire. But this will provide essential background information for the subsequent identification of Satan's final beast empire in chapter 7.

The most striking characteristic of all the beast empires is their hatred and subjugation of the Jews, God's chosen nation, the natural line of Abraham through which Messiah would come. Because the earth's ultimate King of kings and Lord of lords would arise from that divinely blessed and protected nation, Satan has continually sought ways to destroy Israel in his vain attempt to frustrate Christ's rightful and sovereign rule over the earth.

As we look back through biblical history, six nations, or empires, were temporarily successful in subjugating the Hebrew people. They first persecuted the Hebrews even before they became an actual nation and took possession of the Promised Land under the leadership of Joshua.

(1) *Egyptian (Hamitic)*. The first beast empire was Egypt, a country descended from Mizraim,* a son of Ham (Gen. 10:6). A certain Egyptian king "who did not know Joseph" saw the rapidly growing numbers of the Hebrews as a threat to his throne and his people. Consequently he enslaved and severely persecuted them in their adopted land, the very land which the Lord, through Joseph, had spared from great famine (see Exod. 1:8-14). The pharaoh twice attempted infanticide. First he ordered the Hebrew midwives to kill all male babies at birth, and when that scheme failed because the godly midwives refused to obey that heinous order, the king ordered all male Hebrew infants drowned in the Nile (Exod. 1:15-22; cf. Acts 7:19, 20). God, however, protected the infant Moses from death and even caused him to be raised as a grandson of that pharaoh — protected, educated, and favored in the very household of the heartless king. The Lord

* Hebrew for Egypt.

eventually used Moses to lead His nation out of Egypt and to give them His sacred law at Sinai. And when the pharaoh and his great army were miraculously drowned in the Red Sea while attempting to overtake the fleeing Hebrews, Egypt fell into decline and never fully regained her former glory and power.

(2) *Assyrian (Semitic).* The second beast empire was Assyria, a Semitic nation descended from Asshur, a son of Shem (Gen. 10:22). The national god of Assyria was named after their forefather, Asshur, and was supremely a god of war and arrogant brutality. Under King Shalmaneser, Assyria conquered the northern kingdom of Israel in 722 B.C. Because Israel's King Hoshea conspired with Egypt against Shalmaneser, "the king of Assyria captured Samaria and carried Israel [the northern kingdom, ten of the twelve tribes] away into exile to Assyria, and settled them in Halah and Habor, on the river of Gozan, and in the cities of the Medes" (2 Kings 17:6).

(3) *Babylonian (probably Semitic).* The third beast empire was Babylon, who conquered Jerusalem, the heart of the southern kingdom representing two of the twelve tribes of Israel, in 597 B.C. and destroyed Solomon's Temple in 586 B.C. This beast empire was in control of Jerusalem when the prophetic book of Daniel was written. The citizens of Babylon possibly descended from Ham, through Cush and Nimrod, and settled "in the land of Shinar," later called Babylonia (see Gen. 10:8, 10). There is some question today about the Hamitic lineage of Nebuchadnezzar, however, since the Chaldeans are Semitic and it was their language and literature that dominated the Babylonian Empire (Dan. 1:4). Likewise, Abraham, the father of the Hebrews (Semitic), was from "Ur of the Chaldeans" (Gen. 11:31), Ur being a city approximately one hundred miles southeast of Babylon. Either way, Babylon is the first empire depicted in Nebuchadnezzar's statue and, as Daniel makes explicit in his interpretation, the magnificent head of gold represented the king himself (Dan. 2:38; cf. v. 32).

(4) *Medo-Persian (Japhethite).* This fourth beast empire is represented in Nebuchadnezzar's statue as the chest and arms of silver, a "kingdom inferior to" that of Nebuchadnezzar (Dan. 2:39). The Medes and Persians descended from Japheth, the two separate nations making up this fourth beast empire being pictured perfectly by the two arms of Nebuchadnezzar's statue. In 474 B.C., during the reign of Xerxes (called Ahasuerus in Esther 1:1), Haman the Agagite was given authority by the king over all the princes of the kingdom. Haman, "the enemy of the Jews" (Esther 3:10), was clearly an instrument of Satan.

Immediately upon receiving that almost unlimited authority, Haman sent letters "by couriers to all the king's provinces to destroy, to kill, and to annihilate all the Jews, both young and old, women and children, in one day, the thirteenth day of the twelfth month, which is the month Adar, and to seize their possessions as plunder" (3:13). It is interesting to note that the modern Iranian (Persian) name Khomeni is derived from the ancient name Haman. It was during the rule of this fourth beast empire (445 B.C.) that the "seventy weeks" of Gentile domination of Israel (predicted by Daniel) began.

(5) *Greek (Japhethite).* The fifth beast empire was also descended from Japheth and is represented in Nebuchadnezzar's statue as the "third kingdom [from the time of Daniel's writing] of bronze, which will rule over all the earth" (Dan. 2:39). After the death of Alexander the Great, his empire was divided among his four generals. It is from the line of General Seleucus, who was given Syria to rule, that Antiochus Epiphanes descended. Antiochus came to the throne in 175 B.C. and, like Haman, almost immediately began severe persecution of Jews (Dan. 8:23-25; 1 Macc. 1 – 6). His most heinous acts were to plunder the Jerusalem Temple and to sacrifice swine flesh on its altar. As this volume continues, we will see that the life and career of Antichrist will perfectly parallel the life and career of Antiochus.

(6) *Roman (Japhethite).* Like the two preceding beast empires, Rome was also from the line of Japheth. The territories it eventually conquered and ruled were by far the most extensive the world had seen until that time. And once again, in the same manner that the two arms of silver perfectly reflected the dual leadership of the fourth beast empire (the Medes and the Persians), the two legs of iron perfectly reflect the Roman Empire at its peak, with its Western Division (Rome) and its Eastern Division (Constantinople). This sixth beast empire (the fourth one in Nebuchadnezzar's statue) was "as strong as iron; inasmuch as iron crushes and shatters all things, so, like iron that breaks in pieces, it will crush and break all these in pieces" (Dan. 2:40). It is to this sixth beast empire that John referred when he wrote, "five have fallen, one [the Roman Empire] is" (Rev. 17:10). This is also the beast empire that fulfilled Daniel's prophecy that "the Messiah will be cut off and have nothing, and the people of the prince who is to come will destroy the city and the sanctuary" (Dan. 9:26) — which is clearly a reference to the Roman general Titus (son of an emperor and an emperor himself for a brief time), who destroyed the city of Jerusalem and Temple in A.D. 70, slaughtering over a million Jews in the process.

Careful examination of the first six empires reveals several clues concerning the identity of the seventh, which, like the first two empires (the Egyptian and the Assyrian), is not depicted in Nebuchadnezzar's statue. All six empires exerted direct and dominant control over Israel, taking away her independence and physically persecuting her citizens, often to death. The empires became progressively larger geographically and progressively more ruthless in their treatment of Israel. And, of course, all six empires were pagan and worshiped false gods.

But another significant reality begins to emerge. The first three beast empires of Satan (before the beginning of the "seventy weeks" of Daniel in 445 B.C.) were all descendants of either Ham or Shem. However, beginning with the fourth beast empire (the Medo-Persian), the empire in existence when the seventy weeks of Gentile domination predicted by Daniel began, the fourth, fifth and sixth beast empires of Satan were all from the line of Japheth. In other words, through the end of the sixty-ninth week (483 years) of Daniel's seventy-week "curse" on Israel, all of the beast empires that Satan has used have all been from the same ancestral background — namely, Japhethite. As we will see very soon below, the seventh beast empire was no exception.

THE MYSTERIOUS SEVENTH BEAST EMPIRE

When we come to identify the seventh beast empire mentioned in Revelation 17:10, 11, we encounter a potential problem. It is of great importance to note that there is no mention or even hint of the seventh beast empire in either the statue of Nebuchadnezzar's dream or in Daniel's vision of the four beasts recounted earlier in this chapter. As we will see, the seventh empire would have to appear in the statue after the legs of iron (the sixth beast empire, Rome), but before the feet with its ten toes of iron and clay representing the final ten-nation beast empire of Satan (Dan. 2:40, 41).

In direct parallel to the dream of Nebuchadnezzar, the final beast in Daniel's later vision represents the ancient Roman Empire (Dan. 7:7a), from whose descendants at some unspecified later time there will arise a ten-nation confederacy ruled by "another horn, a little one." This "little horn" will rise up among the ten-nation confederacy, overthrow three of the original "horns," and then rule over all ten nations (Dan. 7:7b, 8, 24), clearly a reference to the eighth and final beast empire (see

Rev. 17:12, 13). Again there is no mention of a seventh beast empire which would have to exist between the Roman Empire and the final beast empire of ten nations ruled by Antichrist (the little horn).

Yet Christ's revelation to John clearly identifies a mysterious seventh beast empire that appears *before* the eighth and final beast empire, but *after* the Roman Empire (see Rev. 17:10). This seventh empire would have to come *before* the ten toes of clay and iron in Nebuchadnezzar's dream and *before* the ten horns in Daniel's vision. This is seen clearly in Revelation, which was written about A.D. 90 during the time of the sixth king (representing the Roman Empire). John is told: "They are seven kings [representing seven separate beast empires]; five have fallen [the first five beast empires], one is [the Roman Empire], the other [the seventh] has not yet come; and when he comes, he must remain a little while. And the beast which was and is not [Antichrist], is himself also an eighth [the leader of the final beast empire], and is one of the seven, and he goes to destruction. And the ten horns [the eighth beast empire] which you saw are ten kings [representing the eighth beast empire], who have not yet received a kingdom, but they receive authority as kings with the beast for one hour [during the seventieth week]" (Rev. 17:10-12).

In other words, after the Roman Empire (the sixth beast empire) but before the final ten-nation beast empire (the eighth beast empire), there is a seventh empire never even hinted at in the Old Testament. Before considering why the seventh beast empire is missing in both passages in Daniel, it would be helpful to see clearly how the empires identified in these passages relate to the eight beast empires of Satan described in Revelation 17, as shown in the following chart.

With this chart in mind, we can now begin to see why the seventh beast empire of Revelation 17 is omitted from both Nebuchadnezzar's dream and Daniel's vision of the beast empires. And for the key to this explanation we need to consider this in light of God's revelation to Daniel of the seventy weeks as discussed in the preceding chapter.

As mentioned above, Daniel wrote his book after the Babylonians under Nebuchadnezzar had already conquered Jerusalem, plundered the Temple, and exiled most Israelites, including Daniel himself. During the first year of King Darius (539-538 B.C.) Daniel became deeply burdened about the plight of his people and the unrepentant wickedness that had brought that plight upon them. He therefore made earnest intercession on their behalf, acknowledging their distress as a consequence of the curse (see Dan. 9:11, 13, 18).

SATAN'S EIGHT BEAST EMPIRES

THE REVELATION TO JOHN CONCERNING THE EIGHT BEAST EMPIRES Revelation 17:3, 9–12	NEBUCHADNEZZAR'S DREAM OF THE STATUE Daniel 2:31–43	DANIEL'S VISION OF THE BEAST Daniel 7:1–28	SEVENTY WEEKS OF DANIEL Daniel 9:24–27
1st Beast Empire Egyption (Hamitic)	The first two empires are not mentioned here because this dream concerned only things in the future, after Daniel's time—things that "will take place in the later days" (Dan. 2:29).	The first two empires also are not mentioned here because this vision concerned only future events—"kings who will arise" (Dan. 7:17).	
2nd Beast Empire Assyrian (Semitic)			
626 B.C.			
3rd Beast Empire Babylonian (Semitic)	Head of gold	A beast like a lion	
539 B.C.			
4th Beast Empire Medo-Persian (Japhethite)	Breast and arms of silver	Another beast resembling a bear	445 B.C. Decree of Artaxerxes
330 B.C.			The 69 "weeks" 483 prophetic years
5th Beast Empire Greek (Japhethite)	Belly and thighs of bronze	A beast lke a leopard	
63 B.C.			
6th Beast Empire Roman (Japhethite)	Legs of iron	A dreadful and terrifying beast	33 A.D. Messiah "cut off"
70 A.D.			The gap
7th Beast Empire The other beast which "has not yet come [and] must remain a little while" (Rev. 17:10)	Not mentioned	Not mentioned	70 A.D. "the city and the sanctuary destroyed" 1948 A.D. Israel restored
8th Beast Empire "The ten horns which . . . receive authority as kings with the beast" (Rev. 17:12)	Ten toes partly iron and partly clay	Ten horns and the little horn	The 70th "week" 7 years

The Lord responded to that cry for mercy by revealing to Daniel the length of time in which the disobedient nation would continue to endure the hardships of foreign oppression: "Seventy weeks [i.e., seventy seven-year periods, or 490 years] have been decreed for your people and your holy city, to finish the transgression, to make an end of sin, to make atonement for iniquity, to bring in everlasting righteousness, to seal up vision and prophecy, and to anoint the most holy" (Dan. 9:24). This seventy "weeks" (490 years) would begin with "a decree to restore and rebuild Jerusalem" (v. 25). Israel was looking for an immediate reprieve, but God told her through Daniel that she would have to endure 490 more years of Gentile domination — domination of both the nation and her holy city, Jerusalem, *while Israel, or at least a remnant of Israel, remained in or at least had free access to her own land — in particular their holy city of Jerusalem.*

THE INTERVENING GAP

As we saw in the last chapter, the "decree to restore and rebuild Jerusalem" was actually given by Artaxerxes Longimanus in 445 B.C. (see Neh. 2:5). And when we calculate the exact time between the date of this decree to Christ's arrival in Jerusalem on Palm Sunday, it comes to exactly 483 prophetic years, after which "the Messiah will be cut off and have nothing" (Dan. 9:26a). This then leaves seven years (one "week") until the 490 years of Gentile domination of Israel will be complete.

This intervening gap, therefore, came about as the result of Israel rejecting her Messiah, thereby delaying the last seven-year period. Because Israel rejected her Messiah, she also suffered God's ultimate curse as foretold by Moses in his warnings to the nation of Israel concerning the blessings or the curses of God — the curse of being scattered to the ends of the earth without access to her holy land, to her holy city, or to her holy Temple.

The reason now becomes clear as to why the mysterious seventh beast empire is not depicted in Nebuchadnezzar's dream of the statue (Dan. 2), nor in Daniel's vision of the beast empires (Dan. 7), but only in the book of Revelation, written circa A.D. 90, twenty years *after* the *Diaspora* began. If Israel had not rejected her Messiah, the great *Diaspora* would have never occurred, and the seventieth "week" would have begun without the seventh beast empire ever coming into existence, the final beast empire coming directly out of the Roman Empire. It would have most likely appeared sometime during the first century A.D. — *after* "Messiah [is] cut off [33 A.D.]" and the desctruction of "the city and the sanctuary [70 A.D.]" (Dan. 9:26).

The seventh beast empire, therefore, is radically different from the first six beast empires. Unlike the others, it would brutalize the people of Israel during the intervening gap between the sixty-ninth and seventieth week — *when Israel is out of her land, dispersed among the nations to the ends of the earth.* Even the early church did not fully understand the interval, until after the *Diaspora* actually began with the destruction of Jerusalem and the Temple in A.D. 70. Moreover, the first scriptural reference to the seventh beast empire is in the book of Revelation, which was written some twenty years after the *Diaspora* had begun, after the church began to realize that Christ was not going to return soon after His resurrection.

THE SEVENTH BEAST EMPIRE IDENTIFIED

We can now summarize the essential characteristics of the seventh beast empire:

(1) It must come after the sixth beast empire (Rome).

(2) It must persecute the Jewish people while they are out of their land, dispersed "from one end of the earth to the other."

(3) It "must remain a little while" (Rev. 17:10b).

(4) It would be hideously cruel in its persecution and slaughter of the Jewish people as prophesied in the curses recorded in Deuteronomy (see 28:64-67).

(5) It must exist and come to an end *before* Israel would return to her land.

(6) And finally, since Israel returned to her land as a nation in 1948, there is only one thing we can conclude — *the seventh beast empire had to have existed sometime between A.D. 70 and 1948.*

The shocking reality is that only one nation in history fits these criteria — Nazi Germany, the Third Reich, under the absolute and demonic dictatorship of Adolf Hitler! The two overriding ambitions of Hitler were, first, to establish a thousand-year reign over the entire world — the counterfeit millennium of a demonic messiah; and, second, to totally exterminate all Jews. As we will see further in the next chapter, Hitler's ancestry was Aryan-European, from the line of Japheth — like all the beast empires that have dominated or will dominate Israel during the seventy weeks (490 years) of Gentile domination.

A PREVIEW OF THE EIGHTH BEAST EMPIRE

In his attempt to destroy the elect nation of God, Satan has already employed seven of the eight beast empires, as described earlier in this chapter. With Israel now in control of all her land, in particular the city of Jerusalem, the rise of the eighth beast empire is imminent. This eighth empire will be the last and by far the worst. It will be a unique composite of the previous beast empires since the time of Daniel and will be driven primarily by the descendants of Japheth, properly called Aryans, who historically have been anti-Semitic in the extreme. It will also somehow be tied to the same ancestry that drove the Roman Empire (the iron legs), becoming the iron component of the toes of iron and clay, as depicted in Nebuchadnezzar's statue.

Satan's ultimate objective will be to provide the world with a totally ungodly king and a totally ungodly and worldwide kingdom over which to rule. That scheme includes his intent to annihilate all Jews — especially "the woman" — that is, those within the nation of Israel who refuse to yield to his ultimate leadership — and "the rest of her offspring [including believing Gentiles], who keep the commandments of God and hold to the testimony of Jesus" (Rev. 12:17). By worshiping the beast (Antichrist) or his image, or by taking his mark on their right hand or forehead (Rev. 13:16-18), those who declare their allegiance to Antichrist will forfeit all possibility for salvation (Rev. 14:9-11). This satanically inspired and supremely arrogant tyrant will establish the eighth and final beast empire in a desperate last attempt to gain complete and permanent control of earth for himself. Thus Antichrist will attempt to destroy every man, woman, or child in the nation of Israel and anyone else who will refuse to worship him or his image and thereby become a potential citizen of the millennial kingdom over which Christ has promised to rule.

God has promised Israel that the ten nations that will someday comprise the eighth and final beast empire of Satan will be harvested by fire during the day of the Lord's wrath (see chapter 18 of this book). But before that time of final accounting, those nations will be under the demonic and powerful leadership and control of Antichrist and will wreak unimaginable havoc on the elect of God (Matt. 24:21, 22). Having unwittingly made a covenant with Antichrist at the beginning of the seventieth week (see chapter 10), many of the Jews living in Israel will feel secure and will be unsuspecting for three and a half years — until Antichrist conquers Jerusalem, enthrones himself in a rebuilt temple or sanctuary, and demands and receives the worship of a demonically controlled earth. Then he and his confederacy will inaugurate the time of Jacob's trouble, referred to by Christ as the great tribulation by Antichrist (Matt. 24:21). As Daniel states, this "will be a time of distress such as never occurred since there was a nation until that time" (12:1).

What will be the composition of the eighth and final beast empire? As we will see further in the next chapter, the critical issue is not so much a matter of geographic location as it is of their ancestry as given in the table of nations in Genesis 10. In other words, those ten "nations" or "kingdoms" that will make up the final beast empire will represent ten specific lines of ancestral descent, all of which can be traced back to the table of nations. As we will see, the final beast empire will be a composite of all the other beast empires of Satan that have existed during Daniel's seventy weeks and during the interlude between the sixty-ninth and seventieth weeks. As with the others, it will be dominated by the Japhethite, Indo-European peoples properly called Aryan, and both its leadership and its people will be totally and completely anti-Semitic.

The Eighth and Final Beast Empire

With Israel now back in her own homeland, there is much speculation concerning events taking place in Europe, especially as they may seem to pertain to the final ten-nation confederation of nations that will comprise the eighth and final beast empire of Satan. Although certain historical events, such as the restoration of Israel as a nation in 1948, have indisputable end-times significance, it is foolish and futile to attempt to relate all major contemporary events or circumstances to biblical prophecy — even when they profoundly involve Israel or other parts of the Middle East. History should never determine prophetic interpretation, but rather prophetic truth should always be the basis for understanding the events of history. And even when one starts with biblical revelation, identifying current events with specific biblical end-time events should be done with tentativeness and the utmost caution.

Attempts, for example, to equate the modern European Common Market, now called the European Community (EC), with the final ten-nation empire of the last days are at best risky and, in this author's mind, completely out of touch with what Scripture clearly teaches, as we shall see in the remainder of this chapter. The makeup of that coalition has changed numerous times, and many of the member nations do not correspond to any territorial, political, or people group spoken of in end-time prophecies concerning the final beast empire. Whether or not the composition and nature of the EC will someday change sufficiently to make it a candidate for the prophetic ten-nation empire, only time will tell. But I wouldn't hold my breath.

WHAT WE CAN KNOW

Some things about the final beast empire, however, can be known with certainty. The following passage from the book of Daniel, quoted in part in the preceding chapter, gives the first scriptural mention of this eighth and final beast empire of Satan and reveals a number of specific characteristics about it.

After this I kept looking in the night visions, and behold, a fourth beast [the Roman Empire], dreadful and terrifying and extremely strong; and it had large iron teeth. It devoured and crushed, and trampled down the remainder with its feet; and it was different from all the beasts that were before it, and it had ten horns [the ten kingdoms comprising the final beast empire]. While I was contemplating the horns, behold, another horn [Antichrist], a little one, came up among them, and three of the first horns were pulled out by the roots before it; and behold, this horn possessed eyes like the eyes of a man, and a mouth uttering great boasts.

. . . Then I desired to know the exact meaning of the fourth beast, which was different from all the others, exceedingly dreadful, with its teeth of iron and its claws of bronze, and which devoured, crushed, and trampled down the remainder with its feet, and the meaning of the ten horns that were on its head, and the other horn which came up, and before which three of them fell, namely, that horn which had eyes and a mouth uttering great boasts, and which was larger in appearance than its associates.

. . . Thus he [Gabriel] said: "The fourth beast [the Roman Empire] will be a fourth kingdom on the earth, which will be different from all the other kingdoms, and it will devour the whole earth and tread it down and crush it. As for the ten horns, out of this kingdom ten kings will arise [representing the final beast empire]; and another [Antichrist] will arise after them, and he will be different from the previous ones and will subdue three kings. And he will speak out against the Most High and wear down the saints of the Highest One, and he will intend to make alterations in times and in law; and they [the saints] will be given into his hand for a time, times, and half a time [three and a half years]. (Dan. 7:7, 8, 19, 20, 23-25; cf. v. 21)

Several closely related verses in the book of Revelation clearly indicate that the ten-nation satanic empire seen in Daniel's vision (the ten horns) is the same ten-nation beast pictured in the revelation of Christ to John, which is also described symbolically as ten horns:

And he [the dragon] stood on the sand of the seashore. And I saw a beast coming up out of the sea, having ten horns [the final beast empire] and seven heads [leaders of the first seven beast empires], and on his horns were ten diadems, and on his heads were blasphemous names. . . . And I saw one of his heads [Antichrist] as if it had been slain, and his fatal wound was healed. And the whole earth was amazed and followed after the beast; . . . And it was given to him to make war with the saints and to overcome them; and authority over every tribe and people and tongue and nation was given to him. And all who dwell on the earth will worship him. (Rev. 13:1, 3, 7, 8)

As seen in the last chapter, this eighth beast empire is also portrayed in Nebuchadnezzar's dream by the ten toes of iron mixed with clay, again reflecting the ten separate kingdoms that comprise the final beast empire. Interpreting King Nebuchadnezzar's dream, Daniel explained that "the feet and toes, partly of potter's clay and partly of iron . . . will be a divided kingdom; but it will have in it the toughness of iron, inasmuch as you saw the iron mixed with common clay. . . . And in that you saw the iron mixed with common clay, they will combine with one another in the seed of men; but they will not adhere to one another, even as iron does not combine with pottery" (Dan. 2:41-43).

The significance of all three of these passages that describe the final beast empire of Satan is that the strength of the final beast empire, the iron, will come from its *ancestry* in the "legs of iron" — in other words, from *the ancestry of the Roman Empire*. Therefore, before we can identify which nations will be part of Antichrist's final ten-nation confederacy, it is necessary to have at least some understanding of what the ancestry of Rome was. We know in general that Rome is Japhethite, rather than Hamitic or Semitic. But Japheth had seven sons, and having an understanding of which of these sons drove the Roman Empire will give us a better understanding of the final beast empire. As background for gaining this insight into the ancestry of Rome, one must have a clear understanding of the table of nations given in Genesis 10. A proper view of this table avoids the common trap of trying to make Scripture fit current events, movements, and political entities, instead allowing current events to fit themselves into prophetic Scripture.

THE TABLE OF NATIONS

The table of nations tracks the ancestry of Noah after the Flood through his three sons, Shem, Ham, and Japheth, who are therefore the fathers of all nations in the world today. The many references in this book to Semitic, Hamitic, or Japhethite peoples pertain to the descendants of Shem, Ham, and Japheth respectively. Understandably there are differences of opinion about the ancestry of the various ethnic groups that exist today, but the biblical descriptions of the nations that will comprise the final beast empire leave no doubt about their ancestry, despite any possible uncertainty about precise geography. As a general rule of thumb, in relation to the eight beast empires of Satan, the Semitic peoples are considered Jewish or Arabic, the Hamitic peoples the blacks, and the Japhethite peoples the fair-skinned Caucasian races.

The following table gives a complete listing of *all the sons* of Shem, Ham, and Japheth, but lists *only those grandsons* which have a direct bearing on the ten kingdoms that will comprise the eighth beast empire of Satan. (The sons of Shem, Ham, and Japheth are placed directly under the father's name, while grandsons are indented to the right immediately after their father.)

THE HISTORICAL MOVEMENTS OF THE NATIONS

Understanding the movement of these nations or people groups over the centuries is critical for identifying the participants in Satan's eighth beast empire. It was indeed God's sovereign will that the nations would, over time, move throughout the world and settle in places determined beforehand by God Almighty. Thus, after the ark came to rest on Mt. Ararat, in what is now eastern Turkey, "God

---

TABLE I

THE TABLE OF NATIONS

JAPHETH	HAM	SHEM
(Japhethite Nations)	(Hamitic Nations)	(Semitic Nations)
Gomer	Cush	Elam
Togarmah	Nimrod	Asshur
Magog	Mizraim	Arpachshad
Madia	Put	Lud
Javan	Cannan	Aram
Tubal		
Meshech		
Tiras		

(The present locations of the nations or peoples shown in this table are discussed later in the sections on the "three power-base nations" and the "seven secondary nations." See further note 1 for a brief description of where these nations seem to have settled and the cautions that must be made concerning the certainty of present locations.)[1]

---

blessed Noah and his sons and said to them, 'Be fruitful and multiply, and fill the earth'" (Gen. 9:1). In other words, with their wives and forthcoming children they were to spread throughout the world and not remain in one area.

Yet after some three hundred years they had not dispersed. Instead of "filling the earth," they had established themselves together in and around the ancient city of Babylon, a city founded by Nimrod, a grandson of Ham (see Gen. 10:6-10), located in the region of Babylonia (modern-day southern Iraq). Scripture specifically tells us that Shem was still alive at this time and that he did not die until several hundred years later, at the age of six hundred, more than five hundred years after the Flood (Gen. 11:10, 11). And so, even though the ages of Ham and Japheth are not recorded in Scripture, it is fair to assume that they too were alive in the ancient city of Babylon, as well as their sons and grandsons.

These direct descendants of Noah said to themselves, "Come, let us build for ourselves a city, and a tower whose top will reach into heaven, and let us make for ourselves a name; lest we be scattered abroad over the face of the whole earth" (Gen. 11:4). In other words, they made plans to deliberately disobey God's command to disperse throughout the world. Greatly angered by their rebelliousness, God declared that the name of that place would become Babel, because it was there that "the Lord confused the language of the whole earth; and from there the Lord scattered them abroad over the face of the whole earth" (v. 9). Because there were no roads, because even nearby lands were virtually unknown, and because the various tribal groups no longer shared a common language, this divinely forced dispersion was necessarily slow, arduous, and nomadic.

The Japhethite tribes of Magog, Meshech, and Tubal, usually considered to have been especially nomadic, probably were among the first to push out the fringes of civilization — especially to the north, where the weather and terrain were more difficult to overcome. As will be discussed later, the exact locations of the final settlements of those three peoples are of considerable importance to eschatology. But it is important to remember that at different times in history the ancestry of these nomadic families can be traced to different parts of the world, as they continued to conquer new frontiers. Eventually, however, even they finally settled down in a particular location. (Normally when the table of nations ends its chronology at a grandson of Noah — for example, Magog or Tiras, sons of Japheth [Gen. 10:2] — this seems to indicate that this particular family traveled together and finally settled together in the same general area. On the other hand, when great grandsons of Noah are listed — for example, Togarmah, the son of Gomer, the grandson of Japheth, the great grandson of Noah [Gen. 10:3] — his parents settled in one location and stayed, while Togarmah moved on to new territories alone.)

It was not by human determination but by divine decree that those particular people groups, as well as all others throughout history, eventually settled in the areas where they did. As Paul made clear to the philosophers on Mars Hill (the Areopagus), "[God] made from one every nation of mankind to live on all the face of the earth, having determined their appointed times, and the boundaries of their habitation" (Acts 17:26). Many centuries earlier Moses had explained to Israel that "when the Most High gave the nations their inheritance, when He separated the sons of man, He set the boundaries of the peoples . . ." (Deut. 32:8).

Therefore, as we look at who the beast empires of Satan represented, especially the empire still future that will be comprised of ten separate nations, it is important to remember that *the key issue is ancestry, not geography*. It is also important to remember that, depending on whose ancestry is being tracked, some people moved a ways and then stayed there, some stayed in one particular area while their sons settled in new and different areas, and others kept moving and did not finally settle down until after much of the Old Testament was written. But ancestry is the crucial issue — in fact, the only issue — especially as we examine the eighth and final beast empire, with its ten-nation (ancestral) coalition.

IRON MIXED WITH CLAY

As we have seen, the "iron" depicted in the legs of iron in Nebuchadnezzar's statue extends down into the toes where the iron is mixed with clay. As such the iron represents the strength or leadership of the ten-nation coalition with its iron roots extending back to Rome. Clay, on the other hand, is a composite of various minerals which perhaps may bond together "in the seed of men," but nevertheless will not bond to the iron, "even as iron does not combine with pottery"; the clay ancestry, therefore, maintains its own separate characteristics. In other words, ten such ancestry groups will combine with each other for the final campaign against God's elect during the last days, but they will still maintain their separate ancestral identities under the absolute iron grip of leadership that traces its roots back to ancient Rome.

Thus, it will be from the "iron" represented in the legs of iron in Nebuchadnezzar's statue that the leadership — the strength, so to speak — of the ten-nation eighth and final beast empire will arise. And because Rome was driven by Japhethite ancestry (like all the other beast empire nations during the seventy weeks of Daniel, as well as the interlude between the sixty-ninth and seventieth weeks), so the iron of the final beast empire will again represent Japhethite lineage. And just as the iron is found in all ten toes of the statue, so this same Japhethite ancestry will be present in all of the kingdoms that unite to form the final beast empire of Satan.

TRACING THE ROMAN ANCESTRY

But just where did the Roman people originate, those people who empowered the legs of iron that became the sixth beast empire? There seems to be no question that when the Roman Empire came into existence in the first century B.C. the descendants of Kittim, the son of Javan and grandson of Japheth, dominated what is now the country of Italy.[2] But Rome *began* as a powerful city-state — long before it ever became a nation, much less an empire; and it does not seem to be the Kittim ancestry who dominated Roman ancestry. Rome became a republic near the end of the fifth century B.C. and expanded into an actual empire — the largest and strongest in history until that time — in the beginning of the first century B.C. But it was the inhabitants of the *city-state*, not the various inhabitants of the Italian peninsula, who were considered true Romans. As Cyril Robinson explains in his book *A History of Rome*:

> In immemorial days volcanos were both numerous and active along this western coast [of Italy]; and its plains were for this reason left almost untenanted by the primitive inhabitants [the Kittim] of the peninsula. Of these [people with a] rudimentary culture, very little is known. In historic times their descendants were still to be found in the Ligurian mountains above Genoa and in moorlands of Apulia and Calabria in the southeast. Elsewhere, however, *at a very early date they were either absorbed or evicted by invaders [the Roman ancestry] coming from beyond the Alps — [who are] the true Italian race. The original home of this extremely virile people appears to have been in the Danube basin or even farther north. They were, in fact, a branch of that great Indo-European stock, tribes of which in the process of migration found their way into many lands.* For from the language that they spoke was derived not merely the Italian tongue, but Greek, German, Anglo-Saxon.[3]

The Alps are located just north of modern Italy, in what is now Austria and Switzerland, and the Danube River flows just north of the Alps in the southern region of modern-day Germany. The Danube River basin and the region just north and south of it would therefore be entirely Germanic. According to Robinson, then, the ancestry of Rome is rightly traced to the Indo-European nomadic peoples who came from the area in central Europe that we today recognize as Germanic and therefore is Japhethite in its lineage.

In the same way, Walter Wallbank and Alastair Taylor have written about the early settlers of Italy and the founders of Rome as follows:

> The Greeks and Romans were offshoots of a common Indo-European stock [Japheth], and settlement of the Greek and Italian peninsulas followed stages that were broadly parallel. Between 2000 and 1000 B.C., when Indo-European peoples invaded the

Aegean world, a western wing of this nomadic migration filtered into the Italian peninsula, [which was] then inhabited by indigenous Neolithic tribes. . . . One group [of these nomadic Indo-European peoples], the Latins, settled in the lower valley of the Tiber River, a region which became known as the plain of Latium.

. . . Modern scholars believe that early in the eighth century B.C. the occupants of some small Latin settlements on hills in the Tiber valley united land and established a common meeting place, the Forum, around which the city of Rome grew up.[4]

It is well established that these tribes of nomadic Indo-European peoples, whom this historian refers to as Aryans,[5] were of Japhethite descent. It is clear from the previous quotation that these peoples moved westward from the areas of the Black Sea and Caspian Sea, on to what later became the German-speaking countries of Europe, and then down into the Italian peninsula.

In other words, Rome was founded by northern nomadic Japhethite tribes who came down from European areas north of the Alps and the Danube basin. It is known that they traveled down the west coast of the Italian peninsula to the Latinus plain, in which the city of Rome was established and still remains. Both the Germanic regions of Europe and the former western U.S.S.R. are north of the Alps and were settled by nomads of Japhethite extraction. It is therefore probable that the founders of Rome were descendants of Magog, Meshech, or Tubal — although Magog seems most likely because it was these people who finally settled in the area (central Europe) from which the migration into the Italian peninsula originated.

It therefore seems certain that the ancestry of those nomadic peoples will be part of the final beast empire, the iron found in the toes of iron and clay, even though their lineage cannot unequivocally be traced back to a particular son of Japheth. Yet, if one carefully studies the movement of the Japhethite tribes after God's confusion of tongues at the tower of Babel, only the descendants of three sons of Japheth — Magog, Meshech, and Tubal — are the logical candidates for the tribes who moved north from the city of Babylon, over the Caucasus Mountains, and then west over a region north of the Black Sea into the Danube valley. Although Magog, as we shall see in the next section, is the most likely ancestral line, it is possible that actual ancestry is a combination of all three, as a result of the three lines having been combined in "the seed of men." It is not critical, however, to identify which of those three sons fathered the people who made the migration that gave birth to Rome, because all those people were Aryan descendants of Japheth — which, in this author's opinion, is the critical issue.

As we saw earlier, there is a direct continuity between the empire of iron represented by the legs of Nebuchadnezzar's statue and the later ten-nation empire described as iron mixed with clay. We can therefore expect to find this same continuity between the Aryan/Japhethite peoples who founded Rome (the sixth beast empire) and the Aryan/Japhethite ancestry of the ten kingdoms that will make up the final beast empire — especially in the dominant three nations that will drive the other seven.

With this in mind, we turn now to see how the Scriptures identify which nations — or more correctly, which *people groups* from the table of nations — will make up the ten-nation coalition of Satan's final beast empire. As emphasized earlier, the critical issue is not so much the *location* of specific geographic nations as it is the *ancestry of those peoples* who will comprise the ten-nation coalition. In some cases this may in fact involve all of a specific modern-day nation, but in other cases it may include only a specific people group with a specific ancestry within a nation. We begin by considering first what the Scriptures reveal concerning the identity of the three power-base nations and will then turn to consider the remaining seven secondary nations.

THE THREE POWER-BASE NATIONS IDENTIFIED

As he beheld the final beast in his vision, Daniel wrote, "While I was contemplating the [ten] horns, behold, another horn, a little one, came up among them, and three of the first horns were pulled out by the roots before it; and behold, this horn possessed eyes like the eyes of a man, and a mouth uttering great boasts" (Dan. 7:8). Later the prophet explains that "As for the ten horns, out of this kingdom ten kings will arise; and another will arise after them, and he will be different from the previous ones and will subdue three kings" (Dan. 7:23, 24). The "little horn" of verse 8 is the same as "another" king of verse 24 and is a depiction of Antichrist, who will come up from "among them," over-throwing the rulers of three nations, what this author calls the power-base nations that will drive the final beast empire.*

Identifying those three nations is critical. Because Israel is presently

* See chapter 9, endnote 25.

firmly established back in all of her own land with possession of her holy city, Jerusalem, in this writer's opinion the unification of those three nations is the only prophetic event that must yet occur before the seventieth week of Daniel can commence. Chapters 38, 39 of Ezekiel speak directly to end-time events[6] and for that reason reveal significant information about the events in and surrounding the seventieth week of Daniel, including crucial clues as to the identity of those dominant three nations. The key material is found in the first few verses of chapter 38. This passage definitely identifies two of the three ancestral groups and allows for two options for the third, both of which should be thoroughly considered.

In a key passage found in Ezekiel 38, the Lord tells the prophet, "Son of man, set your face toward Gog of the land of Magog, the prince of Rosh, Meshech, and Tubal, and prophesy against him, and say, 'Thus says the Lord God, "Behold, I am against you, O Gog, prince of Rosh, Meshech, and Tubal"'" (vv. 2, 3). That wording suggests that Gog (who, as we shall see, is Antichrist) is a Magogite and will rule over three nations, Rosh, Meshech, and Tubal — in perfect consistency with the critical prophetic passage in Daniel 7 that pictures the little horn overthrowing the three larger horns (v. 8).

But unlike Magog, Meshech and Tubal, the name Rosh is found nowhere in the table of nations. Therefore an immediate problem arises because, as has been clearly established, the final beast empire of Satan will be composed entirely of peoples whose lineage can be traced back to the table of nations. The solution to this seems to be found in a better rendering of the Hebrew given in the *King James Version*, which translates Ezekiel 38:2 as, "Son of man, set thy face against Gog, the land of Magog, the *chief prince* of Meshech and Tubal, and prophesy against him" (emphasis added). Some Jewish Talmudic scholars give similar translations of the Hebrew.[7] These renderings do not take Rosh to be a country (which explains why it does not appear in the Genesis 10 table of nations), but rather a title of leadership. The Hebrew term behind Rosh is often translated "head" or "chief" (as in Num. 31:26 ["heads"]; 1 Chron. 5:7 ["chief"]; Neh. 7:70, 71 ["heads"]). The idea therefore seems to be that Gog is the national leader of Magog. But Gog is also the international leader of Meshech and Tubal, thereby making him the ruler of a three-nation confederacy — Magog (not Rosh) being the other nation over which Gog rules.

We know with certainty from our key passage in Ezekiel that Gog (Antichrist) will definitely come from the line of Magog (one of the nomadic sons of Japheth) and that he will rule over three nations. Those three nations, then, will be *Magog* (or possibly Rosh, depending on how the Hebrew term *Ro'sh* is understood[8]), *Meshech*, and *Tubal*.

The overthrow of the three nations by a man of Magogite lineage will doubtless be a well-known public event when it occurs. This event itself will immediately identify the three nations and is the only major event remaining before the seventieth week can commence. Israel will then make a covenant with the leader of this newly formed, three-nation confederation for the sake of national security. (See further chapter 10 where this is discussed in detail.) Understanding who this Japhethite ancestry represents provides the best clue as to why Israel will be so anxious to become an ally rather than the enemy of this power-base confederation of nations when it actually does come together.

THE IDENTITY OF MAGOG

Josephus, the great Jewish historian of the first century A.D., identifies the Magogites as Scythians who branched eastward and westward from the region north of the Black Sea. This is in agreement with the writings in the Jewish Talmud[9] (for example, *Yerushalmi Megillah* 3:9) which identifies Magog as the Goths, a group of Nomadic tribes who destroyed the Scythians and made their homes in Scythian territory. This source also comments, "considering that the Goths were a Germanic people, the identification of Magog's descendants as the Goths is in accord with *Targum Yonasan* to Genesis 10:2."[10] *The Encyclopedia Britannica* notes that the Gothic language was the most certain base of the language spoken by the eastern Germanic tribes (Visigoths) in Europe.[11] It seems beyond doubt, therefore, that the Germanic line as we know it today is descended from Magog.[12]

We cannot be adamant about whether or not the Germanic ancestry of Magog will represent one of the three ancestral lines that come together to form the three-nation power base of Antichrist (because of the use of the Hebrew word *ro'sh* in our key passage), but this author is inclined to think that this will be the case. It does seem certain, however, that Gog (Antichrist) will come from the Germanic line of Magog, which seems most probably to be the iron ancestry of the Roman Empire. In this respect, it is interesting to note that Nazi Germany under Adolf Hitler claimed the title "The Third Reich" (The Third Empire) — and in so doing claimed to be a direct extension and heir to the rule of Rome as expressed over the centuries in the Holy Roman

Empire (The First Reich) and the empire of Kaiser Bismarck (The Second Reich).

However, as clear as the *ancestry* of the Magogites may be, *the exact geographical location* is much less clear. Obviously the majority of the Magogite ancestry is concentrated in modern-day Germany. But large numbers are also concentrated in other countries in Eastern and Western Europe — for example, in Austria, which was responsible for the slaughter of up to two million Jews during Hitler's Holocaust. But even within the former Soviet Union, there is a large concentration of people with Magogite/Germanic ancestry. Remarkably, these Germanic people are presently making an aggressive appeal to have a Germanic country of their own within the borders of the old Soviet Union, which would be located in the Volga River region, south and a little east of Moscow.[13] Thus it could be that the people representing the Magogite/Germanic ancestry could come entirely from within the borders of the former Soviet Union. This is a significant possibility, especially since the other two power-base peoples are also located today within the boundaries of the former Soviet Union.

THE IDENTITY OF ROSH

If Magog only describes the ancestry of Gog and is not a reference to one of the three power-base nations, then Rosh must be considered a specific ancestral group and should not be translated "chief prince" as rendered in the *King James Version*. Many interpreters, holding to the view that Rosh represents a people, maintain that Rosh is the name from which "Russia" is derived (cf. Henry M. Morris, *The Genesis Record* [Grand Rapids: Baker, 1976], p. 248). But it is more likely that the name Russia was derived from "Rus," which had its origins in the eighth or ninth century A.D. and is believed to be Scandinavian in derivation. We will probably never know whether or not the name Russia is derived in any way from the Hebrew *ro'sh*. But all interpreters who do identify Rosh with a people group always trace its forward lineage to Russia, probably because of its association with Meshech and Tubal in Ezekiel 38.

THE IDENTITY OF MESHECH AND TUBAL

The identity of the other two nations, Meshech and Tubal, is relatively simple. Certain Jewish writings indicate that by the eighth century A.D. the descendants of Meshech and Tubal were located in what is the former western portions of the U.S.S.R.,[14] with Meshech in the west near Moscow, and Tubal in the far western sections of Siberia near the city of Tobolsk, which is located in the former west central U.S.S.R., more than a thousand miles east of Moscow. It must be remembered that the Russian republic (which includes Siberia) measures over five thousand miles from east to west, and so even though Tobolsk is a thousand miles east of Moscow, this area is still considered western Russia. "Meshech clearly is preserved in the name Muskovi (the former name of Russia) and in Moscow. Tubal is known in the Assyrian monuments as the Tibareni, and probably has been preserved in the modern Russian city of Tobolsk."[15]

If this is true, it is obvious that sometime before the seventieth week of Daniel begins, the U.S.S.R. must divide,* and at least two of the resulting provinces, or states, must be ruled independently by at least two of the three horns that will be uprooted by the "little horn" (Antichrist) when he comes into power (Dan. 7:8). Or, if the U.S.S.R. does not completely dissolve, but instead becomes a loosely unified confederation, it will be the presidents of those former U.S.S.R. states who will become the rulers of those peoples when they give their allegiance to Antichrist. Or perhaps it will be just the leaders of particular peoples of common ancestry within those republics — not unlike the situation of the Palestinians and their distinct, separate leadership within the nation of Israel today.

In any case, those distinct lines of descent already exist in the former U.S.S.R. and are heavily Japhethite in ancestry — in contrast to the eastern provinces and peoples of the U.S.S.R., which have distinct and totally different ancestry.

THE ROMAN CONNECTION

With the identification of the power-base ancestry, several interesting facts begin to come to light. As discussed earlier in this chapter, the three nations that drive the eighth and final beast empire of Satan will have a connection with the ancient Roman Empire, as depicted by the legs of iron from which the feet and toes of iron and clay are partially derived. The Japhethite lineage that will dominate those three nations will in part represent the iron in the toes of iron and clay — the iron

---

* This paragraph was originally written prior to the breakup of the former U.S.S.R. in the fall of 1991. It was startling to see this breakup occur as required by the position presented here, and so this paragraph was left in its original form for the purpose of emphasis.

representing *ancestry* rather than *geography*, as stated numerous times already.

None of these three power-base nations, however, will be descended from ancient Italy because it was not the native Italians but the nomadic Japhethite descendants who founded the ancient Roman Empire. The most likely candidate for the founders of Rome would seem to be the line of Magog (rather than one of the lines of Japheth's other six sons) for the two reasons already discussed in some depth earlier in this chapter: first, because the people who established the city-state of Rome came from the Danube basin; and second, because the Danube basin is part of the area in Central Europe where the Magogites were the primary settlers. (We will see in chapter 11 that this assumption holds true, even when arrived at from a completely different direction.) The logical conclusion, then, is that the Magogites, from which the Germanic lineage descended, were the founders of the Roman Empire, which grew out of the city-state they had founded earlier. It is more than coincidental that the German title *kaiser* is derived from *caesar* and that so much of today's German culture can be traced directly back to the old Roman Empire.

On the other hand, the Roman Empire eventually dominated almost all of the Japhethite world of its time. The two legs of iron thus represent both the western division of the Roman Empire centered out of Rome and the eastern division (including most of Eastern Europe) out of Constantinople — in the same way that the two arms of silver represented two separate peoples, the Medes and the Persians. Just as *kaiser* is a derivative of *caesar*, so also is the Russian title *czar*. The "iron" in the toes of iron and clay will be, in this author's opinion, at least partially Germanic. But more than this, I believe that the "iron" better represents the *powerful ancestry* of all these other Japhethite peoples who will not "combine" with the "clay" ancestry of the final beast empire. The "iron," therefore, may be representative of all three of the rugged nomadic Japhethite peoples that will drive the final beast empire; or it may even be a broader representation of all the Japhethite ancestry represented in the final ten-nation coalition; or it may represent just the Japhethite ancestry that has dominated Israel during Daniel's seventy weeks. This author will not be adamant except to say that the "iron" certainly *includes* Germanic lineage from Magog, and to the degree that it is broader in scope, it may include all the Japhethite ancestry of Noah, as we shall see below.

In summary, then, the three-nation confederacy that Antichrist will use to control the final beast empire of Satan will be comprised of the three Japhethite and formerly strong nomadic peoples of the remote north — whose ancestry can be traced to the same people who both established and ruled the ancient Roman Empire. All three nations will be zealously anti-Semitic. And in this respect these nations will continue the consistent pattern followed by all of the beast empires who have dominated Israel during the seventy weeks of Daniel and the interlude as well — all of which have been driven by anti-Semitic leaders of Aryan/Japhethite ancestry.

THE SEVEN SECONDARY NATIONS IDENTIFIED

During John's vision on Patmos, the angel spoke of a later stage in the same series of events: "And the ten horns which you [John] saw are ten kings, who have not yet received a kingdom, but they receive authority as kings with the beast [Antichrist] for one hour. These have one purpose and they give their power and authority to the beast" (Rev. 17:12, 13). "For God has put it in their hearts," the angel goes on to explain, "to execute His purpose by having a common purpose, and by giving their kingdom to the beast, until the words of God should be fulfilled" (v. 17). By surrendering their nations to the rulership of Antichrist, those rulers unwittingly will fulfill God's own purposes and at the same time seal their own doom.

We have determined that the dominant three nations that comprise the final beast empire will include some if not all of the same Japhethite lineage that drove the ancient Roman Empire. The origin and identity of the other seven nations can also be clearly determined, as seen in additional passages taken from the prophetic books of Daniel and Ezekiel.

THREE SECONDARY NATIONS IDENTIFIED BY DANIEL

In order to identify three of the seven secondary nations, we need to look carefully again at the explanation of Nebuchadnezzar's dream given by Daniel.

You, O king, were looking and behold, there was a single great statue; that statue, which was large and of extraordinary splendor, was standing in front of you, and its appearance was awesome. The head of that statue was made of fine gold, its breast and its arms of silver, its belly and its thighs of bronze, its legs of iron, its feet partly of iron and partly of clay. You continued looking until a stone was cut out without hands, and it struck the statue on its feet of iron and clay, *and crushed them. Then the iron, the clay, the bronze, the silver and the gold were crushed all at the same time*, and became like chaff from the summer threshing floors; and the wind carried them away so that not a trace of them was found. But the stone that struck the statue became a great mountain and filled the whole earth. . . . And in the days of those kings the God of heaven will set up a kingdom which will never be destroyed, and that kingdom will not be left for another people; *it will crush and put an end to all these kingdoms*, but it will itself endure forever. Inasmuch as you saw that a stone was cut out of the mountain without hands and that *it crushed the iron, the bronze, the clay, the silver, and the gold*, the great God has made known to the king what will take place in the future; so the dream is true, and its interpretation is trustworthy. (Dan. 2:31-35, 44, 45, emphasis added)

This passage from Daniel tells us that before Christ (the stone "cut out without hands") establishes His millennial kingdom on earth, He will crush the final ten-nation beast empire (the "feet of iron and clay"), which will include "the bronze, the silver and the gold" — that is, the Greeks, the Medes and Persians, and the Babylonians (spoken of here in the reverse order of Daniel 2:32). In other words, the first three empires depicted in Nebuchadnezzar's statue (the Babylonian, the Medo-Persian, and the Greek) will all be incorporated into the final beast empire as part of the feet of iron and clay, along with the Roman Empire. As explained in the previous chapter, the Babylonian, Medo-Persian, and Greek empires were respectively the third, fourth, and fifth beast empires of Satan. Although seemingly invincible, direct ancestry from that awesome multinational empire will be utterly and permanently destroyed by God just before the Millennium, when rule over the earth comes back under His rightful and sovereign control.

In Daniel's vision of the four future beasts that would dominate both the nation of Israel and the city of Jerusalem (Dan. 7:4-7), we find exactly the same truth that was illustrated by Nebuchadnezzar's statue five chapters earlier. First he saw a lion with wings like an eagle (Babylon; cf. Jer. 4:7, 13), then a bear (Medo-Persia; cf. Isa. 13:17, 18), and then a leopard (Greece). After Alexander's death, the Greek empire was divided into four regions — Asia Minor, Syria, Egypt, and

Macedonia — represented by the leopard's four wings and four heads. The final beast of this vision represents the Roman Empire, from which the eighth beast empire of Satan will emerge.

Likewise, when we turn to Revelation we again find total consistency to our Old Testament passage — the first three beasts in Daniel correspond exactly to the composite beast that John saw in his vision on Patmos. Thus Revelation 13 refers to the final beast empire of Satan as having "ten horns and seven heads" and states further that this final beast empire "was like a leopard [Greece], and his feet were like those of a bear [Medo-Persia], and his mouth like the mouth of a lion [Babylon]. And the dragon [Antichrist] gave him his power and his throne and great authority" (vv. 1, 2).

A few verses later in Daniel 7 we are given further insight into the destiny of the eighth and final beast empire. "Then I kept looking," the prophet reports, "because of the sound of the boastful words which the horn [Antichrist, the "little" but dominant horn of Daniel 7:8] was speaking; I kept looking until the beast [Antichrist] was slain, and its body was destroyed and given to the burning fire. As for the rest of the beasts, their dominion was taken away, but an extension of life was granted to them for an appointed period of time" (Dan. 7:11, 12).

"The rest of the beasts" who were given a temporary extension of life (Dan. 7:12) seem certain to represent the first three kingdoms of the statue as they existed in ancient times. The temporary extension of life "for an appointed period of time" then refers to two things: first, the dominion of these three kingdoms would be taken away (i.e., each of these three kingdoms came to an end before Christ); but, secondly, each of these kingdoms would have "an extension of life" in the sense that they would continue to exist as a people (but not as a kingdom) until the defeat of Antichrist when the ancestry of these original beast empires will be utterly destroyed and burned along with all the other components in the feet of iron and clay — that is, when Christ, the stone "cut out of the mountain without hands," destroys the entire statue (Dan. 2:45) during His great day-of-the-Lord judgment.

In part, then, the final beast empire will be a composite of every previous beast empire that has dominated both Israel and God's holy city, Jerusalem, at the same time (chapter 6 looked at these in some detail). Daniel gives some insight into the importance of Jerusalem to God when he refers to Jerusalem as "Thy [God's] city Jerusalem, Thy holy mountain" (Dan. 9:16). It is for that reason that the 490-year curse was "decreed for your people and your holy city" (Dan. 9:24). In other words, all of the previous beast empires that have dominated Israel and God's holy city of Jerusalem will without exception be a part of the final beast empire of Satan that God will personally destroy.

In summary, then, we see that the final beast empire of Satan will include the *descendants* of the Babylonian (Semitic [Arpachshad], from the general vicinity of modern-day Iraq), the Medo-Persian (Japhethite [Madia, Tiras], from the general vicinity of modern-day Iran), and the Greek (Japhethite [Javan]) empires of ancient times (as well as the Romans who are directly represented by the iron). Like their forefathers, the descendants of these three former beast empires will once again align themselves with Satan to form his final evil empire, which Christ will destroy with a single blow when He returns for judgment.

FOUR SECONDARY NATIONS IDENTIFIED BY EZEKIEL

In addition to the three power-base nations of Magog (or possibly Rosh), Meshech, and Tubal, and the three nations represented in Nebuchadnezzar's statue just discussed (Babylon, Medo-Persia, and Greece), four additional nations of the ten-nation confederacy have yet to be identified.

After declaring God's judgment against Magog (Rosh), Meshech, and Tubal, Ezekiel goes on to include "Persia, Ethiopia, and Put with them, all of them with shield and helmet; Gomer with all its troops; Beth-togarmah from the remote parts of the north with all its troops — many peoples with you" (Ezek. 38:5, 6). If Magog (Rosh), Meshech, and Tubal are the three power-base nations of the ten-nation eighth beast empire, it seems reasonable to assume that the other four nations mentioned in this passage (Ethiopia, Put, Gomer, and Beth-togarmah) will also be member nations, representing the remaining clay kingdoms of Nebuchadnezzar's statue (with Persia already having been included in the previous group of nations just discussed).

When we trace the ancestry and present locations of these four nations or peoples we find the following: *Ethiopia* is descended from Cush, a son of Ham, and corresponds to modern Ethiopia and probably eastern Sudan in East Africa. *Put* was another son of Ham and corresponds to modern Libya. *Gomer* was a son of Japheth and corresponds generally, it is believed, to the Ukraine province in the western portion of the former U.S.S.R. *Togarmah* (Beth-togarmah, *Beth* in the Hebrew meaning "house of") was a grandson of Japheth and again corresponds in general to the province of Armenia in the southwestern portion of the former U.S.S.R. and perhaps the far eastern portion of Turkey and the northwestern portion of Iran.

OVERVIEW OF THE TEN NATIONS

If all of the above identifications are correct, ten nations (or people groups) comprising the final beast empire may be summarized in terms of their ancestry and present location as follows:

TABLE II

THE TEN NATIONS OF THE FINAL BEAST EMPIRE

Name of Nation or People Group	Modern Location	Ancestry (Son of)
THE THREE POWER-BASE NATIONS		
Magog (or Rosh)	Germanic areas* (or Russia prov.)	Japhethite (Magog)
Meshech	Russia prov.,western U.S.S.R.†	Japhethite (Meshech)
Tubal	Russia prov.,west-central U.S.S.R.†	Japhethite (Tubal)
THE SEVEN SECONDARY NATIONS		
Babylon	Iraq	Semitic (Arpachshad)
Medo-Persia	Iran	Japhethite (Madia, Tiras)
Greece	Greece	Japhethite (Javan)
Ethiopia	Ethiopia, including eastern Sudan	Hamitic (Cush)
Put	Libya	Hamitic (Put)
Gomer	Ukraine prov., western U.S.S.R.†	Japhethite (Gomer)
Togarmah	South-western U.S.S.R.†/eastern Turkey	Japhethite (Togarmah)

*This includes areas in the former U.S.S.R. where there is heavy Germanic ancestry.
†All references to the U.S.S.R. are, in fact, references to the "former" U.S.S.R.

SIGNIFICANCE OF THE TEN NATIONS

What, then, is the significance of those ten nations that will join to form the final beast empire of Satan? Of primary importance is the fact that *all seven sons and one grandson of Japheth* will be represented in the final composition of the nations. It is not possible to determine with certainty whether the iron of the "toes of iron and clay" represents only the nomadic line of Japheth (i.e., Magog, Meshech, and/or Tubal) that drove the ancient Roman Empire, or whether it represents the entire Aryan/Japhethite line that will dominate the final beast empire. But there is no doubt that the three-nation consortium that will drive the final beast empire will be as powerful as they are anti-Semitic. The significant fact to keep in mind, however, is that all of the beast empire nations of Satan that have dominated Israel during the seventy weeks — as well as the seventh beast empire (Germany) that sought to destroy Israel while she had no control of Jerusalem during the interlude of some two thousand years when she had no homeland — have been of Japhethite descent. The final beast empire will be no exception because, as just emphasized above, all seven sons of Japheth and one grandson will be represented in the final ten-nation consortium.

Of equal importance is the fact that the final beast empire of Satan will include all of his previous beast empires that have dominated God's holy city, Jerusalem. It is for this reason that Moses told the nation Israel that when "your outcasts are at the ends of the earth, from there the Lord your God will gather you . . . and the Lord your God will bring you into the land which your fathers possessed. . . . *And the Lord your God will inflict all these curses on your enemies and on those who hate you, who persecuted you*" (Deut. 30:4, 5, 7, emphasis added). Only two of the previous seven beast empires (the first two — Egypt and Assyria) will not be a part of the eighth and final beast empire of Satan. As will be seen in chapters 19 and 21 of this book, God will still have a remnant within those two nations, both Jewish and Gentile, and for that reason those nations are not a part of Antichrist's ten-nation consortium.

It is also of importance, as well as of interest, that the ancestral lines of the three power-base nations are all located in central or far eastern Europe (or perhaps far western Asia, as it were), though all are north of Israel. In this regard, the general location of these peoples fits the descriptions given by other prophets at various times. For example, the Lord promised His people Israel through the prophet Joel that He would deliver them from the evil coalition which will come upon Israel from the north: "Then the Lord will be zealous for His land, and will have pity on His people. . . . I will remove the northern army far from you, and I will drive it into a parched and desolate land, and its vanguard into the eastern sea, and its rear guard into the western sea. And its stench will arise and its foul smell will come up, for it has done great things" (Joel 2:18, 20). Similarly through Ezekiel, the Lord tells Gog, the leader of Satan's last empire, "You will come from your place out of the remote parts of the north, you and many peoples with you, all of them riding on horses, a great assembly and a mighty army" (Ezek. 38:15).

All three of the power-base nations certainly can be considered as being from the "remote parts of the north," especially so if the Magogites should rise up as a particular nation out of the former U.S.S.R. boundaries. The territories represented by Meshech and Tubal perfectly fit that description; and, as already established, the third nation — whether Magog or Rosh, whether in the former U.S.S.R. or in modern-day Germanic countries in Central Europe — is also from the north. As revealed through Ezekiel, this army will include "you and many peoples with you" (38:15). Those "many peoples" represent the other seven nations that will come together to form the final beast empire of Satan, most of them coming from north of Israel as well.

Another striking fact comes to light when we consider Joel 3:11, 12 and Zechariah 12:6, which indicate that the nations surrounding Israel will come up against her during a campaign just prior to the day of the Lord. When the geographic locations of the seven secondary nations are noted, the phrase "surrounding nations" takes on remarkable significance. As seen in the map on the facing page, those seven secondary nations will literally surround Israel, while the armies of the other three nations, which will be from the north, may already be in Jerusalem with their leader, Antichrist.

There is one last significant detail to keep in mind. It would appear as best as we can ascertain today that the ancestry of at least four of the final ten nations (Meshech, Tubal, Gomer and Togarmah) are all located in the western portion of what was once considered the Soviet Union. (To these four nations a fifth could be added if either Rosh should be included or if the Magog ancestry were to come out of a newly formed Germanic country in the former U.S.S.R., as is being proposed today.) It is remarkable to see that the Soviet Union has recently come apart (after this chapter was first written) — which is exactly what needed to happen before the final ten-nation coalition could come together. The former Soviet Union will nonetheless be heavily represented in the final beast empire, especially through the Japhethite ancestry located in the far western portion of this once powerful region.

When God assaults that eighth and final empire, He will be confronting the strongest force that Antichrist, with Satan's direct help, can muster. But the outcome of that conflict has been divinely

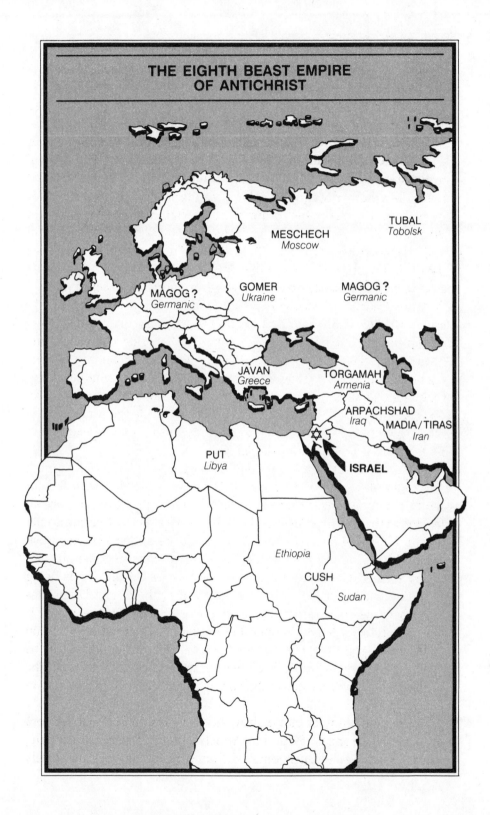

THE EIGHTH BEAST EMPIRE
OF ANTICHRIST

TUBAL
Tobolsk

MESCHECH
Moscow

MAGOG?
Germanic

GOMER
Ukraine

MAGOG?
Germanic

JAVAN
Greece

TORGAMAH
Armenia

ARPACHSHAD
Iraq

MADIA/TIRAS
Iran

PUT
Libya

ISRAEL

Ethiopia

CUSH

Sudan

ordained since eternity past and is foretold in Daniel's interpretation
of Nebuchadnezzar's dream:

> And in the days of those kings the God of heaven will set up a
> kingdom which will never be destroyed, and that kingdom will
> not be left for another people; it will crush and put an end to all
> these kingdoms, but it will itself endure forever. (Dan. 2:44)

8

Antichrist and His Foreshadow

Who will lead this "dreadful and terrifying" final beast empire of Satan? Scripture uses many terms to describe this ruthless international ruler. His best-known title is Antichrist, although Ezekiel knew him as Gog. He will be the supreme human destroyer in the history of the world. Careful exegesis reveals the startling truth that this most powerful and destructive of all human despots will be the ruler of one of the previous seven beast empires, a man who has already died but will be supernaturally brought back to life by Satan for the express purpose of commanding the final assault against Christ and His people. In order to gain the world's support and to consolidate all political and military power under his personal control, Antichrist will operate incognito prior to and throughout the first half of the seventieth week. During this time many will throw their lot in with him, only to find it impossible to extricate themselves once his true identity is revealed. (See further chapters 11 and 12 where this is covered fully.)

AN OVERVIEW OF ANTICHRIST'S STRATEGY

The beginning of Antichrist's strategy, as seen in the preceding chapter, will center on the creation of a ten-nation confederation. This will be heavily Aryan/Japhethite in its ancestry and vehemently anti-Semitic in all its objectives. Before the final consolidation of these ten nations, however, it is the opinion of this writer that Antichrist will first overthrow three nations in the far north which will become the power base by which he will drive his final empire.

This powerful and generally respected world leader will then make a covenant with the nation of Israel, ostensibly for her protection (see chapter 10). After Antichrist breaks his covenant with Israel, conquers Jerusalem, and establishes his throne in the rebuilt Temple, and after the age-long protector of the nation of Israel (the archangel Michael) is withdrawn, thereby giving Antichrist direct and unrestricted access to Israel — then, and only then, will Antichrist reveal his true identity and demand the world's worship as the only true god. He then will seek to destroy every Jew, every genuine Christian, and even every Gentile unbeliever who will not worship the beast (Antichrist) or his image or accept his soul-damning mark. Since Satan failed to eliminate or disqualify the King when He came as Redeemer, his only hope now is to eliminate the King's elect, "the woman [that portion of Israel that refuses to worship Antichrist] and . . . the rest of her offspring [Christian believers within the church], who keep the commandments of God and hold to the testimony of Jesus" (Rev. 12:17; see further chapter 13 of this book where this is covered fully).

THE PAST FORETELLS THE FUTURE

Students of Scripture have long noted the striking parallels between the character and activities of Antichrist during the end times and those of another despot, Antiochus Epiphanes, who conquered and ravaged Israel and the Temple during the second century B.C. Although from Daniel's perspective even the events referring to Antiochus were future, it is clear from the following verses that Daniel's focus moves even further into the future, specifically to the last days in the time of Antichrist: "And some of those who have insight [Jewish believers] will fall, in order to refine, purge, and make them pure, until the *end time*; because it is still to come at the appointed time. *Then the king [Antichrist] will do as he pleases, and he will exalt and magnify himself above every god*, and will speak monstrous things against the God of gods; and he will prosper until the indignation is finished, for that which is decreed will be done" (Dan. 11:35, 36, emphasis added).

Daniel, then, establishes the parallelism by referring to both Antichrist and Antiochus as "a small horn." But it is clear from the context of these two references that the "small horn" of Daniel chapter 7 (see vv. 8-27) is in reference to Antichrist, while the "small horn" of chapter 8 (see vv. 9-26) is in reference to Antiochus. The parallelism between Antichrist and Antiochus is indeed striking. We know, however, that it is more than coincidence and in fact reveals the intended meaning of Scripture because Christ Himself refers to Daniel's prophecy and draws upon this parallelism with His reference to the "abomination of desolation" in the Olivet Discourse (see Matt. 24:15). The "near" fulfillment of this event, as first predicted centuries earlier by Daniel, was of course in 168 B.C., with the ancient desecration of the Temple by Antiochus. The parallel, "far" fulfillment of this event will come at the midpoint of the last seven years of the end times, when Antichrist desecrates the rebuilt Temple in the last days. Thus, by looking at the ancient despot Antiochus we gain considerable insight into Antichrist and his strategy for the last days, as well as the many events that will occur during the seventieth week. We turn then to a brief overview of the parallels we find in Antiochus IV (Epiphanes) and the way in which he foreshadows Antichrist in the end times.

In ancient Israel, long after the end of her own monarchies and after most of the exiles had returned to the Promised Land, God's chosen nation, the natural line of Abraham, persisted in ever-increasing apostasy. Because of their blatant disbelief and disobedience, the Lord not only allowed His nation to be conquered and persecuted by an exceedingly cruel pagan oppressor named Antiochus Epiphanes, the Greek king of Syria, but He even permitted His own holy Temple in Jerusalem to be profaned.

An informative and vivid picture of Antiochus is found in the apocryphal book of 1 Maccabees — which, although not being inspired Scripture, nonetheless provides reliable historical information of that time. The writer gives the following account of the invasion of Israel by Antiochus and of Israel's willingness to make peace with him at any cost: "And there came out of them a wicked root, Antiochus surnamed Epiphanes, son of Antiochus the king. . . . In those days went there out of Israel wicked men, who persuaded many [fellow Israelites], saying, 'Let us go and make a covenant with the heathen that are round about us: for since we departed from them we have had much sorrow'" (1 Macc. 1:1a-11).

That covenant with Antiochus closely parallels the covenant that Daniel predicted Antichrist will make with Israel at the beginning of the seventieth week: "And he [Antichrist] will make a firm covenant with the many [Israel] for one week" (Dan. 9:27) — that is, for the final seven-year period, during the last half of which Antichrist will wreak his greatest persecution upon the earth.

Many Jews were so eager to please Antiochus and to avoid persecution that they not only forsook the Mosaic law but even their racial identity and heritage, considering themselves from then on to be Gentiles. "Then certain of the people were so forward herein, that they went to the king, who gave them licence to do after the ordinances of the heathen; and made themselves uncircumcised, and forsook the holy covenant, and joined themselves to the heathen, and were sold to do mischief" (1 Macc. 1:13-15).

That great apostasy of ancient Israel parallels the apostasy their far-distant descendants will fall into after making the ungodly covenant with the secular world leader at the beginning of the seventieth week. During the first half of the week (i.e., during the first three and one half years), that leader's true identity as Antichrist will not be known, and Israel will fall into greater and greater apostasy. During that time Israel will enjoy the worldly security (Ezek. 38:8, 14) they obtained through their covenant with Antichrist (Dan. 9:27), which the prophet Isaiah calls their "covenant with death" (Isa. 28:15, 18). This will be a false security, however, that perfectly parallels the early days of ancient Israel's conquest by Antiochus when, because of their compromise with that pagan ruler, they lived "in a time of tranquility" (Dan. 11:21). As Paul explained to the believers at Thessalonica, Israel would once again in the future commit a great apostasy paralleling the one committed by Israel under Antiochus, after which Antichrist will reveal his true identity and, like Antiochus of old, proclaim himself as god. "Let no one in any way deceive you, for it [the day of the Lord] will not come unless the apostasy comes first, and the man of lawlessness is revealed, the son of destruction, who opposes and exalts himself above every so-called god or object of worship, so that he takes his seat in the temple of God, displaying himself as being God" (2 Thess. 2:3, 4).

We learn also from the historical record of the book of Maccabees what God had predicted through Daniel centuries earlier. After his conquest of Israel was complete and presumed secure, Antiochus then turned his eyes to Egypt. "Now when the kingdom [over Israel] was established before Antiochus, he thought to reign over Egypt, that he might have the dominion of two realms . . ." (1 Macc. 1:16). This again exactly parallels the actions of Antichrist in the last days, as predicted by Daniel: "He [Antichrist] will also enter the Beautiful Land [Israel]. . . . Then he will stretch out his hand against other countries, and the land of Egypt will not escape" (Dan. 11:41a, 42).

In the meanwhile Israel considered herself safe under the despotic but thus far lenient rule of Antiochus. Again from the historical book of 1 Maccabees, we see that after conquering Egypt, Antiochus moved his troops back northward into Israel and began a treacherous and merciless campaign of murder, pillaging, destruction, and sacrilege. "And after Antiochus had ravaged Egypt in the hundred and forty-third year, he returned and went up against Israel. . . . And he made a great slaughter of [Israelite] men, and spoke very proudly. And there was great mourning in Israel, and in every place where they were " (1 Macc. 1:21, 25, 26).

The foregoing passage from First Maccabees is actual recorded history. In the book of Daniel, however, we see the *prediction* of that historical event centuries before it ever came to pass:

Then he [Antiochus] will return to his land [from Egypt] with much plunder; but his heart will be set against the holy covenant [between God and Israel], and he will take action and then return to his own land. At the appointed time he will return and come into the South, but this last time it will not turn out the way it did before. For ships of Kittim [Italy] will come against him; therefore he will be disheartened, and will return and become enraged at the holy covenant [between God and Israel] and take action; so he will come back [to Israel] and show regard [favor] for those who forsake the holy covenant. And forces from him will arise, desecrate the sanctuary fortress, and do away with the regular sacrifice. And they will set up the abomination of desolation. And by smooth words he will turn to godlessness those who act wickedly toward the covenant, but the people who know their God will display strength and take action. And those who have insight among the people [the spiritual descendents of Abraham] will give understanding to the many [the natural line of Abraham]; yet they will fall by sword and by flame, by captivity and by plunder, for many days. (Dan. 11:28-33)

That sacrilege was the culmination of Antiochus' initial plan to completely eradicate Jewish religion. He had already forbade Jewish worship on the Sabbath, the rite of circumcision, the observance of religious festivals, and the offering of the Mosaic Temple sacrifices. He ordered the destruction of all copies of the Hebrew Scriptures that could be found. He commanded all Jews to eat pork and had numerous altars erected throughout Israel at which Jews, under pain of death, were ordered to offer sacrifices of swine. Had it not been for the successful Jewish revolt under Judas Maccabaeus, Antiochus doubtless would have destroyed this second (Zerubbabel's) Temple, just as Nebuchadnezzar had done with the Temple of Solomon several centuries earlier (see 2 Kings 25:8, 9).

That most blasphemous of all desecrations of the Jerusalem Temple occurred in 168 B.C., when Antiochus ordered that swine, the most ceremonially unclean of all animals, be offered on the Temple altar of burnt offerings. And to make the sacrilege still worse, he insisted that those animals be offered to the pagan god Zeus. Because he had declared himself to be Theos Epiphanes (meaning, "the manifest god"), and even more explicitly Zeus Epiphanes ("the manifestation of Zeus"), he was actually demanding worship of himself in place of Almighty God.

Continuing in perfect parallel to the historical Antiochus, Daniel predicts that Antichrist "will stretch out his hand against other countries, and the land of Egypt will not escape" (Dan. 11:42); that "he will pitch the tents of his royal pavilion between the seas and the beautiful Holy Mountain" (Dan. 11:45); and that then "there will be a time of distress such as never occurred since there was a nation until that time" (Dan 12:1). "In the middle of the [seventieth] week he [Antichrist] will put a stop to sacrifice and grain offering; and on the wing of abominations will come one [Antichrist] who makes desolate, even until a complete destruction, one that is decreed, is poured out on the one who makes desolate" (Dan. 9:27b). Referring to the prophecy of Daniel, Christ warns those Jews who will again be living in Jerusalem to flee "when you see the abomination of desolation which was spoken of through Daniel the prophet, standing in the holy place" (Matt. 24:15). Paul adds that when "the man of lawlessness is revealed, the son of destruction, who opposes and exalts himself above every so-called god or object of worship . . . [then] he takes his seat in the temple of God, displaying himself as being God" (2 Thess. 2:3b, 4).

It was this first "abomination of desolation" by Antiochus that led to the eventual revolt of Jews under the Maccabees. That rebellion so incensed Antiochus that he not only was more determined than ever to eradicate Jewish religion, he also wanted to eradicate the entire Jewish race. Through numerous means, the Lord frustrated that satanic scheme against His chosen people.

It will be the second "abomination of desolation" — that is, Antichrist — who will demand worship by the entire world, with death being the cost of refusal. And again there will be Jews unwilling to worship the beast or his image, like the Maccabeans in the days of Antiochus. When the great tribulation of Antichrist is "cut short" by the appearance of Christ's coming, these Jews, like the Maccabeans dwelling in the Judean wilderness, will revolt against Antichrist and his armies in a campaign this author refers to as the Jehoshaphat Campaign (see Glossary). As Zechariah predicted, "In that day I will make the clans of Judah like a firepot among pieces of wood and a flaming torch among sheaves, so they will consume on the right hand and on the left all the surrounding peoples [armies of Antichrist], while the inhabitants again dwell on their own sites in Jerusalem" (Zech. 12:6).

SEVEN SIGNIFICANT PARALLELS

As the activities of Antichrist are followed carefully as this volume progresses, we will see many parallels between the careers of those two satanic rulers acted out against God's elect nation of Israel. Understanding the sequence of events during the reign of Antiochus will therefore give considerable insight into the sequences of events that will occur in the days of Antichrist.

The following seven similarities or parallels of Antiochus and Antichrist perhaps are the most significant and should be watched for as the sequence of events begins to unfold.

First, under the guise of friendship and the promise of protection, both men make covenants with the nation of Israel.

Second, as in the days of Antiochus, many in Israel will again commit great apostasy after the signing of the covenant, as they again seek to gain the favor of this powerful world leader, who is the Antichrist, yet to be "revealed."

Third, after making their treaties with Israel, while Israel lives under a false sense of security, both men seek to conquer Egypt and then return to ravage Israel and desecrate her Temple.

Fourth, both men proclaim themselves to be gods and demand worship from their subjects, and those Jews who refuse become the primary target of his wrath.

Fifth, both tyrants have to contend with groups of Jews who refuse to worship or serve them and who foment considerable dissension and opposition from the rural areas surrounding the city of Jerusalem when they learn of the despots' true character and intentions regarding Israel.

Sixth, the parallel significance of Antiochus and Antichrist is further underscored by the fact that the only two blowings of the trumpet of God are related to these two men. The first trumpet of God is prophesied in Zechariah 9:13-16 in a near/far prophecy which says that "the Lord God will blow the trumpet" when He would come centuries later to intervene on Israel's behalf against the Greeks and defeat Antiochus.[1] The second trumpet of God is at the Rapture when "the Lord Himself will descend from heaven . . . with the trumpet of God" (1 Thess. 4:16; cf. 1 Cor. 15:51, 52) to deliver the church and to "slay [Antichrist] with the breath of His mouth and bring to an end by the appearance of His [Christ's] coming" (2 Thess. 2:8).[2]

Seventh and finally, following the defeat of Antiochus and the cleansing of the Temple that had been defiled by him, the nation of Israel initiated the feast of Hanukkah (the Festival of Lights, or of Dedication). This festival commemorates Israel's deliverance from that ungodly tyrant Antiochus, and celebrates the restoration of the Temple and the purification of its altar. It also looks forward to the eventual return of God's glory to the Temple. In a remarkable way this prefigures what will happen after the end of the "seventieth week," forty-five days after the defeat of Antichrist. For as will be shown in detail in chapter 22 and the Epilogue, the redeemed nation of Israel will once again observe Hanukkah in a unique and resplendent way — this time in remembrance of the defeat of Antichrist, in celebration of the rebuilding of the Temple by Christ Himself, and in recognition of the permanent return of God's glory to the Temple.

THE RISE OF ANTICHRIST

The world's political, moral, and spiritual state (discussed in chapter 9) will provide the perfect conditions for Antichrist to establish Satan's eighth and final beast empire. And for a few brief years, in the guise of a benevolent world ruler, he will dominate the entire world except for the select peoples whom God will divinely protect. As the world collapses into chaos preceding and during the first half of the seventieth week, masses of people will welcome Antichrist as their "leader." But by its midpoint the entire world will welcome Antichrist as their "savior," falling under Satan's "deception of wickedness" and the "deluding influence" sent by God Himself (2 Thess. 2:10, 11).

Thus, Antichrist's strategy will be to offer the world a false savior, a false king, and a false kingdom — satanic counterfeits of God's true Savior, true King, and true kingdom — knowing that those who do not serve Antichrist become potential citizens of the kingdom of Christ. And because Satan failed to kill or disqualify the rightful Savior and King of the earth, Jesus Christ, Satan's only remaining hope will be to destroy all potential citizens of that divine, future millennial kingdom.

We will return to an in-depth discussion of Antichrist in chapter 11, especially to consider in detail his purpose in remaining incognito until the middle of the seventieth week — until "he who now restrains . . . is taken out of the way . . . [and the] lawless one [Antichrist] will be revealed" (2 Thess. 2:7, 8). If Israel would have the slightest notion of the true identity of this seemingly benevolent ruler, the covenant with him never would be made. But when he makes his true identity known, when "the man of lawlessness is revealed" (2 Thess. 2:3), unbelieving Israel, as well as the rest of the unbelieving world, will immediately realize their deception and their frightening plight. Particularly for the Jews living in Jerusalem, "it will be sheer terror to understand what it means" (Isa. 28:19).

9

The Stage
Is Set

The world is in an unprecedented state of change. The last few years have seen governments rise and fall overnight. Who could have predicted the sudden collapse of the Berlin Wall or the reunification of Germany? Who could have foreseen the sudden, dramatic disintegration of the Soviet Union? These and other unimagined changes in world events have brought a new sense of immediacy to prophetic Scripture — and the realization that prophetic events can unfold literally overnight.

If changes of this magnitude can happen so suddenly, should we be surprised if the "seventieth week of Daniel" were to begin sometime soon or in the near future? As we study Scripture carefully, we see that the seventieth week cannot begin until certain conditions and events have first occurred. But the first of these critical events — i.e., the return of Israel to her own land and her more recent control over Jerusalem in 1967 — *has already occurred*, as noted earlier in this volume. And Christians today are therefore the first generation of Christians since the early church who can genuinely look daily for the commencement of the seventieth week. Quite literally, the stage is set.

Since certain conditions and events must first occur, the questions we must honestly ask ourselves are these: Do the conditions of the world today match the *prophetic conditions* revealed in Scripture, as these relate to the conditions of the world just preceding the commencement of the seventieth week? And, What *prophetic events* must still occur before the seventieth week can occur?

As we will see below, *all of the prophetic conditions already exist*, and *all of the prior events except one have already happened* — and this single remaining event could occur almost overnight. It is essential, therefore, that we have a clear understanding of what these prior conditions and prior events are. If ever there was a time for the church to "be alert and sober," the time is now.

PRIOR CONDITIONS

The prior conditions of the world, as seen in Scripture, may be summarized in terms of three main categories. The first involves *a general spiritual and moral decay in culture*; the second involves *a general climate of thought*; the third involves *a general condition of the church*. Each of these conditions, as we will see below, is already widely evident — giving the serious Christian who is looking for Christ's return an indication that the time of His return is approaching rapidly.

(1) THE GENERAL DECAY IN CULTURE

Paul predicted in his second letter to Timothy that the end times will be characterized by pervasive spiritual and moral decay. "But realize this," he wrote,

> that in the last days difficult times will come. For men will be lovers of self, lovers of money, boastful, arrogant, revilers, disobedient to parents, ungrateful, unholy, unloving, irreconcilable, malicious gossips, without self-control, brutal, haters of good, treacherous, reckless, conceited, lovers of pleasure rather than lovers of God; holding to a form of godliness, although they have denied its power; and avoid such men as these. (2 Tim. 3:1-5)

There could hardly be a more accurate description of the moral and spiritual condition of the world today. Everywhere in culture we see this catalog of perversion celebrated as the path to self-gratification and personal fulfillment. This mentality of perversion dominates the visual images of television and film, the pages of popular magazines, the music of the day, and even the fine arts. As mirrors of the world, the media and popular culture as a whole reflect the distorted image of moral and spiritual perversion of the last days so clearly captured in the Scripture passage just quoted.

The Music of the Day   It is remarkable to see just how far our culture is willing to go in tolerating and condoning the most offensive material. For example, a recent article in the *Chicago Tribune* surveyed more than two dozen current rock albums, encouraging parents to be open-minded and appreciative of the music their kids are listening to. Rock critics Brenda Herrmann and Greg Kot write:

> Here's a quick primer on some recent popular albums and what parents should listen for:
> — *Danzig*, "Lucifuge" [the group's name followed by the album title]. The liner notes fold out into an inverted crucifix, and leader Glenn Danzig's lyrics are obsessed with religion, death, doom and other light-hearted topics. Then again, you'd only know that by studying the lyric sheet, because his voice is swallowed up by the loud, distorted music. The effect is strangely cathartic, and the young headbanger in your household is probably enjoying this rather than considering a conversion to Satan worship.
> — *Death metal roundup*: Although no death-metal releases have made the top of the charts, plenty of kids are bringing these albums home, much to their parents' apprehension. Cover art is invariably bloody and repulsive, obsessed with mutilated internal organs.
> The lyrics are also often graphic descriptions of murder, mutilation, cannibalism; if it has to do with death and pain, it's here. Although every death-metal group sings of violence and death, some clearly have something to say about life while others are just trying to out-gore one another. Cannibal Corpse is useless gore, almost to the point of silliness, and too extreme for most parents and some kids to handle.
> The band Death limits the kill-o-rama on its new album, "Human," to discuss social issues, including the right-to-die movement (the group is for it). Sepultura, the most popular of death groups, sings about living through poverty, and Slayer

sings about the devil but more in terms of a theology lesson than an endorsement.

Deicide are Satanists and proud of it, right down to the inverted cross branded into the bassist's forehead. Rather than judging these albums by their cover art, parents should evaluate each band on its own merits. They may find that not all death-metal bands are deadly to their kids' growth.[1]

The article goes on to sing the praises of *The Geto Boys* album "We Can't Be Stopped," despite a profusion of profanity "and some horribly violent and misogynous imagery"; to commend *Prince's* "Graffiti Bridge" as "a considerable work of substance about sex, spirituality and temptation"; and to laud *Ozzy Osborne*, known for his songs on Satanism and suicide, for his concentration "on emotions and fine instrumentation."[2]

Current Films   In the area of film, the moral and spiritual decay of our culture is equally pervasive. But the impact of film on people's minds and behavior goes far beyond popular music with its ability to create a total experience of sight and sound, of image and emotion. As with popular music, some of the most highly acclaimed movies in recent years are unimaginably perverse. This is not to say there are no movies of real value and beauty. But there is something fundamentally wrong in a society which creates, condones, and commends behavior and ideas which are in contemptuous rebellion against God's moral standards and openly blasphemous to His Name. It is hard to imagine how such films (for example, a brutal "slasher movie") could be watched for entertainment. We should hardly be surprised, however, when we see the same scenes played out in the streets of our cities.[3] And they are. One needs only to look at the daily newspaper or watch the evening news on television to confirm this sad commentary on mankind, made in the "image of God."

Contemporary Art   A similar picture is repeated in the area of contemporary art. Whereas art once expressed the highest aspirations of man, today it is often a vehicle for the most debased ideas imaginable. The art of ancient Israel, for example, found its highest expression in relation to the worship of God, as seen in the magnificent adornment of the Tabernacle and the Temple. Even up to the time of the Renaissance, art was primarily created as an expression of faith. The *avant garde* of contemporary art, by contrast, has a radically different objective. A good example is the art of AIDS-martyr Robert Mapplethorpe, whose explicit photographs of homosexual erotica include masochism, sadism, pedophilia, and scatology. Although his work, *financed in part by tax dollars* (the National Endowments to the Arts), has outraged many who have seen the exhibit, the artistic establishment has rallied aggressively to defend and promote his work.[4] Perhaps the single most offensive example of contemporary art, again financed by the NEA, is the work of Andres Serrano, often described as "postmodern blasphemy," in which "he displays a photograph of a crucifix immersed in urine."[5]

The spiritual and moral decay of culture today is dramatically captured in the distorted mirrors of contemporary art and the media. And although it is true that every culture since the Fall has been thoroughly affected by sin, it seems clear that a radical shift has taken place in recent years. In this regard Dr. Francis Schaeffer's insight is especially relevant. "As evangelical, Bible-believing Christians," Dr. Schaeffer wrote,

> we have not done well in understanding this. The world spirit of our age rolls on and on . . . crushing all that we cherish in its path. Sixty years ago could we have imagined that unborn children would be killed by the millions here in our own country? Or that we would have *no freedom of speech* when it comes to speaking of God and biblical truth in our public schools? Or that every form of sexual perversion would be promoted by the entertainment media? Or that marriage, raising children, and family life would be objects of attack? Sadly we must say that very few Christians have understood the battle we are in. . . .[6]

And in the last decade since Dr. Schaeffer wrote these words the decay has accelerated all the more rapidly. Certainly the first condition as described in 2 Timothy 3:1-5 — that is, the general spiritual and moral decay of culture in the last days — is present today in a way that clearly corresponds to the prophetic warnings of Scripture.

(2) THE GENERAL CLIMATE OF THOUGHT

The second condition which must exist before the last seven-year period of the end times will begin has to do with *the general climate of thought* that will prevail in the last days. The main features of this climate of thought are described in a number of related Scripture passages. Some of these speak specifically to conditions in the church, as we will see later, but they also have a certain application to conditions in the culture generally.

As already quoted above, Paul wrote that "in the last days . . . men will be . . . lovers of pleasure rather than lovers of God" (see 2 Tim. 3:1-5), and that "the time will come when they will not endure sound doctrine; but wanting to have their ears tickled, they will accumulate for themselves teachers in accordance to their own desires; and will turn away their ears from the truth, and will turn aside to myths" (2 Tim. 4:3, 4). One further passage may be related more to events during the seventieth week, but nonetheless gives a clear picture of *the kind of thinking that will pave the way* for the rise of Antichrist. Thus Paul wrote in his first letter to Timothy, "the Spirit explicitly says that in later times some will fall away from the faith, paying attention to deceitful spirits and doctrines of demons" (1 Tim. 4:1), and a few verses later warned against having anything to do with "old wives' fables" (1 Tim. 4:7, KJV).

The general climate of thought we see in these verses is characterized by: the desire for self-love and self-gratification; believing false doctrine and false teachers; turning from the truth to believe in myths; and coming under the influence of deceitful spirits, doctrines of demons, and old wives' tales. Thus before Antichrist secretly comes on the international scene, this kind of thinking will be widespread, setting the stage for the greatest of all counterfeit christs to capture the hearts and minds of men. With their hearts set on self-love and their minds perverted by false teachers and demonic doctrines, the world will be prepared to receive Antichrist as a god.

The New Age Movement   Is there a common philosophy that reflects this general climate of thought? A clear example of this is the New Age Movement, which is rapidly gaining adherents under the guise of many different cults, both new and old. Most such groups have a philosophical-religious orientation largely based on eastern mysticism. Because much of the movement is nebulous and changing, it is unwise and dangerous to try to relate specific groups to specific end-time prophecies. But the New Age Movement in general cannot be ignored because many of its basic tenets and practices correspond to biblical teaching about the end times.

Satan is the supreme deceiver and counterfeiter — and so the New

Age Movement offers him a ready means in his grand strategy. As demonstrated so clearly in his wilderness temptation of Jesus Christ, Satan's most dangerous tactic in relation to Israel and the church has always been to promote falsehood under the guise of biblical truth, and the following excerpts from contemporary writing give helpful insights into Satan's use of the New Age Movement.

In an article entitled "Selected Scenes from the End of the World," secular writer Jill Pearlman comments,

> Popular among both the New Age faithful and religious fundamentalists is the spectacular story line that unfolds, broadly, as follows: The decades after the year 2000 will usher in a Golden Age. People will subdue their violent tendencies and become humane and downright delightful. But it will occur after a period of cataclysmic destruction during which many will die and the earth will be radically altered. . . . [Certain] interpreters have Nostradamus predicting that the Third World will be wrought by the Third Antichrist (Napoleon was the first and Hitler the second), who will be a mysterious man from Asia.[7]

New Age leader John Randolph Price, author of *The Planetary Commission* and *The Superbeings*, claims that "more than half a billion [New Age] believers are on the planet at this time working in various religious groups." Price further asserts that "New Thought (New Age) concepts are spreading more rapidly than any other spiritual teaching."[8]

Of particular significance is the connection of the New Age with Hitler and Antichrist which Texe Marrs makes in his book *Dark Secrets of the New Age*:

> In the New Age view, their concept of unity, love, and peace marks Christians as members of an inferior race. It doesn't take much foresight to recognize the dangers in a doctrine that artificially creates two races and sets one up as superior. Hitler's poisonous racial theories were not far afield from those of the New Age extremists. The Aryan race was to become the man-god race of a thousand-year Reich founded by Hitler and his monstrous SS troops. It is no coincidence that, like those of New Age leaders today, Hitler's theories were grounded in the occult and in the teachings of Theosophy and Hinduism. Furthermore, like [New

Age prophetess] Alice Bailey, Hitler, too, believed in the Masters of Shamballa and in the superiority of a Tibetan occultism. . . .[9]

What New Age evangelists are teaching their converts is that their "God" (the demon hierarchy) has a Plan. This Plan will result in the ascension to power of the superior root race composed of New Agers with higher, Cosmic (Christ- or God-) Consciousness. Men will at that point become gods, and the Antichrist, the Great Teacher, will inaugurate his wondrous reign of planetary unity, peace, and love.[10]

Douglas Groothuis, another Christian expert on the New Age, explains:

The New Age movement teaches that we are poised on the edge of a quantum leap in consciousness as evolution surges upward. . . . Some New Agers sound apocalyptic tones, warning that without a massive raising of consciousness, the planet will face severe catastrophes that will "cleanse" it from error. (Exactly what is meant by *cleansing* varies. Some think in terms of a peaceful transition; others believe that non-New Agers must be somehow disposed of. . . .) [Thus] New Age utopians envision a New World Order sometimes described as involving a one-world government, global socialism or New Age religion. . . . Some . . . expect a world leader sometimes (falsely) called "the Christ," to show us the way to the New Age.[11]

This is only a brief look at some of the basic beliefs of the New Age. What this author has tried to show in these few quotes is the fact that New Age teaching is preparing New Age followers for what God says will definitely occur. The consensus of New Age teaching is that Antichrist and his world system is the system everyone must follow.

It should be obvious by now that there is nothing new about the New Age. Instead it is the same ancient lie offered by Satan, the father of lies, to Adam and Eve in the Garden of Eden. There Satan's strategy was first to raise doubts about God's Word: "Indeed, has God said . . . ?" (Gen. 3:1), and then to deceive Eve with cleverly appealing lies: "You surely shall not die! For God knows that in the day you eat from [the tree] your eyes will be opened, and you will be like God, knowing good and evil" (Gen. 3:4b, 5).

And the strategy Satan found so effective in the Garden of Eden is the same strategy he has used through the centuries and is exactly the same strategy he employs to promote the myth of New Age philosophy. As Walter Martin has written, "The New Age cult is a revival of this ancient occultism [with] . . . historical ties to Sumerian, Indian, Egyptian, Chaldean, Babylonian, and Persian religious practices."[12]

The New Age Movement, then, is in direct continuity with Satan's strategy through the centuries, extending back through ancient empires of the past to his original deception in the Garden of Eden.[13] What is new today is that New Age thinking is filtering into every area of modern culture and spreading so rapidly. Thus if the seventieth week were to begin soon, the groundwork for the world's acceptance of Antichrist will already have been extensively and strategically laid. By the middle of that last seven-year period, when Antichrist reveals his true identity and demands the world's worship, the New Age "Plan" will have prepared a great part of the unbelieving world to eagerly assist Antichrist in his immediate and horrendous persecution and annihilation of the "inferior" Jews and Christians when the great tribulation by Antichrist begins.

Evolutionary Thinking The impact of evolutionary thinking, as suggested already in the beliefs of the New Age Movement, is equally important in creating a *general climate of thought* that will characterize the last days. This was predicted explicitly by the Lord, as seen in the Apostle Peter's second letter:

> Know this first of all, that *in the last days* mockers will come with their mocking, following after their own lusts, and saying, "Where is the promise of His coming? *For ever since the fathers fell asleep, all continues just as it was from the beginning of creation.*" For when they maintain this, it escapes their notice that by the word of God the heavens existed long ago and the earth was formed out of water and by water, through which the world at that time was destroyed, being flooded with water. But the present heavens and earth by His word are being reserved for fire, kept for the day of judgment and destruction of ungodly men. (2 Pet. 3:3-7, emphasis added)

That passage gives a perfect description of scientific uniformitarianism. This is the modern scientific belief that all physical laws and principles — as well as all psychological and sociological laws and principles after the appearance of man — have operated in exactly the same way throughout time. This theory is the driving force of modern evolutionism, and the only position taught in the world's leading scientific institutions today. Thus Satan's lie concerning the origins of man is used to deceive man in the one area that God holds all men accountable. Paul warned the church at Rome that "the wrath of God is revealed from heaven against all ungodliness and unrighteousness of men, who suppress the truth in unrighteousness, *because that which is known about God is evident within them*; for God made it evident to them. *For since the creation of the world His invisible attributes*, His eternal power and divine nature, *have been clearly seen, being understood through what has been made, so that they are without excuse*" (Rom. 1:18-20, emphasis added).

In other words, Satan's greatest deception in the last days is a deceptive substitution for God's creative acts, the one area in which all men are "without excuse." If man can be deceived in this area, as is so often the case, man's membership in the kingdom of Satan can be assured.

Scientific uniformitarianism obviously leaves no room for supernatural intervention, including especially intervention by God. In the above passage, Peter's words "escapes their notice" includes the idea "is contrary to their thinking." Most unbelievers today consider the notion of a literal, worldwide flood in Noah's day to be mythical and legendary because they refuse to accept a literal creation by God. Remarkably, many science teachers in professing Christian colleges hold to that view as well, in their attempt to be acceptable in the scientific community at large. But they do so at the expense of the clear teaching of the Word of God, if the hermeneutics outlined in chapter 1 are followed. Even though they profess to take the Ten Commandments of God as very literal, they rationalize the Fourth Commandment ("Remember the sabbath day, to keep it holy . . . for *in six days* the Lord made the heavens and the earth, the sea and all that is in them, and rested on the seventh day; therefore . . ." [Exod. 20:8, 11a, emphasis added]) with their non-literal view of Genesis 1 and 2.

In their book *The Genesis Flood*, John C. Whitcomb, Jr., and Henry M. Morris make a significant comment on the passage just cited from 2 Peter:

In this passage of Scripture, Peter speaks of a day, yet future from his standpoint, when men would no longer think seriously of Christ's Second Coming as a cataclysmic, universal intervention by God into the course of world affairs. And the reason for this skeptical attitude would be none other than a blind adherence to the doctrine of uniformitarianism — a doctrine which maintains that natural laws and processes have never yet been interrupted (or newer and higher laws introduced) so as to bring about a total destruction of human civilization through the direct intervention of God. And since this has never been the case in past history, there should be no cause to fear that it will ever occur in the future!

In answering the skeptics of the end-time, the Apostle Peter points to two events in the past which cannot be explained on the basis of uniformitarianism. The first of these events is the creation of the world: "there were heavens from of old, and an earth . . . by the word of God"; and the second event is the Flood: "the world [kŏsmŏs] that then was, being overflowed with water, perished [apŏlĕtŏ]."

But it is the second of these two events, the Flood, which serves as the basis of Peter's comparison with the Second Coming and the final destruction of the world. For even as "the world that then was" perished by *water*, so "the heavens that now are, and the earth," protected as they are by God's eternal promise from another aqueous cataclysm (Gen. 9:11-19), have nevertheless "been stored up for *fire*, being reserved against the day of judgment and destruction of ungodly men."[14]

Throughout this century, as it will be again in the last days, the idea of superior and inferior races has been strongly undergirded by the theory of evolution. Much of Hitler's philosophy was shaped by Darwin's *Origin of the Species*. Commenting on that influence, Henry M. Morris writes:

As a result, evolution — especially of the Darwinian and Lamarckian varieties — has long been used as the supposedly scientific basis of racism. All of the nineteenth-century evolutionists, in fact Darwin, Huxley, and all the rest, well up into the first quarter of the twentieth century — were convinced proponents of white [Aryan] supremacy. . . .

The most vicious of the racist philosophies that were built on evolutionism, however, was probably Adolf Hitler's Nazism. The background for this is found especially in the teachings of Darwin's contemporary propagandist in Germany, Ernst Haeckel, who was probably the most influential evolutionist in continental Europe. [As historian Daniel Gasman has shown . . .] "Along with his social Darwinist followers, [Haeckel] set about to demonstrate the 'aristocratic' and non-democratic character of the laws of nature. . . . Up to his death in 1919, Haeckel contributed to that special variety of German thought which served as the seed-bed for National Socialism. He became one of Germany's main ideologists for racism, nationalism, and imperialism."[15] When Hitler came along, he used Haeckel's so-called scientific evolutionism as the basis of his own racist philosophy. [Thus Gasman writes . . .] "Hitler stressed and singled out the idea of biological evolution as the most forceful weapon against traditional religion and he repeatedly condemned Christianity for its opposition to the teachings of evolution. . . . For Hitler, evolution was the hallmark of modern science and culture, and he defended its veracity as tenaciously as Haeckel."[16, 17]

In other words, as the passage in 2 Peter 3:4, 5 predicts, evolution will be the dominant thought of the world as it goes into the seventieth week of Daniel. Moreover, it will be used in part to justify racism when Antichrist demands that every person worship the beast (Antichrist) or his image. In the same way that Hitler used his evolutionary reasoning to justify his ruthless anti-Semitism, so will Antichrist use that same atheistic philosophy to his own advantage in Satan's final attempt to kill the entire nation of Israel who refuse to take his mark or worship his image, those whom he knows are destined by God to become the inhabitants of Christ's millennial kingdom on earth.

(3) The General Condition of the Church

Parallel to the moral and spiritual decay and destructive thinking in the world, we now turn to the general condition of the church, which will be characterized by pervasive heresy and compromise. Speaking specifically of the church in the last days, Paul continued to warn Timothy,

For the time will come when they [nominal Christians] will not endure sound doctrine; but wanting to have their ears tickled, they will accumulate for themselves teachers in accordance to their own desires; and will turn away their ears from the truth, and will turn aside to myths. (2 Tim. 4:3, 4; cf. 3:1-5)

In the context of the last days, when "the Lord knows how to rescue the godly from temptation [testing], and keep the unrighteous under punishment for the day of judgment [the day of the Lord]" (2 Pet. 2:9), the Apostle Peter further warned that

there will also be false teachers among you, who will secretly introduce destructive heresies, even denying the Master who bought them. . . . And many will follow their sensuality, and because of them the way of truth will be maligned; and in their greed they will exploit you with false words. . . . They are stains and blemishes, reveling in their deceptions, as they carouse with you; having eyes full of adultery and that never cease from sin; enticing unstable souls, having a heart trained in greed, accursed children; forsaking the right way they have gone astray, having followed the way of Balaam, the son of Beor, who loved the wages of unrighteousness. (2 Pet. 2:1b-3a, 13b-15)

Because of moral decay in society at large, many who claim the name of Christ will choose to capitulate rather than suffer criticism and possible persecution for His name's sake. Many churches will not have the courage or commitment to maintain doctrinal purity. Consequently, many local churches, denominational bodies, and parachurch organizations not only will condone but will even promote every sort of false teaching and practice imaginable. Likewise, the prophetic views of many will promote a false security in the church — giving a false assurance that the afflictions revealed in the book of Revelation either do not apply to them, having been taught that the church will be "raptured away" before that time (see Glossary, "Pretribulationalism") or that those afflictions are simply allegorical or historical and should therefore be "spiritualized away" (see Glossary, "Amillennialism"). Much of this decline in commitment and doctrinal purity is already evident in the church today, even among those who claim to be evangelical and conservative.

This is seen for example in the following analysis of the condition of the modern church in the United States by a secular writer in *Time* magazine:

> Traditional strictures against homosexuality, premarital sex (once called fornication), even adultery, are up for theological debate. The Presbyterians in conclave assembled gave thumbs down to the new morality; the Episcopalians gave thumbs sideways; the United Methodist Church and the Evangelical Lutheran Church in America will not be far behind in giving their thumb signals. . . .
>
> Roman Catholics have caught the bug too (as in so many other areas, liberal American Catholics find themselves playing catch-up with their Protestant soul mates). . . .
>
> The obvious secular explanation for this hubbub is that America's churches are internalizing the mores of a developed society. . . . It was . . . inevitable that the churches would adjust to the new morality. If that meant adjusting traditional interpretations of the Ten Commandments, so be it.[18]

In a similar vein, *Newsweek* carried an article titled "Roll Over, John Calvin" concerning the debate in the Presbyterian Church (USA) over rethinking the sexual revolution. The article explains that

> until now no Christian denomination has seriously considered the wholesale rejection of traditional sexual ethics as outdated and oppressive — much less blessing homosexuality, fornication and other behavior that it once found sinful. . . .
>
> Prepared by a committee of 17 ministers, academics and health professionals, [the Presbyterian report] reads like a sermon on Eros prepared in the heat of politically correct passion. . . .
>
> If the committee has its way, the Presbyterian church will liberate itself from an unsophisticated reading of the Bible, beginning with Adam and Eve, and re-evaluate its definition of sin to reflect "the changing mores of our society."[19]

Nor have conservative churches been exempt from moral and spiritual decline. The behavior of certain prominent TV evangelists, for example, reads like a page out of 2 Peter: "[they] follow their sensuality, and because of them the way of truth [is] maligned . . . having eyes full of adultery . . . having a heart trained in greed." Similarly Christian researchers have found very little difference between Christians and the world in matters of sexual morality and other areas of moral behavior.

The Seven Churches of Revelation While the foregoing examples are instructive, Jesus' letters to the seven churches reveal much additional truth about the condition of the church in general just before the seventieth week begins. Those seven churches existed in Asia Minor (Western Turkey) at the time of John's writing of Revelation. But the letters to those specific historical churches contain *both near and far* prophetic truth, as the language of these letters indicates.

The "near" message to the seven churches was specifically addressed to the apostle's contemporaries in the seven first-century churches and applied in every detail to them. But future relevance of the "far" message becomes plainly evident when the context is studied. As discussed in chapter 2 of this book, not only is the book of Revelation written to the churches in general (Rev. 22:6), but readers of Revelation are told to read, hear, and heed the prophecies about to be given them (1:3). At the end of each prophetic warning given to the seven churches, readers are again admonished to "hear what the Spirit says to the churches." And although all seven of those historical churches were out of existence before the end of the second century, the messages to five of them contain direct language that is only appropriate to the end times.

The theme of the book of Revelation is the return of Christ. That in itself is certainly an end-time event. This great prophetic book begins with a reference to Christ's return: "Behold, He is coming with the clouds, and every eye will see Him, even those who pierced Him" (Rev. 1:7), and it ends with the same emphasis: "Yes, I am coming quickly" (Rev. 22:20). Therefore the warnings given to the seven churches in chapters 2 and 3, although having a near-term application, are *primarily* given as a warning to the church going into the seventieth week. Consequently, the language used to address the seven churches should bear out the theme of the book in general, as it clearly does. To Ephesus, Pergamum, Thyatira, Sardis, and Philadelphia, Jesus foretold *His personal coming to them* to chastise (2:5; 3:3), to judge (2:16), or to bless and deliver (2:25; 3:11). This can only be a direct reference to His second coming, because His first coming was already history when these words were penned. And even His words to the other two churches suggest an end-time context. To believers at

Smyrna, Christ speaks of giving them the crown of life (2:10), as He also does to believers in Philadelphia (3:11; cf. 2 Tim. 4:8; Jas. 1:12). Even in His message to the lukewarm and self-satisfied church at Laodicea, Christ promises overcomers a place beside Him on His heavenly throne (3:21), but also warns them that "those whom I love, I reprove and discipline" (3:19).

The exact proportion of faithful to unfaithful churches in the last days cannot be deduced from the seven letters in Revelation 2, 3, but it is clear that the vast majority of latter-day churches will be far from pure and holy. Only two of the seven, Smyrna and Philadelphia, do not reflect the moral and spiritual decay of the unbelieving world around them, and a case can be made that the church of Smyrna will "suffer" and undergo "tribulation" (2:10) because of her tolerance of "the blasphemy by those who say they are Jews and are not, but are a synagogue of Satan" (Rev. 2:9).

Summing up the messages to the seven churches, we find only one that is unmistakably faithful — the church at Philadelphia. We find three churches that have been infected or influenced by false teachers. The church at Smyrna permits "blasphemy by those who say they are Jews and are not" (2:9). The church at Pergamum holds "the teaching of the Nicolaitans" (2:15). The church at Thyatira tolerates "the woman Jezebel, who calls herself a prophetess, and she teaches and leads My bond-servants astray" (2:20), for which reason the church is told that she will be thrown into "great tribulation" (2:22). The other three churches also fall far short of faithfulness to Christ. The condition of the church at Ephesus can be summed up in Christ's declaration, "I have this against you, that you have left your first love" (2:4). To the church at Sardis Christ says, "I know your deeds, that you have a name that you are alive, and you are dead" (3:1). To the church at Laodicea He says, "I know your deeds, that you are neither cold nor hot; I would that you were cold or hot. So because you are lukewarm, and neither hot nor cold, I will spit you out of My mouth" (3:15, 16).

This then is what we know the church in the last days will be like — as revealed by Christ's own descriptions of the churches that will go into the seventieth week. For the most part they will be weak, insipid, and compromising — with low moral standards and poor and even false doctrine, and without spiritual leadership. It is no wonder that Paul warns that "the time will come when they will not endure sound doctrine; but wanting to have their ears tickled, they will accumulate for themselves teachers in accordance to their own desires; and will turn away their ears from the truth, and will turn aside to myths" (2 Tim. 4:3, 4).

Paul's phrase, "will turn away their ears from the truth" is significant, especially in light of the admonition with which the book of Revelation begins, calling believers to "hear the words of the prophecy, and heed the things which are written in it; for the time is near" (1:3), and in light of Christ's closing warning to all seven churches: "He who has an ear, let him hear what the Spirit says to the churches" (2:7, 11, 17, 29; 3:6, 13, 22).

The almost identical phrase, "everyone who has an ear, let him hear" is found in only one other place in John's writings. This other place is also in the book of Revelation, in the context of Satan's war with the saints during the great tribulation by Antichrist against "the woman, and . . . the rest of her offspring, who keep the commandments of God and hold to the testimony of Jesus" (12:17). A few verses later the apostle adds what amounts to a parenthesis for emphasis: "If anyone has an ear, let him hear. . . . Here is the perseverance and the faith of the saints" (13:9, 10). The warning is repeated because, as Christ had declared earlier, the churches will directly undergo "the hour of testing, that hour which is about to come upon the whole world, to test those who dwell upon the earth" (3:10).

And so the seven churches represent a mostly sad commentary on the condition of the churches that will go into the seventieth week. They also are an explicit warning that only overcomers, real Christians, will survive the "fiery testing" that is about to occur. Peter exhorts his readers, "Beloved, do not be surprised at the fiery ordeal among you, which comes upon you for your testing [the same Greek word as used in Revelation 3:10], as though some strange thing were happening to you. . . . For it is time for judgment to begin with the household of God; and if it begins with us first, what will be the outcome for those who do not obey the gospel of God? And if it is with difficulty that the righteous is saved, what will become of the godless man and the sinner?" (1 Pet. 4:12, 17, 18).

Because of the corrupt nature of the church at large in the last days, the church must of necessity go through the "fiery testing" in order to cleanse the compromising bond-servants of Christ and prepare her for becoming the bride of Christ, just before the earth's wicked are destroyed by the day-of-the-Lord wrath.

That is why the church at Laodicea is warned, "Those whom I love, I reprove and discipline; be zealous therefore, and repent" (Rev. 3:19).

That is why Christ tells the church at Thyatira that, because His bond-servants are led astray (2:20), He "will cast her upon a bed of sickness, and those who commit [spiritual] adultery with her into great tribulation" (v. 22), until "all the churches will know that I am He who searches the minds and hearts; and I will give to each one of you according to your deeds" (v. 23). That is why the church at Smyrna is told that "the devil is about to cast some of you into prison, that you may be tested, and you will have tribulation" (2:10), brought on because of "the blasphemy by those who say they are Jews and are not, but are a synagogue of Satan" (v. 9). Only the faithful church at Philadelphia is promised protection during "the hour of testing, that hour which is about to come upon the whole world, to test those who dwell upon the earth" (3:10).

Those within *compromising churches* will quickly show their true colors, and many will align themselves with Antichrist rather than face persecution for something they truly do not believe. The *dead church* can expect only the wrath of God, along with the rest of the wicked world. The *faithful church* will experience the special protection of God within the sphere of danger, "that hour which is about to come upon the whole world, to test those who dwell upon the earth." And, although it will bear the full brunt of Antichrist's fury, the true Christians within the *compromising church* will be delivered "from the wrath to come" (1 Thess. 1:10), literally "saved, yet so as through fire" (1 Cor. 3:15). But this will happen only after they have been made pure by the fiery testing — so that God Almighty might present them to Christ "as a pure virgin" (2 Cor. 11:2), so that Christ will also confirm them to the end, "blameless in the day of our Lord Jesus Christ" (1 Cor. 1:7, 8), and so they may "stand in the presence of His glory blameless with great joy" (Jude 24).

Called to Be Overcomers In each of His letters to the seven churches, the Lord explicitly exhorts believers to be overcomers — to be those "who overcome" (see Rev. 2:7, 11, 17, 26; 3:5, 12, 21), who resist the powerful temptations and pervasive pressures that Christians will face as Satan makes his last great onslaught against God's people. The Greek verb translated "overcome" in the above verses is *nikaō*, which comes from the Greek noun *nikē* ("victory" or "conquest").

A *nikē*, therefore, to coin a word we all have some familiarity with, is an overcomer, one who never quits until complete victory is attained. This was the same idea expressed by Sir Winston Churchill when he gave the final charge to a graduating class. His remarks were brief but pointed: "Never, I say never, give up." With that he sat down. That is exactly the idea carried in Christ's charge to the seven churches who will face the trials of the seventieth week: "Be a *nikē*, an overcomer, and never, never give up."

The overcomer, then, is the true child of God. "For whatever is born of God overcomes the world," John testified, "and this is the victory that has overcome the world — our faith. And who is the one who overcomes the world, but he who believes that Jesus is the Son of God?" (1 John 5:4, 5).

Through His repeated admonition to be *overcomers*, Christ makes clear that the church will go through great testing and purification during the great tribulation of Antichrist. But "to him who overcomes," Christ promises, "I will grant to eat of the tree of life, which is in the Paradise of God" (Rev. 2:7b; cf. vv. 11, 17, 26; 3:5, 12, 21). It is interesting to note that the book of Revelation ends its sequential narrative with a glimpse of the millennial kingdom (21:4). But it is the verses that follow that should give the church (comprised of both wheat and tares) great pause: "He who overcomes shall inherit these things, and I will be his God and he will be My son. But for the cowardly and unbelieving . . . their part will be in the lake that burns with fire and brimstone . . ." (21:7, 8). Certainly the "fiery ordeal" described in the pages that follow in this volume will distinguish the true overcomers from the cowardly and unbelieving.

So far in this chapter we have surveyed the *prior conditions* which must exist before the seventieth week of Daniel will begin — and we have seen that each of these conditions are already widely evident. Thus the media, film, popular culture, and the fine arts reflect a thoroughgoing *spiritual and moral decay*. As mirrors of our culture as a whole, these specific areas reflect the distorted image of moral and spiritual perversion of the last days, as this is so clearly captured in 2 Timothy 3:1-5.

Likewise, *the general climate of thought* which dominates our culture today corresponds so clearly to what the Scriptures teach concerning how people will think during the last days. On one hand there is Satan's age-old deception repackaged for a "New Age" looking for "a golden age . . . after a period of cataclysmic destruction during which many will die . . . wrought by the Third Antichrist . . . a mysterious man from Asia" (see endnote 7). On the other hand, there is the evolutionary mind-set that scorns the supernatural in general and specifically denies that Christ will ever return or come "for the day of judgment and destruction of ungodly men" (2 Pet. 3:7). Moreover, we have seen that evolutionary thought leads necessarily to the racist philosophies that advocate the extermination of "unacceptable" people.

Lastly, we have seen that *the general condition of the church* today corresponds explicitly to what the Scriptures teach the church will be like during the last days. Thus we find widespread accommodation to the spiritual and moral decay of the wider culture, along with false teaching and a lack of spiritual leadership.

These three *prior conditions*, which must exist before the last seven-year period of the end times can begin, *do in fact already exist*. More than this, when they are taken together, they pave the way for the ready acceptance of Antichrist and Satan's final strategy. The conditions exist; the stage is set. The beginning of the seventieth week only awaits the completion of the prior events outlined in Scripture.

PRIOR EVENTS

What then are the *prior events* that must occur before the seventieth week can begin? Immediately we should note that all of these have already occurred, except for one that is yet to come. That one, the fulfillment of which is imminent, should be watched for daily by every believer! To be forewarned is to be forearmed. We should therefore look with special care at the events that will initiate the seventieth and final week of Daniel's prophecy, as summarized below.

(1) THE RETURN OF UNBELIEVING JEWS TO ISRAEL

Israel's overall prophetic timetable was predicted by Daniel as seen in the following passage:

Seventy weeks [490 years] have been decreed for your people and your holy city, to finish the transgression, to make an end of sin, to make atonement for iniquity, to bring in everlasting righteousness, to seal up vision and prophecy, and to anoint the most holy. . . . And he [Antichrist] will make a firm covenant with the many [Israel] for one week [the seventieth], but in the middle of the week he will put a stop to sacrifice and grain offering. (Dan. 9:24, 27)

The "seventy weeks" prophesied by Daniel (7 x 70 years = 490 years) all pertain to "your people" (the Jews) and their "holy city" (Jerusalem). In other words, Daniel's prophecy refers only to that period of time (490 total years) when the chosen people of God are *back in the land of Israel and have control over their land, including their holy city of Jerusalem.* Because the "everlasting righteousness" of the nation does not occur until after the seventieth week is complete, their return to the land must then be in unbelief. And as mentioned several times earlier, after almost two thousand years these events (i.e., coming back into the land and again having control of Jerusalem) were initiated in 1948 and completed in 1967 during the Six-Day War. All end-time events revolve around the small piece of real estate called Israel, God's land of promise to His chosen nation. But it was not possible for the events of the seventieth week (the last seven-year period of the end times) to begin until the natural line of Abraham had already returned to the land (though still refusing to accept their true Messiah) and until Israel had begun again to rule over the entire land as their own sovereign nation, bringing to an end the great *Diaspora* begun in A.D. 70.

This can be seen further in God's revelation to Moses as follows:

So it shall be when all of these things have come upon you, the blessing and the curse which I have set before you, and you call them to mind in all nations where the Lord your God has banished you [the *Diaspora*] . . . [then] the Lord your God will bring you [back] into the land which your fathers possessed, and you shall possess it; and He will prosper you and multiply you more than your fathers. Moreover the Lord your God will circumcise your heart and the heart of your descendants, to love the Lord your God with all your heart and with all your soul, in order that you may live. And the Lord your God will inflict all these curses on your enemies and on those who hate you, who persecuted you. And you shall again obey the Lord, and observe all His commandments which I command you today. (Deut. 30:1, 5-8)

The sequence of events in that passage is of great significance. Verse 1 speaks of the Jews' blessings and curses, as they obeyed or disobeyed the Lord. Verse 5 foretells their physical restoration to the Promised Land, verse 6 their spiritual restoration to God, verse 7 the divine defeat of their enemies, and verse 8 their rule with the Messiah in His earthly, millennial kingdom. (Each of those end-time events, in exactly that sequence, will be dealt with in depth as this book develops.)

This sequence is also reflected in Ezekiel's prophecy: "For I will take you from the nations, gather you from all the lands, and bring you into your own land. Then I will sprinkle clean water on you, and you will be clean; I will cleanse you from all your filthiness and from all your idols. Moreover, I will give you a new heart and put a new spirit within you; and I will remove the heart of stone from your flesh and give you a heart of flesh" (Ezek. 36:24-26).

As is clear from both passages, Israel will first be brought back to the land in unbelief. The fact that she would need purification of heart (Deut. 30:6) and cleansing from sinfulness (Ezek. 36:25) indicates that she would *not* return in faith and righteousness. She would initially return as "dry bones," a lifeless spiritual skeleton (Ezek. 37:11). As modern history bears witness, the present nation of Israel was established in a spirit of self-reliance — by what Jews considered to be the power of their own strategy, industriousness, and alliances. Although .the nation has experienced great economic and military successes after reentering the land, she also looks on these successes as her own doing rather than as the supernatural provision of her gracious God.

(It should be noted that *this* return of the Jews to the land of Israel should not be confused by a later return of the *believing* remnant after going into hiding in Azel [Zech. 14:5], returning to the land of Israel on the Highway of Holiness [see Isaiah 35:8-10], which will occur during the forty-five-day restoration period just prior to the millennial rule of Christ [see further chapter 21 which deals with this in more detail.])

For many centuries, devout Christians have looked anxiously for their Lord's return, only to be frustrated by the knowledge that He could not return until His ancient people Israel were reestablished in their land. Because of the anti-Semitic bias of most of the world and even much of professing Christianity, the likelihood of Israel's again becoming a recognized state in her own ancient land, much less of ever accepting Christ as their Messiah, seemed remote indeed. Consequently, many Christians were inclined to "spiritualize" or "allegorize" the scriptural promises so that they no longer would apply in a literal way to Israel.

But the literal, historical nation of Israel is the absolute focal point of all end-time prophecy, and therefore to allegorize or spiritualize away the promises to Israel is to spiritualize *all* end-time "events" —

which, of course, is exactly what many biblical interpreters have done through the centuries. Even now that Israel has returned to her land in perfect fulfillment of many Old Testament prophecies and has been politically reestablished in the international community, nonliteral interpretations of the last days unfortunately still persist and in fact are increasing!

Although such spiritualized views are still prevalent and influential in the church, it is not within the intent or scope of this present study to debate those who hold to such views — but only to warn those of that nonliteral persuasion that such an approach is unbiblical and accomplishes nothing but to fulfill the desire of Satan to keep the true church misinformed about the last days. In doing so, Satan will have some control over what will happen, when it is "given to him to make war with the saints and to overcome them" (Rev. 13:7). In His letters to the seven churches, Christ also warns: "If anyone has an ear, let him hear" (v. 9). The overriding intent of this author is the same overriding intent behind the warnings given to the seven churches of Revelation — to warn the genuine Christian that what he or she thinks about the last days is of critical importance and that the price of faulty doctrine will be high. Prophecy that need not be fulfilled literally is not prophecy at all, but mere "wishful thinking," especially as it pertains to the genuine church entering into the last days.

It is important, then, to acknowledge that there are many who spiritualize or allegorize prophetic Scripture and to severely warn them of the consequences of holding false doctrine about the last days — consequences both for the teachers who persist in this false teaching (2 Pet. 3:16; Rev. 22:19) and to the spiritual sheep who are under their care (see Rev. 2:22). Paul exhorts the "misled" Thessalonians to "let no one in any way deceive you" (2 Thess. 2:3) and then proceeds to carefully describe a very literal Antichrist (vv. 3, 4) and pinpoint the exact timing of His literal return in relationship to the activities of Antichrist (v. 8).

The great *Diaspora* from the Promised Land that began in 70 A.D. was the ultimate curse, scattering Israel to the ends of the earth. As a result, Jews had no homeland for nearly two thousand years. In 1897 a group of Jews met to discuss their common dream of a homeland — not a homeland just anywhere in the world, but back in the land God had promised to their forefather Abraham, where they had lived for many centuries in ancient times. The movement born from that gathering was called Zionism, after the name of the holy mountain on which the city of Jerusalem was built.

Zionism has never gained wholehearted support from all Jews, and certainly not universal recognition, much less support from Gentiles. Nevertheless, the Zionist movement that began in the late nineteenth century gradually gained recognition from various world powers, especially Great Britain and the United States. After the First World War, the Balfour Declaration by Great Britain (1917) gave Jews land in Palestine to which they could emigrate and live under Britain's protection. It was not until the middle of the twentieth century, however, that the divinely prophesied and long-awaited reestablishment of the *nation* of Israel materialized, when in 1948 the United Nations officially recognized Israel as a sovereign state.

Although several more events must come together before the seventieth week of Daniel can begin, the return of the Jew to the land of Israel, I believe, was *the critical occurrence that set the stage for all else that is to happen.* For that reason, with all of the *prior conditions* outlined earlier in this chapter having already become historical reality, today's church should be in an attitude of expectancy as never before. In other words, this is now the first generation of the church since the early church *before* the *Diaspora* that could conceivably see all the remaining events come together almost overnight. In the same way that the *Diaspora* "triggered" the interlude between the sixty-ninth and seventieth weeks, so the return of Israel to their homeland was the event that "cocked the trigger," as it were, for the events that will initiate the seventieth week.

(2) The Control of Jerusalem by Israel

Not until after the Six-Day War of 1967, however, were all of the city of Jerusalem and the west bank of the Jordan incorporated into the nation. And because the seventy week prophecy of Daniel deals with "your people [Israel] *and your holy city* [Jerusalem]" (Dan. 9:24), the prophecies of the seventieth week could not be fulfilled until Israel regained control of God's "holy city." It was not until 1967, therefore, that the greatest and last historical "barrier" to the second coming of Christ was completely removed. If the return of Israel to her homeland "cocked" the prophetic trigger in preparation for the end times, then her gaining control over the entire city of Jerusalem took off the "safety," preparing the weapon for firing — in other words, for the initiation of the seventieth week of Daniel when the final conflict between God and Satan will be played out on earth.

As an aside, a question frequently asked this writer concerns the rebuilding of the Temple on Mount Zion, a Temple that has not existed since it was destroyed by Titus in A.D. 70, at the beginning of the *Diaspora*. Because Antichrist, in his abomination of desolation, "will put a stop to sacrifice and grain offering" (Dan. 9:27), it is clear that there must be an existing Temple in which those sacrifices and grain offerings will be made. And we learn from Paul that after Antichrist commits that great abomination, he will oppose and exalt "himself above every so-called god or object of worship, so that he takes his seat in the temple of God, displaying himself as being God" (2 Thess. 2:4).

At the time of the first printing of this volume (1992), no Temple has been rebuilt in Jerusalem, and if Israel plans such a rebuilding, those plans have not been made public — although numerous articles (even in secular magazines) have reported on the desire of many Israelis to rebuild their temple.[20]

The Muslim Dome of the Rock mosque is presently on the Temple mount, although the actual site of the original Temple is thought to be several hundred yards north of that mosque. Therefore it may be that after Antichrist persuades Israel to make the "covenant of death" with him, he will seize that site from the Arabs and permit Israel to build a Temple there. Or he may allow both structures of worship to exist. Moreover, if Antichrist were to allow the Temple to be rebuilt, this would further endear him to Israel and make his diabolical deception of that nation less suspected.

It is also possible that an entire Temple will not be built, but only a Tabernacle-like structure that could be erected quickly to provide a place for sacrifice. The Greek word used to describe the Temple Antichrist will desecrate at the midpoint of the seventieth week fully permits that view.[21]

In any case, *a place of sacrifice is not a necessary precursor to the seventieth week,* and in reality may not be built until shortly before the midpoint of that week.

Only one last event must occur before the seventieth week can commence. It is this event for which every Christian should be watching daily. If the return of the Jew to the land of Israel can be compared to cocking the trigger of a gun, and the regaining control of all Jerusalem compared to taking off the safety, then this final event could be compared to pulling the trigger! Because all of the *prior conditions* necessary for that to happen have already become reality, there is only *one event* yet to occur before Antichrist signs the covenant of death with the nation of Israel, thereby initiating the seventieth week of Daniel. That remaining event is *the overthrow of three separate Aryan nations by a new and powerful world leader to form the three-nation coalition that will drive the final beast empire.*

(3) THE THREE-NATION POWER BASE

In chapter 7 of this volume, Daniel's vision was discussed at some length. In particular we saw that while Daniel "was contemplating the horns, behold, another horn, a little one, came up among them, and three of the first horns were pulled out by the roots before it; and behold, this horn possessed eyes like the eyes of a man, and a mouth uttering great boasts" (Dan. 7:8). When Daniel asked for an explanation of what he had just seen in this prophetic vision he was told, "As for the ten horns, out of this kingdom ten kings will arise; and another will arise after them, and he will be different from the previous ones and will subdue three kings" (v. 24). Daniel had just envisioned Antichrist's overthrow of the three nations that would become his three-nation power base, which he will then use to dominate the ten-nation confederacy of Satan's final beast empire. We further learn from the angel's explanation to the Apostle John that "the ten horns which you saw are ten kings, who have not yet received a kingdom, but they receive authority as kings with the beast for one hour. These have one purpose and they give their power and authority to the beast" (Rev. 17:12, 13).

The seventieth week will begin with the signing of a covenant* between the incognito Antichrist and the nation of Israel. As in the days of Antiochus Epiphanes, this covenant will be made for the protection of Israel from a group of nations Israel would otherwise consider to be a threat. Since the power-base nations will be Germanic/Russian in their ancestry, one can quickly understand how Israel (not realizing that the "covenant maker" is Antichrist incognito) would think that a covenant with the leader of these Aryan nations would be in her best interests. *Therefore, just before the seventieth week begins, we can expect to see the overthrow and consolidation of those three nations to form the three-nation power base that Antichrist will use to build his empire.* Whether some of the other seven nations line up immediately with

---

* See further the full discussion of this in the first section of the following chapter.

Antichrist, I am not sure. But the overthrow of the "power-base three" is a specific event that will be immediately recognizable to those looking for it, and it will occur before the covenant is signed initiating the seventieth week.

For this reason close attention should be given to the events occurring in Germany and the former Soviet Union nations, since it is from some combination of these peoples that the "power-base three" will come (see chapter 7 of this book). In this regard it is worth noting a very interesting article in the April 13, 1992, edition of *Time* magazine, which came to my attention just as I was putting the finishing touches on the manuscript for this book. Although it would be easy to editorialize on this article, I will let the reader come to his own conclusions. The following excerpts from this article in *Time* are indeed worthy of attention:

> At U.N. headquarters in New York City there has been talk of giving Germany a permanent role on the Security Council — either directly, with a seat of its own, or by establishing a European seat, which the Germans would almost certainly dominate. "What we see — some among us with a shudder — is Germany taking the helm in Europe," says James Rollo of London's Royal Institute of International Affairs.
>
> An Istanbul newspaper caricatured Foreign Minister Hans-Dietrich Genscher wearing a swastika, and Turkish President Turgut Ozal darkly warned that "Germany changed a lot after unification. It is as if it is trying to intervene in everything, interfere with everyone, trying to prove it is a great power. In the past, Hitler's Germany did the same thing."
>
> These signs of assertiveness are the more unsettling because they represent such a departure from Germany's postwar behavior.
>
> By contributing about 70% of all assistance pledged by the industrialized world to the new entities rising from the wreckage of the old Soviet Union, Germany has emerged as the point nation for managing the economic development of the Commonwealth of Independent States [the former U.S.S.R.]. The same holds for the rest of the old East bloc, where German business is overwhelmingly in front. "The more the East is emptied of Soviet power, the more it is being replaced by Germany's," observes French historian Georges Valance.

"Indisputably, Germany is going to occupy a totally dominant position in the years to come," says Simon Petermann, professor of international relations at Brussels Free University.

"Except for Hitler you have to go back a long way to find a German head of government who speaks so provocatively and insensitively about the outside world," says Heinrich Jaenecke, a columnist for the weekly *Stern*. "Hubris has led this nation astray more than once. The old symptoms are reappearing."[22]

As will be discussed in the next chapter, there is strong reason to believe that some of the other seven nations will not align themselves with Antichrist until sometime after the seventieth week begins.[23] This author, however, is not adamant about the initial size of the final beast empire. It may consist only of the three power-base nations, or these three Aryan nations plus several others, or perhaps all ten at the same time, although this does not seem as likely. Whatever the alignment of these particular ten nations in the days immediately preceding the seventieth week, it is the only event that needs to occur before the covenant can be signed with Israel.

The conclusions that we can draw from the material in this chapter have far-reaching significance for every believer and non-believer as well. We have seen, first, that there are certain *prior conditions* which must exist before the seven-year period of the end times can begin — *and that each one of these prior conditions already exists.* In addition to this, we have seen that there are certain *prior events* which must occur before the seventieth week can begin — *and that each of these events except one has already taken place.* This one last event involves the rise of a world leader and the three-nation power base from which he will begin his domination of the world — an event that can occur as quickly as any government can be overthrown by a new regime. And as history tells us, this can happen practically overnight.

Therefore, it should go without saying that every believer who longs for the return of Christ should watch with anticipation for this development. Soon after this power-base confederacy is formed, its leader will initiate the seventieth week by making a "covenant of death" with Israel, who will despair in "sheer terror" (Isa. 28:15, 19) when the true identity of that leader is later revealed. Thus we turn now *from* the realm of prior conditions and events and *to* what will actually happen when the seventieth week begins.

Countdown to the
End of the Age

W hen the seventieth week begins, it will happen unexpectedly, suddenly — as it were, overnight. The prophetic timetable — after standing still for nearly two thousand years during the gap — will begin to move forward with measured precision. First a powerful world leader will arise out of a Germanic state, taking control of his three-nation, Aryan/Japhethite power base. And then Israel will make the disastrous decision that will set in motion the final seven-year timetable of the end times. These indeed will be the last days, leading the world a step at a time to the end of the age, the day of the Lord.

And so the seventieth and last "week" of Daniel's prophecy will begin, starting the countdown to the end of the ages. It will be a time of great persecution by Antichrist, a time when God allows the spiritually dead nation of Israel to be purged and purified, a time when the church will be made pure and spotless and absolutely worthy to be the bride of Christ, a time that will culminate with Christ's return and rescue of His elect and His eternal destruction of the wicked during the day of the Lord (2 Pet. 2:9; 2 Thess. 1:4-6).

A COVENANT WITH DEATH

What is this event that will initiate the seventieth week of Daniel, this disastrous decision that Scripture calls a "covenant with death," a "pact with Sheol" (Isa. 28:15, 18)?

As so often in the past, unbelieving Jews in Israel will eagerly trust other men instead of God for protection. When the powerful world leader (Antichrist incognito) arises out of Europe and takes control of three Aryan/Japhethite nations to serve as his power base, Israel unwittingly will make a covenant with him, again thinking (as in the days of Antiochus Epiphanes) such a treaty will be her only hope for peace and security. Because of their unbelief — and their resulting intellectual and spiritual blindness — Israelis will look to that seemingly invincible leader as a great protector and will quickly develop a false sense of security. As Isaiah predicts, however, they will instead encounter "sheer terror" (Isa. 28:19) when, three and one half years later, they discover their presumed protector to be their supreme destroyer.

This "protector," however, will be none other than Antichrist — "the prince who is to come . . . [who] will make a firm covenant with the many for one week" (Dan. 9:26, 27). And this covenant that Israel makes with Antichrist will initiate the seventieth week. The "many" are the majority of Jews who will be living in Israel in the last days. And although many Jews will have come back to the Promised Land long before the seventieth week begins, they will not yet, as a nation, have been brought back to faith in God, who promised to give them the land as an eternal inheritance. Thus it will be the time of Israel's ultimate unfaithfulness, and a time that will result in Israel's greatest apostasy (2 Thess. 2:3).

During this first three and a half years of the last "week," the archangel Michael, the divinely appointed and empowered protector of Israel (Dan. 12:1), will not yet have been withdrawn by God. For that reason Antichrist will not yet be able to instigate his unparalleled persecution of Israel, through which he will intend to annihilate every Jew on earth that refuses to worship the beast or his image. Consequently, during the first half of the seventieth week he will not reveal his true identity but will carefully maintain his ruse as Israel's benefactor.

As seen earlier in chapter 8, there is a direct parallel between the persecution of Israel under Antiochus Epiphanes in 168 B.C. and the strategy of Antichrist in the end times. And because Christ Himself confirms this parallel, much of what we learn about Antiochus has direct relevance to understanding the strategy of Antichrist. Thus we can expect that "near" prophecies about Antiochus will also be fulfilled as "far" prophecies about Antichrist, as seen in the following passage from Daniel: "And after an alliance is made with him he will practice deception. . . . [He will] become enraged at the holy covenant and take action; so he will come back and show regard [favor] for those who forsake the holy covenant. . . . And by smooth words he will turn to godlessness those who act wickedly toward the covenant" (Dan. 11:23, 30, 32).

This prediction from Daniel was literally fulfilled as a "near" prophecy under Antiochus Epiphanes, as we see in the historical record of 1 Maccabees:

> In those days there arose out of Israel lawless men, who persuaded many, saying, "Let us go and make a treaty with the heathen around us, for ever since the time we became separated from them, many misfortunes have overtaken us." The plan seemed good in their eyes, and some of the people went eagerly to the king, and he authorized them to introduce practices of the heathen. And they built a gymnasium in Jerusalem, in the heathen fashion, and submitted to uncircumcision, and disowned the holy agreement; they allied themselves with the heathen and became the slaves of wrongdoing. (1 Macc. 1:11-15)

The sequence of events in that passage is significant. First the covenant with a pagan nation is made, and then the apostasy worsens as more and more Israelites forsake God's law and emulate the idolatry and immorality of their new ally. Israel's covenant with Antichrist will follow the same pattern. Once the pact is made, more and more Jews will forsake whatever formalities of Judaism remain and will become virtually indistinguishable from the rest of unbelieving mankind. This will be the beginning phase of Israel's final great apostasy.

Speaking of that time of false security, Isaiah wrote,

> Therefore, hear the word of the Lord, O scoffers, who rule this people who are in Jerusalem, because you have said, "We have made *a covenant with death*, and with Sheol we have made a pact. [Deceiving ourselves, we mistakenly believe that] the overwhelming scourge

will not reach us when it passes by, for we have made falsehood our refuge and we have concealed ourselves with deception." (Isa. 28:14, 15, emphasis added; cf. v. 18).[1]

Once Satan has induced Israel to make this covenant with his earthly minion Antichrist, Satan will be in a perfect position to begin his campaign of slaughter against the Jews; and the moment Michael's protection is removed, Satan will begin. As already noted, Satan's primary hatred is of God, and his primary objective is to completely and permanently wrest control of earth from its Creator. But because Jesus' refusal of the kingdom offered by Satan and His resurrection forever thwarted Satan from deceiving or killing the divine and rightful King of earth, his only remaining hope is to exterminate all potential subjects of the true King's domain.

We cannot be adamant as to whether or not Christians will know when this covenant is made, but, as will be seen in the Epilogue, I believe the whole world will in fact know. Scripture gives no indication that it will be made in secret. Really, can Israel do anything today without making the headlines of practically every newspaper in the free world? How much more so when Israel makes a covenant with this emerging world leader! Therefore it would seem that all of the world will be aware of it, though not aware of its enormous significance. Surely the entire world, including Christians, will at least be aware of the three-nation Aryan power base that will have come under the control of one powerful leader. It will be, then, out of self-interest that Israel will enter into the covenant with death with this man, once again thinking, like ancient Israel, that this powerful human leader will be her friend and can protect her from her enemies. But three and a half years later Israel will discover to her sheer horror that the covenant of safety was in fact a covenant with death.

A FALSE SECURITY

For the first forty-two months, or three and a half years, the nation of Israel will live in relative security because of the attractive but unholy alliance she has made with the most powerful world leader of that day. In their false sense of safety, they will say confidently, "calamity will not overtake or confront us" (Amos 9:10). The context of that statement (see Amos 9:9-15) clearly indicates that the prophet was speaking of Israel's situation in the last days, just before she is almost destroyed — and would be destroyed but for her divine rescue at the last moment. In a similar way Ezekiel describes the Israel of that day as "those who are at rest, that live securely, all of them living without walls, and having no bars or gates" (Ezek. 38:11), thinking she will be protected by her seemingly benevolent and invincible ally.

THE JEWISH WITNESSES

But a small group of Jews living in Israel at that time will know the truth and will use every opportunity to warn their fellow countrymen of their tragic mistake. These Jewish Christians will be motivated more than ever to witness to unbelieving Jews, pointing them to the true Messiah, who will soon come, and warning them of the impending disaster about to occur and their need to flee Israel and go to a safe place. Just as John the Baptist preached to the Jews of his day, "Repent, for the kingdom of heaven is at hand" (Matt. 3:2) and just as he prepared the way for Christ's first coming, so these latter-day witnesses will proclaim the same message to Jews of their day in preparation for Christ's second coming (Matt. 10:16-23).[2]

THE BEGINNING OF "BIRTH-PANGS"

The signing of Israel's covenant with death, as we have seen, will set in motion the last seven-year timetable of the end times. The first half of this last "week" is made up entirely of the events resulting from the opening of the first four seals (Rev. 6:1-8). As each seal is broken, one of the four horsemen of the Apocalypse (see Glossary) is released to carry out a specific form of deception or affliction on earth, the last three of which will result in certain death for one quarter of the earth. These events — false christs, wars, famines and plagues — correspond to Christ's description of these same events in the Olivet Discourse (see Matt. 24:4-8; cf. Luke 21:8-11). Yet Christ refers to these afflictions as "merely the beginning of the birth-pangs" (v. 8) which occur *before* the great tribulation — for as Christ clearly states, it will only be *after* these afflictions that "they will deliver you up to tribulation" (v. 9). Or as He explains a few verses later, "then there will be a great tribulation, such as has not occurred since the beginning of the world until now, nor ever shall" (v. 21). The first three and a half years, then, are "merely the beginning of the birth-pangs," with the great tribulation by Antichrist not occurring until the second half of the seventieth "week" begins.

Directly related to this, it is essential to understand that the great calamities brought on by the four horsemen *are not the beginning or any part of God's day-of-the-Lord wrath*; the same is true even of the great tribulation which will follow during the second half of the last week. Although this is contrary to the interpretation of many Christians who attempt to keep the church out of the seventieth week by equating the seventieth week with the wrath of God, it is essential to understand that these events do not correspond to the day-of-the-Lord wrath and that the church will not be raptured before these events occur. Because of the drastic consequences of holding that position, I feel compelled to warn the church of the grave error of such thinking. That view has been partly responsible for lulling much of the conservative, evangelical church of today into spiritual complacency, making her an unwary and unprepared target for Antichrist's deceit and destruction. If Christians believe these events of the seventieth week (i.e., the birth pangs and the great tribulation) are somehow a part of *God's wrath*, then quite naturally they must believe that those frightening events could not involve them — because, as the Scriptures unquestionably teach, "God has not destined us for wrath, but for obtaining salvation through our Lord Jesus Christ" (1 Thess. 5:9).

The problem is *not* in believing that the Rapture will occur before God's wrath (this is an undisputed truth among all conservative Christians who interpret Scripture literally), but that His wrath begins with the seventieth week and the opening of the first seal. No matter how sincerely pretribulationalism is taught and believed, it unintentionally plays into the hands of Satan by giving the church a false sense of security from end-time affliction. It teaches that the church will be a "heavenly onlooker" to that time of tribulation, whereas in truth God has ordained that His church will very much be an earthly participant. As Paul explains to the church of Thessalonica, persecution of the church will be a prior condition to the wrath of God:

We ourselves speak proudly of you among the churches of God *for your perseverance and faith in the midst of all your persecutions and afflictions which you endure.* This is a plain indication of God's righteous judgment so that you may be considered worthy of the kingdom of God, for which indeed you are suffering. *For after all it is only just for God to repay with affliction those who afflict you, and to give relief to you who are afflicted and to us as well when the Lord Jesus shall be revealed from heaven with His mighty angels in flaming fire, dealing out retribution* to those who do not know God and to those who do not obey the gospel of our Lord Jesus. (2 Thess. 1:4-8, emphasis added)

THE SEVENTIETH WEEK NOT THE DAY OF THE LORD

There are any number of reasons, all of them biblical and logically sound, that show why the entire seventieth week *cannot* be equated with the day of the Lord (although, as we will see, the day of the Lord does begin at the seventh seal, sometime during the second half). First, Christ tells us explicitly that the reaping of the "tares" at the end of the age (the day of the Lord) will be accomplished by the angels of God (Matt. 13:39, 40) — which is exactly what is portrayed in the passage quoted above. But with the first four seals, it is the *four living creatures* who surround the throne of God (not the angels) who are involved with the opening of each seal (Rev. 6:1, 3, 5, 7). These "living creatures" are clearly distinguished from the angels who are associated with the blowing of the trumpets and the pouring out of the bowls (Rev. 8:1-6; 15:5-8) — all of which will be a part of God's wrath when the day of the Lord occurs. (See chapters 18 and 20.)

Second, although some of the natural events depicted in the second, third, and fourth seals are used in the Old Testament to describe the wrath of God, *nowhere in Scripture* are the first four seals of Revelation referred to as manifestations of His wrath during the day of the Lord. Careful study of the use of the various Hebrew words translated "wrath" in the Old Testament clearly indicates that the strong Hebrew word explicitly used in connection with God's day-of-the-Lord wrath against the nations is not the same Hebrew word used in relation to God's chastisement of Israel through these natural disasters. Milder terms are invariably used.[3]

Third, God's wrath is not spoken of in Revelation until *after the sixth seal is broken* and the great cosmic disturbances are displayed as the sign of the end of the age (see Matt. 24:3, 29) — this sign being the event which God has told His people will announce the beginning of the day of the Lord (see chapter 14). Thus, after the sixth seal is broken we are told that "the wrath of the Lamb [Christ]" is about to commence (Rev. 6:15-17). When the seventh seal is broken, initiating the wrath of God, His angelic reapers will directly administer His wrath; and Revelation records that indeed it is the angels who carry out the trumpet and the bowl judgments, exactly as explained by Christ in the parable of the wheat and the tares (Matt. 13:30, 39).

Fourth, it is clear that Christ associates the activities of the first seal with false christs (Matt. 24:5). If the four horsemen are instruments of God's wrath, then God would be in the unthinkable position of sending "false christs" as His own agents to deceive His own elect! Such a logical contradiction is excluded not only by common sense, but explicitly by Christ Himself. When accused by the Pharisees of casting out demons by the power of Satan, the Lord said, "Any kingdom divided against itself is laid waste; and any city or house divided against itself shall not stand. And if Satan casts out Satan, he is divided against himself; how then shall his kingdom stand?" (Matt. 12:25, 26).

Fifth, if the entire seventieth week is the day of the Lord, the wrath of God would be directly responsible for the fifth-seal martyrdom of "the souls of those who had been slain because of the word of God, and because of the testimony which they had maintained" (Rev. 6:9). Such a position directly contradicts the divine assurance, already mentioned above, that *all* who believe in Him (not just believers before the seventieth week) have the unconditional "hope of salvation [deliverance]."[4] "For God has not destined us for wrath, but for obtaining salvation [deliverance] through our Lord Jesus Christ" (1 Thess. 5:8, 9). On the other hand, the fifth-seal martyrdom of these faithful saints is a result of wrath that has its roots in the heavenlies — not God's wrath but Satan's. "Woe to the earth and the sea, because the devil has come down to you, *having great wrath*, knowing that he has only a short time" (Rev. 12:12, emphasis added).

Sixth, and perhaps most significantly, if the day of the Lord were to begin at the opening of the seventieth week, Antichrist would prevail over the Lord for the majority of those seven years! While God was supposedly venting His wrath on the earth, Antichrist would be expanding his satanic kingdom. And after Michael's restraint is removed at the midpoint of the week, Satan's minion would have still greater reign over the earth, even to the point of setting up his throne in God's Temple and demanding worship from the world. If the day of the Lord were to include the entire seventieth week, it would be a mockery of God's omnipotence. Isaiah speaks directly to that issue:

> For *the day of the Lord* of hosts shall be upon every one that is proud and lofty, and upon every one that is lifted up; and he shall be brought low. . . . And the loftiness of man shall be bowed down, and the haughtiness of men shall be made low; and *the Lord alone shall be exalted in that day.* (Isa. 2:12, 17, KJV, emphasis added)

If "the Lord alone shall be exalted" in the day of the Lord, as Isaiah so explicitly states, it is an irrational contradiction to believe that during the Lord's own day an unhindered Antichrist will be demanding and receiving the world's worship of himself!

Seventh, Christ Himself confirms in answering His disciples that when the second seal of the "beginning birth pangs" is in process, "the end" — or "the end of the age" — will not yet have come. Christ had already explained to His disciples that "the end of the age" will be when the tares are harvested and burned (Matt. 13:40) — which is, in other words, a direct reference to the day of the Lord. Jesus then continues to tell His disciples that the day of the Lord ("the end" of the ages) will not occur until *after* their tribulation. "You will be hearing of wars and rumors of wars," Christ explains, but "see that you are not frightened, for those things must take place, but *that is not yet the end.* . . . Then they will deliver you to tribulation, and will kill you, and you will be hated by all nations on account of My name. . . . *But the one who endures to the end*, it is he who shall be saved [delivered]" (Matt. 24:6, 9, 13, emphasis added).

And finally, in perfect keeping with the previous teaching of Christ given in point 7, Christ specifically says that "when you see all these things, recognize that He [Christ] is near, right at the door" (Matt. 24:33). In the context of His promise, "these things" refers to all of the events up to and including the sign of the end of the age which comes "immediately after the tribulation of those days" (v. 29). Therefore, the wrath of God cannot occur until after "these things" occur, making it impossible to equate the seventieth week with the wrath of God.

In my own opinion, it is a contradiction to claim that the seventieth week and the day of the Lord are one and the same. This false teaching is explicitly refuted by the very words of our Lord, and it is therefore impossible for these two events to be the same. Those, then, that hold to this view in an attempt to keep the church out of the seventieth week are preparing the sheep that they shepherd for the slaughter of Antichrist. Those of you sitting under that teaching are warned to "let no one in any way deceive you" (2 Thess. 2:3), and then Paul proceeds to pinpoint the exact timing of the day of the Lord, explaining that it will not come until *after* Antichrist "takes his seat in the temple of God, displaying himself as being God . . . whom the Lord will slay with the breath of His mouth and *bring to an end at the appearance of His coming*" (vv. 4, 8).

THE FIRST FOUR SEALS

The events that ensue, as the first four seals are opened, correspond closely to the events spoken of by Jesus in the beginning of His Olivet Discourse (see Matt. 24:6, 7; Luke 21:9-11). As mentioned earlier, it is important to interpret the book of Revelation *of Christ* by the Olivet Discourse *of Christ*. Both speak directly to end-time events, both describe events that exactly parallel one another, and both are given to us directly by Christ. Because they speak of exactly the same events during the same time period, and because they are clearly intended to teach the same truths concerning the end times, the book of Revelation and the Olivet Discourse are clearly intended by our Lord to complement each other. Thus as we consider in the section below what will happen when each of the first four seals are broken, it will be instructive to understand the "seals" in light of the parallel truths revealed in the Olivet Discourse.

THE FIRST SEAL — FALSE CHRISTS

When Christ, the Lamb, breaks the first seal, "one of the four living creatures [will say], 'Come.'" At that moment, a rider mounted on a white horse and carrying a bow will emerge, and he will go out "conquering, and to conquer" (Rev. 6:1, 2).

The white horse can only represent one thing. In His Olivet Discourse Christ tells us, "Many will come in My name, saying, 'I am the Christ,' and will mislead many" (Matt. 24:5). In Luke's account of the first seal, the Lord warns His elect: "Take heed that you be not misled; for many will come in My name, saying, 'I am He,' and, 'The time is at hand'; do not go after them" (Luke 21:8). Thus the first seal, the white horse, must represent the proliferation of false messiahs, or christs, that will suddenly appear on the scene right after the covenant with death is signed by Israel.

It is interesting to note that this is the only one of the first four seals about which Christ personally warns and exhorts His listeners, using the personal pronoun: "Take heed that *you* be not misled; for many will come in My name, saying 'I am he,' and 'the time is at hand'; do not go after them" (Luke 21:8). Why the personal exhortation here? Christ uses it here, and only here, because He is speaking of the only seal during the first half of the seventieth week that will have direct significance for Christians. The next three seals relate to an entirely different group. Christians need to understand these next three events, but they will not affect Christians with the same impact as the first seal.

The *false* christs represented by the first seal will convince many people within the professing church that they (the false christs) are indeed the *true* Christ who has now returned to earth. They will claim His second coming! For this reason, the Lord's warning about those counterfeit messiahs is a clear and stern command to every believer: "*You* . . . do not go after them."

To understand how the church can be deluded by those false christs, we must look once again at the characteristics of the typical church that will go into the seventieth week. As pointed out in the previous chapter, severe spiritual and moral decay will have gripped the world long before Antichrist begins to operate. Because their leadership will lack spiritual discernment, because they will not have the resolution to teach the truth when it is unpopular, and because they will refuse to take the necessary measures to protect their congregations, many churches will be infested with false teaching. As a consequence, those spiritually weak and compromising churches will never have the desire, or will lose their desire, to accurately learn and understand God's truth and to act accordingly, including their understanding of the end times and how these last days will directly affect them.

When Antichrist begins his world conquest, all the world will watch the overthrow of three powerful Aryan nations by one man. That in itself should be enough to arouse concern in everyone who bears the name of Christ. But the great majority of the visible church, being spiritually dead, will watch those events unfold with little, if any, reaction. In addition, because a great percentage of people in the "believing" Christian church today allegorizes or simply dismisses prophetic Scripture, many of these will likewise be totally unprepared for what is about to happen. Disregarding the fact that all of the prophecies of Christ's first coming were fulfilled literally and in every detail, they will prefer to follow their traditional methods of interpretation and spiritualize, allegorize, or otherwise explain away the prophecies concerning His coming again. As for the rest, the majority of the evangelical churches are taught that they will be raptured before the seventieth week even begins, and for that reason they will be equally unprepared for the events of the seventieth week — even though this position, in the words of one of its strongest proponents, is not even an "explicit teaching of the Scriptures . . . [it is] logically invalid or at least unconvincing."[5]

Therefore, the great majority of those who bear the name of Christ will be totally unprepared for the events that will occur once the covenant with Israel is made. But even though they have been taught that the events of prophetic revelation are not to be taken literally, or that those events do not apply to the church, most genuine believers will quickly become aware of the historical realities of the last days, including the destructive work of Antichrist and his covenant with Israel. When the events of the seventieth week actually begin to materialize, the untaught and the improperly taught members of these compromising churches will be panic-stricken. They will frantically begin looking for the *literal* return of Christ to rescue them from the *literal* persecution by a *literal* Antichrist that they know will soon follow. The genuine believer, no matter how poorly taught, knows the consequences of refusing to worship the beast or his image and refusing his mark (Rev. 13:15-17). Distrusting the leaders who have led them astray, they will search desperately for teachers and preachers they can trust. Or they will look for the immediate return of Christ Himself to deliver them from the wrath of Satan that they know will soon follow (see Rev. 12:12). It is to those poorly taught and unprepared Christians that Christ gives the warning mentioned earlier: "Take heed that you be not misled; for many will come in My name, saying, 'I am He,' and, 'The time is at hand'; do not go after them" (Luke 21:8).

But many undiscerning believers will be led astray to follow one or another of the false christs, being unable to distinguish God's real truth from Satan's counterfeits. Consequently, they will follow false deliverers, who will "deliver" them unknowingly and unwittingly into the very jaws of Antichrist during his great tribulation against God's people.

It should be noted that many prophetic writers mistakenly try to relate "false christs" to the supreme false christ, Antichrist. The untaught church that becomes panic-stricken when the covenant is made with Antichrist will not run directly into the arms of the very one they know has caused their dilemma. They may be poorly prepared for the seventieth week, especially the great tribulation by Antichrist that is soon to follow. But they all will know that Antichrist is the covenant maker; it will be his covenant with Israel that brings the compromising church abruptly to their senses. It will, of course, be Antichrist from whom they will be trying to escape. On the other hand, because of their confusion and panic, many will turn to one of the various false christs, thinking him to be the true Christ — which will play perfectly into the scheme of Antichrist.

If the compromising church is so unprepared, what then of the faithful church — the church which has carefully and accurately taught the Word of God and has not been polluted by false or compromising teachers? They will be prepared to survive the great persecution by Antichrist just as Noah and his family were before the Flood and just as Lot and his family were before the destruction of Sodom and Gomorrah (see 2 Pet. 2:4-9; Luke 17:26-30; Matt. 24:36-41). These saints will accurately read the signs and will fully realize what is happening and what is about to happen. They will recognize the first certain sign of the end times when the great leader gains control over the three powerful Aryan nations. They will know that he is Antichrist and that those three nations will be the power base of the ten-nation empire he will subsequently form. They will also understand the significance of Israel's signing a covenant with that leader — that the seventieth week has begun and that they will have but three and a half years to prepare themselves for the great tribulation by Antichrist. They will understand who the false Christs are and the Lord's warning concerning them. Yet they will also know that their Lord has promised to protect them while within the sphere of danger, the great "hour of testing, that hour which is about to come upon the whole world, to test those who dwell upon the earth" (Rev. 3:10).* And, just as a remnant of Israel will flee into the wilderness before that terrible tribulation, so the faithful church will go into hiding — to the ridicule of the ungodly world and even to the ridicule of many Christians who have been mistaught.[6]

We do not know *how* the Lord will keep those who have been faithful in their doctrine and their lives, but we have the assurance of His promise. Those who are prepared can rest assured in the promise of God's protection — that He will be faithful to those who have been faithful to Him in purity of doctrine and holy living. Likewise, there is no need to panic or build bomb shelters or become extremists. In fact, it is essential that we *not* panic, but that we instead faithfully continue to carry out the calling the Lord has given to us — whether as a businessman, a homemaker, a teacher, a laborer, or whatever — until we are called to do otherwise at the beginning of the seventieth week. When we see that Israel has signed the covenant of death, faithful believers will know that they have three and a half years until

* See chapter 2, endnote 1.

Antichrist will be revealed and three and a half years before the saints will come under his direct attack. During this time those who have remained faithful will have time to go their way and quietly prepare for the persecution that will come to all who do not take the mark of the beast or worship his image (Rev. 13:14-18). But that preparation will be made in the full confidence that the Lord knows how to safely keep His own during "the hour of testing, that hour which is about to come upon the whole world, to test those who dwell upon the earth" (Rev. 3:10), and that He will "rescue the godly from *temptation* [i.e., from *testing*]"* — as He did in the days of Noah, as He did in the days of Lot, as He will do again in the days of Satanic testing (2 Peter 2:5-9; cf. Matt. 24:37-39; Luke 17:26-36).

THE SECOND SEAL — WARS

The first seal, then, will only be the *beginning* of the "beginning birth pangs." With the second seal the "birth pangs" will continue, bringing great destruction on "a fourth of the earth" (Rev. 6:8). As the Apostle John wrote, "And when He [Christ, the Lamb] broke the second seal, I heard the second living creature saying, 'Come.' And another, a red horse, went out; and to him who sat on it, it was granted to take peace from the earth, and that men should slay one another; and a great sword was given to him" (Rev. 6:3, 4).

At this point, Antichrist and his "power-base three" will begin to consolidate the complete ten-nation empire. Although he will still hide his true identity, his actions will prove that whoever he may be, he is not a deliverer but a conqueror. The second seal will usher in a time of intense warfare. Because his true intentions to rule the world, to demand the world's worship, and to annihilate God's people will not yet be evident, Antichrist will still be viewed by much of the world as a beneficent warrior who uses his military might to bring order to a chaotic world.

During this time Antichrist will establish his position as a world leader by the defeat of his enemies, and he will try to consolidate the various nations and political factions who are willing to give him their allegiance. Describing that effort for consolidation, Daniel says of Antichrist: "He will take action against the strongest of fortresses with the help of a foreign god; he will give great honor to those who

---

* This is the same Greek word as used in Revelation 3:10.

acknowledge him, and he will cause them to rule over the many, and will parcel out land for a price" (Dan. 11:39).

There can be no question that the consolidation of the eighth beast empire takes place with the help of a "foreign god." This writer cannot be adamant about who this "foreign god" will be, but the most likely candidate in this writer's opinion is the Babylonian Harlot — that is, the false religious system or systems that originated in Babylon, that system which Satan has used and will use *to deceive the nations* concerning Christ (the true seed of the woman [Gen. 3:15]) in Satan's attempt *to destroy the elect of God*.[7] With its roots in ancient Babylon, that system through the centuries has subtly replaced "the seed of the woman" (Christ) with the mother/child or "Queen of Heaven" worship that was denounced so strongly by the prophets of old (see Jer. 44:16-19; 24:28). As described by John in the book of Revelation, the great harlot is "drunk with the blood of the saints, and with the blood of the witnesses of Jesus" (Rev. 17:6); likewise she is the one "with whom the kings of the earth committed acts of [spiritual] immorality, and those who dwell on the earth were made drunk with the wine of her [spiritual] immorality" (17:2). In the next verse John sees the harlot "sitting on a scarlet beast . . . having seven heads and ten horns" (v. 3). Adding these two verses together comes up with only one conclusion. The harlot will be a powerful religious force that over the ages has controlled the kings of the nations. In like manner, in the last days she will also have the same relationship with the final beast empire of Satan, using her international influence developed in the past to help Antichrist assemble his ten-nation coalition and eventually rule the world.

In addition, the passage just quoted above from Daniel reveals that Antichrist will "give great honor to those who acknowledge him . . . and will parcel out land for a price." The price, of course, will be total allegiance to their benefactor. John confirms this in chapter 17 of the book of Revelation:

> And the ten horns which you saw are ten kings, who have not yet received a kingdom, but they receive authority as kings with the beast for one hour. These have one purpose and they give their power and authority to the beast. (vv. 12, 13)

As in New Testament times, the center of international power in the last days apparently will be in the Mediterranean area, with the dominant nations being in Eastern Europe, the Middle East, and north

Africa. Impossible as it seems from the perspective of modern times, North and South America, Australia, the British Isles, most of the Far East, and most of Africa will have insignificant roles, if any, in the major international events of the last days. But as we shall see in chapter 12 of this book, during the second half of the seventieth week Antichrist nevertheless will have absolute demonic control over all those nations and all their inhabitants as well.

During the time represented by the second seal Daniel predicts that:

> the king of the South will collide with him [Antichrist], and the king of the North will storm against him with chariots, with horsemen, and with many ships; and he will enter countries, overflow them, and pass through. He will also enter the Beautiful Land, and many countries will fall; but these will be rescued out of his hand: Edom, Moab and the foremost of the sons of Ammon. Then he will stretch out his hand against other countries, and the land of Egypt will not escape. But he will gain control over the hidden treasures of gold and silver, and over all the precious things of Egypt; and Libyans and Ethiopians will follow at his heels. But rumors from the East and from the North will disturb him, and he will go forth with great wrath to destroy and annihilate many. And he will pitch the tents of his royal pavilion between the seas and the beautiful Holy Mountain. (Dan. 11:40-45)

The king of the South is probably the ruler of Egypt, and the king of the North is most probably the ruler of Assyria or Babylon or of both — the general areas of modern Syria and Iraq. The "Beautiful Land" is, of course, the Promised Land of the Jews, and "the beautiful Holy Mountain" is Mount Zion in Jerusalem.

It is evident from this passage that, just as Antiochus did in the second century B.C. (see 1 Macc. 1:16-24), Antichrist will loot Egypt before he plunders and desecrates the Temple in Jerusalem. And while quelling the southern and northern uprisings against him, he will attempt to conquer the region of modern Jordan that in ancient times was comprised of Edom, Moab, and southern Ammon. But those lands will be divinely protected, "rescued out of his hand." It will be to this safety zone that a portion of the "woman" (the unbelieving remnant of Jews who refuses to bow down to Antichrist) will be able to flee (see Ezek. 20:34, 35; Rev. 12:6, 14) before Antichrist breaks his covenant with Israel, reveals his true evil identity, and begins his merciless persecution of those Jews who refuse to worship him. This terrifying time, the great tribulation by Antichrist, will make even the Nazi Holocaust pale by comparison. It is for that reason that Jesus calls the afflictions of the first half of the seventieth week, destructive as they are, only "the beginning of birth pangs."

THE THIRD SEAL — EARTHQUAKES AND FAMINES

While Antichrist and his forces are wreaking military havoc, there will also be tremendous food shortages: "And when He [Christ] broke the third seal, I heard the third living creature saying, 'Come.' And I looked, and behold, a black horse; and he who sat on it had a pair of scales in his hand. And I heard as it were a voice in the center of the four living creatures saying, 'A quart of wheat for a denarius, and three quarts of barley for a denarius; and do not harm the oil and the wine'" (Rev. 6:5, 6). When the corresponding descriptions in the Olivet Discourse are examined, the emphasis of the third seal is stated clearly: "In various places there will be famines . . ." (Matt. 24:7).

Whether or not Antichrist in some way causes these shortages, they will at least play into his hands. As this part of the world's political and economic plight becomes progressively worse, its people will become increasingly more willing to offer their loyalty, and even to surrender their freedom, to a leader who promises political stability and famine relief.

THE FOURTH SEAL — PLAGUE AND DEATH

And when He broke the fourth seal, I heard the voice of the fourth living creature saying, "Come." And I looked, and behold, an ashen horse; and he who sat on it had the name "Death"; and Hades was following with him. And authority was given to them over a fourth of the earth, to kill with sword and with famine and with pestilence and by the wild beasts of the earth. (Rev. 6:7, 8)

Death will be the overriding consequence of the fourth seal, with specific authority given to kill "over a fourth of the earth." Upon careful scrutiny of that text and comparison of it with other passages, it seems likely that the phrase "a fourth of the earth" refers to *the amount of the earth's inhabited surface* that will be subject to unusual death, coming as a result of war, famines, plagues and even wild animals — that is, from all of the first four seals except the first one (false christs). With this interpretation, the specific theaters of conflict mentioned in Scripture concerning the first half of the seventieth week (namely, most of Eastern Europe, the Middle East, Western U.S.S.R., North Africa, plus the "rumors from the East and from the North" [Dan. 11:44]) could quite conceivably cover a fourth of the earth's inhabited land. By contrast, the great slaughter during the day of the Lord's wrath, mentioned in Revelation 9:15, is said to affect "a third of mankind," clearly referring to *inhabitants* of the earth, not to the *portion* of the earth that will be affected.

The famine in the affected fourth of the world will be so extreme that "the wild beasts of the earth" will compete with men for food, and many of them, it would seem, will be driven by hunger to attack and devour human beings. Therefore, during the time of the second, third, and fourth seals, men not only will be killed by warfare (the sword), by starvation (famine), and by disease (pestilence),[8] but also by animals (wild beasts).

As the end of the first half of the seventieth week nears its conclusion, the remaining unbelieving inhabitants of that "fourth of the earth" will be so desperate that they will be more than ready to submit to Antichrist's rule and even to worship him when he demands it. At that time his forces will be poised just outside Jerusalem, ready to conquer the city, to reveal his true identity, to desecrate the Temple, and to rule the whole world. In the meantime, the compromising churches throughout the world, untaught and unprepared, will now be in complete turmoil. Having been rent asunder, their congregations will go off in many different directions, many of them following whichever false christ seems most appealing and promises the most protection from the great persecution of Antichrist that they now will know is coming soon. Some of those that don't follow after the false christs will, like the faithful church, go into some sort of seclusion. But unlike the faithful church, they will be totally unprepared for the system of world control that Antichrist will soon exercise over the entire world. They will be safe for a while, but because they have not been taught, they will eventually pay the price with their life. The spiritually dead members of the church for the most part will be oblivious to the real meaning of what is going on, but the faithful believers will be unobtrusively going into hiding totally prepared for what is to come, under the protection God has promised to give.

All is now ready for the revealing of Antichrist and his true identity — as we shall discover in the following chapter.

Antichrist Revealed

T he midpoint of the seventieth "week" will mark a dramatic turn of events in the end times. The first three and a half years of "birth-pangs" will come to an end, and the last three and a half years — the "great tribulation, such as has not occurred since the beginning of the world until now, nor ever shall be" (Matt. 24:21) — will be initiated by Antichrist.

PREPARING THE WAY

Just prior to the midpoint, Antichrist will have risen to become the most powerful leader in the world. He will, in fact, be viewed by the unbelieving world (including Israel) as a great deliverer and protector. He will have crushed oppressive regimes throughout the world. He will seem to have brought peace and order in the place of international conflict and chaos. He will have amassed a seemingly invincible coalition of ten nations that will encompass the leading powers of Eastern Europe, North Africa, and the Middle East. And he will concentrate the best of his massive armies in the Middle East, posing as the benevolent protector of Israel.

THE JERUSALEM CAMPAIGN

But without warning the tables will be dramatically turned. The treaty of protection made three and a half years earlier will turn out to be a "covenant of death." The defending armies will launch a ruthless assault on Israel and her holy city, Jerusalem, intent on total destruction. As Antichrist carries out his "Jerusalem Campaign,"* he will invade the Holy City, and at this irreversible point in time (the midpoint of the seventieth week) Antichrist, "the man of lawlessness," will enter the holiest part of the Temple and reveal himself for who he really is — "the son of destruction, who opposes and exalts himself above every so-called god or object of worship, so that he takes his seat in the temple of God, displaying himself as being God" (2 Thess. 2:3, 4). This will be "sheer terror" for Israel when she understands what this really means.

Jesus Himself foretold the events that will inaugurate the great tribulation by Antichrist. As recorded in Matthew's account of the Olivet Discourse the Lord warns His people:

> "Therefore when you see the ABOMINATION OF DESOLATION which was spoken of through Daniel the prophet, standing in the holy place (let the reader understand), then let those who are in Judea flee to the mountains; let him who is on the housetop not go down to get the things out that are in his house; and let him who is in the field not turn back to get his cloak. But woe to those who are with child and to those who nurse babes in those days! But pray that your flight may not be in the winter, or on a Sabbath; for then there will be a great tribulation, such as has not occurred since the beginning of the world until now, nor ever shall." (Matt. 24:15-21)

Christ warns those living specifically in Jerusalem to flee, because Antichrist's purge of the natural line of Abraham will begin in the city of Jerusalem. Eventually two out of three Jews living in Israel will die

---

* The term "Jerusalem Campaign" is used to describe this first invasion of Israel by Antichrist in order to distinguish this from the other two military campaigns that will take place in the land of Israel before the Millennium. For further information, see the Glossary.

at his hands (Zech. 13:8), preferring death rather than submission to the worst Jew-hater in history.

These same events — Antichrist's betrayal of Israel and his invasion of her holy city — are vividly foretold in a number of Old Testament prophecies. Thus Isaiah warned, "your covenant with death shall be canceled, and your pact with Sheol shall not stand; when the overwhelming scourge passes through, then you become its trampling place" (Isa. 28:18).

Ezekiel portrayed the invasion of Antichrist (Gog) with similar graphic intensity:

> . . . *in the latter years* you [Antichrist] will come into the land that is restored from the sword, whose inhabitants have been gathered from many nations to the mountains of Israel which had been a continual waste; but its people were brought out from the nations, and they are living securely, all of them. And you [Antichrist] will go up, you will come like a storm; you will be like a cloud covering the land, you and all your troops, and many peoples with you . . . and you will say, "I will go up against the land of unwalled villages. I will go against those who are at rest, that live securely, all of them living without walls, and having no bars or gates." . . . And you will come up against My people Israel like a cloud to cover the land. It will come about *in the last days* that I shall bring you against My land, in order that the nations may know Me when I shall be sanctified through you before their eyes, O Gog. (Ezek. 38:8, 9, 11, 16, emphasis added)

Likewise, Zechariah gives further description of what awaits Israel: "For I will gather all the nations against Jerusalem to battle, and the city will be captured, the houses plundered, the women ravished, and half of the city exiled, but the rest of the people will not be cut off from the city" (Zech. 14:2).

As these passages show, during the first half of the seventieth week Israel will be living securely, untouched and possibly little concerned about Antichrist's conquests of the surrounding countries. Israel's false sense of security will be founded on the covenant she has made with the great world leader whose true identity and true intentions will have been concealed.

However, when the people of Israel see their beloved holy city surrounded by a massive army, they will begin to realize that they have been betrayed and that the time of Jacob's distress, the great tribulation by Antichrist, is at hand. For Antichrist will keep his pact with Israel only as long as he is prevented by the archangel Michael from pursuing the real intent of Satan. But after Satan is cast down to earth with great wrath and little time (Rev. 12:12), the restrainer will be removed, and Satan will begin his counteroffensive against those of the natural line of Abraham who refuse to submit to his leadership (Rev. 12:13). After the Jewish people have been lulled into complacency and a false sense of security, Antichrist will attack Israel without warning and with relentless, merciless brutality.

For most, if not all, of the previous three and a half years, Jewish witnesses will have pleaded with their fellow inhabitants of Israel to repent of their great apostasy, to accept and to wait for their true Messiah, Jesus Christ, and to flee from the treachery and tribulation that will soon fall upon them with astonishing swiftness. Some of those witnesses will have forfeited their lives because of their godly and fearless testimony to their beloved but largely unresponsive countrymen. Some of the hearers, however, will have heeded the warning and already fled into the wilderness for protection.

During this terrible period of affliction of God's people, Antichrist "will speak out against the Most High and wear down the saints of the Highest One, and he will intend to make alterations in times and in law; and they will be given into his hand for a time, times, and half a time" (Dan. 7:25; cf. 12:7). The exact meaning of Antichrist's intent to alter times and law is not clear. It might well mean that he will attempt to completely revise the modern calendar, eliminating all Jewish and Christian observances (such as Passover, Christmas, and Easter), or it might mean that he will attempt to overturn commonly accepted codes of ethics and morals that have prevailed throughout history in most societies. In any case, his supreme purpose will be to do everything within his power "against the Most High and . . . the saints."

Antichrist's intense hatred of Jews, as we have seen, stems from Satan's intense hatred of God, who chose the Jews to be His channel for the redemption of the world and for the eventual defeat of Satan. But because God Himself is out of the reach of Satan and his minion Antichrist, the only way left for Satan to thwart God's plan would be to destroy God's chosen nation. First he would seek to destroy "the woman" (an obedient remnant within the natural line of Abraham who refuse to worship Antichrist); and if unable to do that, he would then seek to destroy "the rest of her offspring [believing Christians], who keep the commandments of God and hold to the testimony of Jesus" (Rev. 12:17). For if Antichrist can either destroy those who refuse to worship him from within the natural line of Abraham (the woman) or obliterate God's people (the spiritual line of Abraham), he could still prevent God's reclaiming the rule over earth.

Antichrist, therefore, will virtually be the devil incarnate, and during this final three and a half years of his usurped rule over the earth he will manifest unparalleled "wrath, knowing that he has only a short time" (Rev. 12:12; cf. 13:4, 5).

"THE FAITHFUL WOMAN" WHO FLEES

Some Jews in Israel, however, in particular those who have distrusted the covenant with Antichrist from the beginning, will heed the warning of their fellow countrymen, the Jewish witnesses. And when the armies of Antichrist begin to move around the city of Jerusalem during the Jerusalem Campaign, they will flee the city and hide in the wilderness place provided by God. As John writes, "And when the dragon [Satan] saw that he was thrown down to the earth, he persecuted the woman [those refusing to worship Antichrist]. . . . And the two wings of the great eagle were given to the woman, in order that she might fly *into the wilderness* to her place, where she was nourished for a time and times and half a time [three and a half years], from the presence of the serpent" (Rev. 12:13, 14; cf. v. 6, emphasis added).

God also predicted through Ezekiel that He would bring Jews from other lands into the wilderness as well:

> *I shall bring you out from the peoples and gather you from the lands where you are scattered,* with a mighty hand and with an outstretched arm and with wrath poured out; and I shall bring you *into the wilderness of the peoples,* and there I shall enter into judgment with you face to face (Ezek. 20:34, 35, emphasis added)

In the book of Isaiah, God even reveals the general location of that wilderness:

> Send ye the lamb *to the ruler of the land from Sela* [Petra, capital of Edom] *to the wilderness,* unto the mount of the daughter of Zion. . . . Take counsel, execute judgment; make thy shadow as the night in the midst of the noonday; hide the outcasts; bewray

[betray] not him that wandereth. *Let mine outcasts dwell with thee, Moab*; be thou a covert to them from the face of the spoiler. (Isa. 16:1-4a, KJV, emphasis added)

It is interesting to note that the wilderness into which a remnant of Israel will flee is the one area that Antichrist and his armies will be unable to overthrow during the first half of the seventieth week (Dan. 11:41).* God will protect this region for the Jews who flee there.

But God also warns the inhabitants of Edom about exulting in the plight of the Jews who flee to their land for safety or of taking advantage of them, as seen in this graphic description in Obadiah of the remnant of Israel fleeing into the wilderness:

Do not gloat over your brother's day, the day of his misfortune. And do not rejoice over the sons of Judah in the day of their destruction; yes, do not boast in the day of their distress. Do not enter the gate of My people in the day of their disaster. Yes, you, do not gloat over their calamity in the day of their disaster. And do not loot their wealth in the day of their disaster. And do not stand at the fork of the road to cut down their fugitives; and do not imprison their survivors in the day of their distress. *For the day of the Lord draws near on all the nations.* As you have done, it will be done to you. Your dealings will return on your own head. (Obad. 12-15, emphasis added)

In this very specific warning to the descendants of Esau, God threatens the Edomite with his *impending* day of the Lord (v. 15), *still to come after* "the woman" flees to the wilderness to avoid the great tribulation by Antichrist. Unfortunately, most of the Edomites, consistent with their historical attitude about Israel, will not heed that divine warning. Consequently, the prophet predicts that "because of violence to your brother Jacob, you will be covered with shame, and you will be cut off forever" (Obad. 10). This is exactly what happens, as we shall see in chapter 20 of this book.

After carefully examining all relevant Scripture, this author believes that the only Jewish group that fits the description of the woman who flees to the wilderness during the Jerusalem Campaign,

---

* Edom was located in the southwestern portion of modern Jordan, just south and east of the Dead Sea, whereas Moab was immediately north of Edom, on the east bank of the Dead Sea.

will be a special group of 144,000 faithful Jews referred to only twice in Scripture, in Revelation chapters 7 and 14.[1] The 144,000 will be a small remnant of Israel, twelve thousand coming from each of the twelve tribes of Jacob (7:4-8). All of these will have refused to apostasize to Antichrist during the first half of the seventieth week, although they will still be unsaved when they flee to the wilderness at the midpoint of the week.[2]

John explains further in Revelation 14 that these 144,000 are those "who have not been defiled with women, for they have kept themselves chaste" (v. 4). In other words, in context, this refers to those who have kept themselves spiritually pure by refusing to "adulterate" themselves with Antichrist in any way.[3] "These are the ones," John continues, "who follow the Lamb wherever He goes. These have been purchased from among men as first fruits to God and to the Lamb" (v. 4). In a similar vein Isaiah refers to these as the "righteous" Jews who have not made the adulterous "agreement" with Antichrist (Isa. 57:1, 8). It seems probable, therefore, that these are the ones who flee into the wilderness rather than subject themselves to the false messiah. Thus these 144,000 faithful Jews will have refused to apostatize themselves by approving the covenant with Antichrist at the beginning of the seventieth week, and they therefore represent "the woman [who] fled into the wilderness where she had a place prepared by God, so that there she might be nourished for one thousand two hundred and sixty days" (Rev. 12:6).

Once in the wilderness, "the faithful woman" will be *judged and purged by God*. As the Lord promised long ago through Ezekiel, "I shall bring you into the wilderness of the peoples, and there I shall enter into judgment with you face to face. . . . And I shall purge from you the rebels and those who transgress against Me; I shall bring them out of the land where they sojourn, but they [the rebels] will not enter the land of Israel. Thus you will know that I am the Lord" (Ezek. 20:35, 38).

But "the faithful woman" will eventually be *saved*. Because God has sovereignly chosen them — just as He has chosen all believers "before the foundation of the world" (Eph. 1:4) — He will cause "the faithful woman" to "pass under the rod, and . . . bring [them] into the bond of the covenant" (Ezek. 20:37) so that they become the first fruits of the natural line of Abraham.

SATAN THROWN DOWN TO EARTH

After "the woman" has fled, or perhaps as she is fleeing into the wilderness "prepared by God" (Rev. 12:6), John records that there will be

war in heaven, Michael and his angels waging war with the dragon. And the dragon and his angels waged war, and they were not strong enough, and there was no longer a place found for them in heaven. And the great dragon was thrown down, the serpent of old who is called the devil and Satan, who deceives the whole world; he was thrown down to the earth, and his angels were thrown down with him. And I heard a loud voice in heaven, saying, "Now the salvation, and the power, and the kingdom of our God and the authority of His Christ have come, for the accuser of our brethren has been thrown down, who accuses them before our God day and night." (Rev. 12:7-10)

With Satan's sudden exit from the heavenlies to a new earthly abode, the battleground has shifted from Heaven to earth for the final showdown between God and Satan, which will bring the cosmic conflict to a predetermined and eternal end. The time for the fiery testing of all mankind, including the church (1 Pet. 4:12; cf. v. 17), will have begun, and Satan will soon be given access to "the elect of God," knowing that he must convince them, by whatever means, to take the mark of Antichrist or else kill them if they refuse. He fully understands that *any who refuse his test* become potential citizens of Christ's millennial kingdom. So every inhabitant on earth, without exception, must pass Satan's test or die.

Because all of God's true elect will refuse that mark by the power of the indwelling Holy Spirit, "the loud voice in heaven" will declare that

They overcame him because of the blood of the Lamb and because of the word of their testimony, and they did not love their life even to death . . . rejoice, O heavens and you who dwell in them. Woe to the earth and the sea; because *the devil has come down to you, having great wrath,* knowing that he has only a short time. (Rev. 12:11, 12, emphasis added)

Here we see unequivocally that the great tribulation is *not an expres-*

sion of the wrath of God, but of the "great wrath" of the devil and his persecution carried out through Antichrist.

SATAN EMPOWERS ANTICHRIST

From the time that Antichrist is brought back to life, he will be inspired and controlled by Satan. But at some point near the beginning of the second half of the seventieth week, after Satan has been cast to earth for the final conflict, Antichrist will be *empowered by Satan* in a supernatural and extremely powerful way. The unbelieving world will worship "the dragon [Satan], because *he gave his authority to the beast* [Antichrist]; and they worshiped the beast, saying, 'Who is like the beast, and who is able to wage war with him?'" (Rev. 13:4, emphasis added).

MICHAEL (THE RESTRAINER) REMOVED

When Satan is thrown down to earth, one obstacle will stand between Satan and his scheme to unleash his wrath upon any in the world who refuse to worship the beast (Antichrist) or his image. This one remaining obstacle will be the archangel Michael, the great restrainer who has been the heavenly protector of God's people since ancient times (see Dan. 10:21).[4]

In a crucial prophetic passage, Paul describes the exact sequence of events involving the removal of the restrainer and the revealing of Antichrist (all of which take place *before* "the appearance of [the Lord's] coming" [2 Thess. 2:8]). As seen in 2 Thessalonians 2:1-9, this sequence may be outlined as follows:

(1) "The apostasy comes first" (v. 3) — i.e., the signing of the covenant with Antichrist and the subsequent apostasy of Israel to the "covenant-maker."

(2) Then "he who now restrains [Michael]" will be "taken away" (v. 7) so "that lawless one [Antichrist] will be revealed" (v. 8).[5]

(3) Then "the man of lawlessness [Antichrist] is revealed, the son of destruction" (v. 3b).

(4) Whereupon Antichrist "exalts himself above every so-called god or object of worship, so that he takes his seat in the temple of God, displaying himself as being God" (v. 4).

In other words, we see that Michael, the great restrainer, will be removed at the midpoint of the seventieth week, and only after the restrainer is removed will Antichrist reveal his true identity to the world.

This is exactly what we see, but with more detail, when John writes: "And I saw one of his heads [a previous beast empire leader] as if it had been slain, and his fatal wound was healed [a dead man come alive]. And the whole earth was amazed [that their leader is a dead man come alive] and followed after the beast" (Rev. 13:3). First comes the revealing of Antichrist's true identity — a dead man come back to life — and then worship by everyone worldwide when they realize who this man is. But this cannot happen, of course, until the restrainer is first removed — "and then that lawless one will be revealed" (2 Thess. 2:8).

The idea that God would remove Israel's protection at their hour of greatest need is not a punishment foreign to the nation of Israel. This exact consequence for their rebellion against God is substantiated in the prophetic parable of the vineyard found in Isaiah 5:1-7. First Isaiah describes God's loving care for His vineyard, Israel. Yet in spite of this, Israel produced only worthless fruit (v. 2b). "So now," the Lord proclaims, "let me tell you what I am going to do to My vineyard. I will *remove its hedge* and it will be consumed; I will break down its wall and it will become trampled ground. And I will lay it waste" (vv. 5, 6a). The Lord's prediction that He will first remove Israel's "hedge" and that Israel will then become trampled ground clearly parallels the removal of the restrainer and the beginning of the "great tribulation, such as has never [before] occurred" (Matt. 24:21). The relevance of this passage in Isaiah is further underscored by Christ's own use of this parable in Matthew 21, where He relates the parable's message to the judgment of Israel in the end times "when the owner of the vineyard comes" (see Matt. 21:33-44, esp. v. 40).

Regardless of the restrainer's identity, however, it is clear that his restraining hand must be removed before Antichrist can reveal himself, take his place in the Temple, and be able to execute his satanic plan and powers to their fullest extent.

THE ABOMINATION OF DESOLATION

Jesus admonishes believers in the last days: "Therefore when you see the ABOMINATION OF DESOLATION which was spoken of through Daniel the prophet, standing in the holy place (let the reader understand) . . . then there will be a great tribulation, such as has not occurred since the beginning of the world until now, nor ever shall.

And unless those days had been cut short, no life [of the elect] would have been saved" (Matt. 24:15, 21, 22).

The Holy Spirit reveals through the prophet Daniel that *"in the middle of the week"* — that is, three and a half years after he has made his deceptive covenant with Israel — Antichrist "will put a stop to sacrifice and grain offering; and on the wing of abominations will come one who makes desolate" (Dan. 9:27, emphasis added). At that time Satan (the dragon) will give Antichrist (the beast) "his power and his throne and great authority. And I saw one of his heads as if it had been slain, and his fatal wound was healed. And the whole earth was amazed and followed after the beast; and they worshiped the dragon, because he gave his authority to the beast; and they worshiped the beast, saying, 'Who is like the beast, and who is able to wage war with him?'" (Rev. 13:2-4).

Antichrist will be the unequaled "man of lawlessness . . . the son of destruction, who opposes and exalts himself above every so-called god or object of worship, so that he takes his seat in the temple of God, displaying himself as being God" (2 Thess. 2:3, 4). His "coming [will be] in accord with the activity of Satan, with all power and signs and false wonders" (2 Thess. 2:9).

THE IDENTIFICATION OF ANTICHRIST

Who is Antichrist? Can we in fact identify who he actually is, or will be? Perhaps the most startling fact concerning Antichrist is that he is (or will be) a dead man brought back to life, one whose "fatal wound was healed" (Rev. 13:3).

Yet the true identity of Antichrist will remain scrupulously concealed to the world until the middle of the seventieth week. If he were to be revealed before this irreversible midpoint in the last seven years — before he took over the three-nation power base, before he made his covenant with Israel, before he put together his ten-nation beast empire, before he assembled his massive military strength, before being supernaturally empowered by Satan — he would be killed or imprisoned long before he could set his diabolical strategy in motion.

But as soon as Satan is cast down to earth and the restrainer is removed, Antichrist will be emboldened and empowered by Satan to carry out the most hideous blasphemies and atrocities the world has ever known. Israel, as we have seen, will suddenly realize who this man is and will be filled with terror, while the rest of the world — also recognizing who this dead man brought back to life really is — will be compelled to give him their absolute allegiance and worship.

DESCRIPTIONS OF ANTICHRIST

Scripture refers to Antichrist by numerous names or titles: *Antichrist* (1 John 2:18); *the beast* (Rev. 13:4); *the man of lawlessness* and *the son of destruction* (2 Thess. 2:3); *Gog* (Ezek. 38:2); the *little horn* (Dan. 7:8); an extremely powerful and ungodly *king* (Dan. 11:36); *the destroyer* and *extortioner* (Isa. 16:4); *the head of the house of evil* (Hab. 3:13); and even the personified *abomination of desolation* (Matt. 24:15).

But the exact identity of Antichrist has long been the subject of debate among Bible scholars. Although Scripture does not identify him by a historical name, as we shall see, careful study of all the relevant passages would seem to lead to only one conclusion. As we consider these various passages in more detail below, a vivid picture of Antichrist begins to emerge.

Looking first at Jesus' own description, the Lord speaks of Antichrist as the personified "abomination of desolation which was spoken of through Daniel the prophet, standing in the holy place" (Matt. 24:15). (This is clearly a reference to a person, not a nation, since only an individual could *stand* in the holy place.)

Daniel describes the blasphemous actions of Antichrist by prophesying that he "will do as he pleases, and he will exalt and magnify himself above every god, and will speak monstrous things against the God of gods; and he will prosper until the indignation is finished" (Dan. 11:36).

These same words are echoed in the Thessalonians passage quoted earlier, where Paul describes Antichrist as "the son of destruction, who opposes and exalts himself above every so-called god or object of worship, so that he takes his seat in the temple of God, displaying himself as being God" (2 Thess. 2:3, 4).

From the book of Ezekiel we learn that Antichrist (Gog) will come "[from] the land of Magog . . . from the remote parts of the north" (Ezek. 38:2, 6), and that he will descend upon the land of Israel "like a storm . . . like a cloud covering the land" with a vast army and massive weapons of war (vv. 4, 8, 9).

In addition to these, we find the most comprehensive and complex picture of Antichrist in the book of Revelation. It is especially important to carefully discern the different ways the term "beast" is used — sometimes referring specifically to Antichrist as the leader of the final beast empire and sometimes referring to Satan's beast empire itself — depending on how the term is used in each specific context. (In addition to this, it should be noted that there is one additional passage in Revelation that speaks of "another beast." In this context "another beast" does *not* refer to either Antichrist or the final beast empire but to a subordinate of Antichrist who acts on his behalf [see Rev. 13:11-17].)

In Revelation 17, John describes the "beast" as "having seven heads and ten horns" (v. 3), which is almost exactly the way he had described the beast earlier ("a beast coming up out of the sea, having ten horns and seven heads" [13:1]). In this context the "beast" is the final beast empire of Satan which represents all the previous seven beast empires of Satan. Thus the seven heads represent the leaders of the first seven empires, and the ten horns represent the ten nations (or peoples) that will comprise the eighth and final beast empire over which Antichrist will rule.

From Revelation 17:10, 11 we learn that the seven heads "are seven kings; five have fallen, one is, the other has not yet come; and when he comes, he must remain a little while. And the beast [Antichrist in this context] which was and is not, is himself also an eighth, and is one of the seven, and he goes to destruction."

It is important to look carefully at these two verses. When Revelation was written by John at the end of the first century A.D. we see that five beast empires of Satan had come and gone ("five have fallen"), "one is" (i.e., the Roman Empire), one was still to come in the future and would "remain for a little while" (i.e., the Nazi Empire of the Third Reich).* Also, there will be an eighth leader who will lead the final ten-nation confederation — namely Antichrist, who "was and is not," and who is also "one of the seven" rulers of the preceding seven beast empires. In other words, this last reference to the eighth beast clearly refers to a *man*, not an empire as some interpret. This is seen in John's careful choice of words stating that "the beast [Antichrist] . . . is *himself* also an eighth [head or king], and is one of the seven [heads or kings]" (v. 11). "Himself" is obviously a reference to Antichrist as a *man*. The other startling truth about this passage is the fact that this eighth king (Antichrist) will be one of the previous seven kings "who was and is not" — in other words, he has already died. Which one of the previous seven is not revealed to us in this critical passage — only

* For a full discussion of the first seven beast empires, see further chapter 6.

that he will be one of the previous seven leaders who has ruled over one of the first seven beast empires and has since died. By definition, therefore, in order for this dead ruler to rule over the final beast empire, he will have to be a dead man brought back to life.

Therefore, it will be the fact that Antichrist has come back to life that will bring the world to submission. John writes that he saw one of the seven beast's heads "as if it had been slain, and his fatal wound was healed. And the whole earth was amazed and followed after the beast" (Rev. 13:3). Notice in particular that the whole world follows after the beast *because they are "amazed"* — and the cause of their amazement clearly is the fact that Antichrist is a dead man whose "fatal wound [is] healed." This same cause and effect is stated later when it is explained to John, "The beast that you saw *was and is not, and is about to come up out of the abyss* and to go to destruction. And *those who dwell on the earth will wonder*, whose name has not been written in the book of life from the foundation of the world, when they see the beast, that *he was and is not and will come*" (Rev. 17:8, emphasis added).

When Antichrist is revealed, after Michael the restrainer is removed at the midpoint of the seventieth week, the whole earth will be amazed — both at who he actually is and that he is a dead man come back to life. And this shocking reality will cause most of the world to give their full allegiance to him.

EIGHT STARTLING FACTS

When we bring these passages together and add several others that are self-explanatory, a startling picture of Antichrist's true identity begins to come into sharp focus. The facts are that Antichrist is:

(1) A man who will claim to be God incarnate (Dan. 11:36; 2 Thess. 2:3, 4).

(2) A man who will be an extremely powerful and ungodly military leader (Ezek. 38:4, 8, 9; Dan. 11:38).

(3) A man who will be given the diabolical power of Satan himself (Rev. 13:12; 2 Thess. 2:9).

(4) A man who is the dead leader of one of the seven previous beast empires of Satan (Rev. 17:11).

(5) A man who was killed by a fatal wound to the head (Rev. 13:3) with a military weapon or "sword" (Rev. 13:14).

(6) A dead man who will come back to life to rule the final beast empire of Satan (Rev. 13:3, 12; 17:8, 11).

(7) A man who will receive the absolute allegiance and worship of the world when they realize that he is a dead man brought back to life (Rev. 13:12; 17:8; 2 Thess. 2:3, 4).

(8) A man who is from the ancestral line of Magog (Ezek. 38:2).

Can we determine the specific identification of Antichrist? In this regard, these last four facts about Antichrist are of crucial significance, especially the last one.

Since Antichrist must be one of the leaders of the seven previous beast empires of Satan brought back to life, then the list of possible candidates is limited to only seven men who have ever lived in all of history. Out of these seven leaders from the past, we can further eliminate all those who are not from the ancestral line of Magog. This fact, therefore, immediately eliminates the first five beast empires — namely the leaders of the Egyptian (Mizraim), Assyrian (Asshur), Babylonian (Nimrod or Arpachshad), Medo-Persian (Madia-Tiras), and Greek (Javan) empires — because none of these leaders were from the line of Magog.*[6] The only logical conclusion, therefore, is that *Antichrist must be either the dead ruler of the sixth beast empire (ancient Rome) or of the seventh beast empire (Hitler's Third Reich) who is somehow brought back to life to rule over the eighth and final beast empire of Satan.*

The Sixth and Seventh Beast Empires

If Antichrist was the leader of the ancient Roman Empire who will live again as the ruler of the final beast empire, which specific Roman leader would this be? One of the first names that comes to mind is Herod the Great, who ruled over Israel at the time of the birth of Christ. Herod, of course, is notorious for ordering the ruthless slaughter of all male Jewish babies in and around Bethlehem, hoping to kill the prophesied Redeemer and King (Matt. 2:16). But although he ruled Israel at the behest of Rome, he was far from being a Roman emperor. Herod, in fact, was not even of Roman ancestry, but was an Edomite, a descendant of Esau, and therefore a Semite. Not being from Antichrist's ancestral line of Magog, Herod must also be eliminated from consideration.

Because of his fierce hatred of both Jews and Christians, Nero is probably the best candidate for ruler of the Roman beast empire. It

---

* See endnote 6 for a detailed discussion of each of the first five beast empires and why each of these does not qualify as a candidate for being Antichrist.

was under his instruction that Titus began his systematic campaign against Israel in A.D. 67. As a Roman leader, moreover, Nero's ancestral lineage was possibly from the line of Magog, as discussed in detail in chapter 7.

Another possible Roman candidate is Vespasian, who succeeded Nero as caesar and who ordered his son Titus to intensify the campaign against Israel, destroying Jerusalem, the Temple, and most of the city's inhabitants in A.D. 70. But Titus himself, more than his father Vespasian, seems to be a more likely candidate. He followed Nero's and then Vespasian's orders with relish and absolute thoroughness, virtually exterminating the Jews, and he himself became caesar for about three years some time later. His ancestry, as discussed in detail in chapters 6 and 7, seems also to be possibly from the line of Magog.

Thus a Roman Antichrist would have to be selected from these three possible candidates. But as we saw above, Antichrist, in his earlier role as leader of one of Satan's previous beast empires, was killed by a fatal wound to the head with a military weapon, and none of those three died in military battle. Vespasian died of an unspecified illness, and Titus died of a fever. But because he committed suicide by stabbing himself in the neck with a dagger (a military weapon but not in a military setting), Nero would be the only Roman prospect.[7]

The only other possible ruler would be the leader of the seventh beast empire which did not emerge until almost two millennia after Rome. The diabolical leader of this most recent and ravenous beast empire was, of course, Adolf Hitler, who persecuted the Jews while they were scattered throughout the world without a homeland. Hitler's empire was known as the Third Reich, or the third empire of Germany, which Hitler boasted would last a thousand years, "and in Nazi parlance . . . was often referred to as the 'Thousand-Year Reich.'"[8] Although the empire lasted only twelve years, it perpetrated the worst persecution of the Jews in all of history. For this reason it is still referred to by Jews and most of the civilized world as *the* Holocaust. Notably, Hitler's ancestry is Japhethite, from the line of Magog — thereby giving him the necessary ancestral lineage to qualify him as a candidate for Antichrist.

Adolf Hitler, like Nero, also killed himself with a military weapon — in Hitler's case a pistol. Unlike Nero, however, Hitler took his life in the context of a military battle, as the Allies liberated Berlin at the end of World War II.

More than a dozen witnesses who saw Hitler's corpse shortly after his death testify to the fatal bullet wound to his head. Although a pistol is not a sword per se, the word "sword" is used in Scripture and in much of ancient literature to represent warfare or deadly violence in general. And because Jesus Himself used "sword" in this figurative sense — when He said, "All who take up the sword shall perish by the sword" — it seems clearly legitimate to consider a pistol as a kind of "sword" or military weapon in the broader sense.

Lastly, as H. R. Trevor-Roper wrote in his fascinating book *The Last Days of Hitler*, it is of interest to note that the bones of Hitler have never been found. "Whatever the explanation," Trevor-Roper concludes, "Hitler achieved his last ambition. Like Alaric, buried secretly under the river-bed of Busento, the modern destroyer of mankind is now immune from discovery."[9]

WHICH ONE?

As shown above, we are left with only two candidates that fit the description of Antichrist as outlined in Scripture. Let us compare these two men, then, in terms of their scriptural qualifications for being the "resurrected" Antichrist of Satan's last beast empire.

First, both Nero and Hitler fit the three crucial criteria discussed above. By way of review we have seen that:

(1) *Antichrist must have been a leader of a former beast empire* (Rev. 13:3; 17:11). Both Nero and Hitler meet this criterion.

(2) *Antichrist must have died by a "wound of the sword"* (Rev. 13:14). Neither Nero nor Hitler died literally by the sword, but both died by weapons used in warfare, and Hitler in particular took his life during battle rather than surrender.

(3) *Antichrist will be from "the land of Magog"* (Ezek. 38:2), which is a perfect description of Hitler, who not only was from the geographical area of Magog, but also came from the ancestral lineage of Magog. Nero, however, was not from the land of Magog. And because Rome was founded by the nomadic tribes of Magog, Meshech, or Tubal, it is uncertain as to which of these peoples he descended from, although this author would be inclined to think that Nero was Magogite as well.

Two further considerations, however, make the choice between Nero and Hitler virtually indisputable. These additional considerations are:

(1) *Antichrist will be a notorious anti-Semite* (Matt. 24:15-21; Rev. 12:13-17). Hitler is the supreme anti-Semite of history. Nero despised Jews,

but he hated all non-Romans in general, and unlike Hitler, he had no consuming desire to specifically destroy all Jews.

(2) *Antichrist will be immediately recognized* — and it will be the immediate recognition of this man when his true identity is revealed as a dead man brought back to life that will amaze the world to the point that the world will follow after him (Rev. 13:3; 17:8). Hitler would easily qualify in that regard, whereas Nero would not.

There is little doubt in the author's mind as to which of those two will return as the Antichrist. Without question, Hitler alone fully and unquestionably meets all the requirements,[10] and he certainly was the historical embodiment of Antichrist's supremely evil nature.*[11]

Is there any man better known to the entire world than Adolf Hitler? One cannot watch television for very long without coming across a direct or indirect reference to Hitler. His picture still appears frequently on the covers of popular novels and historical works. Hardly a year goes by without producing another book or film on World War II, the Third Reich, or specifically on Hitler himself. What historical figure could more readily come to mind when one reads, "The beast [Antichrist] that you saw was and is not [lived and died], and is about to come up out of the abyss [i.e., to be brought back to life as the leader of the final beast empire] and to go to destruction [at Armageddon]. And those who dwell on the earth will wonder [be astonished] . . . when they see the beast, that he was and is not and will come" (Rev. 17:8)? In other words, they will recognize him immediately and be shocked by the reality of what they see. Who could better fit the person John earlier describes, saying, "I saw one of his heads as if it had been slain, and his fatal wound was healed. And the whole earth was amazed and followed after the beast" (Rev. 13:3)?

WHO IS THIS MAN?

Who was this man Hitler? Could he in fact be brought back from the dead to become Antichrist? Although we cannot be dogmatic about this, it would be hard to imagine that any other man could better fit the Scripture's description of this diabolical world leader. Hitler's hatred of the Jews and his extermination of more than six million in gas chambers is of course well-known. But it is much less widely

---

* To all of the foregoing conclusive considerations, a number of other secondary considerations could be added, as summarized in endnote 11.

known that Hitler took part in Satanic practices and that he was venerated as God incarnate.

This can be seen clearly in the book *Riddle of the Reich*, written by Wythe Williams during the Second World War and based on firsthand information obtained by the author:

> Deification of Hitler is a very earnest business with Nazi writers and orators. There is no doubt that many of them spread the unique incense, not with a tongue to their cheek, but in a sincere ecstasy. . . . Said Reverend Dr. Leutheuser in February, 1934: "Adolf Hitler is the voice of Jesus Christ, who desired to become flesh and blood of the German people and did become flesh and blood." Echoed the editor of *Der Deutsche Buero und Handelsangestellte*, an official publication of Berlin, in July, 1934: "Two thousand years ago the Creator revealed himself to mankind in the person of Jesus Christ. Today God reveals Himself to the German people in the person of His Messiah, Hitler." Herr Spaniol, the Nazi leader in Saarbruecken, exclaimed in January, 1935: "The churches will not go on existing in their present form. Its prophet, its pope, its Jesus Christ will be Adolf Hitler."[12]

"It is no wonder, then," Williams continues, "that the latest Nazi versions of Christmas carols substitute Hitler for the holy family" — as in the case of "Silent Night" which Williams quotes — where "the Savior is no longer Jesus Christ but Fuehrer Hitler."[13]

In their book *The Morning of the Magicians*, Louis Pauels and Jacques Bergler reveal some fascinating and little-known facts about Adolf Hitler. The cover blurb reads, *"The Morning of the Magicians* reads like an adventure story. It has shaken the convictions of hundreds of thousands of educated people in France, Italy, Germany, Portugal, Holland, and England. The work of its authors has been supported by such eminent scientists as J. Robert Oppenheimer, Julian Huxley, Bertrand Russell; by such writers as Robert Graves, Henry Miller, Jean Cocteau, Aldous Huxley. Fourteen volumes of a new encyclopedia have appeared in Europe as a direct consequence of this one book!"[14] The following excerpts from that book speak for themselves:

> Apart from [Hitler's] conviction that there was no department of human activity that could be saved without the intervention of a

Messiah, there was also the banal and crude idea of a "strong man" Messiah who would put everything to rights by force. In the event it was not just a single Messiah who was going to appear, but, so to speak, a whole society of Messiahs who had appointed Hitler as their chief.[15]

[Hitler's associate] Rauschning, who did not possess a key to the Fuhrer's way of thinking and had never been anything but a good aristocratic humanist, was alarmed by the things Hitler sometimes allowed himself to say in his presence. "A theme which constantly recurred in his conversations," Rauschning relates, "was what he called the 'decisive turning-point in the history of the world.' There would be an upheaval on our planet of which we, the uninitiated, would be unable to understand the full implications." . . . *The only way in which he could explain the miracle of his own destiny was by attributing it to the action of unseen forces* — the same forces to which he owed his superhuman vocation of having to preach a new Gospel to humanity.[16]

The probable explanation for all this in our opinion is the existence of a magic "puzzle," *a powerful and Satanic mystical current* such as we have tried to describe in the course of the preceding chapters. This could explain a great many terrible facts in a more realistic way than that of the conventional historians who are ready to attribute so many cruel and irrational acts [to other reasons].[17]

This "powerful and satanic mystical current," as Pauels and Bergler describe it, found its strongest expression in Hitler's satanic desire to annihilate every living Jew. Thus Hitler describes the Jewish people as

another species of humanity which does not deserve the name and no doubt came into being on the globe during some dark and dismal epoch when, after one of the Moons had descended on the Earth, vast portions of the Earth's surface were nothing but a desolate swamp. [They were] probably created along with other crawling and hideous creatures, the relics of a baser form of life. The . . . Jews are not men, in the true sense of the term. . . . [They] imitate man and are envious of him, but do not belong to the same species. They are as far removed from us as animals are from humans. . . . I do not mean . . . that I look upon Jews as animals; they are much further removed from animals than we are. Therefore, it is not a crime against humanity to exterminate them, since they do not belong to humanity. They are creatures outside nature.[18]

Another of [Hitler's] dreams, which was also an obsession, was to change life on Earth everywhere. He sometimes alluded to it or, rather, was unable to prevent what he was thinking from escaping now and then in some casual remark. He once said to Rauschning: "Our revolution is a new stage or, rather, the final stage in an evolution which will end by abolishing history. . . ." Or, again: "You know nothing about me; my party comrades have no conception of the dreams which haunt me. . . . The world has reached a turning point; we are now at a critical moment in time. . . . The planet will undergo an upheaval which you uninitiated people cannot understand. . . . What is happening is something more than the advent of a new religion."[19]

One of those strange dreams that haunted Hitler was relayed in this chilling report by Rauschning:

. . . he [Hitler] woke up nights shouting convulsively. He yells for help. Sitting on the edge of his bed, he is as though paralyzed. He is seized with a panic which makes him tremble so violently that the bed shakes. He utters confused, unintelligible vociferations. He gasps for breath as though about to suffocate. The same person told me some details about one of these crises, which I would not have believed were my source of information not as sure as it is. Hitler was standing there in his bedroom, stumbling about, looking around him with a distraught look. He was muttering: "It's him! It's him! He's here!" His lips had turned blue. He was dripping with sweat. Suddenly, he uttered some numbers which made no sense, then some words, then bits of sentences. It was frightening. He used terms which were strung together in the strangest way and which were absolutely weird. Then he again became silent, although his lips continued to move. . . . Then, all of a sudden, he screamed: "There! Over there! In the corner! Who is it?" He was jumping up and down, and he was howling. They reassured him that everything was all right, and he gradually calmed down.[20]

Perhaps the most shocking aspect of Hitler's dreams, however, is not even such hysterical outbursts, but the blasphemous aspirations that he and his confidants shared, as reported for example by Pauels and Bergler in *The Morning of the Magicians*:

"I will tell you a secret," said Himmler to Rauschning; "I am founding an Order. . . . It is from there that the second stage will emerge — the stage of the Man-God, when Man will be the measure and the center of the world. The Man-God, that splendid Being, will be an object of worship. . . ."[21]

Finally, and of particular interest, is a direct quote from a film made by the personal aide to Hitler, the last man to see him alive, just before Hitler shot and killed himself. Hitler's last words to his aide were to break up and scatter to the West. In response to this statement, the aide replied to Hitler, "For whom should we fight now?" With that, Hitler said in a monotone, "For the coming man."[22] With those final words, Hitler closed the door and shot himself in the forehead with his own gun.

THE DREAM BECOMES REALITY

The parallels between Hitler and what the Scriptures reveal about Antichrist are almost too obvious to point out. Hitler's pact with the devil, his delusion as the new messianic savior, his veneration "above every so-called god or object of worship" (see 2 Thess. 2:4), his dream of a "thousand year Reich," his satanic desire to annihilate every one of God's chosen people — all correspond precisely to the character of the man who will be the Antichrist of the end times. But as the ruler of Satan's seventh beast empire, Hitler, of course, was not Antichrist — or to put it another way, he had not yet become Antichrist. This would have to wait, first until all of the events in God's prophetic timetable have taken place, and second, until Antichrist would be supernaturally empowered with the authority of Satan himself (Rev. 13:4, 12). In the end times Hitler's dream will become Satan's reality.

Like his demonic mentor Satan, Antichrist will be a great deceiver. His true identity will be scrupulously concealed — from the time three nations of the world again yield to his leadership, during the time when Israel initiates her second great apostasy by signing the covenant of death, throughout the first three and a half years of the seventieth week when Antichrist will rise to power and consolidate his massive military forces, until Satan is cast down to earth and Michael the great angelic restrainer is removed.

Only then — at the midpoint of the seventieth week — will Antichrist reveal his true identity, just before he commits the abomination of setting up his throne in the rebuilt Temple. And when the world first becomes aware of who this great world leader is, this dead man come back to life, the vast majority of the unbelieving world will be so awed that they will willingly or out of fear worship the beast or his image. And with this astounding revelation it is no wonder that for Jews everywhere, as Isaiah predicted, "it will be sheer terror to understand what it means" (28:19b).

At that point Antichrist will unleash his full fury against the "woman" whom he had earlier (in the seventh beast empire of Nazi Germany) tried to annihilate during the Jewish Holocaust. Tragically the end-time Jewish holocaust will be immeasurably worse. Were not this time of Antichrist's deadly persecution cut short, no Jew or "any of the other offspring of the woman who keep the commandments of God and hold to the testimony of Jesus" would survive. "But for the sake of the elect," Christ has graciously promised, "those days shall be cut short" (Matt. 24:22).

12

Counting the Cost

S cripture clearly teaches that the whole world will worship the beast (Antichrist) and his image, and those who do not will be sought out and killed. If we believe what the Scriptures teach, this fact should be a matter of grave concern to every Christian. Revelation 13 states explicitly that the power of the beast will extend over "the whole earth" (v. 3), "over every tribe and people and tongue and nation" (v. 7), and over "those who dwell on the earth" (v. 14; cf. vv. 13, 16) and that all who do not worship the beast or his image will be killed (v. 15).

ANTICHRIST'S CONTROL OF EARTH

How will Antichrist be able to extend his satanic power and allegiance from his blasphemous throne in Jerusalem to the far corners of the earth? What will this mean for Christians living in America or Europe or other places in the world? We know that even Satan, despite his pervasive powers, is not omnipresent; likewise his minion Antichrist, even with his satanically bestowed supernatural powers, will be a mere human being. How then will Antichrist keep those in the remote regions of the world, as well as in the Middle East and the rest of the world, under his satanic power?

For years I wondered and puzzled over this question.

While studying other seemingly contradictory passages regarding another prophetic issue, I discovered what seemed to be the only harmonizing solution. To my great surprise, the solution not only harmonized the apparently contradictory passages concerning the other issue, but it also answered the question regarding Antichrist's ability to control the whole earth, including the most remote regions of the world, thousands of miles from the center of Antichrist's operations. That discovery was so unexpected and frightening that I immediately consulted several theologian friends to see if my conclusions had exegetical integrity. When they carefully studied the texts and evaluated my reasoning, they confirmed that the conclusions were exegetically sound and that the consequences were indeed terrifying — for the entire world, not just for the localized areas occupied by Antichrist and his armies specifically identified in end-times prophecy.

The apparent contradiction alluded to above, which brought understanding regarding Antichrist's control of the world, was this: If the whole world is worshiping Antichrist after he gains control of it at the midpoint of the seventieth week, why would men also be worshiping their *own* demons and idols?

There is no question that the whole world will worship Antichrist when he gains control of the earth at the midpoint of the seventieth week. As God's Word reveals, "*the whole earth* was amazed and followed after the beast [Antichrist]" (Rev. 13:3, emphasis added). Later we learn through John that a second beast (the enforcer for Antichrist) "makes the earth and those who dwell in it to worship the first beast [Antichrist], whose fatal wound was healed" (Rev. 13:12). This parallels Paul's reference to Antichrist as he "who opposes and exalts himself above every so-called god or object of worship, so that he takes his seat in the temple of God, displaying himself as being God" (2 Thess. 2:4). This is a perfect description of what Daniel foretold about Antichrist: "Then the king [Antichrist] will do as he pleases, and he will exalt and magnify himself above every god . . ." (11:36).

But while Antichrist is receiving the world's worship, mankind will *also be worshiping demons and idols of their own making*. Thus, when a third of mankind is killed during the sixth trumpet judgment of the day of the Lord, at the very time Antichrist is receiving the world's worship, John reports that "the rest of mankind, who were not killed by these plagues, did not repent of *the works of their hands, so as not to worship demons, and the idols of gold and of silver and of brass and of stone and of wood,* which can neither see nor hear nor walk" (Rev. 9:20, emphasis added). Isaiah uses remarkably similar language when he describes the same period of idolatry, during the reign of Antichrist, just prior to the day of the Lord:

> For the Lord of hosts will have a day of reckoning, against everyone who is proud and lofty, and against everyone who is lifted up, that he may be abased . . . and the Lord alone will be exalted in that day. But the idols will completely vanish. And men will go into caves of the rocks, and into holes of the ground before the terror of the Lord, and before the splendor of His majesty, when He arises to make the earth tremble. In that day men will cast away to the moles and the bats *their idols of silver and their idols of gold, which they made for themselves to worship.* (Isa. 2:12, 17-20, emphasis added)

When the day of the Lord is announced at the sixth seal, plunging the universe into darkness (Rev. 6:12-17), men will then cast the idols of gold and silver that they have made for themselves to the moles and bats in the caves in which they will hide when, as Isaiah announced, the Lord "arises to make the earth tremble."

In other words, when the world is supposedly worshiping only Antichrist, Scripture tells us that the world is worshiping demons and idols. How can this seeming contradiction be resolved? How can the world *both* give worship to the beast (Antichrist) *and* be worshiping demons and the idols they have made with their own hands? Is there any way to harmonize these two seemingly contradictory objects of worship?

Because God's Word is inerrant and therefore consistent in every detail, there is always a biblical explanation that will reconcile any seeming self-contradictions or inconsistencies. The biblical answer to the dilemma just mentioned, though frightening, is rather simple. John informs us that the second beast (Rev. 13:11), the enforcer for the first beast (Antichrist), "makes the earth and those who dwell in it to worship the first beast, whose fatal wound was healed. And he [the second beast] performs great signs, so that he even makes fire come down out of heaven to the earth in the presence of men. And he deceives those who dwell on the earth because of the signs which it was given him to perform in the presence of the beast" (vv. 12, 13).

But an immeasurably more frightening revelation immediately follows. The second beast then tells "those who dwell on the earth to *make an image to the beast* [Antichrist] who had the wound of the sword and has come to life. And [then] there was given to him [the second beast] to give *breath to the image* of the beast, that the image of the beast might even speak and cause as many as do not worship the image of the beast to be killed" (13:14, 15, emphasis added). The most common interpretation of that passage is that all the inhabitants on earth are commanded to make one single image of the beast. But since the Greek word for "image" is a collective noun, it is more likely that each person is commanded to *make* his own individual image,[1] and that everyone will *have* his own personal image or images of the beast. Suddenly what seemed at first to be a contradiction became instead a confirmation of the incredible accuracy of Scripture.

To understand this passage better, two words — "image" and "breath" — need to be examined carefully. The Greek term for the first of these, "image," can be rendered just as appropriately as "statue." Similarly, it is the Greek term from which the English word "icon" is derived. These images, then, that the second beast commands the earth to make in the image of the first beast will be the idols that mankind is worshiping when the day of the Lord begins. We do not know exactly what these images will be or look like, but a wide variety of possibilities would be consistent with the Scriptures. We do know that these are images people will make themselves, with their own hands, and that they will be made out of a variety of materials (gold, silver, bronze, stone, wood — see Rev. 9:20; cf. Isa. 2:20). In other words, everyone will be commanded to make some kind of image or statue or other symbolic representation *of* the beast or *to* the beast (see. Rev. 13:14). Whatever the form, however, such "images" will proliferate to the ends of the earth and will be in the personal possession of the vast majority of people everywhere — because they will have made these images with their own hands, out of allegiance to Antichrist, for the specific purpose of worshiping them. These images, then, will be made under the deceptive influence of the second beast, when "he makes the earth and those who dwell in it to worship the first beast" (Rev. 13:12), by performing "great signs, so that he even makes fire come down out of heaven to the earth in the presence of men" (v. 13). "He deceives those who dwell on the earth . . . telling those who dwell on the earth to make an image to the beast" (v. 14).

The second word, "breath," however, should cause every man, woman, and child alive — in particular those who refuse to worship "the beast or his image" — tremendous concern and even greater fear when one understands the full meaning and implications of this word. The second beast, then, was given power *"to give breath* to the image of the beast [Antichrist]." The Greek term here rendered "breath" is rarely translated that way but is usually rendered as "spirit" (even in "Holy Spirit" or in "evil spirit") and sometimes as "life" (as in the KJV of Rev. 13:15).[2] The meaning of this passage, then, is that *after* the world is commanded to build their own "images" to Antichrist, some form of spirit or life will be put within these "images," so "that the image of the beast might even speak and cause as many as do not worship the image of the beast to be killed" (Rev. 13:15)!

Worshiping the "the idols of gold and of silver and of brass and of stone and of wood" spoken of in Revelation 9:20 is specifically said to involve the worship of demons, which are of course spirit beings. In other words, the idols of 9:20 and the images of 13:14, 15 will be indwelt by Satan's demons, to form a worldwide monitoring system to enforce the worship of Antichrist (whose likeness the images will bear) and to destroy any human being who refuses to comply with that worship.

Fortunately those demonic images, despite their fearsome powers, will be blind, deaf, and immobile — unable to see, hear, or walk (Rev. 9:20). The idols in themselves are nothing more than immaterial creations of man's own making. It is the demons that give these inanimate objects life. And although the demons are limited to these inanimate objects, they *can see* and they *can hear*, even though their movement is restricted to the objects they indwell. For this reason the passage makes no reference to the idols' inability to speak. The reason is clear. They *will* be able to talk once the false prophet of Antichrist gives "breath [spirit, life] to the image of the beast, that the image of the beast might even speak and cause as many as do not worship the image of the beast to be killed" (Rev. 13:15). Each demon's movement being limited by the inanimate object it indwells would seem to allow the possibility that Christians, as well as others who refuse to bow down to the images, will have some chance to avoid detection and destruction. But if they *do* come into the presence of those images, the demons will know it, and those persons will be killed for their failure to worship the images.

A passage in Matthew sheds considerable light on the power and limitations of demons who manifest themselves on earth.

> And when He [Jesus] had come to the other side into the country of the Gadarenes, two men who were demon-possessed met Him as they were coming out of the tombs; they were so exceedingly violent that no one could pass by that road. And behold, they cried out, saying, "What do we have to do with You, Son of God? Have You come here to torment us before the time?" Now there was at a distance from them a herd of many swine feeding. And the demons began to entreat Him, saying, "If You are going to cast us out, send us into the herd of swine." And He said to them, "Begone!" And they came out, and went into the swine. (Matt. 8:28-32)

That familiar passage reveals several important truths about the nature and operation of demons that will shed light on the end-times demon-indwelt idols or images. First, demons require some physical object, animate or inanimate, through which to operate. In the Gadarene instance, the multitude of demons originally inhabited two men. When the demons realized Jesus was about to cast them out of the men, they pleaded with Him for permission to enter a nearby herd of swine, so they would have some place to reside. Because the demons indwelt animate objects, they had movement. In the end times, however, the demons will indwell inanimate objects and therefore will have no movement on their own.

Second, we learn that the demons spoke *through* the men they indwelt. To my knowledge, there is no instance in Scripture of demons speaking apart from the physical object they were indwelling. During the great tribulation by Antichrist, a time of affliction for all who will not worship the beast or his image *throughout the world*, Satan's demonic monitors will speak through the images they indwell.

Third, although demons are restricted to the objects they indwell, they are able to create great havoc both within and through those objects. The demons who indwelt the two men in the country of the Gadarenes took over those men's minds and gave their bodies superhuman strength (see Mark 5:3, 4). In Matthew's account the demons are described as being "exceedingly violent" (8:28). During the time of

Antichrist's rule, the demons within the images will "cause as many as do not worship the image of the beast to be killed" (Rev. 13:15). Whether or not they do the killing themselves, or merely see to it that those bearing the mark of Antichrist carry out their orders for them, this author is not adamant. Either way those that come into the presence of these demon-possessed images, and then refuse to worship them, will be killed.

Fourth and finally, demons seem to have no ability to choose their physical abodes. The demons who indwelt the men at Gadarenes had to have Jesus' permission to enter the swine. In the end times, the demons will be assigned to their respective images by the second beast (Rev. 13:15).

How then will these images suddenly be indwelt and empowered by demonic spirits? The first part of the answer is found in a careful reading of Revelation 13:15. This passage seems to indicate that the "image" — or more correctly the "images," since this is a collective noun — will not be empowered when they are made by individuals around the world. They only come to "life" later, when the "second beast" (Antichrist's deputy) gives a "spirit" to these images. People therefore will initially fashion their individual images without even knowing the diabolical purpose for which they will soon be used.

The second part of the answer is found in Revelation 12:9. When "the great dragon was thrown down, the serpent of old who is called the Devil and Satan, who deceives the whole world; he was thrown down to earth, and his angels were thrown down with him." This event occurs at the midpoint of the seventieth week — just before Antichrist (the first beast) demands the world's worship, just before "the second beast" deceives mankind throughout the world into worshiping the beast and making an image of him for their own personal use.

In these two passages we see, then, that people will make their images during the euphoria of the world's initial worship of Antichrist, and that the images will then, without the world's knowledge or understanding, be suddenly indwelt by the horde of Satan's fallen angels and demonic spirits that will have been cast down to earth just prior to that time. It is obvious, therefore, that the demonic spirits that indwell the man-made images of Antichrist will already have come down to earth with Satan when they are commanded to take control of the images. By that supernatural and pervasive scheme,

Antichrist will exercise universal control over all unbelievers, even those living in the most remote regions of the earth.

As an aside, images, idols, and statues *abound* in every nation of the world — even in America. Ask yourselves what would happen if all of these statues, images, or whatever, no matter how pious our purpose may have been for having them initially, were suddenly demon-possessed, with the power to kill any and all who did not worship them on the spot. *Bedlam!* The world, to say nothing of America, would be in the absolute vise-grip of the one who controlled the demons. In the last days it will be Satan who has the control of these demons, the same Satan "who has come down to you, having great wrath, knowing that he has only a short time" (Rev. 12:12).

As Christians, therefore, it will be absolutely essential that we do not go near these images or enter any place where they are present — so that the images have no opportunity to "speak" and identify us, or to "cause [us who] do not worship the image of the beast to be killed" (Rev. 13:15b).

THE TWO-FOLD TEST

Antichrist, as we have seen, will be revealed as a dead man come back to life at the midpoint of the seventieth week, whereupon he will enthrone himself in the rebuilt Temple in Jerusalem, claim to be divine, and demand the worship of the world. Antichrist (the "first beast") will then initiate *a two-fold test* to identify those who do — and those who do not — truly worship Antichrist and give him their full allegiance. This two-fold test will be carried out by "another" or "second beast" (as discussed in some detail in the previous section) who is Antichrist's enforcer and "exercises all the authority of the first beast" (Rev. 13:11).

This test will consist of two specific things: *First*, everyone will be required to *"worship the image of the beast* [or] be killed" (Rev. 13:15). This first test has already been developed thoroughly in the first half of this chapter. *Second*, everyone will be required to take the *mark of the beast* or he will be unable to buy or sell anything. As John wrote in Revelation:

> And he [the second beast] causes all, the small and the great, and the rich and the poor, and the free men and the slaves, to be given a mark on their right hand, or on their forehead, and he provides

that no one should be able to buy or to sell, except the one who has the mark, either the name of the beast or the number of his name. Here is wisdom. Let him who has understanding calculate the number of the beast, for the number is that of a man; and his number is six hundred and sixty-six. (Rev. 13:16-18)

We do not know how the mark will be imprinted on the hand or the forehead. Given modern technology, however, there are numerous ways this could be accomplished. A tiny microchip, for example, could be imbedded just under the skin in the palm of the hand. Whenever anyone wanted to buy or sell something, he could be required to wave his hand over a scanning device that would "read" the chip, identify the buyer or seller, and validate or invalidate the sale. In any case, it seems unlikely that the mark would be a series of numbers crudely branded on the hand or forehead, but it will be a mark nonetheless that clearly identifies the man with either the name of the beast or the number of his (Antichrist's) name.

Again we see the critical dilemma facing every Christian — the potential of death for not worshiping the beast or one of his images, and the inability to purchase or sell anything unless one has taken Antichrist's mark on his hand or forehead. But even more critical, as we shall see, all who do worship the beast or take his mark will come under God's holy judgment and be damned forever. Satan will, therefore, use this two-fold test to try to exclude everyone he possibly can from God's millennial kingdom. The primary target of Antichrist will be that part of the nation of Israel that refuses Antichrist, since it is to these Israelites that the promise of national salvation has been given (Rom. 11:26). Satan knows that those who worship him cannot qualify for the millennial rule of Christ. But in addition, the true church will equally incur Antichrist's wrath when he goes out "to make war with . . . [all] who keep the commandments of God and hold to the testimony of Jesus" (Rev. 12:17b).[3]

These last three and a half years of the end times — the satanically inspired great tribulation by Antichrist — are described variously in Scripture as "the hour of testing" (Rev. 3:10; see chapter 2, endnotes 1 and 2), the "test[ing] by fire" (1 Pet. 1:7), the "fiery ordeal" (1 Pet. 4:12), and the judgment of "the household of God" (1 Pet. 4:17). The great tragedy is that many within the compromising church will pass the test of Satan, failing the commands of God, and will succumb to the demands of the demonic idols of Antichrist. Timothy warns the church that "the Spirit explicitly says that in later times some will fall away from the faith, paying attention to deceitful spirits and doctrines of demons" (1 Tim. 4:1). In view of what we know about Antichrist and his control of the earth through the demon-indwelt images of the beast during the "later times," this passage takes on frightening meaning. In like manner, Ezekiel warns the natural line of Abraham concerning the images of Antichrist that they will worship before God's wrath destroys them: "They shall fling their silver into the streets, and their gold shall become an abhorrent thing; their silver and their gold shall not be able to deliver them in the day of the wrath of the Lord . . . they made the images of their abominations and their detestable things with it; therefore I will make it an abhorrent thing to them" (Ezek. 7:19, 20).

The test will essentially parallel the test that Adam and Eve faced in the Garden of Eden. Because they failed the test, their nature became sinful, and they immediately experienced spiritual death and became subject to physical death. This sinful nature and those two deaths became the heritage of all their progeny. And because God had given Adam and Eve dominion over the earth as His stewards (Gen. 1:28), their dominion became subject to the power of Satan — in a limited but devastating way — because Adam and Eve chose to trust Satan above God. When Antichrist demands the worship of the world and requires everyone to take the mark, mankind will once again be confronted with a monumental choice with eternal consequences — the choice between allegiance to the only true and holy God, at the cost of physical death, or allegiance to Antichrist, the supreme counterfeit god established by Satan, at the cost of eternal death.

At that time "the perseverance and the faith of the saints" will be tested as never before in the history of the church (Rev. 13:10; cf. 14:12). Nevertheless, the Lord gives His faithful saints the certain promise that "Because you have kept the word of My perseverance, I also will keep you from [protect you within the sphere of danger and rescue you out from within] the hour of testing, that hour which is about to come upon the whole world, to test those who dwell upon the earth" (Rev. 3:10).[4]

The contrast between those who *do not* persevere and those who *do* is made dramatically clear in a later passage of Revelation. For those who do not persevere, "The smoke of their torment goes up forever and ever; and they have no rest day and night, *those who worship the beast and his image, and whoever receives the mark of his name.*" For those who do persevere, "Here is the perseverance of the saints who keep the commandments of God and their faith in Jesus"; they will be called blessed and find eternal rest (Rev. 14:11, 12; also see v. 13). Those saints will not experience the eternal punishment soon to be meted out on the unbelieving world at the day of the Lord. For before the time of God's judgment, God will rapture His persevering church, rescuing them out from within "the hour of testing, that hour which is about to come upon the whole world, to test those who dwell upon the earth. I [Christ] am coming quickly" (Rev. 3:10b, 11a).

The promise of protection during the hour of testing, however, is conditional — just as were God's promises to Israel regarding the blessings and the curses (see chapter 4). In both cases the condition is faithfulness. The blessing of Israel would be according to their "loving the Lord your God, by obeying His voice, and by holding fast to Him" (see Deut. 30:20). Likewise, the protection of believers during the great tribulation by Antichrist will be on the condition of their persevering in devotion to the Lord and refusing to bow down to Antichrist or his images. Because believers in *faithful churches* will have been prepared, they will have gone into hiding. And because the demonic images of Antichrist will be incapable of moving about, Antichrist's control through his host of demons will be limited to those people who display those images, in disobedience to God and obedience to Antichrist. True believers in *compromising churches* will refuse both to worship or to take the mark of Antichrist, but they will pay a great price, because they will be totally unprepared for the testing that is to come. Members of *dead churches*, however, will likely take the mark in order to survive and escape persecution by Antichrist — only to face an immeasurably worse fate during God's day-of-the-Lord judgment, which will come upon them like a thief in the night.

THE THREE-ANGEL ANNOUNCEMENT

When all these things begin to occur at the beginning of the second half of the seventieth week, God will graciously give advance warning to every inhabitant on earth about the dreadful and irreversible consequences of worshiping the beast or his image and of receiving his mark. The central message of this warning will be one final presentation of the gospel. This will come in the form of three divine announcements from the Lord, each given by a separate angel, and will occur during a short period of time at the beginning of the last three and a half years when every man, woman, and child on the face of this planet is making his or her choice. Through the three angels, then, the message of the gospel will be graciously proclaimed, giving the world a final opportunity to repent and trust in Christ for eternal salvation.

THE FIRST ANGEL

The first of three divinely dispatched angels will proclaim the promise of eternal life for those who worship the true God and Him alone, and he will also warn of the eternal wrath awaiting those who turn to the false god of this world, Antichrist. The first angel, "flying in midheaven, [had] an eternal gospel to preach to those who live on the earth, and to every nation and tribe and tongue and people; and he said with a loud voice, 'Fear God, and give Him glory, because the hour of His judgment has come; and worship Him who made the heaven and the earth and sea and springs of waters'" (Rev. 14:6, 7). ("Has come" carries the meaning of "is at hand," indicating its impending arrival.)

What is the "eternal gospel" proclaimed by the first angel? It is the gospel of Jesus Christ, the same gospel proclaimed throughout Scripture. In His own words, Christ explains how a person becomes a child in God's family and a citizen in God's kingdom:

> "As Moses lifted up the serpent in the wilderness, even so must the Son of Man be lifted up [crucified]; that whoever believes may in Him have eternal life. For God so loved the world, that He gave His only begotten Son, that whoever believes in Him should not perish, but have eternal life. For God did not send the Son into the world to judge the world, but that the world should be saved through Him. He who believes in Him is not judged; he who does not believe has been judged already, because he has not believed in the name of the only begotten Son of God.... He who believes in the Son has eternal life; but he who does not obey the Son shall not see life, but the wrath of God abides on him." (John 3:14-18, 36)

In order for a man to become right before God, he must *turn from* his sin (repent) and *turn to* (believe in) Jesus Christ as his only means of salvation (2 Cor. 7:9, 10). Christ used the word *believe* six times in the passage quoted above. The Greek term translated as *believe* carries the idea of putting one's trust in something or someone, not merely acknowledging that something is right or true.[5] Many people acknowledge that Christ *is* the Savior and the only way to salvation, but are not saved, because they have not placed their personal trust in Him. That is exactly the kind of false, or incomplete, belief Jesus spoke of when He said,

> "Not everyone who says to Me, 'Lord, Lord,' will enter the kingdom of heaven; but he who does the will of My Father who is in heaven. Many will say to Me on that day, 'Lord, Lord, did we not prophesy in Your name, and in Your name cast out demons, and in Your name perform many miracles?' And then I will declare to them, 'I never knew you; depart from Me, you who practice lawlessness.'" (Matt. 7:21-23)

In other words, when we compare the words of Christ in John's Gospel quoted above with His words from Matthew, it is clear that putting one's trust in Christ as Savior cannot be separated from accepting Him as Lord. Genuine belief is much more than mere assent to the truth of the gospel; it also requires the total commitment of one's heart to follow Christ — even if it means facing the onslaught of Satan's wrath through Antichrist. Those who claim the name of Christ, but who then take the mark of Antichrist, will prove with absoluteness that they never belonged to Him at all and were Christians in name only. On the other hand, those who claim Christ's name and truly belong to him will be like the faithful overcomers in Philadelphia who refused to deny the name of their Lord; and as overcomers they will be divinely enabled to keep the word of Christ's perseverance (Rev. 3:8, 10). No matter what the cost, including martyrdom, true believers (the overcomers) will not identify themselves with Antichrist in any way — not even by the seemingly superficial act of taking his mark on their right hands or foreheads in order to survive (see Rev. 13:16).

A story from some years back dramatically illustrates the difference between true and false belief or faith. A renowned aerialist had a steel cable stretched across Niagara Falls, with one end anchored in the United States, the other in Canada. After successfully pushing a wheelbarrow across the wire from the United States side, using the wheelbarrow for balance, he asked two young men standing nearby if they believed he could push the wheelbarrow back safely to the other side — this time with someone riding in the wheelbarrow. Both men unhesitatingly said they believed he could. But when he asked the first man to volunteer as a rider, he quickly declined. Turning to the second man, the aerialist posed the same question — and to the astonishment of the crowd the second man volunteered. The point, of course, is that both men *acknowledged* that the aerialist could perform such a feat, but only the second man *truly believed* as demonstrated by his act of *total trust*, by placing himself in the care of the aerialist.

Acknowledging Christ's power to save from sin is the first step of faith, but by itself it accomplishes absolutely nothing. Instead, such head knowledge *about* Christ and the gospel gives a person a false sense of spiritual security and becomes a barrier rather than a bridge to salvation. Pointing out this truth, Jesus said, "He who believes in the Son has eternal life; but he who does not obey the Son shall not see life, but the wrath of God abides on him" (John 3:36).

In other words, it is not the one who assents to a list of doctrines about Christ who is saved, but the one who puts his entire confidence and trust in Him as Savior and Lord. They, and they alone, can claim the promise that "God has not destined us for wrath, but for obtaining salvation [deliverance] through our Lord Jesus Christ" (1 Thess. 5:9). Only this genuine relationship to Christ will make "overcomers" out of weak, compromising believers who enter the last seven years of the end times. But for those genuine Christians who have lived a life of personal or doctrinal compromise, the cost will be great. For although the Scriptures teach that compromising believers will be saved, it will only be "as through fire" (1 Cor. 3:15).

Jesus predicted during the Olivet Discourse that before God's final wrath is meted out in the day of the Lord, He will give assurance of deliverance to those who belong to Him, that He will make a final appeal for men to trust in His Son for salvation, and that He will give a final warning to those who persist in rejecting Him. Only "the one who endures to the end . . . shall be saved. And this gospel of the kingdom shall be preached in the whole world [by the first angel] for a witness to all the nations, and then the end [the day of the Lord] shall come" (Matt. 24:13, 14).

THE SECOND ANGEL

The second of the three angels will announce to the world that the Babylonian Harlot — Satan's false religious system — has been destroyed by Antichrist. "And another angel, a second one, followed, saying, 'Fallen, fallen is Babylon the great, she who has made all the nations drink of the wine of the passion of her immorality'" (Rev. 14:8). Later John refers to the Babylonian Harlot as "BABYLON THE GREAT, THE MOTHER OF HARLOTS AND OF THE ABOMINATIONS OF THE EARTH" (17:5). Because of the way "Babylon the Great" is described in Revelation 17 and 18, this author believes that "Babylon the Great" refers to *both* a false religious system(s) (the mother/child worship that originated in Babylon*) *and* to the corrupt city situated on seven hills** from which this mother/child worship will emanate in the last days. The announcement here by the second angelic messenger, however, refers to Satan's false religious system ("Babylon the Great, the Mother of Harlots") because this announcement occurs at the midpoint of the seventieth week. Later, at the seventh bowl judgment just before the battle of Armageddon,*** "Babylon the Great, the great city" will be destroyed, along with the rest of the cities of the world. And like the earlier announcement of the Great Harlot, this judgment of the great city will also be proclaimed to the world by another angel of God (Rev. 18:2, 3).

Antichrist, of course, *must* destroy his temporary ally, the Babylonian Harlot, because in his claim to deity, Antichrist cannot tolerate any rival. That harlot, whatever her end-times identity might be, will represent the culmination of the false religion that Satan himself first inspired in ancient Babylon. As the name "Babylonian Harlot" indicates, this counterfeit religious system(s) has been characterized from the very beginning by the elevation of the "Queen of Heaven" to a status of worship. But once Antichrist sets himself up as God, even this false religious system, and those representative of her false system(s), must and will be destroyed since Antichrist will allow nothing to compete with him for the world's worship and absolute allegiance. He and his ungodly coalition of ten nations will "hate the harlot and will make her desolate and naked, and will eat her flesh and will burn her up with fire" (Rev. 17:16). Thinking they are acting freely out of their own self-will, they will in fact be fulfilling the will of God, "For God has put it in their hearts to execute His purpose" (Rev. 17:17).

* See chapter 10, endnote 6.
** See chapter 20, endnote 3
*** See chapter 20.

THE THIRD ANGEL

The last of the three angels will make the final worldwide announcement. This will be the most sobering warning possible to those who are considering taking the mark of the beast or worshiping his image, thereby giving irrevocable allegiance to Satan's counterfeit savior and king. Because the "whole earth" will be amazed by the recognition of who Antichrist really is and will "follow after the beast" (Rev. 13:3), this warning has incredible significance to absolutely everyone who has refused the gospel of Christ:

> And another angel, a third one, followed them, saying with a loud voice, "If anyone worships the beast and his image, and receives a mark on his forehead or upon his hand, he also will drink of the wine of the wrath of God, which is mixed in full strength in the cup of His anger; and he will be tormented with fire and brimstone in the presence of the holy angels and in the presence of the Lamb. And the smoke of their torment goes up forever and ever; and they have no rest day and night, those who worship the beast and his image, and whoever receives the mark of his name." (Rev. 14:9-11)

The pronouncement of the third angel will set forth the only two alternatives about which all living souls will be compelled to decide. Put in the starkest contrast, the message of the third angel is: *Worship the beast or his image* and you will live today but will spend eternity in the Lake of Fire; or *refuse the beast or his image* and you risk death today but will spend eternity with Christ. This, then, is the test, the choice everyone must make, the same choice God gave Adam and Eve in the Garden. And every man, woman, and child upon the face of the earth will know the consequences, in advance, for following Antichrist.

As Christ explained in the Olivet Discourse, those who worship the beast or his image and take his mark will suddenly, but too late, become aware of their fatal mistake when the Lord returns "as a thief in the night" (1 Thess. 5:2, 3; cf. 2 Pet. 3:10). For when they see the sign of the Son of Man, they will say "to the mountains and to the rocks, 'Fall on us and hide us from the presence of Him who sits on the throne, and from the wrath of the Lamb; for the great day of their wrath has come; and who is able to stand?'" (Rev. 6:16, 17; cf. Matt. 24:30; Luke 21:25, 26). Thus when the sign of the day of the Lord appears in the heavens (see chapter 14 in this book), and the earth is rocked with earthquakes (Rev. 6:12-14), there will be no question in anyone's mind as to what is about to occur. Every unbeliever will have heard the angelic warnings and will know the eternal consequences of their choice — the day of the Lord's wrath and eternity in the Lake of Fire "for ever and ever" for taking the mark of the beast rather than turning to Christ for salvation.

THE TWO WITNESSES

In addition to the witness of the three angels at the beginning of the last three and a half years, God will also graciously provide "two witnesses" who will minister throughout this last period.[6] As Christ revealed to John in the eleventh chapter of Revelation:

> And I will grant authority to my two witnesses, and they will prophesy for twelve hundred and sixty days, clothed in sackcloth. These are the two olive trees and the two lampstands that stand before the Lord of the earth. And if anyone desires to harm them, fire proceeds out of their mouth and devours their enemies; and if anyone would desire to harm them, in this manner he must be killed. These have the power to shut up the sky, in order that rain may not fall during the days of their prophesying; and they have power over the waters to turn them into blood, and to smite the earth with every plague, as often as they desire. (Rev. 11:3-6)

Although the two witnesses are not specifically identified, it seems most likely that they are Elijah and Moses brought back to life. We know that Elijah must come back to earth before the day of the Lord, just as Malachi predicted: "'Behold, I am going to send My messenger, and he will clear the way before Me. . . . Behold, I am going to send you Elijah the prophet before the coming of the great and terrible day of the Lord'" (Mal. 3:1; 4:5).

Just as John the Baptist was a type of Elijah, preparing the way for Christ's first coming, so this latter-day witness will almost certainly be Elijah himself brought back to life, who will prepare the way for Christ's second coming. Jesus Himself predicted that "Elijah is coming and will restore all things" (Matt. 17:11). In doing so, Elijah will zealously strive to point Jews to their true Messiah, to prepare their hearts to trust in Him in anticipation of the day when Israel's spiritual blinders are finally removed and the repentant nation "will look on

[Him] whom they have pierced; and they will mourn for Him" (Zech. 12:10).*⁷

The most important truth about the two witnesses, of course, is that God will use them to do two things. *First*, He will use them to "prophesy" — to proclaim the approaching condemnation on those who submit to Antichrist and to call their fellow Jews to repentance and faith in Jesus Christ, their true Messiah, Redeemer, and King. This they will do for "twelve hundred and sixty days" (Rev. 11:3). The rest of the unbelieving world, however, who have heard and rejected the angelic proclamations from God discussed earlier in this chapter, will have been deceived by Satan and deluded by God, "so that they might believe what is false, in order that they all may be judged who did not believe the truth, but took pleasure in wickedness" (2 Thess. 2:11, 12). *Second*, He will use them "to smite the earth with every plague, as often as they desire" (v. 6). In this regard they will be part of God's counteroffensive against Antichrist — especially after Satan's two-fold test is complete and the day of the Lord's wrath is poured out upon those who pass — that is, upon the wicked that remain after the overcomers have been rescued.

There really is just one central theme to this chapter. It is a warning I would express to you, my readers, with all of my heart. If we should be the generation that enters the last seven years of the end times, I would urge you first to be sure of your relationship to Christ — not just acknowledging Him as your Savior, but acknowledging Him as Lord of your life and walking in obedience. And second, I would urge you to understand the monumental test that Antichrist will use in trying to destroy God's own elect. The consequences to God's elect of being unprepared for the great tribulation by Antichrist will be that they will receive the full brunt of Antichrist's fury, a time of persecution which will make the Holocaust pale in comparison. And if Antichrist doesn't get those who are unprepared, his demons will! But for all who are genuinely "in Christ," they will nevertheless still stand right before God, even if only "so as through fire" (1 Cor. 3:15).

On the other hand, to the "tares," the counterfeit Christians, and to the world in general, the consequences for worshiping Antichrist or his images, or for taking the mark of the beast, are eternal damnation — to be forever separated from God, where "the smoke of their

* With regard to the reasons why Moses seems most likely to be the second witness, see endnote 7.

torment goes up forever and ever; and they have no rest day and night" (Rev. 14:11). But the gracious gift of God, to all who refuse Antichrist and truly trust in God, is eternal life. "We also urge you not to receive the grace of God in vain . . . behold, now is 'the acceptable time,' behold now is 'the day of salvation'" (2 Cor. 6:1b, 2b). To you I must caution that there will come a time when you will be "deluded" by God Himself, so that you might believe what is false, in order that you may be judged for not believing the truth when you could. Behold, *now, right now* is the day of salvation. Tomorrow may be too late.

The Great Tribulation by Antichrist

The great tribulation has been mentioned frequently in the foregoing chapters. But because it is of such great importance — to
every Christian, to every Jew, and indeed to every person who
will live through these threatening years — we now turn specifically
to a careful consideration of this period of time.

Many questions come immediately to mind. What exactly is the
great tribulation? When will it occur? Who will go through it? What
will happen to them? Who will be behind it? Why will God allow it to
happen? Although many of these questions have already been
touched on, we will attempt to bring this critical timeframe into clearer
focus in the following pages.

TRIBULATION WITH NO EQUAL

The name *great tribulation* is derived from Jesus' Olivet Discourse,
in which He warns of "a great tribulation, such as has not occurred
since the beginning of the world until now, nor ever shall" (Matt. 24:21;
cf. Luke 21:22, 23). Jeremiah refers to this period of intense suffering

as the time of Jacob's distress or trouble. "Alas! for that day is great," the prophet says, "there is none like it; and it is the time of Jacob's distress" (Jer. 30:7). Daniel calls it "a time of distress such as never occurred since there was a nation until that time" (Dan. 12:1).

For many these words have become so familiar that we lose the magnitude of what they really mean. Thus we would do well to reflect again on these words of Scripture. This will be a time of distress and persecution that is greater than the world has ever known before — greater than the massive persecution of Christians in Nero's Rome; more lethal than Stalin's slaughter of twenty million Russians; more inhumane and brutal than the extermination of six million Jews in Hitler's Holocaust. We shudder at the idea of such unimaginable inhumanity and rampant evil — and we are right to do so. But it is even more sobering to realize that the great tribulation by Antichrist will go far beyond anything that has ever "occurred since the beginning of the world" (Matt. 24:21), and the target of this incredible persecution will be those who refuse to worship the beast or his image.

It would be hard to overemphasize the urgency of what this will mean for every person who is alive during these days — especially for every Jew and Christian who will be the primary targets of Satan's wrath through his minion, Antichrist. Does it not behoove us to do everything in our power, relying on God's grace, to be prepared for these days?

When will the great tribulation of Antichrist occur? As we have seen already, it will begin at the midpoint of the seventieth "week" of Daniel. The start of the great tribulation will come when Antichrist's forces treacherously invade Israel in a military incursion which, for the sake of identification and clarification, this author has chosen to call the Jerusalem Campaign. The great tribulation will last for an unknown period of time, but will doubtless last through a substantial part of the second half (three and a half years) of the seventieth week, until God brings it to an abrupt end. At some point unknown to any man but only to the Father alone, God will mercifully "cut short" Antichrist's great persecution *before* the completion of the seventieth week, for "unless those days had been cut short, no life would have been saved; but for the sake of the elect those days shall be cut short" (Matt. 24:22).

Yet there are those within the evangelical church today who teach that this terrible persecution of God's elect is in reality the wrath of God. In this writer's opinion, that is a seriously mistaken teaching. The

Word of God could not be more clear that this terrible time of persecution occurs "because the devil has come down to you, having great wrath, knowing that he has only a short time . . . and the dragon [Satan] gave him [Antichrist] his power and his throne and great authority" (Rev. 12:12; 13:2). It is true, God does permit it. The very existence of Satan and his host of demons, since the day they rebelled against God, is solely by the permissive will of God. But God is not, nor has ever been, *the source* of this terrible end-time inhumanity and brutality against the elect of God. Satan is.

ANTICHRIST'S PERSECUTION PRIORITIES

Because Satan failed to deceive or destroy the Redeemer and King when He came the first time, his purpose now will be to destroy all potential citizens of the King's millennial kingdom before Christ comes the second time. These individuals will be readily recognizable because they will have failed Satan's two-fold test: refusing to worship the beast or his image and for that reason refusing his mark as well. Satan's objective then will be to destroy, primarily through his demon-possessed idols, all who refuse Antichrist. He will not succeed, but before he is finally thwarted by God at the day of the Lord, he will have attempted to carry out his plan of total annihilation of all who refuse to bow down, and he will have inflicted upon these the worst suffering the world has ever known. The primary intent of Satan is revealed in Revelation 12 where John writes:

> [W]hen the dragon [Satan] saw that he was thrown down to the earth, *he persecuted the woman* who gave birth to the male child. And the two wings of the great eagle were given to the woman, in order that she might fly into the wilderness to her place, where she was nourished for a time and times and half a time, from the presence of the serpent. . . . *And the dragon was enraged with the woman, and went off to make war with the rest of her offspring, who keep the commandments of God and hold to the testimony of Jesus.* (vv. 13, 14, 17, emphasis added)

The primary objects of Satan's wrath, which by definition become the targets of Antichrist's intense persecution, are indicated in these verses. In verse 13 Satan's persecution is first directed against "the woman who gave birth to the male child." In this first instance, "the woman" (v. 13) refers to Israel in general as the people through whom Christ ("the male child") was born, but more specifically, in the last days, to those Jews who refuse to bow down to Antichrist and who resist his reign of terror launched against Israel.[1] It is this resistance and the refusal of many Jews to give their allegiance to Satan that will result in the massive slaughter predicted by the Lord's prophets long ago. As the Lord told Zechariah concerning this time, "two parts [of Israel] in it [the land] will be cut off and perish; but the third [part] will be left in it" (13:8).

In the second reference to "the woman" (v. 14), we see the focus of Satan's wrath shift specifically to "the woman" *who flees into the wilderness* — which in this context refers to the faithful 144,000 from within the nation of Israel who specifically did not apostacize to Antichrist during the first half of the seventieth week; and for this reason, in part, they are divinely protected by God in the wilderness during the second half.[2]

Then as Satan is unable to find and destroy those who flee, we see that "the dragon was enraged . . . and went off to make war with the rest of her offspring, who keep the commandments of God and hold to the testimony of Jesus" (v. 17) — which refers to genuine Christians, the true church, both Jew and Gentile. (See endnote 3 for an in-depth defense of this position.)[3]

These three groups, then, will encounter Satan's wrath in an unprecedented way, meted out through the great tribulation by Antichrist, as we shall see in considering each of these below. Failing the test of Satan will have its greatest consequences on those unprepared (i.e., the compromising church and those Jews who fail to heed the warnings of the Jewish witnesses), the consequences of which will literally make the Jewish Holocaust pale in comparison.

This author has referred to that specific atrocity several times. The reason that I do is because most everyone who wades through this volume is familiar with the extreme brutality of that particular event. Yet our Lord specifically says that this time of intense persecution "will be a great tribulation, such as has not occurred since the beginning of the world until now, nor ever shall" (Matt. 24:21). That statement of Christ puts all the other atrocities in the history of mankind into second place. Because the stakes are so high, and the price for refusing to worship Antichrist so great, most of the world will reject the warning of the third angelic messenger (Rev. 14:9-11), preferring instead to take their chances with God in the future rather than with Satan here and now.

Perhaps this is what Christ had in mind when He promised His disciples, "Shall not God bring about justice for His elect, who cry to Him day and night, and will He delay long over them? I tell you that He will bring about justice for them speedily. However, when the Son of Man comes, will He find faith on the earth?" (Luke 18:7, 8).

John has already told his readers that "the whole earth was amazed [when Antichrist is revealed as a dead man come back to life] and followed after the beast" (Rev. 13:3). And even though the first angelic messenger from God proclaims the gospel to every living creature, "God will send upon them [those who refuse the angel's message] a deluding influence so that they might believe what is false [in Antichrist], in order that they may be judged [at the day of the Lord] who did not believe the truth, but took pleasure in wickedness" (2 Thess. 2:11, 12). Obviously the majority of the natural line of Abraham will know only too well the real motive of Antichrist when his identity is revealed and, in this author's opinion, will then refuse the mark. Likewise, the genuine Christian "whose name has . . . been written from the foundation of the world in the book of life of the Lamb who has been slain" (Rev. 13:8) will refuse the mark. And like "the woman," those prepared will survive Antichrist's slaughter in hiding, but the rest will pay the price for compromise. And so the target of Satan's wrath will be limited — limited because the world in general will worship the beast and his image, and limited because only the true "overcomer" and "the woman" will fail Satan's test, knowing in advance that their refusal to worship Antichrist will make them the direct target of Satan's wrath.

"THE COMPROMISED WOMAN"

Antichrist's most intense — and successful — persecution will be against "the compromised woman," those who supported the covenant with Antichrist initially, shunning their opportunity to flee when they could, and yet who will not bow down and worship the beast or his image once his true identity is known. As Antichrist turns his fury against these Jews living in the city of Jerusalem or in the land of Israel, he will probably first use his exclusively Gentile military forces that are with him in Jerusalem to unleash his final, devastating onslaught. Most of Israel, in this writer's opinion, will refuse to worship the beast, which is why two out of three of all Jews living in the land of Israel will eventually die at the hands of Antichrist (Zech. 13:8). Those of "the woman" who do survive will somehow escape into the rural areas of Israel or into remote, protective areas in either the land of Egypt or the land of Assyria* (Hos. 11:11).

Speaking of Israel's covenant with Antichrist, Isaiah gives this frightening prediction:

> Your covenant with death shall be canceled, and your pact with Sheol shall not stand; when the overwhelming scourge passes through, then you become its trampling place. As often as it passes through, it will seize you. For morning after morning it will pass through, anytime during the day or night. And it will be sheer terror to understand what it means. (Isa. 28:18, 19)

Unbelieving Jews will be in "sheer terror" as they realize that their treaty with the beguiling world leader was indeed a "covenant with death," a "pact with Sheol," as Antichrist openly begins his systematic program to exterminate every Jew who fails the test.

As would be expected, Antichrist's first onslaught will be against Jews living in and near Jerusalem. For this reason, therefore, Christ warned:

> "When you see the ABOMINATION OF DESOLATION which was spoken of through Daniel the prophet, standing in the holy place (let the reader understand), then let those who are in Judea flee to the mountains; let him who is on the housetop not go down to get the things out that are in his house; and let him who is in the field not turn back to get his cloak. But woe to those who are with child and to those who nurse babes in those days! But pray that your flight may not be in the winter, or on a Sabbath." (Matt. 24:15-20)

But there will be some Jews — not a part of "the woman" — who, living in Jerusalem, will find some excuse, most likely out of fear, to worship the beast and his image and take the mark of Antichrist. Perhaps the memories of the Holocaust will be fresh on their minds, and they will again choose submission rather than confrontation. These are perhaps the temporary survivors of whom the Lord spoke through Zechariah: "For I will gather all the nations against Jerusalem

---

* The ancient land of Assyria would be located in an area just east of and a bit north of modern-day Syria, between the headwaters of the Euphrates and Tigris Rivers.

to battle, and the city will be captured, the houses plundered, the women ravished, and half of the city exiled, *but the rest of the people* [those who worship the beast or his image] *will not be cut off from the city*" (Zech. 14:2, emphasis added).

As suggested in this passage, apostate Jews who choose to worship Antichrist may receive the temporary protection of Antichrist, although it seems highly probable that even many of these will eventually be exterminated, as in the Nazi Holocaust, simply because they are Jews — despite their taking Antichrist's mark of allegiance.

"THE FAITHFUL WOMAN"

However, there will be a relatively small group of faithful Jews who refuse to acknowledge the covenant made with Antichrist and therefore heed the warnings to flee from Jerusalem (as well as from other nations of the world). These will be divinely protected from the grasp of Antichrist. After the general persecution is begun upon all of those in Israel who have refused to flee, but have nonetheless refused to bow down to Antichrist — "the compromised woman" — Antichrist will shift his focus to the select faithful few (144,000) of "the woman" who do flee to the Edomite wilderness. As we see in the following, however, Antichrist will be unable to harm them:

> And the two wings of the great eagle were given to the woman, in order that she might fly into the wilderness to her place, where she was nourished for a time and times and half a time, from the presence of the serpent. And the serpent poured water like a river out of his mouth after the woman, so that he might cause her to be swept away with the flood. And the earth helped the woman, and the earth opened its mouth and drank up the river which the dragon poured out of his mouth. (Rev. 12:14-16)

"The faithful woman," then, will include those who refuse to apostacize to Antichrist during the first half of the seventieth week and who flee "into the wilderness" where they are protected by the Lord and "nourished for one thousand two hundred and sixty days" (Rev. 12:6). It seems clear that only those who flee to the wilderness will have this special protection that God will provide to the natural line of Abraham during these difficult days of persecution, not unlike the protection God will extend to the "faithful church" during this same time of intense persecution. This protection will go to those who have not apostacized to Antichrist when the covenant is made, but will instead have heeded the warnings of the Jewish witnesses and will therefore flee to the wilderness before Antichrist establishes his throne in the Temple and begins his unrelenting annihilation of "the woman" in general. It is for this reason that this particular group will become the "first fruits to God and to the Lamb" because these will be the ones who "have kept themselves [spiritually] chaste" (Rev. 14:4).

THE JEWISH WITNESSES

There is one further Jewish group, although very small, that will be the special object of persecution during the great tribulation by Antichrist. This group will be the Jewish witnesses who will call their fellow countrymen to repentance, starting at the beginning of the seventieth week. The witnesses will warn others of the danger they are in, pointing them to the true Messiah soon to come. These are the ones about whom Christ said:

> "Behold, I send you out as sheep in the midst of wolves; therefore be shrewd as serpents, and innocent as doves. But beware of men; for they will deliver you up to the courts, and scourge you in their synagogues. . . . And brother will deliver up brother to death, and a father his child; and children will rise up against parents, and cause them to be put to death. And you will be hated by all on account of My name, but it is the one who has endured to the end [of the age] who will be saved [delivered]. But whenever they persecute you in this city, flee to the next; for truly I say to you, you shall not finish going through the cities of Israel, until the Son of Man comes." (Matt. 10:16, 17, 21-23)

This passage describes a small courageous band of men totally committed to the Lord and willing to risk everything for the sake of Christ. They will be hauled into court, beaten, betrayed by their own parents and by their own children, hated by their fellow Jews, forced to flee from one city to the next, yet will faithfully proclaim the name of Christ to their fellow countrymen in Israel until the end of the age. Before the Son of Man comes on the day of the Lord, many of these will be martyred.

Fifth Seal Martyrs In this author's opinion, those Jewish witnesses who die in pursuit of their fellow countrymen are the martyrs to whom Christ refers in His Olivet Discourse (Matt. 24:9) and to which John refers when he describes the opening of the fifth seal, a scene which takes place entirely in Heaven:

> And when He broke the fifth seal, I saw underneath the altar the souls of those who had been slain because of the word of God, and *because of the testimony which they had maintained*; and they cried out with a loud voice, saying, "How long, O Lord, holy and true, wilt Thou refrain from judging and avenging our blood on those who dwell on the earth?" And there was given to each of them a white robe; and they were told that they should rest for a little while longer, until the number of *their fellow-servants and their brethren who were to be killed even as they had been*, should be completed also. (Rev. 6:9-11, emphasis added)[4]

These martyrs may also include other faithful Christians ("their fellow servants") who, before the day of the Lord commences, likewise choose to lay down their lives for the sake of the lost or the compromising church in other parts of the world, paralleling the work of the Jewish witnesses in the land of Israel. These will be men who could claim the protection promised the faithful church, but instead heed the call of God to minister to those who are unprepared for the intense persecution of Antichrist. Many of these faithful men will die assisting their fellow countrymen. In my opinion, this group *does not* include the multitudes of believers who will die from within the compromising church because of their complete lack of preparedness for the great tribulation by Antichrist. The martyrs underneath the altar refer to this particular group as "their brethren who were to be killed even as they had been," separate and distinct from "their fellow servants." Although many of these compromising believers will suffer martyrdom, it will not be because "of the testimony which they had maintained," but rather because of the testimony they compromised in their unfaithfulness in both life and doctrine. Even less will these martyrs include the faithful Christians per se, since they are promised protection "within a sphere of danger,"* or new converts to Christianity, because during the great tribulation "God will send upon [the world] a deluding influence so that they might believe what is false, in order that they all may be judged who did not believe the

---

* See chapter 2, endnote 1.

truth" (2 Thess. 2:11, 12). I realize that precisely identifying the fifth seal martyrs involves some speculation, but because of the special attention that is given these martyrs on the first day of the Millennium, at least to those who have been beheaded, this author is comfortable with (but not adamant about) the position he takes when all the passages are taken together.*

THE "REST OF HER OFFSPRING"

After ravaging Jerusalem and demanding and receiving the world's worship, after beginning his persecution of "the compromised woman" who remains in Israel, and after unsuccessfully trying to reach "the faithful woman" who has fled safely to the wilderness, Antichrist will next begin the unrelenting persecution of Christians, both Jewish and Gentile — that is, persecution directed at those who have refused his mark and "who keep the commandments of God and hold to the testimony of Jesus" (Rev. 12:17).** Satan will have become enraged by God's protection of "the faithful woman" who flees, and so will cause Antichrist to "make war with the saints" (Rev. 13:7a; see also 12:17). With the assistance of the second beast (the enforcer), who "makes the earth and those who dwell in it to worship the first beast, whose fatal wound was healed" (Rev. 13:12), and using the demon-indwelt images to control the world, he will have now attained universal "authority over every tribe and people and tongue and nation" (Rev. 13:7b), and no human effort will be able to withstand him.

How will the unrelenting persecution of Antichrist against Christians affect the church? This will depend directly upon how well Christians are prepared for Antichrist's onslaught — that is, upon how well we understand what is actually happening and upon whether we are living a life of genuine obedience to the Lord. In general, the organized church will be torn by dissension and thrown into chaos, for spiritually dead Christians will have privately given homage to the image of Antichrist and even taken his mark in order to buy and sell in the marketplace. These will be the ones about whom Timothy warned when he wrote that "the Spirit explicitly says that in the later times some will fall away from the faith, paying attention to deceitful spirits and doctrines of demons" (1 Tim. 4:1). For the most part, these spiritually dead Christians will actually *escape* the persecution of

---

* See chapter 22, "Third Event" section.
** See again endnote 2 for the author's defense of this.

Antichrist, because they have given their allegiance to him. But the price for their temporary escape will be too high when they face the day-of-the-Lord judgment and eternal damnation as the consequence of their fatal choice.

By contrast, genuine children of God (those who are totally committed to Christ, not merely having a head knowledge of Christ) will fail the test of Satan by refusing to worship the image of the beast and refusing to take his mark. But the price of their faithfulness to God will be costly. With demon-empowered images that have the ability to speak and kill virtually everywhere, and with everyone required to take the mark of the beast in order to buy and sell, genuine Christians will be at enormous risk.

Depending on how well prepared these Christians are, this risk will affect them to a greater or lesser degree. As explained in chapter 2, God will give the *faithful church* protection *"within* the sphere of danger"; and eventually God will rescue the faithful church "out from within this sphere of danger" at the rapture of the church. As with "the faithful woman" that flees, God's hand of protection will likewise be upon the faithful within the church.

But genuine Christians within the compromising church will be thrown into the teeth of the great tribulation by Antichrist — not unlike "the compromised woman" — as a holy God purifies and refines His disobedient children in preparation for becoming the pure and blameless bride of Christ. Refusing to take the mark, yet unprepared for the destructive power of the demon-possessed images, they will suffer dearly for the bad doctrine and compromised lifestyles that will characterize the church in general as it goes into the seventieth week of Daniel. Those believers may or may not survive the worst persecution known to man. But before the Lord takes them to Himself, by death or by rapture, they will have paid a high and unnecessary price. Many will be led into the deadly hands of Antichrist by the many false christs, whom the true Christ warns His church not to follow (Luke 21:8; cf. Matt. 24:24). Many others no doubt will suffer martyrdom as they are lured out of hiding (Matt. 24:25) into the presence of demon-empowered images of Antichrist worldwide. Others, totally unprepared, will pay the price, never knowing what hit them until too late. "But he himself shall be saved, yet so as through fire" (1 Cor. 3:15).

Accomplishing God's Purposes Why will God allow His church to undergo this intense time of persecution? The primary reason is so the church will be presented to Christ as His bride "in all her glory, having no spot or wrinkle . . . that she should be holy and blameless" (Eph. 5:27). Thus the *compromising church* will experience the full force of Antichrist's persecution, but at the same time God will graciously use this persecution to purify Christ's bride and to draw such compromising believers back to godly living and purity of doctrine. In this regard Peter admonishes Christians how important it is that we be prepared for the coming day of the Lord: "Therefore, beloved, since you look for these things, be diligent to be found by Him in peace, spotless and blameless" (2 Pet. 3:14). Most of the church today is not looking for "these things" — at least, not looking for these things to happen to *them*. Most think they will perhaps happen to unbelieving Israel, or perhaps to the unrighteous world at large, but certainly not to the church. And yet Peter specifically warns "*you*" (i.e., every Christian) to look for these things, and then admonishes every Christian "to be diligent to be found by Him in peace, spotless and blameless." Although the untaught, compromising church will not be removed from among the elect, they will know the purifying fires of persecution and be saved only "as through fire."

In a different way, faithful believers will also have to suffer, although they will not take the brunt of Antichrist's fury as will unfaithful and unprepared believers. Faithful believers will suffer for a number of other reasons — because of Antichrist's demonic control of the earth and the harsh living conditions brought on them for refusing the mark; because of concern for their loved ones and friends who are under direct affliction by Antichrist; because of remorse for those who have taken his mark and therefore forfeited salvation; because of the faithful believers who openly preach the gospel or assist the compromising church and are martyred for it; and because of the hardship, suffering, and evil that will then pervade the earth. But at the same time, faithful believers will also know God's protection in the midst of danger and God's sustaining grace as they face persecution.

But there are other more subtle reasons as to why God allows His church to endure suffering. Perhaps the most important of these is that the suffering of the saints for Christ's sake is certain evidence of their salvation. It proves beyond doubt that they belong to God, because only a true child of God has the motive to be persecuted for His sake and, even more importantly, because only a true child of God has the power of Christ's indwelling Holy Spirit to sustain and encourage him in that suffering. Thus the Apostle Paul wrote to the church in Thessalonica:

> We ourselves speak proudly of you among the churches of God for your perseverance and faith in the midst of all your persecutions and afflictions which you endure. This is a plain indication of God's righteous judgment so that you may be considered worthy of the kingdom of God, for which indeed you are suffering. (2 Thess. 1:4, 5)

Paul went on to encourage these believers that God would indeed bring relief at the Rapture and judgment on the day of the Lord to those who afflict the saints.

> For after all it is only just for God to repay with affliction those who afflict you, and to give relief to you who are afflicted and to us as well when the Lord Jesus shall be revealed from heaven with His mighty angels in flaming fire, dealing out retribution to those who do not know God and to those who do not obey the gospel of our Lord Jesus. (2 Thess. 1:6-8)

In addition to the assurance of salvation, another reason for persecution is the *assurance of glory*. Thus Peter wrote, "If anyone suffers as a Christian, let him not feel ashamed, but in that name let him glorify God. For it is time for judgment to begin with the household of God . . ." (1 Pet. 4:16, 17a). Later in the same letter he said, "I exhort the elders among you, as your fellow elder and witness of the sufferings of Christ, and a partaker also of the glory that is to be revealed . . . and when the Chief Shepherd appears, you will receive the unfading crown of glory" (1 Pet. 5:1, 4). His point was that if they, like him, suffered for Christ's sake, they, like him, would partake of the glory of Christ, which is doubtless a reference to the Rapture.

One last reason why God will allow genuine believers to undergo the persecution of Antichrist is so that we might develop *patience and endurance*. Christ told His disciples that "The days shall come when you will long to see one of the days of the Son of Man, and you will not see it. And they will say to you, 'Look there! Look here!' Do not go away, and do not run after them. For just as the lightning, when it flashes out of one part of the sky, shines to the other part of the sky, so will the Son of Man be in His day" (Luke 17:22-24). He was clearly speaking of a coming time in the last days just prior to the return of Christ when God's elect would yearn for the return of their Lord because of the intense persecution they would be undergoing. Christ goes on to explain concerning His return, "just as it happened in the days of Noah, so it shall be also in the days of the Son of Man: they [the world] were eating, they were drinking, they were marrying, they were being given in marriage, until the day that Noah entered the ark, and the flood came and destroyed them all. . . . It will be just the same on the day that the Son of Man is revealed" (vv. 26, 27, 30). A few verses later (18:1-8), Christ gave the disciples the parable of the persistent widow to teach them that during this coming time of distress, "when you will long to see one of the days of the Son of Man, and you will not see it" (v. 22), you "ought to pray and not to lose heart" (18:1). Then He gave them a comforting promise, asking rhetorically, "Shall not God bring about justice for His elect, who cry to Him day and night, and will He delay long over them? I tell you that He will bring about justice for them speedily. However, when the Son of Man comes, will He find faith on the earth?" (vv. 7, 8).

This theme of patience and endurance is also proclaimed powerfully by Paul in a triumphant passage in Romans on the results of justification. Paul writes that we can

> exult in our tribulations, knowing that tribulation brings about perseverance; and perseverance, proven character; and proven character, hope; and hope does not disappoint; because the love of God has been poured out within our hearts through the Holy Spirit who was given to us. . . . Much more then, having now been justified by His blood, we shall be saved [delivered] from the wrath of God through Him. (Rom. 5:3-5, 9)

Yet in the infirmity of our flesh, in the heartbreak of the world around us, and much more in the midst of the great tribulation of Antichrist, we yearn for the return of our Lord. The human cry is impatient, scarcely seeing reality from our extremely limited perspective. But because it is stated in God's Word, we can sincerely acknowledge the truth of Peter's statement "that with the Lord one day is as a thousand years, and a thousand years as one day," and that "the Lord is not slow about His promise, as some count slowness. . . . But the day of the Lord [bringing relief to the genuine Christian] will come like a thief, in which the heavens will pass away with a roar and the elements will be destroyed with intense heat, and the earth and its works will be burned up" (2 Pet. 3:8-10). Because of our human limitations, we cannot possibly comprehend such a truth but only accept it by faith.

On the other hand, the faithful church will indeed be protected from Antichrist's greatest fury during his great tribulation. Those who are biblically taught and who genuinely seek to obey the Lord will have a three and a half year period in which to seek refuge, prior to the beginning of the great tribulation by Antichrist. Some men, no doubt, will choose to risk persecution and death for the sake of the compromising churches and in order to carry a true witness of the gospel to those "who are perishing." But because the faithful church in general will be in hiding and will know what the true sign of their Lord's coming will be, they will not succumb to being deceived by the many false signs that the second beast will supernaturally display (Rev. 13:13, 14) or by the false claims that Antichrist will make (Matt. 24:23-26). The faithful church will patiently await the Lord's return, when "the Lord Himself will descend from heaven with a shout, with the voice of the archangel, and with the trumpet of God; and the dead in Christ shall rise first. Then we who are alive and remain shall be caught up together with them in the clouds to meet the Lord in the air, and thus we shall always be with the Lord" (1 Thess. 4:16, 17). Paul then follows this great passage with the same words this writer has for the faithful church, "therefore comfort one another with these words" (v. 18).

NEW TESTAMENT EXPECTANCY VS. BIBLICAL REALITY

Every genuine believer longs for the day of the Lord's return. It is true today as we look with expectation for the beginning of the last days, as they seem to be approaching before our very eyes. It will be true of the end-times martyrs under the altar who cry out to the Lord, "How long, O Lord?" It will be true of those undergoing the great persecution of Antichrist, of whom Christ spoke when He said, "you will long to see one of the days of the Son of Man" (Luke 17:22). Believers in the early church knew that God's people would endure intense suffering just before the return of Christ. And because so many of them were then being falsely accused, imprisoned, tortured, and martyred for the sake of their faith, it is understandable why they often thought the end times were near.

In the pages of the New Testament we find a delicate balance between a strong expectancy that the end times would begin very soon and a call to patience and endurance because certain events must take place first.

There are many reasons why the early Christians had such a strong sense of expectancy. For example, just after Christ ascended to Heaven, two angels told the disciples that Jesus would return "in just the same way as you have watched Him go into heaven" (Acts 1:11). It seems certain that those disciples expected their Lord to return very soon, perhaps in a few weeks, or even a few days. They had no comprehension of the great gap between the sixty-ninth and the seventieth weeks of Daniel's vision. With the last week of Gentile domination being only seven years, many early Christians expected to witness Christ's return in their lifetimes. Part of their expectation for Christ's soon return came as a result of Christ's instruction to Peter on how he would die. Peter, more concerned about how John would die, said to Jesus, "'Lord, and what about this man?' Jesus said to him 'If I want him to remain until I come, what is it to you? You follow Me!' This saying therefore went out among the brethren that that disciple would not die [before Christ's return] . . ." (John 21:21-23a).

Those believers were then living during the time of the sixth beast empire (depicted in Daniel 7 as the fourth beast) and fully expected the "little horn" (v. 8), Antichrist, to soon arise out of Rome. The Babylonians (the head of gold in Daniel's statue, Dan. 2:32-45), the Medes and Persians (the breast and arms of silver), and the Greeks (the belly and thighs of bronze) had been quickly overthrown, almost overnight as it were. Consequently, many Christians in the early church expected the overthrow of Rome (the legs of iron and the empire that then oppressed them) to be the next major event in God's prophetic calendar. Thus they thought that the overthrow of Rome could occur at any moment, never even suspecting the long gap between the impending destruction of both the city and the sanctuary and the commencement of the seventieth week (Dan. 9:26, 27). And, of course, they had no knowledge of a seventh beast empire that had to first arise between the Roman Empire and the final ten-nation beast empire of Satan, as this teaching was introduced almost twenty years after the *Diaspora* had begun in A.D. 70. Indeed, because of the intense persecution the churches were undergoing, these faithful believers genuinely believed that all systems were "go" and the seventieth week was imminent. Christians in the early church, therefore, had many good reasons to think that *they* were the "generation [that would] not pass away until all these things take place" (Matt. 24:34) — not unlike the church today, now that Israel is back in the land with control again of the city of Jerusalem.

In view of the early church's strong sense of expectancy that the end times would begin immediately, it is extremely important to see how this expectancy is addressed by Christ and the New Testament in general. It would be helpful to look briefly at a number of passages where the issue is raised, to see how God's Word handles this.

As a first example, there is the question Jesus' disciples asked Him just before His ascension: "Lord, is it at this time You are restoring the Kingdom to Israel?" Jesus was very careful not to answer either yes or no, but simply stated, "It is not for you to know times or epochs which the Father has fixed by His own authority" (Acts 1:6, 7). A similar point is made in the Gospel of John — a point mentioned earlier — when Jesus tells Peter how he will die and then rebukes Peter for thinking that John was receiving preferential treatment. Thus Jesus told Peter,

> "If I want him [John] to remain until I come, what is that to you? You follow Me!" This saying therefore went out among the brethren that that disciple [John] would not die; *yet Jesus did not say to him that he would not die, but only, "If I want him to remain until I come, what is that to you?"* (John 21:22, 23, emphasis added)

In both of these passages the point is generally the same: We are to look expectantly for the last seven years to begin and for the events that will then lead up to the return of Christ. But at the same time, Jesus did not teach that His return *would* be soon. In either case, the most important thing is that we (like Peter) *follow Him.*

Two additional passages also give important insight into the early church's sense of expectancy and God's balanced response. The first has to do with the church at Thessalonica and their concern that the day of the Lord was at hand when the church would be gathered together to Him. Theirs had become an exaggerated and misinformed expectancy which Paul quickly corrected. Thus Paul writes that certain very specific things must happen first:

> Let no one in any way deceive you, for it will not come unless the apostasy comes first, and the man of lawlessness is revealed . . . [who] takes his seat in the temple of God, displaying himself as being God. (2 Thess. 2:3, 4)

In a similar way, Peter admonished those who had *abandoned* any sense of expectancy. Peter begins by reminding his readers that the Lord will indeed return, but certain things must take place first:

> Know this first of all, that in the last days mockers will come with their mocking, following after their own lusts. . . . But do not let this one fact escape your notice, beloved, that with the Lord one day is as a thousand years, and a thousand years as one day. The Lord is not slow about His promise, as some count slowness, but is patient toward you, not wishing for any to perish. (2 Pet. 3:3, 8, 9)

The clear teaching of Scripture, then, is that the church in *every* age is to live with a strong sense of expectancy — always being alert and sober, always looking with anticipation for the events that will lead up to the end times, and always being prepared for the day of the Lord once these events have come to pass. The fact that the early church had this sense of expectation, then, was *not a mistake*, but the proper attitude of believers in every age. For it is true that in any generation after the *Diaspora* of A.D. 70 the Lord *could have* brought His people back to the land, even if it is only in our generation that this critical event preceding the end times has actually taken place.

Lastly, we should consider why Christ and the writers of the New Testament often used verbs in the present tense and pronouns in the first or second person when speaking of Christ's second coming. Paul, for example, promises believers: "We who are alive, and remain until the coming of the Lord, shall not precede those who have fallen asleep" (1 Thess. 4:15). Jesus assured His disciples, "If I go and prepare a place for you, I will come again, and receive you to Myself; that where I am, there you may be also" (John 14:3). In the Olivet Discourse He warned, "If therefore they say to you, 'Behold, He is in the wilderness,' do not go forth, or, 'Behold, He is in the inner rooms,' do not believe them. For just as the lightning comes from the east, and flashes even to the west, so shall the coming of the Son of Man be" (Matt. 24:26, 27).

The obvious question is, why do these passages use first- and second-person pronouns? When Jesus and the New Testament writers used the pronoun "you," was the intended meaning that "you" should refer only to those who specifically heard the words of Jesus or who first read the words of Paul? Or was the intended meaning something much broader — meant for the teaching and instruction of the church in *every* age? There is always a sense in which any generation *could* be the last generation — depending on when the Lord in His sovereign timing permits the events of the last days and the end times to unfold. But more importantly, Christians through the ages have always understood the words of Christ to have a much broader meaning. Thus, Christ went to prepare a place for "you" (the disciples), but just as much for "us" (believers today). And when Christ returns to receive the disciples to Himself, He will just as much receive every other Christian believer to Himself as well. In other words, the present tense can best be explained as a means of rhetorical inclusiveness that does not exclude those who are not specifically addressed, but embraces a much wider meaning (i.e., every believer in every age).

But as the centuries have unfolded since the time of Christ, we can now look back in retrospect and see that today's church, as never before in history, stands on the threshold of the end times and the return of Christ. The Roman Empire is long gone. The seventh beast empire has risen and been destroyed. The Jews are back in their own land and again have control of all Jerusalem. Just one major event awaits fulfillment before the beginning of the end times. And this event — the rise of Antichrist disguised as a powerful world leader who overthrows and takes control of three Aryan nations — this event could happen overnight. If ever there was a time for the church to be prepared and watch expectantly for the signs of the end and the coming of Christ, the time is *now*.

The Sign of the End
of the Age

There is a longing in the heart of everyone who truly loves the Lord — a longing for the day when every wrong will be made right, when every tear will be wiped away, when there will be no more mourning or crying or pain or death (Rev. 21:4). We long to be rescued from the terrible effects of sin. Even the whole creation groans in anticipation of the day when it will be set free from Satan's reign and the bonds of corruption (Rom. 8:19-22). In a sense the cry of Paul is the cry of every believer: "Wretched man that I am! Who will set me free from the body of this death?" (Rom. 7:24).

TIMELESS QUESTIONS

"How much longer, Lord?" "When will You return?" Even before the end times these questions burn in the thoughts of every genuine Christian. How much more will they burn in the hearts and minds of Christ's church during the great tribulation by Antichrist in the last half of the seventieth "week."

Indeed, these questions were raised by the disciples even while

Christ was here on earth at His first coming: "When will these things be," they asked, "and what will be the sign of Your coming, and of the end of the age?" (Matt. 24:3). It was the afternoon of the third day of Passover Week. Christ would die at the hands of the Roman government with the approval of the Jewish multitudes just three days later. He had just told the multitudes, "For I say to you, from now on you shall not see Me until you say, 'Blessed is He who comes in the name of the Lord!'" (Matt. 23:39). Slowly but surely the disciples were beginning to realize that Christ was indeed going to leave them, but that He would also return the next time to judge the nations (Luke 17:22-37). Uppermost in their mind, then, was the question, "What will be the sign of Your coming?" and, "What will be the sign of the end of the age?" They knew by the very words of Christ that "Just as the tares are gathered up and burned with fire, so shall it be at the end of the age" (Matt. 13:40). They knew that the end of the age would be the day of God's judgment of the wicked, that prophetic day referred to over and over again in the Old Testament — the day of the Lord — the day when their Lord would return. Thus the disciples wanted to know the answers to their two burning questions:[1]

1. "What will be the sign of Your coming?"
2. "What will be the sign . . . of the end of the age?"

It is interesting to note that the disciples asked their questions in the specific order that these *events* will occur — i.e., first Christ will return, and then God will pour out judgment. Likewise, in Matthew 24:1-29 Christ answers these questions in the order asked by the disciples. But in verse 30 Christ makes it clear that the *signs* will occur in the reverse sequence of the events; i.e., the *sign* of the end of the age actually precedes the *sign* of Christ's coming. It is essential to understand the order of this sequence according to how Christ taught this will actually occur. We will, therefore, look at these questions in the order that they will occur as taught by our Lord — by first considering in this chapter *"What will be the sign of the end of the age?"* and then in the next chapter turning to the second question, *"What will be the sign of Christ's coming?"*

Christ's answers to the disciples' questions are given along with one of our Lord's strongest warnings — a warning that every Christian who enters the seventieth week needs to heed with utter seriousness. This warning comes at the end of Christ's explanation of the specific things that will occur before the sign of the end of the ages is given in the heavenlies, and it is directed especially to those faithful Christians who have gone into hiding prior to the great tribulation by Antichrist, out of reach of his demonic control over the earth. Hoping to lure those believers out of hiding, Antichrist will dispatch many false christs and false prophets, who will show such seemingly divine signs and wonders that if God did not secure them in the faith, many of His own elect would be ensnared and executed. Thus Jesus warned of that day, saying, "Then if anyone says to you, 'Behold, here is the Christ,' or 'There He is,' do not believe him. For false christs and false prophets will arise and will show great signs and wonders, so as to mislead, if possible, even the elect. Behold, I have told you in advance. If therefore they say to you, 'Behold, He is in the wilderness,' do not go forth, or, 'Behold, He is in the inner rooms,' do not believe them" (Matt. 24:23-26).

Christ's warning here is very specific. It is a warning to the church *not to be deceived* by the "great signs and wonders" that false christs and false prophets will perform during the great tribulation by Antichrist. We do not know what these false signs and wonders will be, but they will most certainly be awesome displays of power — so awesome, in fact, that even the elect will be tempted to come out of hiding where they would fall into the deadly grasp of Antichrist. Thus Christ commands His own with the strongest words, "Do not go forth . . . do not believe them" (v. 26). In other words, do not be deceived by any of these false signs no matter how impressive they may be. *Wait instead for the real sign of the end of the age.* Then, and only then, will you see the sign of Christ's coming.

Christ had just explained to His disciples that "when you see the ABOMINATION OF DESOLATION which was spoken of through Daniel the prophet, standing in the holy place . . . then there will be a great tribulation, such as has not occurred since the beginning of the world until now, nor ever shall. And unless those days had been cut short, no life [of those opposed to Antichrist] would have been saved" (Matt. 24:15, 21, 22a). That is why Christ's warning was so specific. "Do not go forth . . . do not believe them." But with the warning comes the promise of Christ, ". . . but for the sake of the elect those days shall be cut short" (Matt. 24:22b). This one little promise is indeed pregnant with meaning! If the persecution of Antichrist were permitted to run its full course, throughout the forty-two months allotted him (Rev. 13:5), "no life would have been saved." But Christ promises to "cut short" the great tribulation by Antichrist — not his forty-two-month time allotment, but rather his persecution of God's elect, including both the spiritual and natural lines of Abraham. The Greek word literally means "to amputate."[2] Thus the promise of Christ is that the great tribulation by Antichrist will not be permitted to run the full course of the time allotted to him. Instead it will be amputated, cut short, even though Antichrist himself will continue on until he meets with "complete destruction, [and] one that is decreed, is poured out on the one who makes desolate" (Dan. 9:27b).

What Will Be the Sign?

If the counterfeit signs created by the false christs and false prophets will be stunningly impressive, what of the true sign that will mark the end of the age? In describing this sign, Christ begins by saying that this sign will occur "immediately after the tribulation of those days" (Matt. 24:29a). He then goes on to quote the classic day of the Lord passage in Isaiah, which explains that on this fearful day "the sun will be darkened, and the moon will not give its light, and the stars will fall from the sky, and the powers of the heavens will be shaken" (Matt. 24:29b; see Isa. 13:10). This corresponds identically to the classic day of the Lord passage in Joel, where the Lord proclaims through the prophet that "The sun will be turned into darkness, and the moon into blood, *before* the great and awesome day of the Lord comes" (2:31, emphasis added). In other words, from these passages we see that the sign of the end of the age is the same sign that the Lord gave to Joel, the same sign the Lord gave to Isaiah, and also the same sign Christ gave His disciples so they'd know when "the end of the age" *was about to occur*, when Christ would return to earth for the judgment of the inhabitants of Satan's earthly kingdom. (Later in this chapter, we will see that it is also the same sign Christ gave John in the book of Revelation announcing the day of the Lord at the sixth seal.) Thus there is total agreement in Scripture as to *what* the sign will be, but there also is complete consistency as to *when* this sign will occur — that is, "immediately *after* the tribulation of those days" (Matt. 24:29a) and *"before* the great and awesome day of the Lord" (Joel 2:31). Christ therefore explicitly links together the sign of the end of the age which occurs "immediately after the tribulation" (Matt. 24:29a) and the day of the Lord, which therefore must occur when the great tribulation by Antichrist is "cut short." Then in the next verse Christ explains that the second sign — "the sign of the Son of Man will appear in the sky" (v. 30) — will follow in immediate succession to the sign of the end of the age. Our passage then continues to explain that after these two signs are given back to back, "then all the tribes of the earth will mourn, and they will see the Son of Man coming on the clouds of the sky with power and great glory."

From this we may conclude three things: First, the day of the Lord will be preceded by two successive stunning signs — the sign of the end of the age and the sign of Christ's coming. Second, both of these signs (and the events they announce) will occur *after* the tribulation — or more correctly, *when* the tribulation is cut short (see Matt. 24:22). And third, both these signs are given *before* the coming of the Son of Man on the clouds of the sky. This conclusion is of major theological significance, for it clearly shows that the Rapture will not occur until *after* the tribulation, at the point when the great tribulation of Antichrist is cut short sometime during the second half of the last "week" of Daniel. With the relationship of these two cataclysmic signs now clearly in mind, we will now consider the first sign more extensively and will return to the second sign in the next chapter.

It is hard to imagine the stunning effect of this first sign — the sign of the end of the age. The Bible uses the most dramatic language in numerous places to describe this sign which is, in effect, a portent indicating that the day of the Lord is about to begin. The Lord repeatedly told His people of a sign that would announce that terrible day of vengeance, a spectacle in the heavens that will pale everything that human eyes have seen before. It will be a sign of such magnitude and awesomeness that the most confirmed atheist will acknowledge its divine origin and attempt to flee in terror.

Those alive on earth at that time will see "the heavens tremble, the sun and the moon grow dark, and the stars lose their brightness" (Joel 2:10). "And I will display wonders in the sky and on the earth," the Lord says; "blood, fire, and columns of smoke. The sun will be turned into darkness, and the moon into blood, before the great and awesome day of the Lord comes" (Joel 2:30, 31). The major theme of the book of Joel is the day of the Lord, and near the end of his message the prophet reiterates that when certain divinely preordained events transpire, "the day of the Lord is near in the valley of decision. The sun and moon grow dark, and the stars lose their brightness. And the Lord roars from Zion" (Joel 3:14-16). Isaiah also predicts that "the day of the Lord is coming, cruel, with fury and burning anger, to make the land a desolation; and He will exterminate its sinners from it. For the stars of heaven and their constellations will not flash forth their light; the sun will be dark when it rises, and the moon will not shed its light" (Isa. 13:9, 10).

It is hard for us to fully comprehend the monumental significance of the sign that will signal the end of the age and the beginning of the day of the Lord. For these cataclysmic events are not simply metaphors; *they will really happen.* It is no wonder that it will be this sign that cuts short the great tribulation by Antichrist. In essence, the sign of the end of the age will simultaneously extinguish all natural lights in the heavens,[3] plunging the earth into total darkness. This sign will also be accompanied by tremendous worldwide earthquakes, so that "every mountain and island were moved out of their places" (Rev. 6:14). When that bewildering event occurs, unbelieving mankind will panic and desperately seek hiding places among rocks and in caves — because they will then know with horrifying certainty that the wrath of God, about which they had been so often and graciously warned, is about to commence. As vividly portrayed in Luke's Gospel: "there will be signs in sun and moon and stars, and upon earth dismay among the nations, in perplexity at the roaring of the sea and the waves, men fainting from fear and the expectation of the things [God's wrath soon to follow] which are coming upon the world" (Luke 21:25, 26). In striking contrast, however, God's children, the overcomers, will look up with great joy and expectancy, knowing that "when these things begin to take place . . . your redemption is drawing near" (Luke 21:28).

AS "THAT DAY" APPROACHES

The unbelieving world will be oblivious to what God is doing. The world will have been warned by the third angel of their impending disaster if they worship the beast or its image. They will have been told that they will "drink of the wine of the wrath of God, which is mixed in full strength in the cup of His anger" (Rev. 14:10). And yet, that warning, until it is too late, will go totally unheeded — in part because of Satan's "deception of wickedness for those who perish" (2 Thess. 2:10), in part because "God will send upon them a deluding influence so that they might believe what is false, in order that they all may be judged who did not believe the truth, but took pleasure in wickedness" (2 Thess. 2:11, 12). For these reasons most people will, in fact, not take God into account at all. Having given their allegiance to Antichrist, they will bask in physical peace and safety and have a great sense of well-being, being completely unaware of what is about to happen. As Jesus warned in the Olivet Discourse: "For the coming of the Son of Man will be just like the days of Noah. For as in those days which were before the flood they were eating and drinking, they were marrying and giving in marriage, until the day that Noah entered the ark, and they did not understand until the flood came and took them all away; so shall the coming of the Son of Man be" (Matt. 24:37-39). Similarly Paul informs us that "the day of the Lord will come just like a thief in the night. While they are saying, 'Peace and safety!' then destruction will come upon them suddenly like birth pangs upon a woman with child; and they shall not escape" (1 Thess. 5:2b, 3).

But believers, undergoing great tribulation, longing for the return of Christ and looking for the signs, must remember that the *exact* time of the day of the Lord is *not* known, even to the most godly and discerning of saints. It was not even known by Jesus during His incarnation and is not known by the heavenly angels. "Of that day and hour no one knows," Jesus said, "not even the angels of heaven, nor the Son, but the Father alone" (Matt. 24:36). Christ explained to the disciples that "The days shall come [during the great tribulation by Antichrist] when you will long to see one of the days of the Son of Man. And you will not see it. And they will say to you, 'Look there! Look here!' Do not go away, and do not run after them. For just as the lightning, when it flashes out of one part of the sky, shines to the other part of the sky, so will the Son of Man be in His day" (Luke 17:22-24). Christ then told His disciples, in a parable, that during this time of great persecution, "they ought to pray and not to lose heart" (18:1). For if the unrighteous judge in the parable will eventually heed the cries of the widow, seeking legal protection from her opponent, "shall not God bring about justice for His elect, who cry to Him day and night, and will He delay long over them? I tell you that He will bring about justice for them speedily. However, when the Son of Man comes, will He find faith on the earth?" (18:7, 8). In other words, the return of Christ *cannot* be imminent* until two conditions exist. The first of these is the great tribulation by Antichrist. The second is the beginning of a second military campaign against the nation of Israel, undertaken by the surrounding Gentile nations.

---

* See chapter 16 and the Glossary for more discussion on the imminent return of Christ.

THE JEHOSHAPHAT CAMPAIGN

The major event, then, that believers will see happen just before the sign of the end of the age is given will be what this author calls the Jehoshaphat Campaign. The "Jehoshaphat Campaign" refers to the gathering of the nations in the valley of Jehoshaphat in preparation for a second military attack against Jerusalem, the first being the Jerusalem Campaign that occurred when Antichrist was revealed and took the throne in the Temple, demanding the worship of the world. As prophesied in the book of Joel, God will once again draw the nations surrounding Israel into the valley of Jehoshaphat, this time just before the day of the Lord actually begins. Thus the Lord proclaimed through the prophet Joel:

> For behold, in those days and at that time, when I restore the fortunes of Judah and Jerusalem, I will gather all the nations, and bring them down to the valley of Jehoshaphat. Then I will enter into judgment with them there on behalf of My people and My inheritance, Israel, whom they have scattered among the nations; and they have divided up My land. (Joel 3:1, 2; cf. Zech. 14:2)

A few verses later Joel continues,

> Proclaim this among the nations: prepare a war; rouse the mighty men! Let all the soldiers draw near, let them come up! . . . Let the nations be aroused and come up to the valley of Jehoshaphat, for there I will sit to judge all the surrounding nations. Put in the sickle, for the harvest is ripe. Come, tread, for the wine press is full; the vats overflow, for their wickedness is great. Multitudes, multitudes in the valley of decision! For the day of the Lord is near in the valley of decision. The sun and moon grow dark, and the stars lose their brightness. And the Lord roars from Zion and utters His voice from Jerusalem, and the heavens and the earth tremble. But the Lord is a refuge for His people and a stronghold to the sons of Israel. (Joel 3:9, 12-16)

As seen in these verses, the *Jehoshaphat Campaign* will begin when "the day of the Lord is near" (v. 14), and this distinguishes this battle from the two other military campaigns that will occur at different points during the end times.[4] The first of these, as discussed earlier, is the *Jerusalem Campaign* which will occur at the midpoint of the seventieth week — at which time Antichrist will move his armies against Jerusalem, set up his throne in the Temple, and demand the world's worship.

The second is the *Jehoshaphat Campaign* itself, a precursor to the day of the Lord and the return of Christ. This campaign will involve Gentile nations that surround the nation of Israel (see Zech. 12:6; Joel 3:11, 12). It is possible that these surrounding nations are actually the seven secondary nations that join the three-nation power base coalition of Antichrist. When the general locations of these seven nations are studied in relation to the city of Jerusalem, it becomes evident that they form a complete circle around the nation of Israel.* As prophesied by Joel, God will draw these nations together in the valley of Jehoshaphat just prior to the day of the Lord. This campaign will occur sometime during the second half of the seventieth week, just prior to when the great tribulation by Antichrist is cut short by God's day-of-the-Lord wrath.

The third campaign will be the *Armageddon Campaign*, which will take place after the seventieth week is complete, at the end of the day of the Lord. This will involve primarily the ungodly armies of the eighth beast empire and their battle against the righteous forces of Christ.

These three military campaigns, then, will occur at different points in the end times, and they must be properly distinguished and understood in order to avoid serious confusion. For the sake of clarity, therefore, these campaigns have been given these three different names, based on how they are described in Scripture.

The valley of Jehoshaphat is considered by most scholars to be the valley referred to in the Gospels as the Kidron Valley, which borders Jerusalem on the east side. Jehoshaphat means "Yahweh (or Jehovah) judges" and is therefore a particularly fitting designation. In Old Testament times, however, no valley was called Jehoshaphat, so Joel may therefore have been referring to the valley of Beracah — located about six miles southwest of Bethlehem — where King Jehoshaphat of Judah successfully fought against the forces of Ammon, Moab, and Mount Seir (see 2 Chron. 20:20-26). Whatever the exact location, the Lord will throw down His gauntlet against those arrogant and ungodly nations.

* See map on page 133.

As Zechariah reveals, "'In that day,' declares the Lord, 'I will strike every horse with bewilderment, and his rider with madness. But I will watch over the house of Judah, while I strike every horse of the peoples with blindness. . . . In that day I will make the clans of Judah like a firepot among pieces of wood and a flaming torch among sheaves, so they will consume on the right hand and on the left all the surrounding peoples, while the inhabitants of Jerusalem again dwell on their own sites in Jerusalem'" (Zech. 12:4, 6). This counteroffensive by the clans of Judah will be studied in greater depth in chapter 18.

For our purposes right now, the important thing to remember is that the Jehoshaphat Campaign will begin shortly before the day of the Lord, and that will be a further indication that this fearful day is about to come. This, then, is the last prophetic event given in Scripture that must occur before the return of Christ at the day of the Lord. And for that reason the sign of the end of the age, which is followed by the sign of Christ's coming, cannot occur until the Jehoshaphat Campaign has been initiated against Jerusalem. Then, and not before, will the return of Christ be "imminent."

THE SIXTH SEAL

The book of Revelation gives a perfect summary of the sign of the end of the age — that is, the sign which will "cut short" the great tribulation of Antichrist, which immediately precedes the day of the Lord, the end of the age, and which will be coupled perfectly with "the sign of Christ's coming." Immediately before the Lord takes His saints to be with Himself, the unbelieving world will be living in peace and security under Antichrist's protection. Suddenly and without warning, an astounding sign in the heavens will appear, announcing God's day of wrath and bringing terror into every person's heart except the elect of God. At that moment no human being, no matter how ungodly and skeptical, will fail to realize that God Almighty is about to take full control of His creation and render final judgment against evil. This will be the sign of the end of the age, vividly described in Revelation as the breaking of the sixth seal:

And I looked when He broke the sixth seal, and there was a great earthquake; and the sun became black as sackcloth made of hair, and the whole moon became like blood; and the stars of the sky fell to the earth, as a fig tree casts its unripe figs when shaken by a great wind. And the sky was split apart like a scroll when it is rolled up; and every mountain and island were moved out of their places. And the kings of the earth and the great men and the commanders and the rich and the strong and every slave and free man, hid themselves in the caves and among the rocks of the mountains; and they said to the mountains and to the rocks, "Fall on us and hide us from the presence of Him who sits on the throne, and from the wrath of the Lamb; *for the great day of their wrath has come;*[5] and who is able to stand?" (Rev. 6:12-17, emphasis added)

The earth's wicked will immediately recognize the awesome significance of the heavenly signs, because they will have been warned by the third angel's announcement, at the midpoint of the seventieth week. Thus John explains later, "If anyone worships the beast and his image, and receives a mark on his forehead or upon his hand, he also will drink of the wine of the wrath of God, which is mixed in full strength in the cup of His anger; and he will be tormented with fire and brimstone in the presence of the holy angels and in the presence of the Lamb" (Rev. 14:9, 10).

It is that "hour of His judgment," heralded to all the world by the first angel (Rev. 14:7), of which Isaiah prophesied long ago: "In that day men will cast away to the moles and the bats their idols [images of the beast] of silver and their idols of gold, which they made for themselves to worship, in order to go into the caverns of the rocks and the clefts of the cliffs, before the terror of the Lord and the splendor of His majesty, when He arises to make the earth tremble" (Isa. 2:20, 21).

There will be great terror for the wicked on earth who have been repeatedly warned of the consequences of worshiping the image and taking the mark of Antichrist. Thus "men [will faint] from fear," Jesus said, "and the expectation of the things which are coming upon the world" (Luke 21:26).

But for the overcomer, the genuine believer who has survived the onslaught of Antichrist and who has carefully watched for the signs of Christ's return, there will be blessed hope, great expectation, and a completely different response. "When these things begin to take place," Jesus said, "straighten up and lift up your heads, because your redemption is drawing near" (Luke 21:28). And just as the end of the age will be heralded by this first cataclysmic sign in the heavens, so an even more stunning sign will immediately follow — the sign of Christ's coming for the redemption of the elect — to which we now turn in the following chapter.

15

The Sign of Christ's Coming

With the earth cast into utter darkness and the world still in terror at the sign of the end of the age, the second sign — the sign of Christ's coming — will immediately follow. "Then the sign of the Son of Man will appear in the sky," Jesus said, "and . . . all the tribes of the earth will mourn, and they will see the Son of Man coming on the clouds of the sky with power and great glory" (Matt. 24:30). And Jesus explained just a few verses earlier, "For just as the lightning comes from the east, and flashes even to the west, so shall the coming of the Son of Man be" (v. 27).

SUPERNATURAL BRILLIANCE

Just as the disciples' question linked these two signs together — "What will be the sign of Your coming, and [what will be the sign] of the end of the age?" (v. 3) — so these two signs will be interlocked with each other, the first leading immediately to the second. For first, all the *natural* lights in the heavens will be extinguished by the sign of the end, plunging the world into total darkness; and then in stunning contrast the darkened natural lights will be replaced by the *supernatural* brilliance of the sign of the Son of Man when He comes.

It is, of course, the sign of the Son of Man, the sign of the coming of the Lord Jesus Christ, which all believers long to behold. But the sign of the end of the age must appear first — as a warning to the unbelieving world of the imminent day of the Lord's judgment, but also as the first divine evidence to believers, in hiding or directly undergoing the terrible persecution of Antichrist, that the return of their Lord and therefore their "rescue" is at hand (2 Pet. 2:9).

Every Eye Will See

After the natural lights are turned off all over the world, the supernatural light of God's holy splendor will return to earth from the east, flooding the world with the radiance of Christ as He returns in power and great glory. The majesty glory of Christ's second coming is the sign every true overcomer has looked for since Christ ascended to His Father some forty days after His resurrection. Every eye on earth — even the despicably evil eyes of Antichrist and his wicked hosts — will clearly witness the return of Christ. Thus John describes the return of Christ with these words: "Behold, He is coming with the clouds, and every eye will see Him, even those who pierced Him" (Rev. 1:7). His return will be anything but secret or unobtrusive. It will be an unequaled spectacular event that "every eye shall see" and that every ear will hear, when "the Lord Himself will descend from heaven with a shout, with the voice of the archangel, and with the trumpet of God" (1 Thess. 4:16).

When Christ returns, He will come to judge the unrighteous of the earth, all who have rejected His grace by passing Satan's test, choosing rather to worship the beast or his image. But when Christ returns He will also come to bring final redemption to the overcomers, to all those who have put their unwavering trust in Him.

So that all would know the true sign of His coming and be able to distinguish it from the many false signs that will abound in the last days (Matt. 24:26), Jesus declared that "just as the lightning comes from the east, and flashes even to the west, so shall the *coming* of the Son of Man be" (v. 27, emphasis added). Immediately after all natural light in the heavens is extinguished (v. 29), the true sign of the coming of Christ will exhibit itself in an immeasurably immense flash of supernatural light that will come from the east and encompass and illumine the earth in an instant. Astounding and indescribable as it will be, that vast radiance will be but the precursor and partial reflection of the infinite divine glory which will be revealed in the heavenlies when Christ appears, when every man, woman, and child on earth "will see the Son of Man coming on the clouds of the sky with power and great glory" (Matt. 24:30).

THE GLORIOUS APPEARING OF CHRIST

In describing Christ's second coming, Scripture uses a number of dramatic words and descriptions. For example as recorded in Luke, Jesus said: "For just as the lightning, when it flashes out of one part of the sky, shines to the other part of the sky, so will the Son of Man be in His day. . . . It will be just the same on the day that the Son of Man is revealed" (Luke 17:24, 30). The word rendered "is revealed" in this passage is the Greek verb *apokaluptó*, which refers basically to a revealing or uncovering, but may also express the idea of manifestation. Similarly Paul frequently speaks of Christ's "appearing," which in the Greek is *epiphaneia* and expresses the idea of "a shining forth," "a brightness," or "a manifestation." Thus Paul exhorts Timothy, "I solemnly charge you in the presence of God and of Christ Jesus, who is to judge the living and the dead, and by his appearing [*epiphaneia*] and His kingdom . . . in the future there is laid up for me the crown of righteousness, which the Lord, the righteous Judge, will award to me on that day; and not only to me, but also to all who have loved his appearing [*epiphaneia*]" (2 Tim. 4:1, 8). Lastly, "appear" is often used to translate the Greek word *phaneroó*, which can carry the idea of "lighten" or "shine" as well — as, for example, when the Apostle John admonishes believers, "And now, little children, abide in Him so that when He appears [*phaneroó*], we may have confidence and not shrink away from Him in shame at His coming" (1 John 2:28).

When we take these terms together, we get a sense of how dramatic and spectacular the coming of Christ will be. His coming will be a "manifestation," a "revealing," a sudden "appearance"; it will be accompanied by a shining brightness, His glory. Although the second coming of Christ will be a physical and literal return, it will also be profoundly different from His first coming. It will not be a "coming" in the sense of going from one place to another, but rather the brilliant, shining manifestation of Christ, sweeping instantaneously across the earth's atmosphere when He comes for His own. When the sign of the Son of Man is seen in the heavens, God's glory will shatter the vast blackness caused by the sign of the day of the Lord. As Jesus said in His own words, then "they will see the Son of Man coming in a cloud with power and great glory" (Luke 21:27).

PARTAKERS OF HIS GLORY

For nearly two thousand years, faithful saints of God have been "looking for the blessed hope and *the appearing of the glory* of our great God and Savior, Christ Jesus" (Titus 2:13, emphasis added). Upheld in that hope by the power of the indwelling Spirit, they willingly *"share the sufferings of Christ*, [and] *keep on rejoicing; so that also at the revelation of His glory*, [they] may rejoice with exultation" (1 Pet. 4:13, emphasis added). Because of God's superabundant grace, believers not only will rejoice in the manifested glory of their Savior and "stand in the presence of His glory blameless with great joy" (Jude 24), but will even be actual partakers of that glory (1 Pet. 5:1; cf. Col. 3:4). Even compromising believers who enter the seventieth week will share in that glory, having been made pure and blameless by the refining persecution of the great tribulation by Antichrist.

Yet the same divine glory that will infuse God's saints will obliterate His enemies, commencing with Antichrist, "whom the Lord will slay with the breath of His mouth and bring to an end by the appearance of His coming" (2 Thess. 2:8).

CONFIRMED IN THE OLD TESTAMENT

Numerous Old Testament passages reveal that the Messiah will come to judge the world, restore the nation of Israel, and establish His earthly kingdom. Although many messianic prophecies were a mystery even to faithful Jews in Jesus' day, they did clearly understand that the Lord's coming to judge and to reign would be accompanied by great glory. They were well acquainted with Isaiah's warning to the ungodly that "in the last days" (Isa. 2:2), during God's "day of reckoning" (v. 12), "men will go into caves of the rocks, and into holes of the ground before the terror of the Lord, and before *the splendor of His majesty*, when He arises to make the earth tremble" (v. 19, emphasis added). They were also well acquainted with, and greatly rejoiced in, that same prophet's promise to God's faithful people in the last days: "Arise, *shine; for your light has come*, and *the glory of the Lord* has risen upon you. *For behold, darkness will cover the earth, and deep darkness the peoples* [the sign of the end of the age]; but the Lord will rise upon you, and *His glory will appear upon you* [the sign of Christ's coming]. And nations will come to your light, and kings to the brightness of your rising" (Isa. 60:1-3, emphasis added).

Both the warning and the promise vividly depict the awesome divine glory that will accompany the return of the Lord. But whereas "the splendor of His majesty" will fill the godless with unspeakable terror, it will fill the Lord's faithful with unspeakable joy and gladness, as Christ's own glory not only comes upon them but shines through them for all the world to see.

Other prophets also speak of the manifestation of God's glory at the return of the Lord, and they disclose the same sequence of events. In his vision of the angelic surveyor Zechariah was told:

> "'For I,' declares the Lord, 'will be a wall of fire around her [Jerusalem], and *I will be the glory* in her midst.'" "Ho there! Flee from the land of the north," declares the Lord, "for I have dispersed you as the four winds of the heavens," declares the Lord. "Ho, Zion! Escape, you who are living with the daughter of Babylon." For thus says the Lord of hosts, "*After glory* He has sent me against the nations which plunder you [during the day of the Lord], for he who touches you, touches the apple of His eye. . . . Then you [Israel] will know that the Lord of hosts has sent Me. Sing for joy and be glad, O daughter of Zion; for behold I am coming and I will dwell in your midst," declares the Lord. (Zech. 2:5-10, emphasis added)

Even the Psalms portray the interrelationship of God's glory and the judgment of the wicked and the final redemption of His people. Speaking of the end times as if they had already transpired, the psalmist wrote:

> The Lord reigns; let the earth rejoice; let the many islands be glad. Clouds and thick darkness surround Him; righteousness and justice are the foundation of His throne. *Fire* goes before Him, and burns up His adversaries round about. His *lightnings lit up the world*; the earth saw and trembled. The mountains melted like wax at the presence of the Lord, at the presence of the Lord of the whole earth. The heavens declare His righteousness, and all the peoples have seen His *glory*. (Ps. 97:1-6, emphasis added)

GOD'S GLORY IN ANCIENT ISRAEL

Further evidence that the sign of Christ's coming is the supernatural manifestation of God's glory is found in the scriptural history of Israel.

From the time the Tabernacle was built under the direction of Moses until an unspecified time later (probably during the Babylonian Captivity in the sixth century B.C.), God's glory was present in the Tabernacle and later in the Temple. God's glory was present in a way that was unique (localized and restricted) and by its very nature beyond human understanding. Moreover, God's glory was not visible even to the high priests, because to have beheld His glory would have been to die (Exod. 33:20).

The prophet Ezekiel had the heartrending task of reporting the departure of God's glory from the Temple because of the continued and unrepented sinfulness of Israel. In his vision of the four wheels, Ezekiel witnessed the glory of the Lord going "up from the cherub to the threshold of the temple, and the temple was filled with the cloud, and the court was filled with the brightness of the glory of the Lord" (10:4). But the glory continued to move further away, as it "departed from the threshold of the temple and stood over the cherubim. When the cherubim departed, they lifted their wings and rose up from the earth in my sight with the wheels beside them; and they stood still at the entrance of the east gate of the Lord's house." Moving with the cherubim, "the glory of the God of Israel" now hovered with them over the east gate, still further from its original dwelling place (10:18, 19). Finally "the cherubim lifted up their wings with the wheels beside them, and the glory of the God of Israel [still] hovered over them. And the glory of the Lord went up from the midst of the city, and stood over the mountain which is east of the city" (11:22, 23).

At that point Ezekiel's vision ended, and we can safely assume that the glory ascended from the Mount of Olives ("the mountain which is east of the city") to Heaven, from which it came.

Ezekiel later had the privilege of also predicting the return of God's glory to earth. Ezekiel is given a supernatural tour, as it were, of the restored Temple. After an extensive tour of the Temple Ezekiel reports that he was led "to the gate, the gate facing toward the east; and behold, the glory of the God of Israel was coming from the way of the east. And His voice was like the sound of many waters; *and the earth shone with His glory*" (43:1, 2a, emphasis added). It becomes quickly evident that the Lord's glory will return in exactly the reverse order and path by which it departed! It will return first when Christ is revealed at His second coming and later when He returns to rule over Israel.

The prophet goes on to say that "the glory of the Lord came into the house [that is, the Temple] by the way of the gate facing toward the east. And the Spirit lifted me up and brought me into the inner court; and behold, *the glory of the Lord filled the house*" (vv. 4, 5, emphasis added). And so the glory will return "from the way of the east . . . and the earth [will shine] with His glory"; and then "the glory of the Lord [will come] into the house by the way of the gate facing toward the east."

In the Olivet Discourse, Jesus clearly described those two separate, glorious events. First, "Just as the lightning *comes from the east*, and flashes even to the west . . . then the sign of the Son of Man will appear in the sky, and then all the tribes of the earth will mourn, and they will see the Son of Man coming on the clouds of the sky *with power and great glory*" (Matt. 24:27, 30, emphasis added). This glorious coming of Christ *"from the east"* will occur at the beginning of the day of the Lord. Second, "When the Son of Man comes *in His glory*, and all the angels with Him, then He will sit on His glorious throne" (Matt. 25:31, emphasis added). This glorious coming of Christ will occur on the first day of the Millennium.

YOUR REDEMPTION DRAWETH NIGH

As we have seen in the last three chapters, the great tribulation by Antichrist will be a time of great suffering for the true church of Christ. The faithful church is promised protection "within the sphere of danger," the great hour of testing that is to come on the whole earth. On the other hand, many within the compromising church will be unprepared for the events that occur during the seventieth week and will be thrown into "great tribulation," as Christ "searches the minds and hearts" of every person naming His name (Rev. 2:22, 23).

Those who are well taught will be forewarned and will have opportunity to be prepared as Antichrist tries to lure them out of hiding with false christs and false prophets. Christ specifically warns them not to move until they see the "sign of the end of the age" and "of His coming," which will occur in immediate succession, back to back. First, the natural lights in the heavens will be extinguished, and that fearsome event will be accompanied by worldwide earthquakes, in order that

274 ■ *The Sign*

every person alive will know that it is the sign of the day of the Lord. Then the glory of the Lord will return "just as the lightning comes from the east, and flashes even to the west," illuminating the pitch blackness with a brilliance so that "every eye will see Him."

In summary then, the signs given for the end of the age and for Christ's return will have different effects upon different individuals during the great tribulation by Antichrist. Those who have passed the test of Satan — that is, those who have worshiped the enemy — will be gripped by incredible fear; those who have chosen to be true to Christ, no matter how severe the persecution, will know incredible joy. Although already quoted several times in the past two chapters, Christ's summary as recorded in the Gospel of Luke says it best:

> "... there will be signs in sun and moon and stars, and upon the earth dismay among nations, in perplexity at the roaring of the sea and the waves, *men fainting from fear and the expectation of the things which are coming upon the world;* for the powers of the heavens will be shaken. And then they will see the Son of Man coming in a cloud with power and great glory. *But when these things begin to take place, straighten up and lift up your heads, because your redemption is drawing near.*" (Luke 21:25-28, emphasis added)

Charles Haddon Spurgeon, the great English preacher of the nineteenth century, has never been known to be a preacher who spoke extensively concerning the end times. But what he did say showed a remarkable understanding concerning the interrelationship of the events developed in the past several chapters and summed up beautifully in the passage above. The following are excerpts from his sermon entitled "Joyful Anticipation of the Second Advent."

> I must leave this first point, concerning the terrible time [a time of fearful national trouble] when this precept is to be carried out, by just reminding you that, when the Lord Jesus Christ shall come, the heavens shall tell us: "There shall be signs in the sun, and in the moon, and in the stars." ...
> Now I come to THE REMARKABLE PRECEPT itself: "Then look up, and lift up your heads." ...
> Let there be no looking down because the earth is quaking and shaking, but let there be a looking up because you are going to rise from it; no looking down because the graves are opening;

why should you look down? You will quit the grave, never more to die. "Lift up your heads." The time for you to hang your heads, like bulrushes, is over already, and will certainly be over when the Lord is coming, and your redemption draweth nigh. Wherefore, "look up, and lift up your heads."[1]

Hallelujah!

16

The Prewrath Rapture
of the Church:
Part I

The scene is set for the return of Christ — for the deliverance of the righteous and the judgment of the wicked — events which will be so closely connected as to be virtually simultaneous. And so the day of the Lord will begin — as Christ returns for rapture and judgment.

The timing of the Rapture is of the utmost importance to the church. Sadly, much of the church today is seriously mistaken about the specific timing of the Rapture as it relates to the great tribulation of Antichrist or else is inclined to historicalize or spiritualize this essential teaching. The correct timing of the Rapture, however, is *clearly revealed* by Christ in His Olivet Discourse, is confirmed through Paul in his Thessalonian epistles, and verified further by John in the book of Revelation.

As mentioned in the first chapter of this volume, all the prophecies concerning Christ's first coming were fulfilled literally in every detail, and the prophecies of His second coming will, of course, be fulfilled just as perfectly and completely. This writer cannot understand how any Christian who acknowledges the inerrancy of Scripture could believe otherwise. Yet many sincere Bible students, who are careful to interpret God's Word in its literal and normal sense in most areas of doctrine, modify that standard in various degrees when dealing with the timing of the Rapture and other closely related end-time events.*

Rightly understood, the prewrath view is the only view supported by the New Testament if one's hermeneutic is truly literal. The essence of the prewrath position is that Christ will rapture His church *immediately after* He cuts short the great tribulation by Antichrist and *immediately before* He unleashes His day-of-the-Lord judgment on the ungodly world. In other words, the church *must* be prepared for the fiery testing that the whole earth will undergo since those who fail Satan's test will be subject to the great persecution by Antichrist. As discussed at some length in the previous two chapters, the sign of the end of the age and the sign of Christ's coming occur back to back — the first sign precipitating the second, both signs cutting short the great tribulation by Antichrist against God's elect, both signs precipitating "the Son of Man['s] coming on the clouds of the sky with power and great glory."

This is the heart of the issue. Either the church goes through the severe persecution by Antichrist or it doesn't. This entire volume has tried to warn the believer that he (or she) must be prepared for this time of unparalleled distress. So far we have worked through the biblical sequence of events, including the persecution of Antichrist against "the woman and the rest of her offspring who keep the commandments of God and hold to the testimony of Jesus," right up to the sign of Christ's coming. Every biblical passage developed in some depth thus far has supported the concerns of this writer. If our premise is correct, the very next event in this sequence of events must be the Rapture; but more than this, it must be a clear teaching of the New Testament, not a position such as pretribulationalism whose defenders admit in writing that it is not "an explicit teaching of the Scriptures" that "the Bible does not, in so many words, state" or whose "proof at times has been logically invalid or at least unconvincing" (see chapter 10, endnote 5). Because the majority of the church's teaching today either removes the church before the great tribulation or simply allegorizes this critical truth, I have chosen at this point to slow the movement of this book and focus on this critical issue, carefully going through the biblical defense for the prewrath

* See further chapter 10, "The Seventieth Week Cannot Equate with the Day of the Lord" section.

position. To those who are more concerned about the clear teaching of Scripture than clinging to a system with no clear biblical support, the prewrath position does indeed offer "an explicit teaching of Scripture, logically valid and convincing." If the prewrath position *is* the biblical position, which it is, the consequences of faulty thinking will be devastating.

The purpose, then, of this present chapter is to understand the unequivocal teaching of Scripture as to when the Rapture will occur. Thus we will see, *first*, that the Rapture occurs on the same day that the Lord begins to pour out His wrath of judgment on the world; and, *second*, that these back-to-back events (rapture and judgment) can only occur when God cuts short the great tribulation of Antichrist. Although these conclusions have been developed already throughout the preceding chapters, we now turn to an explicit and systematic presentation of what the Scriptures consistently teach concerning these truths.

RAPTURE AND WRATH ON THE SAME DAY

The previous two chapters have established the interrelationship of the sign of the end of the age and the sign of Christ's coming and have already given considerable evidence that the Rapture and the day of the Lord must occur on the same day, sometime during the second half of the seventieth week. As we study the Scriptures further, we see conclusively that when Christ comes again He will first rescue His church and then destroy the world, both actions occurring back to back, on the very same day. *The Rapture will, in effect, activate the wrath.*

This is an important issue to understand. If these two events occur on the same day, this fact destroys the imminency of Christ's return, the heart of the pretribulationalist position. The imminency of Christ's return, as understood and taught today by those who attempt to keep the church out of the seventieth week, means that Christ could return "any moment" since His departure recorded in Acts 1:9-11. According to the imminency view, nothing prophetically has had to occur since the Ascension, since Christ's second coming has always been imminent and could occur at any moment. On the other hand, if both these events (rapture and judgment) occur on the same day, the doctrine of imminency is destroyed since important events would need to occur prior to our Lord's return. In this case the day of the Lord cannot occur until Israel is back in her own land. And as the wrath of God is against the unrighteous inhabitants and armies of Satan's earthly kingdom, Antichrist and his eighth beast empire must likewise be on the world's scene when Christ returns for rapture and judgment. Therefore, if the Rapture of the church and the day of the Lord occur on the same day, the imminent return of Christ has been impossible for the past two thousand years. Therefore, the fact that rapture and wrath occur on the same day is important. We will begin by looking at the teaching of Christ on this issue.

TAUGHT SPECIFICALLY BY CHRIST

In a discussion Christ had with His disciples prior to His Olivet Discourse, He specifically told them that the two events, the Rapture and the wrath, will occur *on the very same day*. The discussion begins with a passage we have already looked at several times — a passage which refers specifically to the time when the true disciples of Christ will undergo great persecution, looking anxiously for the return of Christ. It is the perfect summary of all we have worked through in the past several chapters.

> "The days shall come when you will long to see one of the days of the Son of Man, and you will not see it. And they will say to you, 'Look there! Look here!' Do not go away, and do not run after them. For just as the lightning, when it flashes out of one part of the sky, shines to the other part of the sky, so will the Son of Man be in His day. . . . *And just as it happened in the days of Noah, so it shall be also in the days of the Son of Man*: they were eating, they were drinking, they were marrying, they were being given in marriage, *until the day that Noah entered the ark*, and the flood came and destroyed them all. *It was the same as happened in the days of Lot*: they were eating, they were drinking, they were buying, they were selling, they were planting, they were building; *but on the day that Lot went out from Sodom it rained fire and brimstone from heaven and destroyed them all. It will be just the same on the day that the Son of Man is revealed*." (Luke 17:22-24, 26-30, emphasis added)

In this writer's opinion, it could not be clearer. Christ explains that the Son of Man will be revealed (referring directly to the sign of Christ's coming [v. 24]), *on the same day* that God's judgment of the unrighteous will begin — just as in the days of Noah and as in the days of Lot. Yet some interpreters refuse this clear, simple teaching of Christ, attempting to show a time gap between the Rapture and the day-of-the-Lord judgment by attempting to "explain away" the clear teaching of Christ's illustration concerning Noah and the Flood.[1] In this attempt, then, they appeal to the Flood story in Genesis where God commanded Noah:

> "Enter the ark, you and all your household; for you alone I have seen to be righteous before Me in this time. You shall take with you of every clean animal by sevens, a male and his female; and of the animals that are not clean two, a male and his female. . . . For after seven more days, I will send rain on the earth forty days and forty nights; and I will blot out from the face of the land every living thing that I have made." (Gen. 7:1, 2, 4)

The argument is made that the phrase "after seven more days, I will send rain on the earth" means that Noah and his family entered the ark seven days before God's wrath came.[2] Therefore, what Christ specifically says occurred on the same day, they maintain, did not actually happen on the same day, but instead included a seven-day gap. Such a conclusion, however, not only contradicts the clear teaching of Christ, it is based upon Scripture taken out of context. For as the Genesis text goes on to explain, Noah's entering the ark with his family was in fact "on the very same day" that "the fountains of the deep burst open."

> In the six hundredth year of Noah's life, in the second month, on the seventeenth day of the month, *on the same day* all the fountains of the great deep burst open, and the floodgates of the sky were opened. And the rain fell upon the earth for forty days and forty nights. *On the very same day Noah and Shem and Ham and Japheth, the sons of Noah, and Noah's wife and the three wives of his sons with them, entered the ark.* (Gen. 7:11-13, emphasis added)

In other words, the rescue of Noah and his family occurred *on the same day* that the rains of judgment began to fall — which "will be just the same," Jesus said, "on the day that the Son of Man is revealed" (Luke 17:30).

The disciples understood that truth, as we see in their question to Christ that generated the Olivet Discourse: "Tell us, when will these things be, and what will be the sign of Your coming, and of the end of the age?" (Matt. 24:3). Again, as mentioned in chapter 14, the disciples understood the right sequence of events even though the signs will occur in reverse order of the events — something they had no way of knowing until Christ explained the interrelationship of the two signs to them. They knew that Christ's coming and the end of the age were inseparably connected — that His coming initiated the end of the age (the day of the Lord). Doubtless the disciples recalled the teaching of Christ that these two events would occur on the same day, and they therefore wanted to know how to recognize the signs that would signal that great two-part event.

CONFIRMED BY PETER

It would almost seem as if the Holy Spirit intended to underscore the importance of this truth when we see the same illustrations used by Peter:

> . . . and [if God] did not spare the ancient world, but preserved Noah, a preacher of righteousness, with seven others, when He brought a flood upon the world of the ungodly; and if He condemned the cities of Sodom and Gomorrah to destruction by reducing them to ashes, having made them an example to those who would live ungodly thereafter; and if He rescued righteous Lot, oppressed by the sensual conduct of unprincipled men . . . then the Lord knows how to rescue the godly from temptation [i.e., from testing],[3] and to keep the unrighteous under punishment for the day of judgment. (2 Pet. 2:5-7, 9)

Peter simply repeats what he had been taught by his Lord — the truth that when Christ returns, He will come to simultaneously rescue His saints and destroy the wicked.

One "Taken" and the Other "Left"   As we have just seen in the foregoing sections, the illustration of Noah's rescue before the world was destroyed by water is used to describe the back-to-back timing of the rapture of the church and the judgment of God. Peter uses it in the passage quoted just above, and Christ used the illustration to show that both events occurred on the same day (Luke 17). When He delivered His Olivet Discourse a few days later, He used the same illustration once again. Yet some, in order to preserve a system unsupported by

Scripture, must again somehow distort the clear intent of Christ's illustration, making it applicable to the battle of Armageddon instead of the Rapture, and thereby claiming that the one "taken" is taken to judgment and the one "left" is left behind to enter into the millennial kingdom of Christ.[4]

In response to this position, we need only to look carefully at the illustration itself, in particular the very words of Christ. In response to the disciples' question "What will be the sign of your coming?" Christ illustrates His teaching concerning His "coming" by giving the example of Noah and the Flood. "For the coming of the Son of Man will be just like the days of Noah. . . . And they [the world] did not understand until the flood came and took them all away, so shall the coming of the Son of Man be. Then [at His coming] there shall be two men in the field; one will be taken, and one will be left. Two women will be grinding at the mill; one will be taken, and one will be left" (Matt. 24:37, 39-41; cf. Luke 17:34-36). When the one is "taken," the other is "left."

The meaning of this passage in this context clearly is that those who are "taken" are taken to be with the Lord at the Rapture when He comes (see 1 Thess. 4:15), and those that are "left" are left for judgment "like [in] the days of Noah" — again indicating that the Rapture and judgment will occur back to back. This is exactly as Peter understood it, as seen in the previous section, when the godly are "rescued" and the unrighteous are left for "punishment."

This is confirmed further when we look at the Greek term translated as "taken." In both instances the word "taken" is *paralambanō*, which means to "receive near, that is, to associate with oneself (in any familiar or intimate act or relation)."[5] Christ uses the term only six times in reference to future events. He uses it twice in Matthew 24:40, 41 and three times in Luke 17:34-36, each instance referring to one person being taken and another being left behind. The other time Christ uses the word is in the beautiful promise to His followers that

> "In My Father's house are many dwelling places; if it were not so,
> I would have told you; for I go to prepare a place for you. And if
> I go and prepare a place for you, I will come again, and *receive*
> *[paralambanō] you to Myself*; that where I am, there you may be
> also." (John 14:2, 3, emphasis added)

In light of the meaning of *paralambanō* as found in John 14, we see that, in these verses from Luke and Matthew, "taken" carries the sense of "being received" — that is, of being received by Christ, as in the case of John 14:2, 3. As we continue, we will see that when believers are received by Christ in the clouds at the Rapture of the church, it will be the angels of God who "gather the wheat into My barn" (Matt. 13:30) and who "gather together His elect from the four winds, from one end of the sky to the other" (Matt. 24:31), and that "we who are alive and remain shall be caught up together with them in the clouds, to meet the Lord in the air" (1 Thess. 4:17). Then, as in the days of Noah, God will destroy those who are "left" during His fiery day-of-the-Lord judgment of the world, "when the Lord Jesus shall be revealed from heaven with His mighty angels in flaming fire, dealing out retribution to those who do not know God" (2 Thess. 1:7, 8).

CONFIRMED BY PAUL

The classic rapture passage in the New Testament, quoted in part just above, is found in 1 Thessalonians 4. In this passage Paul begins by comforting the confused Thessalonian believers concerning their believing loved ones who had died:

> But we do not want you to be uninformed, brethren, about those who are asleep, that you may not grieve, as do the rest who have no hope. For if we believe that Jesus died and rose again, even so God will bring with Him those who have fallen asleep in Jesus. For this we say to you by the word of the Lord, that we who are alive, and remain until the coming of the Lord, shall not precede those who have fallen asleep. (1 Thess. 4:13-15)

Here Paul explains that not only those believers who had recently died but *all* believers who had or would die before Christ's second coming will be taken by resurrection to their Lord just before the living are raptured. Paul gives greater weight to that promise by declaring that he is speaking "by the word of the Lord," which is undoubtedly a reference to Jesus' teaching in the Olivet Discourse and in His earlier discourse recorded in Luke 17.

After first mentioning "the coming of the Lord" in verse 15, Paul goes on to describe the Rapture in detail in verses 16 and 17. In anticipation of the obvious question of the church, "When will this happen?" Paul replies "Now as to the times and the epochs, brethren, you have no need of anything to be written to you" (5:1). Paul then immediately links the return of Christ to the day of the Lord, when Christ will come in judgment — "like a thief in the night" — as seen in the verses that follow: "For you yourselves know full well that the day of the Lord will come just like a thief in the night. While they are saying 'Peace and safety!' then destruction will come on them suddenly . . ." (vv. 2, 3a). It is noteworthy, in fact, that this reference to "a thief in the night" links together four other passages all of which refer to the Lord coming in judgment, as found in Luke 12:39, 40, 2 Peter 3:10, Revelation 3:3, and 16:15.

Again, the sequence of events recorded in 1 Thessalonians 4 and 5 is both critical and clear. Paul clearly teaches that the taking of believers and the destruction of unbelievers will occur on the same day. Similarly, as in Jesus' and Peter's comparisons to the times of Noah and Lot, the judgment of unbelievers will come upon them totally unexpected, just like a thief in the night.

In summary then, based on the unequivocal teaching of the New Testament — as seen by the teaching of Christ in both the Olivet Discourse and His earlier discussions with His disciples recorded in Luke 17, and as confirmed by Peter in his second epistle and again by Paul to the church of Thessalonica — the only possible conclusion is that Christ will return to simultaneously rapture the church and unleash His wrath of judgment upon the ungodly. We must therefore conclude that nothing will separate the Rapture and the beginning of judgment when Christ returns on the day of the Lord. Therefore, by definition all of the conditions and events discussed in chapter 9 *must be in place, at a minimum*, before the Christian can expect to see the return of Christ. The return of Christ has never been imminent and will never be imminent until the great tribulation of Antichrist begins and the surrounding Gentile nations come together against Jerusalem in the valley of Jehoshaphat. Only then are the elect of God told to look for the sign of Christ's coming, which will be seen in the heavens. And that sign will not be given until the earth is first plunged into darkness by the sign of the end of the age. Thus the unequivocal teaching of Scripture is that back-to-back signs will announce back-to-back events — first the rescue of the true church and then the destruction of the wicked. But none of this will happen until after the great tribulation of Antichrist has begun. "For after all it is only just for God to repay with affliction those who afflict you, and to give relief to you who are afflicted and to us as well when the Lord Jesus shall be revealed from heaven with His mighty angels in flaming fire, dealing out retribution to those who do not know God and to those who do not obey the gospel of our Lord Jesus" (2 Thess. 1:6-8).

CHRIST'S COMING FOLLOWS THE GREAT TRIBULATION

It is important to understand that the Rapture and the day of the Lord occur on the same day, but it is far more important to understand, as the New Testament clearly teaches, that Christ's second coming will not occur until after the great tribulation by Antichrist has begun. *The return of Christ will be imminent only during the great tribulation by Antichrist, only after the Gentile nations begin to assemble in the valley of Jehoshaphat, and not one day before.* As pointed out in chapter 1,* the position not only of the New Testament church but also of the leading church fathers of the first several centuries (with the exception of Origen and Clement of Alexandria, who allegorized much of Scripture) was that *the church would go through the great tribulation by Antichrist.* Since this is indeed true, the true church of Christ must be prepared for these terrible days of persecution.

THE COMING (*PAROUSIA*) OF CHRIST

Before we look at the clear teaching of the New Testament concerning the timing of Christ's return, one word of clarification must be made which will bring incredible simplicity to this critical defense. When referring to the second coming of Christ, invariably the Greek word *parousia* is used. This particular word does not indicate movement from one place to the next, but, as a noun, speaks more to the overall event of Christ's second coming. It carries the basic meaning of "presence." Therefore, within the scope of the second coming (*parousia*) of Christ as an event, there will be various comings and goings of Christ, but in those cases a different Greek word is used.[6] However, the *parousia* of Christ *always* refers to the event in general. There will only be one "second coming" or "*parousia*" of Christ, not two.** Keeping that simple fact in mind will bring total harmony to the teaching of the New Testament concerning the timing of Christ's *parousia*.

TAUGHT SPECIFICALLY BY CHRIST

In the last two chapters, which describe the signs of the end of the age and of Christ's coming, we carefully followed the sequence of events Christ gave in His Olivet Discourse.[7]*** First of all, in response

* See especially chapter 1, endnote 3.
** See further chapter 1, endnote 2.
*** See the extensive defense in endnote 7 of this chapter, which establishes that the teaching of the Olivet Discourse is intended for the church and not just for the Jews as claimed by some interpreters.

to the disciples' question, "What will be the sign of Your coming [*parousia*], and of the end of the age?" (Matt. 24:3), Jesus said,

> "For just as the lightning comes from the east, and flashes even to the west, so shall the coming [*parousia*] of the Son of Man be. . . . But immediately after the [great] tribulation of those days the sun will be darkened, and the moon will not give its light, and the stars will fall from the sky, and the powers of the heavens will be shaken, and then the sign of the Son of Man will appear in the sky, and then all the tribes of the earth will mourn, and they will see the Son of Man coming on the clouds of the sky with power and great glory. And He will send forth His angels with a great trumpet and they will gather together His elect from the four winds, from one end of the sky to the other. (Matt. 24:27, 29-31)[8]

This critical passage from the Olivet Discourse recorded by Matthew virtually sums up everything developed thus far in this book relating to "the blessed hope and the appearing of the glory of our great God and Savior, Christ Jesus" (Titus 2:13). The *timing* of His return that Christ gave the disciples in response to their question clearly placed His coming (*parousia*) *after* the great tribulation by Antichrist. The sequence of events described in the Olivet Discourse could not be more explicit. First Jesus described the "birth-pangs" (Matt. 24:4-8), then He described the "great tribulation" (vv. 9-26), and then He described His glorious *parousia* (vv. 27-30) for rapture (v. 31) and for judgment (vv. 32-51). In Jesus own words, the timing of His *parousia* is "immediately after the tribulation of those days" (v. 29), which, as Christ had already promised, would be "cut short . . . for the sake of the elect" (v. 22).

The only viable conclusion, based on Christ's own teaching in the Olivet Discourse, is that the church will indeed go through the great tribulation by Antichrist and that the great tribulation will be cut short[9] by the day of the Lord, at Christ's coming (*parousia*) to rapture the church and judge the world.

CONFIRMED BY PAUL

Paul's critical teaching about the timing of the Rapture in his two epistles to the Thessalonians also perfectly coincides with Jesus' teaching in the Olivet Discourse. But whereas the first letter to the

Thessalonians deals with the fact that the Rapture and the day-of-the-Lord judgment will occur at the coming (*parousia*) of Christ (4:15) — i.e., back to back, at the same time — Paul's second letter to this church specifically pinpoints the exact timing of those two events in relation to the activity of Antichrist.

The Thessalonian Christians understood from Paul's previous teaching in his first epistle and his ministry in their church that they would endure severe persecution before being graciously raptured by the Lord just before His day-of-the-Lord judgment (see 2 Thess. 1:4-10). But, not unlike today, false teachers had come into the church and had seriously confused the believers about those truths. And so Paul cautions the Thessalonian believers,

> Now we request you, brethren, with regard to the coming [*parousia*] of our Lord Jesus Christ, and our gathering together to Him, that you may not be quickly shaken from your composure or be disturbed either by a spirit or a message or a letter as if from us, to the effect that the day of the Lord has come. (2 Thess. 2:1, 2)

Paul began by establishing again the connection of the coming (*parousia*) of Christ with "our gathering together to Him" (the Rapture) and the day of the Lord (God's judgment). He then unequivocally tells them, as well as the church today, *exactly* what must occur before the *parousia* of Christ ("the coming [*parousia*] of our Lord . . . and our gathering together to Him") at "the day of the Lord." Continuing his discourse on the end times, Paul cautions,

> Let no one in any way deceive you, for it [the coming (*parousia*) of our Lord at the day of the Lord] will not come unless the apostasy comes first, and the man of lawlessness [Antichrist] is revealed, the son of destruction, who opposes and exalts himself above every so-called god or object of worship, so that he takes his seat in the temple of God, displaying himself as being God. Do you not remember that while I was still with you, I was telling you these things? And you know what restrains him now, so that in his time he may be revealed. For the mystery of lawlessness is already at work; only he who now restrains will do so until he is taken out of the way. And then that lawless one [Antichrist] will be revealed whom the Lord will slay with the breath of His mouth and bring to an end by the appearance of His coming

[*parousia*]; that is, the one whose coming is in accord with the activity of Satan, with all power and signs and false wonders. (vv. 3-9)

The events spoken of in that passage are in exact parallel order to those given in the Olivet Discourse, where the "coming" (*parousia*) of Christ is clearly stated as occurring after the great tribulation by Antichrist is "cut short" by the sign of the day of the Lord and just before God's elect are gathered to Christ by His angelic reapers. In perfect harmony with the Olivet Discourse, Christ's coming (*parousia*) at the day of the Lord will only occur *after* the apostasy (v. 3a), *after* the man of lawlessness (Antichrist) is revealed (v. 3b), and *after* Antichrist takes his seat in the temple and demands the world's worship (v. 4). Only then will Christ bring Antichrist "to an end by the appearance of His coming [*parousia*]" (v. 8). Clearly the purpose of Christ's coming (*parousia*) includes both the deliverance of His saints (v. 1) and the judgment of His enemies (vv. 2, 8). And clearly the coming of Christ can occur only *after* the great tribulation by Antichrist — as the Scriptures teach with precise consistency.

THE RAPTURE DESCRIBED

The heart of Christ's Olivet Discourse is the glorious depiction of His return. After the universe is plunged into total darkness and the sign of Christ's coming is seen by every eye, everyone living on earth "will see the Son of Man coming on the clouds of the sky with power and great glory. And He will send forth His angels with a great trumpet and they will gather together His elect from the four winds, from one end of the sky to the other" (Matt. 24:30, 31). Coming "with power" refers to judgment, and coming in "great glory" refers to the sign of His return — for which every true believer will have been anxiously watching and yearning, especially once the great tribulation by Antichrist begins.

Those two verses also contain several other important truths about Christ's return. *First*, the context of the last two verses is Christ's coming, His *"parousia"* (see vv. 3, 27). *Second*, His coming will be associated with "the clouds" (see v. 30). *Third*, His coming will be associated with a "great trumpet" (see v. 31). *Fourth*, His coming will involve "His angels" who will gather "His elect from the four winds, from one end of the sky to the other" (see v. 31).[10] As shown below, this is the exact same sequence consistently taught throughout the New Testament.

It will be helpful to look at those four truths in light of the undisputed classic passage on Christ's rapture of His church:

> For this we say to you by the word of the Lord, that we who are alive, and remain[11] until *the coming [parousia] of the Lord,* shall not precede those who have fallen asleep. For the Lord Himself will descend from heaven with a shout, with the voice of the archangel, and with *the trumpet of God;* and the dead in Christ shall rise first. Then we who are alive and remain *shall be caught up together with them in the clouds to meet the Lord in the air,* and thus we shall always be with the Lord. (1 Thess. 4:15-17, emphasis added)

In this beautiful and well-known rapture passage we discover the same four truths just mentioned above and emphasized by Jesus in Matthew 24:27, 30, 31. First, the events described here also occur at the "coming" (*parousia*) of Christ.

Second, His coming will, in like manner, be announced "with the trumpet of God."

Third, both passages teach that at the coming (*parousia*) of Christ, the Lord will come "in the clouds" (cf. Acts 1:9-11).

The fourth parallel truth is implied by Paul's passive phrase "shall be caught up together." Because believers will be "caught up . . . *to meet the Lord . . . in the air*" it is implied that someone or some ones will "catch them up" and carry them to Him. As Jesus clearly stated, it will be His angels who will "gather together His elect from the four winds, from one end of the sky to the other" (Matt. 24:31). Earlier, in His parable of the wheat and the tares, Christ had already taught His disciples that "in the time of harvest I will say to the reapers . . . 'gather the wheat into my barn'" (Matt. 13:30), and He later explained to His disciples that "the reapers are [His] angels" (v. 39).

In other words, Paul's teaching in 1 Thessalonians 4 perfectly parallels Jesus' teaching about the Rapture in the Olivet Discourse. Moreover, Paul's expression of being "caught up . . . to meet the Lord in the air" perfectly reflects the idea behind Christ's statement in Matthew 24 that "one will be taken [*paralambanō*; see endnote 5], and one will be left" (v. 40), which in the context directly refers to Christ's second coming (*parousia*, see vv. 27, 30, 37, 39, 42, 44).

Four specific truths, then, may be gleaned from these three passages (Matt. 24:27, 30, 31; 1 Thess. 4:15-17; and Matt. 13:24-30, 36-43). First, the Rapture occurs at the coming (*parousia*) of Christ. Second, it occurs at the sounding of "the trumpet of God." Third, it occurs when Christ comes in the clouds. And, fourth, God's angelic reapers (Matt. 13:30; cf. v. 40) will "gather together His elect from the four winds, from one end of the sky to the other" (Matt. 24:31) "to meet the Lord in the air" (1 Thess. 4:17). In other words, all three of these passages consistently teach the exact same sequence and truths concerning the return of Christ.

A CONCLUDING WORD OF ENCOURAGEMENT

In the foregoing sections of this chapter, we have seen the essential teachings of Scripture concerning the coming or *parousia* of Christ. These are:

(1) The Rapture of the church and the day of the Lord will occur back to back, on "the same day that the Son of Man is revealed."

(2) The coming (*parousia*) of Christ occurs immediately after the great tribulation by Antichrist is cut short by God.

(3) The exact same truths are taught consistently in the New Testament concerning how and when these events will take place.

But these truths are much more than abstract doctrine — they are the living truths of God's holy Word, given by our loving Father in Heaven for our teaching and encouragement. In this regard we see how beautifully the Apostle Paul has woven these truths together to encourage the Thessalonian believers, but just as much for the encouragement of Christians in every age:

> Therefore, we ourselves speak proudly of you among the churches of God for your perseverance and faith in the midst of all your persecutions and afflictions which you endure. This is a plain indication of God's righteous judgment so that you may be considered worthy of the kingdom of God, for which indeed you are suffering. For after all it is only just for God to repay with affliction those who afflict you, and to give relief to you who are afflicted and to us as well when the Lord Jesus shall be revealed from heaven with His mighty angels in flaming fire, dealing out

292 ■ *The Sign*

retribution to those who do not know God and to those who do not obey the gospel of our Lord Jesus. And these will pay the penalty of eternal destruction, away from the presence of the Lord and from the glory of His power, when He comes to be glorified in His saints on that day, and to be marveled at among all who have believed — for our testimony to you was believed. To this end also we pray for you always that our God may count you worthy of your calling, and fulfill every desire for goodness and the work of faith with power. (2 Thess. 1:4-11)

Having carefully considered the teaching of Scripture concerning the prewrath position on the timing of the Rapture as taught consistently by Christ, by Paul, and by Peter, we turn now to Revelation — the most comprehensive prophetic book in the Bible — where we find further confirmation and precise consistency.

The Prewrath Rapture of the Church: Part II

If the truths so clearly taught by Christ in the Olivet Discourse and by Paul in 1 and 2 Thessalonians are taken at face value, the Rapture will follow the great tribulation by Antichrist and will occur immediately before the day of the Lord — on the same day. That being so, we would expect this glorious deliverance of believers to be depicted in the book of Revelation as well — which, as we will see, it clearly is. This last book of the Bible — which contains the most prophetic writing concerning the end times in all of Scripture — perfectly substantiates what was taught by Christ in His Olivet Discourse and by Paul in his second letter to the Thessalonians.[1]

CONFIRMED BY REVELATION

The critical passage that parallels the specific teaching of Christ and the Apostle Paul concerning the end times is found in Revelation chapter 6 through the beginning of chapter 8. Chapter 6 outlines the events of the first half of the seventieth week (the first four seals), as well as the martyrdom of faithful Christians that comes as a result of the great tribulation by Antichrist that initiates the second half of the seventieth week (the fifth seal). The sixth seal recorded in chapter 6 then depicts the sign of the day of the Lord (when the natural light of the sun, moon, and stars is extinguished), when the great tribulation is cut short by God. All of those events, as discussed in previous chapters, harmonize precisely with Christ's teaching in the Olivet Discourse and Paul's confirmation of Christ's timing in 2 Thessalonians.

The seventh chapter of Revelation, however, discloses an interesting break in the sequence. The first six seals (all described in chapter 6) are given in succession, one right after the other. Then the sequence is broken by a full chapter interlude (chapter 7). This interlude occurs between the account of the sixth seal at the end of the sixth chapter (the sign of the day of the Lord) and the account of the seventh seal which actually initiates the day of the Lord at the beginning of chapter 8.* Chapter 7 then begins with John's vision of four angels (God's reapers) who will have the responsibility to bring divine affliction on the earth. But they will be instructed by another angel to withhold their destructive work (the day of the Lord) until they "have sealed the bond-servants of our God on their foreheads" (Rev. 7:1-3).

Two events will occur during that seventh-chapter interval. The first of these (the sealing of the 144,00) will be studied later in this chapter. It is the second intervening event — the great heavenly multitude's praising God before His heavenly throne (Rev. 7:9-17) — that is of profound significance and should bring great joy and delight to every true believer reading this volume.

THE GREAT HEAVENLY MULTITUDE

Who is this great heavenly multitude? Where did they come from? The text in Revelation gives the following vivid description:

> . . . I [John] looked, and behold, a great multitude, which no one could count, from every nation and all tribes and peoples and tongues, standing before the throne and before the Lamb, clothed in white robes, and palm branches were in their hands; and they cry out with a loud voice, saying, "Salvation to our God who sits on the throne, and to the Lamb." (Rev. 7:9, 10)

* The seventh seal will be discussed in detail in chapter 18.

The text goes on to describe three groups of beings who are *already* in Heaven, gathered around the heavenly throne, and *already* present when the great multitude arrives on the scene. As seen in verse 11, those who are already present include "all the *angels* [who] were standing around the throne . . . and the *elders* and the *four living creatures.*" The arrival of this new group, the great multitude, is apparently sudden and unexpected, as seen by the questions asked by an elder: "And one of the elders answered, saying to me [John], 'These who are clothed in the white robes, who are they, and from where have they come?'" (v. 13).

Before seeing how the Scriptures answer these questions, it is important to remember the sequence of events that lead up to the arrival of this great multitude in Heaven. As we have already seen in great detail in prior chapters, all of this leads up to the arrival of "a great multitude, which no one could count, from every nation and all tribes and peoples and tongues." The first four seals correspond to what will happen during the first half of the seventieth week — that is, during the "birth pangs" of the Olivet Discourse. The fifth seal will occur during the second half of the seventieth week — that is, during the great tribulation by Antichrist. And the sixth seal corresponds to the sign of the day of the Lord — that is, the sign which will cut short the great tribulation, immediately preceding the rapture of the church and the beginning of God's wrath on the ungodly. And then we see the arrival of the great multitude. Can there be any doubt in anyone's mind on who this great multitude must be, especially in light of the clear teaching of Christ and Paul?

"'Who are they, and from where have they come?'" (Rev. 7:13b).[2] Based on the sequence just outlined above, there is only one possible conclusion. As stated succinctly in the next verse: "*'These are the ones who come out of the great tribulation'*" (v. 14). In an earlier verse we are told that *these are the ones* "from every nation and all tribes and peoples and tongues" (v. 9), a direct reference to the previous passage in Revelation where this same multitude is described as those for whom Christ "wast slain, and didst purchase for God with Thy [Christ's] blood from every tribe and tongue and people and nation" (Rev. 5:9) — the elect of God from all ages. Therefore, *"these ones," this great multitude, can only be the elect of God for whom Christ died who have just been raptured out of the great tribulation by Antichrist, after the sign of the end of the age is given at the sixth seal.*

The magnificent splendor of the scene — especially in contrast to

the great tribulation out of which the church will have just been raptured — is beautifully described in the verses that follow:

> ". . . they have washed their robes and made them white in the
> blood of the Lamb . . . they are before the throne of God; and they
> serve Him day and night in His temple; and He who sits on the
> throne shall spread His tabernacle over them. They shall hunger
> no more, neither thirst anymore; neither shall the sun beat down
> on them, nor any heat; for the Lamb in the center of the throne
> shall be their shepherd, and shall guide them to springs of the
> water of life; and God shall wipe every tear from their eyes."
> (Rev. 7:14b-17)

What unspeakable joy the church will know upon being raptured
out of the great tribulation by Antichrist! What unspeakable joy every
believer knows in anticipation of that day!

Although the parallels between the teaching of Christ, the teaching
of Paul, and the teaching of John seems conclusive by itself, there is
one inescapable proof that *this multitude must be the church*, not martyrs who have died during the great tribulation by Antichrist.
Remember, this great multitude can only be one or the other. If it is
not the church, by definition it has to be believing martyrs who refuse
to worship the beast or his image.[3] However, even without the teachings of Christ, Paul, and Peter, the context demands, in a unique and
interesting way, that this great multitude be the church. Follow along
with me carefully.

As noted in several other places in this book, the fifth-seal martyred
saints pictured under the altar in Heaven (Rev. 6:9) are described as
"souls" who do not yet have their resurrection bodies. As explained in
Revelation 20, these martyred saints will not be given their resurrection bodies until the Millennium begins: "And I [John] saw thrones,
and they sat upon them, and judgment was given to them. And I saw
the souls of those who had been beheaded because of the testimony of
Jesus and because of the word of God, and those who had not worshiped the beast or his image, and had not received the mark upon
their forehead and upon their hand; and they came to life [that is, were
resurrected] and reigned with Christ for a thousand years" (Rev. 20:4).[4]
(See chapter 22, endnote 4.)

The saints depicted in Revelation 7:9, on the other hand, are *standing* before the throne, *clothed* in white robes, *holding* palm branches in

their hands — indicating conclusively that they already possess resurrected bodies. This great multitude then can only be the resurrected saints who have been raptured out of the great tribulation of Antichrist — and it must be exactly the same heavenly group (who also have bodies) referred to in Revelation 15:2 as "those who had come off victorious from the beast . . . *standing* on the sea of glass, *holding* harps of God" (emphasis added).

This conclusion becomes certain when we consider what the Scripture teaches about the spiritual bodies of resurrected believers. Scripture is explicit that except for Enoch and Elijah, who were taken bodily to Heaven, no believer in Heaven will have a resurrected spiritual body until the first resurrection of believers (see Luke 14:14; John 5:28, 29; 1 Thess. 4:16; Rev. 20:4; cf. Dan. 12:2).[5] Therefore, since this group of men and women standing before the throne clothed in white robes and holding palm branches in their hands obviously have resurrected bodies, this great multitude can only be the church[6] — not the martyred fifth-seal souls who will not receive their resurrection bodies until the first day of the Millennium.

This conclusion is further confirmed by looking at one last Scripture passage written by Paul to the church of Corinth. In this passage Paul shows that believers will receive their resurrection bodies immediately at the Rapture — "in a moment, in the twinkling of an eye, at the last trumpet" (1 Cor. 15:52a). Shedding much light on the resurrection of the righteous, Paul wrote:

But someone will say, "How are the dead raised? And with what kind of body do they come?" . . . So also is the resurrection of the dead. It is sown a perishable body, it is raised an imperishable body; it is sown in dishonor, it is raised in glory; it is sown in weakness, it is raised in power; it is sown a natural body, it is raised a spiritual body. If there is a natural body, there is also a spiritual body. . . . Behold, I tell you a mystery; we shall not all sleep, but we shall all be changed, in a moment, in the twinkling of an eye, at the last trumpet;[7] for the trumpet will sound, and the dead will be raised imperishable, and we shall be changed. For this perishable must put on the imperishable, and this mortal must put on immortality. But when this perishable will have put on the imperishable, and this mortal will have put on immortality, then will come about the saying that is written, "Death is swallowed up in victory." (1 Cor. 15:35, 42-44, 51-54; cf. 1 Thess. 4:13-17; Phil. 3:21; 1 John 3:2)

These verses have been a tremendous comfort to the church in every age. But they also clearly teach that believers in Heaven, who have a resurrected spiritual body, will receive their spiritual body at the Rapture.

When all of this is taken together and applied to the great heavenly "multitude, which no one could count, from every nation and all tribes and peoples and tongues," there are eight logical conclusions which of necessity must follow. These conclusions are:

First, the great multitude arrives in Heaven immediately after the sign of the end of the age (the day of the Lord) is given at the sixth seal.

Second, this multitude is made up of those "who come out of the great tribulation" (Rev. 7:14), when the great tribulation is "cut short" by Christ (Matt. 24:22).

Third, the next event following the arrival of the great multitude in Heaven is the seventh seal (Rev. 8:1-6), the day of the Lord. (The next chapter will discuss this in greater detail.)

Fourth, both Christ and Paul taught that the Rapture will occur when the great tribulation is cut short, just before the day of the Lord.

Fifth, Paul taught that the church and the dead in Christ will receive their resurrection bodies at the Rapture.

Sixth, the great heavenly multitude has bodies.

Seventh, because this great multitude has bodies, it cannot represent the fifth-seal souls (great-tribulation martyrs), because they do not receive their resurrection bodies until the first day of the Millennium.

Eighth, the only possible conclusion is that this great multitude must be both the "rapture church" and the "dead in Christ" for whom Christ "wast slain . . . from every tribe and tongue and people and nation."

In summary, then, we find a perfect harmony between the teachings of Christ in Matthew and Luke, the teaching of Paul, particularly in Second Thessalonians as well as First Corinthians, the teaching of Peter in both 1 and 2 Peter, and the teaching of John in Revelation — all of which lead to the compelling conclusion that the church *will go through* "the hour of testing" (Rev. 3:10), "the fiery ordeal among you, which comes upon you for your testing" (1 Pet. 4:12), which will be "cut short" by the return of Christ for the rapture of His church and the beginning of wrath for the ungodly.

WHEN WILL THE RAPTURE OCCUR?

A question that concerns every mature believer who is looking for the Lord's return is, "When exactly will the Rapture occur?" Jesus said, "Of that day and hour no one knows, not even the angels of heaven, nor the Son, but the Father alone" (Matt. 24:36). Obviously we know that it will occur during the great tribulation by Antichrist. But of that exact day and hour, we are not to know, but only the Father in Heaven. That is why the tribulation martyrs under the throne of God ask, "How long, O Lord, holy and true, wilt Thou refrain from judging and avenging our blood on those who dwell on the earth?" (Rev. 6:10). And that is why the disciples of Christ, during the last days "will long to see one of the days of the Son of Man, and you will not see it" (Luke 17:22). Instead they are told simply to look for the sign of Christ's return: "For just as the lightning, when it flashes out of one part of the sky, shines to the other part of the sky, so will be the Son of Man in His day" (v. 24). In other words, we are not to know when; we are told only to watch for the sign: "But when these things begin to take place, straighten up and lift up your heads, because your redemption [deliverance] is drawing near" (Luke 21:28).[8]

THE "DEAD IN CHRIST" RISE FIRST

When the church is raptured, the dead in Christ will be resurrected first. "For the Lord Himself will descend from heaven with a shout, with the voice of the archangel, and with the trumpet of God; and the dead in Christ shall rise first. Then we who are alive and remain shall be caught up together with them in the clouds to meet the Lord in the air . . ." (1 Thess. 4:16, 17).

Who are these dead in Christ? Many believers in the Thessalonian church, and doubtless many believers elsewhere, were confused and unduly concerned about the eternal destiny of both Old and New Testament believers who had already died or would die before the Lord's return. For this reason Paul first gives them a general word of assurance: "We do not want you to be uninformed, brethren, about those who are asleep, that you may not grieve, as do the rest who have no hope" (v. 13). He then explains the order in which the Lord will take His people to Himself in this beautiful and awesome event. The first ones to be taken will be those about whom the Thessalonians were so concerned: "The Lord Himself will descend from heaven with a shout, with the voice of the archangel, and with the trumpet of God; and *the dead in Christ shall rise first*" (v. 16, emphasis added).

When "the dead in Christ" are raised, this group will definitely include the Old Testament saints. A number of Old Testament passages give a prophetic preview of the rapture of Old Testament saints. For example, the Lord inspired Isaiah to write, "Your dead will live; their corpses will rise. You who lie in the dust, awake and shout for joy, for your dew is as the dew of the dawn, and the earth will give birth to the departed spirits. Come, my people, enter into your rooms, and close your doors behind you; hide for a little while, until indignation [the great tribulation] runs its course. For behold, the Lord is about to come out from His place to punish the inhabitants of the earth for their iniquity [the day of the Lord]; and the earth will reveal her bloodshed, and will no longer cover her slain" (Isa. 26:19-21).

Remarkably, this ancient passage seems to speak specifically about the Rapture and related events of the end times. Thus verse 19 describes the resurrection of all the believing dead; verse 20 gives a warning to "my people" that in the end times they will have to hide from Antichrist until rescued by the Lord; and verse 21 tells of the day-of-the-Lord wrath that immediately follows — which is the exact sequence of events developed in chapters 16 and 17 of this book. The dead in Christ will be resurrected when the great tribulation is "cut short" on the same day that the day of God's wrath will begin.

A somewhat expanded sequence of the same end-time events is found in Daniel. Speaking of the midpoint of the seventieth week, the prophet says,

And he [Antichrist] will pitch the tents of his royal pavilion between the seas and the beautiful Holy Mountain; yet he will come to his end, and no one will help him. Now at that time Michael, the great prince who stands guard over the sons of your people, will arise. And there will be a time of distress [the great tribulation] such as never occurred since there was a nation until that time; and at that time your people, everyone who is found written in the book, will be rescued. And many of those who sleep in the dust of the ground will awake, these to everlasting life [the first resurrection], but the others to disgrace and everlasting contempt [the second resurrection]. And those who have insight will shine brightly like the brightness of the expanse of heaven, and those who lead the many to righteousness, like the stars forever and ever. (Dan. 11:45; 12:1-3)

In addition to its clear teaching concerning the resurrection of the Old Testament saints, this passage from Daniel gives many other details of the end times. Thus we see that Antichrist establishes his forces near Jerusalem ("the Holy Mountain"); that the archangel Michael, the great protector of Israel, will arise or stop; that the great tribulation by Antichrist (the "time of distress such as never occurred since there was a nation until that time") will commence; that God's sovereignly chosen remnant will be rescued; that the Old Testament saints ("those who sleep in the dust") will be resurrected; that some will go "to everlasting life"; and that others (at the Great White Throne judgment of sinners) will go "to disgrace and everlasting contempt." Verse 3 then refers to those who will have insight — the spiritual line of Abraham, who "will shine brightly . . . forever and ever," which is clearly a reference to resurrected saints being with Christ during eternity future.

Daniel's prophecy does not specifically denote the timing of the resurrection as occurring immediately before the day of the Lord, but it does clearly indicate that the resurrection (v. 2) will *follow* the time of great distress and God's rescue of the Jewish believing remnant "found written in the book [of life]" (v. 1).

Although these two passages from Isaiah and Daniel are not identical in the events they portray, the *sequences of the various events* are perfectly compatible. Isaiah teaches that the Old Testament saints will be resurrected just before the day of the Lord,[9] while the great tribulation is in process, and Daniel's passage confirms the fact that the resurrection will follow "a time of distress such as never occurred since there was a nation until that time" (cf. Matt. 24:21).

Therefore, when "the dead in Christ shall rise first," before the living church is raptured, the dead in Christ will include both Old and New Testament saints "found written in the book [of life]." Taken together, these Old and New Testament passages provided a tremendous hope for the early church, as they do for believers today.

THE SEALING OF THE 144,000

Either simultaneously or immediately following the Rapture, God will seal unto salvation and protection "the faithful woman" who flees to the wilderness — i.e., the 144,000.

After this I saw four angels [God's reapers] standing at the four corners of the earth, holding back the four winds of the earth, so that no wind should blow on the earth or on the sea or on any tree. And I saw another angel ascending from the rising of the sun, having the seal of the living God; and he cried out with a loud voice to the four angels to whom it was granted to harm the earth and the sea, saying, "Do not harm the earth or the sea or the trees, until we have sealed the bond-servants of our God on their foreheads." And I heard the number of those who were sealed, one hundred and forty-four thousand sealed from every tribe of the sons of Israel. (Rev. 7:1-4)

From the only other passage that refers explicitly to the 144,000, we learn that "these are the ones who have not been defiled with women [i.e., have not committed spiritual adultery], for they have kept themselves [spiritually] chaste. These are the ones who follow the Lamb wherever He goes. These have been purchased from among men as first fruits to God and to the Lamb" (Rev. 14:4).

When the church is raptured, the 144,000 will not be taken with the saints because they will not as yet have been brought into a saving relationship with their Messiah, Jesus Christ. Just as God prophesied through Ezekiel: "I shall bring you into the wilderness of the peoples, and there I shall enter into judgment with you face to face. . . . And I shall make you pass under the rod, and I shall bring you into the bond of the covenant" (Ezek. 20:35, 37).

Therefore, when the sign of the end of the age extinguishes the heavenly lights, and the sign of Christ's return fills the darkened universe with the glory of Christ, the angels of God will gather His elect from the four corners of the earth to meet the Lord in the air. Then, and only then, will the 144,000 persevering Jews (those who have kept themselves spiritually chaste during the first half of the seventieth week) be brought "into the bond of the covenant" described by Ezekiel. It is at this point, then, that "the faithful woman" who flees to the wilderness, "the faithful woman" who has been made to "pass under the rod," will be sealed by God with the seal of God on their foreheads (Rev. 9:4) and will become the first fruits of unbelieving Israel, brought into "the bond of the covenant." However, "the compromised woman" who remained behind, who survived the great tribulation by Antichrist, will be saved only after God's day-of-the-Lord refinement of them, when "the fulness of the Gentiles has come in" (Rom. 11:25) — that is, after the seventieth week is complete and God brings in "everlasting righteousness" (Dan. 9:24). Once the church is removed, "the faithful woman" who flees will become the first fruits of Israel, given special protection from the wrath of God that will begin on the same day. (See, in particular, Revelation 9:4 where God's wrath is directly against *all* "the men who do not have the seal of God on their foreheads.")

We also learn from Ezekiel that *shortly before* God's *shekinah* glory departed from the first Temple, God placed His "mark on the foreheads" of faithful Jews — on those "who sigh and groan over all the abominations which are being committed in its midst" (Ezek. 9:4; cf. vv. 5-11; 10:18). That is a fascinating parallel to the 144,000 who have kept themselves spiritually chaste by not succumbing to the apostasy of the covenant with death — for they too will receive the seal of God "on their foreheads" (Rev. 7:3), but in this case *not before the glory departs*, but *immediately after the glory returns* to the heavenlies.

The *shekinah* glory probably departed in 606 B.C. This occurred just before God wreaked terrible judgment on Israel by means of the Babylonians under Nebuchadnezzar who conquered Judah and took most of her inhabitants into exile in 586 B.C. The glory will not return to the heavenlies until God is ready to unleash His wrath upon the wicked nations of the world. Shortly before God unleashes His final end-time judgment on Israel and the rest of the world, He will again place His own divine mark on the foreheads of Jews who, like their forefathers, "sigh and groan over all the abominations" being committed by their fellow countrymen.

IN SUMMARY

As we bring together the conclusions of these two chapters on the prewrath Rapture of the church, we see first and foremost that there is a complete consistency in Scripture concerning the sign of the end of the age and the sign of Christ's coming; concerning the coming (*parousia*) of Christ and the great tribulation of Antichrist; concerning the rapture of the church and God's judgment of the ungodly; concerning the resurrection of believers both in the Old and New Testaments. This consistency is found throughout the New Testament — in the Gospels, in the letters of Paul, in the writings of Peter, in the book of Revelation — as well as in the prophecies of the Old Testament.

By way of summary from the last chapter we have seen that Scripture clearly teaches:

(1) The rapture of the church and the day of the Lord will occur back to back, on the same day.

(2) The coming (*parousia*) of Christ occurs immediately after the great tribulation by Antichrist is cut short by God.

(3) The exact same truths are taught consistently throughout the New Testament concerning how and when these events will take place.

Carrying these conclusions further in this present chapter, with its focus especially on the book of Revelation, we have seen that the Rapture occurs in Revelation, between the sixth and seventh seals, exactly where the teachings of Christ, Paul, and Peter put it — namely, after the persecution of Antichrist but before the day of the Lord.

Christ is indeed coming! But His return will not be imminent until the church is undergoing the fiery testing of Antichrist. These last two chapters have shown consistently and conclusively that the teaching of the New Testament writers warns the church that it will go through the great tribulation by Antichrist before she will see the back-to-back signs of Christ's return. What is imminent today is the last event that must occur before the covenant can be signed with Antichrist — namely, the rise of a powerful leader who will gain control of three Aryan nations and position them in such a way as to become the power-base nations of the final beast empire of Satan. The church today is the first generation of the church since the early church before the *Diaspora* which can genuinely look for the start of the seventieth week of Daniel. Israel again is back in her homeland — still in unbelief, but with control once again of the city of Jerusalem. Therefore the stakes are high. What we believe concerning the last days will directly affect how well we survive the persecution of Antichrist. If we allegorize all that we have worked through up to now, or if we deny the clear teaching of Christ, of Paul, of Peter, and of John, we will never know what has hit us when the seventieth week begins.

Because of the severity of what is taught and how it effects every believer in the last days, perhaps now the warning of Paul to the church of Thessalonica takes on more meaning. When confused about when Christ would gather together the church and begin the day of the Lord, Paul warned, "Let no one in any way deceive you . . ." (2 Thess. 2:3). He then tells the Thessalonians that Christ *will not return until* after Antichrist "takes his seat in the temple of God, displaying himself as being God" (v. 4). Indeed, it is at "the appearance of His coming" that Christ will "bring [Antichrist] to an end" (v. 8).

But to the faithful church Christ has promised that He will guard her while within this sphere of danger, the great tribulation by Antichrist — safe deliverance out from within "the hour of testing, that hour which is about to come upon the whole world, to test those who dwell upon the earth" (Rev. 3:10).

With this warning to the compromising church, and with this specific promise of protection to the faithful, we now leave the church "standing before the throne and before the Lamb, clothed in white robes, and palm branches in their hands; and they cry out with a loud voice, saying, 'Salvation to our God who sits on the throne, and to the Lamb'" (Rev. 7:9b-11). For both the faithful and the compromising will have been made ready to "stand in the presence of His glory blameless with great joy" (Jude 24).

> . . . and He who sits on the throne shall spread His tabernacle over them. They shall hunger no more, neither thirst anymore; neither shall the sun beat down on them, nor any heat; for the Lamb in the center of the throne shall be their shepherd, and shall guide them to springs of the water of life; and God shall wipe away every tear from their eyes. (Rev. 7:15b-17)

The Day of
the Lord

What is the day of the Lord? What will this momentous day be like? Some of the most vivid writing in all of Scripture is used to describe this awesome event. It will be an event like none that has ever happened before, or like any that will ever happen again. The day of the Lord is described in graphic detail by eight prophets in the Old Testament and mentioned explicitly by three New Testament writers (Luke, Paul, and Peter), and it is essential that we have a thorough understanding of the day of the Lord in order to have a clear understanding of the end times. The importance of the day of the Lord — the time which Christ calls the end of the age — cannot be overstated.[1] It is the focal point of the end times.

THE BEGINNING OF JUDGMENT

In reality, the second coming (*parousia*) of Christ and the day of the Lord are one and the same. It will occur suddenly and unexpectedly when God intervenes to cut short the great tribulation by Antichrist. The *parousia* of Christ will simultaneously involve the deliverance of the righteous and the beginning of God's judgment on the wicked, as Christ returns as both Savior and Judge. Though we have already seen that the day of the Lord will begin with the glorious deliverance of the saints, it remains to understand clearly what this day will mean for the ungodly who remain on earth after the great tribulation is cut short and the church is raptured.

One of the most powerful day of the Lord passages in the Old Testament is found in the book of Zephaniah:

Near is the great day of the Lord, near and coming very quickly; listen, the day of the Lord! In it the warrior cries out bitterly. A day of wrath is that day, a day of trouble and distress, a day of destruction and desolation, a day of darkness and gloom, a day of clouds and thick darkness, a day of trumpet and battle cry, against the fortified cities and the high corner towers. And I will bring distress on men, so that they will walk like the blind, because they have sinned against the Lord; and their blood will be poured out like dust, and their flesh like dung. Neither their silver nor their gold will be able to deliver them on the day of the Lord's wrath; and all the earth will be devoured in the fire of His jealousy, for He will make a complete end, indeed a terrifying one, of all the inhabitants of the earth. (Zeph. 1:14-18)

As seen in Zephaniah, the day of the Lord will be that climactic event in history when God will pour out His wrath in judgment on the wicked world. When we bring Old Testament passages such as this alongside the day of the Lord passages in the New Testament, we find in the New Testament the same graphic description of God's judgment, explicitly linked there to the return of Christ. Thus, in response to mockers who ask, "Where is the promise of His coming [*parousia*]," Peter writes,

The present heavens and earth by His word are being reserved for fire, kept for *the day of judgment* and destruction of ungodly men. . . . The Lord is not slow about His promise, as some count slowness, but is patient toward you, not wishing for any to perish but for all to come to repentance. But the *day of the Lord* will come like a thief, in which the heavens will pass away with a roar and the elements will be destroyed with intense heat, and the earth and its works will be burned up . . . looking for and hastening the coming of *the day of God*, on account of which the heavens will be destroyed by burning, and the elements will melt with intense heat! (2 Pet. 3:4-7, 9, 10, 12, emphasis added).[2]

Simply stated, the day of the Lord will be unlike any day that has occurred before in history. Indicating something of the total devastation accompanying the day of the Lord, Christ gives only two illustrations, both from Old Testament times. The first is the total destruction of the world by the Flood in Noah's day, and the second is the complete and awesome destruction of Sodom and Gomorrah by fire and brimstone (see Luke 17:26-30). The Flood was a judgment by water, after which God gave the rainbow as a guarantee that He will never again destroy the earth by that means (see Gen. 9:12-15). But God has never promised that He would not destroy the world by fire, and instead predicted unequivocally and unconditionally that "the present heavens and earth by His word are being reserved for fire, kept for the day of judgment and destruction of ungodly men" (2 Pet. 3:7).

A FIERY, SUPERNATURAL JUDGMENT

The day of the Lord will clearly be a judgment by fire. Scripture often depicts fire as symbolic of judgment. But as we look closely at passages pertaining to the day of the Lord, we see an almost constant association between this final judgment and punishment by fire that Scripture clearly intends to be taken literally.

It is of great importance to understand that although God has often used natural disasters and human means as His instruments of judgment — as when he used "Assyria [as] the rod of [His] anger" (Isa. 10:5) — His end-time judgment will be entirely supernatural, administered directly by Himself, through His avenging angels. It will not be executed through any human or natural means. The entire world will know that the calamity upon earth is the judgment of God, not an offensive strike by a hostile government or an act of nature (Ezek. 38:23; cf. Isa. 2:17; Rev. 6:16, 17).

The prophets repeatedly identified the day of the Lord with fire. For example, Isaiah proclaimed: "Behold, the Lord will come in fire and His chariots like the whirlwind, to render His anger with fury, and His rebuke with flames of fire. For the Lord will execute judgment by fire and by His sword on all flesh, and those slain by the Lord will be many" (Isa. 66:15, 16). Joel said of God's enemies, in "the day of the

Lord [that] is coming . . . a fire consumes before them, and behind them a flame burns" (Joel 2:1, 3). Likewise, Joel warned that the Lord "will display wonders in the sky and on the earth, blood, fire, and columns of smoke . . . before the great and awesome day of the Lord comes" (vv. 30, 31). In his warning to the ungodly in the end times, Zephaniah declared: "'Therefore, wait for Me,' declares the Lord, 'for the day when I rise up to the prey. Indeed, My decision is to gather nations, to assemble kingdoms, to pour out on them My indignation, all My burning anger; for all the earth will be devoured by the fire of My zeal'" (Zeph. 3:8).

In the New Testament John the Baptist spoke of Jesus burning "up the chaff with unquenchable fire" (Matt. 3:12). Similarly, in His parable of the wheat and tares, Jesus spoke of the angels gathering the tares to be "burned with fire . . . at the end of the age" (Matt. 13:39, 40), and He spoke of Himself as having "come to cast fire upon the earth" (Luke 12:49). Likewise, Paul declared that in the last days "the Lord Jesus shall be revealed from heaven with His mighty angels in flaming fire" (2 Thess. 1:7).

THE OPENING OF THE SEVENTH SEAL

The day of the Lord corresponds specifically to the seventh seal described in the initial verses of Revelation 8. But it is important to understand it in the context of the stunning signs that will immediately precede the breaking of the seventh seal.

By way of review, the sixth seal initiates the two signs discussed in chapters 14 and 15 of this book, which will occur in immediate sequence. First comes the sign of the end of the age when there will be "a great earthquake; and the sun [will become] black as sackcloth . . . and the whole moon [will become] like blood" (Rev. 6:12). Second will be the sign of Christ's coming with a brilliant blaze of light flashing like lightning from the east to the west (see Matt. 24:27, 30). When they see these two staggering signs, the wicked who remain on earth will be stricken with terror. They will say "to the mountains and to the rocks, 'Fall on us and hide us from the presence of Him who sits on the throne, and from the wrath of the Lamb; for the great day of their wrath has come; and who is able to stand?'" (Rev. 6:16, 17). But in like manner Christ tells the church that "when these things begin to take place, straighten up and lift up your heads, because your redemption is drawing near" (Luke 21:28).

Paul explains that then "the Lord Himself will descend from heaven with a shout, with a voice of the archangel, and with the trumpet of God; and the dead in Christ shall rise first. Then we who are alive and remain shall be caught up together with them in the clouds to meet the Lord in the air . . ." (1 Thess. 4:16, 17).

Chapter 7 of Revelation then portrays the sealing of the "woman who flees," the 144,000 "first fruits" of Israel, and then the heavenly arrival of the raptured saints, the great multitude "from every nation and all tribes and peoples and tongues . . . before the throne and before the Lamb" (v. 9).

It is hard to find words that properly express the magnitude of these events, all of which occur in a very short timeframe, on the very same day. And it is only against this backdrop that we can begin to comprehend the equally breath-taking events that are initiated by the breaking of the seventh seal. Clearly the Scriptures intend to convey something of the awesome significance of the day of the Lord. As John wrote in Revelation: "And when He broke the seventh seal, there was silence in heaven for about half an hour" (8:1). Surely one purpose of this solemn period of silence is for all of Heaven and earth to contemplate the eternal significance of what is about to happen.

HEAVENLY ANGELS, BLAZING FIRE

The description that follows in Revelation perfectly fits Jesus' own teaching concerning the day of the Lord as found in the parable of the wheat and the tares. There we saw that the *heavenly angels are the reapers* of both the wheat and the tares, and that after the wheat has been harvested into the barn, the angels will harvest the tares which are "gathered up and burned with *fire*" (see Matt. 13:37-42).

The seventh seal's being opened initiates God's day-of-the-Lord wrath, and this is exactly what we find in Revelation 8. Immediately after the solemn period of silence, seven heavenly angels are given the task of reaping the earth. As John writes, "seven angels who stand before God" were given the "seven trumpets" of God's judgment (see Rev. 8:2, 6-13; 9:1-21; 11:15-19). Likewise, the central significance of *fire* in carrying out God's judgment is seen as John writes: "And another angel came and stood before the altar, holding a golden censer. . . . And the angel took the censer; and he filled it with the fire of the altar and threw it on the earth; and there followed peals of thunder and sounds and flashes of lightning and an earthquake. And the seven angels who had the seven trumpets prepared themselves to sound them" (Rev. 8:3, 5, 6).

THE FIRST SIX TRUMPET JUDGMENTS

As the first six trumpets sound in succession, the great wrath of God will be released in progressively more destructive afflictions upon mankind. When the trumpet of the first angel sounded, "there came hail and *fire*, mixed with blood, and they were thrown to the earth; and a third of the earth was *burnt up*, and a third of the trees were *burnt up*, and all the green grass was *burnt up*. And the second angel sounded, and something like a great mountain *burning* with *fire* was thrown into the sea; and a third of the sea became blood" (vv. 7, 8). Similarly, when "the third angel sounded . . . a great star fell from heaven, *burning like a torch*, and it fell on a third of the rivers and on the springs of waters" (v. 10). And when "the sixth angel sounded . . . this is how I saw in the vision the horses and those who sat on them: the riders had breastplates the color of *fire* and of hyacinth and of brimstone; and the heads of the horses are like the heads of lions; and out of their mouths proceed *fire* and smoke and brimstone. A third of mankind was killed by these three plagues, by the *fire* and the smoke and the brimstone, which proceeded out of their mouths" (9:13, 17, 18, emphasis added). Only the fourth and fifth trumpet judgments will involve no fire.

On a minute scale, but with equal realism, the fire-and-brimstone destruction of Sodom and Gomorrah portends this judgment, just as Jesus said: "It will be just the same on the day that the Son of Man is revealed" (Luke 17:29, 30).

GOD'S PURPOSE FOR THE DAY OF THE LORD

As seen repeatedly in the Old and New Testaments, the day of the Lord will see the unleashing of God's wrath on the wicked world in a final, total, and climactic way. Although this is the unequivocal teaching of Scripture, many today, even in the church, are unwilling to accept the reality of God's wrath. God is indeed a God of love — He loved us so much that He gave His only Son to suffer and die for our own sins; God is not willing that any should perish, but that all might come to repentance and salvation (2 Pet. 3:9). God is long-suffering and compassionate, as the Scriptures teach repeatedly. But God is equally a God of holiness, righteousness, and judgment; and because of this, He cannot and will not let wickedness, sin, and rebellion go unpunished. Even the context of the classic statement, God is "not wishing for any to perish" is given within the larger context of the day of the Lord, when "the present heavens and earth by His word are being reserved by fire, kept for the day of judgment and destruction of ungodly men" (2 Pet. 3:7).

TO JUDGE THE UNGODLY

The wrath of God poured out on the ungodly during the day of the Lord, therefore, is the righteous consequence of God's character as a God of love and holiness. Every opportunity will have been given to the ungodly to repent and call upon God for mercy until they choose instead to worship the beast or his image. Just as the Scriptures reveal, those who will be killed during the day of the Lord "did not repent of the works of their hands, so as not to worship demons, and the idols of gold and of silver and of brass and of stone and of wood . . . and they did not repent of their murders nor of their sorceries nor of their immorality nor of their thefts" (Rev. 9:20, 21). The wrath of God is the necessary consequence of man's blatant, unrepentant rebellion against a holy, loving God; and if we ignore or minimize the reality of God's wrath, we do so to our own eternal peril.

TO PURIFY ISRAEL

But in addition to inflicting judgment on the ungodly world in general, the day of the Lord will be used to purify the nation of Israel, discarding the dross, those who have compromised to Antichrist, refining "the compromising woman," that part of the natural line of Abraham that refused to flee but also refused to bow down to Antichrist and by God's grace survives his intense persecution. Thus Isaiah wrote: "Therefore the Lord God of hosts, the Mighty One of Israel declares, 'Ah, I will be relieved of My adversaries, and avenge Myself on My foes. I will also turn My hand against you [Israel], and will smelt away your dross as with lye, and will remove all your alloy. Then I will restore your judges as at the first, and your counselors as at the beginning; after that you will be called the city of righteousness, a faithful city. Zion will be redeemed with justice, and her repentant ones with righteousness. But transgressors and sinners will be crushed together, and those who forsake the Lord shall come to an end'" (Isa. 1:24-28).

Like all others who worship the beast or his image, Jews who do so will escape the great tribulation by Antichrist only to be cast into the wrath of God. Then "they shall fling their silver into the streets, and their gold shall become an abhorrent thing; their silver and their gold shall not be able to deliver them in the day of the wrath of the Lord . . . they made the images of their abominations and their detestable things with it; therefore I will make it an abhorrent thing to them" (Ezek. 7:19, 20). For this reason the prophet Amos warned the nation of Israel, "you who are longing for the day of the Lord, for what purpose will the day of the Lord be to you? It will be darkness and not light; as when a man flees from a lion [the great tribulation of Antichrist], and a bear meets him [the day of the Lord], or goes home, leans his hand against the wall, and a snake bites him" (5:18, 19). Likewise, as the prophet Zechariah wrote, "'It will come about in all the land,' declares the Lord, 'that two parts in it will be cut off and perish [during the great tribulation by Antichrist]; but the third will be left in it. And I will bring the third part [of Israel] through the fire, refine them as silver is refined, and test them as gold is tested [during the day of the Lord]. They will call on My name, and I will answer them; I will say, "They are My people," and they will say, "The Lord is my God"'" (Zech. 13:8, 9; cf. Mal. 3:1-3).

And so God will use His wrath to purify the nation Israel, as He did the 144,000 in the Edomite wilderness. He will preserve for Himself only that portion of the nation that survives the persecution of Antichrist, the third who have refused to worship the beast or his image. It will be this remnant of "the compromising woman" who stays, then, along with "the faithful woman" that flees (the first fruits), that will become the heart of His earthly millennial kingdom, as we shall see in more detail in the coming chapters. God will bring this "third" through His own refining fires, leading the remnant that survives into saving faith when "the fulness of the Gentiles has come in" (Rom. 11:25), when they will acknowledge, "The Lord is my God" (Zech. 13:9).

THE BEGINNING OF THE END

When the day of the Lord begins, Christ brings about a very significant change in the amount of "freedom" that Antichrist has exercised since Michael, the restrainer, has been removed. At the appearance of Christ's coming (*parousia*), Antichrist will again feel the effects of restraint, but this time the one who restrains will be Christ, not Michael. And with this restraint "the woman" who stays will begin to fight back, not unlike the Maccabean revolt in the days of Antiochus Epiphanes, the foreshadow of Antichrist.

SATAN "RENDERED USELESS"

The Scriptures reveal that Satan will be cast down from Heaven at the midpoint of the seventieth "week," and that he will exercise "great wrath, knowing that he has only a short time" (Rev. 12:12). Satan's divinely permitted but restricted presence and power on earth will continue throughout his allotted forty-two months plus thirty days until Christ's final defeat of Antichrist and his armies at Armageddon.[3] But even before Antichrist's final destruction there will be a decisive change in the limits of his power with the return of Christ on the day of the Lord. This can be seen by carefully studying Paul's teaching that the "lawless one [Antichrist] will be revealed *whom the Lord will slay with the breath of His mouth and bring to an end by the appearance of His coming;* that is, the one whose coming is in accord with the activity of Satan, with all power and signs and false wonders" (2 Thess. 2:8, 9, emphasis added).

Paul seems to be redundant when he says that Christ will both *slay*[4] Antichrist (the "lawless one") and *put him to an end*. Anyone who is slain obviously is put to an end. When examined carefully, however, verse 8 in reality describes separate and distinct results of Christ's second coming. Ultimately Christ will destroy Antichrist at the final battle of Armageddon (the last event of the day of the Lord), but first, "by the appearance of His coming [*parousia*]," Christ will *render him helpless*, as the first event of the day of the Lord. Christ will in effect "handcuff" Antichrist and his forces and "render him useless" (a better translation of the Greek term rendered "bring to an end" is given in Rotherham's Bible which translates this more precisely as "paralyzed").[5] This restriction of Antichrist's power will happen "at the appearance of His coming" — in other words, when "every eye will see Him" (Rev. 1:7), when the church is gathered to Christ in the clouds and the wrath of God begins. Antichrist will be "rendered useless" until the time of final judgment and destruction, when he will be slain.

This interpretation gives greater understanding to Jesus' statement that "unless those days had been cut short, no life would have been saved; but for the sake of the elect those days shall be cut short" (Matt. 24:22). "Those days" is frequently taken to refer to the second half — the last three and a half years — of the seventieth week. But the context makes clear that Jesus was talking specifically about the great tribulation by Antichrist (v. 21), not about his allotted time upon earth. If God were to cut short the three and a half years, the seventieth week would no longer be a "week," since the last half would be less than three and a half years. Thus, it is the *persecution* of the great tribulation that will be cut short when Christ's renders Antichrist (the perpetrator of the tribulation) helpless, idle, or paralyzed.

This interpretation also fits well Isaiah's classic day of the Lord prophecy: "For the Lord of hosts will have a day of reckoning. . . . And the pride of man will be humbled, and the loftiness of men will *be abased*, and *the Lord alone will be exalted in that day*" (Isa. 2:12, 17, emphasis added). During this period of the Lord's "day of reckoning" (the day of the Lord), the ungodly will "be abased" before they are judged and destroyed.

The key truth is that during the day of the Lord only He will be exalted! Satan will still rule over earth through his minion Antichrist, but only within new and much narrower limitations defined by God, until Antichrist's final destruction at the battle of Armageddon.[6]

The Jewish Counterattack

With Antichrist greatly restricted, persecuted Jews, for the first time since Antichrist took control of Jerusalem and the world, will have some opportunity to carry on a resistance movement against Antichrist. Thus those Jews who have escaped the persecution of Antichrist by hiding in the remote areas of Israel, a part of "the compromising woman" who stayed, will venture out to launch guerrilla attacks against the surrounding nations which have come against Israel in the valley of Jehoshaphat just before the day of the Lord begins. The strategy, in fact, will be much like the ancient resistance movement of Judas Maccabaeus, who lived in the hills of Judea with his forces during the Jewish rebellion against Antiochus Epiphanes in the second century B.C. (see chapter 8). This end-time strategy, moreover, was described clearly when Zechariah prophesied: "In that day [the day of the Lord] I will make the clans of Judah like a firepot among pieces of wood and a flaming torch among sheaves, so they will consume on the right hand and on the left all the surrounding peoples, while *the inhabitants of Jerusalem again dwell on their own sites in Jerusalem*" (Zech. 12:6, emphasis added).

In this passage, of course, "that day" refers to the day of the Lord, when Antichrist will be "rendered useless" or "paralyzed." As a result some Jews who have been so fiercely persecuted will "*again* dwell on their sites in Jerusalem," while others (the clans of Judah) will turn against the restricted forces of Antichrist and return havoc for havoc.

Zechariah goes on to say that the clans of Judah will receive "some help" from the Lord:

> Now this will be the plague with which the Lord will strike all the peoples who have gone to war against Jerusalem; their flesh will rot while they stand on their feet, and their eyes will rot in their sockets, and their tongue will rot in their mouth. And it will come about in that day that a great panic from the Lord will fall on them; and they will seize one another's hand, and the hand of one will be lifted against the hand of another. And Judah also will fight at Jerusalem. (Zech. 14:12-14a)

THE FINAL EVENT OF THE SEVENTIETH WEEK

The final event of the seventieth week of Daniel will be the martyrdom of the two witnesses of Israel — probably Moses and Elijah whom God will bring back to life as his special witnesses during the great tribulation by Antichrist (see chapter 12). God will have sent those two men to make one last proclamation of the gospel, especially to apostate Jews living in Israel, and to give one last proclamation of God's judgment upon those who have not heeded the call to repentance and faith. Those two men will have stood in direct opposition to Antichrist, the false king, and to his false prophet, the enforcer. And when their work is finished, when the seventieth week is complete, God will permit their lives to be taken.

These two men of God will be highly visible during the day of the Lord and will be given supernatural powers "to shut up the sky, in order that rain may not fall during the days of their prophesying; and . . . have power over the waters to turn them into blood, and to smite the earth with every plague, as often as they desire" (Rev. 11:6). Because of this, they will be greatly feared by the unbelieving world, and many of the events of God's wrath probably will be credited to them as God's ambassadors of terror. Consequently, when those two witnesses are killed at the end of the three and a half years (the second half of the seventieth week), the world will rejoice, utterly deluded by the diabolical belief that the end of those "troublemakers" will bring an end to the wrath of God they have been experiencing.

And when they [the two witnesses] have finished their testimony, the beast that comes up out of the abyss will make war with them, and overcome them and kill them. And their dead bodies will lie in the street of the great city which mystically is called Sodom and Egypt, where also their Lord was crucified. And those from the peoples and tribes and tongues and nations will look at their dead bodies for three days and a half, and will not permit their dead bodies to be laid in a tomb. And those who dwell on the earth will rejoice over them and make merry; and they will send gifts to one another, because these two prophets tormented those who dwell on the earth. (Rev. 11:7-10)

As we have seen, Antichrist will have been rendered generally helpless at the return of Christ (2 Thess. 2:8), thereby cutting short his great tribulation persecution of God's elect (Matt. 24:22). Satan, however, will still have spiritual rule over the earth and will, solely upon the permissive will of God, enable Antichrist to kill the two witnesses as his last act of defiance against God, before Antichrist's complete authority is taken away at the conclusion of the seventieth week. By the death of the two witnesses, Antichrist will be deluded into thinking his rule is secure when in reality it is over and will, like the rest of the ungodly world, believe that his battle with the forces of God is finally won. But the only two things God will permit Antichrist to do after he is "rendered useless" will be, first, to kill the two witnesses and, second, to assemble his forces for his predetermined defeat at Armageddon, which is still to come thirty days later.

Although the seventh trumpet will not yet have sounded, the literal sequence of the book of Revelation unequivocally shows that the death of the two witnesses will bring the seventieth week to an end. And despite the fact that the vast majority of prophetic scholars believe that all of the events in the book of Revelation associated with the seals, the trumpets, and the bowls must be completed by the end of the seventieth week, Scripture clearly teaches otherwise. The natural study of the book of Revelation demands that the seals, trumpets, bowls, Armageddon, and the Millennium be taken sequentially, one following the other, without overlap, if we take Scripture at face value. There is nothing in Revelation to suggest any overlap of the various events, but rather that they clearly will occur in sequential order. When this is done, the seventieth week closes with the death of the two witnesses, which must still be followed by the seventh trumpet judgment, the seven bowl judgments, and the battle of Armageddon. Taking these events in that sequence perfectly harmonizes the book of Revelation with the numerous prophetic passages in both the Old and New Testaments, as we shall see in the remaining chapters of this volume.[7]

In light of all this we see that the final event of the seventieth week will be the martyrdom of the two witnesses, their work having been accomplished. Yet to come will be the all-important blowing of the seventh trumpet, the bowl judgments, and the defeat of Antichrist at the battle of Armageddon.

THE FULFILLMENT OF DANIEL 9:24

Way back in chapter 5 of this book, a critical prophetic passage (Daniel 9:24-27) was introduced as one of the most critical prophetic passages of all Scripture. Because of the nation's continued disobedience to God, the nation of Israel had been subjugated to Babylon in 586 B.C., the Temple of Solomon had been destroyed, and their great Defender was withdrawing the protection He had so often provided in the past. Seeing the tragic condition of Israel, Daniel poured out his heart in prayer, pleading with God Almighty to forgive and act on behalf of His chosen nation. In response, God sent His angel Gabriel to Daniel with this message, in part, outlining six things God would do and when He would do them, for the natural line of Abraham.

> Seventy weeks [490 years] have been decreed for your people and your holy city, [1] to finish the transgression, [2] to make an end of sin, [3] to make atonement for iniquity, [4] to bring in everlasting righteousness, [5] to seal up vision and prophecy, and [6] to anoint the most holy. (Dan. 9:24)

With the deaths of the two witnesses, the seventieth week is finished, and three of the six issues (the bad news, so to speak) will be history. Then, and not before, (1) the nation's transgression against God will be finished, (2) their sin against God will be ended, and (3) full atonement (satisfaction given for wrongdoing — *Webster's New World Dictionary*) for their iniquity will be satisfied before God. The "jail sentence" is over; the price has been paid. It is exactly to this issue that Paul explained, "I say then, they [the natural line of Abraham] did not stumble so as to fall, did they? May it never be! But by their transgression [completed at the end of the seventieth week] salvation has come to the Gentiles, to make them jealous. Now if their [Israel's] transgression be riches for the world and their failure be riches for the Gentiles, how much more will their [Israel's] fulfillment be! . . . For I do not want you, brethren, to be uninformed of this mystery, lest you be wise in your own estimation, that a partial hardening has happened to Israel [because of her transgression, her sin, her iniquity] until the fulness of the Gentiles has come in [the end of the seventieth week]; and thus all Israel will be saved . . ." (Rom. 11:11, 12, 25, 26a).

The bad news, then, was that Israel must first atone for her sin, in order to satisfy God for (1) her transgression, (2) her sin, and (3) her iniquity. God will be satisfied at the completion of the seventieth week, but until that time the natural line of Abraham will continue to be spiritually blinded by God. (The reference here is not to the remnant, the spiritual descendants of Abraham raptured as part of the church, but to the nation of Israel that has been spiritually "hardened . . . until the fulness of the Gentiles has come in.") This is why the nation of Israel had to return to the land of Israel as "dry bones," spiritually blinded to the truth of God. Not until the seventieth week is over, not until the natural line of Abraham has fully atoned for their iniquity, will God take off their spiritual blinders and (4) "bring in everlasting righteousness." Then, and only then, will (5) the vision and prophecy of Daniel be sealed up, and (6) the anointing of the most holy will occur.

The good news, then, is that once Israel's iniquity has been atoned for, at the close of the seventieth week, the time has come to "bring in everlasting righteousness" for the remnant of Israel that survived the purge of Antichrist and the refinement of Christ. The time has come to seal up the vision and prophecies of Daniel, and the time has come to anoint the most holy (Christ), in preparation for the first day of the Millennium when "His kingdom will be an everlasting kingdom, and all the dominions will serve and obey Him" (Dan. 7:27).[8]

And so, even though the wrath of God is not yet complete, the seventieth week of Daniel will have ended. The time of the Gentiles will be fulfilled, the fulness of the Gentiles will have come in, and Israel's sin will be atoned for. The time "to bring in" her salvation will have come. The work of the two witnesses will be over, and in his last act of evil defiance Antichrist will have them put to death. For a brief period the world will rejoice, thinking God's wrath has ended. In reality, however, it will be but the beginning of the end for Satan's dominion over the earth. It will be time to "bring in righteousness" for every Jew who has survived the persecution of Antichrist and the wrath of God; it will be time to return the reign over earth to its rightful Ruler, God Almighty, and to anoint the most holy, Jesus Christ; and it will be the time to begin the millennial rule of Christ when "the Lord will be king over all the earth; [when] in that day the Lord will be the only one, and His name the only one" (Zech. 14:9).

The Mystery of God
Is Finished

I t is hard for us to comprehend the monumental importance of the events that begin immediately after the close of the seventieth week. One small verse, pregnant with meaning, outlines truths of such eternal significance that they can only be described as the "mystery of God." As the Lord revealed to John: "In the days of the voice of the seventh angel, when he is about to sound, then the mystery of God is finished, as He preached to His servants the prophets" (Rev. 10:7).

To understand this critical passage, we must look carefully at the events that will occur during the first six days following the close of the seventieth week. These events, associated in and around the blowing of the seventh trumpet, are the heart of the cosmic conflict between God and Satan. In essence they are the focal point of our entire end-times study. A proper understanding of these events is crucial to a proper understanding of *all end-time events*. For this reason we will carefully study each of these, taking the time necessary to clearly understand the eternal significance of each one.

THE SMALL SCROLL

The sequence of events which transpire during the seventieth week of Daniel are recorded in proper chronological order in Revelation 5:1 — 9:21. The seventieth week ends with the death of the two witnesses, as discussed in some detail in the last chapter, after the sixth trumpet judgment kills a third of mankind. Having been "tread under foot . . . for forty-two months" (Rev. 11:2), "until the times of the Gentiles be fulfilled" (Luke 21:24), Israel's purging and purifying will now be complete. Now that the "fulness of the Gentiles has come in . . . all Israel will be saved" (Rom. 11:25, 26). The time of her full redemption, "to bring in everlasting righteousness" (Dan. 9:24), will begin with the opening of the "small scroll" or "little book" as recorded in Revelation 10:2.

The contents of the little book reveal bittersweet truths. John reports, "I took the little book out of the angel's hand and ate it, and it was in my mouth sweet as honey; and when I had eaten it, my stomach was made bitter. And they said to me, 'You must prophesy again concerning many peoples and nations and tongues and kings'" (vv. 10, 11). As we will see in this chapter, the sweetness represents God's gracious redemption of Israel and the return of the kingdom of earth to God Almighty. The bitterness represents the final wrath of God, the worst ever to be poured out, that will be as swift as it is devastating upon unrighteous mankind. This will be looked at more carefully in the next chapter.

But first we must understand a very simple, yet incredibly significant prophetic truth — the piece of the puzzle that makes all the rest fit together perfectly! The seventh trumpet judgment, the seven bowl judgments that follow, and the climactic battle of Armageddon *all occur after* the seventieth week is complete, in the following thirty days. Whereas the large scroll represented the events of the seventieth week, the little scroll with its bittersweet contents is a record of the events that occur *after* the seventieth week is complete.

THE THIRTY-DAY RECLAMATION PERIOD

This thirty-day period, which begins immediately at the end of the seventieth week, may be best described as the "Thirty-Day Reclamation Period." Simply stated, this will be the time when Christ reclaims the nation of Israel that survives the seventieth week to Himself, when God Almighty reclaims the rule over earth from Satan, and when Christ reclaims physical possession of earth at the battle of Armageddon.

To understand this all-important truth, it is necessary to look carefully at Daniel 12:11: "And from the time that the regular sacrifice is abolished, and the abomination of desolation is set up, there will be 1290 days [three and a half years plus thirty days]." Christ speaks of the "ABOMINATION OF DESOLATION which was spoken of through Daniel the prophet" as "standing in the holy place" (Matt. 24:15) when the great tribulation by Antichrist begins, at the midpoint of the seventieth week. Therefore, it is apparent that the "abomination of desolation" referred to by Daniel is, in fact, Antichrist when he "opposes and exalts himself above every so-called god or object of worship, so that he takes his seat in the temple, displaying himself as being god" at the midpoint of the seventieth week (2 Thess. 2:4). However, the wording would appear to say that 1,290 days will separate the end of the regular sacrifice from the abomination of desolation. But we know explicitly from other Scripture that those two events are both initiated at the same time, at the middle of the seventieth week. Thus, Daniel revealed earlier that Antichrist "will make a firm covenant with the many for one week [i.e., seven years], but *in the middle of the week he will put a stop to sacrifice and grain offering; and on the wing of abominations will come one who makes desolate,* even until a complete destruction, one that is decreed, is poured out on the one who makes desolate" (9:27, emphasis added; cf. Matt. 24:15; 2 Thess. 2:4). In other words, Daniel 9:27, as well as the other passages referred to, clearly indicate that the regular sacrifices and the abomination of desolation will be initiated at the same time, at the midpoint of the seventieth week.

How can we reconcile these passages which seem contradictory — several of which clearly teach that these two events will occur at the same time — and our critical text, Daniel 12:11, which would seem to indicate a 1,290 day interval between these two events? The solution lies in the simple fact that Daniel was referring to the *"duration" of the abomination,* not to the "interval" between setting up the abomination and the abolishing of the regular sacrifice. In other words, Antichrist's desecration of the Temple (by stopping the sacrifice and demanding the world's worship from "the holy place") will continue from the middle of the week — that is, from the point when Antichrist "puts a stop to sacrifice and grain offering" for 1,290 days "until a complete destruction, one that is decreed, is poured out on the one who makes desolate" (Dan. 9:27). This, of course, corresponds to three and a half prophetic years of 360 days each (3.5 x 360 = 1,260 days) *plus a thirty-day period immediately following* the last half of the seventieth week of years. This is exactly the position that the noted Old Testament and Hebrew scholar C. F. Keil has proposed for this critical passage:

> The angel gives to the prophet yet one revelation more regarding the *duration of the time of tribulation and its end. . . .* All interpreters *therefore have found in these two verses statements regarding the duration of the persecutions. . . .* Since all interpreters rightly understand that the 1,290 and the 1,335 days have the same "terminus a quo," and thus that the 1,290 days are comprehended in the 1,335, the latter period extending beyond the former by only forty-five days; then *the oppression cannot properly last longer than 1,290 days,* if he who reaches to the 1,335 days is to be regarded as blessed.[1]

We therefore know with certainty that Antichrist will be destroyed on the last day of the thirty-day period — exactly 1,290 days (three and a half years plus thirty days) after he desecrates the Temple by abolishing the sacrifice and demanding the world's worship at the midpoint of the seventieth week.

As we shall see, this is in perfect keeping with a literal sequential view of the book of Revelation. A literal hermeneutic of Revelation *demands* that the day of the Lord will continue after the seventieth week is complete, culminating later in the great battle of Armageddon.* The key, then, to making the obvious sequence of the book of Revelation fit Daniel's seventieth week is to understand one simple fact — that *Antichrist will not be defeated and evicted from earth's premises until the end of the thirty days that follow the close of the seventieth week.* Then the sequence of the seals, the trumpets, the bowls, and Armageddon move smoothly, one after the other, perfectly harmonizing the prophecies of Daniel given some seven hundred years earlier.

During this brief thirty-day period, Christ will accomplish much, as we shall see below, with every day building up steadily to the climactic ending at the battle of Armageddon, when the abominator of God's "holy place" is destroyed and the physical possession of earth is reclaimed by Christ for eternity.

* See chapter 18, endnote 7.

FORETOLD BY HOSEA

A critical passage that gives understanding to the events that *immediately follow the seventieth week* is found in the book of Hosea. This prophet reveals that

> . . . you have played the [spiritual] harlot, Israel has defiled itself. Their deeds will not allow them to return to their God. For a spirit of [spiritual] harlotry is within them, and they do not know the Lord. Moreover, the pride of Israel testifies against him, and Israel and Ephraim stumble in their iniquity; Judah also has stumbled with them. They will go with their flocks and herds to seek the Lord, but they will not find Him; He has withdrawn from them. (Hos. 5:3-6)

Israel had committed spiritual adultery, an offense so serious in God's eyes that "they will go with their flocks and herds to seek the Lord, but they will not find Him; He has withdrawn from them." A few verses later the Lord declares directly through the prophet, "I will go away and return to My place until they acknowledge their guilt and seek My face; in their affliction they will earnestly seek Me" (v. 15).

In the passage from Daniel discussed at some length in the last chapter, the Lord reveals *when* "in their affliction they will earnestly seek Me." "Seventy weeks have been decreed for your people and your holy city, to finish the transgression, to make an end of sin, to make atonement for iniquity" (Dan. 9:24). Paul tells us that this "partial hardening [that] has happened to Israel" will continue "until the fulness of the Gentiles has come in" (Romans 11:25). In other words, Israel as a nation will not "acknowledge their guilt and seek My face" (Hos. 5:15) *until after the seventieth week is complete.* Only then can and will "all Israel . . . be saved; just as it is written, 'The Deliverer will come from Zion, He will remove ungodliness from Jacob'" (Rom. 11:25, 26).

Hosea goes on to reveal the exact day when Israel will acknowledge her sin and the exact day the Lord will bring salvation to Israel. Immediately after the seventieth week is complete — on the first day following, when Israel has atoned for her sin — that chastened and repentant generation will say, "Come, let us return to the Lord. For He has torn us, but He will heal us; He has wounded us, but He will bandage us. He will revive us *after two days*; He will raise us up *on the third*

day that we may live before Him" (Hos. 6:1, 2, emphasis added). After
the completion of the seventieth week, when the sin of Israel has
finally been atoned for, Israel will repent of her sin and two days later
will be reunited spiritually with their Messiah. Then "they will look on
Me whom they have pierced; and they will mourn . . ." (Zech. 12:10).
In other words, Christ will personally return to earth for the salvation
of His nation.

CHRIST'S PHYSICAL RETURN TO EARTH

The thirty-day reclamation period will commence, therefore, when
Christ once again literally returns to earth in physical form, descending to earth from the heavenly Zion for the face-to-face salvation of
Israel. "Christ also, having been offered once to bear the sins of many,
shall appear a second time for salvation without reference to sin, to
those who eagerly await Him [as their King]" (Heb. 9:28). This passage
is not talking about "the appearance [*ĕpiphanĕi*] of His [Christ's] coming [*parousia*]" (2 Thess. 2:8), when the righteous are raptured, but
about when He will physically "appear" again on earth for the spiritual salvation of the nation;[2] that is, when "they will look on Me
whom they have pierced" (Zech. 12:10). The literal meaning of "shall
appear" as used in Hebrews 9:28 comes from an entirely different
Greek verb (*ŏptŏmai*), meaning "to see" or "to be seen." This passage,
then, is speaking about the Jewish remnant that will "see" Christ when
He comes to earth for the second time for the salvation of Israel, the
first time being when Christ "offered [Himself] once to bear the sins of
many" at His first coming (Heb. 9:28a).

When Christ physically comes back to earth specifically for the salvation of the natural line of Abraham that survives the seventieth
week, it will be the first time He will have been physically present on
earth since His departure forty days after His resurrection. The significance of this is taught in a number of Scriptures. First, this is the physical return to earth which the book of Acts refers to, when Christ "will
come in just the same way as you have watched Him go into heaven"
(Acts 1:11). This second time, however, He will come for the spiritual
salvation of the nation of Israel, who will have been spiritually blinded
up until then. Literally, therefore, their "Redeemer will come *to Zion,*
and to those who turn from transgression in Jacob" (Isa. 59:20, emphasis added). But first "the Deliverer will come *from Zion,* [when] He will
remove ungodliness from Jacob" (Rom. 11:26, emphasis added). In

other words, first Christ comes *from* the heavenly Zion down to earth, and then on His way *to* the earthly Zion, the surviving remnant of Israel will be saved![3]

THE "STRONG ANGEL"

Christ's coming down to earth for the salvation of Israel is pictured beautifully in the book of Revelation, exactly where and when it should occur. This then is the first recorded event after the completion of the seventieth week and is depicted clearly in the passage about the "strong angel" with "the little book" who comes down from Heaven:

> I saw another strong angel coming down out of heaven, clothed with a cloud; and the rainbow was upon his head, and his face was like the sun, and his feet like pillars of fire; and he had in his hand a little book which was open. And he placed his right foot on the sea and his left on the land; and he cried out with a loud voice, as when a lion roars; and when he had cried out, the seven peals of thunder uttered their voices. . . . And the angel whom I saw standing on the sea and on the land lifted up his right hand to heaven, and swore by Him who lives forever and ever, who created heaven and the things in it, and the earth and the things in it, and the sea and the things in it, that there shall be delay no longer. (Rev. 10:1-3, 5, 6)

Who is this "strong angel" that John beheld? For several reasons it seems certain that this angel is none other than Christ Himself when He physically comes back to earth for the spiritual salvation of Israel. When we consider the context of the book of Revelation, we see in chapter 5 that only the Lamb of God, Christ (v. 9), is worthy to open the scroll (v. 2) and break its seals. With this in mind, we then see that the "strong angel, coming down out of heaven . . . had in his hand a little book *which was open*" (10:1, 2, emphasis added). If Christ will be the only one permitted to open the large scroll, it is highly probable that He will be the only one worthy to open the smaller scroll as well.

However, probability becomes reality when we compare the "strong angel" of Revelation 10 with a number of Old Testament passages. Bible students throughout the history of the church have generally agreed that unless the context clearly indicates otherwise, Old Testament references to "the angel of the Lord" are references to the appearance of God in visible form to men before the Incarnation. For example, as the *Wycliffe Bible Encyclopedia* states, "it is often inferred that the angel [of the Lord] is, in the Old Testament, a preincarnate appearance of the Second Person [Christ] of the Trinity."[4]

Sometimes the Old Testament text itself makes clear that the angel of the Lord is divine, although the specific person of the Godhead is not stated. Thus when the angel of the Lord appeared to Hagar in the wilderness, she recognized Him as "the Lord . . . a God who sees" and was amazed that she had actually seen God and lived (Gen. 16:7-13). Likewise, the "angel of the Lord" who appeared to Moses in Midian is explicitly called "the Lord" and "God" (Exod. 3:1-4; cf. Judg. 13:21, 22).

With this in mind, it is remarkable to see the similarity between the strong angel in Revelation and Ezekiel's vision of Jehovah during his vision of the four living creatures. Thus the prophet Ezekiel saw that

> above the expanse that was over their heads there was something resembling a throne, like lapis lazuli in appearance; and on that which resembled a throne, high up, was a figure with the appearance of a man. Then I noticed from the appearance of His loins and upward something like glowing metal that looked like fire all around within it, and from the appearance of His loins and downward I saw something like fire; and there was a radiance around Him. As the appearance of the rainbow in the clouds on a rainy day, so was the appearance of the surrounding radiance. Such was the appearance of the likeness of the glory of the Lord. And when I saw it, I fell on my face and heard a voice speaking. (Ezek. 1:26-28)

The "figure with the appearance of a man" clearly refers to Christ, who had "the likeness of the glory of the Lord." The prophet later sees the same figure, described in almost the exact same way: "The hand of the Lord fell on me there. Then I looked, and behold, a likeness as the appearance of a man; from His loins and downward there was the appearance of fire, and from His loins and upward the appearance of brightness, like the appearance of glowing metal" (8:2). Previously, like John in our Revelation account, the Lord gave Ezekiel a scroll to eat, which the prophet says "was sweet as honey in my mouth" (3:3).

Speaking clearly within the context of Christ's appearing for the salvation of Israel, Hosea declares that "they [Israel] will walk after the Lord, He will roar like a lion; indeed He will roar, and His sons will come trembling from the west. They will come trembling like birds from Egypt, and like doves from the land of Assyria; and I will settle them in their houses, declares the Lord" (Hos. 11:10, 11). Hosea uses exactly the same language as John when the apostle explains that the strong angel "cried out with a loud voice, as when a lion roars" (Rev. 10:3).

Putting all these pieces together, it seems incontestable that "the figure with appearance of a man" depicted by Ezekiel corresponds to the angel described by John in Revelation 10, and that both passages correspond to the coming of the Lord for the salvation of Israel exactly as described by Hosea. When we take these passages together, then, there are at least four reasons why these passages from Ezekiel, Hosea, and Revelation refer to the literal return of Christ to earth for the salvation of Israel. First, the strong angel is shown "coming down out of heaven," initiating the thirty-day reclamation period with His "open" little book or scroll. Second, Ezekiel's description of a "figure with the appearance of a man" who had "the likeness of the glory of the Lord" and John's description of the "strong angel" of Revelation are remarkably similar (Ezek. 1:27, 28; 8:2; Rev. 10:1). Third, the heavenly persons give the two human witnesses of these events (the prophet Ezekiel and the Apostle John) small scrolls to eat that were sweet to the taste (Ezek. 3:1-3; Rev. 10:9). And finally, the voices of the heavenly persons are compared to the roaring of lions (Hos. 11:10; Rev. 10:3; cf. 5:5), which, as we shall see, is directly associated with the salvation of the remnant of Israel that survives the seventieth week.

THE ITINERARY OF CHRIST'S EARTHLY JOURNEY

Therefore, as so beautifully pictured in the book of Revelation, Christ will come down to earth at the beginning of the thirty-day reclamation period to bring the salvation of Israel and to reclaim rule over earth for God Almighty. In doing this, not only will Christ physically come back to earth *from* the heavenly Zion (Rom. 11:26), but He will also be going *to* the earthly Zion (Isa. 59:20), bringing everlasting righteousness to the seventieth-week survivors of Israel. It is this triumphant activity of Christ during this thirty-day period that we will now consider.

DAYS ONE AND TWO: EDOM TO ISRAEL

Israel, having atoned for her sin, will now "acknowledge their guilt and seek My face; in their affliction they will earnestly seek Me"

(Hos. 5:15). Therefore, "The Deliverer [Christ] will come from Zion, [in order to] remove ungodliness from Jacob [Israel]" (Rom. 11:26). Immediately then after the close of the seventieth week, Christ will physically come back to earth — specifically to Edom. Out of Edom — "where she had a place prepared by God, so that she might be nourished for one thousand two hundred and sixty days" (Rev. 12:6) — Christ will personally gather together the 144,000 (the first fruits of Israel) who were saved immediately after the rapture of the church (see chapter 17).

Isaiah graphically depicts Christ's return to earth when he asks rhetorically, "Who is this who comes from Edom, with garments of glowing colors from Bozrah [a capital of Edom], this one who is majestic in His apparel, marching in the greatness of His strength? 'It is I who speak in righteousness, mighty to save.' Why is Your apparel red, and Your garments like the one who treads in the wine press? 'I have trodden the wine trough alone, and from the peoples there was no man with Me. I also trod them in My anger, and trampled them in My wrath; and their life blood is sprinkled on My garments, and I stained all My raiment. For the day of vengeance was in My heart, and My year of redemption [for Israel] has come'" (Isa. 63:1-3).

Christ is pictured coming from Edom in garments sprinkled with the lifeblood of those enduring His wrath that has already begun. Later He will be clothed in those same blood-stained garments when He returns to earth with His armies at the final battle of Armageddon (Rev. 19:11), the last event of the day of the Lord some thirty days later. In addition to this, the text clearly states that He is going forth because "My year of redemption has come." Hosea says that "His going forth [for the salvation of Israel] is as certain as the dawn; and He will come to us like the rain" (Hos. 6:3). The time will have come for the salvation of the natural line of Abraham that survives the seventieth week.

Although this passage does not mention the 144,000, it clearly shows Christ coming out of Edom after the day of the Lord has begun. The reference to marching seems to suggest a large group, since that activity is not normally associated with a single individual. Because the Lord promises He will return to His "place" until His people "acknowledge their guilt and . . . earnestly seek [Him]" (Hos. 5:15); because Christ will not go forth to bring salvation to Israel until after the seventieth week is complete; because the 144,000 will be leaving Edom at the same time that Christ will come "from Zion" to Edom (their wilderness sojourn limited to forty-two months — Rev. 12:6);

and because the 144,000 will follow Christ wherever He goes — it therefore seems reasonable to conclude that the 144,000 will follow Christ on His triumphal march from Edom to Mount Zion in the city of Jerusalem. Just five days later, as we shall see, the 144,000 will be seen with Christ on Mount Zion for a very special occasion.

The prophet Habakkuk also vividly describes Christ's coming from Edom: "God comes from Teman [a village in Edom], and the Holy One from Mount Paran [which borders Edom and Sinai]. Selah. His splendor covers the heavens, and the earth is full of His praise. His radiance is like the sunlight; He has rays flashing from His hand, and there is the hiding of His power. Before Him goes pestilence, and plague comes after Him. He stood and surveyed the earth; He looked and startled the nations. Yes, the perpetual mountains were shattered, the ancient hills collapsed. His ways are everlasting. . . . In indignation Thou didst march through the earth; in anger Thou didst trample the nations " (Hab. 3:3-6, 12). Significantly the phrase "His radiance is like sunlight" (Hab. 3:4) is the same description John gives of the "strong angel" whose "face [is] like the sun" (Rev. 10:1), further confirming that Christ is indeed the "strong angel."

Habakkuk goes on to declare, "Thou didst go forth for the salvation of Thy people, for the salvation of Thine anointed. Thou didst strike the head of the house of the evil to lay him open from thigh to neck" (Hab. 3:13). This single verse reveals two extremely significant truths. First, it mentions Christ's going "forth for the salvation of His people" — in other words, for the ultimate salvation of the nation of Israel. The second significant truth found here is that Christ will "strike the head of the house of the evil to lay him [Antichrist] open from thigh to neck." The order of events is both specific and significant. During the day of God's indignation Christ will come forth from Edom (i.e., from Teman, a village in Edom; v. 3) first for the salvation of His people (v. 13a) and then for the final destruction of Antichrist (v. 13b), "whom the Lord will slay with the breath of His mouth" (2 Thess. 2:8), at the end of the thirty-day period, when Christ reclaims physical possession of the earth.

It is truly remarkable to understand the significance of these vivid prophetic passages — for these passages describe in graphic detail what will literally happen immediately after the close of the seventieth week. Christ will come physically to Edom in majestic garments, sprinkled with the lifeblood of the enemies He has just trampled with His wrath. He will come to gather together the 144,000 divinely hidden in Edom, and for the next two days they will follow Christ on foot north along the east side of the Dead Sea, west across the Jordan River, southwest up into the Judean wilderness, and finally in a triumphal procession into the city of Jerusalem, where He will bring everlasting righteousness to the natural line of Abraham that survives the seventieth week of Daniel. The scene will bring shouts of joy to the clans of Judah and to the house of Israel who are in mourning — to all who are looking for the physical return of their Messiah — as they see this multitude coming from the east and returning to the holy city of Jerusalem and its holy mountain.

DAY THREE: THE MYSTERY IS COMPLETE!

"Come, let us return to the Lord. For He has torn us, but He will heal us; He has wounded us, but He will bandage us. For He will revive us after two days; He will raise us up on the third day that we may live before Him" (Hos. 6:1, 2). We now come to one of the most profound truths of all of Scripture — "the mystery of God" — God's plan for the spiritual salvation of Israel that goes back to God's covenant with Abraham, that is woven throughout the pages of Scripture, and that indeed was sovereignly ordained by God in eternities past.

To understand this monumental truth, we need to consider it in light of a number of Scripture passages both in the Old and New Testaments. Turning first to Revelation, John makes an ever so small comment that has an ever so large significance to all end-time prophecy. He simply says that "in the days of the voice of the seventh angel, when he is about to sound, then *the mystery of God* is finished, as He preached to His servants the prophets" (Rev. 10:7). What is this mystery to which John refers? What is the significance of this mystery to end-time events?

First, what is this mystery to which John refers? It refers to one of the most significant of all prophetic events. As Paul explains this mystery in his letter to Rome, he first reminds Gentile believers that they "were cut off from what is by nature a wild olive tree, and were grafted contrary to nature into a cultivated olive tree" (Rom. 11:24). In other words, the Gentiles were not the physical descendants of God's chosen nation Israel, through whom the Messiah was divinely ordained to come (John 4:22). And although the vast majority of Jews had not received their Messiah at His first coming — but, in fact, participated in His crucifixion — believing Gentiles nevertheless are spiritually grafted into the tree of salvation which God originally planted in

Abraham. Believing Gentiles, therefore, become Abraham's *spiritual* descendants, but are not a part of the natural line of Israel.

Paul's point was that despite Israel's rejection of Christ, God had not forever rejected the natural line of Abraham (Israel). "I do not want you, brethren, to be uninformed of this mystery," the apostle explained, "lest you be wise in your own estimation, that a partial hardening has happened to Israel until the fulness of the Gentiles has come in" (Rom. 11:25). As we have seen, the fullness of the Gentiles refers to the period of Daniel's seventy weeks of years, including the unspecified but already long interval between the sixty-ninth and seventieth weeks.

Israel's "partial hardness" refers to her spiritual blindness — her inability as a people and a nation to perceive divine truth. Earlier in the same passage Paul had already explained that "that which Israel is seeking for [salvation], it has not obtained, but those who were chosen obtained it, and the rest were hardened" (v. 7). In this regard, Jews and Gentiles are essentially the same: The majority of Jews have been spiritually blind for exactly the same reason that the majority of Gentiles are also blind to God's truth. As Paul warned believers in Ephesus, "walk no longer just as the Gentiles also walk, in the futility of their mind, being darkened in their understanding, excluded from the life of God, because of the ignorance that is in them, because of the hardness of their heart" (Eph. 4:17, 18).

Stated concisely, then, the mystery of God referred to in Revelation 10:7 and Romans 11:25 is this: it is God's divine plan to bring Israel's spiritual blindness and alienation from God to an end precisely at His appointed time, which is not meant to be "until the fulness of the Gentiles has come in" (Rom. 11:25) — that is, after the end of the seventy weeks of Gentile domination which He required of the nation as a penalty for their sin. Only then will God "bring in everlasting righteousness" (Dan. 9:24). By God's sovereign power and provision, at a particular moment several days after the seventieth week is complete "all Israel will be saved; just as it is written, 'The Deliverer will come from Zion, [and] He will remove ungodliness from Jacob'" (Rom. 11:26). Similarly, the writer of Hebrews assures us that Christ "shall appear a second time, not to bear sin, to those who eagerly await Him" (Heb. 9:28). And although the hearts of most Jews were unprepared to receive Christ at His first coming, the hearts of the Jewish remnant will "eagerly await Him" when He comes the second time.

The second question, what is the significance of this mystery to end-time events? is answered by the timing John gives as to when "the mystery of God is finished." The mystery will be finished "in the days of the voice of the seventh trumpet, when he is about to sound." In other words, Israel is saved just before the seventh trumpet sounds; and since the seventh trumpet does not sound until after the two witnesses have been resurrected on the fourth day following the close of the seventieth week (Rev. 11:11, 15), the timing of Israel's salvation given by John in the New Testament substantiates exactly the timing of Israel's salvation given by Hosea in the Old Testament: "He will revive us after two days; He will raise us up on the third day" (6:2).

"Why," we might ask, "the third day?" Perhaps we can gain insight into this question by looking at how God gave the Old Covenant to Israel. When the natural line of Abraham (still in the wilderness by Mount Sinai) were instructed by God through Moses to "obey My voice and keep My covenant" (Exod. 19:5), they responded, "All that the Lord has spoken we will do" (v. 8). Then in reply the Lord told Moses, "Go to the people and consecrate them today and tomorrow, and let them wash their garments; and let them be ready for the third day, for on the third day the Lord will come down on Mount Sinai in the sight of all the people" (vv. 10, 11). "So it came about on the third day, when it was morning, that there were thunder and lightning flashes and a thick cloud upon the mountain and a very loud trumpet sound, so that all the people who were in the camp trembled. And Moses brought the people out of the camp to meet God, and they stood at the foot of the mountain" (vv. 16, 17). "Then God spoke all these words . . ." (20:1), and the Old Covenant was made with the natural line of Abraham. The New Covenant clearly parallels the Old Covenant. Three days after Israel has atoned for her sin, saying, "Come, let us return to the Lord" (Hos. 6:1), the New Covenant will be established. Then "He will raise us up on the third day that we may live before Him" (v. 2).

In any event, after Christ physically comes to Edom and escorts the 144,000 to Mount Zion in the city of Jerusalem, probably on foot, they will pass through the eastern Judean hills. During this time they will be joined by other surviving Jews — namely, the "clans of Judah" who have not taken the mark of the beast, those who have instead been fighting against the surrounding Gentile nations in the valley of Jehoshaphat. These will be the first group of the remnant that survives the seventieth week — "the compromising woman" — to put their faith in Christ as Savior and to join their Messiah on His way to Jerusalem with the 144,000 — "the faithful woman" — His first fruits. Unlike the 144,000 who will be protected by God in the wilderness because they never will have apostacized during the first half of the seventieth week, these "clans of Judah" will have survived the initial onslaught of Antichrist at the midpoint of the seventieth week and will have sought refuge in the remote areas of Israel when Antichrist's true identity is revealed. These will have been fighting the armies of the surrounding Gentile nations since Antichrist was "rendered useless" at the beginning of the day of the Lord. The salvation of the remnant in the Judean hills is confirmed further by the prophet Zechariah who wrote that "the Lord also will save the tents of Judah *first* in order that the glory of the house of David and the glory of the inhabitants of Jerusalem may not be magnified above Judah" (Zech. 12:7, emphasis added).

Along the way to Jerusalem, perhaps in the hills of Judea, one more group — a part of "the compromising woman" — will be added. These are the Jews who, like the clans of Judah, survived the initial onslaught of Antichrist and will return to Israel from the lands of Egypt and Assyria where they have been hiding. As Hosea explains, "They will walk after the Lord, He will roar like a lion; indeed He will roar, and His sons will come trembling from the west. They will come trembling like birds from Egypt, and like doves from the land of Assyria . . ." (Hos. 11:10, 11a).

In order to assist their return from the remote areas of Egypt and Assyria where they have been in hiding, "a highway will be there, a roadway, and it will be called the 'highway of holiness.' The unclean will not travel on it, but it will be for him who walks that way, and fools will not wander on it" (Isa. 35:8), for "your God will come with vengeance; the recompense of God will come, but He will save you" (v. 4). As recorded earlier in Isaiah, "It will come about in that day, that the Lord will start His threshing from the flowing stream of the Euphrates to the brook of Egypt; and you will be gathered up one by one, O sons of Israel. It will come about also in that day that a great trumpet will be blown; and those who were perishing in the land of Assyria and who were scattered in the land of Egypt will come and worship the Lord in the holy mountain at Jerusalem" (Isa. 27:12, 13; cf. Jer. 31:21, 31). God's roaring will be a last call of repentance to Israel, which they will heed. And as they return from Assyria and from

Egypt, they will join the Lord with His great entourage marching triumphantly to Jerusalem.

After the clans of Judah are saved, the Lord "will pour out on the house of David and on the inhabitants of Jerusalem, the Spirit of grace and of supplication, so that they will look on Me whom they have pierced; and they will mourn for Him, as one mourns for an only son, and they will weep bitterly over Him, like the bitter weeping over a first-born" (Zech. 12:10). "The house of David and . . . the inhabitants of Jerusalem" suggest that many other Jews in Israel — all a part of "the compromising woman" — will have returned to Jerusalem after Christ appeared initially and incapacitated Antichrist. Further confirmation of this is seen when Zechariah refers to "the inhabitants of Jerusalem [who] *again* dwell on their own sites in Jerusalem" when "the clans of Judah . . . consume on the right hand and on the left all the surrounding peoples" (12:6, emphasis added). These will be among those who will "eagerly await Him" when He "shall appear a second time" (Heb. 9:28).

It will be an unequaled majestic procession. As Christ begins His journey northwestward from Edom with the 144,000, an ever-increasing army of the faithful brand-new believers will join the triumphant procession — first the fighting remnant in the hills of Judah, then those from Egypt and Assyria, and finally a multitude living "again" in the city of Jerusalem. As in His triumphal entry a few days before His crucifixion, Christ will again approach and enter Jerusalem from the east with a great throng praising His name. But unlike that previous crowd, those who follow Him at the future triumphal entry will not be fickle followers whose acclaim quickly turns to derision. These instead will be men, women, and children who have had their spiritual blinders removed and, with the "mystery of God" now finished, have come into a saving relationship with their true Messiah. They will be genuine believers and true children of God, the spiritual as well as the physical descendants of Abraham, the father of all the faithful (Rom. 4:11; cf. John 8:39-44; Gal. 3:7).

And so the Lord will graciously save a remnant of His chosen nation Israel. "*I will bring the third part through the fire,*" the Lord declared long ago, "refine them as silver is refined, and test them as gold is tested. They will call on My name, and I will answer them; I will say, 'They are My people,' and they will say, 'The Lord is my God'" (Zech. 13:9). As prophesied through Moses over three thousand years ago, the Lord proclaims: "when their uncircumcised hearts are humbled and they pay [make atonement] for their sin, I will remember my covenant with Jacob and my covenant with Isaac and my covenant with Abraham.... I will not reject them or abhor them so as to destroy them completely, breaking my covenant with them. I am the Lord their God. But for their sake I will remember the covenant with their ancestors.... I am the Lord" (Lev. 26:41b, 42, 44b, 45, NIV).

DAY FOUR: THE TWO-WITNESS RESURRECTION

The next event that occurs will be the resurrection of the two witnesses (probably Moses and Elijah), whose martyrdom will be the last event of the seventieth week.* The time of their resurrection is stated specifically in Revelation: "And after the three and a half days the breath of life from God came into them, and they stood on their feet; and great fear fell upon those who were beholding them" (Rev. 11:11). Their resurrection is therefore three and a half days into the thirty-day period — that is, probably sometime in the afternoon or early evening of the fourth day, three and a half days (eighty-four hours) after the two witnesses are martyred. The phrasing "the breath of life from God came into them" suggests the possibility that Christ Himself will resurrect the two witnesses while He is in Jerusalem.

Without being dogmatic, it seems that God will raise up the two witnesses and take them back to Himself in this way for several reasons: their mission will be accomplished; the seventieth week will be complete; the rule of Antichrist will be destroyed; the surviving remnant of Israel will all be saved; and Christ will be present personally to breathe life into their breathless bodies and send them "up into heaven in the cloud," where their enemies will behold them (Rev. 11:12). What a powerful testimony and time of rejoicing for the believing remnant of Israel as together with Christ they will see these things happen firsthand.

During that very hour there will be a great earthquake, and a tenth of the city will fall, seven thousand people will be killed by the earthquake, and the rest will be terrified and give "glory to the God of heaven" (Rev. 11:13).

And so we come to the climactic turning point in God's sovereign plan decreed in eternities past. "The second woe is past," John writes, "the third woe is coming quickly" (Rev. 11:14). This third woe will be the sounding of the seventh trumpet, bringing about the most

* See chapter 12, endnote 7 and chapter 18.

significant transformation the world will have ever known since its corruption by the sin of Adam and Eve.

DAY FIVE: THE SEVENTH TRUMPET!

It is hard for us to comprehend the full importance of the sounding of the seventh trumpet, which will most probably occur on the fifth day following the completion of the seventieth week. To capture some sense of its overwhelming significance, we must see that it is in one sense the culmination of God's sovereign plan of redemption determined in eternities past. It must be seen in the context of one of the most monumental events ever revealed by God to man — on a level with creation, the Fall, the Incarnation, the death and resurrection of Christ, and His second coming, for the sounding of the trumpet marks the point at which God Almighty reclaims divine authority over the earth from Satan, the great usurper and consummate enemy of God.

This significance is captured with beautiful simplicity in the words of Scripture:

> And the seventh angel sounded; and there arose loud voices in heaven, saying, "The kingdom of the world has become the kingdom of our Lord, and of His Christ; and He will reign forever and ever." And the twenty-four elders, who sit on their thrones before God, fell on their faces and worshiped God, saying, "We give Thee thanks, O Lord God, the Almighty, who art and wast, because Thou hast taken Thy great power and hast begun to reign." (Rev. 11:15-17)

It is particularly important to note that "the kingdom of the world [will] become the kingdom of our Lord [God the Father], and of His Christ" immediately *after* the seventh trumpet is blown but *before* the beginning of the bowl judgments (i.e., before "the third woe" [Rev. 11:14]). For as our text in Revelation continues to say, "the nations [still in existence] were enraged, and Thy wrath [the third woe] came . . ." (v. 18). This same sequence is seen in Daniel's prophecy: "In the days of those kings the God of heaven will *set up a kingdom which will never be destroyed*, and that kingdom will not be left for another people; *it will crush and put an end to all these kingdoms*, but it will itself endure forever" (Dan. 2:44, emphasis added).

As important as the sounding of the seventh trumpet will be, it is also interesting to note where this event will occur. This event will occur on top of Mount Zion. Remember, Isaiah has specifically stated that the "Redeemer will come to Zion" (59:20) when Israel is saved, and later Mount Zion will become the throne room of Christ when He rules over the millennial kingdom (see chapter 21 of this book). Therefore, Mount Zion is where Christ will be when the seventh trumpet sounds, when the voices in Heaven will say, "The kingdom of the world has become the kingdom of our Lord, and of His Christ, and He will reign forever and ever" (Rev. 11:15).

We are given an Old Testament glimpse of this truth, as well as a New Testament confirmation of the same. Obadiah gives the first clue when he prophesies that "the deliverers will ascend Mount Zion to judge the mountain of Esau, and the kingdom will be the Lord's" (Obad. 21). And who are the "deliverers"? There is only one group that "follow the Lamb wherever He goes" (Rev. 14:4). If they have followed Christ from Edom through the hills of Judea into the city of Jerusalem, they are sure to have followed Him to the top of Mount Zion as well. Thus John, in the book of Revelation, makes clear who the "deliverers" are:

> And I looked, and behold, *the Lamb was standing on Mount Zion, and with Him one hundred and forty-four thousand*, having His name and the name of His Father written on their foreheads. And I heard a voice from heaven, like the sound of many waters and like the sound of loud thunder, and the voice which I heard was like the sound of harpists playing on their harps. And they [the voice in heaven] sang a new song before the throne and before the four living creatures and the elders; and no one could learn the song except the one hundred and forty-four thousand [on Mount Zion] who had been purchased from the earth. (Rev. 14:1-3, emphasis added)

And the song that the voice from Heaven sings — the song "like the sound of harpists playing on their harps" — is sung by

> those who had come off victorious from the beast and from his image and from the number of his name, standing on the sea of glass, holding harps of God. And they sang the song of Moses the bond-servant of God and the song of the Lamb, saying, "Great and marvelous are Thy works, O Lord God, the Almighty; righteous and true are Thy ways, *Thou King of the nations*. Who will not

fear, O Lord, and glorify Thy name? For Thou alone art holy; for all the nations will come and worship before Thee, for Thy righteous acts have been revealed." (Rev. 15:2-4, emphasis added)

As an aside, this writer is absolutely convinced that the "Psalm of Ascension," Psalm 118, will be sung by the 144,000 as they walk to the summit of Mount Zion. It is this particular psalm that is sung by Israel in connection with the Feast of Tabernacles when, once a year, they travel to the top of Mount Zion, where the celebration is held even today. This feast, which occurs exactly five days after the Day of Atonement, is celebrated only on Mount Zion. Although Psalm 118 is used in the Feast of Tabernacles to represent God's protection during their forty-year wilderness sojourn and God's provision in the harvest, in reality this psalm is clearly prophetic, looking forward to the national salvation of Israel after undergoing great distress and the severe discipline of the Lord.[5*] No psalm, then, could be more fitting for Israel to sing as Christ and the 144,000 make their way to the top of Mount Zion for the sounding of the seventh trumpet.

At the sounding of the seventh trumpet, the rule over earth will be reclaimed by God Almighty, its rightful Ruler (Rev. 11:15). As far as His enemies are concerned, all that remains will be the devastating bowl judgments upon wicked mankind and the final conquest of Antichrist and his armies by Christ and His reapers at the battle of Armageddon (Rev. 19:17-21), when Christ reclaims physical possession of the earth.

DAY SIX: REMNANT TO AZEL

The final wrath of God, which will be "poured out" upon the nations during the seven bowl judgments, will culminate in the battle of Armageddon at the end of the thirty-day period. During that time of final wrath (Rev. 15:1), the newly saved nation of Israel will be divinely hidden and protected, probably for no longer than three weeks. "Come, my people, enter into your rooms, and close your doors behind you," the Lord will bid them; "hide for a little while, until indignation runs its course. For behold, the Lord is about to come out from His place to punish the inhabitants of the earth for their iniquity; and the earth will reveal her bloodshed, and will no longer cover her slain" (Isa. 26:20, 21).

* See further the Epilogue, where this is developed in full.

These believers will need to flee Jerusalem, probably on the sixth day of the thirty-day reclamation period, because the seventh bowl judgment will completely destroy the city of Jerusalem. The final battle of Armageddon will extend far beyond the plains of Esdraelon, covering most, if not all, of the land of Israel. As a result of that last great battle alone, the blood from the divine "wine press" will reach "up to the horses' bridles, for a distance of two hundred miles" (Rev. 14:20).

Zechariah perhaps gives a clue as to how God will preserve these believers. "For I will gather all the nations against Jerusalem to battle," the Lord says,

> and the city will be captured [the Jerusalem Campaign], the houses plundered, the women ravished, and half of the city exiled, but the rest of the people will not be cut off from the city. Then the Lord will go forth and fight against those nations [the day of the Lord], as when He fights on a day of battle. And in that day [on the sixth day after the seventieth week is complete] His feet will stand on the Mount of Olives, which is in front of Jerusalem on the east; and the Mount of Olives will be split in its middle from east to west by a very large valley, so that half of the mountain will move toward the north and the other half toward the south. And you will flee by the valley of My mountains, for the valley of the mountains will reach to Azel; yes, you will flee just as you fled before the earthquake in the days of Uzziah king of Judah. Then the Lord, my God, will come [at Armageddon], and all the holy ones [His armies] with Him! (Zech. 14:2-5)

In this depiction of the day of the Lord, we see Christ's provision for His people's escape. After He miraculously splits the Mount of Olives, the remnant escapes through the "valley of the mountains" to a place called Azel — a place whose location is not identified in Scripture and is only known by God. Although Satan would never be able to penetrate a shield created by God, he will not have even the opportunity to try to harm that righteous remnant protectively hidden in Azel. There is no historical area in Israel known as Azel. God intended it this way, for it will be here that the nation of Israel, now the spiritual descendants of Abraham, will hide until the wrath of God is complete, until physical possession of earth has been taken by Christ (v. 5), and until the millennial inhabitants of Christ's earthly kingdom, soon to begin, can return safely to the city of Jerusalem.

LATER: CHRIST RETURNS TO HEAVEN

After Christ splits the Mount of Olives and provides the believing Jews a way of escape to Azel, He will return to Heaven. Scripture is not explicit as to the exact time that Christ will return to the heavenlies, except that it obviously must occur *after* He splits the Mount of Olives, but *before* He comes back to earth with His holy ones to defeat Antichrist and his forces at Armageddon, at the end of the 1,290 days allotted to Antichrist.

THE BEMA-SEAT JUDGMENT

After Christ returns to Heaven, He will hold court at the divine "Bema Seat,"[6] where all the elect who have been resurrected or raptured will be judged according to their *faithfulness to God*. This is in great contrast to the Great White Throne judgment at the end of the Millennium, when the unsaved of all ages will be judged and condemned according to their *faith in God* — or, more exactly, according to their lack of faith in Him (Rev. 20:11-15).

In his second letter to Corinth, Paul reminds every believer that "We must all appear before the *judgment-seat* of Christ, that each one may be recompensed for his deeds in the body, according to what he has done, whether good or bad" (2 Cor. 5:10, emphasis added; see also Rom. 14:10, 12). In his first letter to the Corinthians, however, the apostle gives a vivid and somber picture of what that judgment will be like. Paul warns, "let each man be careful how he builds upon" the foundation we have been given in Jesus Christ. "For no man can lay a foundation other than the one which is laid, which is Jesus Christ. Now if any man builds upon the foundation with gold, silver, precious stones, wood, hay, straw, each man's work will become evident; for the day will show it, because it is to be revealed with fire; and the fire itself will test the quality of each man's work. If any man's work which he has built upon it remains, he shall receive a reward. If any man's work is burned up, he shall suffer loss; but he himself shall be saved, yet so as through fire" (1 Cor. 3:9-15). Many of these, sad to say, will be those within the compromising church, untaught and thus unprepared for the fiery testing of Antichrist. Needlessly, these will suffer the full brunt of Antichrist's persecution, but nonetheless will be saved "as through fire" (1 Cor. 3:15).

The timing of the bema-seat judgment is clearly pinpointed in the book of Revelation as occurring right after the seventh trumpet is sounded:

> And the seventh angel sounded; and there arose loud voices in heaven, saying, "The kingdom of the world has become the kingdom of our Lord, and of His Christ; and He will reign forever and ever." And the twenty-four elders, who sit on their thrones before God, fell on their faces and worshiped God, saying, "We give Thee thanks, O Lord God, the Almighty, who art and who wast, because Thou hast taken Thy great power and hast begun to reign. And the nations were enraged, and Thy wrath came, *and the time came for the dead to be judged . . . to give their reward to Thy bond-servants the prophets and to the saints and to those who fear Thy name*, the small and the great, and to destroy those who destroy the earth." (Rev. 11:15-18)

The significance of this is clearly evident: When the seventh angel sounds (v. 15a), rule over all earthly kingdoms will be returned to God Almighty (vv. 15b-17), and believers will then be rewarded at the bema-seat judgment on the basis of their faithfulness (v. 18a). Immediately following will be the destruction of "those who destroy the earth" (v. 18b) as carried out in the final bowl judgments of God's great wrath.[7]

While Christ holds court over the church at the bema seat, another Judge will be holding an immeasurably more severe court over Satan and his final beast empire. Describing that divine tribunal, Daniel tells how he "kept looking in the night visions" until he saw the final beast who was "dreadful and terrifying and extremely strong."

> I kept looking until thrones were set up, and the Ancient of Days took His seat; His vesture was like white snow, and the hair of His head like pure wool. His throne was ablaze with flames, its wheels were a burning fire. A river of fire was flowing and coming out from before Him; thousands upon thousands were attending Him, and myriads upon myriads were standing before Him; the court sat, and the books were opened. Then I kept looking because of the sound of the boastful words [spoken

by the beast]; I kept looking until the beast [Antichrist] was slain, and its body was destroyed and given to the burning fire. (Dan. 7:9-11)

The execution of the sentence handed down by this divine "Supreme Court" will begin with God's final wrath in the bowl judgments. While His angelic reapers prepare themselves to administer that final punishment of God's enemies (in particular Antichrist and Satan's final beast empire), the saints of God will receive their rewards and be made ready to become the purified and spotless bride of Christ.

The Final Wrath
of God

At the beginning of the day of the Lord, as we saw in chapter 18, Antichrist will be "rendered useless" — in effect "paralyzed" with regard to his ability to inflict further destruction, except within the very narrow limits allowed by God. Antichrist and his satanic forces, therefore, will still be in existence, though "paralyzed," even after the rightful reign over the earth has been returned to God Almighty. This corresponds specifically to Daniel's prophecy that "in the days of those kings [the kings of the final beast empire] the God of heaven will set up a kingdom which will never be destroyed, and that kingdom will not be left for another people; it will crush and put an end to all these kingdoms, but it will itself endure forever" (Dan. 2:44). The sequence expressed here is critical. This verse makes clear that God will *first* establish His indestructible kingdom *and then* He will utterly crush the end-times nations that oppose Him. In other words, the kingdoms of Antichrist will be destroyed *after* God has established His everlasting kingdom at the seventh trumpet.

A PREVIEW OF GOD'S JUDGMENT

The sequence of what will happen — from the sounding of the seventh trumpet to the final destruction of the satanic nations of Antichrist — is outlined concisely and with remarkable precision in Revelation 11:15-19. Using an outline form, the sequence is clearly evident as follows:

I. *The Seventh Trumpet Is Sounded*
"And the seventh angel sounded" (v. 15a).

II. *Almighty God Reclaims His Reign Over the World*
"And there arose loud voices, in heaven, saying, 'The kingdom of this world has become the kingdom of our Lord and of His Christ; and He will reign forever and ever.' And the twenty-four elders, who sit on their thrones before God, fell on their faces and worshiped God, saying, 'We give thanks, O Lord God, the Almighty, who art and who wast, because Thou hast taken Thy great power and hast begun to reign'" (vv. 15b-17).

III. *Still on Earth After God's Reign Begins, the Nations Respond with Rage*
"And the nations were enraged'" (v. 18a).

IV. *God Pours Out His Wrath on the Nations*
"'And Thy wrath came'" (v. 18b).

V. *The Bema-seat Judgment Takes Place*
"'And the time came for the dead to be judged, and the time to give their reward to thy bond-servants the prophets and to the saints and to those who fear thy name'" (v. 18c).

VI. *The Time Has Come to Destroy the Nations*
"'. . . and [the time came] to destroy those who destroy the earth'" (v. 18d).

VII. *A Preview of the Bowl Judgments Is Given*
"And the temple of God which is in heaven was opened; and the ark of His covenant appeared in His temple, and there were flashes of lightning and sounds and peals of thunder and an earthquake and a great hailstorm" (v. 19).

This vivid preview of the dreadful bowl judgments — with the heavenly temple opened to the accompaniment of lightning, thunder, an earthquake, and a great hailstorm — is described further when John continues to recount this awesome vision, after a three-chapter interlude, later in the book of Revelation:

> I saw another sign in heaven, great and marvelous, seven angels who had seven plagues, which are the last, because in them the wrath of God is finished. . . . After these things I looked, *and the temple of the tabernacle of testimony in heaven was opened*, and the seven angels who had the seven plagues came out of the temple, clothed in linen, clean and bright, and girded around their breasts with golden girdles. And one of the four living creatures gave to the seven angels seven golden bowls full of the wrath of God, who lives forever and ever. And the temple was filled with smoke from the glory of God and from His power; and no one was able to enter the temple until the seven plagues of the seven angels were finished. (Rev. 15:1, 5-8, emphasis added)

The description of God's judgment as being poured out from bowls is especially fitting. The Greek word used in Revelation refers to a shallow bowl or saucer out of which the contents can be rapidly poured.[1] Additional insight is given us by Old Testament scholars:

> A common idiom is the use of *shapak* [*Strong's*, 8210 — "pour out"] in connection with the building of siege ramps (II Sam 20:15; Isa 37:33; Jer 6:6; Ezk 4:2). This usage may derive from the fact that soldier workmen carried dirt in baskets to the designated spot, then poured the dirt out. In the category of metaphoric uses, that of the outpouring of God's wrath is most frequent. Thus in Isa 42:25 God is depicted as pouring out on Israel the heat of this anger. The symbolism is certainly obvious but nevertheless intensely sobering, and underlies the imagery of the bowls or vials of wrath in Revelation.[2]

This concept — i.e., of God's final wrath being poured out of relatively shallow but wide-rimmed bowls — indicates that God's final judgment will be both swift and pervasive, which is the general understanding reflected in both the Old and New Testaments. For example, Jeremiah pleaded to God, "*Pour out Thy wrath on the nations* that do not know Thee, and on the families that do not call Thy name; for they have devoured Jacob; they have devoured him and consumed him, and have laid waste his habitation" (Jer. 10:25, emphasis added).

Likewise, the psalmist wondered aloud how long God would wait to take vengeance on the ungodly nations, for His own sake as well as theirs:

> O God, the nations have invaded Thine inheritance; they have defiled Thy holy temple; they have laid Jerusalem in ruins. They have given the dead bodies of Thy servants for food to the birds of the heavens, the flesh of Thy godly ones to the beasts of the earth. They have poured out their blood like water round about Jerusalem; and there was no one to bury them. . . . How long, O Lord? Wilt Thou be angry forever? Will Thy jealousy burn like fire? *Pour out Thy wrath upon the nations* which do not know Thee, and upon the kingdoms which do not call upon Thy name. For they have devoured Jacob, and laid waste his habitation. (Ps. 79:1-7)

As if in response to those very pleas, the Lord promised through Zephaniah, "'Therefore, wait for Me,' declares the Lord, 'For the day when I rise up to the prey. Indeed, My decision is to gather nations, to assemble kingdoms, *to pour out on them My indignation*, all My burning anger; for all the earth will be devoured by the fire of My zeal'" (Zeph. 3:8).

As explained earlier in chapter 18, the fifth trumpet judgment will last five months and the sixth perhaps as long as thirteen months. The bowl judgments, however, will be extremely brief by comparison — because all of them will have to occur within the remaining twenty-four days of the thirty-day reclamation period, *after* the newly saved survivors of Israel have been safely hidden away in Azel. Unlike a pitcher which takes a few moments to empty, these shallow bowls of God's final divine wrath will be emptied almost instantaneously, one immediately after another, climaxing at the battle of Armageddon.

THE ARK OF THE COVENANT

Before the bowl judgments are studied directly, it will be helpful to consider a significant event that will occur in Heaven while those judgments are being meted out on earth. As already mentioned above, the final wrath of God will be preceded by the opening of the heavenly temple (Rev. 11:19a; cf. 15:5), from which the last seven avenging angelic reapers of God will later depart (15:5, 6). Once the heavenly temple is opened, the ark of God's covenant will be revealed (11:19b). This will be the first public display of the ark since it was lost when Nebuchadnezzar, king of the Babylonian beast empire, destroyed Solomon's Temple in 586 B.C. (2 Kings 25:8-17). No, the ark is not in a warehouse somewhere in New Jersey or in a hiding place in Ethiopia. It is in the heavenly temple of God, and it will be revealed precisely at this time.

For the nation of Israel, the ark was the supreme symbol of God's covenant. It was also the visible symbol of God's presence and was even referred to as the throne of God (see 1 Sam. 4:4; 2 Sam. 6:2). Similarly, the ark symbolized the power of God's presence when Israel went into battle (see Josh. 6:12, 13). The ark contained the tablets of the Ten Commandments given by God to Moses on Mount Sinai, and its cover, made of pure gold, was called "the mercy seat" (Exod. 25:17).

It is especially significant that the ark of the covenant was closely associated with the holiest day of the Jewish year, the Day of Atonement (Yom Kippur). On that day, only once a year, the high priest entered the Holy of Holies, the innermost sanctuary of the Tabernacle and later of the Temple. There he made a sacrifice for his own sins, the sins of his family, and the sins of all Israel. As God instructed Moses, the ark played a central part in the Day of Atonement. Thus the Lord told Moses that the priest is to "take some of the blood of the bull and sprinkle it with his finger on the mercy seat," the cover of the ark (Lev. 16:14). The priest was commanded further to slaughter a bull as an atoning sacrifice "for the sons of Israel for all their sins once every year" (Lev. 16:34). That sacrifice, of course, had no redemptive power in itself but was a reminder of the perfect sacrifice that one day would be paid through the blood of God's Son, the Messiah, Jesus Christ.

After the destruction of Solomon's Temple and the exile of the rest of Israel in 586 B.C., we hear nothing more of the ark in Old Testament Scripture. It is of more than a little significance, therefore, that the ark of God's covenant reappears in Scripture just before Christ returns to execute the bowl judgments against the enemies of His chosen people Israel and right after the end of the seventieth week — that is, right after the end of the time specifically set apart by God for Israel "to make atonement for iniquity, to bring in everlasting righteousness" (Dan. 9:24). The ark of the covenant disappeared when the time of the Gentiles began, and it will reappear only after that time is finished, when the "fulness of the Gentiles has come in" (Rom. 11:25). Thus the ark of the covenant, the great symbol of God's power and presence, will become a reality for Israel once again only after her spiritual eyes have been opened, after she has repented of her sins and received atonement through trust in her Redeemer and King, and after Almighty God will begin His reign in great power over all the earth (Rev. 11:17) — all of which will take place just prior to the bowl judgments and the final battle of Armageddon.

THE BOWL JUDGMENTS

The text of Revelation 16:1-21, which recounts the actual pouring out of the seven bowls, not only indicates that each judgment will come upon the earth quickly and completely, but also that the judgments will follow one another in rapid succession. Although the exact time and duration of the bowl judgments is not specified, all seven, along with the battle of Armageddon, must transpire within a timeframe that is less than four weeks in total. This brief four-week period represents the time remaining in the thirty-day grace period that God will give the wicked before "a complete destruction, one that is decreed, is poured out on the one who makes desolate" (Dan. 9:27), when physical possession of the earth is reclaimed by Christ. Christ then will exercise His unrestricted and supreme authority to evict the usurper Satan from a kingdom now rightfully belonging to God.

Although the final wrath of God, the bowl judgments, and Armageddon will be against the world in general, the last three bowl judgments and the battle of Armageddon will, in part, single out the beast empire nations which under the direction of Antichrist will have brutalized Israel in the last days. As seen in chapters 6 and 7 of this book, those ten nations — more accurately, the people groups who dominate those nations — will include, in part, *descendants of all the beast empires depicted in Nebuchadnezzar's statue* (all of which dominated both the people of Israel and their holy city of Jerusalem), as well as the one beast empire nation (the seventh) that brutalized Israel during the gap between the sixty-ninth and seventieth weeks of Daniel.

THE FIRST FOUR BOWL JUDGMENTS

Since the first four bowl judgments (Rev. 16:1-9) are not critical to this study, we need only mention them here in summary. The *first bowl* will bring loathsome sores on those who have taken the mark of Antichrist and worshiped him (vv. 1, 2), which by definition means practically every man, woman, and child upon the face of the earth except for a very small remnant. The *second bowl* will be poured in the sea, causing it to become like the blood of a dead man (v. 3). The *third bowl* will pollute all the rivers and springs, causing those bodies of water also to become like blood (vv. 4-7). The *fourth bowl* will scorch all ungodly men with intense heat (vv. 8, 9). These first four bowl judgments, it should be noted, are inflicted on the whole earth in general, in contrast to the first four trumpet judgments that afflict only a third of the earth (see Rev. 8:7, 8, 10, 12). Moreover, in the same way that the final three trumpet judgments will be the most severe of the trumpet judgments of God, so also the remaining three bowl judgments will be the most severe, as seen below.

THE FIFTH BOWL JUDGMENT

The emphasis of God's final wrath now shifts to the final beast empire of Satan which, in part, includes all of the previous beast empires that have sought to destroy Israel while she had access to the land and her holy city of Jerusalem. The *fifth bowl*, then, will be upon "the throne of the beast" and will bring total darkness on the evil earthly kingdom of Antichrist, causing men to "gnaw their tongues because of pain" (v. 10). But all these excruciating afflictions will not bring men to repentance, the opportunity for which they will have forfeited when they took the mark of Antichrist (v. 11).

THE SIXTH BOWL JUDGMENT

Just before the seventh and last bowl judgment, the ungodly nations of the "whole world," under the leadership of Antichrist, will be preparing for Satan's desperate last-chance battle against God — the "Armageddon Campaign" of Antichrist. To bring them more quickly to their ultimate destruction, God will assist Satan's forces by drying up the Euphrates River, giving the wicked kings in the east more rapid access to Israel (Rev. 16:12; cf. Zeph. 3:8). That divine "assistance," which will probably occur sometime near the middle of the thirty-day period following the seventieth week, will be accomplished by the sixth bowl judgment. As John reports:

> The sixth angel poured out his bowl upon the great river, the Euphrates; and its water was dried up, that the way might be prepared for the kings from the east. And I saw coming out of the mouth of the dragon and out of the mouth of the beast and out

of the mouth of the false prophet, three unclean spirits like frogs; for they are spirits of demons, performing signs, which go out to the kings of the whole world, to gather them together for the war of the great day of God, the Almighty. . . . And they gathered them together to the place which in Hebrew is called Har-Magedon [or Armageddon]. (Rev. 16:12-14, 16)

After God begins to unleash His final wrath upon the earth immediately after the sounding of the seventh trumpet (after rule over the earth is returned to God Almighty), the wicked nations of the "whole world" will become hopelessly desperate. Rallied by the satanic messengers ("three unclean spirits . . . of demons"), those nations will begin to dispatch their legions of fighting men from throughout the world to the plains of Esdraelon near the city of Megiddo, some sixty miles or so north of Jerusalem. There they will engage in the military conflict commonly known as the battle of Armageddon, in one last effort to win back what they already will have lost.

As will be discussed in some detail later, the ensuing battle there will be Satan's last effort to regain his rule over the earth, a rule that he lost to God Almighty at the sounding of the seventh trumpet. Although he will have lost every previous battle, Satan's futile desperation will drive him to amass the largest army ever assembled in the history of mankind, from the "whole world," to face the forces of God in a final counteroffensive against Christ and His heavenly armies. This, then, will be Satan's last attempt to foil the prophetic plan* of God, which will have been fulfilled perfectly and literally right up to this final battle of Armageddon.

THE SEVENTH BOWL JUDGMENT

But before the final battle of Armageddon, there will be one more bowl judgment — the seventh and last, and by far the worst. Again John reports:

The seventh angel poured out his bowl upon the air; and a loud voice came out of the temple from the throne, saying, "It is done." And there were flashes of lightning and sounds and peals of thunder; and there was a great earthquake, such as there had not

* See further chapter 3, "The Cosmic Conflict," where God's prophetic plan and Satan's counterattack are presented in full.

been since man came to be upon the earth, so great an earthquake was it, and so mighty. And the great city was split into three parts, and the cities of the nations fell. And Babylon the great was remembered before God, to give her the cup of the wine of His fierce wrath. And every island fled away, and the mountains were not found. And huge hailstones, about one hundred pounds each, came down from heaven upon men; and men blasphemed God because of the plague of the hail, because its plague was extremely severe. (Rev. 16:17-21; cf. 11:19; 15:5)

In this writer's opinion, this will be the most severe judgment of God, not only upon the nations of the final beast empire, but upon the whole world in general. First, the world will undergo the worst earthquake known to man. It is hard to comprehend how massive and extensive this earthquake will be. We get a small sense of this when we think of the earthquakes in the early 1990s in Iran and Armenia (only a few hundred miles from Israel) which took the lives of upwards of two hundred thousand people in the very localized areas affected by them. But the toll taken by the seventh bowl judgment will make these others pale in comparison — when there will be "a great earthquake, such as there had not been since man came upon the earth" (16:18). This specific judgment will be worldwide, and for that reason all the cities of the nations will fall and every island will be destroyed and all the mountains will be leveled — total devastation of the world!

And then, in the midst of this worldwide chaos hundred-pound hailstones will climax the total devastation of the earthquakes. The cities will have already been leveled; homes, apartments, and the like will most certainly lay in ruins, offering little protection, if any, to those who survive the earthquakes. And then will come the hail — hundred-pound hailstones rocketing down upon earth from the heavens, killing everyone and every living thing that it hits. There should be no question in any one's mind as to the severity of this judgment. "Men blasphemed God because of the plague of the hail, because its plague was extremely severe" (v. 21). In view of this devastation, we may wonder how the armies of the whole world, on their way to the final battle against God in the plains of Armageddon, are able to survive this seventh bowl judgment. Although we do not know *how*, we do know that these armies *will* be spared for the specific destruction by Christ at Armageddon, when "in righteousness He judges and wages war . . .

[against] the kings of the earth and their armies, assembled to make war against Him . . ." (Rev. 19:11, 19).

Directly related to the seventh bowl judgment, another extremely significant event will occur. This will be *the leveling of all Jerusalem*, which is seen in the passage just quoted where "the great city was split into three parts" (v. 19). Although the words "the great city" are not used exclusively in reference to Jerusalem, it seems that Jerusalem is clearly intended here. This is confirmed, for example, by the earlier reference to "the great city" as the place "where also their Lord was crucified" in Revelation 11:8, which of course can only refer to Jerusalem.

Jerusalem, the great city, *like all the rest of the cities of the world*, will be "split into three parts" and will be completely destroyed by this great earthquake. Is it any wonder Christ had His people Israel "flee by the valley of My mountains, for the valley of the mountains will reach to Azel . . . just as you fled *before the earthquake* in the days of Uzziah king of Judah" (Zech. 14:5, emphasis added)?

Jerusalem's destruction is only in preparation for an even more awesome event that will occur after Jerusalem is leveled. Whether it occurs at this moment, near the end of the thirty-day reclamation period, or sometime later, during the forty-five day restoration period that follows, this author will not be adamant. All I know for sure is that when the millennial kingdom begins less than two months from this time, the mountains upon which Jerusalem sets, leveled at the seventh bowl judgment, will take on a new look.

A number of prophetic passages give details of this awesome event which will occur just before the Millennium begins. Thus Zechariah writes: "All the land will be changed into a plain from Geba to Rimmon south of Jerusalem; *but Jerusalem will rise* and remain on its site from Benjamin's Gate as far as the place of the First Gate to the Corner Gate, and from the Tower of Hananel to the king's wine presses" (Zech. 14:10, emphasis added).

By contrast to the rest of the world where "the mountains were not found [i.e., they were leveled]," after the great city is split three ways, the mountain upon which the city of Jerusalem sets "will rise" and be elevated to become the highest point on earth. Thus Isaiah writes that this mountain "will be established as the chief of the mountains, and will be raised above the hills; and all the nations will stream to it" (Isa. 2:2; see further Mic. 4:1). And Ezekiel refers to the new elevated Mount Zion as "a very high mountain" (40:2), "'for on My holy mountain, on the high mountain of Israel,' declares the Lord God, 'there the whole house of Israel, all of them, will serve Me in the land'" (20:40).

To briefly summarize this last point, the earthquakes associated with the seventh bowl judgment will level the mountains of the world ("and the mountains were not found"), making hills and plains out of what were once mountain ranges. During the course of these events the mountain upon which Jerusalem sits, Mount Zion, will be thrust up and "established as the chief of the mountains, and will be raised above the hills." It will become the high point of the earthly kingdom over which Christ will soon rule. It will be on the top of Mount Zion that the millennial Temple will be built.

Finally we read that "Babylon the great [city] was remembered before God, to give her the cup of the wine of His fierce wrath" (16:19). And so when God destroys "the cities of the nations," He also destroys the city of Jerusalem *and* "the great city" (17:18; 18:18, 19, 21) built upon "seven mountains" (17:9) upon which the Babylonian harlot sits (17:3).[3]

When it was all over, "a loud voice came out of the temple from the throne, saying, 'It is done'" (16:17).

THE MARRIAGE OF THE LAMB

While the foregoing events are taking place on earth, another scene is taking place in Heaven. In this resplendent scene we see a great multitude lifting their voices in praise to God and saying, "'Hallelujah! For the Lord our God, the Almighty, reigns. Let us rejoice and be glad and give the glory to Him, for the marriage of the Lamb has come and His bride has made herself ready.' And it was given to her to clothe herself in fine linen, bright and clean; for the fine linen is the righteous acts of the saints" (Rev. 19:6b-8).

With the bema-seat judgment just concluded, the time has now come for the marriage of the Lamb (Christ) to His bride! This will be an occasion of magnificent splendor beyond anything we can begin to imagine! Think of the occasion! The very Son of God will be the bridegroom. Surely the Father will spare nothing in the celebration of His only Son's marriage. Surely the God of the heavens and the earth and every galaxy in the universe will display His glories as never before at the wedding of His only Son. And what of the bride? Can we begin to comprehend what it means to be the bride of Christ, the bride of the only Son of God? This astounding reality should bring every Christian to his or her knees in awe and reverence and gratitude. Although utterly unworthy in our own right, as believers we will come before Christ, washed in the blood of the Lamb — *in the blood of the One who gave His life for us that we might be His bride* — and "stand in the presence of His glory blameless with great joy" (Jude 24b).

In this regard, Peter's admonition is especially relevant. As we look forward to the coming of the Lord and to becoming His pure and holy bride, should we not make every effort to live worthy of our high calling? As Peter writes, "Therefore, beloved, since you look for these things, be diligent to be found by Him in peace, spotless and blameless" (2 Pet. 3:14). And so, out of deep love and gratitude to the Savior, every believer should seek to live in purity of life and doctrine so that he or she might be "blameless in the day of our Lord Jesus Christ" (1 Cor. 1:8b) and "stand in the presence of His glory blameless with great joy" (Jude 24). Sadly, however, we know that many will not live this way — and for these, as we have seen in chapters 2 and 14, the last days before the return of Christ will be a time of great trial and testing, a time when the compromising church will be permitted to directly undergo the great persecution of Satan's wrath (Rev. 12:12), in order to purify her in preparation for becoming the pure and spotless bride of Christ.

It is commonly thought that Christ's bride will consist only of the church, but careful study of the Old as well as the New Testament clearly indicates that His bride will include *all* the saints, the redeemed of Israel as well as the church — in other words, the same group that was raptured and resurrected on the same day that God's wrath began, the same group that has just been rewarded for their faithfulness at the bema seat of Christ.

The classic New Testament passage, of course, which teaches that the church will be the bride of Christ is in Paul's letter to the Ephesians: "For the husband is the head of the wife, as Christ also is the head of the church, He Himself being the Savior of the body. But as the church is subject to Christ, so also the wives ought to be to their husbands in everything. Husbands, love your wives, just as Christ also loved the church and gave Himself up for her" (Eph. 5:23-25).

There are, however, several Old Testament passages that make similar claims to this elevated position, which refer to *Israel* as the bride of the Lord. For example, the Lord instructed Hosea to take the morally corrupt Gomer to be his wife as a symbol that the Lord would ultimately take spiritually unfaithful Israel back as His eternal bride: "I will betroth you to Me forever," the Lord said to Israel; "Yes, I will betroth you to Me in righteousness and in justice, in lovingkindness and in compassion, and I will betroth you to Me in faithfulness. Then you will know the Lord" (Hos. 2:19, 20).

In a similar way Isaiah declared to Israel, "'For your husband is your Maker, whose name is the Lord of hosts; and your Redeemer is the Holy One of Israel, who is called the God of all the earth. For the Lord has called you, like a wife forsaken and grieved in spirit, even like a wife of one's youth when she is rejected,' says your God. 'For a brief moment I forsook you, but with great compassion I will gather you. In an outburst of anger I hid My face from you for a moment; but with everlasting lovingkindness I will have compassion on you,' says the Lord your Redeemer" (Isa. 54:5-8; cf. 62:4, 5).

Finally, a passage from Hebrews gives further evidence that Christ's bride not only will include the church but also the redeemed of all ages. Speaking of Abraham, the physical forefather of the natural line of Israel and the spiritual forefather of all true believers (Rom. 4:11), the writer of Hebrews states:

> By faith he [Abraham] lived as an alien in the land of promise, as in a foreign land, dwelling in tents with Isaac and Jacob, fellow-heirs of the same promise; for he was looking for the city which has foundations, whose architect and builder is God. . . . But as it is, they desire a better country, that is a heavenly one. Therefore God is not ashamed to be called their God; for He has prepared a city for them. (Heb. 11:9, 10, 16)

The heavenly city that God has prepared for Abraham and his spiritual descendants can be none other than the same heavenly city He has prepared for the church — that is, the New Jerusalem — because, like all other believers, the church is among the spiritual descendants of Abraham. Thus Jesus described this same heavenly city when He promised, "In My Father's house are many dwelling places; if it were not so, I would have told you; for I go to prepare a place for you. And if I go and prepare a place for you, I will come again, and receive you to Myself; that where I am, there you may be also" (John 14:2, 3).

Scripture nowhere speaks, or even hints, of two classes of believers, two heavenly households, two heavenly cities, or two brides of Christ. Believers who lived before Christ was crucified and resurrected are just as much saved by the redeeming blood of Christ as believers who live after He came to earth as God incarnate. As just noted, Abraham is the forefather of all believers in all ages (Rom. 4:11). For the saints in every age there is only one way of salvation — by grace, through faith — either in anticipation of Christ's atoning death in the future or in acceptance of Christ's completed work. As Jesus explained, "Your father Abraham rejoiced to see My day; and he saw it, and was glad" (John 8:56).

When "the dead in Christ shall rise first" (1 Thess. 4:16) at the rapture of the church, all believers of all ages will comprise that "great multitude." Likewise, when "the time came for the dead to be judged, and the time to give their rewards to Thy bond-servants the prophets and to the saints and to those who fear Thy name" (Rev. 11:18), again all believers of all ages will comprise that "great multitude" at the bema seat of Christ. And finally, when "the holy city, new Jerusalem, [comes] down out of heaven from God," then, as before, all believers of all ages will comprise that glorified "bride adorned for her husband" (Rev. 21:2).

THE FINAL SHOWDOWN

At the end of the thirty-day reclamation period, after the marriage of the Lamb, Christ will come back to earth with His army of angels (His reapers) to defeat the remainder of the ungodly forces on earth, thereby reclaiming physical possession of the earth. This momentous event will occur subsequent to the seventh bowl judgment and will conclude the day of the Lord. Using the most vivid description, John depicts Christ's return to earth to lead in the final battle of Armageddon:

And I saw heaven opened; and behold, a white horse, and He who sat upon it is called Faithful and True; and in righteousness He judges and wages war. And His eyes are a flame of fire, and upon His head are many diadems; and He has a name written upon Him which no one knows except Himself. And He is clothed with a robe dipped in blood; and His name is called The Word of God. And the armies which are in heaven, clothed in fine linen, white and clean, were following Him on white horses. And from His mouth comes a sharp sword, so that with it He may smite the nations; and He will rule them with a rod of iron; and He treads the wine press of the fierce wrath of God, the Almighty.

And on His robe and on His thigh He has a name written, "KING OF KINGS, AND LORD OF LORDS." (Rev. 19:11-16)

CHRIST AND HIS ARMIES

Who are "the armies which are in heaven, clothed in fine linen, white and clean" (Rev. 19:14)? The identity of these "armies . . . in heaven" is not made explicit in the text, but when this is examined in light of other Scriptures it seems there can be no question, in this writer's opinion, as to their identity.

First, as we have already seen in the parable of the wheat and the tares, Christ Himself states that "the harvest is the end of the age; and the reapers are angels" (Matt. 13:39). The Lord's own description, in fact, sounds very similar to the coming of the Son of Man as just quoted above. As Christ explains, "Just as the tares are gathered up and burned with fire, so shall it be at the end of the age. The Son of Man will send forth His angels, and they will gather out of His kingdom all stumbling blocks [the tares], and those who commit lawlessness [the unrighteous world], and will cast them into the furnace of fire. . . . Then the righteous will shine forth as the sun in the kingdom of their Father" (Matt. 13:40-43a). The sequence of what will happen could hardly be more clear: the Son of Man will come with His angels; He will send forth His angels to harvest the wicked; the "stumbling blocks" will include the counterfeit Christians who have infiltrated the church and "all those who commit lawlessness" (i.e., the unrighteous world, in particular "the man of lawlessness" [2 Thess. 2:3]); both groups will be utterly destroyed and cast into the eternal fire, whereupon the Millennium will begin and "the righteous will shine forth . . . in the kingdom of their Father."

This, of course, is in perfect harmony with Revelation 15:6, where the seven angels are identified as the ones who will mete out the final wrath of God. It is consistent as well as with Paul's description of Christ during the day of the Lord, when He "shall be revealed from heaven with His mighty angels in flaming fire, dealing out retribution to those who do not know God" (2 Thess. 1:7, 8).

When all this is taken together, the only possible conclusion is that "the armies which are in heaven, clothed in fine linen, white and clean" who accompany Christ at the final battle of Armageddon are in fact the angels of Matthew 13:37-43 and of Revelation 15:6 and that these angels, as Christ explains in His own words, will be the reapers at the end of the age.[4]

THE BATTLE OF ARMAGEDDON

We have just seen the vivid picture of Christ coming with His "armies . . . in heaven" for the final battle of Armageddon. Meanwhile the counterpart to this heavenly scene will have taken final shape on earth, as Antichrist has assembled the most massive army of all time in his one last futile attempt to defy and defeat Almighty God. During the sixth bowl judgment, Satan will have initiated the call to the armies of the "whole world," in one last attempt to win back what he has already lost.

And so the most devastating battle of all time, the cosmic conflict that has raged from the time when Satan first chose to defy God, is about to come to an end. Again it is hard to capture the magnitude of this, and for this reason it is perhaps best just to let Scripture powerfully speak for itself as seen so clearly in the following passages:

Writing vividly of that dreadful day, Isaiah said,

> Draw near, O nations, to hear; and listen, O peoples! Let the earth and all it contains hear, and the world and all that springs from it. For the Lord's indignation is against *all the nations*, and His wrath against *all their armies*; He has utterly destroyed them, He has given them over to slaughter. So their slain will be thrown out, and their corpses will give off their stench, and the mountains will be drenched with their blood. (Isa. 34:1-3, emphasis added)

In a parallel account, Ezekiel gives this graphic description of the defeat of "Gog" (the prophetic name of Antichrist):

> "Thus says the Lord God, 'Behold, I am against you, O Gog, prince of Rosh, Meshech, and Tubal;* and I shall turn you around, drive you on, take you up from the remotest parts of the north, and bring you against the mountains of Israel. . . . You shall fall on the mountains of Israel, you and all your troops, and the peoples who are with you; I shall give you as food to every kind of predatory bird and beast of the field. You will fall on the open

---

* For the identification of Gog and his final beast empire, see chapter 7.

field; for it is I who have spoken,' declares the Lord God. . . . For seven months the house of Israel will be burying them in order to cleanse the land. Even all the people of the land will bury them; and it will be to their renown on the day that I glorify Myself,' declares the Lord God." (Ezek. 39:1-5, 12, 13)

John completes his description of Armageddon with the following account of Antichrist's final destruction and eternal destiny:

And I saw the beast and the kings of the earth and their armies, assembled to make war against Him who sat upon the horse, and against His army. And the beast was seized, and with him the false prophet who performed the signs in his presence, by which he deceived those who had received the mark of the beast and those who worshiped his image; these two were thrown alive into the lake of fire which burns with brimstone. And the rest were killed with the sword which came from the mouth of Him who sat upon the horse, and all the birds were filled with their flesh. (Rev. 19:19-21)

Lastly, two passages from Daniel provide a clear description of the sequence of events as well as a vivid portrayal of Antichrist's eternal end. Thus Daniel writes,

And in the days of those kings [the final beast empire] the God of heaven will set up a kingdom which will never be destroyed, and that kingdom will not be left for another people; it will crush and put an end to all these kingdoms, but it will itself endure forever. (Dan. 2:44)

Later Daniel reports:

I kept looking until thrones were set up, and the Ancient of Days took His seat; His vesture was like white snow, and the hair of His head like pure wool. His throne was ablaze with flames, its wheels were a burning fire. . . . Then I kept looking because of the sound of the boastful words which the horn [Antichrist] was speaking; I kept looking until the beast was slain, and its body was destroyed and given to the burning fire. (7:9, 11)

In these two prophetic passages from Daniel, we see again the clear sequence of Scripture — that first the kingdom of God will be "set up" (at the sounding of the seventh trumpet), and then God's final wrath will totally destroy Antichrist and the final beast empire of Satan. And thus with the defeat of Antichrist, Christ will forever reclaim the physical possession of earth.

FINAL DESTINATION OF THE BEAST AND HIS PROPHET

What will happen to Antichrist at this point? To understand this we need to look carefully at a number of related Scriptures. First in Revelation we read, "And the beast was seized, and with him the false prophet who performed the signs in his presence . . . *these two were thrown alive into the lake of fire* which burns with brimstone" (Rev. 19:20).

In the book of Ezekiel, however, Antichrist (Gog) is seen being buried in the land of Israel:

And it will come about on that day that I shall give Gog a burial ground there in Israel, the valley of those who pass by east of the sea, and it will block off the passers-by. So they will bury Gog there with all his multitude, and they will call it the valley of Hamon-gog. (39:11)

In a seeming discrepancy, Ezekiel speaks of Antichrist (Gog) being buried in Hamon-gog with the multitude of his army (v. 11), whereas in Revelation 19 he is shown being cast alive with the false prophet into the lake of fire (v. 20). There is no doubt that both these passages refer to Antichrist. The problem is that one says he is cast alive into the lake of fire, and the other says he was slain and buried, a position clearly supported by other passages of Scripture as well (see 2 Thess. 2:8; Isa. 11:4). A possible solution to that seeming discrepancy is found in Isaiah.

Isaiah's reference to the "star of the morning, son of dawn" (Isa. 14:12) is commonly taken as a description of Satan, which it may well be, though personally this writer thinks otherwise. The context of that verse allows for another, far better possibility. The passage is doubtless a near/far prophecy, applying initially to the king of Babylon (v. 4) — that is, to a man. But then at a later date — at the end of the age, in this writer's opinion — the passage applies to Antichrist, also a man. Thus in this case the reference is to "the man who made the earth tremble" (v. 16) — not an angel, not Satan, but "a man" — namely, Antichrist.

At the midpoint of the seventieth week Antichrist certainly will "have weakened the nations" (v. 12) and attempted to raise his throne above God's and make himself "like the Most High" (vv. 13, 14). But at Armageddon Antichrist will be "thrust down to Sheol" (v. 15), where he will be known as "the man who made the earth tremble" and who "shook kingdoms" (v. 16) and who "made the world like a wilderness and overthrew its cities" (v. 17). Isaiah concludes this passage by saying of this "man": "You have been cast out of your tomb like a rejected branch, clothed with the slain who are pierced with a sword, who go down to the stones of the pit, like a trampled corpse. You will not be united with them in burial, because you have ruined your country, you have slain your people" (vv. 19, 20).

The Hebrew word behind "country" in verse 20 is much more commonly translated "earth."[5] With that translation, Isaiah 14:18-20 takes on a quite different meaning. This powerful *world ruler* will be buried, but more importantly he "will be cast out of [his] tomb like a rejected branch" (v. 19). In other words, Antichrist "the man" will not remain buried in his own tomb like the other "kings of nations" who "lie in glory," but instead will be "cast out of his tomb," as it were, "like a rejected branch" (vv. 18, 19) — being cast alive into the lake of fire. This corresponds to Revelation where John again uses a derivative of the same Greek word translated "alive" directly in reference to the resurrection bodies received by the martyrs at the "first resurrection": "And they came to life [alive] and reigned with Christ for a thousand years. . . . This is the first resurrection" (Rev. 20:4, 5).

Although far from certain, it seems possible that Antichrist will be killed and buried at Armageddon, his soul going first to Sheol (Hades); his soul will then be cast alive into the lake of fire, "the second death" (Rev. 20:6; cf. v. 14), along with all those who comprise the first fruits of those still in Sheol awaiting the Great White Throne judgment of the wicked at the end of the Millennium.

After Antichrist is cast into the lake of fire, we are told that "the rest were killed with the sword which came from the mouth of Him who sat upon the horse, and all the birds were filled with their flesh" (Rev. 19:21). The carnage will be so immense that "for seven months the house of Israel will be burying them in order to cleanse the land" (Ezek. 39:12).

FINAL DISPOSITION OF MAGOG

The prophet Ezekiel also predicts the total destruction of the nation Magog. As seen in chapter 7 of this book, Magog is the nation from which Gog (Antichrist) will come, and most probably Magog will be the leading nation among the three-nation power base that Antichrist will use to lead the ten-nation confederacy of the final beast empire of Satan. As quoted earlier, Ezekiel declared that "'You [Gog/Antichrist] shall fall on the mountains of Israel, you and all your troops, and the peoples who are with you; I shall give you as food to every kind of predatory bird and beast of the field. . . . And I shall send fire upon Magog . . . and they will know that I am the Lord" (Ezek. 39:4-6).

In other words, God will specifically destroy Magog with fire. Speaking of this day, the Lord also gave the following prophecy through Isaiah, which as we shall see contains a remarkable revelation: "For I know their works and their thoughts; the time is coming to gather all nations and tongues. And they shall come and see My glory. And I will set a sign among them and will send survivors from them to the nations: Tarshish, Put, Lud, Mashech, Rosh, Tubal, and Javan, to the distant coastlands that have neither heard My fame nor seen My glory. And they will declare My glory among the nations" (Isa. 66:18, 19). The nation that is most noticeably missing from this list is Magog— because it will exist no more.[6]

EDOM BECOMES A MEMORIAL

And so the book is closed on Magog — the nation whose ancestry drove the sixth beast empire, the nation whose ancestry drove the seventh beast empire, the nation who will help drive the final beast empire. But there is another nation that God has not forgotten in His wrath. This is the nation of Edom, which has always been the enemy of God, going back to the time of Jacob and Esau, and will be dealt with in a unique way after the final battle of Armageddon. With Edom* as His unforgettable example, God will make certain that the devastating and permanent outcome of the final defeat of the beast empire nations, as well as the rest of the armies of "the whole world," will be never be forgotten. "Draw near, O nations, to hear; and listen, O peoples!" God will say to the whole world after Armageddon. "Let the earth and all it contains hear, and the world and all that springs from

---

* Edom is located immediately south and east of the Dead Sea, the northwest corner of Edom being approximately sixty miles southeast of Jerusalem as the crow flies.

it. For the Lord's indignation is against *all the nations*, and His wrath *against all their armies; He has utterly destroyed them*, He has given them over to slaughter" (Isa. 34:1, 2, emphasis added).

It is remarkable to see how many times in Scripture Edom is spoken of with regard to its ignoble distinction. Because Edom, comprised of the descendants of Esau, has so fiercely opposed God and His people throughout history, and because Edom will in particular stand against Israel during the second half of the seventieth week (see Obad. 12-14), God will make that nation a symbol of and a memorial to the ignominious defeat of Antichrist and the ungodly forces of the world. "Because of violence to your brother Jacob," the Lord long ago warned Edom, "you will be covered with shame, and you will be cut off forever. . . . For the day of the Lord draws near on all the nations. As you have done, it will be done to you. Your dealings will return on your own head" (Obad. 10, 15). And again, referring to the same betrayal by Edom, Ezekiel records: "Behold I [the Lord] am against you. . . . I will stretch out My hand against you. . . . I will lay waste your cities . . . because you have had everlasting enmity and have delivered the sons of Israel to the power of the sword *at the time of their calamity, at the time of punishment of the end* . . ." (Ezek. 35:3-5, emphasis added).

Through the prophet Isaiah, the Lord declared further:

"And all the host of heaven will wear away, and the sky will be rolled up like a scroll; all their hosts will also wither away as a leaf withers from the vine, or as one withers from the fig tree. For My sword is satiated in heaven, behold it shall descend for judgment upon Edom, and upon the people whom I have devoted to destruction. . . . For the Lord has a day of vengeance, a year of recompense for the cause of Zion. *And its streams shall be turned into pitch, and its loose earth into brimstone, and its land shall become burning pitch. It shall not be quenched night or day; its smoke shall go up forever*; from generation to generation it shall be desolate; none shall pass through it forever and ever." (Isa. 34:4, 5, 8-10, emphasis added)

Through Jeremiah, the Lord repeats the same awesome promise: "'For I have sworn by Myself,' declares the Lord, 'that Bozrah [a major center of sheepherding in Edom] will become an object of horror, a reproach, a ruin and a curse; and all its cities will become perpetual ruins. . . . And Edom will become an object of horror; everyone who passes by it will be horrified and will hiss at all its wounds. Like the overthrow of Sodom and Gomorrah with its neighbors,' says the Lord, 'no one will live there, nor will a son of man reside in it'" (Jer. 49:13, 17, 18). Why is that? Because "its land shall become burning pitch. It shall not be quenched night or day; its smoke shall go up forever" (Isa. 34:9, 10).

It seems more than just interesting that Sodom and Gomorrah, which were divinely destroyed by fire and brimstone, were located in what became northern Edom, at the south end of the Dead Sea. That region originally was so lush and productive that Lot chose to move there when the land near Bethel could no longer support both his flocks and those of his uncle Abraham (Gen. 13:5-11). Yet since the destruction of those two cities almost four thousand years ago, the entire surrounding area has been utterly desolate — making it a historical and geographical reminder of Edom's fate after the battle of Armageddon.

After Armageddon only a small portion of the world's former Gentile population will have survived all of the terrible destruction of the end times. These survivors will then send representatives from all the ungodly Gentile peoples of the world and will "bring all your brethren [the remaining Jews of the *Diaspora*] from all the nations . . . to My holy mountain Jerusalem" (Isa. 66:20). In those days, Mount Zion will rise high above the surrounding region, and from that vantage point, "'All mankind will come to bow down before Me,' says the Lord. . . . 'Then they shall go forth and look on the corpses of the men who have transgressed against Me. For their worm shall not die, and their fire shall not be quenched; and they shall be an abhorrence to all mankind'" (vv. 23, 24).

From Mount Zion, which "will be established as the chief of the mountains, and will be raised above the hills" (Isa. 2:2), anyone will be able to look north and see all the corpses left at Armageddon, which will be so numerous that it will take Israel and the neighboring peoples seven months to bury them (Ezek. 39:12, 13). Looking to the south, they will no longer see the great Jewish fortress of Masada, because it doubtless will have been leveled along with all other mountains in the area. But looking almost directly over the previous site of that fortress, observers will plainly see the smoking ruins of Edom — an unforgettable memorial to the eternal defeat of God's enemies for their persecution of God's people.

The Restoration Period

At the conclusion of the battle of Armageddon, the day of the Lord will have come to a close, and the wrath of God will be complete; Antichrist and his final beast empire will have been destroyed; and the thirty-day reclamation period will have come to an end. With the completion of these decisive events, the last period of time immediately preceding the Millennium — that is, the restoration period — will begin.

THE FORTY-FIVE-DAY RESTORATION PERIOD

What is the *restoration period*, and what will happen during this time? In the pages that follow we will first look carefully at the Scripture passage where this period is specifically described; second, we will briefly summarize what will happen during this period; and then in the rest of the chapter we will look in greater depth at the main things that will happen during this time, in climactic preparation for the Millennium that will immediately follow.

WHAT IS THE RESTORATION PERIOD?

The restoration period is a forty-five-day period of time revealed in the book of Daniel, in the same series of verses studied earlier in chapter 19. As we saw there, the book of Daniel teaches first that there will be a *thirty-day period* immediately following the seventieth week of Daniel. This is based on Daniel 12:11 which speaks of a 1,290-day period from the time that the "abomination of desolation is set up" (i.e., at the middle of the seventieth week) "until a complete destruction . . . is poured out on the one who makes desolate" (9:27), when Antichrist is destroyed at Armageddon. As seen in chapter 19, these 1,290 days break down as follows: the first 1,260 days correspond to the last half of the seventieth week (i.e., 3 1/2 years x 360 days per prophetic year = 1,260 days); to these 1,260 days a thirty-day period must then be added, bringing the total to 1,290 days between the time that Antichrist desecrates the Temple and his defeat at Armageddon.*

The next verse in this same passage then reads: "How blessed is he who keeps waiting and attains to the 1,335 days!" (v. 12). In other words, there is an additional forty-five-day period which takes place immediately after the thirty-day period and immediately before the Millennium begins (1,260 + 30 + 45 = 1,335). Thus we see that the 1,335 day total is achieved by adding together the 1,260 days (the last half of the seventieth week) *plus the thirty day reclamation period plus an additional forty-five day restoration* extending right up to the first day of the Millennium.

WHAT THINGS WILL HAPPEN?

During this forty-five day-period two magnificent things will happen. The first is the return of Israel to her own land, the land promised to the nation going all the way back to Abraham more than four thousand years ago. (We will consider specifically who will be included in this return in the next section.)

The second magnificent thing will come at the end of the forty-five days, when Christ will receive the reign over earth from God the Father Almighty. The significance of this, of course, goes far beyond even the return of Israel, for it marks the point at which the rule of earth is restored to its rightful ruler, Jesus Christ, by the Father for the

---

* See chapter 19, the section entitled "The Thirty-Day Reclamation Period."

first time since the beginning of Satan's cosmic conflict with God Almighty.

In addition to these two magnificent events we should also mention that the forty-five-day restoration period will include the return of the surviving Gentiles to Jerusalem in preparation for the Sheep and Goats Judgment, and that it will be the time when Christ rebuilds the Temple.

It seems best, then, to describe this additional time of forty-five days as the *restoration period*, for as we shall see in more detail below this will be a time in which Israel will be *restored* back to God's holy mountain, Zion; a time when the Temple will be *restored* also on the summit of God's holy mountain, Zion; and a time when Gentile survivors will be brought to God's holy mountain, Zion. All of this will take place during the forty-five-day restoration period that occurs just before the start of the Millennium. However, the most important event of all will occur at the very end of this period — not on earth where the other events will occur, but back up in Heaven. This will be the anointing of the "most holy" (Dan. 9:24), when the rule *upon* earth is *restored* back to its rightful King. The restoration period, therefore, is a forty-five-day period of time during which the last necessary events will take place in preparation for the first day of the Millennium.

THE RESTORATION OF ISRAEL

As just mentioned, this is the time when Israel will be restored back to her holy land, to God's holy mountain, Zion, now elevated high above all the surrounding land. It is a time of profound significance, fulfilling the promises of God to Israel over thousands of years — indeed fulfilling God's covenant with Abraham more than four thousand years ago. During this time Israel will return to the land — not in unbelief, not in self-reliance, not in defiance, not shaking her fist at God — but this time in *belief*. This then is the time that Israel has waited for and that God has longed for — when Israel will come to her land and her holy city, but more importantly in the name of her Messiah, redeemed by Him, saved by His grace, in believing faith! This is the joyous occasion prophesied so beautifully by Jeremiah:

> Hear the word of the Lord, O nations . . . and say, "He who scattered Israel will gather him, and keep him as a shepherd keeps his flock." For the Lord has ransomed Jacob, and redeemed him

from the hand of him [Antichrist] who was stronger than he. And they shall come and shout for joy on the height of [Mount] Zion. . . ." (Jer. 31:10-12a)

Who are these who will come? They will be primarily those who have been divinely protected by the Lord, safely hidden in a place called "Azel" (see chapter 19) during the final battle of Armageddon with its unimaginable devastation. They will return then with shouts of joy to the holy land and to the "height of Zion." But the joy of the occasion will be mixed with somber awareness, as they make their way back through the terrible destruction left behind from the day of the Lord and the final battle of Armageddon. Even their return is to the "height of Zion," not to the city of Jerusalem that lies in ruins as a result of the seventh bowl judgment (see chapter 20). But those who come will include in addition small numbers of Jews scattered to the far corners of the world who will survive the day of the Lord and return at this time.

This return of Israel — at last in faith! — has tremendous significance, as noted already. This can be seen further in looking carefully at a number of Scripture passages which proclaim these truths. For example, Jeremiah was told, "Thus says the Lord, the God of Israel . . . 'behold, days are coming,' declares the Lord, 'when I will restore the fortunes of My people Israel and Judah.' The Lord says, 'I will bring them back to the land that I gave to their forefathers, and they shall possess it'" (Jer. 30:2, 3). Later, the Lord continues, "I will be the God of all the families of Israel, and they shall be My people . . . the people who survived the sword [and] found grace in the wilderness" (31:1, 2).

Who are these who, as Jeremiah says, have "survived the sword"? They are *those of Israel* ("the faithful woman," Rev. 12:6) *who fled* the land and "found grace in the wilderness" because of their refusal to sell out to Antichrist when the covenant with death was signed. These are the first fruits of Israel — the first of those out of the seventieth week who returned to God. They are also those of Israel ("the compromised woman," Rev. 12:13) who initially stayed behind because they honored the covenant with Antichrist, but refused to worship him or his image when his true identity was revealed. Those who survive the sword, then, did so *in the wilderness* — in particular in the rural areas of Israel and the remote areas of Egypt and Assyria. Their very survival in the wilderness, until their salvation three days after the close of the seventieth week, was by the grace of God and God alone.

These, then, are those — "the faithful woman" who fled and "the compromised woman" who stayed — to whom God spoke through his prophet Jeremiah: "I will bring them back to the land that I gave to their forefathers, and they shall possess it" (30:3).

As Isaiah predicted, "It will come about in that day that the remnant of Israel, and those of the house of Jacob who have escaped [to Azel], will never again rely on the one who struck them [Antichrist], but will truly rely on the Lord, the Holy One of Israel. A remnant will return, the remnant of Jacob, to the mighty God" (Isa. 10:20, 21). These will be those Jews whom God will sovereignly protect from Antichrist's fierce persecution (those who were given God's grace in the wilderness). They will have been purged and purified, and they will have placed their trust in their true Redeemer and King. The tragic side of that truth, of course, is that only a *remnant* of the nation that entered the seventieth week will survive that traumatic seven-year period and be saved. "For though your people, O Israel, may be like the sand of the sea," the prophet goes on to explain, "only a remnant within them will return [to Israel for the millennial reign of Christ]; a destruction [upon the nation Israel] is determined, overflowing with righteousness. For a complete destruction, one that is decreed, the Lord God of hosts will execute in the midst of the whole land" (Isa. 10:22, 23). But of this remnant of Israel that does survive this "complete destruction," God has given these words of comfort: "Do not fear, for I have redeemed you; I have called you by name, you are Mine! . . . I am the Lord your God, the Holy One of Israel, your Saviour. . . . I will bring your offspring from the east, and gather you from the west. I will say to the north, 'Give them up!' And to the south, 'Do not hold them back. Bring My sons from afar, and My daughters from the ends of the earth, everyone who is called by My name, and whom I have created for My glory, whom I have formed, even whom I have made'" (Isa. 43:1, 3, 5, 6).

And "so the ransomed of the Lord will return, and come with joyful shouting to [Mount] Zion; and everlasting joy will be on their heads. They will obtain gladness and joy, and sorrow and sighing will flee away" (Isa. 51:11).

GENTILE NATIONS TO MOUNT ZION

As incredible as it may seem, there will also be some people from the Gentile nations of the world who will survive the day of the Lord. Many of these will bear the mark of Antichrist, though some will not.

374 ■ *The Sign*

But all of these will also be brought to Mount Zion during the forty-five-day restoration period, to stand before Christ at the "Sheep and Goat Judgment" which will occur on the first day of the Millennium (see chapter 22).

This gathering of the surviving Gentile peoples to God's holy mountain is once again clearly described by Isaiah. Isaiah first describes God's wrath and then tells how the survivors of the day of the Lord, in particular the battle of Armageddon, will go out to the nations of the world to assist them on their journey to Israel:

> For the Lord will execute judgment by fire and by His sword on all flesh, and those slain by the Lord will be many . . . the time is coming to gather all nations and tongues. And they shall come and see My glory [on Mount Zion]. And I will set a sign among them and will send survivors from them to the nations: Tarshish, Put, Lud, Mashech, Rosh [a questionable translation], Tubal and Javan, to the distant coastlands. . . . (66:16, 18, 19).

As noted in the previous chapter, Magog is notably missing from that list of nations because she will have been totally destroyed by fire (Ezek. 39:6).

In some way not fully explained in Scripture, God will bring the survivors of those nations of the world to God's holy mountain in the land of Israel. This will include all those who have survived the trumpet judgments, in particular the sixth trumpet when a third of mankind is killed; those who have survived the bowl judgments, in particular the seventh bowl where all the cities, the mountains, and the islands of the world are destroyed; plus the few that survive the final battle of Armageddon, when all the armies of the whole world will be destroyed. The prophet Micah tells how these people who "trampled down [Israel], like mire of the streets . . . will see and be ashamed of all their might. They will put their hand on their mouth, their ears will be deaf. They will lick the dust like a serpent, like reptiles of the earth. They will come trembling out of their fortresses; to the Lord our God they will come in dread, and they will be afraid before Thee" (7:10, 16, 17).

On the other hand, a remnant will also return to Jerusalem, especially from Egypt and Assyria where small groups of "the compromised woman" hide out during the persecution of Antichrist. These will also have refused to worship the beast or his image, and as Isaiah records they are the ones who "will cry to the Lord because of oppressors, and He will send them a Savior and a Champion, and He will deliver them" (Isa. 19:20). These too, like the Jews they protected, will return to Mount Zion on the "highway from Egypt to Assyria" (v. 23) that God had provided for this remnant of Israel — when Christ "roared like a lion" on His way to Mount Zion for the salvation of the "tents of Judah" and the "inhabitants of Jerusalem." Isaiah also speaks of "the foreigners who join themselves to the Lord . . . even those I will bring to My holy mountain. . . . The Lord God, who gathers the dispersed of Israel, declares, 'Yet others I will gather to them, to those already gathered'" (56:6-8).

THE RESTORATION OF THE TEMPLE

The restoration of the Temple on the very summit of Mount Zion will be the last event to be completed on earth during this forty-five-day period preceding the Millennium. This restored Temple is described in considerable detail in the book of Ezekiel, as well as in other prophetic books in the Old Testament. Thus Ezekiel writes that he was brought to the "nave"[1] (i.e., the sanctuary) of the Temple where he was told by the Lord: "Son of man, this is the place of My throne and the place of the soles of My feet, where I will dwell among the sons of Israel forever. And the house of Israel will not again defile My holy name, neither they nor their kings, by their [spiritual] harlotry and by the corpses of their kings when they die" (Ezek. 41:1; 43:7).

The millennial Temple then will be the throne room in which Christ not only "will dwell among the sons of Israel forever" but from which He will rule over the nations of the earth — that is, over all those peoples who will survive both the day of the Lord and the Sheep and Goat judgment of Christ on the first day of the Millennium. As the prophet Zechariah writes, "Yes, it is He [Christ] who will build the temple of the Lord, and He who will bear the honor and sit and rule on His throne. Thus, He will be a priest on His throne, and the counsel of peace will be between the two offices" (Zech. 6:13).

The millennial Temple will be built by Christ as a final restoration of sorts of the Temple built initially by Solomon in the city of Jerusalem. The seventieth-week Temple, profaned by Antichrist, will have been destroyed by the day of the Lord, most probably at the seventh bowl judgment when all the cities of the nations are destroyed by the worldwide earthquake, including the city of Jerusalem where the

376 ■ *The Sign*

Temple will have been located. The work will need to be done quickly, but as a supernatural act of the Lord this will pose no difficulty. Compared with His complete restoration of the heavens and earth on the first day of the Millennium, the rebuilding of the Temple will be as nothing. The important truth is that Christ Himself, not the redeemed Jews, will build that final Temple, and He will do so during the forty-five-day restoration period immediately preceding the Millennium in preparation for His millennial reign over earth. Exactly as the Lord predicted through Zechariah, "Behold, a man whose name is Branch . . . will build the temple of the Lord. Yes, it is He who will build the temple of the Lord, and He who will bear the honor and sit and rule on His throne" (Zech. 6:12, 13). The Branch in verse 12, of course, can be only one man, Jesus Christ, the Son of David. Isaiah also speaks of Christ as the divine Branch, while describing the redeemed remnant of Israel:

> In that day the Branch of the Lord [Christ] will be beautiful and glorious, and the fruit of the earth will be the pride and the adornment of the survivors of Israel. And it will come about that he who is left in Zion and remains in Jerusalem will be called holy — everyone who is recorded for life in Jerusalem. . . . [For] the Lord has washed away the filth of the daughters of Zion, and purged the bloodshed of Jerusalem from her midst, by the spirit of judgment and the spirit of burning. . . . (Isa. 4:2-4).

And so Christ will build the Temple — His throne room from which He will "dwell in the midst of the sons of Israel forever" and rule over the nations of the earth — that will sit on top of Mount Zion, that "high mountain" now thrust above all the mountains of the land.

THE LAYOUT OF MOUNT ZION

We have made mention a number of times that this new Temple will be on Mount Zion, the "holy mountain of God." But it will not be in the city of Jerusalem like the previous Temple. It will be located instead *near* the new city of Jerusalem after it is rebuilt — not in the city itself, however, but rather on the very top of elevated Mount Zion north of the city.

The book of Ezekiel gives us a clear picture of how the mountain of God will be subdivided during the Millennium. The last nine chapters of Ezekiel contain many prophecies concerning Israel in the millennial kingdom of Christ. It is not this author's intent to discuss in depth the millennial kingdom of Christ, other than the events that occur on day one of the Millennium when we take these up in the next chapter. But for now we need a general picture of how the new Mount Zion, "the mountain of the house of the Lord . . . established as the chief of the mountains . . . raised above the hills" (Isa. 2:2), will be laid out. Although this brief summary only provides an outline, it will give the reader the general "lay of the land" concerning the particulars we will be concerned with in the last chapter of this volume.

(1) The entire top of the mountain is holy (43:12).

(2) In the middle of this holy area on the top of Mount Zion will be "the sanctuary, the most holy place" (45:2, 3).

(3) South of the summit, down the mountain a ways, will be the new city of Jerusalem (40:2; cf. 48:15), rebuilt by "My people Israel" who are restored from captivity (Amos 9:14; cf. Isa. 58:12; 61:4).

(4) And, "on the one side and on the other [side] of the holy allotment and of the property of the city . . . shall be [property] for the prince" (48:21).

Who is "the prince"? The Lord Himself identifies this prince as David. "I will be their God, and My servant David will be king over them. . . . And they shall live on the land that I gave to Jacob My servant, in which your fathers lived; and they will live on it, they, and their sons, and their sons' sons, forever; and David My servant shall be their prince forever" (Ezek. 37:24, 25).

In the next chapter these four points will take on greater significance. In the meantime, an event of monumental importance is about to take place.

RESTORING THE RULE UPON EARTH

The close of the forty-five-day restoration period will be marked by an event of tremendous significance, by far the most important event since the blowing of the seventh trumpet. This will be the return of Christ back to Heaven in preparation for receiving everlasting dominion over "all peoples, nations and men of every language" from God Almighty. God had reclaimed the reign over earth at the blowing of the seventh trumpet approximately two months earlier (see chapter 19), and the time has now come for God Almighty to restore the rule upon earth back to its rightful King, Jesus Christ. In several days Christ will return to earth, this time as its King. Then "His kingdom will be an everlasting kingdom, and all the dominions will serve and obey Him" (Dan. 7:27). But first the prophetic King must be given the kingdom over which He will rule.

Gabriel foretold of Jesus, when he appeared to Mary and announced the Savior's birth, "He will be great, and will be called the Son of the Most High; and the Lord God will give Him the throne of His father David" (Luke 1:32). That time has now come — the time for "the Lord God" to "give Him [Christ] the throne of His father David," the time "to anoint the most holy" (Dan. 9:24).

Many centuries before Gabriel's announcement, Daniel envisioned this same great moment that would occur after the defeat of Antichrist, when he wrote:

> Then I kept looking . . . until the beast was slain [Antichrist], and its body was destroyed and given to the burning fire. As for the rest of the beasts [the ten leaders of the final beast empire], their dominion was taken away. . . . I kept looking in the night visions, and behold, with the clouds of heaven one like a Son of Man was coming, and He came up to the Ancient of Days and was presented before Him. And to Him [Christ] was given dominion, glory and a kingdom, that all the peoples, nations, and men of every language might serve Him. His dominion is an everlasting dominion which will not pass away; and His kingdom is one which will not be destroyed. (Dan. 7:11, 12, 13, 14)

Providing further insight on this magnificent scene, Paul says,

> Then comes the end, when He [Christ] delivers up the kingdom to the God and Father, when He has abolished all rule [Satan's] and all authority [Antichrist's] and power [the eighth beast empire]. For He must reign until He has put all His enemies under His feet [at the end of the Millennium]. The last enemy that will be abolished is death [at the great White Throne]. (1 Cor. 15:24-26)[2]

With this majestic scene we are given a glimpse into one of the most profoundly significant moments of God's eternal plan. Christ has destroyed the enemies of God; Christ has reclaimed physical possession of earth; the cosmic conflict is over; and now Christ will deliver the physical kingdom of earth to God the Father Almighty (Dan. 7:11, 13; 1 Cor. 15:24). Then Christ will receive "dominion, glory and a kingdom, that all peoples, nations, and men of every language may serve Him . . . an everlasting dominion which shall not pass away" (Dan. 7:14). The work of Christ will be complete, and the great prophetic passage of Daniel will be fulfilled; "vision and prophecy" will be "sealed up," and God Almighty will "anoint the most holy" (Dan. 9:24). Christ's "kingdom will be an everlasting kingdom, and all the dominions will serve and obey Him" (Dan. 7:27).

The Millennium Begins

What will the Millennium be like? We can hardly begin to imagine the splendor and the glory of what God has in store for His own. And when we reflect on this as believers, we can only bow in worship before the sovereign God of the universe, who has called us to be His people and to enjoy the presence of His only Son throughout His eternal reign.

THE LITERAL FULFILLMENT

The word "millennium," in the prophetic sense, refers to one thousand years. Revelation 20 specifically refers five times to this literal thousand-year period of time which follows the battle of Armageddon (see chapter 18). The word "millennium" was therefore coined to describe this specific thousand-year period of time.

Many Scriptures give us a glimpse into what the Millennium will be like. For the believer, these include some of the most wonderful promises in the Bible. Thus the Lord tells us that there will be "a new heaven and a new earth" (Rev. 21:1) and God's "holy city, [the] new

Jerusalem" (v. 2) — where the "river of the water of life [flows] clear as crystal" (22:1), where the "tree of life" bears eternal fruit (v. 2), where the curse is forever gone (v. 3). The bride of Christ will dwell in the heavenly New Jerusalem in the presence of the Lamb, and John proclaims the beautiful promise that God "shall wipe away every tear from their eyes; and there shall no longer be any death; there shall no longer be any mourning, or crying, or pain; the first things have passed. . . . Behold, [God will make] all things new" (21:4, 5a). When we read promises such as these from God's Word — *promises that will be literally fulfilled* — the only response of those who truly know the Lord is to be filled with hope and joy and awe! The church today lives at a time in history when these promises could be literally fulfilled in our lifetime, without our first undergoing physical death!

As we consider what the Millennium will be like throughout this chapter, it will be helpful from the beginning to have an overall picture in mind of how the new heavens and the new earth are interrelated with the bride of Christ who dwells in the heavenly New Jerusalem. On the earthly level, the Millennium might be likened to the earth at the time of Adam and Eve in the Garden of Eden. As we will see further below, the new earth will be populated by "nations," or more correctly by those "peoples" who have survived the day of the Lord and, through faith in Christ, are given the right to live in the earthly millennial kingdom of Christ. Then there will be the nation of Israel, comprised of all those who have survived the seventieth week and have come into a saving relationship with their Messiah, Jesus Christ, after "the fulness of the Gentiles has come in" (Rom. 11:25). These will again dwell in the land of Israel, renewed and restored by God when He makes "all things new." The center will be Mount Zion, now elevated above all the mountains of the world, the top of which will be absolutely pure and holy. Resting on the very top of Mount Zion we see God's spectacular holy city — that is, the New Jerusalem which crowns the new earth, as it were, the magnificent city where His bride dwells in the glory and splendor of her Bridegroom's presence. Stretching the limits of human language, John describes the New Jerusalem as "coming down out of heaven from God, having the glory of God. Her brilliance was like a very costly stone, as a stone of crystal-clear jasper" (Rev. 21:10b, 11). This holy city will, in fact, be the very "throne of God and of the Lamb," the place from which Christ, in the presence of His bride, will rule forever and ever over the new earth (Rev. 22:3; cf. Dan. 7:27).

And we, the Scripture continues — that is, all for whom Christ truly is Lord and Savior, the bride of Christ — we "shall see His face" (Rev. 22:4)! There we shall be with Him forever — dwelling in the glory of His presence, drinking from the waters of life, eating from the tree of life, living in the "mansions" He has prepared for us (John 14:2), serving in His resplendent holy courts! And though we can barely begin to comprehend all God has in store for those who are washed in the blood of the Lamb, we have a hope and reality that cannot be shaken by anything in this life because it is anchored in the sovereign God of the universe and His unchanging Word.

THE MILLENNIAL RULE OF CHRIST

In addition to these beautiful truths, Scripture teaches much more about the Millennium. As we saw in the last chapter, the Millennium will begin seventy days after the blowing of the seventh trumpet, seventy-five days after the close of the seventieth week of Daniel. When Satan's rule over earth is taken from him, God will then "set up a kingdom which will never be destroyed, and that kingdom will not be left for another people; it will crush and put an end to all these kingdoms [of Satan], but it will itself endure forever" (Dan. 2:44). For those who accept the inerrancy and the literal interpretation of Scripture, this kingdom which shall "endure forever" can only refer to that time when Christ will *literally* return to earth in the end times to establish a *literal* kingdom encompassing the entire earth over which He will rule as King of kings and Lord of lords. Clearly this is the intent of Gabriel's announcement to Mary that the child to be born to her "will be great, and will be called the Son of the Most High; and the Lord God will give Him the throne of His father David" (Luke 1:32).

Yet, although God the Father will give full authority to the Son, the Son will still be subject to the Father. As the Apostle Paul explains, "For He [the Father] has put all things in subjection under His [Christ's] feet. But when He [the Father] says, 'All things are put in subjection,' it is evident that He [the Father] is excepted who put all things in subjection to Him [Christ]. And when all things are subjected to Him, then the Son Himself also will be subjected to the one [the Father] who subjected all things to Him, that God may be all in all" (1 Cor. 15:27, 28).

As we shall see further below, Christ will rule earth from His throne in the Temple, on top of elevated Mount Zion. The Father, "the Lord God, the Almighty" (Rev. 21:22), will be present there with the Son, the Lamb, when the New Jerusalem descends from Heaven. And because of the divine glory that will forever encompass all redeemed creation, the New Jerusalem will have "no need of the sun or of the moon to shine upon it, for the glory of God [will illumine] it, and its lamp [will be] the Lamb. And the nations shall walk by its light, and the kings of the earth shall bring their glory into it" (vv. 23, 24).

KING DAVID RULES OVER ISRAEL

In the preceding chapter we saw that an area on either side of the holy area on the top of Mount Zion will be designated for the resurrected David, the prince. From there on Mount Zion, now elevated and completely holy, David will be given political rule over Israel (and only Israel) during the millennial kingdom. As Jeremiah foretold long ago, Jews in Israel will "serve the Lord their God, and David their king, whom I [the Lord] will raise up for them" (Jer. 30:9). Similarly the Lord revealed through Ezekiel, "My servant David will be king over them [Israel], and they will all have one shepherd; and they will walk in My ordinances, and keep My statutes, and observe them" (Ezek. 37:24).

The governing chain of command is seen in a previous passage in Ezekiel, where the Lord declares, "Then I will set over them [Israel] one shepherd, My servant David, and he will feed them; he will feed them himself and be their shepherd. And I, the Lord, will be their God, and My servant David will be prince among them; I, the Lord, have spoken" (Ezek. 34:23, 24). Thus David will rule solely over Israel, whereas Christ will rule supremely over all the earth (including Israel) from His throne in the Temple which Christ shares with the Father in the center of the great and expansive holy area on the summit of Mount Zion. Down the mountain, on either side of the holy area to the east and to the west, will be the area, or more precisely the areas, where Prince David will dwell again and once again rule over his own nation, Israel. The palace from which David will rule will be in the rebuilt earthly city of Jerusalem to the south of the holy area — as foretold by God's prophet Jeremiah: "Thus says the Lord, 'Behold, I will restore the fortunes of the tents of Jacob and have compassion on his dwelling places; and the city shall be rebuilt on its ruin, and the palace shall stand on its rightful place'" (Jer. 30:18).

OTHER KINGS AND OTHER KINGDOMS

Whereas the millennial rule over Israel by David is explicit in Scripture, the leadership of the other nations is only implied. Scripture does make clear, however, that there will be nations during the thousand years and that each will, presumably, have its own ruler and its own particular governmental organization — all under the world rule of Christ. We know, for example, that during the Millennium God's glory will illumine not only Jerusalem but that all other "nations shall walk by its light, and the kings of the earth shall bring their glory [that is, their honor and praise of God] into it" (Rev. 21:23, 24). This universal reign of the Messiah over the kings and the nations of the earth was depicted even by Solomon in what is clearly a "near-far" psalm. Thus Solomon declared: "May he also rule from sea to sea, and from the river to the ends of the earth. . . . And let all kings bow down before him, all nations serve him. For he will deliver the needy when he cries for help, the afflicted also, and him who has no helper" (Ps. 72:8, 11, 12).

The other nations of the world not only will serve and glorify God, but they will also serve His chosen people Israel, rather than afflict them as they had for thousands of years. Speaking through the prophet Isaiah, God revealed: "Thus says the Lord God, 'Behold I will lift up My hand to the nations, and set up My standard to the peoples; and they will bring your sons in their bosom, and your daughters will be carried on their shoulders. And kings will be your guardians, and their princesses your nurses. They will bow down to you with their faces to the earth, and lick the dust of your feet; and you will know that I am the Lord; those who hopefully wait for Me will not be put to shame'" (Isa. 49:22, 23).

Where will these nations come from? As we saw in the last chapter, there will be a remnant of these Gentile nations that will survive the wrath of God and who "will come trembling out of their fortresses; to the Lord our God they will come in dread, and they will be afraid before Thee" (Micah 7:17) at the Sheep and Goat Judgment of Christ on the first day of the Millennium, on His holy mountain. Those who, in addition to surviving God's wrath, survive Christ's judgment of the nations (Matt. 25:31, 32; cf. Rev. 20:4) will become the citizens of the non-Jewish nations that go into the millennial kingdom on earth that will be ruled by Christ.

THE FIRST DAY OF THE MILLENNIUM

Chapters 20 and 21 of the book of Revelation now record a series of events which will occur on the first day of the Millennium. Except for the parenthesis found in Revelation 20:7-15,[1] these events described by John clearly occur in succession, one right after the other.

And I saw an angel coming down from heaven, having the key of the abyss and a great chain in his hand. And he laid hold of the dragon, the serpent of old, who is the Devil and Satan, and bound him for a thousand years, and threw him into the abyss, and shut it and sealed it over him, so that he should not deceive the nations any longer, until the thousand years were completed; after these things he must be released for a short time. *And I saw* thrones, and they sat upon them; and judgment was given to them. *And I saw* the souls of those who had been beheaded because of the testimony of Jesus and because of the word of God, and those who had not worshiped the beast or his image, and had not received the mark upon their forehead and upon their hand; and they came to life and reigned with Christ for a thousand years. . . . *And I saw* a new heaven and a new earth; for the first heaven and the first earth passed away, and there is no longer any sea. *And I saw* the holy city, new Jerusalem, coming down out of heaven from God, made ready as a bride adorned for her husband. (Rev. 20:1-4; 21:1, 2, emphasis added).

These five "And I saw" phrases, then, give the sequence of events that occur at the beginning of the Millennium as follows:

First Event: Satan is bound.
Second Event: The judgment of Christ.
Third Event: The resurrection of the "beheaded" tribulation martyrs.
Fourth Event: The new heavens and earth.
Fifth Event: The descent of the New Jerusalem, the bride, down to earth.

These then are the events that need to be looked at more carefully to complete our discussion of all the preceding end-time events and to have a better appreciation of the millennial kingdom over which Christ will rule.

FIRST EVENT: SATAN BOUND

As we have seen and emphasized from the beginning of this book, the purpose of Christ the Redeemer, in part, was to reverse the consequences of the Fall — when mankind and all the rest of creation were corrupted because of Adam's sin. That corruption allowed Satan to have limited but powerful authority over the earth, and before Christ can have absolute, divine, sovereign control over the earth as King He will have to deal directly with Satan.

Although Satan's forces under Antichrist will have been totally destroyed at Armageddon, Satan himself will still be alive and on earth (see Rev. 12:9). Because God's plan is not to send him eternally into the lake of fire until after the Millennium (Rev. 20:10), Christ will have to neutralize him for that thousand years. Consequently, as John saw in his vision, an angel "laid hold of the dragon, the serpent of old, who is the Devil and Satan, and bound him for a thousand years, and threw him into the abyss, and shut it and sealed it over him, so that he should not deceive the nations any longer, until the thousand years were completed; after these things he must be released for a short time" (Rev. 20:2, 3). Because Satan will be bound for a thousand years, he will, of course, have been bound immediately after the Millennium begins — that is, in the first event of the first day, as suggested by Revelation 20:1, 2.

SECOND EVENT: THE SHEEP AND GOATS JUDGMENT

The last event of the 1,290 days allocated to Antichrist was the destruction of Antichrist and his armies at the battle of Armageddon.* The first event at the beginning of the Millennium, as we have just seen, is the binding of Satan for a thousand years. The only thing left, then, before God will restore the earth back to its original splendor it enjoyed prior to the Fall is to eliminate all the "children of wrath" (Eph. 2:2) who survived the day of the Lord. This will take place at the Sheep and Goats Judgment, which will be the very next event on the first day of the Millennium.

In the Olivet Discourse, Jesus describes the Sheep and Goats Judgment in the following way:

> "But when the Son of Man comes in His glory, and all the angels with Him, then He will sit on His glorious throne. And all the nations [non-Jewish peoples] will be gathered before Him; and He will separate them from one another, as the shepherd separates the sheep from the goats; and He will put the sheep on His right, and the goats on the left. Then the King will say to those on His right, 'Come, you who are blessed of My Father, inherit the

* See chapter 20.

kingdom prepared for you from the foundation of the world. For I was hungry, and you gave Me something to eat; I was thirsty, and you gave Me drink; I was a stranger, and you invited Me in; naked, and you clothed Me; I was sick, and you visited Me; I was in prison, and you came to Me.' Then the righteous will answer Him, saying, 'Lord, when did we see You hungry, and feed You, or thirsty, and give You drink? And when did we see You a stranger, and invite You in, or naked, and clothe You? And when did we see You sick, or in prison, and come to You?' And the King will answer and say to them, 'Truly I say to you, to the extent that you did it to one of these brothers of Mine, even the least of them, you did it to Me.'" (Matt. 25:31-40)

From this passage many things are evident. First, the Lord makes clear that He will personally conduct the judgment from His throne, which is in the Temple in the center of the holy area on top of elevated Mount Zion. Second, "all the angels [will be] with Him" (v. 31) — which seems to indicate that the angels (who have been His reapers during the day of the Lord) will again be part of this final judgment. Third, "all the nations [peoples] will be gathered before" Christ to undergo judgment (v. 32). It is important to note that the word used here for "nations" is the Greek word *ethnos*, which can be translated as "nations," "heathen," or simply "peoples"; it was used by Jews to refer to any non-Jewish people.[2] The Sheep and Goats Judgment, therefore, refers to all those non-Jewish people who may survive the day of the Lord, rather than to "nations" in the modern sense of independent political states. However, no Jews will be judged at this Sheep and Goats Judgment of Christ.

By carefully studying all the related passages, it would seem to this writer that the judgment will be based upon two issues, although the first issue is implied by other texts. The first issue is whether or not the non-Jewish survivors of the day of the Lord have worshiped the beast or his image or have taken his mark. For those who fail this simple test — if indeed any do survive the day of the Lord — their condemnation will have already been established (Rev. 14:9-11), and the second test will be unnecessary.

But for those who pass the first test, the second basis of judgment will be their individual treatment of Israel — that is, their treatment "of these brothers of Mine" (Matt. 25:40). In other words the way in which the "nations" treat the *Jews* will be considered the same as their treatment of *Christ Himself* (Matt. 25:40, 45; cf. Gen. 12:2, 3).

As would be expected, the witnesses at this trial (as it was during the Holocaust trials) will be the survivors of Israel themselves — the very people that the world has so long ridiculed and persecuted (see, e.g., Isa. 54:17). These witnesses will not be a part of Christ's judgment of the nations, but rather, after "all the nations have gathered together" and Christ permits "them [to] present their witnesses that they may be justified," God then declares that "you [Israel] are My witnesses" (Isa. 43:9, 10). Those who have done Israel harm in any way will be condemned. "Then He [Christ] will . . . say to those on His left [the goats], 'Depart from Me, accursed ones, into the eternal fire which has been prepared for the devil and his angels'" (Matt. 25:41). Those who have befriended Israel will be spared: ". . . but the righteous into eternal life" (v. 46).

Obviously everyone present at the Sheep and Goats Judgment will realize who Christ is and, if given a second chance, would be willing to sacrifice all for the sake of Christ rather than spend eternity in the lake of fire. Thus everyone present will recognize who Christ is, as seen in Paul's quote in Romans, taken from Isaiah 45:23: "Every knee shall bow to Me, and every tongue shall give praise to God" (Rom. 14:10, 11). But that belated confession and praise will not bring salvation after the fact, so to speak. The *mere acknowledgment* of Christ's Deity, Saviorhood, and Lordship — whether professed before or during the time of judgment — will not save a person, no matter how outwardly religious he may be. In a similar vein, it is important to note that some who believe they have merited salvation because of their rejection of Antichrist will not be saved and, amazingly, others who believe they have no claim to salvation *will be saved*. Thus some astonished "sheep" whom the Lord calls "righteous" will say to Him with great wonder, "'Lord, when did we see You hungry, and feed You, or thirsty, and give You drink? And when did we see You a stranger, and invite You in, or naked, and clothe You? And when did we see You sick, or in prison, and come to You?' And the King will answer and say to them, 'Truly I say to you, to the extent that you did it to one of these brothers of Mine, even the least of them, you did it to Me'" (vv. 37-40). Similarly, those Gentiles who refused to worship the beast or take his mark, who will not have directly oppressed or harmed the Jews but nonetheless will have stood by indifferently, permitting others to persecute them, will be ranked with the goats. These will have had many opportunities to help the primary target of Satan's wrath, but did not. To them the Lord will say, "'Truly I say to you, to the extent that you did not do it to one of the least of these, you did not do it to Me.' And these will go away into eternal punishment" (Matt. 25:45, 46).

It is essential to understand, however, that the ultimate basis for salvation of the "sheep" as they stand before Christ on the first day of the Millennium is not founded on works. The Scriptures teach without exception that salvation is by grace alone, through faith alone, in response to God's sovereign election before the foundation of the world (Eph. 1:4, 5; 2:8, 9). It would seem that the "sheep" will not have trusted in Christ, however, before coming face to face with Him at the Sheep and Goats Judgment, and yet they will be given their saving faith (that will be accounted unto them as righteousness) "when the Son of Man comes in His glory" (Matt. 25:31) at the Sheep and Goats Judgment. In other words, God chooses before the foundation of the world both *who* the elect will be and *when*, through faith, they will come into right standing with Jesus Christ. Just as the remnant of Israel will be saved at the time God chooses (i.e., after "the fulness of the Gentiles has come in" [Rom. 11:25]; when "they look on Me whom they have pierced" [Zech. 12:10]; when "He will revive us after two days . . . [and] raise us up on the third day" [Hos. 6:2]), so also the sheep will be saved in God's own sovereign timing at the Sheep and Goats Judgment, when they look upon Christ. For the "sheep," chosen by God before the foundation of the world, the time of their salvation is now!

These Gentile peoples who will enter the millennial kingdom will come from "many nations," in particular from Egypt and Assyria[3] because of their assistance to and protection of the small remnant of Israel that fled to the lands of Egypt and Assyria during the great persecution by Antichrist. All of these will hear the wonderful words of Christ the King, spoken to the sheep: "'Come, you who are blessed of My Father, *inherit the kingdom prepared for you from the foundation of the world*'" (Matt. 25:34, emphasis added).

THIRD EVENT: "BEHEADED" MARTYRS RESURRECTED

After Satan is bound and after the judgment thrones appear, the souls of those who have been "beheaded" during the great tribulation by Antichrist will be resurrected. As John writes: "And I saw the souls of those who had been beheaded because of the testimony of Jesus and because of the word of God, and those who had not worshiped the beast or his image, and had not received the mark upon their forehead and upon their hand; and they came to life and reigned with Christ for a thousand years. The rest of the dead did not come to life until the thousand years were completed. This is the first resurrection" (Rev. 20:4, 5).[4]

What does the "first resurrection" refer to? When studied carefully in the context of Revelation 20, it is clear that the first resurrection in this instance refers to the general resurrection of all believers "unto life." At the same time, however, this specific resurrection "unto life" will occur on the first day of the Millennium and is limited to the martyrs who have been "beheaded" because they are the *only ones* referred to in verse 5.

How then can we reconcile what seems to be a contradiction to what other Scriptures teach? In other words, how can we maintain that the church is raptured and resurrected sometime during the second half of the seventieth week, and at the same time maintain that the resurrection of these "beheaded" martyrs is the "first" resurrection even though it occurs much later, on the first day of the Millennium? The answer, in this writer's opinion, is quite simple. There are only two *kinds* of resurrections that this passage speaks directly to — the first resurrection being the resurrection unto righteousness (i.e., unto life [John 5:29]) and the second resurrection which is "a resurrection of judgment" (John 5:29), which is really "the second death" (Rev. 20:6, 14). Scripture teaches that the resurrection unto righteousness (unto life) involves several different phases. First, there is the resurrection of Christ Himself, specifically called the first fruits of this first resurrection (1 Cor. 15:20, 21, 23), then the resurrection of the Old and New Testament saints at the Rapture, and finally the resurrection of the "beheaded" martyrs on the first day of the Millennium. Someday there will be a fourth phase of the first resurrection as well, when the believing men and women who go into the Millennium receive their resurrection bodies. The resurrection of Christ, the resurrection of the church, the resurrection of the "beheaded" martyrs, and the resurrection of the millennial saints, then, are all part of the first resurrection — that is, the resurrection unto life. This first resurrection, then, stands in complete contrast to the second resurrection, which is the resurrection unto death which will take place at the Great White Throne Judgment at the end of the Millennium. It is interesting to note that the first fruits of the second resurrection unto death will be Antichrist and his false prophet who, after the battle of Armageddon, "were thrown alive into the lake of fire which burns with brimstone" (Rev. 19:20).

And who are these "beheaded" martyrs? It is the opinion of this writer, although we cannot be adamant, that these are the martyrs who have died by "beheading" and are seen under the throne of God at the fifth seal. They are the faithful seventieth week witnesses who were "slain because of the word of God, and because of the testimony which they had maintained" (Rev. 6:9). Though they will be hated on account of Christ's name, they will be obedient to their Master, going from city to city in the land of Israel (right under the nose of Antichrist), warning the nation and proclaiming the gospel (Matt. 10:22, 23). For such witness many of them, if not all, will forfeit their lives by beheading. We know their witness will be complete when "the Son of Man comes" (v. 23), but for some reason those witnesses who die before the Son of Man comes will not receive their resurrection bodies at the Rapture of the church (when "the dead in Christ rise first") but later, on the first day of the Millennium.

Without the faithfulness of those martyrs, the remnant of Israel that follows the true Messiah into the Millennium, from man's perspective, would have died in unbelief. But God knows that in those terrible last days He will have faithful Jewish believers to accomplish His will — believers who, at the cost of their own lives by "beheading," will nevertheless continue to steadfastly warn His nation of her impending danger. Because of their faithfulness, these Jewish martyrs will come to life and will reign with Christ for a thousand years over the nation they gave their lives to protect (Rev. 20:4). Daniel, speaking directly to these faithful martyrs, refers to them as "those who lead the many to righteousness, [who will shine brightly] like the stars, forever and ever" (12:3).

FOURTH EVENT: NEW HEAVENS AND NEW EARTH

As mentioned at the beginning of this chapter, the creation of a new heavens and a new earth is among the most beautiful promises in God's Word. More than twenty-five hundred years ago the Lord proclaimed through the prophet Isaiah: "For behold, I create a new heavens and a new earth; and the former things shall not be remembered or come to mind. But be glad and rejoice forever in what I create" (Isa. 65:17, 18a). Likewise, Peter tells of the "new heavens and a new earth, in which righteousness dwells" (2 Pet. 3:13b), while John also tells that he "saw a new heaven and a new earth" in his vision (Rev. 21:1).

Why will the Lord create a new heavens and a new earth? The first reason, of course, is that the earth will be in a state of total devastation when the battle of Armageddon is over and the day of the Lord is completed. As we have seen already, the *type* of destruction is represented by the destruction of Sodom and Gomorrah, and the *extent* of the destruction is represented by the worldwide flood of Noah's day. As Peter writes, "the heavens will pass away with a roar and the elements will be destroyed with intense heat, and the earth and its works will be burned up" (2 Pet. 3:10b). Except for God's protected remnants, the entire earth will be filled with death and destruction. The destruction of the heavens and the earth will be so devastating, in fact, that a new heavens and a new earth will have to rise from the ashes, so to speak, before the millennial kingdom can be inaugurated and the earth made inhabitable. This "creation," however, will not be *ex nihilo*, but rather a radical *renovation* or reconstruction of the remaining creation. The Greek term translated "new," therefore, does not refer to something that has never existed before, but rather to the *renewing* of something that already exists.[5] This radically renovated creation then will bring the heavens and earth back into an interrelationship with one another that was enjoyed by Adam and Eve before the Fall. It will be a "new heavens and a new earth, *in which righteousness dwells*" (2 Pet. 3:13, emphasis added). In other words, the heavens and earth so terribly corrupted by the Fall and devastated by the day of the Lord will be remade and perfected by Christ into a splendid new and uncorrupted form. This, then, will be the time for which all "creation waits eagerly" (Rom. 8:19), the time that Jesus referred to as "the regeneration," the time that Peter called "the period of restoration of all things, about which God spoke by the mouth of His holy prophets from ancient time" (Acts 3:21).

It is important to note that the renovation of the heavens and earth will begin on the first day of the Millennium,[6] but only *after* the wicked who survive the day of the Lord have been sent to their eternal punishment at the Sheep and Goats Judgment. Only then — after the earth has been completely eradicated of any and all who were a part of Satan's kingdom of darkness — will the earth be renovated and reinstated to its original splendor as it existed before the Fall.

Obviously we cannot begin to comprehend how the Lord will renovate the heavens and the earth — especially with the presence of God's elect still upon the earth with their earthly bodies, with the eternal fires still burning in Edom throughout the Millennium, and with the dead from Armageddon still remaining unburied seven months (Ezek. 39:14), well into the millennial reign of Christ. But we do know that "the anxious longings of the creation . . . subjected to futility [at the Fall of Adam] . . . will be set free from its slavery to corruption" (Rom. 8:19-21). As it was in the days of creation, when "God saw all that He had made, and behold, it was very good" (Gen. 1:31), so it will be once again in the re-creation in the Millennium, directly benefiting all of mankind inhabiting the millennial kingdom of Christ.[7] We know that the new heavens and the new earth will be perfect in every detail — yet renovated in such a way that somber reminders will be left behind of God's judgment of the wicked on the earth. However our sovereign and omnipotent God chooses to accomplish this renewal, the result will be a magnificent new heavens and earth, worthy of the New Jerusalem (the mansions of God housing the bride of Christ) that will hover over it, from which Christ will rule with His saints in perfect justice and righteousness.

FIFTH EVENT: THE NEW JERUSALEM

And so we come to the closing scene of Christ's holy work on the first day of the Millennium, the climactic event of human history, the crowning occasion of God's sovereign plan which He in His inscrutable wisdom and grace determined before the foundation of the world. Words cannot begin to capture the significance, the grandeur, the magnificent splendor of this crowning event. For in this final scene something beyond our comprehension will happen. The New Jerusalem, the heavenly mansions prepared for the bride of Christ (John 14:2), in brilliant beauty beyond anything we can imagine, will descend from Heaven. And within this holy city the Old and New Testament saints — those taken to Heaven *together*, and rewarded *together* at the bema seat — will now descend *together* adorned in resplendent garments as Christ's own bride — married to the very Son of God, to the Lamb who shed his precious blood to make us pure and holy, to the One who suffered, bled, and died to redeem us from our sins.

It would have been an amazing thing to have seen all of this in John's magnificent vision recorded in Revelation. How much more when we — that is, all for whom Christ is truly Lord and Savior — take part in the magnificent grandeur of what will actually happen! As seen again in John's account we begin to capture a glimpse of what this will be like:

And I saw a new heaven and a new earth. . . . And I saw the holy city, new Jerusalem, coming down out of heaven from God, made ready as a bride adorned for her husband. And I heard a loud voice from the throne, saying, "Behold, the tabernacle of God is among men, and He shall dwell among them, and they shall be His peoples, and God Himself shall be among them, and He shall wipe away every tear from their eyes; and there shall no longer be any death; there shall no longer be any mourning, or crying, or pain; the first things have passed away." And He who sits on the throne said, "Behold, I am making all things new." And He said, "Write, for these words are faithful and true." And He said to me, "It is done. I am the Alpha and the Omega, the beginning and the end. I will give to the one who thirsts from the spring of the water of life without cost. He who overcomes shall inherit these things, and I will be his God and he will be My son." (Rev. 21:1-7)

There are a number of important truths within these verses — truths which fulfill God's promises to His bride throughout the Scripture, truths which should provide great encouragement to every believer. (Note that above and in the following paragraphs I have used "we" in connection with these wonderful truths, because they apply so intimately to all of us who know Christ as Lord and Savior. The unbeliever, of course, needs to understand that he would not be included in these promises and in the "we" as used here.)

First, we see the truth that *we will be with the Lord forever* in the most intimate kind of relationship. This fulfills the Lord's promise to His own, given through Paul, concerning the Rapture: "Then we who are alive and remain shall be caught up together with them in the clouds to meet the Lord in the air, and thus *we shall always be with the Lord*" (1 Thess. 4:17, emphasis added). Likewise, we have Jesus' own promise that "in My Father's house are many dwelling places; if it were not so, I would have told you; for I go to prepare a place for you. And if I go and prepare a place for you, I will come again, and receive you to Myself; that *where I am, there you may be also*" (John 14:2, 3, emphasis added). This is perhaps the Lord's most heartwarming promise to His own — that we will always be with Him, wherever He makes His home. That home, we see, is in fact the New Jerusalem, where Christ has made "dwelling places" for His bride. "And He shall dwell among them," John writes, "and they shall be His peoples, and God Himself shall be among them" (Rev. 21:3b). As part of this, we see without question that the New Jerusalem must descend from Heaven at the *beginning* of the Millennium (rather than at the end of the Millennium as some have taught). This is true because if the New Jerusalem, the dwelling place of Christ's bride, were to remain in Heaven during the Millennium while Christ is ruling on the earth, then He and His saints would be separated from each other throughout the thousand years, directly contradicting the two divine promises just mentioned.[8]

Second, we see the truth that *there will be "no temple in [the New Jerusalem]*, for the Lord God, the Almighty, and the Lamb, are its temple" (Rev. 21:22). When the New Jerusalem descends from Heaven, it will hover directly above the earth, with its center encompassing the newly built Temple on top of Mount Zion, their bases adjoining at the same elevation on the summit of Mount Zion. The Temple of God will therefore be the focal point both of the New Jerusalem and of the entire earth. In other words, Christ will rule over earth from His throne room in the new Temple, which will be an inseparable part of the New Jerusalem.

The inseparability of the New Jerusalem and its throne from the millennial Temple on earth is of paramount importance. Christ's throne in the Temple is one and the same with His throne in the New Jerusalem[9]* — resting on the entire top of the elevated Mount Zion, all of which is holy. Thus, as we would expect, John "saw no temple" in the New Jerusalem as it descended from Heaven, precisely because the new Temple had already been rebuilt by Christ on top of Mount Zion during the forty-five-day restoration period. And because the area of the new Temple protrudes up into the New Jerusalem as it hovers over the earth, the elect of the earth in their natural physical bodies will have full access to the throne room of Christ via Mount Zion. Finally, in some divinely mysterious way, the millennial Temple is virtually identified with God the Father and God the Son — so much so that John declares that "the Lord God, the Almighty, and the Lamb, are its temple" (Rev. 21:22). As summarized in the beautiful passage in the same chapter: "'Behold, the tabernacle of God is among men, and He shall dwell among them, and they shall be His peoples, and God Himself shall be among them'" (Rev. 21:3).

The third truth we see in these verses is that *we will be the bride of Christ*, having been married already to Christ after the Rapture and

* For a full discussion of this see endnote 9.

resurrection during the reclamation period (see chapter 20). Thus John writes, "And I saw the holy city, new Jerusalem, coming down out of heaven from God, made ready as a bride adorned for her husband" (Rev. 21:2); and a little later in the same chapter "one of the seven angels" tells John, "Come here, I shall show you the bride, the wife of the Lamb" (v. 9b). It is clear that the wedding has already take place because the saints are described as "the wife of the Lamb." But it is also clear that the saints are still dressed as a bride "adorned for her husband" in anticipation of the great marriage supper of the Lamb that will take place immediately on God's holy mountain. In addition to this we see how closely the bride of Christ is also associated with the New Jerusalem, descending together as one, in a way that parallels Christ's own presence in the New Jerusalem — suggesting again the intimacy of the Lamb with His bride, perfect communion as they dwell together in God's holy city, the New Jerusalem.

THE MARRIAGE SUPPER OF THE LAMB

With the bride of Christ now together with her husband in the New Jerusalem, all that remains is the magnificent celebration that will follow — the marriage supper of the Lamb.

What will this celebration be like? Although we can hardly begin to imagine, we are given a small glimpse in the book of Isaiah. "The Lord of hosts will prepare a lavish banquet for all peoples on this mountain," the prophet declares, "a banquet of aged wine, choice pieces with marrow, and refined, aged wine. And on this mountain He will swallow up the covering which is over all peoples, even the veil which is stretched over all nations. He will swallow up death for all time, and the Lord God will wipe tears away from all faces, and He will remove the reproach of His people from all the earth; for the Lord has spoken" (Isa. 25:6-8).

This will indeed be a resplendent scene, rivaled only by the actual marriage of the Lamb and the bride that will have taken place previously in the heavenlies. Once again we would expect God Almighty, the maker of Heaven and earth and every galaxy in the universe, to display His glories in magnificent splendor. It will indeed be a "lavish banquet" which the finite language of even the prophet Isaiah can barely begin to express.

And who will come to the marriage supper? The angel said to John, "Write, 'Blessed are those who are invited to the marriage supper of the Lamb" (Rev. 19:9). The bride of Christ will, of course, be there, "adorned for her husband" (Rev. 21:2) — that is, the raptured and resurrected saints from all ages. But there will also be invited guests in addition to the bride. These will include those who have come to faith in Christ after the day of the Lord begins — those who survive the great tribulation by Antichrist, the day of the Lord's wrath, and the Sheep and Goats Judgment. These too will be invited to the marriage supper; but more than this, they will be invited to spend eternity with the One who has become their Lord and Savior, Jesus Christ. Indeed, "*Blessed* are those who are invited to the marriage supper of the Lamb" (Rev. 19:9, emphasis added).

And so, in celebrating the marriage supper of the Lamb, we have come full circle. The cosmic conflict has forever come to an end; Satan has been defeated, and all who gave their allegiance to him have been destroyed; God Almighty has reclaimed His eternal rule over earth, and Christ in turn has received the kingdom from the Father; the elect of the nation of Israel have been saved; the saints of all ages have become the bride of Christ to live forever in intimate communion with their Lord; and the heavens and the earth have been restored to the original beauty and perfection they once knew. As these now familiar words of Scripture proclaim so powerfully:

"The kingdom of the world has become the kingdom of our Lord, and of His Christ; and He will reign forever and ever" (Rev. 11:15b). "Hallelujah! For the Lord our God, the Almighty, reigns" (19:6b). "Behold, the tabernacle of God is among men, and He shall dwell among them, and they shall be His peoples, and God Himself shall be among them, and He shall wipe away every tear from their eyes; and there shall no longer be any death; there shall no longer be any mourning, or crying, or pain; the first things have passed away" (21:3, 4).

HOW WILL WE RESPOND?

It seems most fitting to end this study of the end times in the same way that the book of Revelation ends — that is, to end with the same triumphant affirmation, the same sober warning, and the same gracious invitation that Christ Himself addresses to the church and to the world in the closing words in His Revelation. Thus the Lord promises John and every believer in every age, "He who overcomes shall inherit these things, and I will be his God and he will be my son" (Rev. 21:7). In these words we have both a challenge and a magnificent promise

— a challenge first *to be an overcomer* by living a life of godly purity in word and deed and action; a challenge *to be prepared* for the last days, especially as they seem to be so rapidly approaching. But in addition to this we have a promise to all who are overcomers that we "shall inherit these things" — things which we know will be more wonderful than anything we can imagine, even to the extent of becoming sons of God Almighty, "fellow-heirs with Christ" (Rom. 8:17) because we will be the bride of Christ!

But the closing words of Revelation also contain a sober warning. In the very next verse the Lord warns, "But for the cowardly and unbelieving and abominable and murderers and immoral persons and sorcerers and idolaters and all liars, their part will be in the lake that burns with fire and brimstone, which is the second death" (21:8). Again in the last chapter of Revelation we find this same dramatic contrast between the Lord's glorious promises and His sober warning: "Blessed are those who wash their robes [in the blood of the Lamb*], that they may have the right to the tree of life, and may enter by the gates into the city. [But] outside are the dogs and the sorcerers and the immoral persons and the murderers and the idolaters, and everyone who loves and practices lying. I, Jesus, have sent My angel to testify to you these things for the churches" (22:14-16a).

How will we respond to the words of Jesus? I would ask each one of us to carefully examine our hearts before the Lord. Will you and will I be overcomers? Will we be prepared for the terrible times that are to come in the last days? Will we live a life of godly purity — in doctrine and in all we do? Will we have access to God's protection "because [we] have kept the word of [Christ's] perseverance" (Rev. 3:10) "and have not denied [Christ's] name" (v. 8)? Or will we be one of His "bond-servants" that He will cast "into great tribulation . . . [so that] all the churches will know that I am He who searches the minds and hearts . . . [who] will give to each one of you according to your deeds" (Rev. 2:20, 22, 23)? This is the question each of us, claiming the name of Christ, must ask of ourselves.

And if you have not received Christ as your Lord and Savior, or if there is no evidence of this in your life, I urge you with all my heart to heed Christ's warning — to cast yourself upon His grace, to place your faith in the finished work of Christ, to have your sins washed away by the blood of the Lamb. In the final analysis this is the whole message

* See Revelation 7:14

of this book — that we would be overcomers, that Christ would indeed be our *Lord* and *Savior*, that we would be sons of the Lord God Almighty, completely prepared for the cataclysmic days of the end times. To this end the last chapter of Revelation includes this beautiful invitation: "And the Spirit and the bride say, 'Come.' And let the one who hears say, 'Come.' And let the one who is thirsty come; let the one who wishes, take the water of life without cost" (Rev. 22:17).

As in the days of Noah, God has given both the church and the world advance written notice of exactly what will occur in the end times. To His own, the inhabitants of the kingdom of light, He promises blessing for obedience and severe persecution for compromise. To the unbelieving world, the inhabitants of the kingdom of darkness, He promises but one thing: "the wrath of God, which is mixed in full strength in the cup of His anger . . . tormented with fire and brimstone . . . forever and ever" (Rev. 14:10, 11). "The seed of the wicked will be cut off [but] the righteous will inherit the land and dwell in it forever" (Psa. 37:28, 29). How will you — how will I — respond?

Epilogue

Over the ages men have always liked to set dates for the return of Christ. A recent book listed "eighty-eight reasons why Christ must return in eighty-eight" (1988). When Christ failed to return during that year, the author recalculated, discovered he had missed one point concerning the exact year of Jesus' birth, and moved the date of His return up to 1989. In the process of making the one-year adjustment, he advertised *eighty-nine* reasons why Christ would return in 1989. Needless to say, the Lord returned during neither of those years.

"WHEN THE FIG TREE . . ."

In the Olivet Discourse Christ spoke directly about the time of His second coming:

"Now learn the parable from the fig tree: when its branch has already become tender, and puts forth its leaves, you know that summer is near; even so you too, when you see all these things, recognize that He is near, right at the door. Truly I say to you, this generation will not pass away until all these things take place." (Matt. 24:32-34)

Taking this passage in its context and at face value, Christ says there will be signs that will indicate "He is near, right at the door" and that the generation who is living when "all these things" begin to unfold, starting with the false christs (v. 5), will not die out until "all these things take place." The Jews of Jesus' day did not realize that their Messiah, the Christ, would come to earth twice and that a lengthy gap, now nearly two thousand years long, would intervene between the sixty-ninth and seventieth weeks of Daniel's prophecy. For that reason, even those who believed that Jesus was indeed the Christ had no comprehension that the generation of which Jesus was speaking would live in the far-distant future during the final seven-year period of Daniel's prophecy. Obviously, none of "these things" to which Christ referred (all of them being events that will occur within the final week of Daniel's prophecy) did actually begin to take place in their lifetime, or for that matter in the lifetime of any generations of the church since then. And so Christ's return cannot yet be considered "near, right at the door" — not until "these things" begin to take place.

Jesus went on to say,

"But of that day and hour no one knows, not even the angels of heaven, nor the Son, but the Father alone. For the coming of the Son of Man will be just like the days of Noah. For as in those days which were before the flood they were eating and drinking, they were marrying and giving in marriage, until the day that Noah entered the ark, and they did not understand until the flood came and took them all away; so shall the coming of the Son of Man be." (Matt. 24:36-39)

In other words, the generation who will be alive to witness "these things" that Jesus mentions in the first part of Matthew 24 will also witness the return of Christ. The exact "day and hour" of His return were known by "the Father alone." As far as the unbelieving world will be concerned, His coming will be at a time when everything seems to be going well for those who have sold out to Antichrist's system — in exactly the same way that the unbelieving people of Noah's day had no inkling of impending destruction until the rain actually started to descend and the opportunity was past for entering the safety of the ark.

The people of Noah's day had a one hundred and twenty year warning (Gen. 6:3), by far the longest warning of any catastrophe in history. But their blindness to God made them blind to that warning. To them it was utter foolishness for Noah to build the ark, and his preaching of righteousness (2 Pet. 2:5) was equally foolish.

The warning signs of Christ's second coming will be of a radically different sort, but they will be ignored in exactly the same way by the unbelieving world. In fact, "in the last days mockers will come with their mocking . . . saying, 'Where is the promise of His coming?'" (2 Pet. 3:3, 4). When Antichrist arises incognito as a great world leader promising peace and prosperity, the world in general will look to him in hope rather than begin to look in fear and repentance for the signs of Christ's coming. And they will ridicule the faithful church, just as Noah's neighbors ridiculed him, eventually taking part in the world-wide persecution of God's elect (Matt. 24:22).

As in the days of Noah, the Lord's witnesses (including three specially sent angels) will warn the world of God's coming wrath (Rev. 14:9, 10). But wicked mankind will be just as unresponsive.

> While they [the world] are saying, "Peace and safety!" then destruction will come upon them suddenly like birth pangs upon a woman with child; and they shall not escape. But you, brethren, are not in darkness, that the day should overtake you like a thief; for you are all sons of light and sons of day. We are not of night nor of darkness; so then let us not sleep as others do, but let us be alert and sober. (1 Thess. 5:3-6)

Noah did not know the exact day and hour the Flood would commence, but he knew when the time was close; and when it began, he was completely prepared according to God's instruction and provision. In a similar way, God's faithful people who enter the seventieth week will not know the exact day and hour of Christ's second coming, but they will know in advance when His return *will be imminent*. When the great tribulation by Antichrist begins and the armies of the surrounding nations move in against Israel for a second time into the valley of Jehoshaphat, they will understand what is happening, and they will likewise be prepared according to God's Word and His provision. They will not know exactly when their Lord's return will "cut short" that persecution, but they will be spiritually "alert and sober" (1 Thess. 5:6) and ready to meet their Lord at any moment.

It is of immense importance to understand certain twin truths. The *first* is that faithful believers *will be able to know* when the seventieth week is approaching and will have considerable understanding of the events that unfold within it. We will know that when the branch of the fig tree has become tender and puts forth its leaves, summer is near. And yet it will only be the generation that sees all "these things" begin to occur that may assume Christ "is near, right at the door." The *second* truth is that even the most faithful believers *will not know* the exact "day or hour" of our Lord's return — to halt the great tribulation by Antichrist, to gather His saints to Himself, and to initiate His day-of-the-Lord wrath upon the unrighteous that are left.

END TIMES AND THREE JEWISH FEASTS

While preparing material for this book, I often consulted with a young friend of mine who is a very fine Old Testament and Hebrew scholar and a devoted student of prophecy. He writes extensively in an evangelical magazine published by an organization whose primary goal is to bring unbelieving Jews to a saving knowledge of their Messiah, Jesus Christ, and to help prepare Christians for the second coming of Christ.

In a recent series of articles concerning Jewish feasts, this young scholar became more and more convinced that certain events associated with Christ's second coming will occur in precise relation to certain Jewish feasts, just as His crucifixion occurred in precise relation to the Passover feast. As he carefully studied the work outlined in this volume concerning Christ's return for the salvation of Israel — first to Edom, and then from Edom to Jerusalem, and then to the top of Mount Zion with the first fruits of Israel where the reign over the earth will be reclaimed by God Almighty — the relationship of those events to Yom Kippur, to the Feast of Tabernacles, and to Hanukkah became overwhelmingly clear in his mind. It did not take him long to convince me that those remarkable relationships should be mentioned in this book.

Some of the similarities were discussed briefly in chapter 19, but the purpose of this Epilogue is to consider them in somewhat more detail.

YOM KIPPUR

Yom Kippur, which means "Day of Atonement," occurs on the tenth day of the Jewish month of Tishri (September-October), the seventh month in the Jewish calendar. It was the supreme Jewish "holy day," the time of national atonement for sin. Originally it was the time when, once a year, the high priest, and the high priest alone, very briefly entered the Holy of Holies and offered sacrifices for himself and for Israel (see Lev. 16; 23:27-32). On that day,

> [the high priest] shall slaughter the goat of the sin offering which is for the people, and bring its blood inside the veil, and do with its blood as he did with the blood of the bull, and sprinkle it on the mercy seat and in front of the mercy seat. (Lev. 16:15)

During this holy period, fasting was mandatory from the evening of the ninth day through the evening of the tenth. God declared that "it is on this day that atonement shall be made for you to cleanse you; you shall be clean from all your sins before the Lord" (Lev. 16:30).

On this day the slaughtered goat was a symbolic offering for the true sacrifice for sin that Jesus Christ made "once for all when He offered up Himself" (Heb. 7:27), when God "made Him who knew no sin to be sin on our behalf, that we might become the righteousness of God in Him" (2 Cor. 5:21).

Speaking of the end times and the end of Israel's sins, Daniel declares,

> "Seventy weeks have been decreed for your people and your holy city, to finish the transgression, to make an end of sin, *to make atonement for iniquity*, to bring in everlasting righteousness, to seal up vision and prophecy, and to anoint the most holy." (Dan. 9:24, emphasis added)

If any one day of the end times could prophetically represent the Day of Atonement for Israel, it would be the last day of the seventieth week, when, as Daniel reveals, her transgression will be finished, her sins ended, and her iniquity atoned for. This then would be the day that God's hostility against them will end, because they would have made "amends for their iniquity" (Lev. 26:41).

It seems perfectly consistent with Scripture that certain events associated with Christ's second coming will therefore correspond to and fulfill Yom Kippur, just as His crucifixion climaxing His first coming corresponded to and fulfilled the Passover. This conclusion does not set the date for Christ's return, but it does reveal the timing of the end of the seventieth week in relation to Yom Kippur. If that conclusion is correct, the end of the seventieth week, and therefore Yom Kippur, should occur 2,520 days (seven prophetic years of 360 days each) from the date that Israel signs the covenant with death at the beginning of that final week (see chapter 10).

That evidence alone, however, was not sufficient in my mind to make one adamant about making Yom Kippur fall on the last day of the seventieth week. But it was a reasonable possibility and, with additional research, would either appear more likely or more improbable.

SUKKOT

Sukkot, the Feast of Tabernacles, always begins five days after Yom Kippur, on the fifteenth day of Tishri, and is one of three feasts that is required to be observed on Mount Zion. Originally lasting for seven days, this festival celebrated two events. First, it was a remembrance of God's protection of a surviving remnant of Israel during the forty years of wilderness wandering after He delivered His people from Egypt. The name of the feast is derived from the fact that it was celebrated in simple tabernacles, or booths, and was meant to remind God's people of His faithfulness, deliverance, protection, and provision during those nomadic years of hardship. Second, Sukkot celebrated the end of the harvest, as the people gathered and stored the grain and other produce God had provided for them. For that reason it was often called the feast of ingathering. Although the figure of harvest is frequently used in Scripture of God's judgment, it is also used of His blessing, in particular in relation to the salvation of the nation after they have atoned for their sin. Through Hosea God gave His people the clearly eschatological promise, "O Judah, there is a harvest appointed for you, when I restore the fortunes of My people" (Hos. 6:11).

As just noted, Sukkot occurs five days after Yom Kippur, it represents the dual celebrations of God's deliverance from their affliction in Egypt and of His provision of the harvest (near-term physical, far-term spiritual), and it is celebrated on Mount Zion. It is surely more than coincidental that those three central aspects of Sukkot perfectly parallel the events of the fifth day after the end of the seventieth week, when

Christ will ascend Mount Zion after the salvation of the remnant of Israel that survives the horrors of Antichrist's great tribulation.

Of additional fascination to me was the discovery that Psalm 118, the psalm I had already concluded will most likely be the psalm sung when Christ and the 144,000 ascend Mount Zion on the fifth day after the conclusion of the seventieth week, is the great psalm of ascension always sung on Sukkot, five days after Yom Kippur.

Psalm 118   Psalm 118 was specifically sung by Jews in the celebration of Sukkot as they traveled to the top of Mount Zion — hence its designation as a psalm of ascent or ascension. Although this feast was associated with Israel's wilderness deliverance and with the ingathering of the harvest, Psalm 118 itself does not directly focus on those two things. The first four verses express general adoration and praise for the Lord's eternal loving-kindness. The next five verses (5-9) acknowledge Him as the only true place of safety in time of distress — which could refer equally well to Israel's wilderness sojourn as to the second half of the seventieth week or, more probably, to both occasions. Verses 10-14 praise the Lord for His deliverance from enemies — which obviously could relate to the persecution by Antichrist and his ten-nation eighth beast empire. The next four verses (15-18) give thanks for His severe but loving discipline of His people Israel, again paralleling the day-of-the-Lord refinement of Israel when "He will purify the sons of Levi and refine them like gold and silver, so that they may present to the Lord offerings in righteousness" (Mal. 3:3).

It is, however, the next six verses that seem of special importance in relation to the last half of the seventieth week.

> Open to me the gates of righteousness; I shall enter through them, I shall give thanks to the Lord. This is the gate of the Lord; the righteous will enter through it. I shall give thanks to Thee, for Thou hast answered me; and Thou hast become my salvation. The stone which the builders rejected has become the chief corner stone. This is the Lord's doing; it is marvelous in our eyes. This is the day which the Lord has made; let us rejoice and be glad in it. (vv. 19-24)

That passage does not relate to the physical deliverance of the nation of Israel, but clearly pertains to her *spiritual salvation*, when "the stone which the builders [Israel] rejected has become the chief corner stone [Christ]." It is the corner stone about whom Paul speaks when he assures believers: "You are no longer strangers and aliens, but you are fellow-citizens with the saints, and are of God's household, having been built upon the foundation of the apostles and prophets, Christ Jesus Himself being the cornerstone" (Eph. 2:19, 20). When Christ ascends Mount Zion, the first fruits who accompany Him will be the redeemed remnant of Israel, singing, as never before, that magnificent Psalm.

When that final Sukkot is celebrated, Psalm 118 will be sung as a song of thanksgiving to God for His protection during the last half of the seventieth week (vv. 5-9); a song of gratitude to God for His deliverance from Israel's enemies, Antichrist's eighth beast empire of Satan (vv. 10-14); a song of thanksgiving for His severe but loving discipline during the day of the Lord (vv. 15-18); and a song of praise to God for His successful harvest of the nation, as it were (vv. 19-24) by her Lord and Savior, the "chief corner stone" (v. 22). This is the glorious day that the Lord promised through Hosea: "O Judah, there is a harvest appointed for you, when I restore the fortunes of My people" (Hos. 6:11).

As the parallels continued to mount, I began to wonder if it were possible to make a biblically defensible case that these particular end-time events will be specifically fulfilled in the final and perfect celebration of these festivals. I became convinced when I studied the third festival and its relationship to the other two.

HANUKKAH

Hanukkah, the Feast of Lights, or of Dedication, is observed in the month of Kislev (November-December), exactly seventy-five days after Yom Kippur and seventy days after the beginning of Sukkot. Hanukkah is not a biblically prescribed feast, but it is perfectly consistent with Scripture, has clear prophetic implications, and has been celebrated by Israel for well over two thousand years.

This feast celebrates an event that occurred in the second century B.C., several hundred years *after* the last book of the Old Testament was written and several hundred years *before* the writing of the first New Testament book. Perhaps for that reason it is not mentioned as such in Scripture. It was, however, an essential element in the religious life of Jews in the time of Christ (see John 10:22). Christ Himself referred to this important feast when He told the scribes and Pharisees, in the context of the Feast of Lights (Hanukkah), that He was "the light of the world" (John 8:12). The feast is still of great significance to Jews today several thousand years later.

Hanukkah commemorates Israel's deliverance from Antiochus Epiphanes (an Old Testament type of Antichrist) by Judas Maccabaeus, including the restoration of the Temple and the purification of the altar, which had been profaned by Antiochus when he committed the first abomination of desolation by sacrificing swine flesh on it. The celebration of lights is directly associated with Hanukkah and is a reminder to Israel of the eventual return of God's *shekinah* glory to the Temple. As already mentioned, this feast has been observed by Israel for well over two thousand years. Ultimately it looks forward to the day that the Messiah Himself will build His Temple that never will be destroyed and to the return of His *shekinah* glory that never again will depart.

Ezekiel was privileged to envision that return of God's glory to the Temple:

> Behold, the glory of the God of Israel was coming from the way of the east. And His voice was like the sound of many waters; and the earth shone with His glory. . . . And the glory of the Lord came into the house by the way of the gate facing toward the east. . . . And He said to me, "Son of man, this is the place of My throne and the place of the soles of My feet, where I will dwell among the sons of Israel forever. And the house of Israel will not again defile My holy name, neither they nor their kings, by their harlotry and by the corpses of their kings when they die." (Ezek. 43:2, 4, 7)

The glory will first return above the earth, announcing the coming of the Son of Man and His destruction of the earth's wicked, and will then come to reside permanently in the Temple, "the place of My throne . . . where I will dwell among the sons of Israel forever."

This is the grand and ultimate scene that Hanukkah depicts — the scene which will be fulfilled when Christ returns to Jerusalem to rule, on the first day of the Millennium when "the Lord will be king over all the earth; in that day the Lord will be the only one, and His name the only one" (Zech. 14:9). As envisioned by John, "the city has no need of the sun or of the moon to shine upon it, for the glory of God has illumined it, and its lamp is the Lamb" (Rev. 21:23). This glorious event will occur exactly seventy-five days after the completion of the seventieth week and exactly seventy days after Christ ascends to the top of Mount Zion accompanied by His first fruits.

CONCLUSION

The ultimate Yom Kippur for the nation of Israel will be on the last day of the seventieth week when they have made "amends for their iniquity," when they have made "atonement for [their] iniquity."

The ultimate Sukkot will occur five days later, two days after the national salvation of Israel, as Christ and His redeemed people ascend Mount Zion singing Psalm 118.

Then, seventy-five days following the final Yom Kippur and seventy days after the final Sukkot, a restored and redeemed Israel will celebrate the ultimate and final Hanukkah when the glory of Christ returns to the Temple, after which Christ's millennial rule upon earth will begin.

I have become convinced that when Christ returns He not only will fulfill the ultimate meaning and significance of those three festivals, but He will also fulfill them chronologically to the exact day and hour — in precisely the same manner that Christ became the Passover Lamb on the exact day the Passover feast was celebrated by Israel at His first coming.

The significance is clear. We cannot know in advance the exact day or hour that Christ will cut short the great tribulation by Antichrist, when He comes to rescue His church and destroy the earth's wicked. We cannot know in advance the year in which the covenant of death will be signed, initiating the seventieth week. But this author believes that to the degree it is possible to know when Yom Kippur will be celebrated by Israel seven years into the future, a good indication of when the covenant will be signed in the current year can be determined.

Christ tells us that we should learn from the parable of the fig tree — "when its branch has already become tender, and puts forth its leaves, you know that summer is near" (Matt. 24:32). Because all the events necessary to initiate the seventieth week are now complete — except for the alignment of three Aryan nations with a powerful leader — every Christian should be aware that the seventieth week could begin, as it were, practically overnight. To that end, if my assumptions are correct, I believe we can determine to some degree in advance what *time of the year* the covenant will be signed in any given year.

In other words, we know that the seventieth week of Daniel is a "week" of prophetic years (that is, seven years), consisting of 360 days each and totaling 2,520 days. We know the covenant of death will be signed on the first day of that seven-year period. We can also determine what day Yom Kippur will be celebrated for any given year in the future. Assuming that Yom Kippur will be celebrated on the last day of the seventieth week, we can obtain from official Jewish sources the future dates set for Yom Kippur and work back from these dates to determine the exact date the covenant of death would need to be signed in any given year.

The real problem is in one's ability to accurately calculate that future date for Yom Kippur. Because the Jewish calendar is both solar and lunar, it is much more complex than the strictly solar Roman calendar which is used today in most of the world. Consequently, the only way to determine the future date of Yom Kippur in a given Roman calendar year is by the use of a comparative Jewish/Roman calendar. Suffice it to say, however, Yom Kippur normally falls in late September or early October of each year, and if one were to delete 2,519 days from the date that the Jewish religious leaders set for that festival seven years into the future, mathematically the covenant would be signed in late October or early November of any current year. In other words, watch the activities of Israel especially during the fall of any one year! If the covenant is going to be signed in any given year, *that is the time of year* in which the covenant, in this writer's opinion, will be signed. What year? I have no idea. But this one thing I do know. Everything that Scripture says should be in place before "these things" can occur is already in place for the first time in almost two thousand years. For that reason, as never before, the true church should be alert and watchful!

CLOSING REMARKS

My deepest desire for this book is that it present prophetic truth concerning the last days in a way that is as faithful to Scripture as humanly possible and that is honoring to God in every way.

My greatest concern is for you, the reader. As mentioned at the beginning of this work — in the first paragraph of chapter 1 — I am fully aware that many of the major views expressed here will never be accepted by the church at large. If they were, some of the prophetic events outlined in Scripture concerning the last days would not be true. Prophecy would become possibility. But we know with certainty, as well as with sadness, that all of the scripturally revealed events mentioned in these pages will indeed literally occur — if not exactly as I have outlined them, then in some other way. But they will occur. Literally!

I abhor sensationalism and have sincerely sought to avoid it. But I realize that many of the ideas expressed here will seem sensational in the eyes of some readers. But I assure you that it has never been my intent to make them so. Ideas that may appear to be sensational are simply the realities that have been discovered by accepting Scripture in its most normal, literal meaning and by comparing Scripture with Scripture until all contradictions resolve themselves. Two plus two is four, and personal predispositions or inclinations have absolutely no bearing on that reality. When a common denominator was discovered that harmonized all Scripture relevant to an issue, I placed myself under the judgment of that truth, never daring to place myself in judgment of that truth.

Many of my statements and conclusions will be at serious odds with some traditional doctrines and systems of theology, but I have studiously tried to avoid controversy for its own sake. Even less have I tried to establish a new system of interpretation or theology.

I am fully aware of the price that will be paid for the positions taken in this book. I know that I will be accused of setting dates, selling books through sensationalism, taking Scripture out of context, misusing Greek and Hebrew, contradicting hundreds of godly scholars whose biblical academic credentials far exceed mine. I can only say that, like the Bereans, I have endeavored only to find God's truth. Scripture was written for us all, and scholars have no corner on its truth. Those who sincerely and diligently seek God's truth can find it. The words of Christ are significant: "I praise Thee, O Father, Lord of heaven and earth, that Thou didst hide these things from the wise and intelligent and didst reveal them to babes" (Matt. 11:25).

Because of the seriousness of the issues presented in this book, and because of the direct consequences that one's beliefs about them will have on himself and his family, each reader must carefully draw his own conclusions based on the Scriptures — checking the positions expressed here by Scripture, not by the views of a denomination, a theological school of thought, or an esteemed pastor or scholar. All men are fallible, whereas God's Word is infallible and inerrant in the most absolute sense. Therefore, the only test of truth is God's Word, and it is against God's Word and His Word alone that I hope the views expressed here will be measured. I cannot in good conscience amend my views for the sake of outward harmony or personal acceptance. I have tried, like Martin Luther, Jonathan Edwards, John Bunyan, Charles Spurgeon, and many others, to stand firm in God's Word, whatever the consequences.

It is my firm conviction that it will be our families — our children or grandchildren — perhaps even we ourselves — who will experience the brunt of false teaching that will characterize the compromising churches that will enter the seventieth week. Are you willing to pay the price for the poor teaching of others? I am married with three daughters and a house full of grandchildren, with several more on the way. We all have those who are very precious to us. Their safety is uppermost in my mind. But I know that wishful thinking about the hard times that are coming will not protect them. Only faithfulness to God's Word will, "rightly dividing the word of truth" (2 Tim. 2:15, KJV). After giving the clearest possible presentation concerning the timing of Christ's return — revealing the sequence of events that will occur prior to Christ's return, the sequence that is carefully adhered to in this volume — it is no wonder Paul admonished the church of Thessalonica not to be deceived, adding that "if anyone does not obey [heed] our instruction [words] in this letter, take special note of that man and do not associate with him, so that he may be put to shame. And yet do not regard him as an enemy, but admonish him as a brother" (2 Thess. 3:14, 15). Paul wrote in such strong terms because he realized the tragic consequences of faulty teaching about issues pertaining to the return of Christ.

With equal conviction, however, I consider every true believer, every genuine "overcomer," to be my brother or sister in Christ, whatever our differences may be. I also quickly acknowledge my own fallibility and the other human limitations that are common to all men, including God's own people. I realize with Paul that "Now we see in a mirror dimly, but then face to face; now I know in part, but then I shall know fully just as I also have been fully known" (1 Cor. 13:12). Also with Paul, I eagerly await our Lord's return, rejoicing in His last great promise to His people: "Yes, I am coming quickly" (Rev. 22:20).

Finally, I feel compelled to end this lengthy volume with a word of caution. The question asked most frequently by Christians who take these warnings of Scripture very seriously is, "What should we do now?" And my answer is always the same: "Nothing yet." Christ clearly stated in His Olivet Discourse that we are to "learn the parable from the fig tree: when its branch has already become tender, and puts forth its leaves, you know that summer is near" (Matt. 24:32). I am convinced that "summer is near." As carefully outlined in chapter 10, every condition has been met and every event necessary is in place except one. The signing of the covenant could occur almost overnight, as it were. As fast as it takes to topple one regime and put a new one in place — this is how soon the last event could be in place, thereby triggering the signing of a covenant with Israel. But needless to say, the events of the seventieth week outlined by Christ in His discourse will not occur until the covenant is actually signed, and that final event has not yet occurred. Summer may be near, but it is not yet here. Christ goes on to say, "when you see all *these things*, recognize that He is near, right at the door. Truly I say to you, this generation will not pass away until all *these things* take place" (vv. 33, 34, emphasis added). In other words, although summer is near, it will only be *the generation that sees "these things" begin to take place* that will see the return of Christ. Since "these things" refer to the events that occur after the covenant is signed (beginning with the false christs), it is the generation that sees "these things" that should take defensive action. *And not before!* Until that time we should continue to carry out the calling that the Lord has given to us — whether in business, as a homemaker, as a teacher, as a student, as an artist — or whatever the Lord has called us to do.

When the covenant is signed, there will be ample time for those who understand what will follow to quietly go about their business and prepare for what is coming — then and only then, and not before. We will have three and a half years in which to prepare, plenty of time to do whatever needs to be done in a quiet and orderly manner. For those in a sound church, this preparation should begin with the church elders. If not, you should plan your strategy with other believers of like mind, recognizing and using the gifts of every individual to their fullest extent — some leadership, some mechanical, others agricultural, others financial, etc. But not until "these things" begin to take place should we, as individuals and as the faithful church, begin to make preparation. Until then, be expectant, be aware of what is going on, but remember that "these things" may — or may not — happen in your lifetime.

GLOSSARY

As the many issues related to eschatology are studied, it is important that certain significant names and terms be clearly defined. A clear understanding of these names and terms as they are used in this book is essential for understanding of the arguments and conclusions. Many of the definitions will differ, in various degrees, from those used in some evangelical circles. However, the definitions of these terms are thoroughly defended from Scripture within the text of this volume.

The following definitions are relatively brief. To locate the more detailed information given in the text and endnotes, consult the various indexes provided in this volume.

144,000, the
The 144,000 Jews (twelve thousand from each of the twelve tribes of Israel) who will refuse to follow or worship Antichrist (see *Apostasy, the*) during the seventieth week and for that reason will flee to the wilderness of Edom before the great tribulation by Antichrist. Referred to also as "the woman," in particular "the faithful woman," who flees. They will become the first fruits of Israel to come to Christ after the rapture of the church and will be sealed for protection and salvation immediately after the Rapture, just before the day of the Lord begins. (See *Woman, the Faithful.*)

30-day Period, the (see also *Reclamation Period*)
The 30-day reclamation period that begins immediately following the seventieth week. This time of reclamation will be initiated by the return of Christ to Edom when He personally comes down to earth to *reclaim* the nation of Israel that has survived the seventieth week. It will be followed by the blowing of the seventh trumpet when God

Almighty *reclaims* the rule over earth, and it will conclude with the battle of Armageddon when Antichrist and his armies are bodily evicted from God's premises and Christ *reclaims* physical possession of earth.

45-day Period, the (see also *Restoration Period*)

The 45-five-day restoration period that immediately follows the 30-day reclamation period. During this time Christ will *restore* the Temple that will have been destroyed during the day of the Lord, and He will *restore* the redeemed nation of Israel back to their homeland, most of which will have been in hiding in Azel or still in exile in other lands. Gentile survivors from all over the world will likewise come to Mount Zion for the Sheep and Goats Judgment by Christ on the first day of the Millennium. The most important event, however, will be when God Almighty will *restore* the rule *upon* earth to its rightful Ruler, Jesus Christ.

Abomination of Desolation, the

A name for Antichrist. This name is used as a reminder of the desecration of the Temple in Jerusalem, first by Antiochus Epiphanes in 168 B.C. and a second time by Antichrist in the end times at the midpoint of the seventieth week, just after he has revealed his true identity and taken his seat in the Temple, demanding the worship of the world.

Abraham, the Spiritual Descendants of

The chosen *people* of God for salvation, the *spiritual* line of Abraham. It will include both Jews and Gentiles, although until Israel rejected her Messiah at His first coming the great majority of the spiritual descendants of Abraham came from within the natural line of Abraham, the nation of Israel. Gentiles were grafted into the promises to Abraham in order to make the Jews jealous after their rejection of their Messiah at His first coming.

Abraham, the Natural Descendants of

The chosen *nation* of God, the *natural* line of Abraham, through which the Messiah came. Although many of the spiritual descendants of Abraham have come and will continue to come from the nation of Israel, all of the *living* natural line of Abraham will not be in the spiritual line of Abraham until after the seventieth week of Daniel is complete.

Amillennialism

An allegoric system of interpretation of prophetic events. The Olivet

Discourse and the greater part of the book of Revelation are largely viewed as past historical events or are spiritualized out of existence. Amillennialism holds that there will be no future, literal, personal Antichrist who will seek to destroy the elect of God in the last days, and Christ will not return until the end of human history as we know it.

Adultery

In regard to prophetic Scripture, the "adultery" of a people or nation normally refers to spiritual rather than moral unfaithfulness.

Antichrist

Also called the man of lawlessness (or sin), Gog, the son of destruction (or perdition), and the abomination of desolation in the critical passages that are studied repeatedly in this volume. Other names are given to him as well, which are obvious in the scriptural contexts in which they are found. This false messiah is the ruler of the seventh beast empire who is brought back to life to rule over the final beast empire of Satan. He will not reveal his true identity until the midpoint of the seventieth week, when he will set up his throne in the Temple at Jerusalem and demand worship by the whole world. He will die for the second and last time at the battle of Armageddon, thirty days after the end of the seventieth week.

Antimony

"A contradiction between two apparently equally valid principles or between inferences correctly drawn from such principles" (*Webster's Collegiate Dictionary*, 9th ed.).

Apocalypse, the

A transliteration of the Greek term for "revelation." It is normally associated with the events of the seventieth week, especially those dealt with in the book of Revelation.

Apostasy and Heresy

The terms *apostasy* and *heresy* are related but not synonymous. Apostasy, which has the literal meaning of falling away, is the deliberate and open abandonment of true biblical faith, whether under the Old or the New Covenant. Heresy, on the other hand, is false doctrine taught under the guise of true biblical faith.

Apostasy, the

Paul uses this term with the definite article (*the* apostasy) to refer to the response of Jews in Israel when they will follow the heathen customs of "the man of lawlessness . . . the son of destruction" —

Antichrist incognito. Many Israelites will become willing subjects of this false protector when they unwittingly make a covenant of death with him at the beginning of the seventieth week in order to secure the nation's protection. The height of the apostasy will come at the midpoint of the seventieth week when Antichrist reveals his true identity and demands worship by all the world, leading some Jews in Israel to actually bow down and worship him or his image. This great apostasy in the last days is clearly parallel to the apostasy of the ancient Israelites who in a similar way sold out to Antiochus IV (Epiphanes) and his paganistic religion before and after he desecrated the Temple in 168 B.C.

Appearance of Christ

Whereas the *second coming* (*parousia*) of Christ refers to the manifestation of Christ's presence in the affairs of mankind during the day of the Lord, the *appearance* of Christ refers to the several times when He will actually *appear* to mankind on earth before He returns to earth permanently to rule over His millennial kingdom. His first appearance will be at His coming in the clouds, when the church is raptured at the beginning of the day of the Lord, when every eye shall behold him. His second appearance will be at His return to earth to gather the 144,000 at Edom and return to the Judean hills and the city of Jerusalem for the salvation of Israel. At that time the nation of Israel will look upon the One whom they have pierced and will mourn. Christ's final appearance will be at the battle of Armageddon, when He returns from Heaven with His armies for the defeat of Antichrist.

Armageddon, Battle of (or Campaign)

The final event of the thirty-day reclamation period that will immediately follow the seventieth week, when Christ will reclaim the physical possession of earth for God Almighty. The rule over earth already will have been reclaimed by God several weeks earlier, and at this battle the usurper, Antichrist, and his armies will be permanently expelled from the kingdom of God. This battle will be the climax of God's destructive wrath which He will initiate at the seventh seal and will result in the destruction of Antichrist and the armies of the whole world, including those of the eighth beast empire who have so severely persecuted Israel.

Azel

The undisclosed location where the newly saved remnant of Israel is taken for protection, shortly after the seventieth week is completed but before the final wrath of God is poured out (the bowl judgments and Armageddon).

Babylon the Great, the "Great City"

Whereas Babylon the Great, the "Mother of Harlots," represents a false religious system(s), Babylon the Great, the "great city," is almost certainly the *city* of Rome (the seat of Roman Catholicism) and possibly Istanbul (Constantinople — the seat of Eastern [Byzantine] orthodoxy), both of which sit on seven hills and are seaports as described in Revelation. A false religion doesn't sit on seven hills and is not a seaport; the city most representative of that false religious system(s), however, does. The "great city" will be destroyed by God Himself during the seventh bowl judgment when all the cities of the nations are destroyed by the great earthquake. This will occur just before the battle of Armageddon at the end of the thirty-day reclamation period. The destruction of the "great city" occurs some forty-three months after those representing the "harlot" are destroyed by Antichrist and his ten-nation alliance at the midpoint of the seventieth week.

Babylon the Great, the "Mother of Harlots"

As is often the case in prophetic Scripture, harlotry here represents false religion. Babylon the Great, the Mother of Harlots, depicts the supreme *system(s)* of false religion that focuses on the "Queen of heaven," with its mother/child worship, which in one form or another has dominated almost all the beast empires of Satan and has sought to deceive Israel and her God-ordained religion. The most visible manifestation of that false religion as a pervasive influence today is seen within the Catholic churches, either Roman (from Rome) or Byzantine/Eastern Orthodox (from Constantinople — Istanbul). At the midpoint of the seventieth week Satan and his Antichrist will compete with *no one* for the worship of the world, including this "foreign god" that had helped Antichrist gain control of the world. Antichrist and the leaders of his ten-nation coalition will destroy "the harlot" when Antichrist demands the worship of the world.

Beast, the

In most of its figurative uses in Scripture this term refers to the various false kingdoms, or beast empires, raised up by Satan against God's elect nation, Israel. In particular, the final ten-nation empire of Satan is called "a beast" or "a scarlet beast." But the term is also used of Antichrist as the leader of the final beast empire, when the beast is given a mouth, speaking arrogant words and blasphemies, after the world recognizes he is a dead man reincarnated. In the book of Revelation, therefore, the term *beast* can refer either to the final beast empire or to the head of that empire, Antichrist, the context always clearly determining which is in view. In one instance the book of Revelation refers to the "second" beast who acts as the enforcer for Antichrist (see further *Beast, the Second*).

Beast Empire, the Final (Eighth)

This empire is depicted by the ten toes of Nebuchadnezzar's statue, the ten horns of Daniel's vision, and the ten horns of Christ's revelation to John. This particular ten-nation confederation represents the last (eighth) beast empire of Satan, which will be created and ruled by Antichrist and will be, in part, a representation of all the previous beast empires of Satan that have sought to destroy Israel while she was in the land with possession of her holy city, Jerusalem.

Beast Empires

The eight satanically inspired empires, or confederacies, that persecute with the objective of destroying God's chosen people, the Jews, until the perfect millennial rule of Christ over the earth. These empires are always satanically empowered; each empire is ruled by a single man, the "head" of the beast empire that he represents, who has extreme hatred of Jews; and each empire has been intractably opposed to the nation of Israel. Chronologically these empires are: Egypt, Assyria, Babylon, Medo-Persia, Greece, Rome, and Nazi Germany. All seven of these are history. The eighth and final empire, however, is still future. It will be composed of descendants of all the previous beast empires except the first two, and it will be ruled by Antichrist, the reincarnated leader of the seventh beast empire.

Beast, the Mark of the

The identifying symbol (the number 666 written on the forehead or on the back of the right hand) that Antichrist will demand of every person on earth at the midpoint of the seventieth week as a mark of allegiance to him. Without such a mark, no person will be allowed either to buy or sell. Those who accept the mark of Antichrist will forfeit any further opportunity for salvation and will discover during the day of the Lord that they are marked irrevocably for God's judgment.

Beast, the Image of the

Idols made in the likeness of Antichrist at the command of the second beast at the midpoint of the seventieth week. Those idols will be indwelt by fallen angels (demons) who will have the power both to speak through the idol and to cause to have killed those who refuse to give it homage, although the demon-possessed idols themselves will have no mobility.

Beast, the Second

The enforcer for Antichrist (the first beast), who "exercises all the authority of the first beast" during the last half of the seventieth week.

Bema-seat Judgment (see *Judgment, Bema Seat*)

Birth Pangs, Beginning of

The afflictions and suffering — predicted by Christ in the Olivet Discourse and represented by the four horsemen of Revelation — that will occur during the first half of the seventieth week. These "birth pangs" will be mild in comparison to what will follow during the second half of the week — i.e., the great tribulation by Antichrist which will be cut short by God's wrath during the day of the Lord.

Blessings and the Curses, the

The promises by God to the nation of Israel, the natural line of Abraham through which Messiah would come, that obedience to His law would bring blessings and that disobedience would bring curses to the people as a nation. If disobedience persisted, the curses would grow progressively worse. The final two curses were by far the most severe. First, as the result of her continued disobedience, Israel was dominated and persecuted by numerous foreign nations (beast empires) while she still had limited access to her land, including the city of Jerusalem. The second and ultimate curse was the scattering of the nation from her homeland (the *Diaspora*) to the ends of the earth because of her rejection of the Messiah and His kingdom at His first coming.

Blinders Removed

God's spiritual illumination of the entire nation of Israel that survives the great tribulation by Antichrist and the refining wrath of God, after the seventieth week is complete and the time of the

Gentiles is over. The blinders will be removed on the third day following the close of the seventieth week, during the thirty-day reclamation period.

Bowl Judgments

The final seven judgments that the angels (reapers) of Christ will mete out during His day-of-the-Lord wrath, all of which will occur during the thirty-day reclamation period that immediately follows the end of the seventieth week. These judgments will all transpire quickly and decisively, one immediately after the other, like liquid poured out of a shallow, wide-brimmed bowl, and will culminate in the battle of Armageddon. The bowl judgments will focus upon any and all who have taken the mark of Antichrist and worshiped the beast or his image, with a special emphasis on the nations of the eighth beast empire.

Bride of Christ, the

Old and New Testament elect who will receive their resurrection bodies on the last day, at the Rapture of the living church and the resurrection of the "dead in Christ."

Christ, Earthly Reign of (see *Millennium*)

Christ, First Coming

Christ's first coming (at His incarnation) was for redemption, to reconcile God's elect to Himself and to reverse the consequences of sin — primarily death (or separation), which is manifested in two ways: the first is spiritual death, man's separation from God; the second is physical death, the separation of man's physical being from his spiritual. At His first coming Christ overcame both deaths. First, He sacrificed Himself on the cross for the sins of the world, providing spiritual life for those who trust in Him. Second, by His resurrection from the dead, He made provision for renewed and eternal bodies for those believers. As a result of His death and resurrection at His first coming, Christ is "counted worthy" to judge the unrighteous and to cast out Satan at His second coming.

Christ, Marriage Supper of

The feast of Christ with His bride, for all the people on Mount Zion, which will be one of the first events celebrated on earth during the millennial rule of Christ; referred to in Revelation as the marriage supper of the Lamb.

Christ, Second Coming

Christ's second coming (*parousia*) is synonymous with the day of the

Lord, during which time He will rapture His saints; refine, save, and restore the natural line of Abraham (Israel); and judge and destroy Antichrist and all of unbelieving mankind. He will thereby reclaim the rule over earth for God, reclaim physical possession of earth from Satan, and then take His rightful throne in the New Jerusalem on top of Mount Zion when the Millennium begins. The second coming will be initiated by the Rapture (between the sixth and seventh seal judgments), when Christ appears the first time, cutting short the great tribulation by Antichrist. He will then physically appear on earth a second time for the salvation of Israel, immediately after the completion of the seventieth week, and again thirty days later at His final conquest of Antichrist and the eighth beast empire of Satan at the battle of Armageddon. Forty-five days after the battle of Armageddon, Christ will permanently return to earth with His bride to rule over His millennial kingdom.

Covenant with Death, the

Predicted by Isaiah and also called a pact with Sheol, this covenant will be made at the beginning of the seventieth week by the unbelieving nation of Israel with Antichrist, being deluded into thinking that this covenant will protect them and give them peace and security. As a result of this covenant, many Jews living in the land of Israel will apostatize to the incognito Antichrist, paralleling the apostasy of Israel to Antiochus Epiphanes in the second century B.C. The covenant with Israel will be broken by Antichrist when he reveals his true identity at the midpoint of the seventieth week and begins his great tribulation against all who will not worship "the beast or his image," primarily within the nation of Israel. To this end he will eventually kill two out of three Israelites then living back in the land.

Curses, Blessings and (see *Blessings and Curses*)

Daniel's Seventieth Week (see *Seventy Weeks of Daniel's Prophecy*)

Day of the Lord

Synonymous with the second coming (*parousia*) of Christ. Also called the "end of the age," the "final harvest," and the "seventh seal," which includes God's trumpet and bowl judgments and is culminated in the battle of Armageddon. The most prophesied event in the Old Testament concerning the last days, the day of the Lord is marked by God's fiery, judgmental wrath against the earth's wicked.

The primary purpose of the day-of-the-Lord wrath will be to

punish all the ungodly of the world, giving specific attention to the final beast empire of Satan which will then dominate the world with the sole purpose of destroying all who refuse to worship the beast or his image. It will begin on the same day that the Rapture occurs, cutting short the great tribulation by Antichrist, sometime during the second half of the seventieth week. It will be announced with a sign divinely displayed in the heavens (see *Sign of the End of the Age*).

A secondary purpose of the day of the Lord will be to refine the third part of the nation of Israel who will survive the great tribulation by Antichrist, in preparation for the salvation of the surviving remnant of the nation after the seventieth week is complete. If the day of the Lord did not cut short the great tribulation by Antichrist, none of God's elect, Jew or Christian, would survive.

The day of the Lord's wrath is composed of two major parts. The first is the series of God's trumpet judgments against the earth's wicked, including unsaved Israel, that will occur while the seventieth week is in progress. The second part is the series of bowl judgments, "which are the last, because in them the wrath of God is finished." These will begin after the seventieth week is complete, after the surviving remnant of Israel is saved and the Lord has hidden them in Azel for protection. The day of the Lord will be climaxed and ended at the battle (or campaign) of Armageddon.

Day of the Lord Sign (see *Sign of the End of the Age*)

Diaspora (or **Scattering**) **of Israel**

The divine judgment of the nation of Israel that resulted in her expulsion from her homeland and being scattered to the ends of the earth. This ultimate curse, foretold in the blessings and the curses, was specifically warned about by the prophet Zechariah and restated by Christ in His Olivet Discourse recorded in Luke. The *Diaspora* began with the destruction of Jerusalem and of the Temple by the Roman general Titus in A.D. 70 and was completed in 132 when every remaining Jew was expelled from the city of Jerusalem. It was part of God's ultimate curse on Israel (see *Blessings and Curses*) because of her refusal to repent and receive Jesus Christ as her Messiah at His first coming.

Eighth Beast Empire (see *Beast Empire, Final*)

Elect, God's

In its broadest sense this term refers to true believers of all ages — past, present, and future. Included are the spiritual descendants of

Abraham, both within the natural line of the nation of Israel and within the church, including Gentiles, all of whom will become the bride of Christ. In the New Testament the term is used by Christ exclusively in relation to the end times. Jesus used it six times in the Olivet Discourse and once in the parable of the widow.

Empires, Beast (see *Beast Empires*)

End, the (see *Day of the Lord*)

End of the Age, the (see *Day of the Lord*)

End of the Age, Sign of (see *Sign of the End of the Age*)

End Times

The prophetic period of time that immediately precedes, includes, and follows the seventieth week of Daniel. During this time, all of the events of the book of Revelation will transpire: the beginning birth pangs; the great tribulation by Antichrist; the rescue, or rapture, of the church; the destruction of the wicked (the day of the Lord); the salvation of the nation of Israel; and the restoration of Israel back to her own homeland a second time. Only after all those things occur will the millennial kingdom of Christ commence.

Eschatology

The study of biblically prophesied events of the end times, especially in relation to God's redemptive and judgmental work.

Fifth Seal Martyrs (see *Martyrs, Fifth Seal*)

Final Harvest (see *Day of the Lord*)

Foreign God, the

The Babylonian Harlot, the false religious system that has dominated many kings and nations of the world. Antichrist, with the help of this "foreign god," will gain control of the world during the first half of the seventieth week. When her usefulness is finished, at the midpoint of the week, she will be destroyed by Antichrist and his ten-nation coalition.

Gentiles, Time (or Fullness) of

The time of or fullness of the Gentiles will be complete when the seventieth week of Daniel is complete, and not before. This period of time begins and ends with the domination of Israel by Satan's beast empires while Jews occupy their homeland, in particular the city of Jerusalem. This period commenced with the Babylonian captivity in 586 B.C. and encompasses the seventy weeks (490 years) of Daniel as well as the unspecified period of time between the sixty-ninth and seventieth weeks. It is prophetically pictured in the statue in Nebuchadnezzar's dream, which, after the kingdom of Babylon, perfectly parallels the seventy weeks of Gentile domination foretold by Daniel. The time of the Gentiles will end when the seventieth week (seven years) ends, but only *after* Israel — back in her own land but still in unbelief — suffers her final and greatest persecution (see *Tribulation, Great*) by Antichrist, the leader of the final beast empire of Satan.

Gog

A prophetic name of Antichrist, who will come from the land of Magog.

Great Tribulation (see *Tribulation, Great*)

Great White Throne Judgment (see *Judgment, Great White Throne*)

Ham (Hamitic Lineage)

One of the three sons of Noah, from whom all mankind since his day has descended. The lineage of Ham is carefully traced in the table of nations given in Genesis 10, and he in part is generally considered to be the father of the African nations, other than Egypt.

Harlotry

In prophetic settings this term normally refers to spiritual unfaithfulness to God, not to physical immorality.

Harlots, Mother of (see *Babylon, Mother of Harlots*)

Harvest, God's Final

Synonymous with the day of the Lord. God's final harvest will be accomplished by His reapers, the angels, and will begin with the rapture of believers (the harvesting of the wheat into God's heavenly barn) sometime during the second half of the seventieth week, followed by the day-of-the-Lord wrath upon the unrighteous (God's harvesting of the tares by fire). In regard to the end times, the term *harvest* is therefore synonymous with *the day of the Lord* and *the end of the age*.

Head, Eighth (see *Toes, Ten*)

Head, Seventh

Depicted in Revelation as representing the dominant ruler of the short-lived seventh beast empire that persecutes God's chosen people Israel while they are *out of* their own land, with *no control* over Jerusalem, *after* the crucifixion of Christ. He appeared during the long interval between the sixty-ninth and the seventieth weeks that occurred because of Israel's rejection of Christ at His first coming. For this reason, the empire he represents is not depicted in the statue of Nebuchadnezzar, which, except for the head of gold (Babylon), represents the nations that would persecute Israel while they are *in* their own land, with *control* of Jerusalem, during the seventy-week (490-year) curse.

Heads, Seven

Depicted in Revelation as representing the first seven leaders of the seven beast empires of Satan that persecute God's elect nation Israel during seven different periods of history. One of those seven heads (leaders) will be brought back to life (as Antichrist) to rule over the eighth and final beast empire of Satan.

Heresy (see *Apostasy and Heresy*)

Hermeneutics

The study and use of methods and principles of biblical interpretation.

Highway of Holiness

A highway from Assyria to Egypt, passing through Israel, that God will provide for a small band of Israelites — part of "the compromised woman" — who will return to Christ for salvation on the third day after the completion of the seventieth week. These men and women (not to be confused with "the faithful woman" who flees) will have escaped the persecution of Antichrist by hiding in remote areas of those two foreign lands and will come "trembling" back to Christ when He will "roar like a lion."

Hope, the Great

The hope of true believers in the present age that Christ is coming again — to resurrect His dead elect and rapture His living church, to judge all evil men and nations, and to establish His perfect kingdom of righteousness in the Millennium.

Horn, Little

A representation both of Antiochus Epiphanes and Antichrist, the context always clearly showing which is in view.

Horns, Ten

A depiction in both the prophetic books of Daniel and Revelation of the ten rulers who, under Antichrist (one of the seven heads), will govern the ten nations (see also *Toes, Ten*) that comprise the eighth and final beast empire of Satan.

Horns, Three

Depicted in Daniel as representing the three Japhethite (Aryan) nations that Antichrist will overthrow and use as his power base to drive the final ten-nation beast empire of Satan.

Horsemen, Four

Depicted in Revelation as representing the first four seal events, which are referred to by Christ in His Olivet Discourse as "the beginning of birth pangs"; these will occur during the first half of the seventieth week.

Imminency, the Doctrine of

The belief as taught and understood today that since Christ's ascension back to Heaven recorded in the first chapter of Acts, no prophetic event needs to be fulfilled before Christ's second coming. In other words, He could return "any moment." This position is the critical cornerstone of pretribulationalism.

Israel, the Natural Line of

The physical lineage of Abraham through which Messiah would come. It is totally apart from, but includes some of, the spiritual lineage of Abraham, which refers to all believers, Jews and Gentiles alike. (See *Abraham, Natural Descendants of.*)

Israel, the Purge of (see *Tribulation, the Great*)

Israel, Purification of

The refinement or purge of the divinely chosen remnant of Israel that will survive the great tribulation by Antichrist. These will be purified further by the day of the Lord, in preparation for the nation's spiritual blinders to be removed. They will then "look on Me [Christ] whom they have pierced" and will be saved as a nation, immediately after the end of the seventieth week. God's purification of the third part of Israel that survives the great tribulation will include His discarding as dross every Jew who takes the mark of Antichrist for his or her personal safety during Antichrist's great tribulation.

Israel, Restoration of

The fulfillment of God's promise to the nation of Israel, the natural line of Abraham through which Messiah would come, that ultimately they will turn to Him in faith and be regathered back to the Promised Land a second time *after* the completion of the seventieth week, *in belief* (the first time being *prior* to the seventieth week, *in unbelief*). This final restoration of the nation will occur during the forty-five-day restoration period between the battle of Armageddon and the inauguration of the Millennium.

Jacob's Trouble, Time of (See *Tribulation, Great*)

Japheth (Japhethite Lineage)

One of the three sons of Noah, from whom all mankind since his day has descended. Japheth's lineage is carefully traced in the table of nations in Genesis 10, and he is generally considered to be the father of Caucasian peoples (Indo-European/Aryan). All of the beast empires that have dominated the nation of Israel during the first sixty-nine weeks (483 years) of Daniel, during the long period between the sixty-ninth and seventieth weeks, and during the seventieth week (seven years) itself have been, or will be, driven by men of this Aryan lineage.

Jehoshaphat Campaign

The campaign undertaken by surrounding nations against Israel, and against Jerusalem in particular, just prior to the day of the Lord, after God has drawn them into the valley of Jehoshaphat. At the appearance of Christ's second coming, which will initiate the day of the Lord and paralyze Antichrist and his forces, there will be great confusion in the ranks of those ungodly nations. Because of this they will suffer destructive retaliation by the clans of Judah (Jewish warriors who have been hiding in the Judean hills), paralleling the Maccabean revolt during the desecration of the Temple by Antiochus Epiphanes in the second century B.C. This campaign comes just *before* the day of the Lord and should not be confused with the *final event* of the day of the Lord, the Armageddon Campaign.

Jerusalem Campaign

While Israel assumes she is living securely — protected by her covenant with the great world leader (incognito) at the beginning of the seventieth week — Antichrist will break that covenant by using the armies of his eighth beast empire to surround and quickly conquer Jerusalem. This will mark the midpoint of the seventieth week, at which time Antichrist will reveal his true identity, will declare himself to be god, and will demand the world's worship. In the process the city of Jerusalem will be captured, its houses plundered, its women ravished, and half of its inhabitants exiled.

Judgment, Bema Seat

Christ's judgment of His saints (both Old and New Testament), who will be rewarded according to their faithfulness to Him while on earth. This judgment will occur in Heaven, during the thirty-day reclamation period that immediately follows the completion of the seventieth week, while the final phase of the day-of-the-Lord judgment (the bowl judgments) is being meted out upon earth by God's reapers, His angels.

Judgment, Great White Throne

The judgment at the end of the Millennium, when all the ungodly, including Satan and his demon angels, are cast into the lake of fire forever. This is the second resurrection that will culminate in the second death.

Judgment, Sheep and Goats

The judgment of the Gentile peoples who survive the day of the Lord. This will take place on the first day of the Millennium, on Mount Zion in the land of Israel. The basis for this judgment will be two-fold. First, those who have worshiped the beast or his image and have taken his mark on their foreheads or right hands (if indeed any do survive the day of the Lord) will be cast aside immediately, their condemnation being written, as it were, on their own bodies. Second, those Gentiles who have refused to worship the beast or his image or to take his mark will be judged on the basis of their treatment of Jews who, like themselves, have refused to worship Antichrist. Some Gentiles will assist Jewish friends in their time of greatest need, and those Jews will testify at this judgment, verifying or contradicting the claims of the Gentiles on trial. Those who have helped the Jews will be saved and will "inherit the kingdom prepared for *you* from the foundation of the world." Those who have not will face eternity in Hell.

Judgments, Bowl (see *Bowl Judgments*)

Judgments, Trumpet (see *Trumpet Judgments*)

Kingdoms, Ten (see *Toes, Ten*)

Kingdoms, Three (see *Horns, Three*)

Lamb, Marriage of

The marriage of the Lamb (Christ) to the bride of Christ (Old and New Testament elect) will occur in Heaven during the thirty-day reclamation period immediately following the seventieth week, after the bema-seat judgment of the elect, but before the final battle of Armageddon which will end the day of the Lord.

Lamb, Marriage Supper of (see *Christ, Marriage Supper of*)

Last Day, the

The day when the church is raptured (see *Rapture*), after which the end of the age, the day of the Lord, will commence. Both events (the Rapture and the end of the age) will occur "on the same day."

Last Days

An unspecified period of time, just prior to the rapture of the church at the end of the age, when the day of the Lord will commence.

Lawlessness, Man of (see *Antichrist*)

Little Horn (see *Horn, Little*)

Magog

The prophetic name of the land from which Gog (Antichrist) will arise and establish the eighth and final beast empire of Satan, which will be composed of descendants of all of the previous beast empires except the first two; specifically the land where the Germanic descendants of Magog, Noah's grandson through Japheth, settled.

Manifestation of Christ (see *Sign of Christ's Coming*)

Man of Sin, or of Lawlessness (see *Antichrist*)

Mark of the Beast (see *Beast, Mark of*)

Marriage Supper of the Lamb (see *Christ, Marriage Supper of*)

Marriage of the Lamb (see *Lamb, Marriage of*)

Martyrs, Fifth Seal

Primarily, the seventieth-week Jewish witnesses in Israel who die for the cause of Christ and their fellow countrymen, calling them to repentance and pointing them to the soon return of their true Messiah. These witnesses become martyrs "because of the testimony they had *maintained*." This position is given further credence when we see that these martyrs will be resurrected on the first day of the Millennium and will rule with Christ over the nation of Israel, whose citizens will have become children of God just after the completion of the seventieth week and will recognize those martyrs as the men who gave their lives that they themselves might live. Daniel refers to these as "those who have insight [who] will shine brightly . . . who lead the many [of Israel] to righteousness."

In addition, these fifth-seal martyrs will include other faithful men outside of Israel who refuse the protection provided the faithful church in order to assist the compromising church undergoing the full brunt of Antichrist's persecution, paralleling the activities of the Jewish witnesses living in the land of Israel.

Midpoint of Seventieth Week (see *Seventieth Week, Midpoint of*)

Millennium, the

The literal reign of Christ on earth for a thousand years. The primary subjects of this kingdom will be the surviving remnant of Israel that is divinely protected from the great tribulation by Antichrist and additionally refined by the day of the Lord and that will eventually turn to Christ as their true Messiah and King just after the completion of the seventieth week. There will also be a remnant in the millennial kingdom from among the surviving Gentile nations, especially from Egypt and Assyria, none of which will have taken the mark or worshiped the beast or his image. The seventieth-week Jewish Christian martyrs, who will have been persecuted and put to death by their fellow Jews, will be resurrected to rule with Christ over the new, divinely established house of Israel.

Nations, Destruction of (see *Judgment, Sheep and Goats*)

Nations, Table of

The Genesis 10 list of seventy nations that descended from the three sons of Noah — Shem, Ham, and Japheth.

Near/Far Prophecy (see *Prophecy, Near/Far*)

Nebuchadnezzar, Statue of

The statue shown by God to King Nebuchadnezzar of Babylon in a dream and interpreted to the king by the prophet Daniel. The time period represented by the statue (except for the head of gold [Babylon] which represented Daniel's era as a prophet to the southern kingdom) exactly parallels the seventy weeks (490 years) of future Gentile domination prophesied by Daniel at a later date.

Olivet Discourse

An extensive message on the end times delivered by Christ to His disciples on the Mount of Olives during the final week of His earthly ministry and recorded, at least in part, in three of the Gospels. Because Matthew addressed his message primarily to believing Jews within the early church, and Mark and Luke addressed theirs primarily to Gentiles, and because the questions that are asked and answered in the two primary accounts (in Matthew and Luke) are different, there are understandable differences in content and in length. But the three accounts harmonize perfectly, with no contradictions or inconsistencies. Because Jesus personally spoke the Olivet Discourse (which deals primarily with end-time events) and because He likewise directly gave the end-time truths outlined in the book of Revelation to John, those two sections of Scripture have a special uniformity of language and emphasis, the one explaining the other.

Overcomer

The genuine believer who perseveres during the great tribulation by Antichrist, who will not bow down to or take the mark of this false god, and who will be raptured (see *Rapture*) when God cuts short the great tribulation by Antichrist, just before the day of the Lord, sometime during the second half of the seventieth week.

Pact with Sheol (see *Covenant with Death*)

Perdition, Son of (see *Antichrist*)

Period, Thirty-day (See *30-Day Period*)

Period, Forty-five-day (See *45-Day Period*)

Persecution

Persecution in the last days refers to the affliction of men by other men. In regard to the end times, it specifically relates to the oppression and slaughter by Antichrist and his followers of all Jews (believing and nonbelieving) and of Gentile Christians. It is important to distinguish between tribulation and God's wrath. Such terms as persecution, tribulation, and distress refer to man's affliction of his fellowman, and specifically that of unbelievers against God's elect nation Israel or His church. The evil source of this wrath against God's elect is Satan, as clearly stated in the book of Revelation. God's wrath, on the other hand, refers to His final, day-of-the-Lord retribution against unbelievers for their ungodliness and their maltreatment of His people.

Pretribulationism

The view that the return of Christ has been imminent since the days of the early church and that the church will be raptured sometime *before* the seventieth week. This is considered by pretribulationists to be the end-time, seven-year period of God's judgmental "tribulation" (hence the term pretribulation). This position generally views the seventieth week as the day of the Lord from which the church is excluded.

Prewrath Rapture

The view espoused in this book that the church will be raptured when the great tribulation by Antichrist inspired by Satan is cut short by God's day-of-the-Lord wrath, which will occur between the sixth and seventh seals of Revelation, sometime during the second half of the seventieth week. The persecution associated with the great tribulation of Antichrist is viewed as the wrath of Satan, whereas the events that follow, beginning with the seventh seal, are considered the wrath of God.

Prophecy, Near/Far
A divinely revealed prediction of a soon-coming event that corresponds to a later event.

Purge of Israel, the (see *Tribulation, the Great*)

Purification of Israel (see *Israel, Purification of*)

Rapture, the
Christ's gathering together, deliverance of, or rescue of the living church (by His angelic "reapers") to Himself in the clouds at His second coming (*parousia*), an event that occurs on the last day, when the day of the Lord commences, between the sixth seal (the sign of the end of the age) and the seventh seal (the day of the Lord). The Rapture cannot occur until sometime during the second half of the seventieth week, when God cuts short the great tribulation by Antichrist. "But of that day and hour no one knows."

Reapers, the
In Jesus' wheat and tares parable, the end-time reapers are His angels who will harvest the wheat (living believers) into His heavenly barn (at the Rapture) just before those same angels harvest and destroy the tares (unbelievers) with fire during the day of the Lord. These angels are depicted in the book of Revelation as God's instruments of judgment during the day of the Lord, administering the trumpet and bowl judgments and coming with Christ for the final battle of Armageddon.

Reclamation Period, the (see also *30-Day Period*)
The thirty-day period that immediately follows the seventieth week, ending with the expulsion of Antichrist (the usurper) and his eighth beast empire at the battle of Armageddon. The first major reclamation during this thirty-day period will be Christ's reclamation (through salvation) of the entire surviving nation of Israel to Himself. The second will be God's reclamation of earth's rule to Himself. The final will be Christ's reclamation of the physical possession of earth, when Antichrist and his armies are defeated and

destroyed at the battle of Armageddon, the last event of the thirty-day reclamation period.

Regathering of Israel (see *Israel, Restoration of*)

Remnant, Jewish

In regard to the last days, the remnant refers to the divinely predetermined number of Jews who will survive the great tribulation persecution by Antichrist, Jews who will be refined and cleansed by God during the day of the Lord, who will come to belief in Christ as their true Messiah and King several days after the completion of the seventieth week, and who will enter His millennial kingdom.

Renovation, the

The renovation of the existing heavens and earth, destroyed by the day of the Lord, after the Sheep and Goats Judgment on the first day of the Millennium. The millennial kingdom over which Christ will rule will be restored back to its original state in the Garden of Eden on the first day of the Millennium.

Repentance, Call to

In regard to the last days, the exhortation by the Jewish witnesses for fellow Jews in Israel to repent and turn from following Antichrist, the false messiah, and to prepare themselves for the return of Christ, their true Messiah. During the reign of Antichrist, however, the rest of the world will be in part deceived by God "so that they might believe what is false."

Restoration of Israel (see *Israel, Restoration of*)

Restoration Period, the (see also *45-Day Period*)

A description of the forty-five-day period between the end of the thirty-day reclamation period and the beginning of the Millennium, a time when Christ will restore the remnant of Israel that survives the seventieth week back to their own land. During this time Christ will also build the millennial Temple (restore the old destroyed Temple, as it were); most importantly, God Almighty will restore the rule *upon* earth to its rightful Ruler, Jesus Christ.

Restrainer, the

The restrainer can only be Michael the archangel, Israel's prince, who stands guard over that nation. Satan will not have complete freedom to persecute Israel through Antichrist until Michael's restraint is removed, permitting the purge of Israel foretold by God through His prophets. Contrary to much popular interpretation, there is no scriptural basis for identifying the restrainer either as the

Holy Spirit or as the church. On the other hand, Michael is called by Daniel the one who "stands firmly against" or "restrains."

Revelation of Christ (see *Sign of Christ's Coming*)

Saints, the

In both the Old and New Testaments this term refers to those who are set apart or separated by God for Himself, those who are holy and elect. It is not a term normally used specifically of the nation of Israel.

Scattering of the Jews (see *Diaspora*)

Scroll (Book), the Large

The book or scroll held by Christ that reveals the seven seal events and the first six trumpet judgments that occur during the seventieth week. The large scroll will be complete when the two witnesses are killed by Antichrist at the end of the seventieth week.

Scroll (Book), the Little

The little book or scroll held by the strong angel who comes down from Heaven, the contents of which encompass the events that *follow* the seventieth week: the salvation of Israel; the seventh trumpet judgment (when rule over the earth will reclaimed by God Almighty); the seven bowl judgments; the battle of Armageddon (when physical possession of earth is reclaimed by Christ); right up to the renovation of the heavens and the earth and the descent of the New Jerusalem to earth, "made ready as a bride adorned for her husband" on the first day of the Millennium. It therefore records all the events of the seventy-five-day period between the end of Daniel's seventieth week up to and including the first day of the Millennium.

Seals of Revelation, the Seven

The seven major events that are initiated during the seventieth week of Daniel. The first four occur during the first half of the week and are referred to by Christ as "the beginning of birth pangs." The last three either occur during or are begun during the second half of the week. The seventh and final seal initiates the day-of-the-Lord judgment on unrighteous mankind which is concluded at the end of the thirty-day reclamation period that follows immediately after the culmination of the seventieth week. It is a picture of God's redeeming back the earth — the reclaiming of its rightful rule and physical possession back from Satan to Himself.

Seal, Sixth (see *Sign of the End of the Age*)

Seal, Seventh (see *Day of the Lord*)

Second Coming of Christ (see *Christ, Second Coming*)

Seventh Head (see *Head, Seventh*)

Seventieth Week

The final seven years of Gentile domination of the nation of Israel and the city of Jerusalem; the last week of the seventy weeks of years (490 years) of Daniel's prophecy, which will begin after the long interval that follows the sixty-ninth week. The events of this week correspond to those of the large scroll. The seventieth week will be initiated when Antichrist (incognito) makes a covenant with Israel. At the midpoint of that week Antichrist will conquer Jerusalem, set up his throne in the sacred part of the Temple, and demand world rule and worship, which he will receive when the restrainer, Michael, is removed and Antichrist's true identity is revealed. These midpoint events will initiate the great tribulation by Antichrist (the time of Jacob's trouble or distress), which Christ will cut short with His day-of-the-Lord wrath on a day and hour no man knows, sometime during the second half of the seventieth week. The seventieth week will end seventy-five days before the Millennium begins, just *before* the salvation of Israel and *before* earth's rule is reclaimed by God at the blowing of the seventh trumpet.

Seventieth Week, Midpoint of

The middle of the seventieth week will begin when Antichrist overthrows Jerusalem, reveals his true identity, desecrates the Temple, and demands the worship of the world.

Seventy Weeks of Daniel's Prophecy

The 490 years of specific Gentile domination of the nation of Israel while she had at least limited access to her own land and the city of Jerusalem; the period depicted in Daniel as seventy weeks, or seventy sevens of years (490 years), during which Israel, particularly their holy city, Jerusalem, will be under the domination of one of the eight Gentile beast empires of Satan. Because of Israel's rejection of her Messiah, Jesus Christ, God placed a long, unspecified period of time between the sixty-ninth and seventieth weeks. During this period, which included the time between A.D. 70/132-1948, the Jews had no control over any part of Israel, including, in particular, the city of Jerusalem. Now that Israel has regained control of her homeland (1948) and has again gained control over the entire city of

Jerusalem (1967), the beginning of the seventieth week could occur almost immediately. The formation of the three-nation power base that will drive the eighth and final beast empire of Satan is the only prophetic requirement yet to occur before Israel makes her covenant with its diabolical leader, thereby initiating the seventieth and last week of Daniel's prophecy.

Sheep and Goats Judgment (see *Judgment, Sheep and Goats*)

Shem (Semitic Lineage)

One of the three sons of Noah, from whom all mankind since his day has descended. The lineage of Shem is carefully traced in the table of nations in Genesis 10, and he is the father of the Semitic peoples, which primarily includes the Jews and the Arabs.

Sign of Christ's Coming (or of the Son of Man), the

This sign immediately follows the sign of the end of the age which will plunge the earth's atmosphere into total darkness. In contrast, the sign of Christ's coming will flood the earth and its atmosphere with the supernatural light of Christ's glory as He descends to earth's atmosphere in the clouds. His glory will come from the east (the direction in which the divine *shekinah* glory departed from the Temple in Old Testament times) and will spread throughout the world. Every eye on earth will behold His magnificent second coming.

Sign of the End of the Age, the

The cataclysmic and terrifying changes in the sun, moon, and stars, with all the natural lights of the world being extinguished, plunging the earth's atmosphere into total darkness. This sign will be accompanied by worldwide earthquakes and will occur at the opening of the sixth seal, immediately before the sign of Christ's coming.

Six Hundred Sixty-six (see *Beast, Mark of*)

Son of Destruction, or Perdition (see *Antichrist*)

Son of Man, Sign of (see *Sign of Christ's Coming*)

Supper, Marriage, of the Lamb (see *Christ, Marriage Supper*)

Table of Nations (see *Nations, Table of*)

Tares, the

In Jesus' wheat and tares parable, the tares are not simply unbelievers, but unbelievers who masquerade as Christians. Although they will be spiritually dead, Jesus makes clear that even a mature, spiritual church is not capable of distinguishing them from true believers and therefore should leave that task to His angelic reapers at the proper time, when the wheat is harvested into the barn and the tares are harvested by fire. It seems certain that many counterfeit Christians will voluntarily leave the church when they begin to face the seventieth-week persecution, especially that of the great tribulation by Antichrist. But the parable makes clear that at least a few unbelievers will manage to endure that great affliction and will have to be identified and removed by Christ's angels before He takes the church to be with Himself at the Rapture.

Temple, Millennial

The Jerusalem Temple that will be gloriously rebuilt, or restored, as it were, by Christ during the forty-five-day restoration period between His return at the battle of Armageddon and the beginning of the Millennium. The Temple will be located in the center of the New Jerusalem, hovering above the earth, while at the same time situated squarely on top of Mount Zion in Israel; it is from here that Christ will rule the earth with his bride.

Temple, Seventieth-week

This Temple in Jerusalem will be rebuilt by unbelieving Jews at some time during or before the first half (three and a half years) of the seventieth week. Judging by the Greek word used to describe this Temple, the structure may be quite small and contain little more than a simple altar upon which sacrifices can and will be made by the nation of Israel until the midpoint of the seventieth week when Antichrist desecrates this sacred place.

Ten Horns (see *Horns, Ten*)

Testing, the Time of

The great time of testing in the last days referred to directly by John and Peter, in particular, will occur during the great tribulation by Antichrist when every human being will be expected to worship the beast or his image and obey him alone. This time of testing will be the test of Satan, not the test of God. Those who refuse to worship the beast or his image will face death and/or persecution that will make the Holocaust pale in comparison. Those who flunk this test will suffer the immediate wrath of Satan through his minion Antichrist, but will live eternally in the presence of their King. *Every* true believer will refuse the mark and refuse to worship Antichrist or his image, but untaught and compromising Christians who will not have prepared themselves during the first half of the week will nevertheless experience the full brunt of Antichrist's fury. Some unbelievers — namely, God's protected remnant of the natural line of Abraham (Israel) and unbelieving Gentiles who assist Israel during her time of great distress — will also refuse the mark and eventually come to salvation after the completion of the seventieth week.

Three Horns (see *Horns, Three*)

Three Nations (see *Horns, Three*)

Three-nation Power Base (see also *Horns, Three*)

The three nations, all Japhethite (Aryan/European) in origin, that will drive the eighth and final beast empire of Satan, which will be composed of ten individual nations, including these three.

Time of Jacob's Trouble (see *Tribulation, Great*)

Time of the Gentiles (see *Gentiles, Time of*)

Toes, Ten

Depicted in Nebuchadnezzar's statue as consisting of iron and clay, representing the ten nations that will form the eighth and final beast empire of Satan during the seventieth week. The iron portion of the toes represent Japhethite ancestry that comes from the Roman Empire (the statue's legs of iron).

Tribulation

In relation to end-time events, *tribulation* refers to man's persecution of other men, inspired by the wrath of Satan, and is not a reference to God's judgment or wrath at the day of the Lord. By far the worst tribulation will be the great tribulation by Antichrist, which will occur during (but is not synonymous with) the second half of the seventieth week.

Tribulation, the Great

This term describes Antichrist's persecution of God's elect beginning at the midpoint of the seventieth week, but it is not synonymous with the entire second half of the seventieth week. This persecution (also called "the time of Jacob's trouble" by Jeremiah and "time of distress such as never occurred" by Daniel) is *man's affliction of other men*, inspired by the wrath of Satan. The great tribulation, spoken of by Christ in the Olivet Discourse and in the book of Revelation, refers to the violent persecution inflicted by Antichrist against all his enemies during most of the second half of the seventieth week, but pertains especially to Antichrist's persecution of God's elect. This time of extreme torment and suffering will begin when Antichrist gains control of the city of Jerusalem, takes his seat in the Temple, reveals his true identity, and demands the worship of the world. It will be the greatest time of persecution Jews will ever experience — surpassing even the Nazi Holocaust — but it will also include persecution of the true church, God's elect (Jews and Gentiles who have not worshiped Antichrist or his image).

The great tribulation by Antichrist will be terminated by God's sovereign intervention at the day of the Lord, sometime before the end of that week. If this slaughter were not divinely cut short, no Jew or any of God's elect would survive. As it is, two out of three Jews living back in Israel will still die during this great tribulation.

Trumpet of God

A heavenly trumpet that is blown by God Himself on two distinct but parallel occasions. The first blowing occurred before God delivered Israel from Antiochus Epiphanes and his armies and is recorded by the prophet Zechariah in a near/far depiction of His second (and last) blowing. The second time God blows His heavenly trumpet will occur just before Christ raptures the church and begins to execute His day-of-the-Lord wrath against Antichrist and his armies, as well as against all of the unrighteous who remain on earth.

Trumpet Judgments, the Seven

The wrath of God that initiates the day of the Lord. The seven judgments (administered by the angels, the reapers of God) will fall upon a totally ungodly earth, as this trumpet judgment will begin immediately *after* the rapture of the church, when all believers are removed before the wrath of God begins. The first six trumpets will occur before the large scroll is closed, at the end of the seventieth week. The seventh will sound just after the little scroll is opened (describing the events that occur *after* the seventieth week is complete); it will include the bowl judgments, which are the final wrath of God. Of all the trumpet judgments, the seventh is by far the most important.

Trumpet, the Seventh

The most critical event of the book of Revelation. Just prior to this trumpet the Lord will remove the spiritual blinders from the eyes of the surviving remnant of Israel and will bring them in faith to Himself, fulfilling the final condition necessary for the return of earth's rule to God Almighty. The seventh trumpet will sound on the fifth day of the thirty-day reclamation period, when Christ is on top of Mount Zion with the 144,000 celebrating the Feast of Tabernacles. At its blowing the reign over earth will be reclaimed by God Almighty, thereby initiating the final wrath of God (the bowl judgments), when Antichrist and his armies are destroyed and the physical possession of earth is reclaimed by Christ.

Weeks, Daniel's Seventy

Units of seven which, depending on the context, could represent seven days, weeks, years, etc. In the context of Daniel's prophecy concerning the seventy weeks, each week represents seven years and seventy weeks represents 490 years. A prophetic year represents 360 days. See *Seventy Weeks of Daniel's Prophecy*.

Wheat and Tares Parable

The first parable taught by Christ, recorded only in the Gospel of Matthew, and one of a few that He explained privately to His disciples. This parable pertains directly to the end times and teaches three major truths pertinent to our study: first, that the wheat (true believers) and the tares (unsaved, counterfeit Christians who have always infiltrated the true church) will exist together in the visible church until the end when they will be separated by God's reapers (His angels); second, that on the last day, when the end of the age commences, God's angelic reapers will harvest the wheat into His barn at the Rapture; third, that the tares will then be harvested by God's angelic reapers for destruction during the day of the Lord, at a time Christ specifically called "the end of the age."

Witnesses, Jewish

Jewish witnesses, Christians, who faithfully witness to their fellow countrymen concerning the return of their true Messiah during the seventieth week. They will be raptured with the church when the end of the age begins. Those of these witnesses who are martyred by Antichrist are in part the martyrs of the fifth seal who will be raised on the first day of the Millennium to rule with Christ on earth.

Witnesses, the Two

Two men, probably the reincarnated Moses and Elijah, whom God will send to prophesy to Israel for a period of forty-two months (1,260 days), during the second three and a half years of the seventieth week, including in part the great tribulation by Antichrist.

These witnesses will preach in sackcloth, a sign of mourning and repentance, and will be killed by Antichrist at the very end of the seventieth week, only to be resurrected by "the breath of God" three and a half days later, one day after the salvation of Israel.

Woes, the Three

The three warnings proclaimed by an eagle flying in midheaven announcing and corresponding to the last three trumpet judgments. The first two occur during the seventieth week; the last occurs on the fifth day after the seventieth week is complete.

Woman, Mother of Harlots (See *Babylon, Mother of Harlots*)

Woman, the

"The woman" in general represents the unsaved remnant of Israel who will refuse to worship Antichrist or his image. For the sake of clarity, "the woman" represents two groups: "the faithful woman" who flees, and "the compromised woman" who stays.

Woman, the Faithful

That part of "the woman" in general who refuses to worship Antichrist or his image; in particular those who have *never* apostacized to Antichrist from the beginning of the seventieth week and who flee to the wilderness, becoming the "first fruits" of unbelieving Israel. "The faithful woman" who flees and the 144,000 are one and the same.

Woman, the Compromised

That part of "the woman" in general who refuses to worship Antichrist or his image at the midpoint of the seventieth week when Antichrist's true identity is revealed. However, during the first half of the seventieth week they will endorse the covenant with Antichrist and refuse to heed the warnings of the Jewish witnesses, and therefore do not flee into the wilderness with the others. Thus the name "the compromised woman." However, when Antichrist's true identity is revealed, they will refuse to worship him or his image, and for this reason two out of three of these will eventually be killed by Antichrist. Those of "the compromised woman" who survive will hide out in the rural areas of Israel or escape to remote areas in the lands of Egypt and Assyria. The survivors will be saved after the seventieth week is complete.

Wrath, God's

God's wrath at the end of the age refers to His acts of judgment against unrighteous men. Its final form will be manifested in His day-of-the-Lord retribution against the final beast empire and the rest of the unbelieving world. It is critical that such end-time terms as *tribulation, distress,* and *persecution,* which are manifestations of Satan's *evil* wrath, not be confused with God's *righteous* wrath at the day of the Lord.

Wrath, Day of God's (see *Day of the Lord*)

ENDNOTES

CHAPTER 1: **Foundations for Understanding Prophetic Truth**

1. *The origins of pretribulationism:* The idea of a pretribulational rapture, or in other words a rapture that occurs before the seventieth week of Daniel, is based on the premise that there must be *two* separate and distinct *"parousias"* or "comings" of Christ, the first *parousia* occurring when Christ comes "for His saints" to take both living and dead believers to be with Himself (1 Thess. 4:13-17) before the seventieth week begins, and the second *parousia* (based on the Olivet Discourse) occurring when Christ comes "with His saints" to conquer Antichrist and his forces at Armageddon at the end of the seventieth week. But the concept of a dual *parousia*, a second and third coming of Christ so to speak, is nowhere supported by Scripture, even though it is essential to the understanding of the pretribulational rapture position. See note 2 for more detail on the use of *parousia* in the New Testament.

   The pretribulational rapture position with its dual *parousias* was unheard of in church history prior to 1830. Although John Darby, founder of the Plymouth Brethren movement, apparently never claimed to have originated pretribulationism — which is based on a strict doctrine of progressive revelation — many of his followers have credited the idea to him.

   In his book *Kept from the Hour*, Gerald B. Stanton has several paragraphs giving his views on the start of pretribulational rapturism. Stanton concludes that "Darby and his associates" originated pretribulationism, but goes on to observe: "In this whole matter concerning the history of the imminent, pretribulational return of Jesus Christ, there is little by way of factual support" ([Grand Rapids, MI: Zondervan, 1956], p. 226).

   One of the most popular and respected books upholding the pretribulational point of view is *The Rapture Question* by John F. Walvoord (Grand Rapids, MI: Zondervan, rev. ed. 1979), pp. 18, 19. He writes: "The third view, which is popular with premillenarians who have specialized in prophetic study, is the pretribulational position, which holds that Christ will come for His church before the entire seven-year period predicted by Daniel. The church in this point of view does not enter at all into the final tribulation period. This teaching was espoused by Darby and the Plymouth Brethren and popularized by the famous *Scofield Reference Bible*."

   Second, there an equal number of scholars who give Edward Irving (considered the father of modern-day Pentecostalism) credit for discovering the dual *parousias* or comings of Christ, and he has been the most logical candidate until recent years. William Kimball, in his book *The Rapture, A Question of Timing* ([Grand Rapids, MI: Baker Book House, second printing, 1987], pp. 35, 36) makes this interesting observation: "However, the concept of a pretribulation rapture did not seem to surface in Irving's teachings until the early 1830s, even though the futuristic groundwork had been carefully prepared at the Albury conferences. However, it has been clearly authenticated that Irving was one of the first to suggest this theory. He is frequently accredited with being a major accomplice in the birth of pretribulational teaching." Similarly, Robert Gundry writes: "Pretribulationism arose in the mid-nineteenth century. The likelihood is that Edward Irving was the first to suggest the pretribulation rapture, or at least the seminal thought behind it" (*The Church and the Tribulation* [Grand Rapids, MI: Zondervan, 1973], p. 185).

The third candidate is Margaret MacDonald. Some believe that the real source of the dual comings of Christ was an ailing, fifteen-year-old girl named Margaret MacDonald, whose two brothers James and George had recently come to know Christ. It is in her first vision, before her "healing," that some find the roots of pretribulationism.

Robert Norton, a medical doctor, perhaps most authoritatively documents the origin of the dual comings theory and gives Margaret MacDonald the credit as the source of this new position. In 1861 he wrote a book entitled *The Restoration of Apostles and Prophets in the Catholic Apostolic Church*, in which he says:

> Marvelous light was shed upon Scripture, and especially on the doctrine of the second Advent, by the revived spirit of prophecy. In the following account by Miss M.M. [Margaret MacDonald] _____, of an evening during which the power of the Holy Ghost rested upon her for several successive hours, in mingling prophecy and vision, we have an instance; for here we first see the distinction between that final stage of the Lord's coming, when every eye shall see Him [the second *parousia*], and His prior appearing in glory to them that look for Him [the first *parousia*].

This writer does not claim to know the original source of the dual second coming (*parousia*) of Christ, the first "for His saints" at their rapture, the second "with His saints" at Armageddon. (The coming of Christ "with His saints" at Armageddon is dealt with in some depth in chapter 20 of this book, this author taking the position that "His armies" must be a reference to the angelic armies of God, not to His bride.) It is certain, however, that prior to 1830 this position was unknown. We also know that Darby popularized this new view, and for that reason he is often considered its originator. But this was not the position of the early church fathers (see note 3), and it clearly was not the position of the Apostle Paul (see 2 Thess. 2).

Contemporaries of Darby in the Brethren Church, in particular Dr. Samuel P. Tregelles, one of the outstanding Greek scholars of his day, rejected Darby's pretribulational rapture theory. Recognizing the unbiblical roots of this position, Tregelles gave Edward Irving the credit:

> I am not aware that there was any definite teaching that there would be a secret rapture of the church at a secret coming, until this was given as an "utterance" in Mr. Irving's church, from what was there received as being the voice of the Spirit. But whether any one ever asserted such a thing or not, it

was from that supposed revelation that the modern doctrine and modern phraseology respecting it arose. *It came not from the Holy Scripture, but from that which falsely pretended to be the Spirit of God* (*The Hope of Christ's Second Coming* [Los Angeles: Ambassadors for Christ, n.d.], p. 35, emphasis added).

After clearly demonstrating that the pretribulational view and the imminency of the Rapture were not the positions of the early church (see note 3), Gundry makes the following observation:

> Appealing to the progress of doctrine, we might think that pretribulation-ism represents a refinement of an early belief in imminence. *However, developments of primitive beliefs had usually come in response to novel and erroneous teachings.* Hence, the undoubted progress of doctrine may be, not a justification for, but an indictment against pretribulationism as a novel and erroneous teaching which now requires in rebuttal an expansion and refinement of the primitive posttribulationism. Since the early Church did not hold to imminence, but to the intervention of the tribulation, pretribulationism appears to be just such an innovation rather than an extension (*The Church and the Tribulation*, p. 182, emphasis added).

2. *One parousia or two?* The *parousia* or coming of Christ describes an event, a "presence" of Christ which is initiated by the Rapture of the church. The term *parousia* is *never directly related* to Christ's literal return to earth for the final battle of Armageddon. (See chapter 16, endnote 6 for a more complete understanding of all the Greek words associated with the second coming of Christ, including *parousia*.)

   To briefly summarize the findings presented in the body of chapter 16: when the Greek word *parousia* is used in association with the return of Christ in the last days, Scripture speaks of only *one* coming (*parousia*) of Christ which is initiated by the Rapture of the church. The Scripture makes no mention of a dual *parousia*, necessitating, by definition, a second and third coming of Christ. The idea of a dual *parousia* was not arrived at until 1830 (see note 1). Both Jesus and Paul make clear that Christ's *single* second coming (*parousia*) — which includes the rapture of His saints and His immediately-following day-of-the-Lord judgment — *follows* the revealing of Antichrist. This occurs after Antichrist has taken his seat in the Temple and demanded the worship of the world sometime during the second half of the seventieth week. Therefore, in light of those plain scriptural truths, the possibility of an extra, pre-seventieth week *parousia* is clearly ruled out on exegetical grounds.

3. *The Rapture Position of the Early Church Fathers.* In his book *The Church and the Tribulation* (Grand Rapids, MI: Zondervan, 1973), Robert Gundry observes that "the antiquity of a view weighs in its favor, especially when that antiquity reaches back to the apostolic age. For those who received their doctrine first-hand from the apostles and from those who heard them stood in a better position to judge what was apostolic doctrine than we who are many centuries removed" (p. 172).

   The prewrath rapture position has been labeled as a product of the late twentieth century. The questions that consequently arise in the minds of many Bible students are: "Why now? If this position is scriptural, why has the church been so long in discovering it? And why have so many godly and capable Bible scholars taught conflicting positions for so many years?" The basic answer is that, far from being a new position, it was rather the position of the early church and of the Ante-Nicene Fathers (the most eminent orthodox leaders of the church from the end of the apostolic age until the Council of Nicea in A.D. 325). The only thing new about the prewrath position is its name, which it is given only to avoid being confused with the other positions.

The critical truth of the prewrath position is that the church will be raptured when the great tribulation of Antichrist is cut short by Christ (Matt. 24:22), which by definition necessitates the church's presence on earth during the great tribulation by Antichrist, and the church's being taken by her Lord immediately before He executes His day-of-the-Lord wrath on ungodly mankind. Sometime thereafter Christ will redeem the remnant of Israel, destroy Antichrist and his eighth beast empire, and establish His literal, thousand-year reign (the Millennium) on earth.

In regard to the early church's views concerning the timing of the Rapture, Gundry gives further helpful information:

> Until Augustine in the fourth century, the early Church generally held to the premillenarian understanding of Biblical eschatology. This chiliasm [millennialism] entailed a futuristic interpretation of Daniel's seventieth week, the abomination of desolation, and the personal Antichrist. And it was posttribulational. Neither mentioned nor considered, the possibility of a pretribulational rapture seems never to have occurred to anyone in the early Church. (p. 173)

> Every Ante-Nicene writer who touches in any detail upon the tribulation, resurrection, rapture, or second coming displays a posttribulational persuasion. The number of those is about equal to those whom we can quote directly in favor of premillennialism. (Some early fathers who cannot be cited by means of direct quotation are claimed premillenarians through inferential and indirect evidence. For example, it is inferred that Polycarp was premillenarian because Irenaeus, his pupil, was so, and that Pothinus was premillenarian from the chiliasm of the churches of Vienne and Lyons over which he presided, and from his association with Irenaeus. We might use such lines of reasoning to swell the ranks of early posttribulationists also. To use the same examples, the posttribulationism of Irenaeus would imply that Polycarp, his teacher, was posttribulational and that Pothinus, whom Irenaeus succeeded, was likewise posttribulational. Almost every time premillennialism and posttribulationalism coincide in the early fathers. (p. 178)

> The fact of the matter is that the writings which are regularly quoted in favor of premillennialism may also be quoted in favor of posttribulationalism. And who among the outstanding early fathers is missing from the list of posttribulationalists? Only Clement of Alexandria and Origen, whose names have become trademarks for the mystical, allegorical method of interpretation and who strongly opposed premillennialism, especially as manifest among the Montanists. The evidence that the early Church was posttribulational needs no apology for lack of numbers. (p. 179)

The term *posttribulational* was never used in the early church simply because there was no pretribulational or other view from which it needed to be distinguished. The issue then and now is simply, "does the church go through the great tribulation by Antichrist (posttribulationalism) or does it not (pretribulationalism)?"

But the fact is that the vast majority of the early church fathers believed the end-time church would go through Antichrist's persecution. That also is the basic tenet of the prewrath position. The prewrath view simply expands on the position of the early church fathers by showing that Christ's day-of-the-Lord judgment (the seventh seal), which immediately follows the Rapture, will cut short the great tribulation by Antichrist before the conclusion of the seventieth week of Daniel.

Such great church fathers as Clement of Rome, Barnabas, Justin Martyr, the Pastor of Hermas, Irenaeus, Hippolytus, Melito of Sardis, Methodius, Tertullian, Cyprian, Commodianus, Victorinus, and Lactantius stated clearly in their writings that the church would undergo the persecution of Antichrist before they were raptured. The following direct quotations from some of those men give further evidence to that truth.

Justin Martyr: The man of apostasy [Antichrist] . . . shall venture to do unlawful deeds on the earth against us the Christians. (*Trypho*, cx)

The Pastor (Shepherd) of Hermas: Happy ye who endure the great tribulation that is coming. (*Pastor of Hermas*, Vision Second)

Those, therefore, who continue steadfast, and are put through the fire, will be purified by means of it. . . . Wherefore cease not speaking these things into the ears of the saints. This then is the type of the great tribulation that is yet to come. (*Pastor of Hermas*, Vision Fourth)

Barnabas: The final stumbling-block (or source of danger) approaches, concerning which it is written, as Enoch says, "For this end the Lord has cut short the times and the days, that His Beloved may hasten; and He will come to the inheritance." And the prophet also speaks thus: "Ten kingdoms shall reign upon the earth, and a little king shall rise up after them, who shall subdue under one three of the kings." . . . Take heed, lest resting at our ease, as those who are the called [of God], we should fall asleep in our sins, and the wicked prince, acquiring power over us, should thrust us away from the kingdom of the Lord. (*The Epistle of Barnabas*, chapter iv)

Irenaeus: And they [the ten kings] . . . shall give their kingdom to the beast, and put the Church to flight. (*Against Heresies*, V, 26, 1)

But [John] indicates the number of the name [Antichrist, 666] now, that when this man comes we may avoid him, being aware who he is. (*Against Heresies*, V, 30, 4)

Hippolytus: Now concerning the tribulation of the persecution which is to fall upon the Church from the adversary [he has been speaking of the Antichrist and the Antichrist's persecution of the saints and continues in the same vein]. . . . That refers to the one thousand two hundred and threescore days [the half of the week] during which the tyrant is to reign and persecute the Church. (*Treatise on Christ and Antichrist*, pp. 60, 61)

Tertullian: That the beast Antichrist with his false prophet may wage war on the Church of God. . . . Since, then, the Scriptures both indicate the stages of the last times, and concentrate the harvest of the Christian hope in the very end of the world. (*On the Resurrection of the Flesh*, xxv; cf. *Scorpiace*, xii)

The Teaching of the Twelve Apostles: Watch for your life's sake. Let not your lamps be quenched, nor your loins unloosed; but be ye ready, for you know not the hour in which our Lord cometh.

Concerning this last quote Gundry observes, "Here Walvoord, Stanton, and Pentecost break off the quotation in an endeavor to make the passage establish a belief in imminence by the early Church" (p. 175). But read the rest of the paragraph!

But often shall ye come together, seeking the things which are befitting your souls: for the whole time of your faith will not profit you, if ye be not made perfect in the last time. For in the last days false prophets and corrupters shall be multiplied . . . and then shall appear the world-deceiver as Son of God, and shall do signs and wonders, and the earth shall be delivered into his hands, and he shall do iniquitous things which have never yet come to pass since the beginning. . . . And then shall appear the signs of the truth; first, the sign of an outspreading in heaven; *then the sign of the sound of the trumpet*; and the third, *the resurrection of the dead*; yet not of all, but as it is said: The Lord shall come and all His saints with Him. Then shall the world see the Lord coming upon the clouds of heaven. (*The Teachings of the Twelve Apostles*, chapter XVI, emphasis added)

The Constitutions of the Holy Apostles: Be watchful for your life. "Let your loins be girded about, and your lights burning, and ye like unto men who wait for their Lord, when He will come, at even, or in the morning, or at cock-crowing, or at midnight. For at what hour they think not, the Lord will come; and if they open to him, blessed are those servants, because they were watching."

"Again," writes Gundry, "Walvoord breaks off the quotation in an endeavor to make the passage teach imminence" (p. 177). Once again we see that the quotation teaches nothing of the sort when taken in its immediate context.

And then shall appear the deceiver of the world, the enemy of the truth, the prince of lies, whom the Lord Jesus "shall destroy with the spirit of His mouth, who takes away the wicked with His lips; and many shall be offended at Him. But they that endure to the end, the same shall be saved. And then shall appear the sign of the Son of man in Heaven;" and afterwards *shall be the voice of a trumpet by the archangel; and in that interval shall be the revival of those that were asleep. And then shall the Lord come*, and all His saints with Him. (*Constitutions*, VII, ii, xxxi, xxxii, emphasis added)

Victorinus: He speaks of Elias the prophet, who is the precursor of the times of Antichrist, for the restoration and establishment of churches from the great and intolerable persecution [followed by a lengthy discussion of the persecution of the Church by the Antichrist]. (*Commentary on the Apocalypse*, VII, 351ff.)

The persecution of the church by Antichrist was clearly the position of the early church. Roman Catholicism under Augustine then moved away from the literal interpretation of end-time events and allegorized prophetic Scripture. This continued up until the pretribulational position (with its dual *parousias* and their imminent rapture *before* the seventieth week and the persecution of Antichrist) was introduced in the early part of the nineteenth century, circa 1830. In this regard Gundry succinctly summarizes the position of this present volume in regard to the prewrath rapture:

We may fairly conclude that both pretribulationists and others who find imminence in the Ante-Nicene fathers are grasping at straws. The early fathers uniformly expected a yet future persecution of Antichrist prior to the Lord's return (*Ibid.*, p. 182).

4. Note that the word used in 2 Thessalonians 1:4, 6 for "affliction" (NASB) is *thlipsis*. This is the same word translated as "tribulation" in both Matthew 24:21 and 29 and in Revelation 7:14, referring to the great tribulation by Antichrist.

5. The Greek word translated "relief" is *"anesis."* Young, in *Young's Analytical Concordance to the Bible*, gives this particular word an interesting definition: "a sending up or back." In the context of 2 Thessalonians 1, the "relief" that will be given those persecuted at the appearing of Christ with His mighty angels will be the Rapture, when "we who are alive and remain shall be *caught up together* with them in the clouds to meet the Lord in the air" (1 Thess. 4:17, emphasis added).

CHAPTER 2: **A Warning to the Church**
1. *Revelation 3:10 (tēreō ek)*: The Greek phrase translated in Revelation 3:10 as "will keep . . . from" is *"tēresō ek,"* a combination of the verb *tēreō*, translated "to keep," and the preposition *ek*, translated "from."

In an article in *Bibliotheca Sacra* (July-September 1980, p. 253), Jeffrey L. Townsend states that

> The preposition *ek* is the focal point of the debate over whether Revelation 3:10 promises internal or external preservation from the hour of testing. The standard Greek lexicons and grammars are in agreement on the basic meaning of the preposition. According to A. T. Robertson, "The word means 'out of,' 'out from within,' not like *apo* or *napa*." (*A Grammar of the Greek New Testament in the Light of Historical Research*, 4th ed. [New York: George H. Doran, 1923], p. 596)

Therefore the basic meaning of *ek* is "out from within" and best carries the idea "deliverance from," rather than the simple idea of keeping "from," giving the reader the false idea of an external preservation from, rather than a deliverance "out from within," an existing condition that the object or subject of the sentence is in the midst of, prior to their deliverance, out from within.

In his book *The Approaching Advent of Christ: An Examination of the Teaching of J. N. Darby and His Followers*, Alexander Reese observes that

> the use of *ek* in Revelation 3:10 distinctly implies that the Overcomer [the genuine believer] would be in the hour of tribulation; the promise refers either to removal from out of the midst of it, or preservation through it. ([London: Marshall, Morgan, & Scott, 1937], p. 205)

In his book *The Church and the Tribulation*, Robert Gundry maintains that *tēreō* means "to keep or protect in a sphere of danger," and that because *ek* means emergence "out from within," the combination of the two Greek words (*tēreō ek*) means "to protect believers in a sphere of danger (the tribulation period), with a final emergence out from within this sphere" (see pp. 54-59).

The sphere of danger from which the believer is promised protection is "the hour of testing, that hour which is about to come upon the whole world, to test those who dwell upon the earth" (Rev. 3:10b). Note 2 that follows explains that "testing" is the Greek word *peirasmos*, better translated "temptation" or "putting to the proof." Revelation 3:10 states we will be protected during this time. The only other time this Greek word is translated "testing" is in the first epistle of Peter.

> The end of all things is at hand; therefore, be of sound judgment and sober spirit for the purpose of prayer. . . . Beloved, do not be surprised at the fiery ordeal among you, which comes upon you for your testing (*peirasmos*), as though some strange thing were happening to you; but to the degree that you share the sufferings of Christ, keep on rejoicing; so that also at the revelation of His glory you may rejoice with exultation. (1 Pet. 4:7, 12, 13)

Again we see exactly the same Greek word, *"peirasmos,"* exactly the same context, "the fiery ordeal *among* you, which comes upon you, for your testing," and exactly the same promise of deliverance at "the revelation of His glory." Thus the clear meaning here concerns protection while within the sphere of danger — not protection "from" the danger — with eventual deliverance "out from within" at the revelation of His glory at His coming.

Only one other time, other than Revelation 3:10, is a form of this phrase, *tēreō ek*, used in the New Testament. Again it is John who uses it, thereby giving us a better understanding of exactly how he meant the phrase to be used. Jesus' great high-priestly prayer was given for the sake of all those in every age who trust in Him. Christ's appeal to His Heavenly Father in this prayer has had and will continue to have the same special meaning to His saints in every age as it will to those who will live during that last great hour of testing: "I do not ask Thee to take them out of the world," He said, "but to keep them from [*tērēsēis . . . ek*] the evil one. They are not of the world, even as I am not of the world. Sanctify them in the truth; Thy word is truth. As Thou didst send Me into the world, I also have sent them into the world" (John 17:15-18).

The context of John 17:15 shows that Christ is praying for the protection of the believer while he is still *in the world*, the "sphere of danger" over which Satan rules. If Christ were referring to keeping the believer while he is *outside* the sphere of danger (which is what many would have us believe is the meaning of *tēreō ek* in Revelation 3:10), then a phrase such as "take them out of the world" (as in the first half of verse 15) would have been far more appropriate. Comparing Scripture with Scripture, we see that protection while within the sphere of danger, during the time that the world is under the control of the evil one, is exactly what Christ was referring to in John 17:15. In his first epistle John explains, "we know that no one who is born of God sins; but He who was born of God [Christ] keeps him [the believer that is in the world] and the evil one does not touch him" (1 John 5:18). The idea is clearly that of protection while within the sphere of danger, not that of keeping the believer outside the sphere of danger.

It may have been those very words of His Lord that inspired Paul to remind us that Christ "gave Himself for our sins, that He might deliver us out of this present evil age, according to the will of our God and Father" (Gal. 1:4), and that "the Lord is faithful, and He will strengthen and protect you from the evil one" (2 Thess. 3:3).

In addition, using this primary interpretation of *tēreō ek*, several critical passages in support of the prewrath position take on special significance. In reply to John's question about the identity of the great multitude "standing before the throne and before the Lamb," one of the elders explained, "These are the ones who come out of [*ek*, out from within] the great tribulation, and they have washed their robes and made them white in the blood of the Lamb" (Rev. 7:9, 14). Peter declares that "the Lord knows how to rescue the godly from [*ek*, out from within] temptation [*peirasmos*, translated testing in Rev. 3:10], and to keep the unrighteous under punishment for the day of judgment" (2 Pet. 2:9). See also note 2 in this chapter.

In summary, if those two Greek words (*tēreō ek*) are taken at face value, with their primary and customary meanings, the inescapable conclusion is that Revelation 3:10 does not refer to divine protection of believers by taking them away from the place of affliction before it occurs, but to their divine protection while they are in the midst of affliction — that is, in the midst of the great tribulation by Antichrist, referred to as "the hour of testing." During the last half of the seventieth week God's people will for a time remain within Satan's worldly sphere of evil, *eventually* to be forever removed from it when God cuts short that great tribulation by Antichrist and takes His saints "out from within" to be with Himself.

2. *Revelation 3:10 (peirasmos)*: In Revelation 3:10, 1 Peter 4:12 and 2 Peter 2:9, the noun *peirasmos* ("testing," NASB) is a key word. The Greek carries the basic idea of putting to a proof. In the same article mentioned in note 1 above, Townsend writes,

> The object of the preposition *ek* in Revelation 3:10 is "the hour of testing." The preservation promised the Philadelphians is in relation to a specific period of time. This is indicated by the inclusion of [original Greek word] as an article of previous reference. Jesus is speaking of the well-known hour of testing which is a reference to the expected time of trouble, the tribulation period before the return of Messiah. . . . This period is graphically portrayed in Revelation 6-18 (cf. "the great tribulation," 7:14; and "the hour of His judgment," 14:7).

In the same article Townsend goes on to state that according to Johnson ([S. Lewis, Jr.], class notes for course #228, on the book of Revelation, taken at Dallas Theological Seminary, Fall 1976), the Greek phrase in Revelation 3:10 ("those who dwell upon the earth") corresponds to the Hebrew idiom which in Isaiah 24:1, 5, 6; 26:9 becomes a technical term for people on the earth ("inhabitants," NASB) during "the time of Jacob's Trouble."

It is to that same time of Jacob's trouble, or distress, that the prophet refers in Daniel 12:1, and which will commence at the midpoint of the seventieth week, when Antichrist breaks the covenant with Israel. It is also to this time of "great tribulation" that Christ refers in the Olivet Discourse (Matt. 24:21).

It is interesting to note how the "hour of testing" that is referred to in Revelation 3:10 is also referred to by Peter, using the identical Greek word: "The end of all things is at hand; therefore, be of sound judgment and sober spirit for the purpose of prayer. . . . *Beloved, do not be surprised at the fiery ordeal among you, which comes upon you for your testing* (*peirasmos*), *as though some strange thing were happening to you; but to the degree that you share the sufferings of Christ, keep on rejoicing; so that also at the revelation of His glory, you may rejoice with exultation*" (1 Pet. 4:7, 12, 13, emphasis added). And then again the second epistle of Peter states, "then the Lord knows how to rescue the godly from temptation (*peirasmos*), and to keep the unrighteous under punishment for the day of judgment" (2 Pet. 2:9). In both cases, the believer is present during the *peirasmos*, the great tribulation of Antichrist, rather than being protected away from it. See further endnote 1 above.

3. In a personal letter, dated December 9, 1991, reprinted with the permission of the writer, Dr. Robert D. Culver states:

> I do not object to the doctrine [the pretribulational rapture position] as certainly false; it is the assumed and unsupported certainty of the usual proclamation of it that has offended me. It is wrong to affirm "Thus saith the Lord" when no Scripture texts or *necessary* inferences derived from them support the affirmation. I don't see how any informed person can read the second chapter of II Thessalonians and then say he is *sure* the church will be "raptured" (I condescend to use the word) before the coming Day of Christ [the day of the Lord] and His *parousia*.

CHAPTER 4: **The Blessings and the Curses**

1. This quote, taken from Luke 21, is part of the Olivet Discourse, also recorded in Matthew 24 – 25 and Mark 13. The rendering in Mark 13 seems to be an abbreviated account of Matthew's account. However, the Luke account, which follows the general overview of Matthew's account, has one section, verses 12-24 (including this passage), that deviates from the general overview given in Matthew's account, although some of the warnings are similar. Nevertheless, a careful reading of both accounts will show that two different events are being described, both including warnings to those in Jerusalem to flee before it happens. The account in Luke may be a near/far passage, but this author cannot be adamant about that. The reason for the deviation is quite simple. The Olivet Discourse was prompted by three questions from Christ's disciples. The first, "When will these things be?" (Matt. 24:3), referred to Christ's statement that "not one stone [of the Temple] here shall be left upon another, which will not be torn down" (Matt. 24:2). The second was, "What will be the sign of Your coming?" And the third was, "What will be the sign of . . . the end of the age?" (Matt. 24:3). The first question was answered in verses 12-24 of Luke's account. The other two questions are answered by both accounts. This is further confirmed when the question of the disciples, recorded in the Luke account, is limited to only the first question given above (Luke 21:7).

CHAPTER 5: **The "Seventy Week" Prophetic Timetable**

1. Sir Robert Anderson, *The Coming Prince* (Grand Rapids, MI: Kregel, 1972), p. iii.
2. See also God's revelation to Moses concerning the future return of Israel to the Promised Land prior to the restoration of Israel in faith and obedience in the last days (Deut. 30:1-8).

CHAPTER 6: **The First Seven Beast Empires**

1. This correlation continues through the sixth empire — i.e., the first empire in Daniel 2 corresponds to the third empire in Revelation 17, the second to the fourth, the third to the fifth, the fourth to the sixth. After the sixth empire, however, the correlation is modified, as is explained later in this chapter in the section entitled "The Intervening Gap." It should be noted further that there is definite reason why the passage in Daniel 2:31-35, 37-44 does not include the first two empires which are mentioned in Revelation 17:3, 9-12. It is clear from the context of these two passages that the Daniel passage is considering only what will happen from the time of Daniel onward (i.e., *after* the first two empires had already come and gone), while the Revelation passage is considering a much broader span extending "from the foundation of the world" (17:8) and on to the time when Christ will become "Lord of lords and King of kings" (17:14).

CHAPTER 7: **The Eighth and Final Beast Empire**

1. The author acknowledges that there is considerable debate among scholars as to where some of Noah's sons and grandsons may have settled. When such locations are of importance to the arguments of this book, nonbiblical historical sources have been cited when they seem helpful. For reliable and more detailed study of the table of nations and the immediate descendants of the sons of Noah, see Henry M. Morris, *The Genesis Record* (Grand Rapids, MI: Baker, 1978), pp. 246-266, and Arthur C. Custance, *Noah's Three Sons* (Grand Rapids, MI: Zondervan, 1975), pp. 52-141.

   After carefully studying the various possibilities it seems most likely to this author that the nations included in Table I of this chapter have settled as briefly described below:

   I. *Japheth (Japhethite Nations)*

   Gomer: Ancient district of Crimea, north of the Black Sea, western portion of the former U.S.S.R. (Ukraine province)

   Togarmah (son of Gomer, grandson of Japheth): Ancient Armenians located in southwest portion of the former U.S.S.R., in the province of Armenia, and perhaps extending down into far eastern Turkey, northwestern Iran, and in the general area northeast of Mt. Ararat.

   Magog: Ancient Scythians and Goths, in Central Europe. Also includes heavy pockets located in the western parts of former U.S.S.R.

   Madia: Ancient Madia, western Iran and eastern Iraq.

   Javan: Ancient Ionia, modern Greece.

   Tubal: West central portion of the former U.S.S.R. (approximately one thousand miles east of Moscow), in far western Siberia (the province of Russia), particularly the area around Tobolsk, a name that some scholars believe was derived from the Hebrew *Tubal*.

   Meshech: Ancient Muskovi, the former name of Russia, located today in the west central portion of the former U.S.S.R. The name Moscow may have been derived from the Hebrew *Meshek*.

   Tiras: Ancient Thracians, or ancient Persia, presently eastern Iran.

   II. *Ham (Hamitic Nations)*

   Put: Libya, northern Africa, west of Egypt.

   Mizraim: Egypt.

   Cush: Ethiopia, eastern Sudan.

   Nimrod (son of Cush, grandson of Ham): Ancient Babylonia (southern Iraq, near the ancient city of Babylon, between the Tigris and Euphrates Rivers, northwest of the Persian Gulf), then north to Nineveh, the land eventually settled by the descendants of Asshur.

   Canaan: Ancient land of Canaan, modern Israel; mostly destroyed by the Israelites under Joshua and Caleb.

III. *Shem (Semite Nations)*

Elam: Ancient land of Elam, located immediately east of the Tigris and Euphrates Rivers, modern far eastern Iraq or far western Iran.

Asshur: Ancient Assyria (Nineveh area in Old Testament times), modern northern Iraq and perhaps the far eastern part of Syria, as well as the northwestern tip of Iran. In very early history this land was invaded by Nimrod, who had just established Babylon to the south.

Arpachshad (great-grandfather of Abraham): Ancient Chaldeans who dominated the Fertile Crescent, in particular the Babylonian area, from which Abraham was called to the land of Canaan, modern Israel.

Lud: Northern Syria.

Aram: Southern Syria.

In analyzing the Genesis genealogies of Noah's sons, it is important to note that grandsons and great-grandsons are not mentioned if the father and his sons remained together in the same geographic area.

2. See *The Zondervan Pictorial Encyclopedia of the Bible*, 5:162, 163.
3. (New York: Thomas Y. Crowell, n.d.), p. 2, emphasis added.
4. T. Walter Wallbank and Alastair M. Taylor, *Civilization Past and Present*, Vol. 1 (Chicago: Scott, Foresman, 1955), p. 130.
5. *Ibid.*, p. 36.
6. *Ezekiel 38 — 39*: Because of the great significance of Ezekiel 38 — 39 in the understanding of all end-time events, it is essential to establish that this passage pertains to the events that occur in association with the seventieth week of Daniel, just prior to the millennial rule of Christ. There are many reasons why this passage can only relate to this timeframe, and when all these different reasons are put together, the serious student of God's Word using the hermeneutics outlined in chapter 1 is left no other option.

First, the passage itself declares explicitly that the events described in it will take place "in the latter years" (38:8) and "in the last days" (v. 16).

Second, these two chapters describe in detail what has been introduced in the previous two chapters — that is, God's prophetic promise of a new covenant with Israel in the end times (chapter 36), and the initial return of Jews to the land of Israel in unbelief, depicted by the dry bones, after which again the national salvation of Israel is foretold (chapter 37).

Third, the divine "wrath" in Ezekiel 38:19 translates the same Hebrew word (*'ebrah*, see *Strong's*, #5678), used twice in Zephaniah 1:14-18, to describe the wrath that will characterize God's day-of-the-Lord judgment of the nations (vv. 15, 18). See chap. 10, endnote 3.

Fourth, the events described in Ezekiel 38 — 39 have many parallels to passages in the book of Revelation that indisputably relate to the seventieth week.

(1) The birds of Ezekiel 39:17-20 correspond to the birds in Revelation 19:17, 18, 21.

(2) Ezekiel's prediction that the Lord's final judgment against the ungodly nations who have persecuted Israel "shall be done" (39:7, 8) corresponds to two passages in Revelation that speak of His final judgment of the nations,

especially those of the eighth beast empire, as already having been accomplished, declaring proleptically but with absolute finality, "It is done" (16:17; 21:6).

(3) The final destruction of Gog and his armies described in Ezekiel 39:1-4 corresponds remarkably to the final destruction of Antichrist and his armies described in Revelation 19:17-21 and Isaiah's prophecy concerning the armies of Antichrist in the last days (Isa. 34:1-3).

Fifth, the ultimate salvation of the entire nation of Israel introduced earlier in both chapter 36 and 37 is portrayed in Ezekiel 39:21-29 as following the events previously outlined in chapters 38 and 39. This is in perfect harmony with Daniel 9:24, where we are told that "everlasting righteousness" will be brought in to Israel *after* the seventieth week is complete (cf. Rom. 11:25, 26). Nowhere in Scripture are we told that the nation of Israel in its entirety will be saved twice. Therefore, by the very fact that Israel's national salvation occurs exactly at this place in Ezekiel 38 — 39, we know that the preceding events must be among the same seventieth-week events described in the prophetic books of Daniel and Revelation, events which occur just before the national salvation of Israel.

Sixth, the ultimate salvation of Israel depicted in Ezekiel 38 — 39 is immediately followed by the detailed prophecies of the millennial kingdom (chapters 40 — 48), when Christ will rule over a redeemed and obedient house of Israel. Commenting on Ezekiel 40 — 48, Charles Ryrie says:

> These chapters are a complement to the many predictions of judgment announced by Ezekiel. He now foresees the rebuilding of the Temple, the establishment of a right relationship between the Lord (Yahweh [or, Jehovah]) and Israel, and the reorganization of her national life. Detailed instructions are recorded for the building of this future Temple and for the service attached to it. The description is not of Solomon's Temple, the specifications being different and larger. If the description was given to help the exiles on their return from Babylon to rebuild the Temple, it is inexplicable why Ezra, Nehemiah, or Haggai do not refer to it. If it is a description of God's relation to the Church, then it is so symbolic as to be meaningless. If understood plainly, the Temple and worship here referred to must relate to Israel when she is reestablished in her land (cf. chapters 47-48) during Christ's millennial kingdom. (*The Ryrie Study Bible* [Chicago: Moody Press, 1978])

Seventh, Gog was considered by many Jewish rabbis (Rashi in particular, who lived in the eleventh century A.D.) and by ancient Hebrew writings (*Targum Jonathan*, an Aramaic paraphrase of the Hebrew Scriptures, written around the time of Christ) as the ungodly king who with arrogant futility will pit himself against Messiah in the end times. That concept perfectly fits the description of Antichrist given in the New Testament.

Interpreting Ezekiel 38 – 39 as relating specifically and exclusively to the seventieth week seems to be demanded by its own context, by parallel passages in other parts of Scripture (especially in the book of Revelation), and by simple logic when all related texts are carefully studied together.

7. See, e.g., *The ArtScroll Tanach Series*, Vol. 2, an annotated translation of Ezekiel (Brooklyn, NY: Mesorah Pub., 1980), p. 582.

8. *Isaiah 66:19 (ro'sh)*: If Rosh is a nation rather than a title of leadership, this nation is almost impossible to ascertain, because it is not found in the Genesis table of

nations. In all fairness, however, some maintain that there may be a reference to Rosh as a nation in Isaiah 66:19, where the survivors of the battle of Armageddon are pictured coming to Jerusalem. But that interpretation is based on a very questionable translation and cannot be used to support the idea that the Old Testament refers to Rosh as a nation. The basic Hebrew word *ro'sh* is not a proper name but rather a title of leadership (cf. K. Keil and F. Delitzsch, *Commentary on the Old Testament*, Vol. 9 [Grand Rapids, MI: repr. 1980], p. 160).

9. Josephus (*Antiquities*, 1:6) identifies the descendants of Magog as the Scythians, who some centuries before the Common Era (i.e., before A.D.), branched out eastward and westward from the region somewhat north of the Black Sea.

10. The *Targum Jonathan* renders Magog as *Geramemaia*, which in *Bereishis Rabbah* 37:1 is given as *Germaniah*. Reference seems to be to the nomads who settled in the Caucasion regions.

   Concerning *Bereishis Rabbah* 37:1, Rabbi Samuel ben Ammi maintains that the sons of Japheth (Gomer, Magog, etc.) correspond to Africa, Germania, and Mysia. (An editorial footnote suggests that Gomer probably represents ancient Phrygia in Asia Minor, not Africa.) Rabbi Samuel ben Ammi writes: "Our identification of Magog as Caucasia, which was at one time inhabited by the Goths, is based on the assumption that the land of Magog is named after Japheth's son. Indeed this seems likely since some of Gog's allies have names identical to, or strikingly similar to, offspring of Japheth. Meshech and Tuval (v. 2) are names of Japheth's sons. . . . *Persia* (v. 5) is identified with Japheth's son Teras, and Togarmah (v. 6) is a grandson of Japheth" (*The ArtScroll Tanach Series*, Yechezkel/Ezekiel, Vol. 2, gen. eds. Rabbis Nosson Scherman/Meir Zlotowitz [Brooklyn, NY: Mesorah Pub., 1980], p. 581).

11. Fifteenth ed., 8:18, 19.

12. See *The Jerusalem Talmud*, Megillah 37:1.

13. See "Spared Immigrant Tide, Europe Remains Wary," in the *Chicago Tribune*, February 16, 1992, pp. 1, 19. The *Tribune* quotes Heinz Scholl, Director of Refugee Affairs in the German Interior Ministry in Bonn, as saying: "The only solution is to help these people [Germans and others in Eastern Europe] live in their own countries. . . . We have given billions of marks to these countries [e.g., 80 billion to Russia] to help them stay put . . ." (p. 19). The article continues by explaining that "German-born Empress Catherine the Great lured her countrymen to the Volga River basin in Russia in the 18th century to help farm the land. . . . Germany currently expressed interest in financing establishment of a German autonomous region along the Volga . . ." (p. 19).

14. "Both Meshech and Tubal are listed in *Genesis* 10:2 as sons of Japheth. Tubal is identified as Beth Unyaki, and Meshech as Mysia in *Yomah* 10a. *Yerushalmi* reads Bithynia instead of Beth Unyaki and, according to *Torah Temimah* to *Genesis* 10:2, there is a province of that name in the Black Sea region. Mysia is also located in Asia Minor. *Chevlei Mashiach BiZemaneinu* quotes a letter which *R'Chisdai Ibn Shaprut* wrote to the king of Khazaria [a Caucasian kingdom which converted to Judaism in the eighth century C.E.] in which he addresses the king as . . . *prince, leader of Meshech and Tubal*. This salutation, drawn from our verse, indicates that the *Gaonim* had a tradition that these countries were indeed located in Russia" (*The ArtScroll Tanach Series*, pp. 582, 583).

15. *Genesis Record*, p. 248.

CHAPTER 8: **Antichrist and His Foreshadow**
1. *Zechariah 9:13 (Javan)*: As explained by Keil and Delitzsch,

> The sons of Javan are the Greeks, as the world-power, the Graeco-Macedonian monarchy (cf. Dan. viii. 21), against which the Lord will make His people into a hero's sword. This took place in weak beginnings, *even in the wars between the Maccabees and the Seleuciadae, to which, according to Jerome, the Jews understood our prophecy to refer*; but it must not be restricted to this, as the further description in verses 14, 15 points to the complete subjugation of the imperial power. Jehovah appears above them, i.e., coming from heaven as a defense, to fight for them (the sons of Zion), as a mighty man of war (Ps. xxiv. 8). His arrow goes out like the lightning. . . . Marching at the head of His people, He gives the signal of battle with a trumpet-blast, and attacks the enemy with terribly devastating violence. (*Commentary on the Old Testament in Ten Volumes* by C. F. Keil and F. Delitzsch, Volume X, *Minor Prophets* by C. F. Keil [Grand Rapids, Mi: Eerdmans, n.d.), p. 341, emphasis added)

2. *Zechariah 9:14 — God's Trumpet*: In his depiction of the defeat of Antiochus during the Maccabean revolution, Zechariah makes clear in a near/far prophecy that the victory would be by God's power and that it would be accompanied by a divine trumpet blown by God Himself: "I will stir up your sons, O Zion, against your sons, O Greece; and I will make you like a warrior's sword; then the Lord will appear over them, and His arrow will go forth like lightning; *and the Lord God will blow the trumpet*, and will march in the storm winds of the south. The Lord of hosts will defend them. And they will devour, and trample on the sling stones; and they will drink, and be boisterous as with wine; and they will be filled like a sacrificial basin, drenched like the corners of the altar. And the Lord their God will save them in that day as the flock of His people; for they are as the stones of a crown, sparkling in His land" (Zech. 9:13-16, emphasis added). The near prophecy is the defeat of Antiochus Epiphanes in 165 B.C. (see note 1); the shift to the future then comes in verse 16 when Israel as a nation will be saved *after* the second and last time God blows His trumpet. This will occur when Christ rescues the church (see 1 Cor. 15:51, 52; 1 Thess. 4:16) and initiates His day-of-the-Lord wrath upon Antichrist (see 2 Thess. 2:8) and those who worship him.

CHAPTER 9: **The Stage Is Set**
1. "Parental Guidance," *The Chicago Tribune*, January 29, 1992, sec. D, pp. 1, 5.
2. *Ibid.*, p. 5.
3. For a very helpful resource with numerous reviews on contemporary films, written from a conservative Christian perspective, see the bi-weekly publication *Movieguide*, published by Ted Baehr, available from Good News Communications, P.O. Box 190010, Atlanta, GA 31119. See also K. L. Billingsley, *The Seductive Image: A Christian Critique of the World of Film* (Wheaton, IL: Crossway Books, 1989) for an insightful introduction and critique of film from a Christian perspective.
4. Gene Edward Veith, Jr., *State of the Arts: From Bezalel to Mapplethorpe* (Wheaton, IL: Crossway Books, 1991), p. 19.
5. *Ibid.*, p. 20.
6. Francis A. Schaeffer, *The Great Evangelical Disaster* (Wheaton, IL: Crossway Books, 1984), p. 23.
7. *Elle*, August 1991, p. 72.

8. John Randolph Price, *The Planetary Commission* (Austin, TX: Quartus Books, 1984), p. 32, cited in Texe Marrs, *Dark Secrets of the New Age* (Wheaton, IL: Crossway Books, 1987), p. 12.

9. *Ibid.*, p. 134.

10. *Ibid.*, p. 161.

11. Douglas R. Groothuis, *Confronting the New Age: How to Resist a Growing Religious Movement* (Downers Grove, IL: InterVarsity Press, 1988), p. 20.

12. Walter Martin, *The New Age Cult* (Minneapolis: Bethany House, 1989), p. 15.

13. For further reading from a Christian perspective on the essential beliefs of the New Age, the following titles, as well as those already cited in the notes above, provide a helpful overview: Douglas Groothuis, *Revealing the New Age Jesus: Challenges to Orthodox Views of Christ* (Downers Grove, IL: InterVarsity Press, 1990); Douglas Groothuis, *Unmasking the New Age* (Downers Grove, IL: InterVarsity Press, 1986); Bob Larson, *Straight Answers on the New Age* (Nashville: Thomas Nelson Publishers, 1989); Paul deParrie and Mary Pride, *Ancient Empires of the New Age* (Wheaton, IL: Crossway Books, 1989); and Paul deParrie and Mary Pride, *Unholy Sacrifices of the New Age* (Wheaton, IL: Crossway Books, 1988).

14. (Philadelphia: Presbyterian and Reformed Publishing Co., 1961), pp. 14, 15.

15. Daniel Gasman, *The Scientific Origins of National Socialism: Social Darwinism in Ernst Haeckel and the German Monist League* (New York: American Elsevier Press, 1971), pp. xvi, xvii, cited in Henry M. Morris, *The Biblical Basis for Modern Science* (Grand Rapids, MI: Baker, 1984), p. 435.

16. Gasman, p. 168, as cited in Morris, *The Biblical Basis*, p. 435.

17. This extract in its entirety is taken from Morris, *The Biblical Basis*, p. 435.

18. Richard Brookhiser, "Of Church Pews and Bedrooms," *Time* Magazine, August 26, 1991, p. 70.

19. Kenneth Woodward with Alden Cohen, "Roll Over, John Calvin," *Newsweek* Magazine, May 6, 1991, p. 59.

20. See, e.g., Richard N. Ostling, "Time for a New Temple?," *Time* Magazine, October 16, 1989, p. 64.

21. *Second Thessalonians 2:4 (naos)*: In Daniel 9:27 the prophet clearly shows that at the midpoint of the seventieth week Antichrist will put an end to sacrifices, which would necessitate a Temple. Second Thessalonians 2:4 reveals that this Temple will be used by Antichrist as a throne room, from which he will demand the world's worship. It is obvious, then, that some sort of man-made Temple will exist and be used by Jews for sacrifices *before* the midpoint of the seventieth week. But Scripture gives no description of that Temple or any indication as to when it will be built.

In this regard it is important to note that two Greek words are translated "temple" in the New Testament. *Hieron* denotes the entire precinct of a place of worship or sacrifice (see James Strong, *Strong's Exhaustive Concordance of the Bible* [Nashville: Abingdon, 1890], #2411; W. E. Vine, *An Expository Dictionary of New Testament Words* [Westwood, NJ: Revell, 1940], 4:115). The term used in 2 Thessalonians 2:4, however, is *naos*, which pertains only to the central sanctuary or holy place (see *Strong's Exhaustive Concordance of the Bible*, #3485; Vine, *An Expository Dictionary of New Testament Words*, 4:115). Therefore the place of Jewish sacrifice just prior to the midpoint of the seventieth week when it will become the throne room of Antichrist could be a relatively small and unpretentious structure that would take but a short while to build, a timeframe that could be measured in months, not years.

22. James O. Jackson, "The New Germany Flexes Its Muscles," *Time* Magazine, April 13, 1992, pp. 34-36.

23. *Three-nation power base precedes ten-nation coalition*: This author takes the position that Antichrist will overthrow the three Aryan/Japhethite nations (two former Soviet and one Germanic or all three former Soviet — see chapter 7) *before* the other seven nations, already in existence, join their ranks to form the final beast empire of Satan. *Although I am not adamant about that view*, there are several significant reasons for taking it. One is purely logical, the other is scriptural.

The logical reason is that if the ten nations all come together as the final beast empire before the three dominant ones are overthrown by Antichrist, there seems no reason why those three would need to be overthrown, because all ten would already be under his control.

The scriptural reason, of course, is by far the most important. To establish that the three dominant nations are overthrown by Antichrist before the other seven join the three-nation power base, it is helpful to look at two prophetic passages from the Old Testament.

First, a key passage in Ezekiel reveals that the Libyans and Ethiopians will be part of Antichrist's army when he moves against Israel at the midpoint of the seventieth week, obviously suggesting they will be included in the secondary seven nations of his empire:

Son of man, set your face toward Gog of the land of Magog, the prince of Rosh, Meshech, and Tubal, and prophesy against him. . . . And I will turn you about, and put hooks into your jaws, and I will bring you out [from your own homelands], and all your army, horses and horsemen . . . Persia, Ethiopia [Cush], and Put [Libya] with them, all of them with shield and helmet. . . . [And] after many days you will be summoned; in the latter years you will come into the land that is restored from the sword, whose inhabitants have been gathered from many nations to the mountains of Israel. (Ezek. 38:2, 4, 5, 8)

The significant truth here is that Put (the Libyans) and Cush (the Ethiopians) will be among the nations that come with Antichrist against Israel at the midpoint of the seventieth week. It is therefore safe to assume that they are a part of the ten-nation final beast empire of Satan. Yet Daniel reveals that those two nations will be conquered by Antichrist sometime just before the midpoint of the seventieth week.

And he will take action against the strongest of fortresses with the help of a foreign god; he will give great honor to those who acknowledge him, and he will cause them to rule over the many, and will parcel out land for a price. . . . Then he will stretch out his hand against other countries, and the land of Egypt will not escape. But he will gain control over the hidden treasures of gold and silver, and over all the precious things of Egypt; and Libyans [Put] and Ethiopians [Cush] will follow at his heels. (Dan. 11:39, 42, 43)

In the sequence just portrayed, Antichrist appears to have some sort of military base established when he "takes action against" and "gains control" of the Libyans and Ethiopians, which, in the chronology of the passage, would seem to take place just before the "time of distress" (Dan. 12:1), which begins at the midpoint of the seventieth week. If he does use military forces to "take action against" and "gain control" of Libya and Ethiopia, then it is also safe to assume that those military forces will come, at least in part, from the three dominant nations he will overthrow initially before the other nations submit to him.

CHAPTER 10: **Countdown to the End of the Age**

1. The "covenant of death" mentioned here by Isaiah does not relate to a historical pact with ancient Assyria, as some would claim, but rather with the covenant Antichrist makes with Israel, initiating the seventieth week (Dan. 9:27). There is no biblical or extrabiblical record of any such covenant with Assyria, and taking that position is clearly out of context when the entire passage is carefully studied.

   On the other hand, Isaiah's "covenant with death" corresponds perfectly with Antichrist's covenant with Israel, for several reasons. First, the message of Daniel 9:24-27 is indisputably eschatological. And careful study of the original Hebrew text indicates that the context of Isaiah 28 is also eschatological. In fact, the three chapters *immediately preceding* chapter 28 are completely prophetic, related directly to end times.

   Second, the section *immediately following* Isaiah 28:18 (which includes the second mention of the "covenant with death") is also, in itself, eschatological, referring specifically to God's end-time "decisive destruction on all the earth" (v. 22b).

   Third, Isaiah 28:5 is unquestionably millennial, referring to the day when "the Lord of hosts will become a beautiful crown and a glorious diadem to the remnant of His people."

   And finally, Isaiah's "covenant with death" corresponds to Antichrist's covenant with Israel because Isaiah 28:16 ("Behold, I [the Lord] am laying in Zion a stone, a tested stone, a costly cornerstone for the foundation, firmly placed. He who believes in it will not be disturbed" — which is directly between Isaiah's two references to the "covenant with death," vv. 15, 18) is quoted by Peter in direct reference to Jesus Christ (1 Pet. 2:6). In a context of purely Old Testament times, Isaiah 28:16 would be meaningless. But in the context of the seventieth week, it is plainly a promise of protection for the end-time remnant of Israel that will "not be disturbed" (Isa. 28:16b) when God "plows and threshes" the nation of Israel (cf. Amos 9:9).

2. As with so much of prophetic Scripture, Jesus' words to His apostles often had both a "near" application and an additional "far" fulfillment. Such is the case in the following passage which applied to the apostles and other witnesses in the early church, but also has special significance for Christ's end-times witnesses to the nation of Israel in the last days. Thus Jesus warned,

   > "Behold, I send you out as sheep in the midst of wolves; therefore be shrewd as serpents, and innocent as doves. But beware of men; for they will deliver you up to the courts, and scourge you in their synagogues; and you shall even be brought before governors and kings for My sake, as a testimony to them and to the Gentiles. But when they deliver you up, do not become anxious about how or what you will speak; for it shall be given you in that hour what you are to speak." (Matt. 10:16-19)

   Although the witnesses in Israel during the seventieth week will be speaking in the Spirit and in the power of God, their message will be largely rejected and they will suffer ever-increasing persecution. In fact, they will be persecuted for the very reason that these godly and faithful Jews *do* speak God's truth in His name and power. In another near/far admonition, Jesus warns that

"Brother will deliver up brother to death, and a father his child; and children will rise up against parents, and cause them to be put to death. And you will be hated by all on account of My name, but it is the one who has endured to the end who will be saved. But whenever they persecute you in this city, flee to the next; for truly I say to you, you shall not finish going through the cities of Israel, until the Son of Man comes." (Matt. 10:21-23)

The Lord's specific references to "the end" (Matt. 10:22) and to the *coming* of the Son of Man (v. 23) clearly indicate that the warnings and promises in this passage apply specifically to His witnesses during the seventieth week. Because the Son of Man was already present on earth as He spoke those words, He had to have been speaking of His coming again. Several chapters later in the book of Matthew, Christ explains to his disciples that "just as the tares are gathered up and burned with fire, so shall it be at the end of the age" (Matt. 13:40), thereby correlating the end of the age (or just "the end") with the day of the Lord. Because the church is raptured on the same day that the day of the Lord begins (see chapter 17 of this book), the Jewish witnesses are told to continue their witness in Israel right up to "the end" (v. 22), when they would be raptured with the rest of the church. Thus Christ tells them that "you shall not finish going through the cities of Israel, until the Son of Man comes" (v. 23).

3. *The Old Testament use of the word wrath*: The entire seventieth week of Daniel is considered by some scholars to depict God's day-of-the-Lord wrath — largely because some of the events associated with the second, third, and fourth seals superficially correspond to His "four severe judgments" mentioned in Ezekiel 14:21 and to the earlier mention of the Lord's wrath (v. 19). Many other Old Testament passages that depict God's wrath being expressed through war, famine, wild animals or plague are also marshaled to support this view (e.g., Lev. 26:21-28; Num. 11:33; 16:46; 25:8-11; Deut. 11:17; 32:22-25; 2 Chron. 29:8, 9; 36:16, 17; Isa. 9:12; Jer. 14:12; 15:1-9; 16:4, 10, 11; 19:7-9, 15; 21:5-7; 24:10; 44:8, 11-13; Ezek. 4:16, 17; 5:11-17; 6:3, 11, 12; 7:3, 8, 14-19; 8:18; 21:19; 33:19-22; 38:19-22; 39:4). There are two flaws to this thinking. The first is a logical flaw, the second is exegetical.

The logical flaw can best be demonstrated from a very practical illustration. The other day on the way to church I saw two teams competing on a playing field, the object of the game being to hit a ball with the wooden object they held in their hand. With the limited information available, unless specifically identified as a particular athletic event, any conclusion as to the game they were playing would be highly speculative based upon the limited information given. More information is needed. The game they were playing could have been any number of games — baseball, field hockey, croquet, or cricket, to name just a few. More information is needed to know exactly which. Even though war, famine, wild animals and plague correspond to the second, third, and fourth seals, we cannot conclude that these refer to the day of the Lord's wrath (which they do not) until all the data concerning the seventieth week is carefully analyzed. Before that conclusion can be made with confidence, we must first look at the other seals, in particular the first and fifth seals, as this writer agrees that the sixth and seventh seals are both directly associated with the wrath of God, indeed even specifically called "the wrath of the Lamb" (Rev. 6:16, 17).

The first seal represents false christs (Matt. 24:5), and the fifth seal represents the "martyrdom" of God's faithful elect (Rev. 6:9), which is associated with the great tribulation of Antichrist (Matt. 24:9, 10; cf. Mark 13:11, 12). To attribute these events (the primary target being the elect of God [Luke 21:8; Matt. 24:21, 22]) to the wrath of God against His own elect is certainly a "kingdom divided against itself" (Matt. 12:25-27). When.the Pharisees attributed the miracles of Christ to Beelzebul (Matt. 12:22-24), Christ called their sin "blasphemy" (v. 31). What will be the response of Christ to those who attribute the "wrath" of Satan (Rev. 12:12) to the "wrath of God"? Though the two sins cannot be equated (I am not saying pretribulationists are committing the unpardonable sin or are guilty of blasphemy), the latter is nevertheless very serious.

In addition to the logical flaw, however, there is more importantly an exegetical flaw that sustains the logical flaw described above.

There is no doubt that all of those references pertain directly or indirectly to the expression of God's anger or wrath. *But those texts translate four different Hebrew words as "wrath" or "anger." Chemah* (*Strong's*, #2534) connotes hot displeasure or indignation. *Charon* (#2740) means heat or burning anger, and *qetseph* (#7110) simply carries the idea of wrath or indignation. *'Ebrah* (#5678), on the other hand, is by far the strongest of those terms and refers to the overflowing fury of God. It is *only this term* that is specifically used of God's day-of-the-Lord wrath, and its context is always the nations, not Israel.

Zephaniah 1:14, 15, 18 uses *'ebrah* of God's judgmental wrath, but the target of that wrath are the inhabitants of earth at large, not the nation of Israel. Ezekiel 14:19-21, mentioned earlier, perhaps the most often used passage to support the idea that the first four seals involve God's wrath during the day of the Lord, uses the milder term *chemah*. God's wrath is here focused on Israel, but, as noted above, this Hebrew term carries the idea of severe discipline but not condemning wrath. (For similar uses of *chemah*, see Lev. 26:21-28; Num. 25:8-11; 2 Chron. 36:16, 17; Jer. 21:5-7; 44:6-8, 11-13; Ezek. 5:11-17; 6:3, 11, 12; 8:18; 21:17-19.) Another milder form (*qetseph*) is used in Numbers 16:46 and 2 Chron. 29:8, 9. The third mild form (*charon*) is used only in Ezekiel 7:14. Here again this milder form of wrath (*charon*) is associated with God's discipline of Israel by Babylon, by use of sword, plague and famine. And once again there is no mention of false messiahs.

The only place that the strong Hebrew word *'ebrah* is used to directly support the view that the entire seventieth week is a time of God's wrath is in Ezekiel 38:19-22. This writer agrees that this passage is certainly a reference to God's wrath during the day of the Lord. But like Zephaniah 1:14-18, the use of *'ebrah* in the Ezekiel 38 context refers to the wrath of God against *the nations* who have come against Israel in the last days (v. 16), just before His wrath is poured out, making absolutely no reference to false messiahs, famines, or wild animals, the persecution of God's own elect which embody the general focus of the first five seals.

4. *First Thessalonians 5:9 (sōtēria)*: The Greek word *sōtēria* can be translated "deliverance" or "salvation," depending upon how and where the word is used (*Strong's*, #4991). The root word actually means "rescue" or "safety," which would be more in keeping with man's physical deliverance than his spiritual salvation; but actually the word can be translated either way, and that is why the context becomes so important. In the context of 1 Thessalonians 5:9, Paul states that "God has not destined *us* for *wrath*, but for obtaining *salvation*" (emphasis added) — the "us" being a direct reference to the believers within the Thessalonian church to which

this letter was written, and the word "wrath" referring to the day of the Lord, the subject of the preceding eight verses. Therefore, the better translation of the Greek word *"sōtēria"* in this context would be deliverance — that is, the physical deliverance of those believers before the wrath of God at the rapture of the church, as the believers in Thessalonica already possessed spiritual salvation. The next verse confirms the context. "That whether we are *awake* or *asleep*, we may live together with Him" (emphasis added). This concluding thought was initiated in the previous chapter when Paul explained to the Thessalonians that the "hope" of dead believers will be the rapture of the church, when the dead in Christ will receive their resurrection bodies along with the living (1 Thess. 4:13-17).

5. *Quotes on pretribulationism by pretribulationists*: John F. Walvoord states: "The fact is that neither posttribulationism nor pretribulationism is an explicit teaching of the Scriptures. The Bible does not, in so many words, state either" (*The Rapture Question*, 1st. ed. [Findlay, OH: n.p., 1957], p. 148). Earlier in that same work he says, "It is therefore not too much to say that the rapture question is determined more by ecclesiology than eschatology" (p. 16).

   In *The Prophet's Watchword, the Day of the Lord* (unpublished doctoral dissertation [Winona Lake, IN: Grace Theological Seminary, 1981]), Richard Mayhue also notes that neither a pretribulation nor a posttribulation rapture is taught directly in Scripture, and that pretribulationists still have problems to solve in regard to their position (p. 181). He goes on to say, however, that "perhaps the position of pretribulationism is correct although its proof at times has been *logically invalid or at least unconvincing*" (p. 182, emphasis added).

6. *Wheat and tares go into hiding together*: This writer takes the position that believers and unbelievers will go into hiding together to escape the persecution of Antichrist. Many unbelievers, Christian in name only, will follow the true Christians into hiding for many reasons. Family ties, friendship, or church ties would be the most logical reasons. This position becomes more obvious when Christ illustrates His coming with the statement that "on that night there will be two men *in one bed*; one will be taken, and the other will be left" (Luke 17:34, 35, emphasis added). Here we see two men, or two women, peacefully sleeping or working together in one place when one is taken and the other is left. Because this identical illustration is given in connection with the coming of Christ discussed in the Olivet Discourse (Matt. 24:36-41), this is clearly an event that occurs after the great tribulation of Antichrist has already begun (vv. 29-31). Therefore, the mark of Antichrist will separate the world in general (those who worship Antichrist) from those in hiding (those who refuse to worship the beast), the two groups being at enmity with one another. But the illustration given by Christ pictures two individuals at peace with one another, together when Christ comes. As one is taken and the other is left, obviously both have already refused the mark. However, this separation of the genuine from the false does not occur until the coming of Christ.

   This is exactly what Christ taught His disciples in the wheat and tares parable, when He explained that genuine believers should "allow both [the wheat and the tares] to grow together [within the kingdom of heaven] until the time of the harvest [the day of the Lord]; and in the time of the harvest I [Christ] will say to the reapers [His angels], 'First gather up the tares; and bind them in bundles [in preparation] to burn them up; but gather the wheat into my barn'" (Matt. 13:30). In other words, when Christ comes to destroy the world at the day of the Lord, first the reapers will separate the tares that have been planted by Satan in the kingdom of heaven (v. 39) from the wheat. Then the wheat will be put into the barn — i.e., raptured before the wrath of God. And finally the tares will be "gathered up and burned with fire . . . at the end of the age" (v. 40), paralleling the illustration of Noah and the Flood given in Luke 17 and Matthew 24. Again, the tares of this illustration are in the context of the "kingdom of heaven" (v. 24), Christian "look-alikes" but not genuine believers. Only the angels of God can tell the difference. This is why the true believer is warned not to make the separation himself, "lest while you are gathering up the tares, you may root up the wheat with them" (v. 29). Obviously warning would not be necessary if the tares bore the mark.

Finally, in the Olivet Discourse of Christ recorded by Matthew, a parallel illustration is given by Christ that can only be understood if one realizes that believers and unbelievers, wheat and tares, will be together in hiding when Christ returns. Christ begins His parable about the ten virgins by saying that "then the kingdom of heaven will be comparable to ten virgins, who took their lamps, and went out to meet the bridegroom. And five of them were foolish, and five were prudent. For when the foolish took their lamps, they took no oil with them" (25:1-3). Christ concludes the parable by explaining that when "the bridegroom came [again a reference to the coming of Christ] . . . those who were ready [the wheat] went in with him to the wedding feast; and the door was shut. And later the other virgins [the tares] also came, saying, 'Lord, lord, open up for us.' But he answered and said, 'Truly I say to you, I do not know you'" (vv. 10-12).

All three of these passages, when put together, lead this writer to believe that the church that goes into hiding and survives the wrath of Satan during the great tribulation by Antichrist will be made up of both genuine believers (the wheat) and counterfeit believers (the tares). Only the angels will know the difference for sure, and before they put the wheat into the barn at the rapture of the church, they will first separate the real from the false. The fact that there are five prudent virgins and five foolish virgins could indicate that as many as 50 percent of those who go into hiding in the name of Christ could in reality be tares — which is something to think about.

7. *The Babylonian Harlot identification*: There has been much speculation about who the Babylonian Harlot is, almost as much as about who Antichrist will be. Although Scripture provides a number of clues, it does not specifically identify the Harlot in so many words. These clues, however, in the opinion of this author, lead to conclusions which nevertheless trouble me greatly because of many close personal relationships that I have. Although the identity of the Babylonian Harlot is not central to the main thrust of the book, I must be true to my conscience. I will therefore try to present my thinking and logic as clearly and concisely as I can, and will let the reader judge for himself the validity of this author's thinking.

The critical passages which contain the main clues concerning the identity of the Babylonian Harlot are as follows:

"Come here, I shall show you the judgment of the great harlot who sits on many waters, with whom the kings of the earth committed acts of immorality, and those who dwell on the earth were drunk with the wine of her immorality." And he carried me away in the Spirit into a wilderness; and I saw a woman sitting on a scarlet beast, full of blasphemous names, having seven heads and ten horns. And the woman was clothed in purple and scarlet, and adorned with gold and precious stones and pearls . . . and upon her forehead a name was written, a mystery, BABYLON THE GREAT, THE MOTHER OF HARLOTS AND OF THE ABOMINATIONS OF THE EARTH. . . . and I saw the woman drunk with the blood of the saints, and with the blood of the witnesses of Jesus. And when I saw her, I wondered greatly. And the angel said to me, "Why do you wonder? I shall tell you the mystery of the woman. . . . The seven heads are seven mountains on which the woman sits, and they are seven kings. . . . The waters which you saw where the harlot sits, are peoples and multitudes and nations and tongues. . . . And the woman whom you saw is the great city, which reigns over the kings of the earth." (Rev. 17:1-7, 9, 15, 18)

All the clues necessary concerning the identity of the Babylonian Harlot are included in the above passages, although chapter 18 of Revelation provides some additional detail concerning the "great city" associated directly with "the harlot." (See chap. 20, endnote 3.) From this quotation, several dominant characteristics are evident.

(1) *The "woman" is a harlot.* Spiritual harlotry, which is what is in mind in this passage, is always a reference to false gods and their false religions. As one Bible dictionary states: "The words harlot and harlotry are used very often, especially in the prophetic books, to describe idolatry. This figurative use was evidently based on the idea that the Lord was the husband of the nation of Israel (see Jer. 3:20). When the people took their allegiance from Jehovah and gave it to idols instead, He called it 'going a whoring after other gods' (KJV) or 'playing the harlot with other gods' (ASV). This expression occurs rather frequently in the prophetic books, and a few times in other books. Also, this spiritual harlotry is mentioned several times in the Book of Revelation, chapter 17" (*The Zondervan Pictorial Bible Dictionary*, Merrill C. Tenney, general editor [Grand Rapids, MI.: Zondervan, n.d.], p. 336).

In other words, the Babylonian Harlot represents, in part, *a false religious system that competes with the true gospel of Christ.*

(2) The woman not only represents an actual false religion, *but a false religion that has its roots in Babylon.* Although this religion has found many expressions through the centuries, it has embodied one religious common denominator that has not only threatened Judaism, but has dominated much of the world since its inception in Babylon. This common denominator is some form of mother/child or mother/goddess (queen of heaven) worship. As explained by the English cleric and scholar Alexander Hislop:

> The Babylonians, in their popular religion, supremely worshipped a Goddess Mother and a Son, who was represented in pictures and in images as an infant or child in his mother's arms. From Babylon, this worship of the Mother and the Child spread to the ends of the earth. In Egypt, the Mother and the Child were worshipped under the names of Isis and Osiris. In India, even to this day, as Isi and Iswara; in Asia, as Cybele and Deoius; in Pagan Rome, as Fortuna and Jupiter-puer, or Jupiter, the boy; in Greece, as Ceres, the Great Mother, with the babe at her breast, or as Irene, the goddess of Peace, with the boy Plutus in her arms; and even in Thibet, in China, and Japan, the Jesuit missionaries were astonished to find the counterpart of Madonna and her child . . . devoutly worshipped. . . . (*The Two Babylons*, 2nd American ed. [Neptune, NJ: Loizeaux Brothers, Inc., n.d.], pp. 20, 21)

In other words, in summary of points 1 and 2, the Babylonian Harlot will be *a false religious system* that traces its roots back to Babylon, of which *mother/child or mother/goddess worship* will play an important part.

(3) *This false religious system will sit upon many waters,* which we are told represent peoples, multitudes, nations, and tongues. In other words, this false religious system will be worldwide, playing a dominant role in the lives of many individuals from one end of the world to the other.

(4) As a dominant religious factor of people worldwide, *it will also have political clout,* so that the Harlot "reigns over the kings of the earth."

(5) This false religious system *will vehemently oppose biblical Christianity* — i.e., it will be "drunk with the blood of the saints and with the witnesses of Jesus."

(6) This false religious system *will also represent "the great city, which reigns over the kings of the earth."* With regard to this point we need to make a careful distinction. We have already seen that the Babylonian Harlot is a false religious system that dominates the world, promoting, in this author's opinion, the mother/child worship that originated in Babylon. But we are also told that it is a "great" or "strong city" (See Rev. 17:18; 18:10, 18, 19, 21). Obviously, a particular city by itself does not classify as a harlot, does not rule over the kings of the earth, and does not kill the saints and the witnesses of Jesus. But a city closely aligned to a particular religious system can do all those things. Thus the Harlot represents both the false religious system promoting the mother/child worship as well as a specific city that specifically identifies with this false religious belief. Together the ideology and the people of the city control many kings of the world.

(7) And, we are told, the seven heads upon which the Harlot sits are not only the seven kings that will provide the leadership for the first seven beast empires, but that they also represent *seven hills upon which this particular great city,* with its religious affiliation to the Harlot, sits.

This particular system has been characterized since the time of Babel with mother/child or mother/goddess (queen of heaven) worship. Even Israel was specifically warned against worshiping the queen of heaven (Jer. 44:16-19, 24-28), with dire consequences for those who disobeyed. Over the centuries this system has also been characterized as being at special enmity with God's chosen nation of Israel, as well as with all the spiritual descendants of Abraham, Jews and Gentiles alike.

When we look especially at the last fifteen hundred years, the facts of history clearly indicate a strong correlation between the characteristics of the Babylonian Harlot, as described above, and the beliefs and practices of the Roman Catholic Church that sits upon the seven hills of Rome. Truly, if there were ever a religious ideology tied uniquely to a city, Roman Catholicism and the city of Rome fit the bill. But in like manner it is also interesting to note that Eastern Orthodoxy, which dominates much of Eastern Europe, not only venerates Mary but originally was closely aligned to and promoted from the Turkish city of Istanbul (formerly Constantinople), Constantine's "new Rome." Like the city of Rome, Constantinople was built upon seven hills and is a seaport. Throughout the Middle Ages and well into the seventeenth century (during the Crusades and Inquisition), Catholicism was notorious for its vicious persecution and slaughter of Bible-believing Christians. Similarly the veneration of Mary has been central to Catholic dogma for many centuries. In addition to this, since the fourth century Catholicism has dominated most of the European nations, through the

Roman church in the west and the Byzantine church in the east — in a direct parallel to the description in Revelation which depicts the Babylonian Harlot as *riding on the final beast empire* with its "seven heads and ten horns."

Having said this, however, a number of careful distinctions need to be made. First, I want to make as clear as humanly possible that the Babylonian Harlot is not the laity or even some of the priestly constituency of the Roman or Byzantine Church. It is instead the ungodly system that dominates its leadership. I have many dear friends who are Roman Catholic, and my sincerest desire is not to give them cause to take personal offense at the positions stated here. Nor do I claim that there are no Christians in either of these religious systems that venerate Mary as the queen of heaven. At the same time, every Bible-believing Christian must recognize that Roman and Byzantine dogma includes much that is in serious contradiction to Scripture — which, of course, is what the Reformation was all about. Thus my prayer is that the material included here, as understood in the context of the end times, will encourage my Roman Catholic friends to carefully examine the system of Catholicism in the light of God's own Word, the Bible, and as far as possible to remove themselves from that system (or from any other system that does not square with God's Word).

Second, we cannot say that the Roman or the Byzantine Church is or will be the Babylonian Harlot per se. The distinction here is that the Babylonian Harlot is a false religious system that *embodies something more comprehensive than any one specific religious system* and that no specific religious system (whether Catholic, Protestant, ecumenical, or otherwise) presently corresponds, or will in the future correspond, directly to the Babylonian Harlot. What we may conclude, however, is the following: To the extent that the Catholic religious system (or any other religious system) affirms the characteristics of the Babylonian Harlot, such a system will certainly be incorporated into the final false religious system represented by the Babylonian Harlot in the book of Revelation. Roman Catholicism and Eastern (Byzantine) Orthodoxy, although sharing the same beginnings, are separate and distinct religious systems today, both of which venerate Mary as queen of heaven and both of which operate through cities seated on seven hills. Both could therefore be a part of the Babylonian Harlot that will associate with Antichrist in the last days, the common denominator being their elevation of Mary alongside of or in place of Jesus Christ.

As stated above, the primary focus of the religious system represented by the Babylonian Harlot is mother/child worship and the related idea of mother/goddess or queen of heaven worship. It is interesting to note how widespread these ideas are in our culture today. For example, *Time* Magazine recently carried a cover story on "The Search for Mary," which made the following observations: "Among Roman Catholics, the Madonna is recognized not only as the mother of God but, also according to modern Popes, as the Queen of the Universe, Queen of Heaven, Seat of Wisdom and even Spouse of the Holy Spirit.... [This includes] the notion that she as well as Jesus was born without sin and that her sufferings at the crucifixion were so great that she participated with her Son in the redemption of humanity [p. 62] ... and that therefore she should be recognized as the Co-Redeemer [p. 66]...." *Time* comments further that "A grass-roots revival of faith in the Virgin is taking place worldwide. Millions of worshippers are flocking to her shrines, many of them young people" (Richard Ostling, *Time*, December 30, 1991, pp. 62-66).

Related to this, *Time* Magazine also chronicles the growing spiritual movement of "goddess worship." In particular *Time* links the "goddess resurgence" to the ecology movement and "worshippers of mother earth." "Though such ancient goddesses as Isis and Astarte are often invoked," *Time* reports, "most worship occurs in the name of a vague generic 'Goddess,' often depicted as Mother Earth or Gaia in line with environmental awareness." *Time* continues, "Despite Christianity's centuries of opposition to paganism, some old-line churches are opening up to the Goddess [sic]. A witch teaches in an institute at the Roman Catholic Holy Names College in California. A book by two United Methodist pastors proposes experimental Bible readings about the crucifixion that replace Jesus with Sophia (Wisdom), a name for the divine personality used by Goddess-minded [sic] Christians" (*Time*, May 6, 1992, p. 73). In addition to this, we might add the widespread presence of goddess worship in the New Age Movement (see further chapter 9).

Although we do not know what specific form the false religion of the Babylonian Harlot will take in the last days, we do know that the groundwork for its acceptance is already being laid by a growing revival of mother/child worship, *especially within the Roman and Byzantine churches*, and through the related widespread influence of mother/goddess worship in the environmental and New Age Movements. This predisposition will surely become the easy prey of the Babylonian Harlot in the last days, which *Antichrist will use* to establish his final beast empire.

8. In the Olivet Discourse of Christ, recorded in Luke, Christ refers to the pestilence of the fourth seal as plague. Scripture does not specify the exact type of pestilence (or plague) that God will permit to run rampant during the fourth seal, except that it will be deadly. The current most dreaded and deadly disease in the world is that of AIDS (Acquired Immune Deficiency Syndrome), which has the potential to destroy large segments of society in virtually every part of the world.

CHAPTER 11: **Antichrist Revealed**

1. *"The faithful woman" who flees identification*: When we look at the description of the 144,000 given to us in Revelation 14, it becomes apparent that "the woman that flees to the wilderness" (Rev. 12:6) and the faithful 144,000 are one and the same. Speaking of the 144,000, John goes on to say, "These are the ones who have not been defiled with women [spiritual chastity], for they have kept themselves [spiritually] chaste. These are the ones who follow the Lamb wherever He goes. These have been purchased from among men as *first fruits* to God and to the Lamb" (v. 4, emphasis added). For several reasons this description of the faithful 144,000 perfectly describes "the woman that flees." First, and most importantly, "the woman that flees" does not become saved until later, when she is in the wilderness (Ezek. 20:37). But the passage is quite clear that this wilderness remnant is saved *before* the house of Israel (Ezek. 20:39). Therefore, "the woman that flees" to the wilderness is by definition the faithful first fruits of unbelieving Israel who enter into the seventieth week, the surviving remainder of the nation not coming to Christ until after the seventieth week is complete (Rom. 11:25, 26; Dan. 9:24).

Secondly, the 144,000 are described as those who have "not been defiled with women, for they have kept themselves chaste" — in this context meaning spiritually chaste, not morally. In other words, they have not sold out to Antichrist, especially during the first half of the seventieth week when most of the nation apostacizes to the covenant maker (see endnote 3). This is a perfect description of "the faithful woman" who "fled into the wilderness where she had a place prepared by God, so that there she might be nourished for one thousand two hundred and sixty days" (Rev. 12:6), thereby refusing the leadership of Antichrist *before* he shows his true intentions at the midpoint of the seventieth week. Therefore, in this writer's opinion the faithful 144,000 and "the woman that flees" must, by definition, be one and the same group. The reference to 144,000 only indicates "how many" and "which tribes" will refuse the covenant with Antichrist, flee to the wilderness, survive the purge of God (Ezek. 20:38), and be brought into the bond of the covenant (v. 37) while in the wilderness.

2. In the Olivet Discourse Christ specifically warns those fleeing to the wilderness, "Woe to those who are with child and to those who nurse babes in those days" (Matt. 24:19). So does the 144,000 refer to just men ("who have not been defiled with women" [Rev. 14:4] — see endnote 3), or does it refer to the men and their families? Scripture often identifies the entire family with the father, and many groups such as clans, tribes, or large multitudes are numbered according to the male "heads of households." On one occasion Moses referred to "the sons of Israel" as numbering "about six hundred thousand men on foot, aside from children" (Exod. 12:37). When God commanded Moses to make a census of the Israelites, He gave explicit instructions about the numbering method to be used: "Take a census of all the congregation of the sons of Israel, by their families, by their fathers' households, according to the number of names, every male, head by head" (Num. 1:2). It seems perfectly legitimate, therefore, to consider the figure of 144,000 as representing the men of Israel, with an additional large number of women and children. An alternative would be to consider 144,000 to be single men only, or men who are given protection but not their families. On the other hand, the two passages describing the 144,000 make no mention directly of their gender, so the 144,000 could be the total size of the group, including men, women, and children. The latter is the position of this writer.

3. *Revelation 14:4 — kept themselves chaste*: Most Jews in Israel will have agreed to the covenant, but some will not participate in the apostasy during the first half of the seventieth week. Those who refuse to join in the covenant with Antichrist, even before they know his true identity, are doubtless "the ones who have not been defiled with women, for they have kept themselves [spiritually] chaste. These are the ones who follow the Lamb wherever He goes. These have been purchased from among men as first fruits to God and to the Lamb" (Rev. 14:4). The references to not being "defiled with women" and keeping "themselves chaste" doubtless represents *spiritual* even more than moral purity.

In the following passage, Isaiah speaks of the righteous man who "perishes" but yet is "taken away from evil [and] enters into peace" (v. 1). Then he speaks of the "sons of a sorceress, offspring of an adulterer and prostitute" (v. 3) who have made a wicked "agreement for yourselves with them" (v. 8) — that is, with the beast empire of Antichrist at the signing of the covenant with death. In context this reference to "an adulterer and prostitute" is a reference to their spirituality, not to their personal morality.

> The righteous man perishes, and no man takes it to heart; and devout men are taken away, while no one understands. For the righteous man is taken away from evil, he enters into peace; they rest in their beds, each one who walked in his upright way. But come here, you sons of a sorceress, offspring of an adulterer and a prostitute. Against whom do you jest? Against whom do

you open wide your mouth and stick out your tongue? Are you not children of rebellion, offspring of deceit? . . . And behind the door and the doorpost you have set up your sign; indeed, far removed from Me, you have uncovered yourself; and have gone up and made your bed wide. And you have made an agreement for yourselves with them, you have loved their bed, you have looked on their manhood. (Isa. 57:1-4, 8)

4. *Daniel 12:1 ('amad):* See *Strong's*, #5975; which, along with the KJV, gives the definition of *'amad* as "stand up." On the other hand, Rashi, one of Israel's greatest scholars, understood "stand up" to literally mean "stand still" (Judah J. Slotki, *Daniel, Ezra, Nehemiah* [London: The Soncino Press, 1978], p. 101). For this reason, the *Midrash*, commenting on this verse, says, "The holy one, Blessed be He, said to Michael, 'You are silent? You do not defend my children'" (Ruth Rabbah I). See other NASB texts where the same Hebrew word is used: 1 Sam. 9:27 ("remain standing"); 2 Sam. 2:28 ("halted"); 2 Kings 4:6 ("stopped"); Judg. 7:21 ("stood in his place"). See also *Theological Wordbook of the Old Testament*, *'amad* (#1637), "stand, remain, endure"; and *Hebrew and English Lexicon of the Old Testament*, 764a.2a. Cf. "stand still, stop, cease moving" (Josh. 10:13; Hab. 3:11; 1 Sam. 9:27; 2 Sam. 2:28; Nah. 2:9); "stop flowing" (2 Kings 4:6), p. 764a, 2d "stop, cease doing" (Gen. 26:35; 30:9; 2 Kings 13:18; Jonah 1:15), p. 764c, 6a.

The verb *'amad* in Daniel 12:1 is ordinarily rendered as "will arise," "will stand up," or the like. But such a rendering makes little sense in the context of what immediately follows in that verse: "And there will be a time of distress such as never occurred since there was a nation until that time; and at that time your people, everyone who is found written in the book, will be rescued."

In the grammatical order of the Hebrew text, as reflected in most English versions, "the time of distress" occurs *between* Michael's "arising" and the rescue of the people. In other words, first Michael arises, next comes an unparalleled time of distress for God's people, and then His people are rescued. But why, one wonders, would the "great prince who stands guard over" Israel arise *before* his people are about to be persecuted but not raise a hand to help them until much later?

The angel who speaks to Daniel in this vision has already told the prophet, "There is no one who stands firmly with me against these forces [the demonic "prince" who empowered Persia] except Michael your prince" (Dan. 10:21; cf. v. 13). This passage describes the ministry of Michael as that of restraint. The Hebrew phrase translated "stands firmly . . . against" has the basic meaning of being strong, holding fast, and restraining. In other words, it is Michael who restrains the demonic forces in their unrelenting attacks against Israel. What, then, would be the point of calling attention to Michael's arising if all he did was to look on as God's people are tormented?

But as demonstrated at the beginning of this endnote, what most translators translate "will arise" for this particular passage in question can equally be translated "stand still." In Joshua 10:13 that same root term is twice translated "stopped" in both the *New American Standard Bible* and the *New International Version* — "So the sun stood still, and the moon *stopped*, until the nation avenged themselves of their enemies. Is it not written in the book of Jashar? And the sun *stopped* in the middle of the sky, and did not hasten to go down for about a whole day" (NASB, emphasis added).

In complete agreement with the noted Jewish rabbi Rashi, this writer takes the position that "stand still" instead of "stand up" seems the most appropriate translation for Daniel 12:1. In other words, Michael will not stand up, or arise, in preparation for later defending Israel, but rather will "stand still" or "stop" doing what he normally does — that is, he will *stop* his activity of restraining the demonic forces of Satan thereby allowing Antichrist to reveal his true identity to the world and to vent his full fury on God's people. As soon as Michael *stops* his work of restraint, the "time of distress such as never occurred since there was a nation" will begin.

In light of that translation and interpretation of Daniel 12:1, Paul's meaning in a remarkably similar passage in 2 Thessalonians becomes much clearer: "And you know what restrains him now, so that in his time he may be revealed. For the mystery of lawlessness is already at work; only he who now restrains will do so until he is taken out of the way" (2:6, 7). From the context, we know that "him" in verse 6 refers back to Antichrist, "the man of lawlessness . . . the son of destruction" (v. 3). In comparing those passages, it seems more than reasonable to identify the restrainer in 2 Thessalonians 2:7 ("he who restrains") as Michael, the restrainer of Daniel 12:1.

Further comparison shows that Daniel's reference to a "time of distress such as never occurred since there was a nation until that time" is almost identical to Jesus' description of the "great tribulation, such as has not occurred since the beginning of the world until now, nor ever shall" (Matt. 24:21), placing the timing of both of these passages at the midpoint of the seventieth week, as the restrainer is removed just prior to the revealing of Antichrist, when he "exalts himself above every so-called god or object of worship, so that he takes his seat in the temple of God . . ." (2 Thess. 2:4).

5. On first reading it may seem as if "the apostasy comes first" and that immediately thereafter "the man of lawlessness [Antichrist] is revealed" (see 2 Thess. 2:3), even before the restrainer is removed. It is clear from verses 7 and 8 ("He who now restrains will do so until he is taken out of the way. And then that lawless one will be revealed . . ."), however, that verse 3 provides an abbreviated overview of the sequence and that "he who restrains" is taken away *before* the "lawless one [Antichrist] is revealed" (v. 3) and "exalts himself" (v. 4).

6. *First — Egyptian.* The Egyptian ruler would be either the pharaoh whom Scripture identifies only as a "new king [who] arose over Egypt, who did not know Joseph" and who began the enslavement and persecution of the children of Israel who had come to dwell there under Joseph (see Exod. 1:8-12) or the pharaoh who opposed Moses and tried to make the Israelites return to Egypt after the Exodus began (see Exod. 4:21). In the first instance secular history would suggest that pharaoh to be Amenhotep I (c. 1546-1525) or Thutmoses I (c. 1525-1508). In the second instance he would most probably be Amenhotep II (c. 1450-1425). In any case, his ancestry was Hamitic, through Mizraim.

Second — Assyrian. The ruler of Assyria would be Tiglath-pileser III, or his son and successor Shalmaneser V, who reigned from 727-722 and is mentioned by name in 2 Kings 17:3-6. His ancestry was Semitic, through Asshur.

Third — Babylonian. The Babylonian Empire ruler is specifically identified as Nebuchadnezzar, the statue's head of gold (Dan. 2:28, 37, 38). His ancestry either was Semitic, through Arpachshad (see Gen. 10:22) or Hamitic, through Cush and Nimrod.

Fourth — Medo-Persian. Neither Scripture nor secular history or archaeology reveal for sure who the Medo-Persian beast empire king may have been (who, in particular, tried to destroy the nation of Israel), but the book of Esther would seem to allow for that leader to have been Haman. Although he was never crowned, the actual king, Ahasuerus, temporarily delegated virtual kingly authority to Haman by giving him the royal signet ring and authorizing Haman's request to exterminate the Jews, whom he had falsely accused of treason (Esth. 3:8-11). Haman is called a descendant of Hammedatha, the Agagite (Esth. 3:1). Agag was king of the Amalekites, who were descendants of Esau (Gen. 36:12), making Haman a Semite. On the other hand, King Ahasuerus (c. 486-465; that name is a Hebrew transliteration of the Persian Khshayarsha; *Xerxes* in Greek) was Persian and therefore a Japhethite through Tiras.

Fifth — Greek. The Greek beast empire ruler was either Alexander the Great, as suggested by Daniel 8:5-8 and 11:13, or Antiochus Epiphanes (c. 175-163), as suggested by Daniel 8:9-14 and 11:21-35. Antiochus seems by far to be the more likely candidate because he is so clearly a type of Antichrist. Like Haman, he was not the most powerful leader in his nation, but he was, also like Haman, the greatest enemy of God's people Israel. His ancestry was Japhethite, through Javan.

7. See Allan Massie, *The Caesars* (New York: Franklin Watts, 1984), p. 171; *The Encyclopedia Britannica*, "Rome, Ancient, Emperors."

8. William Shirer, *The Rise and Fall of the Third Reich* (New York: Simon and Schuster, 1960), p. 5.

9. (New York: Macmillan, 1947), p. 205. Concerning the disposal of Hitler's body, Trevor-Roper gives this remarkable account:

> Linge afterwards told one of the secretaries that they [the bodies of Hitler and Eva Braun] had been burned, as Hitler had ordered, "till nothing remained"; but it is doubtful whether such total combustion could have taken place. 180 litres of petrol, burning slowly on a sandy bed, would char the flesh and dissipate the moisture of the bodies, leaving only an unrecognizable and fragile remainder; but the bones would withstand the heat. These bones have never been found. Perhaps they were broken up and mixed with the other bodies, the bodies of soldiers killed in the defense of the Chancellery, and the body of Fegelein, which were also buried in the garden. The Russians have occasionally dug in that garden, and many such bodies have been unearthed there. Perhaps, as Guensche is said to have stated, the ashes were collected in a box and conveyed out of the Chancellery. Or perhaps no elaborate explanation is necessary. Perhaps such investigations as have been made have been somewhat perfunctory. Investigators who left Hitler's engagement-diary unobserved in his chair for five months may easily have overlooked other relics which were more deliberately concealed. Whatever the explanation, Hitler achieved his last ambition. Like Alaric, buried secretly under the riverbed of Busento, the modern destroyer of mankind is now immune from discovery.

10. As an aside, this author believes that if Christ's offer of the kingdom had been accepted by the nation of Israel at His first coming, Christ would still have been "cut off" and the city and sanctuary destroyed (Dan. 9:26), but the interval between the sixty-ninth and seventieth weeks would have been a matter of years, not centuries. Nero then would have become the Antichrist of the final beast empire of Satan, and the seventh beast empire described in Revelation 17 after the *Diaspora* had begun would have never become reality.

11. As established earlier, in this writer's opinion the seventh beast empire could

have been none other than the Third Reich (third empire), established and ruled by Adolf Hitler. In that dictator's thinking, the Second Reich was the Germanic empire created by Kaiser Bismarck in 1871 and the First Reich was the Holy Roman Empire (*Encyclopedia Britannica*, 15th ed., 8:119). It is also interesting that the German word *kaiser* and the Russian *czar* are both derived from the Latin *caesar* (*Webster's Ninth New Collegiate Dictionary*).

Hitler also had a close relationship to corrupt elements in the Roman Catholic Church, which he may one day use again to his own ends. In his book *Roman Catholicism*, Loraine Boettner observes: "Let it also be noted that both Hitler and Mussolini were Roman Catholics, but that despite their crimes against humanity, neither was ever excommunicated, nor even severely censored, by the Roman Church" ([Philadelphia: Presbyterian and Reformed Pub. Co., 1980], p. 437).

It is also of interest that in Midrashic literature, Gog is referred to by a Hebrew term that is a variant of Romulus, who with his twin brother Remus was the legendary cofounder of Rome in the eighth century B.C. (*The ArtScroll Tanach Series*, Vol. 2 [Brooklyn, NY: Mesorah Pub., 1980], p. 581). With Gog coming from Magog, clearly the Germanic ancestry of Japheth, and tied to Romulus, the legendary founder of Rome, we again find this German-Roman connection perfectly embodied in Adolf Hitler.

In a further description of Antichrist, Daniel makes an interesting observation about the man who will lead the final beast empire of Satan: "He will honor a god of fortresses, a god whom his fathers did not know" (Dan. 11:38). The "god of fortresses" can only refer to a god, as it were, of military might. Yet Daniel states that this will be "a god whom his [Antichrist's] fathers did not know." After the decisive and unconditional World War II victory over Germany and Hitler's suicide, that nation was completely stripped of military power. The armies that developed in East Germany were controlled by the Warsaw Pact under the U.S.S.R., and the small defensive army of West Germany was under the control of the North Atlantic Treaty Organization (NATO). In other words, since 1945 Germany has not possessed an offensive military, not even after its reunification in 1990.

12. Wythe Williams in collaboration with Albert Parry, *Riddle of the Reich* (New York: Prentice-Hall, 1941), p. 142.

13. *Ibid.*, p. 143. As seen from the publisher's introduction, these observations are based on highly reliable sources by men with the highest credentials:

> As main sources for this book, Mr. Wythe Williams and his collaborator Dr. Albert Parry have used reports from inside Germany and other European countries, regularly reaching them, and bearing upon the economic, social, and political conditions and events within the Reich and Nazi-overrun territories. To a certain extent they also relied upon the letters and other documents gathered by the American Friends of German Freedom and the American Committee for International Information. To both these organizations the authors express their lively appreciation. . . .
>
> For much of their material, Mr. Wythe Williams and his collaborator leaned upon the years of their work in the field of international relations. Mr. Williams' experiences with the Axis range from a personal interview with Mussolini to having the distinction of being the first American correspondent to be expelled from Nazi Germany. Dr. Albert Parry served from March, 1939, to September, 1940, as editorial and research director of the American Council

Against Nazi Propaganda, founded by the late Professor William E. Dodd, former United States Ambassador to Germany, on his return to America. He holds a Ph.D. in history from the University of Chicago, and is the author of several books and numerous magazine articles.

14. Louis Pauels and Jacques Bergler, *The Morning of the Magicians* (New York: Stein and Day, 1964). See also Robert Payne, *The Life and Death of Adolf Hitler* (New York: Praeger, 1973), esp. pp. ix, 429, 430, 572, 574.

15. *The Morning of the Magicians*, p. 172.

16. *Ibid.*, p. 176. Hermann Rauschning was a Nazi political leader and president of the Nazi Danzig Senate from 1933-34. See further Joachim C. Fest, *Hitler*, trans. Richard and Clara Winston (New York: Harcourt Brace Jovanovich, 1974), pp. 205, 430, 438.

17. *Ibid.*, p. 192.

18. *Ibid.*, pp. 178, 179.

19. *Ibid.*, p. 195.

20. *Hitler m'a dit* [*Hitler Told Me*], pp. 284, 285, quoted in Jean-Michel Angebert, *The Occult and the Third Reich*, trans. Lewis A. M. Sumberg (New York: Macmillan, 1974), p. 234.

21. P. 204.

22. "The World at War" series on World War II, Vol. 21, by Thames Hamilton Television.

CHAPTER 12: **Counting the Cost**

1. *Revelation 13:14-15 (image)*: In a telephone conversation with Dr. Robert Gundry, a noted New Testament and Greek scholar, he confirmed my position that the Greek text could be interpreted either of the two ways just mentioned. In fact, his own position for some years has been that multiple images of the beast will be made and that everybody will be commanded to worship these images that will be set up for worship in various localities. He went on to say that the Greek term translated "image" in this text can be taken (and here is best taken) as a collective singular, like our English words *crowd* or *people*. That collective noun could therefore represent a great number of separate images. He also noted that the context of the next verse (13:16), which clearly uses the collective singular of "hand," is perfectly in keeping with the preceding collective singular use of "image."

Dr. Gundry strongly emphasized interpreting this passage in light of the culture of John's day. In order to control the diverse peoples and nations of their vast empire and to promote some degree of unification, the Romans erected statues of, and temples to, the caesar, or emperor, in the cities of the lands they conquered and demanded worship of those statues. Certain historical records report that some priests in pagan temples employed a form of ventriloquism to make it appear that the worshiped statues themselves were speaking.

2. *Pneuma*. See James Strong, *Strong's Exhaustive Concordance of the Bible* (Nashville: Abingdon, 1890), #4151; W. E. Vine, *An Expository Dictionary of New Testament Words* (Westwood, NJ: Revell, 1940), 4:62; W. F. Arndt and F. W. Gingrich, *A Greek-English Lexicon of the New Testament* (Chicago: University of Chicago Press, 1957), p. 680.

3. *Revelation 12:17 — Why does Satan persecute the woman's offspring?*: "The rest of her offspring" refers to the true church (see chapter 13, endnote 3). That the church will be present and persecuted during the great tribulation by Antichrist is

absolutely clear from Scripture (see chapters 16 and 17), but Satan's motive for that persecution (knowing that the church will not be a part of the millennial kingdom), other than having great hatred for *all* the people and things of God, is not made clear. Obviously his primary target must be Israel because it is to her that the millennial promises have been given. Perhaps he will think the church will not be raptured before the end of the seventieth week and, in order to be certain, he must destroy all Gentile believers. Otherwise, Satan might reason, they would also become citizens of Christ's millennial kingdom, thereby thwarting his plan to annihilate all potential subjects of the divine kingdom that God has predicted will replace Satan's rule over earth. Or, not being omniscient, he may not know exactly who is Jewish and who is not. Since the great *Diaspora* that began in A.D. 70 and was completed in 132, Jews have been scattered throughout the world, and many have married Gentiles and so lost their original racial and religious identity. Satan may be motivated by the same desperation that drove Herod to order the murder of "all the male children who were in Bethlehem and in all its environs, from two years old and under" to make sure that the predicted newborn King would not be missed (Matt. 2:16; cf. vv. 4-6).

4. *Revelation 3:10 (hupomonē)*: The Greek word, *hupomonē*, translated "perseverance" in this verse (Rev. 3:10), is closely related to the phrase "the hour of testing," found in the same verse. *Hupomonē* has the basic meaning of hiding under (Vine, 3:167), of patient enduring and fortitude (Arndt, p. 854), or of remaining behind. Within the sphere of God's grace, it is the faithful believer's keeping of "My [Christ's] perseverance" that brings believers through "the hour of testing." The hour of testing, as commonly accepted by most conservative evangelical scholars, is the great tribulation by Antichrist. See endnote 2, chapter 2. Unfortunately many interpreters, because of their pretribulational bias, seem to avoid dealing with the full meaning of and implications of *hupomonē*. This specific word is used four times with regard to the churches of Revelation 2 and 3 (2:2, 3, 19; 3:10). The only other uses of this word, *after* its use in connection with the churches, is in Revelation 13:10 and 14:12, where it is directly related to believers' not taking the mark of the beast.

5. The Greek *pisteuō* means "to be persuaded of and have confidence in" and carries the idea of "reliance upon, not mere credence" (Vine, *An Expository Dictionary of New Testament Words*, 1:116).

6. *The timing of the two witnesses' ministry*: Scripture clearly tells us when the two witnesses live in relationship to the seventieth week. As their ministry is for three and a half years, it seems safe to assume that they minister on earth during either the first half or the second half of the seventieth week — not a forty-two month ministry somewhere in between the first and second half of the seventieth week, overlapping both halves. By knowing in advance when they will die (Rev. 11:7-10), it can be shown without question that their ministry is during the second half of the seventieth week if sequences of Revelation are taken literally. The troublesome part of taking Revelation literally, in particular as it pertains to the time of ministry of the two witnesses, is that this literal interpretation of Revelation forces the bowl judgments and Armageddon to occur *after* the seventieth week is complete. As will be demonstrated in chapter 19 of this volume, that is *exactly* the biblical order.

For several reasons, then, the two witnesses must live and minister during the second half of the seventieth week, while Antichrist and his eighth beast empire are demanding the worship and allegiance of the world. One must arrive at this conclusion for the following reasons:

First, the sixth seal will cut short the great tribulation by Antichrist (Matt. 24:22, 29), which therefore must occur *before* the seventieth week is complete but after the middle of the seventieth week, when his great tribulation begins. Consequently, the seventh seal (which follows the sixth seal) and the immediately ensuing trumpet judgments associated with it must also occur after the midpoint of the seventieth week.

Second, the two witnesses are said to have ministered "twelve hundred and sixty days" (Rev. 11:3) — three and a half years; they die after the sixth trumpet judgment (9:13; 11:7), the second woe (9:12), but are resurrected before the seventh trumpet (11:11, 15), the third woe (11:14). Because a literal interpretation of Revelation demands that the trumpet judgments come out of the seventh seal, which by definition must occur during the second half of the seventieth week, the two witnesses therefore must live during the second half of the week. The only assumption this author makes is that the three and a half years that the two witnesses minister is parallel to the three and a half years that make up the last half of the seventieth week. In light of how Revelation and Daniel continually refer to this specific time distinction, always in relation to either the first half or the second half of the seventieth week, this assumption has integrity. With regard to the two witnesses, then, the 1,260 days could only, by definition, refer to the second half of the seventieth week, and for that reason the two witnesses will die at the very end of the seventieth week and will be resurrected three and half days later.

7. Although the first witness is almost certainly the prophet Elijah returned to earth, the identity of the second witness is not as clear. It would seem, however, that Moses is the most likely candidate. At the transfiguration Moses and Elijah appeared with a glorified Christ before the three disciples (Matt. 17:3). In his sermon at Pentecost Peter reminded his mostly Jewish hearers: "Moses said, '*The Lord God shall raise up for you a prophet like me* from your brethren; to Him *you shall give heed in everything He says to you. And it shall be that every soul that does not heed that prophet shall be utterly destroyed from among the people*'" (Acts 3:22, 23, emphasis added; cf. Deut. 18:15, 19).

We know that Moses died alone and was buried by the Lord Himself "in the valley in the land of Moab, opposite Beth-peor; but no man knows his burial place to this day" (Deut. 34:6). We also know that the archangel Michael, the restrainer of Satan and great protector of Israel, "disputed with the devil and argued about the body of Moses" (Jude 9). The bodies of the great patriarchs Abraham, Isaac, and Jacob were interred in Hebron, and as far as we know from Scripture, their bodies were never of interest to Satan. If Moses is to be one of those two end-time witnesses, it is obvious why Satan would want to steal his body and attempt to prevent a resurrected Moses from appearing with Elijah.

The prophet Malachi links those two Old Testament saints in one of his end-time predictions, saying, "Remember the law of Moses My servant, even the statutes and ordinances which I commanded him in Horeb for all Israel. Behold, I am going to send you Elijah the prophet before the coming of the great and terrible day of the Lord" (Mal. 4:4, 5).

A final argument for identifying the second witness as Moses is the fact that he was the human instrument through whom God revealed His law to Israel. Scripture itself frequently refers to the law of God as the law of Moses. The Old

Testament as a whole is often called the law and the prophets, and Moses was the great law-giver and Elijah arguably the greatest prophet.

Based on the text, "But as for you, go your way to the end; then you will enter into rest and rise again for your allotted portion at the end of the age" (Dan. 12:13), some interpreters believe that the second of the two witnesses could be Daniel.

CHAPTER 13: **The Great Tribulation by Antichrist**

1. *"The woman's" identification*: The woman represents the unsaved, natural line of Abraham that exists at the midpoint of the seventieth week and that refuses to worship Antichrist. When Satan is cast down to earth, "he persecuted the woman . . ." (Rev. 12:13). He obviously has no need to persecute those of the natural line of Abraham that take his mark and worship his image. The woman will consist of two groups of Israelites. Those who heed the warning of the Jewish witnesses and flee to the wilderness in Edom (Rev. 12:6) — "the faithful woman" — and those who do not flee to the wilderness but remain in Israel (Rev. 12:13; cf. Zech. 12:6, 7) — "the compromised woman" — only to be slaughtered by Antichrist. Eventually he kills two out of three remaining in Israel, all from the latter group. Those who do survive will escape into the remote areas of Israel, Egypt, or ancient Assyria.

2. Ezekiel explains that the Israelites that flee to the wilderness will be brought "into the bond of the covenant" (20:37), while in the wilderness, *before* the house of Israel, who will be saved *later* (v. 39). Therefore, by definition the wilderness remnant — the "faithful remnant" — is the first fruits of "the woman" in general to come to Christ (see endnote 1). This is the exact definition John gives to the 144,000, who "have kept themselves [spiritually] chaste . . . [and for that reason] have been purchased from among men as first fruits [of Israel] to God and to the Lamb" (Rev. 14:4). See in particular chapter 11, endnote 1 for a more in-depth defense of this position.

3. *The rest of the woman's offspring identification*: "The woman" of Revelation 12:17 represents an obedient "unsaved" remnant within the natural line of Abraham at the midpoint of the seventieth week, who refuses to worship Antichrist or his image, and who in part flees to the wilderness to avoid his persecution. "And the woman fled into the wilderness where she had a place prepared by God, so that there she might be nourished for one thousand two hundred and sixty days" (Rev. 12:6). As explained in endnotes 1 and 2 above, "the woman" includes the 144,000 who become the first fruits of Israel to God — "the faithful woman" — as well as the rest of the nation who refuses to worship Antichrist but is not saved until after "the fulness of the Gentiles comes in" — "the compromised woman."

It is the identification of "the rest of her [the woman's] offspring, who keep the commandments of God and hold to the testimony of Jesus" that is critical to our discussion at this point. This author believes that there can be little doubt that "the rest of her offspring" must refer to the church. Obviously, because the rest of her offspring "keep the commandments of God and hold to the testimony of Jesus," this rules out all of Israel that succumb to Antichrist. It is equally obvious that "the woman" in general must be excluded, not only because she is still unsaved at this point, but also because, by definition, it is her offspring we are concerned with, not her.

Therefore, there is only one group left that can fit the description — that is, Christians, Jews and Gentiles alike who "hold to the commandments of God and the testimony of Jesus" — namely, those who are part of the church and not part of the other groups mentioned above. In several places Paul makes unmistakably clear that every true believer is a spiritual descendant of Abraham, the father of Israel (Rom. 4:11; Gal. 3:7-9, 29), thereby indicating the connection between "the woman" (in part, the first fruits of unsaved Israel that flees in obedience to the wilderness) and "the rest of her offspring." No person can "hold to the testimony of Jesus," which surely includes acknowledgement of His divinity and Lordship, without belonging to Him (1 Cor. 12:3). At the beginning of the book of Revelation, John (a part of the church) identifies himself with the woman's off-spring (i.e., with those who "hold the testimony of Jesus") by referring to himself as one who holds "the testimony of Jesus" (1:9); similarly John is told later by a voice from the throne of God (19:5), "I am a fellow-servant of yours [John's] and your brethren [the church] who hold the testimony of Jesus; worship God. For the testimony of Jesus is the spirit of prophecy" (v. 10).

Later John refers to "the rest of her offspring, who keep the commandments of God and hold to the testimony of Jesus" as "saints" — e.g., "it was given to him [Antichrist] to make war with the saints [the rest of her offspring] and to over-come them" (Rev. 13:7). The same Greek word, *hagios*, translated saints in 13:7, is again used by John in describing the bride of Christ (Rev. 19:8), which certainly includes the church. To emphasize that warning to the saints, John then adds, "If anyone has an ear, let him hear" (v. 9) — which is the same warning, almost word for word, that Christ gave in His letters to the seven churches in chapters 2 and 3. This language is found nowhere else in John's writings. It is found only eight times, all of them in Revelation, seven times addressed to the seven churches and the last time as a final warning to the saints who "keep the commandments of God and hold to the testimony of Jesus" during the great tribulation by Antichrist.

Therefore, the church fits the description perfectly and for that reason will be the secondary target of Antichrist's persecution. (See in addition chapter 17, end-note 3.)

4. It is interesting to note further the plea of the fifth-seal martyrs — in view of the fact that the fifth seal clearly occurs during the great tribulation by Antichrist, after the "beginning of birth pangs" of the first half of the seventieth week. Thus the martyrs beneath the altar ask "with a loud voice, saying, 'How long, O Lord, holy and true, wilt Thou refrain from judging and avenging our blood on those who dwell on the earth?'" (Rev. 6:10). In other words, they were asking when the day of the Lord would begin — that is, when would God's justice be poured out on the wicked in repayment for their afflicting the elect of God.

Speaking about the end times, Jesus gave in advance, as it were, the proper response to the martyrs' question: "Shall not God bring about justice for His elect, who cry to Him day and night, and will He delay long over them? I tell you that He will bring about justice for them speedily. However, when the Son of Man comes, will He find faith on the earth?" (Luke 18:7, 8).

CHAPTER 14: **The Sign of the End of the Age**

1. Although the disciples actually asked their Lord three questions, this chapter is primarily concerned with the last two that deal with Christ's return. The first question, "When will these things be?" refers to the immediately preceding state-ment of Christ in reference to the Temple. "Do you not see all these things? Truly I say to you, not one stone here shall be left upon another, which will not be torn down." The part of the Olivet Discourse recorded in Matthew does not answer this first question; rather it specifically answers the second and third questions.

On the other hand, *still within the framework of the last two questions,* a major part of the Olivet Discourse recorded in Luke deals directly with their first question, as this is the only question being asked by the disciples in Luke's account (21:7) and for that reason is specifically answered by Christ. See Luke 21:12-24.

2. *Matthew 24:22 (koloboō)*: In His Olivet Discourse, Jesus said, "And unless those days had been cut short, no life would have been saved; but for the sake of the elect those days shall be cut short" (Matt. 24:22). The context of that passage is Antichrist's persecution of God's elect during the time Jesus had just referred to as "the great tribulation" (v. 21). Although Satan through Antichrist will be granted forty-two months in which to operate virtually unrestricted (Dan. 9:27; 12:6, 7; Rev. 11:2; 12:6, 14; 13:4, 5), it is not that *time period* that will be cut short but rather *the persecution* by Antichrist against God's elect, which will occur within the forty-two months (starting at the beginning), but will not continue throughout.

   The Greek word translated "cut short" (Matt. 24:22) is *ekolobōthēsan*, from the root word *koloboō*, which was used as a medical term to describe the amputation of a leg, arm, or other body part. In general use, it meant to curtail or to shorten (*Strong's*, #2856; Vine, 4:24). The time originally allotted for Satan to *directly persecute* God's people will therefore be "amputated," as it were, by the sign of the day of the Lord, which will be seen by all the world in the sun, moon and stars, as foretold by Isaiah (13:10; 24:23), Joel (2:10, 31; 3:15), and by Jesus Himself (Matt. 24:29). God will sovereignly and decisively cut short those days by His retaliation against Antichrist and his followers for their persecution of His elect:

   > For after all it is only just for God to repay with affliction those who afflict you, and to give relief to you who are afflicted and to us as well when the Lord Jesus shall be revealed from heaven with His mighty angels in flaming fire, dealing out retribution to those who do not know God and to those who do not obey the gospel of our Lord Jesus. (2 Thess. 1:6-8).

3. It is significant to note that the sign God will give to show mankind that His day of wrath has come will be a sign seen in the heavenlies. This therefore is a perfect counterpart to God's declaration at creation, when He said, "Let there be lights in the expanse of the heavens to separate the day from the night, and let them be for signs, and for seasons, and for days and years" (Gen. 1:14). The lights in the expanse of the heavens were given, in part, for signs. At the first coming of Christ those lights were significant, especially to the magi from the east, who asked, "Where is He who has been born King of the Jews? For we saw His star in the east, and have come to worship Him" (Matt. 2:2). In accord with the purpose for which they were created, those same heavenly lights will be used, along with the sign of His coming (covered in the following chapter), to announce the second coming of Christ when He comes to rescue the righteous and to judge the wicked.

4. *Jehoshaphat/Armageddon campaign comparisons*: There is much confusion about the Jehoshaphat and the Armageddon Campaigns. They do, of course, have numerous similarities. Both occur in the last days, both involve Gentile nations, and both are against Israel; but the similarities end there. The dissimilarities, however, are *far* more numerous and considerably more significant.

   First, the *battlefields* are different, as indicated by the names of the battles themselves. One campaign is fought in "the valley of Jehoshaphat" (Joel 3:2, 12), whereas the other is fought in "the place which in Hebrew is called Har-Magedon" (Rev. 16:16), usually rendered Armageddon in English.

   Second, the *terrains* are vastly different. The Jehoshaphat Campaign is obviously fought in a valley, whereas Armageddon generally refers to the large plain that spans out from the base of Mount Megiddo (the literal meaning of Har-Magedon) and is near the city of Megiddo.

Third, the *timings* of the two campaigns are different in relation to the day of the Lord. The Jehoshaphat Campaign occurs just prior to the day of the Lord, the seventh seal. Joel predicts, "Let the nations be aroused and come up to *the valley of Jehoshaphat*, for there I will sit to judge all the surrounding nations. Put in the sickle, for the harvest is ripe. Come, tread, for the wine press is full; the vats overflow, for their wickedness is great. Multitudes, multitudes in the valley of decision! *For the day of the Lord is near* in the valley of decision" (Joel 3:12-14, emphasis added). Whereas the Jehoshaphat Campaign will be fought before the day of the Lord, Armageddon is clearly the last event of the day of the Lord, naturally following the seven seals, the seven trumpets, and the seven bowls (see chapter 18, endnote 7).

Fourth, the ungodly *enemies* are different. In the Jehoshaphat Campaign Israel is attacked by "surrounding nations" (Joel 3:11, 12), whereas at Armageddon the Lord and His forces are besieged by "the kings from the east" and "the kings of the whole world" (Rev. 16:12, 14).

Fifth, the *defenders* are different. In the Jehoshaphat Campaign Israel will be defended primarily by "the clans of Judah" (Zech. 12:6), although the Lord (without His holy ones) will give assistance (Zech. 14:12). At Armageddon, however, Israel will be defended only by Christ and His holy ones (without the clans of Judah) (Rev. 19:11, 14), while the entire nation of Israel is in hiding in Azel (Zech. 14:5).

Sixth, the *motivation* of the Gentile nations is different. At the valley of Jehoshaphat their "siege [will be] against Jerusalem [and] against Judah" (Zech. 12:2), whereas at Armageddon they will "make war against Him [Christ] who sat upon the horse, and against His army" (Rev. 19:19).

Seventh, the *initiators* of the two campaigns are different. God "will gather all the nations, and bring them down to the valley of Jehoshaphat" (Joel 3:2). At Armageddon, however, Satan and his evil minions — Antichrist, the false prophet, and the three demons — will "go out to the kings of the whole world, to gather them together for the war of the great day of God, the Almighty" (Rev. 16:13, 14).

Eighth, the *proximity* of the two campaigns to Jerusalem is considerably different. As noted above, the valley of Jehoshaphat is adjacent to Jerusalem on the east side, whereas the plains of Armageddon, or Megiddo, are some sixty miles north of the city.

In light of the great differences just described, the need for carefully distinguishing between those two campaigns becomes obvious. Perhaps the most significant difference is that the Jehoshaphat Campaign will occur just before the day of the Lord, whereas the battle of Armageddon will be the last event of the day of the Lord.

5. *Revelation 6:17 (élthen)*: The critical phrase in Revelation 6:17, and in this passage, is "has come," which translates the Greek *élthen*, the aorist tense indicative mood of *erchomai*, the most common Greek verb for "come." See James Strong, *Strong's Exhaustive Concordance of the Bible* (Nashville: Abingdon, 1890), #2064. In order to make the entire seventieth week the day of the Lord, the pretribulationist seeks

to equate this verb with a past action that has already been going on for some time.

In his book *A Grammar of the Greek New Testament in the Light of Historical Research* (Nashville: Broadman Press, 1934), A. T. Robertson says of the aorist indicative: "The caution must be once more repeated that in these subdivisions of the aorist indicative we have only one tense and one root-idea (punctiliar action)" (p. 835). Later he says of the aorist tense as it relates to the future: "It is a vivid transference of the action to the future by the 'timeless aorist'" (p. 846). In other words, the aorist tense speaks to one particular issue that is timeless, the context clearly determining the tense of the action, as against the common belief of some who would make the aorist tense always a past completed action.

In his book *Exegetical Fallacies* (Grand Rapids, MI: Baker Book House, 1984), D. A. Carson writes:

> Frank Stagg wrote an article about "The Abused Aorist." The problem as he saw it was that competent scholars were deducing from the presence of an aorist verb that the action in question was "once for all" or "completed." The problem arises in part because the aorist is often described as the punctiliar tense. Careful grammarians, of course, understand and explain that this does not mean the aorist could be used only for point actions. The aorist, after all, is well-named: it is a-orist, without a place, undefined. It simply refers to the action itself, without specifying whether the action is unique, repeated, ingressive, instantaneous, past, or accomplished. (pp. 69, 70)

In his contribution to *The Rapture: Pre-, Mid-, or Post-Tribulational* (Grand Rapids, MI: Zondervan, 1984), Paul Feinberg makes several observations about the passage in question and adds helpful comments from Robert Gundry concerning the use of the Greek verb *élthen*:

> By far the most important two instances [of *élthen*] are found in Revelation 6:16, 17. The word *wrath* occurs once in each verse. This is the first reference to wrath in the book. . . . Gundry argues two points with regard to this passage. He contends that the wrath spoken of in this text, as well as others, falls only on unbelievers. Further, the aorist verb *élthen* is either an ingressive or dramatic aorist. The ingressive or inceptive aorist expresses a state or condition *just entered*. On the other hand, the dramatic or proleptic aorist functions like a future, taking place after the realization of some condition. This would mean that with the sixth seal the wrath of God has just begun or is about to appear. . . . In support of an ingressive or dramatic aorist interpretation, Gundry argues that "if the wrath of God has already fallen, how could the wicked be yet fleeing for refuge? Rather, the wrath is at the inception of its breaking forth . . . or on the verge of doing so. . . ." Gundry's view is exegetically possible. (p. 59)

In other words, the context determines the tense of an aorist verb. Because the word "wrath" is not mentioned in the book of Revelation prior to the sixth seal, because the signs given in the sun, moon and stars, mentioned in relationship to the sixth seal, perfectly parallel the signs that will occur announcing the day of the Lord's wrath, and because the word "wrath" is mentioned numerous times in the chapters that *follow* in relationship to events directly associated with the seventh seal, the context of our present text (Rev. 6:17) seems self-evident. The wrath of God is *about to begin*. And when the seventh seal is opened, it will.

One final comment which is perhaps the best illustration of the use of *élthen* in our text found in Revelation 6:17. When comparing Scripture to Scripture, we see the use of the identical Greek word, *élthen*, by Christ in the Garden of Gethsemane. The context here, like the context of Revelation 6:17, again clarifies the tense of this aorist indicative verb, describing an event just about to occur. "And He came the third time, and said to them, 'Are you still sleeping and taking your rest? It is enough; the hour has come (*élthen*); behold, the Son of Man is being betrayed into the hands of sinners. Arise, let us be going; behold, the one who betrays Me is at hand!' And immediately while He was still speaking, Judas . . ." (Mark 14:41-43a).

CHAPTER 15: **The Sign of Christ's Coming**
1. *The Treasury of the New Testament*, Vol. 2, "Joyful Anticipation of the Second Advent," Luke 21:28-31 (Grand Rapids, MI: Zondervan, n.d.), p. 130.

CHAPTER 16: **The Prewrath Rapture of the Church — Part I**
1. In an article entitled "Another Look at Rosenthal's Pre-Wrath Rapture," printed in *Bibliotheca Sacra*, October-December 1991, (p. 394), Dr. John A. McLean, Associate Professor of Bible at Grand Rapids Baptist College and Seminary, attempts to rebut the same-day position taken by this writer as follows:

> Rosenthal's argument of a "same day" Rapture with the Day of the Lord does not stand up to biblical scrutiny. After Noah's family and the animals entered the Ark, the Flood waters did not begin for seven days (Gen. 7:7, 10).

2. The most likely explanation is that the seven days referred to here is the length of time it took for all the animals to be gathered into the ark before the rain started.
3. The same word (*peirasmos*) is translated "testing" (NASB) in Revelation 3:10. The Greek carries the basic idea of putting to a proof. For further information on *peirasmos*, see chapter 2, endnote 3.
4. *The dragnet parable*: In an attempt to make the "coming of Christ" in the Olivet Discourse describe the return of Christ at the battle of Armageddon (thereby making the entire Olivet Discourse applicable only to unbelieving Israel entering the seventieth week), some interpreters teach that the person who is "taken" (Matt. 24:40, 41; Luke 17:34-36) is taken for judgment, and the person who is "left" is left to go into the millennial kingdom. This view is commonly justified on the basis of verses 49, 50 of the dragnet parable in Matthew 13:

> "Again, the kingdom of heaven is like a drag-net cast into the sea, and gathering fish of every kind; and when it was filled, they drew it up on the beach; and they sat down, and gathered the good fish into containers, but the bad they threw away. So it will be at the end of the age; the angels shall come forth, and take out the wicked from among the righteous, and will cast them into the furnace of fire; there shall be weeping and gnashing of teeth." (vv. 47-50)

For several reasons this parable is used to justify the position that the one "taken" is taken for judgment and the one left goes into the millennial kingdom. But the most obvious reason is the context of the parable itself. When the verse just before the dragnet parable (13:48) is taken into consideration, there can be little doubt as to what Jesus explicitly states is the proper order: the fishermen first "gathered the good fish into containers, but [then] the bad they threw away." This is the same order described both by John the Baptist and by Jesus when they declared that the wheat is put into the barn (raptured) *before* the tares (or chaff) are burned (judged) (Matt. 3:12; 13:30, 40; cf. 2 Pet. 3:7).

5. *Matthew 24:40 (paralambanō):* James Strong, *Strong's Exhaustive Concordance of the Bible* (Nashville: Abingdon, 1890), #3880. Gerhard Kittel explains that *paralambanō* is best translated "with a personal object, 'to take to or with oneself.' Example: in close fellowship" (G. Kittel, ed. *The Theological Dictionary of the New Testament* (Grand Rapids, MI: Eerdmans, 1964-76), 4:3.

   Pretribulational rapturists who see Armageddon depicted in the Olivet Discourse must do something with the illustrations in Matthew 24:40, 41 to make them fit Armageddon rather than the Rapture. In the text one person is taken and the other left. To make this text, then, fit the events during Armageddon, the ones who are "taken" go to judgment, and the ones that are "left" behind are the believers who enter into the millennial kingdom. But there is no eschatological passage in either Testament that supports the idea that the ungodly are taken or received directly by Christ for judgment at His coming (vv. 37, 39), which will come totally unexpected, as "a thief in the night," after which the godly are left to go into the Millennium. Such broad interpretation is, of course, difficult to counter because no specifics are considered.

   The argument is usually based upon the preceding verse, referring to those left behind in the days of Noah — those who "did not understand until the flood came and *took them all away*" (v. 39, emphasis added). The argument here is that those taken by the Flood (the wicked) are those taken in judgment at the coming of Christ, in the next verse. But the Greek verb (*airō*), translated "took . . . away" in verse 39, carries the ideas of removal and separation. The same word was used by John the Baptist for Christ, whom John called "the Lamb of God who takes away [*airō*] the sin of the world!" (John 1:29). In another example Jesus warned that "every branch in Me that does not bear fruit, He takes away [*airō*]; and every branch that bears fruit, He prunes it, that it may bear more fruit" (John 15:2). In both cases, the idea is clearly that of *taking away from* or *apart from*.

   But the Greek verbs translated "will be taken" in Luke 17:34, 35 and in Matt. 24:40, 41 are from *paralambanō*, which carries the entirely different meaning of *taking near* — in particular the taking of something or someone to oneself. See W. E. Vine, *An Expository Dictionary of New Testament Words* (Westwood, NJ: Revell, 1940), 4:105, 106; Fritz Rienecker, Cleon Rogers, *Linguistic Key to the Greek New Testament* (Grand Rapids, MI: Zondervan, 1980), p. 72; James Strong, *Strong's Exhaustive Concordance of the Bible* (Nashville: Abingdon, 1890), #142, 3880; W. F. Arndt and F. W. Gingrich, *A Greek-English Lexicon of the New Testament* (Chicago: University of Chicago Press, 1957), pp. 23, 24, 625; Gerhard Kittel, ed. *The Theological Dictionary of the New Testament* (Grand Rapids, MI: Eerdmans, 1964-76), 4:3.

   Christ uses this particular verb, *paralambanō*, in only one other context — that is, in the classic rapture passage given in the Gospel of John: "And if I go and prepare a place for you, I will come again and receive you [*paralambanō*] to Myself, that where I am, there you may be also" (John 14:3).

6. *Parousia, hēkō, erchomai interrelationships:* The Greek noun *parousia* (usually translated "coming") has the primary meaning of "presence," and often the derived connotations of "coming or advent" — that is, of *becoming* present by one's arrival or appearance. In other words, the term itself does not carry the idea of movement, although that idea is often implied. See Strong, *Strong's Exhaustive*

Concordance of the Bible, #3952; Arndt and Gingrich, *A Greek-English Lexicon of the New Testament*, p. 635; Vine, *An Expository Dictionary of New Testament Words*, 1:208. It is significant that in Alfred Marshall's highly recognized *Interlinear Greek-English New Testament* (London: Samuel Bagster, 1966), the English "presence" is *always* used beneath *parousia* in the following references (also in the NASB and most English versions): Matt. 24:27, 37, 39; 1 Cor. 15:23; 1 Thess. 2:19; 3:13; 5:23; 2 Thess. 2:1, 8, 9; James 5:7, 8; 2 Pet. 1:16; 3:4, 12; 1 John 2:28.

The verb *hēkō* has the basic meaning of "to come" or "to be present." See Strong, *Strong's Exhaustive Concordance of the Bible*, #2240; Arndt and Gingrich, *A Greek-English Lexicon of the New Testament*, p. 345; and Vine, *An Expository Dictionary of New Testament Words*, 1:204. In reference to Christ's second coming, the term is used only three times in the New Testament, each time in the book of Revelation. It is used once as a word of encouragement to the church at Thyatira and twice as a word of warning to the church at Sardis (Rev. 2:25; 3:3)

The verb *erchomai*, which has no corresponding noun, is always used of persons and specifically connotes movement, either coming or going, from one point to another. It is in contrast to *hēkō*, which denotes only arrival. See Strong, *Strong's Exhaustive Concordance of the Bible*, #2064; Arndt and Gingrich, *A Greek-English Lexicon of the New Testament*, p. 310; Vine, *An Expository Dictionary of New Testament Words*, 1:203. *Erchomai* is rendered as "coming" or "comes" in the following New Testament passages: Matt. 24:30; 26:64; Mark 8:38; 13:26; 14:62; Luke 21:27; Rev. 1:7; 2:5; 22:7, 12, 20.

It is significant that *erchomai*, which always relates to movement, is so often mentioned with Christ's coming *in* or *with* the clouds as he descends from Heaven (Matt. 24:30; 26:64; Mark 13:26; 14:62; Luke 21:27; Rev. 1:7). Clouds are associated with physical movement in the sky, but it was also into a cloud that Jesus was received when He ascended to Heaven from the Mount of Olives (Acts 1:9). After the Lord disappeared from sight, the angels informed the disciples that "this Jesus, who has been taken up from you into heaven, will come in just the same way as you have watched Him go into heaven" (Acts 1:11) — meaning, among other things, that His future descent, like His past ascent, would be through the clouds.

The primary distinction between those three words is that *parousia* refers to an event, *hēkō* to someone's presence, and *erchomai* to someone's movement. The two most significant and most often used of those words are *parousia* and *erchomai* — the former usually encompassing the *entire series of events* of the second coming, the latter accentuating Christ's *movement* during those events. Yet despite their distinctions, they emphasize inseparable facets of the same glorious truth of our Lord's return.

7. *The Gospel of Matthew — for the Church or for Israel?*: It is of the utmost importance to determine whether the Gospel of Matthew was written for the church (which would mean that the Olivet Discourse records the events that must occur before the return of Christ to remove the faithful and to judge the wicked), or whether it was written solely for Israel (which would mean that the Discourse applies only to unbelieving Jews who go into the seventieth week, recording the events that lead up to the battle of Armageddon [see endnote 8]). Many pretribulationists hold the latter view in their attempt to keep the church out of the seventieth week. But the context of the book demands that it is a book written for the church, not unsaved Israel!

The Great Commission (with which the Gospel of Matthew closes) is of great significance. Christ gives the command: "Go therefore and make disciples of all the nations, baptizing them in the name of the Father and the Son and the Holy Spirit, teaching them to observe all that I commanded you; and lo, I am with you always, even to the end of the age" (Matt. 28:19, 20). That passage has always been taken as Christ's commission to His *church*, not to unsaved Israel. It should be obvious that Christ intended for *all* His teaching to be taught to *all* His followers (the church) until "the end of the age" — that is, until He comes again at the day of the Lord.

The church is also in view in other passages in that Gospel. In fact, Matthew is the only Gospel writer to report Jesus' use of the term *church*. Jesus first mentions the church by that name in 16:18, and He gives instruction for church discipline in 18:15-20. The Olivet Discourse (chapters 24, 25) was given on the third day of Passover, three days before He was crucified, just before Jesus' institution of the Lord's Supper (26:26-29), which was given on the sixth day of Passover. Jesus also spoke to His disciples concerning the Rapture (see John 14:1-3) on the sixth day of Passover.

It is obviously of great significance that much of Jesus' most important instruction to His followers — that is, the church — was given during or near Passover, which instruction would be foundational, not simply for the apostles and other church leaders but for all His followers. That is why Christ answered the disciples' question concerning His coming and the end of the age from the standpoint of the church rather than of Israel, who as a nation had just turned her back on her Messiah, refusing the King and forfeiting His kingdom "until the fulness of the Gentiles has come in" (Rom. 11:25), after the completion of the seventieth week (see Dan. 9:24).

8. *Matthew 24:29-31 — Rapture or Armageddon?*: Those who believe that the Gospel of Matthew was written to Israel, not to the church (see endnote 7), must then take the events of Matthew 24:29-31 as applying to Christ's return for judgment at Armageddon rather than to His rapture of the church. But normal, literal translation and interpretation of all the related passages completely undermine such a view.

First, as we have seen, the Olivet Discourse answers the disciples' question about the sign of Christ's coming (*parousia*, Matt. 24:3). The *parousia* of Christ (see endnote 6) is a singular event, with no biblical support for a *parousia before* the seventieth week (at the presumed time of the Rapture) and another *parousia after* the seventieth week, at the battle of Armageddon. Scripture nowhere directly associates Christ's *parousia* with the battle of Armageddon. There is only one *parousia*, and because both 1 Thessalonians 4:15, 16 and the Olivet Discourse speak specifically about the *parousia* of Christ, it is hard to escape the conclusion that both passages refer to the same event.

Second, when all the second-person language in the Olivet Discourse is carefully considered, it becomes clear that Jesus was speaking *to and of believers* who were then alive. Speaking to His disciples, Christ used the word "you" ten times in the sequential portion of His discourse recorded in Matthew (vv. 4-31). See chapter 13, the section entitled "Expectancy of New Testament Churches Concerning Christ's Return." If the church were to be raptured *before* the seventieth week, the events described would have no meaning to believers, not even to the Jews, because the divinely protected remnant of Israel — other than the

144,000 first fruits that are saved after the rapture of the church — are not saved until the seventieth week is complete (see Rom. 11:25, 26). But the second-person language comes alive in the context of the church, which is further supported by the *paralambanō* argument given in endnote 4.

Third, in the opposite way, the third-person language of the Olivet Discourse clearly refers to unbelievers, who are compared to the ungodly people of Noah's day who continued "business as usual" until the Flood swept them away (Matt. 24:37-39). It could hardly be that life will be "going on as usual" up until the battle of Armageddon, which by definition must occur after the trumpet and bowl judgments, bringing the most devastating destruction the world will ever see.

Fourth, the warning to believers to "be on the alert" (Matt. 24:42) would make no sense if all of them will be raptured before the events of the Olivet Discourse transpire. Paul gives a similar warning to the church to "be alert and sober" (1 Thess. 5:4-6, 9).

The fifth argument is similar to the one concerning those who carry on business as usual. It is hard to conceive that Armageddon could come like "a thief in the night" (Matt. 24:43, 44, 50) if it were preceded by all the end-time judgments of God, which would include numerous worldwide disasters on a scale never before known. And how could the nations of the world be surprised by Armageddon when they know they are being assembled on that battlefield for the very purpose of fighting the forces of God? (Cf. the sixth bowl, Rev. 16:12-16.)

Sixth, Jesus states that not even the angels in Heaven or the Son of God know the day or hour of His coming (Matt. 24:36). That would hardly be true if His coming refers to Armageddon, presumably the last event of the seventieth week. His coming would then be easily predictable as occurring 2,520 days (seven prophetic years of 360 days each) after the seventieth week begins, within a margin of perhaps one or two days.

Seventh, if Christ's coming "with power and great glory" at Armageddon can be compared to the times of Noah and Lot (Matt. 24:36-41; Luke 17:26-36), the comparison is exceedingly difficult to comprehend, because the protection offered Noah, Lot, and their families came *before* the judgments, whereas Christ's coming "with power and great glory" will come after the beginning birth pangs and the great tribulation by Antichrist. That would be like Noah's being offered safety in the ark at the end of the forty days and nights of rain, when every person not in the ark was already drowned!

Eighth and finally, in the Olivet Discourse Jesus could not have been referring to unsaved Israel if the illustrations of Noah (Matt. 24:37-39) and of Lot (see the parallel passage in Luke 17:26-30) are seen for what they clearly are — examples of God's protection of the righteous during the manifestation of His wrath. Except for the woman that flees to the wilderness at the midpoint of the seventieth week, Israel will not be directly protected during the day of the Lord. During that time the nation of Israel and most Jews throughout the world will still be in unbelief (Rom. 11:25, 26) and are therefore subject to the full force of God's wrath. "Alas, you who are longing for the day of the Lord," Amos warned his people, "for what purpose will the day of the Lord be to you? It will be darkness and not light" (Amos 5:18). Malachi sounded a similar warning: "Who can endure the day of His coming? And who can stand when He appears? For He is like a refiner's fire and like fullers' soap. And He will sit as a smelter and purifier of silver, and

He will purify the sons of Levi and refine them like gold and silver, so that they may present to the Lord offerings in righteousness" (Mal. 3:2, 3).

9. As carefully developed in chapter 14 and in endnote 2 of the same chapter, *it is not the final forty-two months of Satan's earthly authority that will be cut short, but rather the severe persecution of the great tribulation by Antichrist* that he will inflict on God's people during a portion of the last half of the seventieth week. That satanic persecution will be cut short by the sign given in the sun, moon, and stars, when the lights in the heavenlies are turned off, announcing to the world that the day of the Lord's retaliation is about to begin.

10. *Matthew 24:31 — gathering together His elect*: Those who would make the Olivet Discourse applicable only to Israel must make the gathering "together [of] His elect" (as seen in the last verse of Christ's sequential instruction concerning the last days) a reference to Israel, not to the Rapture of the church. If this gathering can be shown conclusively to refer to the gathering of Israel back to her own homeland after Armageddon, then support is given for the argument that the Olivet Discourse as a whole does not relate directly to the church. By the same token, if the gathering in verse 31 can be shown conclusively to refer to the Rapture, then the Olivet Discourse as a whole must relate to the church and the Rapture must occur *after* the great tribulation by Antichrist (which transpires earlier in the sequence) is "cut short" (vv. 21, 22).

Many pretribulational interpreters use Isaiah 27:12, 13 to support the idea that Matthew 24:31 refers to the regathering of Israel after the battle of Armageddon, just before the millennial kingdom is established. But that Isaiah passage refers to the Lord's gathering the remnant of Israel from Assyria and Egypt and bringing them back to Jerusalem on the highway of holiness. A trumpet is blown, as in Matthew 24:31, but there is no mention of angels. That ingathering is specifically limited to Israel and to those in the two countries just mentioned, whereas the gathering of Matthew 24:31 is just as specifically worldwide and is not limited to any national or racial group, referring only to "His elect."

Deuteronomy 30:1-5 is also frequently used to explain the gathering of Matthew 24:31. But this Deuteronomy passage also pertains to *unbelieving Israel*, gathered *before the seventieth week commences*, as described in the vision of the dry bones in Ezekiel 37. On the other hand, the account in Matthew 24:31 is the gathering of *God's elect* and occurs *after the great tribulation* is cut short. In addition, the Deuteronomy passage depicts God Himself doing the gathering, not His angels — as is clearly depicted in Matthew 24:31 and as taught by Christ when the wheat is harvested into God's heavenly barn (Matt. 13:30) by his angelic reapers (v. 39).

Therefore, if the above two Old Testament passages are used to interpret Matthew 24:31, some immediate problems arise. First, the Isaiah passage is limited to the regathering of Israel from the nations immediately surrounding Israel and therefore cannot apply to the Matthew account, which is worldwide in scope, including all the elect of God. Second, although it is agreed that the Deuteronomy account is worldwide in scope, this event depicts the gathering of unsaved Israel before the seventieth week, whereas the gathering in Matthew 24:31 is of God's elect, after the great tribulation is cut short.

Consequently, the gathering of the elect in Matthew 24:31 is seen to have no relationship to Israel, leaving the inescapable conclusion that it directly answers the question the disciples had just asked Christ about the sign of His coming (*parousia*). Verse 31 must refer to the Rapture, to the gathering of the church by the angels (reapers) of God at the coming (*parousia*) of Christ "with the trumpet of God . . . [when] we who are alive and remain shall be caught up together with them in the clouds to meet the Lord in the air, and thus we shall always be with the Lord" (1 Thess. 4:16, 17).

11. *First Thessalonians 4:15, 17 (perileipō):* The phrase "we who are alive and remain" at first seems to be redundant, but close study of the two Greek verbs indicates that those who remain will have just survived some sort of ordeal, which, of course, would be the great tribulation by Antichrist "out from which" Christ will rescue His saints (2 Pet. 2:9).

   Perileipō ("remain") is used only twice in the New Testament, both times in this classic Rapture passage (vv. 15, 17). Its meaning is broader than *menō*, a frequently used New Testament word that is often rendered "remain." Strong defines *perileipō* as "to *leave* all *around* (i.e., pass.) *survive:-* remain." See James Strong, *Strong's Exhaustive Concordance of the Bible* (Nashville: Abingdon, 1890), #4035.

   It is also significant that the word "and" used just before the word "remain" is italicized in many English translations, indicating that the word is supplied in English but is not in the original language. The only Greek connecting term here is *hoi*, the definite article (the), which places the two verbs in apposition. The text therefore literally reads, "the living, *the* remaining" or "*the* surviving."

CHAPTER 17: **The Prewrath Rapture of the Church — Part II**

1. Peter teaches exactly the same thing. He explains to his readers that "the Lord knows how to rescue the godly from temptation [*peirasmos*], and to keep the unrighteous under punishment for the day of judgment" (2 Pet. 2:9). As explained in chapter 2 (see especially endnote 2), the word "temptation" translates the same Greek term rendered "testing" ("the hour of *testing*") in Revelation 3:10. Peter therefore places the Rapture (the "rescue [of] the godly") in exactly the same sequence as Christ does in the Olivet Discourse, as Paul does in 2 Thessalonians 2:1-8, and as John does in the book of Revelation.

2. *Revelation 7:14 (hoi erchomai):* There is a question as to whether or not this great multitude of Revelation 7 have been arriving over a past period of time, or if they have all arrived at the same time, right before John's eyes. If this great multitude can be shown as arriving over a period of time, their identification as the church becomes more difficult. On the other hand, if this great multitude arrives all at the same time, their identification as the church is greatly enhanced.

   The Greek phrase translated in Revelation 7:14 as "the ones who come" is *hoi erchomenoi.* "This present participle which acts as a substantive, characterizes those 'coming' without reference to time: 'these are such as come'" (Swete, p. 102). Another commentator notes that "the time must be determined by the context" (cf. 15:2; 20:10; Beckwith, p. 545). That being the case, the *prophetically future time* depicted here in John's vision *will already have arrived.* The noted Greek scholar Henry Alford translates the phrase as, "These are they that come," noting that the past tense ("came," as in the KJV) is inappropriate. "Nor again," he says, "must the *present* [participle] be put prominently forward, that *are coming,* as if the number in the vision were not yet complete: still less is it to be taken as a quasi-future, 'that shall come,' . . . but as in the expression *hoi erchomenos,* the present is merely one of *designation.* Their description, generically, is that 'they are they that *come . . . out of the great tribulation.'*" He goes on to point out that the definite article [the] ought not to be omitted" [before "great tribulation"], as it is in some translations (*The Greek Testament* [Chicago: Moody Press, 1958], 4:628).

In his unpublished *Exegetical Digest of Revelation 4-7*, Robert L. Thomas makes several significant comments on *hoi erchomenoi*:

1. The participle with the article simply means "the comers." The present simply expresses the idea of the verb without reference to time. The time must be determined by the context, which shows the act already to have taken place at the time anticipated in the vision (cf. 15:2; 20:10) (Beckwith, p. 545).

2. The *ēlthon* of 7:13 makes it unlikely that they are still arriving. It requires that *hoi erchomenoi* be taken as the equivalent of *hoi ēlthontes* (Charles, I, 202; Mounce, p.173).

3. In 20:4, at the time of the millennium, John has the martyrs coming to life and reigning with Christ. This does not sound as though they have been raised to heaven immediately after physical death (Caird, p. 103).

4. The next verb "they have washed" (*eplunan*) has a past reference, so the same must be true with this participle. The vision is written from the standpoint of the future, after the conclusion of the tribulation, in the happy estate of the kingdom (Beasley-Murray, p. 147).

5. The expression is a mere designation. Their description is generically that "they are they that come" (Alford, IV, 628).

6. The participle is timeless: "such as come" (Swete, p. 102).

There is therefore absolutely no reason to translate this present participle, *hoi erchomenoi*, into the English word "coming," giving the reader the impression that this is an ever-increasing number of martyrs, with the group getting larger and larger as more and more martyrs find their way to Heaven (without being raptured) during the great tribulation, for the following reasons: because the context determines the present participle, and because this context clearly indicates this group is fixed in number, we may conclude that the group is fully arrived and is presently standing before the throne of God as John beheld them (Rev. 7:17).

In summary, *erchomenoi* can properly be translated "come" or "are coming," depending on the context. Because the context of Revelation 17:14 is a great multitude complete in number, *erchomenoi* must here be rendered as "come," not "are coming." Without exception every reputable translator — Wycliffe (1380), Tyndale (1525), Coverdale (1535), John Rogers (1537), Calvin (1565), the *King James* translators (1611), the *English Revised* translators (1881), the *American Standard Bible* translators (1901), and countless others up until the present time, including the *New American Standard* — renders *erchomenoi* in Revelation 7:14 as "come" or "came." Carrying the same basic meaning, the *New International Version* rendering is "have come." Only a few individual translators of the twentieth century, without benefit of a committee of competent scholars, have rendered the word as "coming." Many of those translators' pretribulational tenets were allowed to override the clear biblical context.

3. *Revelation 7:9 (the great multitude)*: Despite the remarkable parallel of Revelation to the Olivet Discourse and to the teaching of Paul, some interpreters take this great multitude before the heavenly throne (Rev. 7:9) to be martyred Gentile believers. According to this view, these Gentile believers are converted in a worldwide revival that occurs during the great tribulation and are subsequently martyred *after* the Rapture, sometime during the seventieth week — which

contradicts their position that the seventieth week is totally Jewish in emphasis and in character. Because the pretribulational school of thought maintains that the church cannot be on earth during the seventieth week, the most incredible Gentile revival of all time would have to occur during a time when their system demands God has returned his emphasis back solely to Israel! Yet, to the contrary, Paul teaches that when Antichrist "takes his seat in the temple of God, displaying himself as being God . . . God will send upon them [the Gentile world] a deluding influence so that they might believe what is false, in order that they all may be judged who did not believe the truth, but took pleasure in wickedness" (2 Thess. 2:4, 11, 12). After Antichrist proclaims himself to be God, demands the world's worship, and inaugurates the great tribulation by Antichrist, the unbelieving and unrepentant world will become more and more spiritually deluded — by Antichrist, by his false prophet, by countless other false teachers, and even by God Himself. That is certainly not the description of the moving of God's Spirit, conducive for a worldwide revival resulting in the conversion of a Gentile multitude too great to count.

Similarly, there is no evidence in the book of Revelation of such a revival occurring at *any* time, and therefore there is no evidence for assuming that the greatest Gentile revival in history would occur at a time, according to pretribulationalists, that God has specifically set aside for His dealing with Israel as a nation. And if that great heavenly multitude were composed of converts after the Rapture, where are the resurrected and raptured saints in that magnificent heavenly scene? If the church were already in Heaven, it is strange that they will not be present to greet this great multitude which comes "out from within" the great tribulation of Antichrist. If this were the case, the great multitude would include many of their loved ones, left behind at the Rapture. If anybody should be in Heaven greeting this multitude, it should be the church, but Scripture portrays this mythical church nowhere in sight when this great multitude arrives.

4. *Revelation 6:9 (psuchē)*: To challenge this necessary conclusion, some theological friends of mine who hold a pretribulational view insist that the Greek word *psuchē*, translated "souls" in Revelation 6:9, does not necessarily refer to the immaterial part of man. It sometimes, they argue, can refer to the entire person, as in our contemporary expression "that poor soul," meaning "that poor *person*." They contend that this Greek term was used to represent the material as well as the immaterial part of man.

But comparison of Scripture with Scripture proves otherwise. In the closing benediction of his first letter to the Thessalonian church, Paul gives clear evidence that the soul (*psuchē*) is a distinct part of man's being: "Now may the God of peace Himself sanctify you entirely; and may your spirit and soul [*psuchē*] and body be preserved complete, without blame at the coming of our Lord Jesus Christ" (1 Thess. 5:23).

5. It should be noted that the resurrection of the unsaved will take place at a different time, at the Great White Throne judgment after the Millennium (see Rev. 20:11-15 and John 5:29).

6. *The great multitude — living church only?*: "These are the ones who come out of the great tribulation" (Rev. 7:14). The question is: Is this group limited to only the living church that is raptured at this point? And if so, where are the "dead in Christ" who rise first (1 Thess. 4:16)? This writer believes that this group includes both the living church and the dead in Christ because both are given their resurrection

bodies and arrive in Heaven at the same time. Therefore, the reference to "the ones who come out of the great tribulation" tells the reader specifically who this group is in relation to the great tribulation. "These are the ones [all with resurrection bodies, whether through rapture of the living or resurrection of the dead] who come out of [*ek;* "out from within"] the great tribulation." "The great tribulation," then, is a reference to when these come up to Heaven, not to whether or not they were living or dead before they received their resurrection bodies.

7. *The last trump of God*: The Rapture will be announced with "the trumpet of God" (1 Thess. 4:16), which Paul also refers to as "the last trumpet," after which "the dead will be raised imperishable" (1 Cor. 15:52). If these passages are taken literally, the solution is easily found to the many problems some Bible students have regarding the identification of this last trumpet.

Contrary to what some interpreters maintain, the "last trumpet" mentioned in that passage *cannot* refer to the last of the seven trumpet judgments. In the first place, those seven trumpets are all blown by angels (Rev. 8:6; cf. 11:15), not by God Himself. Even more significantly, however, if "the last trumpet" were the last of the trumpet judgments, Christians obviously would have to endure the first six executions of God's wrath, from which we are repeatedly assured deliverance (see, e.g., Rom. 5:9; 1 Thess. 1:10; 5:9). However, if the "last trumpet" is the last trumpet blown by *anyone*, it will not be the seventh trumpet of Revelation 11, but rather the trumpet blown initiating the return of Israel from Assyria and Egypt after the seventieth week is complete, just before the millennial kingdom (Isa. 27:12, 13). To have the Rapture occur at this time would again completely negate all the promises to the church that she would not undergo the wrath of God, in that this trumpet is blown *after* the seven trumpet judgments, *after* the seven bowl judgments, and *after* the battle of Armageddon. And yet that is the "last trumpet," technically speaking, of end-time events preceding the Millennium.

However, the text says that this is the "last trumpet" of God! The only other occasion *on which God is said to blow a trumpet* was during the Maccabean period in the second century B.C., when He came to Israel's defense against the blasphemous and merciless Antiochus Epiphanes. (See chapter 8, endnotes 1 and 2.) In predicting that deliverance the prophet Zechariah wrote, "Then the Lord will appear over them, and His arrow will go forth like lightning; and the Lord God will blow the trumpet, and will march in the storm winds of the south. The Lord of hosts will defend them. . . . And the Lord their God will save them in that day as the flock of His people; for they are as the stones of a crown, sparkling in His land" (Zech. 9:14-16).

It is remarkable that in both cases *the Lord* blows the trumpet to announce His direct intervention in order to destroy Antiochus, the foreshadow of Antichrist, or Antichrist himself in the last days. And in both instances God blows the trumpet shortly after His holy temple has been outrageously defiled.

It should be absolutely clear, then, that the trumpet spoken of in 1 Thessalonians 4:16 is precisely what that text says — namely, *the trumpet of God*, His second and last *personal* blowing of a trumpet, which will immediately precede the rapture of His church and which will in turn initiate the final destruction of Antichrist and his followers. Because it will be so unique and worldwide, the "last trumpet of God" may also serve as a warning to the nation of Israel, which at that time will still be in unbelief (see Rom. 11:25) and about to experience the wrath of God.

8. *The timing of the Rapture:* There are several things we do know concerning the timing of the Rapture. Obviously, as explained in the body of this volume, the Rapture comes during the second half of the seventieth week, during the great tribulation by Antichrist, but before the wrath of God. The seventh seal is the day of the Lord and in part includes the seven trumpet judgments. As we shall see in chapter 18, the final trumpet judgment of God *during* the seventieth week will be the sixth trumpet judgment. The only specified time span of the six previous trumpets, which therefore must be between the Rapture and the end of the seventieth week, is that of the fifth trumpet, which will last five months (Rev. 9:5). The maximum length of the great tribulation by Antichrist therefore cannot exceed thirty-seven months (forty-two months less five months). In addition, if the sixth trumpet judgment is thirteen months long (Rev. 9:15) — which seems possible but not probable — then the great tribulation will be shortened by that amount. How much shorter will be determined by the length of the first four and the sixth trumpet judgments.

In Isaiah's description of what is doubtless the seventh seal (the day of the Lord), he speaks of the day of the Lord's vengeance being "a year of recompense for the cause of Zion" (Isa. 34:8). If that figure does indeed apply to the length of the seventh seal, then the great tribulation by Antichrist could last thirty-one months (forty-three months less twelve months), because the final battle of Armageddon, the last event of the day of the Lord, will occur thirty days after the close of the seventieth week. These extra thirty days are carefully and thoroughly defended in chapters 19 and 20 of this book.

9. The prophet Joel gives further insight into the timing of God's deliverance and its general relationship to the day of the Lord:

> The sun will be turned into darkness, and the moon into blood, before the great and awesome day of the Lord comes. And it will come about that whoever calls on the name of the Lord will be delivered; for on Mount Zion and in Jerusalem there will be those who escape, as the Lord has said, even among the survivors whom the Lord calls. (Joel 2:31, 32)

In this writer's opinion, that passage also refers to the rapture of Jewish saints, pinpointing the exact time as just "before the great and awesome day of the Lord comes" (Joel 2:31). As seen in chapter 14, "the woman who flees" is not saved until after the Rapture, and "the woman who stays," not until after the seventieth week is complete. Therefore this must refer to believing Jews who are a part of the church who have been promised that "God has not destined [them] for wrath, but for obtaining salvation [deliverance]" (1 Thess. 5:9).

CHAPTER 18: The Day of the Lord

1. *The day of the Lord overview:* The author believes that all passages dealing with the day of the Lord focus on but one event — the future day when God will unleash His wrath against the unrighteous in general and the beast empire nations of Antichrist in particular. This will be a fiery judgment that can only be compared to the first judgment of the world by water in the days of Noah or, on a more limited basis, to God's complete and devastating destruction of Sodom and Gomorrah. It will result in the complete destruction of the earth as we know it and in the complete devastation of all the wicked living on earth during that time.

Eight prophets use the specific term "day of the Lord" a total of nineteen times. Three New Testament writers (Luke, Paul, and Peter) use that term in four passages that deal incontestably with the end times. Seven additional passages using the phrase "day of Christ" or "day of Jesus Christ" are generally understood as encompassing the same timeframe as the day of the Lord. It is my opinion, and it is a basic assumption of this book, that every reference to the day of the Lord refers only to this single end-time event, *not* two end-time events — one just before the Millennium, one at the end of it (see endnote 2). I have studied all those passages frequently and carefully. In almost every instance the language of the text itself indicates that the context is worldwide and futuristic. In the few cases in which the phrase "day of the Lord" (or the equivalent) is not used explicitly of the end times, the texts and their contexts at least do not exclude association with the end times. And I have discovered that when sufficient time and care are taken, these nonspecific references contribute directly or indirectly to a better understanding of God's revelation regarding the last days.

For example, the most difficult exception is found in Ezekiel, where the prophet declares, "For the day is near, even the day of the Lord is near; it will be a day of clouds, a time of doom for the nations. And a sword will come upon Egypt, and anguish will be in Ethiopia, when the slain fall in Egypt, they take away her wealth, and her foundations are torn down" (Ezek. 30:3, 4). The phrase "day of the Lord" is used here in a passage that at face value seems to refer to the fall of Egypt at the hand of King Nebuchadnezzar of Babylon. Yet, as every other reference to the day of the Lord always has a future eschatological view in mind, I can only conclude that this is again true of this passage. Either the reference to the day of the Lord in this passage as it pertains to Egypt is a near/far prophetic revelation, or else, because of the unusual way the day of the Lord is referred to ("*even* the day of the Lord," as if it is different than "the day that is near"), the reference to the "future" day of the Lord is some sort of comparison to the "present" day that is near, which would then reflect back to the first mention of the day of the Lord by Ezekiel earlier in 13:3-8.

2. *2 Peter 3:3-13:* For a number of reasons the context of 2 Peter 3 demands that the event described here precedes the Millennium and could not occur at the end of it.

First, the phrase "the last days" (v. 3) is nowhere else used in Scripture in reference to the end of the Millennium, but is frequently used in relation to the Rapture (see, e.g., John 6:39, 40, 54), to the resurrection of the dead (John 11:24), and to the end of this present age (Acts 2:17; 2 Tim. 3:1) — all of which coincide with the day of the Lord at the second coming of Christ.

Second, if Peter were speaking of a day of the Lord at the end of the Millennium, no one would be asking questions about Christ's coming (v. 4), because He would then be ruling over the earth as He had been for the previous thousand years.

Third, if the "dual" day of the Lord position were correct, the day of the Lord at the second coming of Christ — the most traumatic event in history — would already have occurred a thousand years earlier, and no one during the Millennium would make the absurd comment that "all continues just as it was from the beginning of creation" (v. 4).

Fourth, Peter's reference to the day of the Lord coming like a thief (v. 10) perfectly parallels Paul's day of the Lord passage given in 1 Thessalonians 5:2-4, where he explains that "the times and the epochs" of the coming (*parousia*) of Christ will come like a thief.

Fifth, Peter's illustrations about the Flood and the destruction of Sodom and Gomorrah (2:4-9; 3:6) are abbreviated versions of identical illustrations given by Christ in the Olivet Discourse, which deals with the wrath of Christ at His second coming (*parousia*).

Finally, Peter concludes the third chapter by saying, "just as also our beloved brother Paul, according to the wisdom given him, wrote to you, as also in all his letters, speaking in them of these things" (2 Pet. 3:15, 16). Obviously the day of the Lord is the main topic of 2 Peter 3. Because Paul teaches more about the day of the Lord than any other New Testament writer (with the exception of the book of Revelation), particularly in his two letters to the church in Thessalonica, Peter's comments here carry special meaning. The day of the Lord of which Paul writes is without exception *always* the day of God's judgment associated with His second coming. Paul's instruction never dealt with a day of the Lord at the end of the Millennium. Peter therefore makes clear that he and Paul are teaching the same truths about the same day of the Lord.

3. The reference here is to Antichrist's total allotted time after Michael, the restrainer, is removed at the midpoint of the seventieth week. When Michael's restraint is removed, Antichrist will immediately stop the Temple sacrifices, and from that point to his final destruction, Antichrist will have 1,290 days (Dan. 12:11). This period of time includes the last three and a half years of the seventieth week (forty-two thirty-day prophetic months), as well as the first interlude period of thirty days. (See chapter 19, the "Daniel 12:11 Text" section.) When Christ returns, He will render Antichrist useless, or paralyzed, and thereby terminate ("cut short") the great tribulation by Antichrist. But Antichrist will not at that time be destroyed, only handcuffed or paralyzed (see note 4).

4. *Second Thessalonians 2:8 (anelei)*: "Whom the Lord will slay." The NASB uses the Greek word *anelei*, from *anaireō* (*Strong's*, #337), which means "to put to death, kill, slay, take away or take up." On the other hand, the KJV uses the Greek word *analō sei*, from *analiskō* (*Strong's*, #355) which means "to consume, to use up or spend up." This verse is in reference to Isaiah 11:4 in the context of the day of the Lord (v. 11), where the prophet states that "with the breath of His [the Lord's] lips He will slay the wicked [singular]." Therefore this writer prefers the NASB manuscripts that render Christ "slaying" Antichrist, not "consuming" him.

5. *Second Thessalonians 2:8 (katargeō)*: "Whom the Lord will bring to an end." The Greek word *katargeō* ("bring to an end") is a compound of two other Greek words, *kata* (down) and *argeō* (to be idle, to reduce in activity, to abolish), and can therefore legitimately be translated as "rendered useless." *Strong's*, #2673, 691; W. E. Vine, *An Expository Dictionary of New Testament Words* (Westwood, NJ: Revell, 1940), 1:13.

6. This truth alone should put to rest the idea that the cruel and ungodly persecutions of the seventieth week (especially those of the great tribulation by Antichrist) could be a part of the day of the Lord. It is even more inconceivable that Antichrist could desecrate the Temple, declare himself to be God, demand the world's worship, and persecute God's elect during a time when only the Lord will be exalted!

7. *Revelation's sequence of events*: The seven seals, seven trumpets, and seven bowls occur consecutively — the trumpets coming out of the last seal and the bowls coming out of the last trumpet — with Armageddon being the final event after

the bowl judgments. The text, if taken literally and naturally, demands this sequence of events for the following reasons:

(1) The seals (chapters 6 — 8) are followed by the trumpets (chapters 9 — 11), which are followed by the bowls (chapters 15, 16), which are followed by Armageddon (chapter 19), in successive chapter order.

(2) The seventh seal (8:1) is nowhere associated with any activity except in relation to the seven trumpet judgments which immediately follow that last seal (8:2).

(3) The seventh trumpet (11:15), which likewise has no judgment directly associated with it, is followed by the opening of the Temple in Heaven (11:19). This opening is again referred to in 15:5, after the interlude of chapters 12 — 14. Out of the Temple, which is opened by the blowing of the seventh trumpet, the seven angels come forth with seven bowl judgments (15:6-8). The seventh bowl judgment is depicted in 16:17-21, and the last thing portrayed before the interlude of chapters 17, 18 is unrepentant mankind still blaspheming God (16:21). Armageddon is described in 19:17-21, where verse 21 concludes the wrath of God with the declaration: "And the rest were killed with the sword which came from the mouth of Him who sat upon the horse, and all the birds were filled with their flesh" (Rev. 19:21).

(4) The three woes refer to specific judgments on unrepentant mankind. The first woe comes at the blowing of the fifth trumpet, when mankind is tormented for five months by God's horse-sized scorpions. The second woe comes at the blowing of the sixth trumpet, at which time a third of mankind is killed. The third woe can be nothing but the final bowl judgments that issue from the blowing of the seventh trumpet, because no other judgment is associated with the seventh trumpet.

(5) The contents of the seals, trumpets, and bowls are distinct and permit no overlap of events without doing injustice to their clear distinctives.

(6) There is an obvious increasing severity of affliction from the beginning trumpet judgments to the end of the bowl judgments, which are specifically called "the last" of the wrath of God (Rev. 15:1).

(7) At the fifth trumpet judgment, the 144,000 are protected by the seal on their foreheads (9:4), a sealing that does not occur until after the sixth seal is opened (7:3). It is obvious, therefore, that the fifth trumpet must occur at least after the sixth seal.

(8) The four living creatures administer the first four seals (6:1-8), whereas angels administer the trumpets (8:6) and the bowls (15:8).

8. *Daniel 9:24 (the Most Holy)*: In the their multi-volume commentary on the Old Testament, C. K. F. Keil and Franz Delitzsch observe that "there is no good ground for referring this expression ["the most holy"] to the consecration of the altar of burnt-offering. Such a reference is wholly excluded by the fact that consecration of Zerubbabel's temple and altar, as well as of that which was desecrated by Antiochus, was a work of man, while the anointing of a 'most holy' in the verse before us must be regarded as a divine act, because the three preceding expressions beyond controversy announce divine actions. Every anointing, indeed, of persons or of things was performed by men, but it becomes a work of God when it is performed with the divinely ordained holy oil by priests or prophets according to God's command, and then it is the means and the symbol of the endowment or equipment with the Spirit of God. . . . Therefore, these consecrations cannot be designated as anointings and as the works of God, and the

angel [Gabriel, v. 21] cannot mean these works of men by the 'anointing of a most holy.'. . . Much older, more general, and also nearer the truth, is the explanation which refers these words to the anointing of *the Messiah*, an explanation which is established by various arguments" (*Commentary on the Old Testament in Ten Volumes*, Vol. IX [Grand Rapids, MI: Eerdmans, repr. 1980], pp. 346, 347, emphasis added).

CHAPTER 19: **The Mystery of God Is Finished**

1. C. F. Keil and F. Delitzsch, *Commentary on the Old Testament in Ten Volumes*, Vol. IX, *Ezekiel, Daniel* by C. F. Keil (Grand Rapids, MI: Eerdmans, n.d.), pp. 496, 97, 98, emphasis added).

    C. F. Keil comes to the identical conclusion that this author has — that the 1,290 days of Daniel 12:11 refer to the duration of the persecution, the tribulation, or the oppression. There is one major difference between our two views, which has no bearing on the basic tenet being argued. This is that the abomination continues for 1,290 days, thirty days more than the three and a half years, which he makes historical, whereas I believe that the context demands that it be considered future. He admits, on page 499, that "verse 7 [of Daniel 12] corresponds . . . with the tribulation which the hostile king of the time of the end . . . shall bring upon the holy people"; in other words, verse 7 is future. But then he flip-flops and makes "vers. 11 and 12 treat of a different, namely, an earlier, period of oppression than ver. 7." This author sees them as referring to the same period of time, *nothing in the context showing a change in subject matter from verse 7 to verses 11 and 12.*

2. Some interpreters suggest that this reference to Christ's appearing for a second time will be for believing Israel's salvation (or deliverance) at the rapture of the church. The context, however, is the spiritual salvation of Israel, not her physical deliverance. A few verses earlier we are told, "For this reason He is the mediator of a new covenant, in order that since a death has taken place *for the redemption of the transgressions that were committed under the first covenant, those who have been called may receive the promise of the eternal inheritance*" (Heb. 9:15, emphasis added). In addition, the context of the first half of verse 28 is likewise directly related to Israel's salvation from sin — that is, to Christ's "having been offered once to bear the sins of many . . . [and He] shall appear a second time . . . for salvation. . . ."

3. We read in Romans that "all Israel will be saved; just as it is written, 'The Deliverer will come *from* Zion, He will remove ungodliness from Jacob'" (11:26). Bibles with cross-references will indicate that Paul is quoting from Isaiah 59:20, which reads, "A Redeemer will come *to* Zion, and to those who turn from transgression in Jacob" (emphasis added). The italicized words indicate the difference. Neither the Hebrew nor the Greek permit any other translation. Therefore, our options are: these two passages are a real antinomy (i.e., Paul misquoted the Old Testament, which causes serious problems with inspiration); or there is another possibility that accommodates both passages.

    One commentator suggests that Paul had in mind the heavenly Zion, from which He will come to earth (Everett F. Harrison, "Romans," in *The Expositor's Bible Commentary*, Vol. 10 [Grand Rapids, MI: Zondervan, 1976], p. 124). This author is comfortable with that position because it is a basic premise of my hermeneutics that there are no antinomies in Scripture. Therefore, Paul was speaking of the "heavenly Zion" *from which* Christ will return to earth, and Isaiah was speaking of the "earthly Zion" *to which* Christ is going, when the nation of

Israel will be saved. Both statements are therefore accurate, and the antinomy is solved.

But is there a biblical basis to make such an assumption? I believe so. The writer of Hebrews makes this statement about the direct access that Christians have to Christ: "But you have come to Mount Zion and to the city of the living God, the heavenly Jerusalem, and to myriads of angels" (12:22). Whereas the Old Testament usage of Zion was always in reference to the earthly Zion, the writer of Hebrews expands the usage of Zion to include the heavenly Zion.

4. *The Wycliffe Bible Encyclopedia* (Chicago: Moody Press, 1975), p. 68.
5. Following are several highlights from that magnificent psalm, followed by brief comments about their appropriateness for that climactic end-time event.

> Give thanks to the Lord, for He is good; for His lovingkindness is everlasting. . . . From my distress I called upon the Lord; the Lord answered me and set me in a large place. . . . It is better to take refuge in the Lord than to trust in princes. All nations surrounded me; in the name of the Lord I will surely cut them off. . . . You pushed me violently so that I was falling, but the Lord helped me. The Lord is my strength and song, and He has become my salvation. . . . The Lord has disciplined me severely, but He has not given me over to death. (Ps. 118:1, 5, 9, 10, 13, 14, 18)

All those verses speak of God's faithfulness during a time of great distress when, in the last days, Israel will be surrounded by all the enemy nations (specifically during the second half of the seventieth week), and both the Jerusalem and Jehoshaphat Campaigns of Satan will take place.

Becoming more specific, the psalmist exults,

> I shall give thanks to Thee, for Thou hast answered me; and Thou hast become my salvation. The stone which the builders rejected [Jesus Christ] has become the chief corner stone. This is the Lord's doing; it is marvelous in our eyes. This is the day which the Lord has made; let us rejoice and be glad in it. (vv. 21-24)

These four verses speak directly of the national salvation of Israel, a redemption that will occur only after her sins have been truly atoned for at the conclusion of the seventieth week.

6. "Bema" is an English transliteration of the Greek *bema*, which literally means "a step or raised platform." It came to be used by the Greeks to refer to a dais from which orations were made. Later the term was used by the Romans to designate a magistrate's tribunal or court, and it is in this sense that Paul uses it.
7. Pretribulationalists often identify the twenty-four elders as being representatives of the church because they are wearing "crowns" received at the bema seat. Therefore, they reason, because the elders wearing their crowns are seen around the throne before the first seal commences (Rev. 4:4), the church, they maintain, had already been raptured and judged before the seventieth week begins. The elders' crowns (4:4, 10) are taken to be bema-seat rewards and thus supposedly prove that the bema-seat judgment must already have taken place. But as the passage (Rev. 11:18) clearly states, that judgment occurs *after* the seventh trumpet, which just as clearly occurs *after* the seventieth week, making that interpretation impossible.

CHAPTER 20: **The Final Wrath of God**
1. Although our English word *vial* is derived from the Greek term *phialē*, used in

Revelation 15:7, 16:1-4, etc. (and is translated "vial" in the *King James Version*), the term in New Testament times denoted a shallow bowl or saucer, a radically different kind of container than a vial. Vine observes that "the word is suggestive of rapidity in the emptying of the contents" (1:144).

2. R. Laird Harris, Gleason L. Archer, Bruce K. Waltke, eds., *Theological Wordbook of the Old Testament* (Chicago: Moody Press, 1980), 2444b, p. 950. See also James Strong, *Strong's Exhaustive Concordance of the Bible* (Nashville: Abingdon, 1890), #8210.

3. *Babylon the great — the "great city"*: A second event of much less importance will also take place during the seventh bowl judgment. This is the final destruction of "Babylon the great" — the great city of Rome which perhaps also includes Constantine's "New Rome," Constantinople (modern-day Istanbul). Constantinople was likewise built upon seven hills and was the original seat of Eastern (Byzantine) Orthodoxy. (See chapter 10, endnote 6.) The context of verse 19 is the destruction of the "cities of the nations." All of the cities of all of the nations of the world, and "Babylon, the great city," "the seven mountains on which the woman sits" (Rev. 17:9), will be destroyed, along with the city of Jerusalem, at this precise time. This "great city" represents the seat of the false religious system(s) of Babylon, distinct from but controlled by "the harlot" (the religious system (or systems) itself), which also will have exerted considerable influence over all ten nations in the final beast empire. Because of her competing efforts for world worship, "the harlot" will already have been destroyed by Antichrist, who will tolerate no rival. As seen earlier, that annihilation will have occurred more than three and a half years previously, at the midpoint of the seventieth week, when Antichrist declares himself to be God and orders all the world to worship him alone. The "great city" of Rome, and possibly Istanbul (Constantinople) as well, will now also be destroyed, but this time by God at the seventh bowl judgment, rather than by Antichrist as in the demise of "the harlot."

The destruction of commercial Babylon, the "great city," is described more fully and vividly in Revelation 18:

> For this reason in one day her plagues will come, pestilence and mourning and famine, and she will be burned up with fire; for the Lord God who judges her is strong. And the kings of the earth, who committed acts of immorality and lived sensuously with her, will weep and lament over her when they see the smoke of her burning, standing at a distance because of the fear of her torment, saying, "Woe, woe, *the great city*, Babylon, *the strong city*! For in one hour your judgment has come." And the merchants of the earth weep and mourn over her, because no one buys their cargoes any more.... And they threw dust on their heads and were crying out, weeping and mourning, saying, "Woe, woe, *the great city*, in which all who had ships at sea became rich by her wealth, for in one hour she has been laid waste!" (Rev. 18:8-11, 19, emphasis added)

Lastly, it is interesting to note that both Rome and Istanbul (Constantinople) are seaports.

4. *Revelation 19:8 (lampros)*: The bride of Christ is spoken of as being clothed "in fine linen, bright and clean" (Rev. 19:8), clearly a reference to believers. It is interesting that when the final wrath of God is poured out (in the bowl judgments) on the nations by the angelic reapers of God, they too will be dressed in "bright" linen (Rev. 15:6). The Greek *lampros* can legitimately be translated either "bright" or "white," as illustrated by the fact that it is rendered as "bright" in the *New*

American Standard texts of 15:6 and 19:8 and as "white" in the *King James* texts of those same verses.

An additional passage in the book of Joshua also gives general support to the idea of the armies of Heaven being the angels — when Joshua sees the "captain of the host of the Lord." Most commentators take this to be a preincarnate appearance of Christ and that the "host of the Lord" are His heavenly angels, prepared for battle (see Josh. 5:13-15).

5. In the Old Testament the Hebrew term *'erets* is overwhelmingly translated as "earth." See R. Laird Harris, Gleason L. Archer, Bruce K. Waltke, eds., *Theological Wordbook of the Old Testament* (Chicago: Moody Press, 1980), #167, p. 74; *Strong's*, #776.

6. *Revelation 21:8 — Gog and Magog:* Gog and Magog are mentioned again at the end of the Millennium (Rev. 21:8), uniting with Satan for war against the millennial rule of Christ — one last shot at Christ before they are totally and finally destroyed. Is this the Gog and Magog referred to in Ezekiel 38? Definitely not, because that Gog and Magog will come against Israel during the seventieth week of Daniel and will be destroyed when Israel is saved (Ezek. 39), *before* the Millennium (Ezek. 40 – 48). Therefore, the Gog and Magog of Revelation *is what the Gog and Magog of Ezekiel 38 represent, not what the Gog and Magog of Ezekiel 38 are* — namely, a false leader and an unrighteous nation of people united, once again, against God and His elect at the end of the Millennium, paralleling the Gog and Magog in the days of Ezekiel 38. And once again, like the Gog and Magog of the seventieth week, they will be totally defeated by God. Who will they be? Scripture doesn't tell us. Therefore we have no more an idea of who they will be — what the makeup of the nations will be comprised of at the end of the Millennium — than Ezekiel had when chapter 38 was written about the end of "this age." We know only that they will be a leader and his people, perhaps again Germanic, with an Aryan mentality. Thus they are a "type," no more, no less; but that's where the parallel ends.

We are given a perfect example of this kind of "type" in the Babylonian Harlot, which does not represent the nation or city of Babylon per se, but rather what the Babylon of old represented and initiated — namely, the false queen of heaven worship introduced by Semiramus, or spiritual harlotry in place of true worship of the only true God of Heaven. When John, in Revelation 17 and 18, refers to the Babylonian Harlot, he had no idea that this Babylonian form of religious rebellion would come out of the very church in Rome that was then under great persecution for her faithfulness to God. Today, looking back, we understand. Then, looking forward, this was not clear. Therefore, as the Babylonian Harlot was no more than a "type" of what was begun in Babylon, yet perfectly descriptive of the spiritual harlotry that has dominated the Japhethite nations for the last two thousand years, so Gog and Magog, *at the end of the Millennium,* are no more than a "type" of the Gog and Magog that will represent Satan during the last days *before the Millennium.*

CHAPTER 21: **The Restoration Period**
1. The Hebrew word *hekal* ("nave"), often translated simply "temple," probably refers here to the main room of the Temple, the "holy place" (see Exod. 26:33).
2. It is important to note, however, that Christ will not "put all His enemies under His feet" and abolish the "last enemy . . . death" (1 Cor. 15:26) until the end of the Millennium. As seen in Revelation 20, "when the thousand years are completed,

Satan will be released from his prison, and will come out to deceive the nations which are in the four corners of the earth, Gog and Magog, to gather them together for the war; the number of them is like the sand of the seashore. And they came up on the broad plain of the earth and surrounded the camp of the saints and the beloved city, and fire came down from heaven and devoured them" (vv. 7-9). (Concerning the reference to Gog and Magog in verse 8, see further chapter 20, endnote 6.) Although this passage extends the rule of Christ only to the end of the Millennium, Daniel states conclusively that "His [Christ's] kingdom will be an everlasting kingdom" (Dan. 7:27; cf. v. 14).

CHAPTER 22: **The Millennium Begins**

1. *Revelation 20:7-15 parenthesis*: The preceding verse (5) introduces the "first resurrection" and verse 6 the "second death." Verses 7 to 15 is a parenthesis that explains in more detail that the "second death" will occur at the end of the Millennium at the Great White Throne. "This is the second death, the lake of fire. And if anyone's name was not found written in the book of life, he was thrown into the lake of fire" (vv. 14, 15). Chapter 21 then continues the flow of events occurring on the first day of the Millennium.

2. *Matthew 25:32 (ethnos)*: See W. F. Arndt and F. W. Gingrich, *A Greek-English Lexicon of the New Testament* (Chicago: University of Chicago Press, 1957), p. 217; James Strong, *Strong's Exhaustive Concordance of the Bible* (Nashville: Abingdon, 1890), #1484; W. E. Vine, *An Expository Dictionary of New Testament Words* (Westwood, NJ: Revell, 1940), 3:102.

3. "In that day," Isaiah continues to explain, "Israel will be the third party with Egypt and Assyria, a blessing in the midst of the earth, whom the Lord of hosts has blessed, saying, 'Blessed is Egypt My people, and Assyria the work of My hands, and Israel My inheritance'" (Isa. 19:23-25).

4. *Revelation 20:4 — they came to life*: When "they came to life" is a hotly debated issue. Do they come to life before John views them in verse 4? Or do they come to life at the time John is viewing them on the first day of the Millennium? The easiest solution would be to assume that this refers to something that has already happened, at the rapture of the church when "the dead in Christ rise first." This interpretation would present no difficulties to the prewrath rapture position espoused in this book. In fact, it would be far easier to explain. But the problem is, it would not be true to the literal, in-context hermeneutic this author has insisted upon from the beginning, nor to the proper Greek usage. The Greek verb, *"ezesan,"* translated "came to life," is in the aorist active tense. Dr. Robert Gundry, the noted Greek scholar, made the following comments to me as to the context and meaning of this particular passage, printed here with his permission:

> The parallelism of the aorist verbs in this passage, for sitting, giving, living and reigning, indicate actions that take place at the same time. Naturally it is the context which determines the time referred to by these verbs, clearly at the beginning of the Millennium because the passage in question ends with "and they came to life [aorist tense] and reigned [aorist tense] with Christ for a thousand years," thus defining exactly when the action takes place."

5. *Revelation 21:1 (kainos)*: Kainos ("new") does not denote that which is "new in time, recent, but new as to form or quality, of different nature from what is contrasted as old." See *Strong's*, #2537; Vine, 3:109. To designate a completely new creation,

a term such as *neos* (new in respect to time, of recent origin) would have been used.

6. *New heavens and new earth*: The Old Testament probably gives the best proof that the new heavens and the new earth are restored before the Millennium. Through Isaiah the Lord declared, "For behold, I create new heavens and a new earth; and the former things shall not be remembered or come to mind. . . . I will also rejoice in Jerusalem, and be glad in My people; and there will no longer be heard in her the voice of weeping and the sound of crying" (Isa. 65:17, 19). The order is explicit: first the new heavens and earth (v. 17), then the millennial kingdom (v. 19).

The same sequence is seen again in the next and final chapter of Isaiah: "'For just as the new heavens and the new earth which I make will endure before Me,' declares the Lord, 'so your offspring and your name will endure. And it shall be from new moon to new moon and from sabbath to sabbath, all mankind will come to bow down before Me,' says the Lord" (Isa. 66:22, 23).

Similarly, some scholars maintain that the remaking of new heavens and earth must occur after the Millennium because of the reference in Revelation 21:1 stating that "there is no longer any sea." The reference here, however, is not to there being no sea in the new earth, but to the sea having been destroyed (turned to "blood," Rev. 16:3, 4) when the "first earth passed away," as seen earlier in Revelation 21:1. The presence of "new seas" in the "new earth" is clearly implied by the fact that streams of living water will pour forth from the throne of God during the Millennium (see Zech. 14:8; 13:1).

7. *Millennial life spans*: It should be noted that it is the *end-time survivors* who go into the millennial kingdom — *not the raptured and resurrected saints* who will live in the New Jerusalem with Christ — and that they will still have earthly bodies, probably like Adam and Eve in the Garden of Eden before the Fall. Although these earthly citizens of the Millennium will not have immortal or resurrection bodies, they will nonetheless enjoy great length of life — much like those who lived before the Flood — because they will live on the renovated earth where the effects of the Fall have been greatly reduced. This new life in the millennial kingdom is described clearly in the following passage from Isaiah where God declares: "For behold, I create new heavens and a new earth; and the former things shall not be remembered or come to mind. But be glad and rejoice forever in what I create; for behold, I create Jerusalem for rejoicing, and her people for gladness. I will also rejoice in Jerusalem, and be glad in My people; and there will no longer be heard in her the voice of weeping and the sound of crying. No longer will there be in it an infant who lives but a few days, or an old man who does not live out his days; for the youth will die at the age of one hundred and the one who does not reach the age of one hundred shall be thought accursed" (Isa. 65:17-20). This passage in Isaiah clearly shows the interrelationship between the "new heavens and new earth" (v. 17), the Millennium (vv. 18, 19), and man's increase in life expectancy (v. 20).

8. The fact that the New Jerusalem must descend to earth at the beginning of the Millennium (rather than at the end, as some hold) is further substantiated as follows: Revelation 21:24, 26, 27a states that "the *nations* shall walk by its light [i.e., the light emanating from the New Jerusalem], and *the kings of the earth* shall bring their glory into it [the New Jerusalem] . . . and they shall bring the glory and the honor of *the nations* into it, and nothing unclean and no one who practices abomination and lying, shall ever come into it." This passage suggests the presence on

earth of some "unclean" things. In other words, verse 27a shows that the earth will still have at least some taint of sin at this time, although the sovereign power of God will not allow its open manifestation. This will be true during the Millennium but not after the Millennium in the eternal state, when there will be no sin of any kind. From this we know that the descriptions of the nations coming to the New Jerusalem in verses 24-27 must be during the Millennium; or conversely, the New Jerusalem must exist during the Millennium in order that the nations may come to it during that time.

9. *Throne room/Temple interrelationship*: The inseparability of the New Jerusalem and its throne room and the millennial Temple of Christ on earth is made absolutely clear when we compare Scripture with Scripture. Follow along with me carefully:

Both places are called the throne of God. It is clear that "the throne of God and of the Lamb [Christ]" are in the New Jerusalem (Rev. 22:1-3). It is just as clear that Christ's throne will be in His millennial Temple. As Ezekiel looked up from the east gate of that Temple, he was told by the Lord, "Son of man, this is the place of My throne and the place of the soles of My feet, where I will dwell among the sons of Israel forever. And the house of Israel will not again defile My holy name, neither they nor their kings, by their harlotry and by the corpses of their kings when they die" (Ezek. 43:7).

Both thrones will seat a King who reigns forever. With His saints in the New Jerusalem, Christ "shall reign forever and ever" (Rev. 22:5); He will also dwell among "the sons of Israel," the inhabitants of the millennial kingdom, and rule them forever from the Temple on Mount Zion (Ezek. 43:7, 9).

Both the throne in the New Jerusalem and the throne in the millennial Temple will display the glory of God. The New Jerusalem will have "no need of the sun or of the moon to shine upon it, for the glory of God has illumined it, and its lamp is the Lamb. And the nations shall walk by its light, and the kings of the earth shall bring their glory into it" (Rev. 21:23, 24). In the same way, the Temple on Mount Zion will radiate God's glory. Zechariah reveals that "it will be a unique day which is known to the Lord, neither day nor night; but it will come about that at evening time there will be light" (Zech. 14:7), and Ezekiel tells us that "the glory of the Lord [will come] into the house [that is, the Temple, the house of God on Mount Zion] by the way of the gate facing toward the east" (Ezek. 43:4).

Both thrones will have water flowing from them. The angel showed John "a river of the water of life, clear as crystal, coming from the throne of God and of the Lamb, in the middle of its street. And on either side of the river was the tree of life, bearing twelve kinds of fruit, yielding its fruit every month; and the leaves of the tree were for the healing of the nations" (Rev. 22:1, 2). Zechariah prophesies that "it will come about in that day that living waters will flow out of Jerusalem, half of them toward the eastern sea and the other half toward the western sea; it will be in summer as well as in winter" (Zech. 14:8). Joel predicts that "a spring will go out from the house of the Lord" (Joel 3:18).

Both thrones will bring life and healing. The water flowing from the New Jerusalem throne will have the tree of life on both sides, and "the leaves of the tree were for the healing of the nations" (Rev. 22:2). The trees nourished by the water flowing from the sanctuary on Mount Zion will bear " fruit . . . for food and . . . leaves for healing" (Ezek. 47:12).

Both thrones will be accessible to "the nations" of the world (Rev. 21:26; Isa. 2:2). Both throne rooms will be entered only by the righteous, "those whose names are written in the Lamb's book of life" (Rev. 21:27), whereas the unright-eous will be excluded (Ezek. 44:9).

Both thrones will swallow up death and wipe away tears (Rev. 21:4; Isa. 25:8).

Finally, both will be adorned with costly jewels (Rev. 21:18-20; Isa. 54:11, 12).

There can be no doubt, therefore, that the throne room of the New Jerusalem and the throne room in the Temple on Mount Zion are one and the same.

SCRIPTURE INDEX

CRITICAL ENDNOTE AND TOPIC INDEX

GENERAL INDEX

To remove chart, tear along perforation.

In order to answer your questions concerning the contents of this book, or to receive additional information, please write:

"The Sign"
P.O. Box 690909
Orlando, FL 32869-0909

OR call toll free:

1-800 MARK 13 4

(1-800-627-5134)